GLENCOE
Writer's Choice
Grammar and Composition
Grade 6

 Glencoe

New York, New York   Columbus, Ohio   Chicago, Illinois   Peoria, Illinois   Woodland Hills, California

ACKNOWLEDGMENTS

Grateful acknowledgment is given authors, publishers, photographers, museums, and agents for permission to reprint the following copyrighted material. Every effort has been made to determine copyright owners. In case of any omissions, the Publisher will be pleased to make suitable acknowledgments in future editions.

Acknowledgments continued on page 703.

 The **Facing the Blank Page** feature in this book was prepared in collaboration with the writers and editors of *TIME*.

6+1 Trait® is a registered trademark of Northwest Regional Educational Laboratory, which does not endorse this product.

Send all inquiries to:
GLENCOE/MCGRAW-HILL
8787 Orion Place
Columbus, OH 43240-4027

ISBN 0-07-829814-8
(Student Edition)
ISBN 0-07-829807-5
(Teacher Wraparound Edition)

2 3 4 5 6 7 8 9 10 071/043 09 08 07 06 05 04

PROGRAM CONSULTANTS

Mark Lester is Professor of English Emeritus at Eastern Washington University. He formerly served as Chair of the Department of English as a Second Language, University of Hawaii. He is the author of *Grammar and Usage in the Classroom* (Allyn & Bacon, 2000) and of numerous other professional books and articles.

Sharon O'Neal is Associate Professor at the College of Education, Texas State University–San Marcos, where she teaches courses in reading instruction. She formerly served as Director of Reading and Language Arts of the Texas Education Agency and has authored, and contributed to, numerous articles and books on reading instruction and teacher education.

Jacqueline Jones Royster is Professor of English and Associate Dean of the College of Humanities at Ohio State University. She is also on the faculty at the Bread Loaf School of English at Middlebury College in Middlebury, Vermont. In addition to the teaching of writing, Dr. Royster's professional interests include the rhetorical history of African American women and the social and cultural implications of literate practices.

Jeffrey Wilhelm, a middle and high school English teacher for thirteen years, is currently Associate Professor of English Education at Boise State University, where he specializes in adolescent literacy, with research interests in struggling readers and writers. He has been a National Writing Project site director for the past eight years. He has written eleven books on literacy education and numerous articles and chapters. He has won the NCTE Promising Research Award for *You Gotta BE the Book* and the Russell Award for Distinguished Research for *Reading Don't Fix No Chevys.*

Denny Wolfe, a former high school English teacher and department chair, is Professor of English Education, Director of the Tidewater Virginia Writing Project, and Director of the Center for Urban Education at Old Dominion University in Norfolk, Virginia. Author of more than seventy-five articles and books on teaching English, Dr. Wolfe is a frequent consultant to schools and colleges on the teaching of English language arts.

Advisors

Educational Reviewers

Student Advisory Board

The Student Advisory Board was formed in an effort to ensure student involvement in the development of *Writer's Choice.* The editors wish to thank members of the board for their enthusiasm and dedication to the project. The editors also wish to thank the many student writers whose models appear in this book.

BOOK OVERVIEW

Part 1   Composition

Unit 1   Personal Writing 2
Unit 2   The Writing Process 36
TIME   Facing the Blank Page 89
Unit 3   Descriptive Writing 100
Unit 4   Narrative Writing 142

Unit 5   Expository Writing 180
Unit 6   Persuasive Writing 216
Unit 7   Troubleshooter 248
Business and Technical Writing 268

Part 2   Grammar, Usage, and Mechanics

Unit 8   Subjects, Predicates, and Sentences 296
Unit 9   Nouns 318
Unit 10   Verbs 332
Unit 11   Pronouns 360
Unit 12   Adjectives 378
Unit 13   Adverbs 394
Unit 14   Prepositions, Conjunctions, and Interjections 414

Unit 15   Subject-Verb Agreement . . . 438
Unit 16   Glossary of Special Usage Problems 454
Unit 17   Diagraming Sentences . . . 464
Unit 18   Capitalization 472
Unit 19   Punctuation 488
Unit 20   Sentence Combining 516

Part 3   Resources and Skills

Unit 21   Library and Reference Resources 526
Unit 22   Vocabulary and Spelling . . . 541
Unit 23   Study Skills 568

Unit 24   Taking Tests 583
Unit 25   Listening and Speaking . . . 616
Unit 26   Viewing and Representing . . 628
Unit 27   Electronic Resources 644

Reference Section

Writing and Language Glossary . . . 658
Spanish Glossary 667
Writing and Research Handbook . . . 677

Index 691
Acknowledgments 703

CONTENTS

Part 1 Composition

UNIT 1 Personal Writing 2

Writing in the Real World 4
Round-the-World Voyage Journal Entries by Bill Pinkney

Instruction and Practice

1.1 **Writing as Self-Expression** 8
Write a Personal Response; Cross-Curricular Activity;
Listening and Speaking; Grammar Link

1.2 **Writing with Confidence** 12
Write a Journal Entry; Using Computers;
Viewing and Representing; Grammar Link

1.3 **Making Personal Connections** 16
Write a Friendly Letter; Using Computers;
Listening and Speaking; Grammar Link

Writing About Literature

1.4 **Responding to a Poem** 20
Write a Poem; Cross-Curricular Activity;
Viewing and Representing; Grammar Link

Writing Process in Action

Personal Writing Project 24
Write a personal account about a special day.
• Prewriting • Drafting • Revising
• Editing/Proofreading • Publishing/Presenting

Literature Model

from **The Invisible Thread** by Yoshiko Uchida 28

Linking Writing and Literature

Collect Your Thoughts; Talk About Reading; Write About Reading. 34

UNIT 1 Review

Reflecting on the Unit
Adding to Your Portfolio
Writing Across the Curriculum 35

UNIT 2

The Writing Process 36

Writing in the Real World 38

from *The Empire Builder: Scenic and Historic Announcements* **Guide** by Curtis Katz

Instruction and Practice

2.1 Exploring the Writing Process 42
Write About Your Writing Process; Using Computers; Listening and Speaking; Grammar Link

2.2 Prewriting: Finding a Topic 46
Explore a Topic; Using Computers; Listening and Speaking; Grammar Link

2.3 Prewriting: Ordering Ideas 50
Write an Ordered List; Cross-Curricular Activity; Viewing and Representing; Grammar Link

2.4 Drafting: Getting It Down on Paper 54
Write a Draft; Cross-Curricular Activity; Viewing and Representing; Grammar Link

2.5 Revising: Reviewing Your Ideas 58
Revise Your Draft; Using Computers; Listening and Speaking; Grammar Link

2.6 Revising: Getting Paragraphs into Shape 62
Use Strong Paragraphs; Cross-Curricular Activity; Viewing and Representing; Grammar Link

2.7 Revising: Achieving Sentence Fluency 66
Smooth Out Paragraphs; Viewing and Representing; Using Computers; Grammar Link

2.8 Editing/Proofreading: Checking Details **70**
Edit Your Draft; Using Computers; Listening and
Speaking; Grammar Link

2.9 Publishing/Presenting: Sharing Your Work **74**
Present Your Work; Viewing and Representing;
Using Computers; Grammar Link

Writing Process in Action

Writing Process Project **78**
Follow a method for writing an explanation.
• Prewriting • Drafting • Revising
• Editing/Proofreading • Publishing/Presenting

Literature Model

from **Coast to Coast** by Betsy Byars **82**

Linking Writing and Literature

Collect Your Thoughts; Talk About Reading; Write
About Reading **87**

UNIT **2** Review

Reflecting on the Unit
Adding to Your Portfolio
Writing Across the Curriculum **88**

Facing the Blank Page **89**

Writing for *TIME* • Prewriting • Drafting • Revising
• Editing/Proofreading • Publishing/Presenting

UNIT 3 Descriptive Writing 100

Writing in the Real World 102
from "Attacking the Nunataks"
Magazine Article by John Boulanger

Instruction and Practice

3.1 **Painting a Picture with Words** 106
Write a Description of a Wolf; Listening and
Speaking; Using Computers; Grammar Link

3.2 **Observing and Taking Notes** 110
Write a Description of Living Things; Listening and
Speaking; Cross-Curricular Activity; Grammar Link

3.3 **Elaborating: Focusing on the Details** 114
Write a Description of Art; Cross-Curricular Activity;
Viewing and Representing; Grammar Link

3.4 **Ordering Descriptive Details** 118
Describe a Scene; Using Computers; Listening and
Speaking; Grammar Link

3.5 **Describing a Place**. 122
Describe a Place; Using Computers; Viewing and
Representing; Grammar Link

Writing About Literature

3.6 **Getting to Know a New Place** 126
Write a Travel Brochure; Using Computers;
Listening and Speaking; Grammar Link

Writing Process in Action

Descriptive Writing Project 130
Describe a memorable experience.
• Prewriting • Drafting • Revising
• Editing/Proofreading • Publishing/Presenting

Literature Model

from **Morning Girl** by Michael Dorris 134

Linking Writing and Literature

Collect Your Thoughts; Talk About Reading; Write
About Reading 140

UNIT 3 Review

Reflecting on the Unit

Adding to Your Portfolio

Writing Across the Curriculum 141

UNIT 4

Narrative Writing 142

MEDIA Connection *Writing in the Real World* 144

from *W. E. B. Du Bois: A Biography*
Biographical Sketch by Virginia Hamilton

Instruction and Practice

4.1 Developing a Real-Life Story 148
Write About the Past; Listening and Speaking;
Viewing and Representing; Grammar Link

4.2 Keeping a Story Organized 152
Write a Real-Life Narrative; Listening and Speaking;
Cross-Curricular Activity; Grammar Link

4.3 Writing Dialogue 156
Write a Dialogue; Cross-Curricular Activity;
Listening and Speaking; Grammar Link

4.4 Writing About an Event 160
Write a Narrative About Learning a Skill; Using
Computers; Listening and Speaking; Grammar Link

Writing About Literature

4.5 Responding to a Biography 164
Write a Brief Biography; Using Computers;
Listening and Speaking; Grammar Link

Writing Process in Action   **Narrative Writing Project**. 168
Write a story about clothes you used to wear.
● Prewriting ● Drafting ● Revising
● Editing/Proofreading ● Publishing/Presenting

Literature Model   **"The Jacket"** by Gary Soto 172

Linking Writing and Literature   Collect Your Thoughts; Talk About Reading; Write
About Reading 178

UNIT 4 Review   Reflecting on the Unit
📼 Adding to Your Portfolio
Writing Across the Curriculum 179

UNIT 5

Expository Writing 180

🌐 *Writing in the Real World* 182

from **"How Does Michael Fly?"**
Newspaper Article by Julie Sheer

Instruction and Practice   **5.1 Writing to Help Others Understand** 186
Write an Explanation of a Game; Cross-Curricular
Activity; Viewing and Representing; Grammar Link

5.2 Comparing and Contrasting Two Things 190
Write a Comparison-Contrast Piece; Using Computers;
Listening and Speaking; Grammar Link

5.3 Explaining How to Do Something 194
Write a "How to" Explanation; Cross-Curricular Activity;
Listening and Speaking; Grammar Link

5.4 Writing a Report 198
Write a Report; Using Computers; Listening and
Speaking; Grammar Link

Writing About Literature   **5.5 Writing a Book Report**. 202
Write a Book Report; Using Computers; Listening and
Speaking; Grammar Link

Writing Process in Action   **Expository Writing Project**. **206**
Write an explanation of a process.
• Prewriting • Drafting • Revising
• Editing/Proofreading • Publishing/Presenting

Literature Model   **"Bathing Elephants"** by Peggy Thomson **210**

Linking Writing and Literature   Collect Your Thoughts; Talk About Reading; Write
About Reading **214**

UNIT 5 Review   Reflecting on the Unit
💼 Adding to Your Portfolio
Writing Across the Curriculum **215**

UNIT 6 **Persuasive Writing**. **216**

Writing in the Real World **218**
from **"A Popular Little Planet"** TV Script by Douglas Anderson

Instruction and Practice   **6.1 Taking a Stand** **222**
Create a Poster; Cross-Curricular Activity; Listening and
Speaking; Grammar Link

6.2 Stating a Position **226**
Write a Proposal; Using Computers; Viewing and
Representing; Grammar Link

6.3 Using Facts and Opinions **230**
Write a Persuasive Letter; Cross-Curricular Activity;
Listening and Speaking; Grammar Link

Writing About Literature   **6.4 Writing a TV Review** **234**
Write a TV Review; Using Computers; Viewing and
Representing; Grammar Link

Writing Process in Action **Persuasive Writing Project** **238**
Write a persuasive newspaper article.
• Prewriting • Drafting • Revising
• Editing/Proofreading • Publishing/Presenting

Literature Model from **"Thanking the Birds"** by Joseph Bruchac **242**

Linking Writing and Literature Collect Your Thoughts; Talk About Reading; Write
About Reading **246**

UNIT 6 Review Reflecting on the Unit
Adding to Your Portfolio
Writing Across the Curriculum **247**

UNIT 7 Troubleshooter **248**

Problems and Solutions 7.1 **Sentence Fragment** **250**
7.2 **Run-on Sentence** **252**
7.3 **Lack of Subject-Verb Agreement** **254**
7.4 **Incorrect Verb Tense or Form** **256**
7.5 **Incorrect Use of Pronouns** **258**
7.6 **Incorrect Use of Adjectives** **260**
7.7 **Incorrect Use of Commas** **262**
7.8 **Incorrect Use of Apostrophes** **264**
7.9 **Incorrect Capitalization** **266**

Business and Technical Writing **268**

Instruction and Practice **Business Letters** **269**
Memos **274**
Application Forms **278**
Instructions **282**
Incident Reports **286**
Multimedia Presentations **290**

Part 2 | Grammar, Usage, and Mechanics

UNIT 8 | Subjects, Predicates, and Sentences.............. 296

Instruction and Practice

8.1 Kinds of Sentences 297

8.2 Sentences and Sentence Fragments 299

8.3 Subjects and Predicates 301

8.4 Finding Subjects 303

8.5 Compound Subjects and
    Compound Predicates 305

8.6 Simple, Compound, and Complex Sentences... 307

Grammar Review   Subjects, Predicates, and Sentences 309

Literature Model   from *A Tree Grows in Brooklyn* by Betty Smith

Writing Application   Compound Predicates and Compound Sentences in Writing;
Techniques with Sentences; Practice 317

UNIT 9 Nouns 318

Instruction and Practice

9.1 Common and Proper Nouns 319

9.2 Singular and Plural Nouns 321

9.3 Possessive Nouns 323

Grammar Review   Nouns 325

Literature Model   from *Black Star, Bright Dawn* by Scott O'Dell

Writing Application   Nouns in Writing; Techniques with Nouns; Practice 331

UNIT 10 Verbs 332

Instruction and Practice

10.1 Action Verbs and Direct Objects 333

10.2 Indirect Objects 335

10.3 Linking Verbs and Predicate Words 337

10.4 Present, Past, and Future Tenses 339

10.5 Main Verbs and Helping Verbs 341

10.6 Present and Past Progressive Forms 343

10.7 Perfect Tenses 345

10.8 Irregular Verbs 347

10.9 More Irregular Verbs 349

Grammar Review   Verbs 351

Literature Model   from **"All Stories are Anansi's"** by Harold Courlander

Writing Application   Action Verbs in Writing; Techniques with Action Verbs;
Practice 359

UNIT 11 — Pronouns 360

Instruction and Practice

11.1 Personal Pronouns 361

11.2 Using Pronouns Correctly 363

11.3 Pronouns and Antecedents. 365

11.4 Possessive Pronouns 367

11.5 Indefinite Pronouns. 369

Grammar Review Pronouns 371

Literature Model from **"The Wise Old Woman"**
a Japanese folktale retold by Yoshiko Uchida

Writing Application Pronouns in Writing; Techniques with Pronouns; Practice . . . 377

UNIT 12 Adjectives...................................378

Instruction and Practice

12.1 Adjectives and Proper Adjectives 379

12.2 Articles and Demonstratives 381

12.3 Adjectives That Compare 383

12.4 Special Adjectives That Compare 385

Grammar Review   Adjectives 387

Literature Model   from *Giants of Jazz* by Studs Terkel

Writing Application   Adjectives in Writing; Techniques with Adjectives; Practice .. 393

UNIT 13 Adverbs....................................394

Instruction and Practice

13.1 Adverbs Modifying Verbs................ 395

13.2 Adverbs Modifying Adjectives and Adverbs .. 397

13.3 Adverbs That Compare 399

13.4 Telling Adjectives and Adverbs Apart 401

13.5 Avoiding Double Negatives............... 403

Grammar Review   Adverbs...................... 405

Literature Model   from *Across Five Aprils* by Irene Hunt

Writing Application   Adverbs in Writing; Techniques with Adverbs; Practice..... 413

UNIT 14 Prepositions, Conjunctions, and Interjections..... 414

Instruction and Practice

14.1 **Prepositions** 415

14.2 **Prepositional Phrases** 417

14.3 **Pronouns After Prepositions** 419

14.4 **Prepositional Phrases as Adjectives and Adverbs** 421

14.5 **Telling Prepositions and Adverbs Apart** 423

14.6 **Conjunctions** 425

14.7 **Interjections** 427

Grammar Review   **Prepositions, Conjunctions, and Interjections** 429

Literature Model   from *One Writer's Beginnings* by Eudora Welty

Writing Application   Prepositions and Conjunctions in Writing; Techniques with Prepositions and Conjunctions; Practice 437

UNIT 15   Subject-Verb Agreement 438

Instruction and Practice

15.1 Making Subjects and Verbs Agree 439

15.2 Problems with Locating the Subject 441

15.3 Agreement with Compound Subjects 443

Grammar Review   Subject-Verb Agreement 445

Literature Model   from *John Muir* by Eden Force

Writing Application   Subject-Verb Agreement in Writing; Techniques with Subjects and Their Verbs; Practice 453

UNIT 16   Glossary of Special Usage Problems 454

Instruction and Practice

16.1 Using Troublesome Words I 455

16.2 Using Troublesome Words II 457

Grammar Review   Glossary of Special Usage Problems 459

Literature Model   from *Exploring the* Titanic by Robert D. Ballard

Writing Application   Usage of Glossary Words in Writing; Techniques with Correct Usage; Practice 463

UNIT 17 Diagraming Sentences......................... 464

Instruction and Practice

17.1 Diagraming Simple Subjects and
Simple Predicates...................... 465

17.2 Diagraming the Four Kinds of Sentences 466

17.3 Diagraming Direct and Indirect Objects..... 467

17.4 Diagraming Adjectives and Adverbs........ 468

17.5 Diagraming Predicate Nouns and
Predicate Adjectives.................. 469

17.6 Diagraming Prepositional Phrases........ 470

17.7 Diagraming Compound Sentence Parts 471

UNIT 18 Capitalization........................... 472

Instruction and Practice

18.1 Capitalizing Sentences, Quotations,
and Salutations 473

18.2 Capitalizing Names and Titles of People 475

18.3 Capitalizing Names of Places 477

18.4 Capitalizing Other Proper Nouns
and Adjectives 479

Grammar Review   Capitalization 481

Literature Model   from *A Secret for Two* by Quentin Reynolds

Writing Application   Capitalization in Writing; Techniques with Capitalization;
Practice.............................. 487

UNIT 19 Punctuation 488

Instruction and Practice

19.1 Using the Period and Other End Marks...... 489

19.2 Using Commas I 491

19.3 Using Commas II. 493

19.4 Using Commas III 495

19.5 Using Semicolons and Colons............ 497

19.6 Using Quotation Marks and Italics 499

19.7 Using Apostrophes and Hyphens 501

19.8 Using Abbreviations 503

19.9 Writing Numbers 505

Grammar Review Punctuation 507

Literature Model from *Harriet Tubman: The Moses of Her People* by Langston Hughes

Writing Application Punctuation in Writing; Techniques with Punctuation; Practice................................. 515

UNIT 20 Sentence Combining 516

Instruction and Practice

20.1 Compound Sentences 517

20.2 Compound Elements 519

20.3 Prepositional Phrases 521

Mixed Review 523

Part 3 Resources and Skills

UNIT 21 Library and Reference Resources 526

Instruction and Practice
21.1 Using a Library 527
21.2 How Books Are Organized 530
21.3 How to Find a Book 532
21.4 Using References 534
21.5 Using a Dictionary..................... 536
21.6 Understanding a Dictionary Entry 539

UNIT 22 Vocabulary and Spelling 541

Instruction and Practice
22.1 Borrowed Words 542
22.2 Clues to Word Meanings................. 544
wordworks WORDS BORROWED
FROM THE FRENCH 546

22.3 Using Word Parts. 547

wordworks WORD ORIGINS 551

22.4 Synonyms and Antonyms 552

wordworks HOMOGRAPHS 554

22.5 Words That Sound Alike 555

22.6 Spelling Rules I 557

22.7 Spelling Rules II 561

wordworks CODED LANGUAGE 564

22.8 Problem Words 565

UNIT 23 Study Skills 568

Instruction and Practice

23.1 Exploring a Book. 569

23.2 Planning Your Study 571

23.3 Using a Study Method 573

23.4 Notes and Outlines 576

23.5 Using Graphic Aids 579

UNIT 24 Taking Tests **583**

Instruction and Practice   24.1 Tips for Test Taking **584**

24.2 Test Items **586**

24.3 Standardized Tests. **588**

24.4 Standardized Test Practice **591**

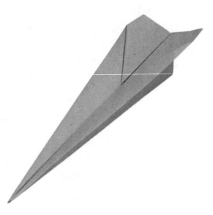

UNIT 25 Listening and Speaking **616**

Instruction and Practice   25.1 Listening. **617**

25.2 Informal Speaking. **621**

25.3 How to Give an Oral Report **624**

UNIT 26 Viewing and Representing 628

Instruction and Practice

26.1 Interpreting Visual Messages 629
26.2 Analyzing Media Messages 635
26.3 Producing Media Messages 640

UNIT 27 Electronic Resources 644

Instruction and Practice

27.1 The Internet 645
27.2 Getting on the Internet 647
27.3 Evaluating Internet Sources 651
27.4 Using E-Mail 654
27.5 Other Electronic Resources 656

Quick Help

Reference Section *Fast answers to questions about writing, research, and language*

Writing and Language Glossary 658

Spanish Glossary. 667

Writing and Research Handbook 677

  Writing Good Sentences 677
  - Using Various Types of Sentences - Revising Wordy Sentences
  - Varying Sentence Structure and Length

  Writing Good Paragraphs 679
  - Writing Unified Paragraphs - Writing Coherent Paragraphs

  Writing Good Compositions 681
  - Making a Plan - Using the 6+1 Trait® Model

  Writing Good Research Papers 685
  - Exploring a Variety of Sources - Preparing the Final Draft
  - Evaluating Sources - MLA Style: Works Cited
  - Giving Credit Where Credit Is Due

Index 691

Acknowledgments 703

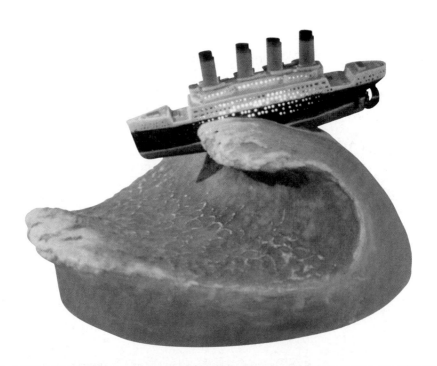

LITERATURE MODELS

Composition Models

Each literature selection is an extended example of the mode of writing taught in the unit.

Yoshiko Uchida, from *The Invisible Thread*   28

Betsy Byars, from *Coast to Coast*   82

Michael Dorris, from *Morning Girl*   134

Gary Soto, "The Jacket"   172

Peggy Thomson, "Bathing Elephants"   210

Joseph Bruchac, from "Thanking the Birds"   242

Skill Models

Excerpts from outstanding works of fiction and nonfiction exemplify specific writing skills.

Terry McMillan, *Breaking Ice*   8

Rosa Guy, *The Ups and Downs of Carl Davis III*   16

William Carlos Williams, "This Is Just to Say"   20

Yoshiko Uchida, *The Invisible Thread*   25

David Kherdian, *Root River Run*   51

Richard B. Lyttle, *The Complete Beginner's Guide to Backpacking*   62

Vicki McVey, *The Sierra Club Wayfinding Book*   63

Marjorie Kinnan Rawlings, *The Yearling*   66

Betsy Byars, *Coast to Coast*   79

Jean Craighead George, *Julie of the Wolves*   106, 107

Maya Angelou, *I Know Why the Caged Bird Sings*   110

Ian Fleming, *Chitty Chitty Bang Bang*   114

Freeman Hubbard, *Great Days of the Circus*   118

Armstrong Sperry, *Thunder Country*   124

Nicholasa Mohr, *Nilda*   126

Michael Dorris, *Morning Girl*   132

LITERATURE MODELS

Skill Models *continued*

Avi, *A Place Called Ugly*   149

Benjamin Tene, *In the Shade of the
    Chestnut Tree*   156

Gary Soto, "The Jacket"   169

Lionel Bender, *Invention*   186

Jack Cowart, *Henri Matisse: Paper Cut-Outs*   196

National Geographic, "Sharks: Magnificent and
    Misunderstood" (a summary)   200

Dr. Ann Squire, *101 Questions and Answers About
    Pets and People*   222

Leda and Rhoda Blumberg, *Lovebirds, Lizards, and
    Llamas: Strange and Exotic Pets*   230

Joseph Bruchac, "Thanking the Birds"   239

Language Models

*Each Grammar Review uses excerpts to link
grammar, usage, or mechanics to literature.*

Betty Smith, *A Tree Grows in Brooklyn*   309

Scott O'Dell, *Black Star, Bright Dawn*   325

Ashanti folktale by Harold Courlander, "All Stories
    Are Anansi's"   351

Yoshiko Uchida, "The Wise Old Woman"   371

Studs Terkel, *Giants of Jazz*   387

Irene Hunt, *Across Five Aprils*   405

Eudora Welty, *One Writer's Beginnings*   429

Eden Force, *John Muir*   445

Robert D. Ballard, *Exploring the* Titanic   459

Quentin Reynolds, *A Secret for Two*   481

Langston Hughes, *Harriet Tubman: The Moses of
    Her People*   507

FINE ART

....

Fine art—paintings, drawings, photos, and sculpture—is used to teach as well as to stimulate writing ideas.

Marsden Hartley, *Hurricane Island, Final Haven, Maine*   xxxii–1

Pieter Bruegel the Elder, *Hunters in the Snow*   23

Paul Cézanne, *Farmhouse and Chestnut Trees at Jas-de-Bouffan*   30

Helen Oji, *Libellule (Memory of My Father)*   32

Tina Dunkley, *Double Dutch Series: Keeping Time*   57

Artist unknown, Navajo, Shiprock rug   65

Robert Delaunay, *Homage to Blériot*   83

Henri Rousseau, *View of the Bridge at Sèvres*   84

Maria Sibylla Merian, *Coral Bean Tree and Saturniid*   113

Kenny Scharf, *Stellaradiola*   117

Louisa Matthiasdottir, *Sheep in Blue Landscape*   121

Pablo Picasso, *Etudes*   135

Paul Gauguin, *Tahitian Women,* or *On the Beach*   137

Glen Rabena, *Mosquito Mask*   152

Edward S. Curtis, *Masked Kwakiutl Dancers*   152

Edvard Munch, *Women on a Bridge*   159

Augustín Lazo, *Head*   173

Carmen Lomas Garza, *Cakewalk*   174

Henri Matisse, *Madame de Pompadour*   197

Andy Warhol, *Endangered Species: African Elephant*   213

Jasper Johns, *Numbers in Color*   225

Amy Cordova, *The Red Dress*   243

Katsushika Hokusai, *Fuji in Clear Weather*   294

Pierre-Auguste Renoir, *The Reading*   315

Rockwell Kent, *The Expedition*   329

Nancy Schutt, *Vanishing*   357

Jacob Lawrence, *Men Exist for the Sake of One Another: Teach Them Then or Bear with Them*   375

Lois Mailou Jones, *The Ascent of Ethiopia*   391

Roger Brown, *Lost America*   411

Janet Fish, *Toby and Claire Reading*   435

Thomas Moran, *Cliffs of the Upper Colorado River, Wyoming Territory*   451

Richard Shaw, *Rough Seas*   461

John Kane, *Across the Strip*   485

Aaron Douglas, *Aspiration*   513

Emile Bernard, *Breton Women with Umbrellas*   524

GLENCOE
Writer's Choice
Grammar and Composition

Welcome to Writer's Choice!

Your writing and your choices are what this book is all about. Take a few minutes to get to know each of the book's four main parts: Composition; Grammar, Usage, and Mechanics; Resources and Skills; and the Writing and Research Handbook.

Part 1

Composition

How do you become a better writer? By writing! Four-page lessons give you the strategies you need to improve your writing skills. Each lesson focuses on a specific writing problem or task. The lessons offer clear instruction, show models of effective writing, and— most importantly—provide a variety of writing activities for you to practice what you've learned.

Part 2

Grammar, Usage, and Mechanics

Short focused lessons make learning grammar easy. Rules and definitions teach you the basics, while examples and literature models show you how the concepts are used in real-life writing.

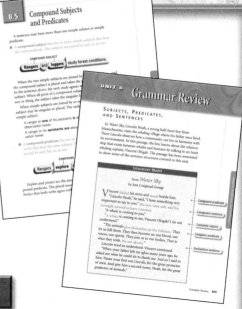

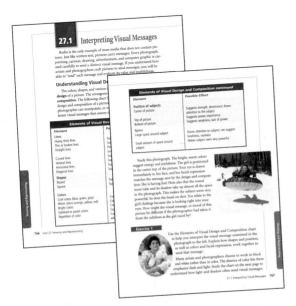

Part 3

Resources and Skills

Would you like to improve your study skills, learn how to give a speech, or get better at taking tests? The lessons in this part give you the skills you need to do all these things and more. Each lesson is complete, concise, and easy to use.

WRITING AND RESEARCH HANDBOOK

This user-friendly handbook gives explanations, examples, and tips to help you write strong sentences, paragraphs, compositions, and research papers. Use it whenever you get stuck!

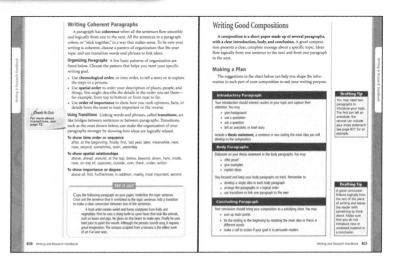

"There was plenty of rain-water in the hollows of soft stones...."

—Louis Untermeyer, "The Dog of Pompeii"

PART 1

Composition

Unit 1   **Personal Writing**   *2*

Unit 2   **The Writing Process**   *36*

TIME   **Facing the Blank Page**   *89*

Unit 3   **Descriptive Writing**   *100*

Unit 4   **Narrative Writing**   *142*

Unit 5   **Expository Writing**   *180*

Unit 6   **Persuasive Writing**   *216*

Unit 7   **Troubleshooter**   *248*

Business and Technical Writing   *268*

Hurricane Island,
Final Haven, Maine,
by Marsden Hartley.
1942

> "I sat perfectly still, with my eyes downcast, daring only now and then to shoot long glances around me."
>
> —Zitkala-Ša, "The Land of Red Apples"

UNIT 1

Personal Writing

Writing in the Real World: *Bill Pinkney*   *4*

Lesson **1.1**   **Writing as Self-Expression**   *8*

Lesson **1.2**   **Writing with Confidence**   *12*

Lesson **1.3**   **Making Personal Connections**   *16*

Lesson **1.4**   **Writing About Literature: Responding to a Poem**   *20*

Writing Process in Action   *24*

Literature Model: from *The Invisible Thread* by Yoshiko Uchida   *28*

Unit 1 Review   *35*

Writing in the Real World

MEDIA
Journal Writing
Connection

In the summer of 1990, Bill Pinkney set out on an adventure that few would ever dream of taking: a solo round-the-world voyage in a sailboat. The excerpts below are from a personal journal that Pinkney kept for most of his remarkable, 32,000-mile trip.

Round-the-World Voyage

by Bill Pinkney

Wednesday, January 15   48° 51′ S 161° 57′ W

Gray overcast morning but near midday the sky cleared completely. I lowered the main sail and set about restrapping the headboard. I had to climb on the boom and straddle it like a horse, with my feet in the lowered sails. I was able to keep my balance and perform the task. It was a challenge because the swell was at least 3 meters. The task completed I felt a great sense of achievement. That problem could have degenerated into a real disaster if left to fester.

Friday, February 7   52° 56′ S 85° 42′ W

I sat in my cocoon (my bunk) and went through all the photos I have on board. The sights and memories made an otherwise grey day a warm and joyful time. It is difficult sometimes to grasp the full scope of the experiences, places and people that have filled my life over the last five to six years.

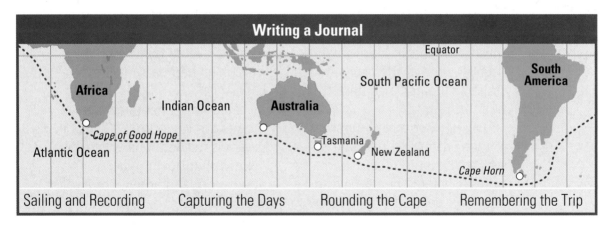

A Writer's Process

Prewriting
Sailing and Recording

Former Chicago businessman Bill Pinkney set sail from Boston on August 5, 1990. Traveling southeastward, he rode the winds to Bermuda and Brazil. After crossing the Atlantic to the Cape of Good Hope, South Africa, he headed to Cape Leeuwin, Australia, and South East Cape, Tasmania. From there Pinkney slipped around South West Cape, New Zealand. Across the Pacific was Pinkney's final goal—Cape Horn. Rounding Cape Horn is one of the most dangerous feats a solo sailor can perform. Once he rounded the Cape, Pinkney sprinted home, arriving twenty-two months after he began.

What was it like to sail this route all alone? "There was no such thing as a typical day," Pinkney said. Good weather or bad, Pinkney rarely became bored. He spent hours fixing sails, cooking, reading, and navigating. He also taped videos for friends, family, and students in Chicago and Boston, who were tracking his voyage. Just as important, Pinkney kept a daily account of the trip.

Between Boston and Tasmania, Pinkney recorded most of his experiences on videotape. But in Tasmania, a friend gave him "a very fancy diary book." From Tasmania onward, it was in this book that Pinkney wrote his daily journal entries.

Drafting
Capturing the Days

After leaving Tasmania, Pinkney hit a string of rough days. Still a month from Cape Horn, he had rough weather and tense moments with the boat. He wrote about many of these moments in his journal. He usually wrote at the navigation station—the nerve center of the boat.

Pinkney began each journal entry by recording the date as well as the latitude and longitude of his location. Then he wrote about his daily adventures. Sometimes, Pinkney says, he drew pictures "of events that happened on a regular basis." These included sightings of whales, dolphins, and ships.

As January eased into February, Pinkney neared Cape Horn, and conditions began to improve. On February 13, Pinkney's dream came true. That night, in pitch blackness, he rounded Cape Horn.

"The anticipation of getting to the Cape was great," recalled Pinkney. "I had in my mind exactly when I was going to arrive. But the weather was getting bad, and my radar went out. I wanted to pass close enough to be able to see the light; it's only visible for about five or six miles. But, because I lost my radar, I couldn't figure my distance, so I kept a general track in an area that would keep me well off. If I wasn't careful, the weather would have blown me up on the Cape."

Pinkney didn't see the Cape Horn light, but he did glimpse the Cape the next morning. "I was exhilarated," Pinkney recalled. "I had completed my mission—I had passed all five capes."

Later Pinkney entered the moment in his journal. "The dream is fulfilled," he wrote. "Not without pain, fear, depression, and anger. But also with love, faith, determination, and humor. I only caught a glimpse of the great 'Rock,' but it will stay in my mind forever."

Presenting
Remembering the Trip

Sailing swiftly north from Cape Horn, Pinkney finished his trip about four months later. He arrived in Chicago to a hometown welcome in June 1992. Pinkney was the first African American to sail solo around the five capes.

"When I started this trip, the object was to finish, and there were days when I would have liked to quit. But I knew that I owed it to myself to stick to my commitment, because once I had done it, no one could ever take the accomplishment away from me."

Thanks to his journal, Pinkney would never lose his life's greatest adventure. "Every time you read your journal you get to do the good things all over again," Pinkney said.

Examining Writing in the Real World

Analyzing the Media Connection

Discuss these questions about the journal entries on page 4.

1. Why do you think Pinkney starts his journal entries by giving the date and his location at sea?
2. Why do you think Pinkney mentions the weather in both of his journal entries?
3. What kind of factual information does Pinkney record? Why do you suppose he includes this information?
4. What feelings does Pinkney express in his journal entries? Why do you think he writes about his feelings in his journal?
5. What things could Pinkney record more effectively in a personal journal than in a videotape?

Analyzing A Writer's Process

Discuss these questions about Bill Pinkney's writing process.

1. What two methods did Pinkney use to record his experiences during his long voyage? Why did he record them?
2. Where on the boat did Pinkney usually go to write in his journal? In what ways might it help a person to keep a journal-writing routine?

3. In his journal, Pinkney recorded both ordinary days as well as high points. What was the advantage of describing both?
4. Why do you think Pinkney didn't revise or edit his journal?
5. What value does Pinkney say the journal is to him now that his trip is over?

Pinkney uses specific nouns to create clear pictures. In this example, he specifies what kind of sail (the main sail) and what part of the boat he adjusted (the headboard).

*I lowered the **main sail** and set about restrapping the **headboard.***

In each sentence below, replace two nouns or pronouns with more specific nouns. (You may need to make other changes too.)

1. They went to the museum in a vehicle.
2. Plants lined the way to the building.
3. Inside, a woman helped them find places.
4. The adults liked an exhibit on weather.
5. The others liked the exhibits about animals the best.

See Lesson 9.1, page 319.

Writing as Self-Expression

Your personal writing expresses the real you. Through personal writing, you can look at yourself, share your feelings with others, or explore your ideas.

You can show any side of yourself in your personal writing, just as you can among friends. Sometimes you might write just for yourself. At other times you might decide to share your writing with others.

Personal writing can also be a way to look at yourself on paper. As the model below shows, novelist Terry McMillan discovered that writing a poem could cheer her up.

Literature Model

I did not sit down and say, "I'm going to write a poem about this." It was more like magic. I didn't even know I was writing a poem until I had written it. Afterward, I felt lighter, as if something had happened to lessen the pain. And when I read this "thing" I was shocked because I didn't know where the words came from. I was scared, to say the least, about what I had just experienced, because I didn't understand what had happened.

Terry McMillan, *Breaking Ice*

Write to Express Your Point of View

Sometimes personal writing can sound like talking to your best friend. When you write about your own experiences, ideas, and interests, just let your ideas come out naturally, as they do in a conversation. Here's one example.

How does Angie make her writing sound friendly?

What details does Angie use to create lively pictures for Sara?

AQUARIUM

Dear Sara,
Wow! My dad took me to see the aquarium today. One of the fish tanks there was so huge it could probably hold a whale. The best part was when a scuba diver fed the tropical fish. They glowed like neon lights—electric blue, lime green, and dazzling gold. The colors were amazing.
— Angie

ADDRESS

Like spending a night in the woods, personal writing can be an adventure. It can be a way of exploring the world around you. Best of all, writing can help you explore your own thoughts and feelings.

Freewrite to Explore Ideas

One of the easiest ways to express yourself in writing is through freewriting. When you freewrite, you explore your thoughts on paper. You don't have to worry about punctuation, spelling, or even making sense. You just start writing—and keep writing, nonstop, for a few minutes. See where your thoughts lead you.

Ideas for freewriting can come from almost anywhere—games, movies, people, or your favorite activity after school. Take a look at the student model to the right. Can you tell what got this student started freewriting?

TIME

For more about exploring ideas, see **TIME Facing the Blank Page,** page 92.

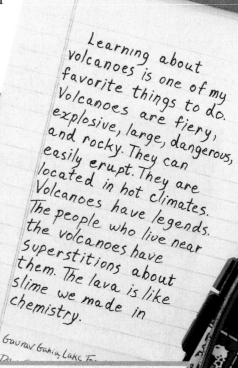

Learning about volcanoes is one of my favorite things to do. Volcanoes are fiery, explosive, large, dangerous, and rocky. They can easily erupt. They are located in hot climates. Volcanoes have legends. The people who live near the volcanoes have superstitions about them. The lava is like slime we made in chemistry.

Gaurav Gahir, Lake Fr...

Journal Writing

Think back on something that happened to you today. Freewrite about it for five minutes. When you finish, look back over your writing. What ideas from your freewriting could you write more about?

Write a Personal Response

Look through this book to find a painting that has people in it. What activities do you see the people doing? Freewrite for five minutes about whatever comes into your mind when you look at the painting.

PURPOSE To express personal thoughts and feelings

AUDIENCE Yourself

LENGTH Write for five minutes

WRITING RUBRICS To freewrite effectively, you should

- write what you see
- write what you think and feel
- use words that create specific images

Cross-Curricular Activity

GEOGRAPHY Pick a place on the globe that you've visited or would like to visit. Do some research on that place. Write a postcard or letter to a friend; describe your real or imaginary adventures there. Try to give a specific feeling of what the place is like.

Listening and Speaking

What is your favorite place in your own community? Tell your classmates about that place and why you like it. If you wish, you can write out what you plan to say before you give your presentation.

Replace nouns with the correct forms of pronouns in your writing.

*The best part was . . . the tropical fish. **They** [the fish] glowed . . . .*

Rewrite the sentences below, replacing the underlined words with pronouns.

1. <u>Jeff and I</u> went to the aquarium.
2. We looked at <u>the tropical fish</u>.
3. <u>The fish</u> were in huge tanks.
4. <u>Jeff</u> has his own tropical fish.
5. The fish were a present to <u>Jeff</u>.

See Lesson 11.1, page 361, and Lesson 11.2, page 363.

LESSON
1.2

Writing with Confidence

A personal journal is meant just for you. You may choose to share it, however. Journal writing doesn't need to be formal. What is important is putting your thoughts on paper.

Like anything else you learn to do, writing seems more natural the more you do it. The more you write, the more confident you'll feel.

One way to build your writing confidence is to keep a personal journal. A journal is usually a notebook or a binder in which you write regularly. It is a place for you to write whatever you want. Look at the journal below. What kinds of things does this writer put in a journal?

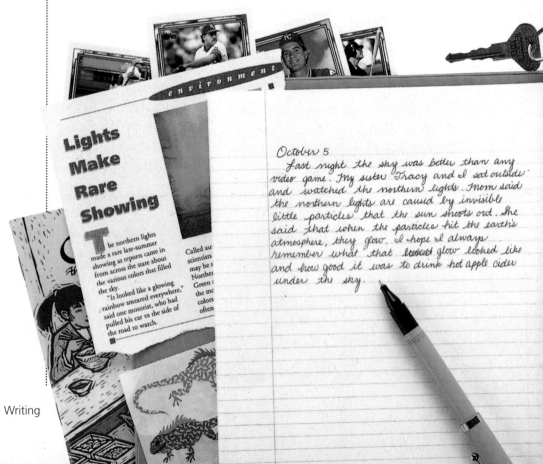

Lights Make Rare Showing

The northern lights made a rare late-summer showing as reports came in from across the state about the various colors that filled the sky.

"It looked like a glowing rainbow smeared everywhere," said one motorist, who had pulled his car to the side of the road to watch.

Called au... scientists may be s... Norther... Green ... the mc... colors... often ...

October 5

Last night the sky was better than any video game. My sister Tracy and I sat outside and watched the northern lights. Mom said the northern lights are caused by invisible little particles that the sun shoots out. She said that when the particles hit the earth's atmosphere, they glow. I hope I always remember what that glow looked like and how good it was to drink hot apple cider under the sky.

Keep a Journal

Your journal is a place where you can take risks with your writing. You might jot down notes about daily events, write poems, or just doodle. You might use your journal to collect things like photos, newspaper clippings, or ticket stubs. You can write about new and different ideas, personal feelings, and special memories. Sometimes you might invite others to share your thoughts and feelings. Here are a few suggestions on keeping a journal:

- Use a notebook or binder that you enjoy writing in.
- Write regularly, even if only for 10 minutes a day.
- Date each entry. Dates can help you find specific entries later.
- Write about whatever you want. Your journal is a place to think freely. Nobody is going to grade you on what you say or how you say it.

Journal Writing

Write down some ideas for things you could write about in a personal journal. They could be an activity you take part in, an experience you have had, or an idea you're thinking about. Remember, you can write about anything that is important to you.

Use a Journal to Help You Study

You can use a type of journal called a learning log to help you study. A learning log is a place to write about what you are studying. It's just for you; no one else will read it.

Learning Log	
Purpose	**Entry**
Summarize.	After Herbert Hoover won the 1928 election, there were signs of economic problems. In 1929, the stock market crashed, marking the beginning of the Great Depression.
Highlight main ideas.	During this time, Americans were going too deeply into debt.
Define problems.	I still don't understand how the economy and the stock market are related.
Ask questions.	Why didn't anyone see the signs and do something before the market crashed?

What did you mean when you wrote, "Last night the sky was better than any video game"?

I was trying to describe what it felt like to watch the northern lights. The way the colors flickered across the sky, it seemed to be raining fire.

Write a Journal Entry

Think about all of the things that happened to you yesterday. Write a journal entry for that day. It might be an entry for a personal journal or a learning log entry.

PURPOSE To explore ideas through journal writing

AUDIENCE Yourself

LENGTH 2–4 paragraphs

WRITING RUBRICS To write an effective journal entry, you should

- write the date for the journal entry
- write about whatever you want
- use your own words

Using Computers

You may wish to keep your personal journal or your learning log on a computer. Many computer programs allow you to set up secured files. You can open secured files only with a secret password. Putting your journal entries in a secured file saves them "for your eyes only."

Viewing and Representing

Pick one of your own journal entries that you especially like. Find an image in a magazine that would make a good illustration for this entry. Show that image to your classmates and explain how the image matches your entry.

Grammar Link

Use forms of *good* correctly in your writing.

Use *good, better,* or *best* to complete each sentence below.

1. Our soccer team is having a _____ year.
2. Of the three players, Jan is the _____ goalie.
3. I am quite _____ at defense.
4. Les is _____ than I am at long kicks.
5. The coach thinks we will do _____ than we did last season.
6. Saturday we play the _____ team in the league.
7. We hope to play _____ than we did last week.
8. Rosa is our _____ scorer.
9. Mr. Chen does a _____ job coaching the team.
10. We hope to end up with the _____ record in the league.

See Lesson 12.3, page 383, and Lesson 12.4, page 385.

Making Personal Connections

*W*hen you write a personal letter, you make a connection. You can tell what you are doing or share your thoughts and feelings. Whether you write a short note or a long letter, what you write should sound like you.

A personal letter is like a gift that lasts a long time. You can hold, reread, and keep a letter. It's not like a telephone call, where the words are gone when you hang up.

In the model below a boy is writing to share his delight about getting a new dog. The boy's name is Carl Davis III, and he's a character in a book by Rosa Guy.

Literature Model

S pots belongs to me! I'm bringing him home! You'll love him. Never in your life have you seen a dog so devoted, so intelligent. How lucky I am. To be seeing my mother, my father, my friend Selena, soon, and to have my very own dog, and to be able to visit Grandma whenever I wish. . . . My life just keeps opening and opening and opening. What a wonderful life.

Rosa Guy
The Ups and Downs of Carl Davis III

Write to Keep in Touch

The writing you send to friends and family can take many forms. You can send thank-you letters, get-well cards, or notes of apology. You can talk about things that interest you. You can ask questions. You can tell your experiences, thoughts, and feelings. Writing a letter is a special way to let other people know what you're doing. Also, if you send a letter, you might get one in return.

Read what one writer included in a letter to his grandfather.

Dear Grandpa,

Are you ready for a surprise? I just started saxophone lessons. I'm going to play you a song when I come visit. Right now my cheeks hurt from practicing so much. Sometimes the only sound I can make is a honk. It sounds like a weird bird. Unfortunately, it's really loud, but I'm working on that. I can't wait to see you.

Marvin

How does Marvin make his letter sound like a conversation?

What kinds of things does Marvin talk about that make his letter friendly?

Journal Writing

Think of a friend to whom you could write a letter. List some activities that both you and your friend enjoy. List some things that you've done lately that you'd like to share with your friend.

Write a Friendly Letter

Getting a letter is like getting a surprise package. It's fun to find out what's inside. Whatever the letter says, it will probably have five main parts: the heading, the greeting, the body, the closing, and the signature.

Look at the letter below. At the top is the heading, which includes the date and usually the writer's address. Next you'll see the greeting, a way of saying hello. Then comes the body, where the writer tells whatever he or she wants to say. Finally, the writer says good-by with a closing such as *Your friend, Love,* or *Sincerely,* and then signs his or her name. No matter what a letter looks like, it's the thoughts and feelings that go into it that are the most important.

Heading

Greeting

Body

Closing

Signature

36 South Drive
Detroit, MI 44444
June 20

Dear Narvin,
Thanks for your letter. I'll have to polish up my old horn for your visit. You might not know this, but I once played for eight straight hours in a traveling bandwagon. After that I couldn't play the whole next day because my cheeks were so sore. I had to sit and suck on "ice cubes," and I'll bet if I had tried to play, I would've sounded like a weird bird, too. Don't worry. It gets easier. I'll show you when you come visit. Don't forget to pack your horn.

Love,
Grandpa

Write a Friendly Letter

Write a brief letter to a friend or relative about something that has happened to you recently.

PURPOSE To share thoughts and feelings

AUDIENCE A friend or relative

LENGTH 2–3 paragraphs

WRITING RUBRICS To write an effective friendly letter, you should

- clearly describe what happened and your feelings about it
- include the five main parts of a friendly letter

Listening and Speaking

Find an issue that you feel strongly about. Write down all of your feelings on the issue and give a speech about it.

Using Computers

You might compose your letter on a computer. After you write the letter, reread and change it until it suits you. If your computer has a spell checker, use it to find any misspellings. Then print out the letter.

Grammar Link

Use clear punctuation and capitalization in letters.

Look at each section of the letter from Marvin's grandfather. Then correct the capitalization and punctuation in the friendly letter below. The letter contains 11 errors.

621 Norton avenue
portland OR 97216
September 18 2001
Dear aunt Lisa
I have just found out that we are going to Boulder, colorado, during the winter vacation. Father says I can bring my best friend, Sung. She will be good company raul will be in school and can't come with us. Maybe we can visit you. Will you be home then. I'll send more details as soon as we're sure of our plans.

Love
Maria

See Lesson 8.6, page 307; 18.1, page 473; Lesson 18.3, page 477; Lesson 19.1, page 489; Lesson 19.3, page 493; and Lesson 19.4, page 495.

Spelling Hints

As you revise your friendly letter, remember that if a word ends with a silent *e* and you want to add a suffix that begins with a vowel (such as *-ing*) you drop the *e*. Examples: *write/writing; hope/hoping*.

Personal Writing

WRITING ABOUT LITERATURE

Responding to a Poem

*P*oems are a way of sharing experiences and feelings. You can read poems, and you can write them. All you need is an idea or feeling to get started.

William Carlos Williams wrote the poem below. In addition to being a poet, he was a doctor. Frequently, he turned everyday experiences into poems.

Literature Model

This Is Just to Say

I have eaten
the plums
that were in
the icebox

and which
you were probably
saving
for breakfast

Forgive me
they were delicious
so sweet
and so cold

William Carlos Williams

Jot down your thoughts about the poem. How would you feel if you received it? Did it make you think of eating plums? What did it make you want to do?

Start with a Poem

One way of responding to a poem is to write. You might write your ideas about the poem in your journal or learning log. In the journal entry below, one student tells how Williams's poem made her feel.

> When I read the poem, I felt like I had actually taken some plums that weren't mine out of the icebox. I have never done that, but I could almost feel what it was like to take something out of the icebox.
>
> Once I stole one of my brother's cookies. He hadn't seen me, but he was so little that I felt bad. I apologized and he said he understood.
>
> Jenny Jeep, O'Plaine Elementary School
> Gurnee, Illinois

Another way to respond to a poem is to draw a picture. The student who drew this was inspired by the poet's description of the plums.

Journal Writing

Reread the notes you jotted down after reading "This Is Just to Say." Think about how you would respond. Would you write something, or would you draw a picture? Write or draw your response.

Respond with a Poem

Another good way to respond to a poem is to write a poem of your own. You might write about the same idea as in the poem you read. You could also write about a different idea.

Read the two poems below. What idea in Williams's poem do you think Shayne Bell is responding to? What different idea is Kim Myers writing about? What similarities or differences can you find between Kim's and Shayne's responses?

How does Shayne help her readers to understand what the plums taste like?

Can you tell how these two poems are similar?

For what I have done,
I will go out and find
the best plums in town.
I will even grow the plums
        that will be as sweet as candy,
that will be sweeter and more delicious.
There will be enough for you to have
at least 10 a day for a year,
to tell you I'm so sorry I ate your plums.

Shayne Bell,
Wauconda Junior High,
Wauconda, Illinois

I'm Sorry

I didn't mean
    to make you mad.
I didn't mean
    to hurt you.

I was just angry
    that was all.
I said some things
    I didn't mean.

Please forgive me.
    Let's not fight.
The fight was not important.

Kim Myers,
Westfield School,
Winthrop Harbor, Illinois

Poets often divide poems into sections called stanzas. Kim's poem has three stanzas, just like the poem on page 20.

Write a Poem

Reread the poem by Kim Myers on page 22.

Then write your own poem in response to Myers's poem.

PURPOSE To respond to a poem with a poem of your own

AUDIENCE Students your age

LENGTH 10 or more lines

WRITING RUBRICS To write an effective poetic response to Myers's poem, you should

- make notes on your ideas about the poem
- make notes on how the poem makes you feel

Cross-Curricular Activity

ARCHITECTURE Observe a house or building near where you live. Take notes on it, going into as much detail as possible. Is the building inviting? Or is it unappealing? Later, turn your notes into a two-paragraph description, using concrete facts to support your opinion.

Grammar Link

Use specific adjectives to create strong, clear images.

In one of her poems, Kim Myers uses the specific adjectives *sweet* and *delicious*.

Add at least one specific adjective to each sentence below.

1. I ate an orange yesterday.
2. I found it in a basket on the table.
3. I peeled the skin.
4. I chewed up each section.
5. Then I wiped my hands and face.

See Lesson 12.1, page 379.

Viewing and Representing

Everybody's interpretation of art is different. Choose a painting in this book. What do you think is happening in the painting? Describe the work in two paragraphs, supporting your interpretation with details and examples.

Pieter Brueghel the Elder, *Hunters in the Snow*, 1565

Writing Process in Action

Personal Writing

In preceding lessons you've learned about various kinds of personal writing. You've expressed your own ideas and feelings in journal entries and personal letters. You've also had the chance to write your responses to poems. Now it's time to make use of what you've learned. In this lesson you're invited to write about a day that became special in your life.

Assignment

Context

You have decided to submit your writing to *Up, Up, and Away*. This is a magazine that publishes student writing about special days, new experiences, or new feelings.

Purpose

To write a brief account of a special day or event in your life

Audience

The readers of *Up, Up, and Away*, ages 10–15

Length

1 page

Visit the *Writer's Choice* Web site at **writerschoice.glencoe.com** for additional writing prompts.

The following pages can help you plan and write your account. Read through them and then refer to them as you need to. Don't feel limited by them, however. You are in charge of your own writing process.

Prewriting

Sometimes keying in on a few single words can help you focus your prewriting thoughts. For example, think of the words *usually, often,* and *always.* Those are words that describe every-day events. Now think of words like *once, seldom,* and *never.* Such words can help you identify the special day or experience that will make a good writing topic. The options graphic at the right will help you with these early, important steps.

Look at page 10 for suggestions on freewriting. Your goal is to choose a topic that fits the assignment and has meaning for you.

Option A
Explore your journal.

Option B
Brainstorm with a friend.

Option C
Freewrite for ideas.

The first time I ever went camping real camping in real woods, far away from streets and sidewalks. All the sounds were new. The intense, black night. What would sleep be like under the stars?

Drafting

As you go over your prewriting notes, think about the specific words and images that will make your readers aware of the special nature of your topic. For example, Yoshiko Uchida writes of riding through vineyards on her first visit to a farm—a wondrous experience for a city girl. Notice the language she uses to give the sense of discovering a new world.

Literature Model

I could hear crickets singing and frogs croaking and all the other gentle night sounds of the country. I felt as though I were in another more immense, never-ending world, and wished I could keep riding forever to the ends of the earth.

Yoshiko Uchida, *The Invisible Thread*

Writing Process in Action

Drafting Tip

For help with getting a flow of your ideas down on paper, see Lesson 2.4, pages 54–57.

Revising Tip

For help with revising your writing, see Lesson 2.5, pages 58–61.

You can bring the same kind of amazement to your own writing if you keep your experience and feelings focused. What made this day important to you?

When you're ready to start your draft, take a deep breath and relax. The most important thing about drafting is to get your ideas down on paper. You can always change things later.

Revising

To begin revising, read over your draft to make sure that what you have written fits your purpose and your audience. Then have a **writing conference.** Read your draft to a partner or small group. Use your audience's reactions to help you evaluate your work.

Question A
Is my writing clear?

Question B
Does the writing sound like me?

Question C
Have I made effective use of details?

The darkness in the forest was ~~amazing~~ awesome. Stars blinked brightly overhead. My aunt and uncle kidded me about and getting lost like some city kid wandering off too far from the camp.

I didn't think I would like the freeze-dried food we had brought along. It was some kind of stew, made by mixing water and these foil envelopes of powder. My uncle cooked it over a portable gas stove. and it looked kind of gross You can't make a fire at this national park.

Editing/Proofreading

At the editing stage you put the finishing touches on your writing. A careful editing job shows your readers that you care about your work and don't want any errors to distract them from your ideas.

The checklist at the right will help you edit your writing. Usually writers **proofread** for only one kind of error at a time. Using this method means that you will read through your work several times, looking for only one kind of error each time.

Publishing/Presenting

Maybe your class wants to make its own special edition of *Up, Up, and Away.* This would give you the chance to have other students read your writing. Likewise, you would have the chance to see how other students tackled this assignment.

Of course, you may not feel ready to share your work with anyone other than your teacher. That's OK. There is some risk involved in sharing with a wider audience. You decide what's best for you.

Editing/Proofreading Checklist

1. Have I used specific nouns and adjectives to create good images?
2. Have I used pronouns correctly?
3. Have I used forms of "good" correctly?
4. Are all sentences complete?
5. Have I used standard spelling, capitalization, and punctuation?

Proofreading Tip

For proofreading symbols, see page 72.

Journal Writing

Reflect on your writing process experience. Answer these questions in your journal: What do you like best about the personal account you wrote? What was the hardest part of writing it? What did you learn in your writing conference? What new things have you learned as a writer?

Literature Model

Yoshiko Uchida

from

The Invisible Thread

In her autobiography, The Invisible Thread, *Yoshiko Uchida focuses on the personal discoveries she made about people and places while growing up. As this passage opens, Uchida and her family are driving off for their first visit to a farm. As you read, note the personal details that the author uses to make her writing clear and appealing to her readers. Then try the activities in Linking Writing and Literature on page 34.*

As we turned off the main highway, it seemed as though we were driving through a vast ocean of vineyards[1] that spread out on both sides of the dusty road. Before long we could see the Okubo waterpump windmill sprouting up among the grapevines.

"There it is!" Keiko shouted. "There's the Okubo farm!"

She reminded Papa of his earlier promise and convinced him there was nothing on the deserted road that she could possibly hit. Papa knew he would never hear the end of it if he didn't give her a chance, so he stopped the car.

---

1 **vineyards** (vin′ yərdz) fields planted with grapevines

Keiko was in heaven as Papa let her slide over behind the wheel. But poor Mama was clutching my arm again.

"Careful, Kei Chan," she cautioned. "Be careful."

Keiko started slowly, like a tired turtle. But by the time she made the final turn toward the farm, she was feeling confident and picking up a little speed.

"Honk the horn to let them know we're here," Papa said.

> " . . . Keiko not only honked the horn, but simultaneously crashed into Jick's dog house. . . ."

At which point Keiko not only honked the horn, but simultaneously[2] crashed into Jick's dog house, knocked it over on its side, and stopped just inches short of the walnut tree.

"Look out, for heaven's sake," we all shouted. "Look out!"

Jick barked furiously at the sudden assault[3] on his territory, and the chickens scrambled in every direction, screeching and cackling as though the end of the world had come.

The startled Okubos rushed from their house, blinking in the sun, surveying with alarm what only moments before had been their peaceful yard.

"We're here!" Keiko shouted, as if they needed to be told. "We're here!"

Because the Okubos' two grown daughters had already left home, they welcomed my sister and me as though we were their grandchildren, and we called them Oji San (uncle) and Oba San (auntie).

Oji San gave us a quick tour of the farm. He showed us how to pump water from the well and put our heads down to gulp the cold water that came gushing out. He pointed to the outhouse, saying, "I guess you've never used one of those before." We certainly hadn't. Whenever I had to use it, I held my breath and got out as fast as I could.

He also let us look for eggs in the henhouse, and took us to the barn where we staggered about in the hayloft, trying to pitch hay with forks that were bigger than we were.

He saved the best for last, taking us to a fenced enclosure where two dusty mules ambled over to greet us.

"Meet Tom and Jerry," he said. Then pulling some scraggly weeds by the fence, he told us to feed them to the mules.

---

2 **simultaneously** (sī′ məl tā′ nē əs lē) occurring at the same time
3 **assault** (ə sôlt′) a violent attack

Paul Cézanne, *Farmhouse and Chestnut Trees at Jas-de-Bouffan*, c. 1885

I thrust some weeds at them and the mules grabbed them hungrily, showing their enormous yellow teeth. They seemed friendly enough, but I was rather glad they were on the other side of the fence.

"They like you," Oji San said. "Maybe they'll do something nice for you later on."

"Like what, Oji San?"

Oji San just grinned and smashed his felt hat down over his forehead. "You'll see," he said. "Wait and see."

Sitting on mats spread out under the walnut tree, we had a wonderful picnic supper of soy-drenched chicken and corn grilled over an out-door pit. There were rice balls, too, sprinkled with black sesame[4] seeds that looked like tiny ants.

Oji San waited until the sun had dipped down behind the dusty grapevines and a soft dusky haze settled in the air. Then he announced he was taking us all on a moonlight ride through the vineyards. It was more than we'd ever hoped for.

Keiko took her usual place up front by Oji San, hoping for a brief chance at the reins. Mama and Papa chatted quietly with Oba San, and I lay stretched out in back, looking up at the enormous night sky.

There seemed to be millions and billions of stars up there. More than I'd ever imagined existed in the

> **" It was as though the entire sky had dropped closer to earth to spread out its full glory. . . . "**

universe. They seemed brighter and closer than they were in Berkeley. It was as though the entire sky had dropped closer to earth to spread out its full glory right there in front of me.

I listened to the slow *clop-clop* of the mules as they plodded through the fields, probably wondering why they were pulling a wagonload of people in the dark, instead of hauling boxes of grapes to the shed under the hot, dry sun.

I could hear crickets singing and frogs croaking and all the other gentle night sounds of the country. I felt as though I were in another more immense,[5] never-ending world, and wished I could keep riding forever to the ends of the earth.

When we got back to the farm, it was time for an outdoor Japanese bath. Oji San built a fire under a

---

4 **sesame** (ses′ ə mē) an Asian plant whose seeds are used for food and oil
5 **immense** (i mens′) without limits; vast

square tin tub filled with water, banking[6] the fire when the water was hot and inserting a wooden float so

---

6 **banking** (bangk′ ing) partially covering a fire with ashes so that it will burn more slowly and for a longer period of time

we wouldn't burn our feet or backsides when we got in.

Oba San hung some sheets on ropes strung around the tub and called out, "*Sah, ofuro!* Come, Kei Chan, Yo Chan. The bath is ready. You girls go first."

Mama gave us careful instructions about proper bathing procedures.

Helen Oji, *Libellule (Memory of My Father)*, 1980

"Wash and rinse yourselves outside before you get into the tub," she reminded us. "And keep the water clean."

> **" As always,
> Keiko was fearless. "**

When we were ready to climb in, I saw steam rising from the water and was afraid I'd be boiled alive. "You go first," I told my sister.

As always, Keiko was fearless. She jumped right in and sank down in the steaming water up to her neck.

"Ooooooh, this feels wonderful!" she said.

I quickly squeezed in next to her, and we let the warm water gurgle up to our chins.

Keiko looked up at the glorious night sky and sighed, "I could stay here forever."

Literature Model

Linking Writing and Literature

 Collect Your Thoughts

Keiko and her sister had never visited a farm before. How do they react? What do they find to be most interesting or memorable? Jot some ideas in your notebook.

 ## Talk About Reading

Discuss the excerpt from *The Invisible Thread* with a group of your classmates. Select one person to lead the discussion and another to take notes. Use the following questions to focus the discussion.

1. **Connect to Your Life** Think about the first time you went someplace special you had never been to before—for example, an art museum or a wild animal park. What do you remember seeing, thinking, and doing that made the visit memorable? Make some notes in your journal about the experience and what it meant to you.

2. **Critical Thinking: Infer** What do you learn about Keiko's character while the family is driving to the farm? How do you know?

3. **6+1 Trait®: Conventions** The excerpt includes a lot of dialogue. What punctuation does the author use to signal dialogue? How do you know when the speaker has changed?

4. **Connect to Your Writing** How does the author's use of dialogue make the characters seem more real?

 ## Write About Reading

Personal Narrative Write a personal narrative describing the first time you and others went to a memorable place. Explain what you found there that made the visit so special. Include dialogue in your narrative.

Focus on Conventions Use appropriate grammar, usage, and mechanics (spelling and punctuation) as you write. Pay special attention to the way you punctuate dialogue in your narrative.

For more information on writing conventions and the 6+1 Trait® model, see **Writing and Research Handbook,** pages 682–684.

6+1 Trait® is a registered trademark of Northwest Regional Educational Laboratory, which does not endorse this product.

Reflecting on the Unit

Summarize what you learned in this unit by answering the following questions.

❶ What are some ways to express your ideas and feelings through personal writing?

❷ How does writing in a personal journal build confidence in your writing skills?

❸ How can a learning log help you make sense of what you study?

❹ What are some important things to remember about writing a friendly letter?

❺ How can you express personal feelings in response to a poem?

Adding to Your Portfolio

Choose a selection for your portfolio.

Look over the personal writing you did during this unit. Select a completed piece of writing to put into your portfolio. The piece you choose should show some or all of the following characteristics:

- grows out of a freewriting idea
- records your personal ideas, experiences, or feelings
- uses specific words that create clear images for your reader
- sounds like you

REFLECT ON YOUR CHOICE. Attach a note to the piece you chose, explaining briefly why you chose it and what you learned from writing it.

SET GOALS. How can you improve your writing?

What skill will you focus on the next time you write?

Writing Across the Curriculum

MAKE A MATHEMATICS CONNECTION. Write down some of your ideas and feelings about mathematics. What do you like most about math? What do you dislike or find difficult? What kinds of math materials do you like to use? What skill or concept would you enjoy teaching to a younger child?

"He listened to the motor, tilting his head from side to side like a parrot, trying to detect any noises that spelled car trouble."

—Francisco Jiménez,
"The Circuit"

The Writing Process

Writing in the Real World: *Curtis Katz*   *38*

Lesson 2.1   **Exploring the Writing Process**   *42*

Lesson 2.2   **Prewriting: Finding a Topic**   *46*

Lesson 2.3   **Prewriting: Ordering Ideas**   *50*

Lesson 2.4   **Drafting: Getting It Down on Paper**   *54*

Lesson 2.5   **Revising: Reviewing Your Ideas**   *58*

Lesson 2.6   **Revising: Getting Paragraphs
into Shape**   *62*

Lesson 2.7   **Revising: Achieving Sentence Fluency** *66*

Lesson 2.8   **Editing/Proofreading:
Checking Details**   *70*

Lesson 2.9   **Publishing/Presenting: Sharing
Your Work**   *74*

Writing Process in Action   *78*

**Literature Model: from *Coast to Coast*
by Betsy Byars**   *82*

Unit 2 Review   *88*

Writing in the Real World

Curtis Katz has always loved trains. Today, his lifelong hobby is part of his job as a coach attendant for Amtrak. As he rides the *Empire Builder,* a train that makes the six-day journey from Chicago to Spokane, Katz tells passengers about the land they see outside the train windows. He has even written a guide for other attendants, so they too can share this information with their riders. The excerpt below is part of an announcement that Katz makes as the *Empire Builder* glides by the Bear Paw Mountains in Montana.

from *The Empire Builder: Scenic and Historic Announcements*

By Curtis Katz

. . . The long trek took its toll on the Nez Percé people, and October of 1877 found them huddled in the mountains you see to the south, with winter weather setting in. By that time the Indians had outdistanced the pursuing General Howard, and Chief Joseph hoped to lead his people over the border into Canada for a rendezvous with Chief Sitting Bull, hardly two days' journey away. But while the Indians regrouped, General Howard sent a telegram to Colonel Nelson Miles, who was stationed to the east of the Indians' location.

Colonel Miles intercepted the Nez Percé in the Bear Paw Mountains. There ensued a fierce three-day battle, at the end of which Chief Joseph, realizing the hopelessness of his situation, surrendered to Colonel Miles. In his speech of surrender, Chief Joseph uttered his most famous quote, "From where the sun now stands, I will fight no more. . . ."

A Writer's Process

Prewriting
Collecting the Ideas

Finding information about the *Empire Builder* route was no problem for Katz. First he collected information from members of the train crew. Carrying a small notebook on all his trips, Katz took notes from conductors and brake operators who lived along the route. He also recorded stories that he heard from passengers.

In addition, Katz did research in books. When he had an overnight stop, he went to used-book shops looking for stories and biographies about people and places in the area. "One thing led to another," he explained. "I'd pick up an out-of-print book. That book contained lists of other books."

Katz also researched facts in railroad magazines, such as *Trains.* As Katz read books and conducted interviews, he recorded the information in his notebook. Eventually, Katz had material on subjects ranging from train robberies to mountain climbing.

Drafting
Writing the Guide

During the week-long breaks between trips, Katz wrote almost constantly. Surrounded by boxes of historical documents, his toy trains, and shelves full of books, he found it easy to get involved in the material. He discovered that in many cases, he had several versions of the same story. So one of the first things he had to do was decide which version to use. Katz explains that he had "to make judgment calls. . . . Sometimes I included several versions."

Katz also had to choose a pattern of organization. He decided to organize his manuscript to follow his route from west to east. Passengers who take the train east to west hear the manuscript in reverse. "I did it kind of straight ahead—from one end of the route to the other," Katz explained. "I wrote each section in the order in which it occurred. It's not like a short story where you write from the middle out. This was strictly written by the way the railroad ran."

As he was drafting, Katz found that he needed to do some additional research to fill in missing facts. He also checked statistics, such as dates and mountain heights.

The drafting process took several weeks. Meanwhile, Katz continued to gather new information during the six-day train trips. To his route folder, he clipped notes and newspaper articles that people gave him.

Revising
Putting the Guide in Final Form

Katz wrote the original manuscript by hand. Then he typed it. He used the typed version to revise, cutting and pasting the manuscript in the order he wanted. Then he combined the typewritten sections with new inserts.

Katz kept his audience in mind as he revised. Since other coach attendants would be learning the announcements, the guide needed to be easy to read. Katz says, "I tried . . . to make things grammatically correct. When you're speaking conversationally, you use phrases. This wouldn't do in a written version."

> 66 *Passengers apparently enjoy being informed about the country that they are passing through. . . . I imagine they find these announcements entertaining and educational, and perhaps such announcements give them a sense of place when in unfamiliar territory.* 99
> —*Curtis Katz*

Editing/Proofreading
Polishing the Manuscript

After retyping all of this material, Katz reread the manuscript. He made corrections in red ink and noted additions in black ink. "Even in the proofreading process," says Katz, "new information came to hand. I couldn't resist adding it."

While proofreading, Katz checked for broad generalizations. He corrected them by adding specific details. Finally, he asked his wife to read the edited manuscript. "She asked me, 'Do you really want to say it that way?'" Katz used his wife's feedback to clarify any parts of the manuscript that were fuzzy or awkward.

Publishing/Presenting
Using the Guide

Katz's manuscript was distributed to his fellow coach attendants. In a cover letter, he encouraged them to have fun with the announcements: "Passengers can always tell the difference between someone reading over the [loudspeaker] and someone speaking ." He also encouraged them to "embellish with your own style and material."

Katz has never stopped working on the guide, continuing to gather stories and update announcements. In his office is a photocopy of the "completed" manuscript. Throughout it, Katz has clipped notes for a later edition.

Examining Writing in the Real World

Analyzing the Media Connection

Discuss these questions about the guide excerpt on page 38.

1. What is the topic of the excerpt from Katz's guide? Why might it interest riders of the *Empire Builder*?

2. What date does Katz mention in the excerpt? What names of historical figures does he provide? Why do you think Katz uses these concrete details?

3. What quotation does Katz use in the excerpt? Explain why you think he used the speaker's exact words, rather than paraphrasing or describing them.

4. What distances and directions does Katz provide in the excerpt? Why might a passenger aboard the train be interested in them?

5. Imagine that you are a passenger on the *Empire Builder*. How would information from the excerpt enhance your trip?

Analyzing a Writer's Process

Discuss these questions about Curtis Katz's writing process.

1. Describe the things Katz did to gather information for his guide. How is your own process of exploring an idea and gathering material like Katz's? How is it different?

2. Did Katz always know exactly what kind of information he was looking for while doing his research? Explain your answer.

3. Did Katz stop researching information when the prewriting stage was done? Why or why not?

4. What kinds of things did Katz surround himself with as he wrote? How did they affect him?

5. What did Katz check for while editing his manuscript? Who helped him in this process? How?

Grammar Link

Use complete sentences in your writing.

Revise each fragment below so that it is a complete sentence.

1. the Lincoln Memorial in Washington, D.C.
2. statue of Abraham Lincoln
3. is a popular tourist attraction
4. the words from the Gettysburg Address
5. the beautiful white building

See Lesson 8.2, page 299.

LESSON
2.1

Exploring the Writing Process

The writing process has five stages: prewriting, drafting, revising, editing/proofreading, and publishing/presenting. Follow this process to create a finished piece of writing.

Maya, a reporter for her school newspaper, was stuck for a topic. While visiting her friend Bernard, Maya watched him cook a pot of gumbo for dinner. She thought that cooking was a topic that might interest other students. She pulled out her notebook and began taking notes.

As soon as Maya got an idea and started taking notes, she had begun the prewriting stage of the writing process.

Begin with Ideas

Most writers take their work through all five of the stages you'll read about here. They often go through some stages more than once. Knowing about each of these stages will be helpful in completing your writing assignment.

PREWRITING Prewriting begins the moment you start to collect ideas. During this stage, writers explore ideas for writing topics. Look at the prewriting notes Maya made as she watched Bernard. Some of her notes are sentence fragments. Notice that she wrote what Bernard did and what she thought. Sometimes she wrote down words Bernard used.

Lots of stages in making gumbo.
Bernard put chicken and sausage into the gumbo. Is there a meatless version?
Whew! Those peppers even smell hot!
Okra—what does it taste like?
Bernard says that in Bantu, an African language, the word for okra is gumbo. Maybe there's a story idea in that.

DRAFTING Drafting involves developing your prewriting notes into connected sentences and paragraphs. During this stage, writers try new ideas and make connections. Sometimes they make some discoveries or even decide to change their topic. That's just part of the adventure of writing.

Journal Writing

What is your family's favorite recipe that has been handed down through the years? What is special about this recipe or food? Jot down ways to turn answers to these questions into a writing topic.

Follow Through

After getting your ideas on paper, you need to make sure they are clear. Look at the follow-through stages.

REVISING The goal of revising is to make your writing clearer and more interesting to your audience. To revise, add or delete information where needed. Read your writing aloud to others to get their reactions. Check to see that sentences and paragraphs fit together.

EDITING/PROOFREADING The object of editing and proofreading is to correct errors in spelling, grammar, and punctuation. To edit, read your draft, watching for mistakes. Use proofreading symbols to mark changes on your draft.

PUBLISHING/PRESENTING Publishing/presenting includes everything from turning work in to your teacher to publishing a class book.

The Writing Process

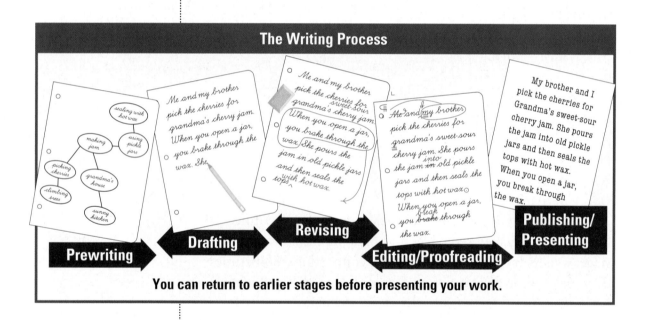

Prewriting → Drafting → Revising → Editing/Proofreading → Publishing/Presenting

You can return to earlier stages before presenting your work.

Write About Your Writing Process

Follow the writing process to write your own paragraph. Describe how you write now and what you might try in the future. For help in organizing your thoughts and for more information on the 6+1 Trait® model, see **Writing and Research Handbook,** pages 679–683.

PURPOSE To describe your own writing process

AUDIENCE Yourself

LENGTH 1 paragraph

WRITING RUBRICS To explore your writing process, you should

- prewrite by making a list of what you do when you write. Organize your list.
- draft a paragraph. Begin with a general statement about what you do when you write.
- revise your paragraph after hearing a peer's comments
- edit and proofread your work

Using Computers

Use a computer to list ideas about your own writing process. Create a table with five columns: one for prewriting, one for drafting, one for revising, one for editing/ proofreading, and one for publishing/ presenting.

Grammar Link

Use correct punctuation at the ends of sentences.

Write each sentence below, ending it with the correct punctuation mark.

1. Have you read the book *The Lion King*
2. How scary parts of it are
3. The book came out after the movie
4. Read me the end of the story
5. Which character did you like best

See Lesson 19.1, page 489.

Listening and Speaking

BRAINSTORMING In a small group, each group member should offer a tip for prewriting. Repeat the process for drafting, revising, editing/proofreading and publishing/presenting. Take notes on helpful ideas. Discuss the writing process. What works for you? How can you help each other with this process?

Prewriting: Finding a Topic

Prewriting techniques can help you explore ideas and pinpoint possible topics that will interest readers. These techniques include listing, questioning, and clustering.

Think About a Topic

Sometimes it is difficult to nail down a topic that interests you. Once you do, you still need to know that your topic will be of interest to your readers.

Before Maya went to Bernard's house, she had struggled to find the right topic for her article. She needed a topic that would catch and hold the attention of her readers. She also wanted a topic she cared about. When people write about topics that truly interest them, that interest energizes the writing. This energy can be felt by the audience.

After her visit with Bernard, Maya knew she was close to pinning down her writing topic. She enjoys cooking, and she thought that others might be interested, too. However, she was not sure. She decided that she needed to do some research to find out if her audience would be as interested in cooking as she was.

Ask Questions

Prewriting techniques can help you explore topics that will interest both you and your readers. Maya combined questioning and listing in her prewriting. She asked herself the following questions:

- What do my friends like to learn about?
- What articles have appeared lately in the school newspaper?
- What things have I done recently?

Maya then took those three questions and made a list to answer each one. Read her notes.

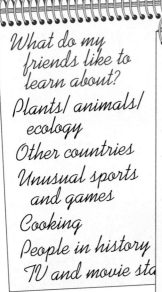

What do my friends like to learn about?
Plants/ animals/ ecology
Other countries
Unusual sports and games
Cooking
People in history
TV and movie sta

What articles have appeared lately in the school newspape
School art show
Interview with the school principal
Plans for fund-raisin carnival
Results of Mr. Chand family-history project

What things have I done recently?
Taught my brother how to dive
Got an A on my science report
Made angel food cake from scratch
Watched Sharon draw a cartoon strip

Journal Writing

Use Maya's lists as an example. Write three questions of your own. Create a list of ideas below each question. Then decide which three ideas might interest you most. Why would you want to write about these ideas? Answer this question in your journal.

Use Cluster Diagrams

When Maya studied her lists, she noticed that some ideas fit together. A few involved collecting things. Others were about her friends' interests. Seeing these connections made Maya decide to write about her friends' hobbies.

Maya further explored her topic, using another prewriting technique called clustering. She began by writing "My Friends' Hobbies" in the center of a piece of paper. Then she drew a circle around the words. As Maya focused on that idea, details popped into her mind. Even though she knew she might not use all the ideas, she wrote them down anyway. She circled each idea, and drew lines to show where the details came from and how they were related.

As her cluster grew, Maya felt more confident about her topic.

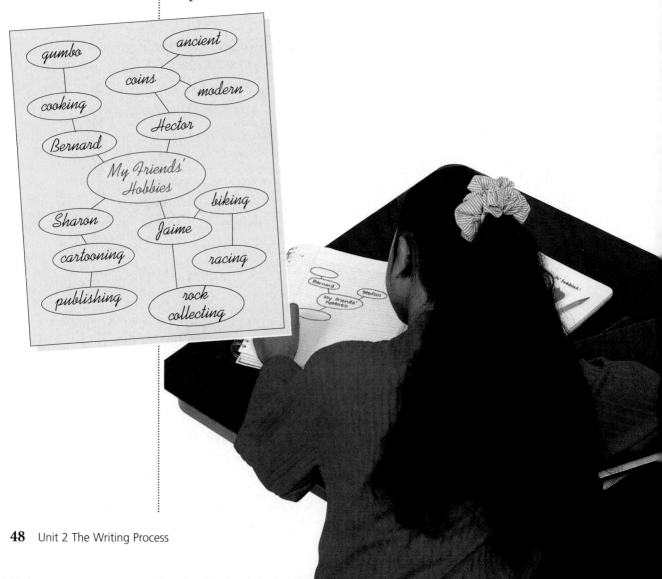

The Writing Process

Explore a Topic

Review the three lists you created for this lesson's Journal Writing. Choose one of your journal ideas that really interests you. Apply prewriting techniques to explore the idea fully. Later in this unit you will develop the topic into a finished piece of writing.

PURPOSE To apply prewriting techniques

AUDIENCE Yourself

LENGTH Lists of varying lengths and a diagram

WRITING RUBRICS To develop a topic, you should

- ask yourself questions about your idea
- use clustering to explore your idea and collect details
- think about why the topic interests you and how you can interest your readers

Using Computers

Consider using a computer drawing program to create your idea cluster. Use the Copy and Paste functions to add circles to your cluster.

Grammar Link

Use possessive nouns correctly in your writing.

Possessive nouns describe ownership and are written with apostrophes.

Mr. Chan's project, or *my friends'* hobbies

Rewrite each sentence, using the correct possessive form of the noun in parentheses.

1. (Sally) hobby is swimming.
2. Sally swims on (Westville) swimming team.
3. Several of her (friends) hobbies also include swimming.
4. Her swim (team) colors are red and blue.
5. Sally's two swim (caps) colors are also red and blue.

See Lesson 9.3, page 323.

Listening and Speaking

COOPERATIVE LEARNING With a small group, choose a topic that interests you. Together, create a cluster diagram to explore the idea and add details to the diagram. Group members should each contribute at least two ideas.

Prewriting: Ordering Ideas

Prewriting notes are much like a collection of baseball cards. These notes need to be ordered so that your readers will understand your message.

Organize Your Ideas

When you write, you can order your ideas in a variety of ways. Knowing your purpose for writing can help you decide what order to use. Most writing has one of four purposes.

- To tell an experience or story
- To describe how something or someone looks or acts
- To explain how something works or how to do something
- To persuade someone of something

Sometimes, one way of organizing works better than others for a certain purpose. For example, if you want to tell a story, you usually put events in the order in which they happened. If you want to convince someone of something, you might put your strongest argument last.

The passage on the opposite page tells about a boy and his mother walking down the street. They're exploring the town where they've just moved. Think about how the author organizes his details so that readers can picture what this town is like.

Literature Model

The first building we had seen when we turned the corner onto State Street was the church. Then we had come to a large house, followed by several stores. Some of the doors were closed, but one was open. There were men inside, talking. The whole next block was one long building. I stared up at all the windows.

David Kherdian, *Root River Run*

How do "first," "then," "followed by," and "next" help you know the order of details?

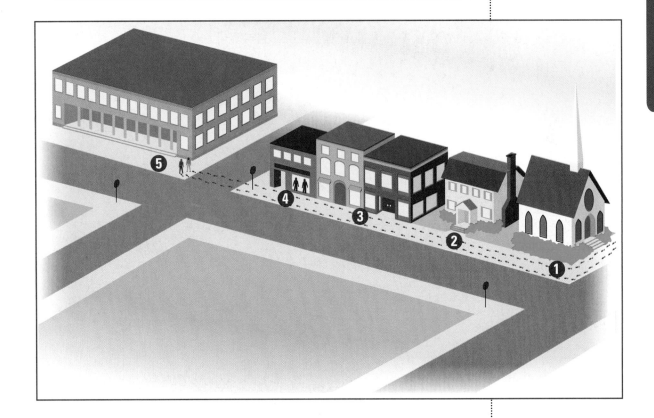

Journal Writing

Look through your journal for an entry that tells a story, describes something, explains something, or persuades someone. Is there a writing purpose you haven't tried yet in your journal? If so, make a list of possible topics for that writing purpose.

Sketch a Plan

Maya looked back at her cluster diagram. Then she chose some of the details and added information to them. To organize her ideas, she made a list. Maya thought about her readers and her purpose for writing. Because she wanted to draw her readers into her article, she reordered her ideas in a way she thought would appeal to the readers. Below, you can see how Maya used her list to order her ideas.

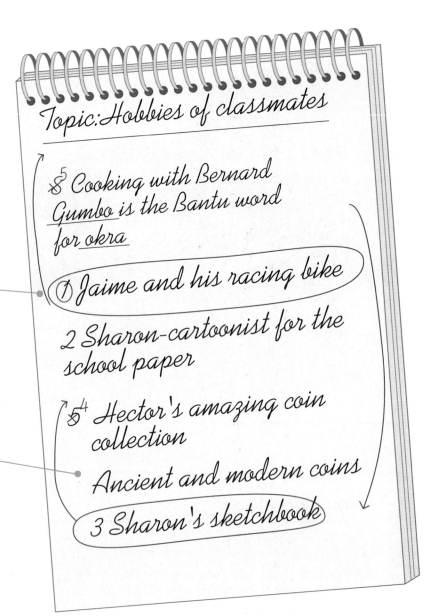

To grab her readers' attention right away, Maya put what she thought was the most interesting hobby first.

This detail sounds interesting. Why didn't Maya list it with a number?

Topic: Hobbies of classmates

~~8~~⁵ Cooking with Bernard
Gumbo is the Bantu word
for okra

① Jaime and his racing bike

2 Sharon-cartoonist for the school paper

~~5~~⁴ Hector's amazing coin collection

Ancient and modern coins

3 Sharon's sketchbook

The Writing Process

Write an Ordered List

Review the cluster diagram that you prepared for your writing topic. Use it to help plan the contents and the structure of your piece of writing.

PURPOSE To order details for writing
AUDIENCE Yourself
LENGTH 1 page

WRITING RUBRICS To plan and structure your writing, you should

- choose details from a cluster diagram and list them
- add information about each detail
- organize the detailed list in the order you think will appeal to your readers

Cross-Curricular Activity

SOCIAL STUDIES Make a cluster diagram to explore a topic from your social studies class. Organize the details that you know about the topic. Check your textbook and other sources for additional details about your topic.

Use past participles correctly in writing.

Past participles must be used with helping verbs.

The first building we **had** *seen . . .*

Rewrite each sentence below using the past participle form of the verb in parentheses.

1. Mr. Akito has (sketch) the scene with charcoal.
2. Earlier he had (make) a watercolor painting.
3. Our art teacher had (tell) us about the artist earlier.
4. We have (look) at much art.
5. What have you (like) best so far?

See Lesson 10.5, page 341.

Viewing and Representing

PLANNING Choose a work of art from this book. Make a cluster diagram with the artwork's title in the circle. Add details to your diagram about what you see. Who or what is in the artwork? What colors does the artist use? How does the work make you feel and why? Number the details in a logical order. Use this order to write a paragraph about the piece of art.

Drafting: Getting It Down on Paper

During drafting, you turn ideas into sentences and paragraphs. When you draft, you just let the words flow. Later you can look for mistakes in grammar or spelling.

Maya couldn't wait to put her prewriting ideas into a first draft. She spread out her latest list, her cluster diagram, and the writing supplies she might need. Then she started to work. Maya thought about some different ways she could organize. She also thought about some things she could say that would make her readers interested right away.

Start the Draft

The act of writing can make you think in new ways. When you begin to write, you may discover new ideas to add to your writing. You may also find that having prewriting notes can help you remember your original ideas and plan.

Maya made those same discoveries as she began to draft her article. Her cluster diagram and numbered list reminded her of the basics. She thought of ways to catch her audience's interest, and she talked to her friends about possibilities. Here's her introduction and part of her second paragraph.

It's time for a Wilson Elementary Wildcats Quiz! Who has attended bike-racing camp in Colorado? Who has boxes full of money in his closet? Whose gumbo can really make your mouth water? Whose name do you see in every edition of the school newspaper? They're all fellow Wildcats, students with some amazing hobbies.

Take Jaime Sánchez, for example. He's been part of a local bike-racing club for two years.

Which details do you recognize from Maya's cluster diagram and numbered list?

How does Maya make her readers want to go on reading the article?

Journal Writing

Look through your journal. Pick out two or three different types of topics. What might be an interesting introduction for each topic? Write your ideas in your journal.

Get Unstuck . . .

Maya got stuck on her introduction. She wasn't sure how to make it interesting. Two things helped. Maya had read that author Betsy Byars often begins writing in the middle of a story idea. So Maya began her draft by writing about Jaime and Sharon. As she wrote, she began to see how she might introduce them.

Maya also talked to her friend Stefan about her article. "Well, nothing makes me as curious as a question does," he told her. His comment helped Maya think of a way to draft her introduction. Maya's draft shows that she wrote her introduction, using the advice from her friend. Most of the introduction, is made up of questions that the rest of her draft will answer.

Sometimes it's hard to keep ideas flowing onto the paper. One or more of the following suggestions may help.

Getting Unstuck

Work on a different part of the piece.

Try other prewriting techniques.

Talk through your writing with a friend.

Take a break.

The Writing Process

Write a Draft

Review the ordered list you prepared about your topic. Use the list to write the first draft of your article or story. For more information on drafting, see **Writing and Research Handbook,** page 681.

PURPOSE To write a first draft
AUDIENCE Yourself
LENGTH 2–3 paragraphs

WRITING RUBRICS To write a draft, you should

- begin by writing an introduction that will catch your readers' attention
- write from your notes and add to them
- if you get stuck, talk with a friend or try a prewriting technique

Grammar Link

Use different kinds of sentences when you write.

Revise each sentence, writing it in the sentence type indicated in parentheses.

1. We will miss the bus. (interrogative)
2. Is everyone ready? (declarative)
3. We would like to go to the zoo. (exclamatory)
4. Will you please wait for me? (imperative)
5. Was this my favorite trip! (declarative)

See Lesson 8.1, page 297.

Cross-Curricular Activity

ART Write about your responses to the picture. What does it remind you of? How does it make you feel?

Tina Dunkley, *Double Dutch Series: Keeping Time,* 1987

Viewing and Representing

SPELLING Make a list of words that describe the girls' actions in *Double Dutch Series: Keeping Time.* Exchange papers with a partner and check each other's spelling.

LESSON
2.5

Revising: Reviewing Your Ideas

The way you think about a piece of writing may change over time. After you've written a draft, you might think of a better way to say something. When you revise, you look for ways to make your draft better or clearer.

Writers aren't the only people who revise their work. While visiting her friend Sharon, Maya watched her study her latest cartoon sketch. Sharon erased a little here and added a little there. Taking a second look helped Sharon make her sketch funnier.

Step Back

When you finish your draft, put it away for a day or two if you can. Then, when you pick it up again, you may see that a point can be restated or that paragraphs can be rearranged.

Questions to Consider

1. Do I keep in mind what my audience knows or needs to know?
2. Do I stick to my topic? If not, why not?
3. Do I give my audience enough information?
4. Do I give my audience too much information?
5. Are the ideas in an order that makes sense?

A good way to check yourself is to ask questions. Read your draft as if you were a member of your audience. Then answer the five questions in the chart above.

The second step of revising is to have a conference to discuss your writing. Maya asked Stefan to comment on her article. His comments helped Maya see her work in a new way.

TIME

For more about knowing your audience, see **TIME Facing the Blank Page,** page 97.

Working with a Peer Reviewer

1. Read your first draft aloud to a partner.

2. Discuss the draft with your partner.

3. Give your peer reviewer an evaluation form to fill out.

Peer Reviewer
Response Sheet

Journal Writing

In your journal, write about some times when you have changed your mind or revised your opinion. What caused the changes?

Make a Mess

Taking a second look at your draft may have given you many new ideas. By asking questions you can decide if you want to make changes. For example, you may discover better ways to direct your writing to your audience. Mark changes on your draft, even if it makes the paper messy. After all, a draft is just a draft; it's not a final copy. Even the draft of the Declaration of Independence became messy when Thomas Jefferson revised it. Maya marked up the draft of her paragraph about Sharon, too.

> Maya deleted these extra details. The phrase "anything else you can imagine" in the next sentence makes them unnecessary.

SOS stands for Sharon Olivia Sanders. Someday you might see the initials SOS in your favorite comic strip. Sharon loves cartooning. She has her own room, which used to belong to her brother. He's away at college now. Sharon can draw animals and spaceships, ~~giraffes, shoes, dinner plates, chairs, fried eggs, toasters, or castles.~~ She can draw anything else you can imagine. Sharon makes cartooning look easy.

She has been drawing pictures since she was three.

DECLARATION OF INDEPENDENCE
In Congress 4th July, 1776.

Revise Your Draft

If possible, put your draft aside for a day or two before you begin this part of the writing process. Reread your first draft carefully. Think about its effectiveness. For more information on revising, see **Writing and Research Handbook,** pages 678–681.

PURPOSE To revise a draft
AUDIENCE Yourself
LENGTH 2–3 paragraphs

WRITING RUBRICS To revise your draft, you should

- ask yourself questions about your draft
- have a partner review and discuss the draft with you
- decide what changes you will make
- make all your changes directly on the first draft

Using Computers

When you are ready to revise, use the Copy or Duplicate function to make copies of your draft. Keep your original unchanged and experiment with changes on the copies. Compare each version with the original. Which version is best? Why?

Grammar Link

Capitalize proper nouns in your writing.

When you write, you often need to capitalize proper nouns that name particular people, places, or things.

Rewrite each sentence below. Use capital letters where needed.

1. We moved from san antonio to houston.
2. Our new home is on saddleback road.
3. My relatives, uncle jack and aunt jessie, live around the corner.
4. I enrolled in a new junior high school, huntington school.
5. My new teacher, mrs. lowery, made me feel welcome.

See Lesson 18.2, page 475 and Lesson 18.3, page 477.

Listening and Speaking

COOPERATIVE LEARNING Work with a partner to discuss the peer review process. Together, make a list of "Do's" and "Don't's" for giving and receiving helpful criticism. Write legibly using cursive writing. Share your list with the class.

The Writing Process

Revising: Getting Paragraphs into Shape

After you have revised your draft, look closely at each paragraph. Be sure each one expresses the main idea in a way that is clear to the reader.

topic sentence

supporting idea

supporting idea

supporting idea

Ask yourself these questions about each paragraph: Does it have a main topic? Does each sentence relate to the topic? Are the sentences in a sensible order? Without realizing it, you think about these questions when you read. When a paragraph is off track or unclear, you notice. The paragraph is difficult to understand. In the model below, how does the writer keep his idea on track?

Literature Model

Which sentence tells what this paragraph is about?

How do the other sentences help make the main idea easy to understand?

You will want several layers of clothing for back-packing. One reason for this is that temperatures can rise or drop several degrees in just a few minutes, particularly in thin mountain air. Stepping from sunlight into shadow can bring a drop of twenty degrees or more. Another reason is that [backpacking] is hard work. Your body will be hot as you hike, but when you stop you will cool off fast.

Richard B. Lyttle
The Complete Beginner's Guide to Backpacking

The Writing Process

Recognize a Paragraph's Shape

Every sentence in a paragraph should have a reason for being there. In Lyttle's paragraph, the main idea is expressed in a topic sentence. Some paragraphs begin with a topic sentence. Others build to a topic sentence that comes at the end.

In a paragraph, all the sentences should work together to develop the main idea in a clear, coherent, way. Lyttle's paragraph on page 62 *begins* with a topic sentence. Other sentences flow from the idea in the topic sentence. Vicki McVey's paragraph below *ends* with a topic sentence. Notice how the topic sentence ties together the sentences that lead to it.

supporting idea

supporting idea

supporting idea

topic sentence

Literature Model

The Pacific Ocean covers almost one third of the earth . . . and there are people who live on tiny islands in the middle of it. They can't see anything from horizon to horizon except water, and yet they set out in canoes for other tiny islands, . . . and get there. These are among the most amazing wayfinders of all time.

Vicki McVey, *The Sierra Club Wayfinding Book*

What do you learn about the people described in this paragraph?

Which sentence is the topic sentence?

Journal Writing

Read a few paragraphs in a library book or textbook, and answer these questions in your journal: Is there a topic sentence that tells the main idea in each paragraph? Where does the topic sentence appear? What do these answers tell you about writing paragraphs?

Shape Up Your Paragraphs

A strong paragraph has a clear main idea even if it does not have a topic sentence. These guidelines can help you find ways to make each paragraph you write stronger. Maya used them to make a few more changes on her draft.

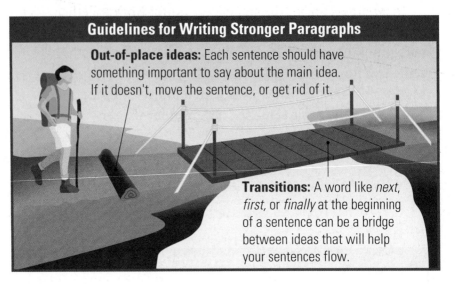

Guidelines for Writing Stronger Paragraphs

Out-of-place ideas: Each sentence should have something important to say about the main idea. If it doesn't, move the sentence, or get rid of it.

Transitions: A word like *next*, *first*, or *finally* at the beginning of a sentence can be a bridge between ideas that will help your sentences flow.

Maya switched the two sentences. She thought the second sentence would work better at the beginning of the paragraph.

Review the guidelines above. Why did Maya take out these two sentences?

Why did Maya change these two sentences?

SOS stands for Sharon Olivia Sanders. Someday you might see the initials SOS in your favorite comic strip. Sharon loves cartooning. She has been drawing pictures since she was three. ~~She has her own room, which used to belong to her brother. He's away at college now.~~ Sharon can draw animals, and spaceships. She can draw anything else you can imagine. Sharon makes cartooning look easy.

Use Strong Paragraphs

Study your draft again. Make each paragraph stronger.

PURPOSE To strengthen paragraphs
AUDIENCE Yourself
LENGTH 2–4 paragraphs

WRITING RUBRICS To make paragraphs stronger, you should

- be sure that each paragraph is about one main idea
- take out any sentence that does not relate to the main idea
- put the ideas in a sensible order
- use transition words

Artist unknown, Navajo, Shiprock rug, c. 1930

Cross-Curricular Activity

ART Look at the photo of a Navajo rug. Write a strong paragraph about what the weaver may have wanted to show. Express your main idea in a topic sentence and support it with details.

Make subjects and verbs agree in sentences with *there.*

Find the subject of each sentence below. Then write the correct form of the verb in parentheses.

1. There (is/are) a new skating rink at the mall.
2. There (is/are) many kids from our class who are good skaters.
3. There (has been/have been) times when the rink was not crowded.

See Lesson 15.2, page 441.

Viewing and Representing

COOPERATIVE LEARNING Find an image in this or another textbook that expresses something about technology in our world. In a small group, share your images. Then discuss how the artist used colors, shapes, figures, or designs.

Revising: Achieving Sentence Fluency

Varying, or changing, the length of sentences can make your writing lively and a pleasure to read. When sentences are the same length, the writing sounds all the same and can be very boring.

In the model below, Marjorie Kinnan Rawlings describes a flock of whooping cranes that seem to be doing a strange dance. Read the paragraph aloud. Does the paragraph have sentence fluency? In other words, do the sentences flow smoothly from one to the other? Think about how sentence length affects the way the sentence sounds.

Literature Model

Would this sentence sound different if it were written as three sentences?

Two stood apart, erect and white, making a strange music that was part cry and part singing. The rhythm was irregular, like the dance. The other birds were in a circle. In the heart of the circle, several moved counter-clock-wise. The musicians made their music. The dancers raised their wings and lifted their feet, first one and then the other. They sunk their heads deep in their snowy breasts, lifted them and sunk again. They moved soundlessly, part awkwardness, part grace. The dance was solemn. Wings fluttered, rising and falling like out-stretched arms.

Marjorie Kinnan Rawlings, *The Yearling*

Write Notes to Yourself

As Maya wrote about her friend Hector Huang, she heard long and short sentences working together to create a pleasing pattern. Maya wanted to be sure that readers would hear this pattern, too.

With her readers in mind, Maya made a plan. She wrote some comments on her draft and put it aside for a day. Read what Maya wrote, and think about how a plan like Maya's might work for you.

Do you agree with Maya's question? How could you avoid repeating these words?

Should I use this word twice?

Too many "Hector's coins" Don't get boring

My friend Hector enjoys biking and canoeing. For his favorite hobby, though, he can stay indoors. You see, Hector is a numismatist. A numismatist is a coin collector. Some of Hector's coins are made of copper. The rest of Hector's coins are made of nickel. They Hector's coins flash white and gold in sunlight. Hector began his collection three years ago when his grandmother gave him a buffalo nickel.

Journal Writing

Choose a paragraph you wrote in a story or an article some time ago, and read it aloud. Listen to the sound of your sentences. Think of ways to improve the sound without changing the meaning of your ideas. In your journal, experiment with different ways of revising your paragraph.

Think About Each Sentence

Maya noticed that her sentences were boring when certain words were repeated again and again. She studied her sentences and decided that she could make her writing smooth by combining some sentences. The point of sentence combining is to join sentences without changing the basic meaning. Combining should help the writing flow more smoothly and sound better.

Another way to make writing more interesting is to vary the beginnings of sentences. Writing also sounds boring if every sentence begins with *I* or *The*. Look at the chart below. How did Maya use these hints to change her writing?

> Notice that changing the repeated words does not change the meaning of the paragraph.

Hints for Sentence Combining
1. Take out repeated words.
2. Use connecting words, such as *and, but,* and *or.*
3. Vary sentence beginnings.

> *Should I use this word twice?*

> *Too many "Hector's coins" Don't get boring*

> How does using a connecting word here make the sentence easier to read?

My friend Hector enjoys biking and canoeing. For his favorite hobby, though, he can stay indoors. You see, Hector is a numismatist. ~~A numismatist is~~ a coin collector. ~~Some of~~ Hector's coins are made of copper. ~~The rest of Hector's coins are made~~ *or* of nickel. *They* ~~Hector's coins~~ flash white and gold in sunlight. Hector began his collection three years ago when his grandmother gave him a buffalo nickel.

The Writing Process

Smooth Out Paragraphs

Improve your draft by revising the sentences within each paragraph.

PURPOSE To improve paragraphs by revising sentences

AUDIENCE Yourself

LENGTH 2–4 paragraphs

WRITING RUBRICS To make your writing more interesting, you should

- vary the length of sentences by combining some of them
- avoid unnecessary repetition
- use connecting words, such as *and*, *but*, and *or*
- vary sentence beginnings

Using Computers

Use a word processing program to compose your paragraph. Write the paragraph's sentences in a list. Check for similar lengths, similar beginnings, and repetitions. Revise your sentences and re-form them into a paragraph.

Viewing and Representing

COOPERATIVE LEARNING Work in a small group to describe a painting in this book. Each member should write one sentence for a group paragraph. Then read your paragraph aloud and revise to improve its flow.

Grammar Link

Combine sentences for smoother paragraphs.

Combine the following pairs of sentences by writing compound subjects or compound verbs. Use the conjunctions in parentheses to combine the sentences.

1. My town is not too big. My town is big enough for me. (but)
2. Colorado has a good baseball team. Cincinnati has a good baseball team. (and)
3. My family can go hiking in the mountains. We can go camping. (or)
4. I like to go to the museum. Ed likes to go to the museum. (and)
5. We ski in winter. We swim in summer. (and)

See Lesson 20.2, page 519.

2.8

Editing/Proofreading: Checking Details

Your writing is not finished until you edit and proofread it. Final checking shows the pride you take in your work.

Checklist

- Check tire pressure
- Oil chain
- Check brakes
- Adjust seat

Maya's friends Jaime and Marta take their biking seriously. Maya watched Jaime and Marta tune up their bikes before a race. Marta showed Maya the checklist they were using. Marta explained that using a checklist gives them confidence during the race. They know they have checked everything and can concentrate on performing well. Maya was surprised. She uses a writing checklist for the same reason.

Polish Your Work

To make sure your sentences are clear, you need to edit your draft. Look for mistakes that might have slipped in. Think about the questions in the checklist on the right. You might want to read the draft one time for each question.

Look at Maya's second paragraph. She used the checklist to edit her draft. For each question she read through her work once. That way, she was more likely to catch errors. Maya will correct errors not covered by this checklist in a later reading.

The Writing Process

Editing/Proofreading Checklist

1. Do I have sentence fragments?
2. Do I have any run-on sentences?
3. Have I used correct punctuation and capitalization?
4. Are my verb forms and tenses correct?

Take Jaime Sánchez for example. He and his sister Marta ~~loves~~ biking. *love* *They both have been* Part of a local bike-racing club for too years. They've even ~~winned~~ *won* some amateur races. This spring, though, Jaime wanted to learn more about racing ~~they~~ *His club* sent him to a four-day racing camp sponsored by the United states Cycling Federation. This was JAime's first trip to Colorado.

Why did Maya change this sentence? Which question on Maya's list covers the problem?

There's more than one way to handle this run-on sentence. How else might you revise it?

Journal Writing

Have you made certain writing mistakes in your papers? In your journal, list questions that can help you catch these mistakes. For more help, see the checklist on page 72.

Use Proofreading Symbols

If you've traveled—by bike, by car, or on foot—you've seen road signs. Some road signs use words to communicate, but many others use pictures. Look at the picture on the left. What does the symbol on the sign tell you?

In a similar way, you can use signs when you edit. The chart below shows a few proof-reading symbols. Use these symbols as you edit your writing. Study both parts of the chart. Then see how Maya used the checklist and the symbols to edit part of her draft.

Proofreading	
Symbols	**Checklist**
∧ insert	**1.** Does each sentence have the right punctuation?
ℒ delete	**2.** Are all words spelled correctly?
⊙ period	**3.** Are possessives and contractions written correctly?
∧ comma	**4.** Are capital letters used as needed?
≡ capital letter	
/ lower-case letter	

Take Jaime Sánchez⌄for example. He and his sister Marta love biking. They both have been part of a local bike-racing club for ~~too~~ ℒ *two* years. They've even won some amateur races. This spring, though, Jaime wanted to learn more about racing⊙His club sent him to a four-day racing camp sponsored by the United states Cycling Federation. This was J_a_ime's first trip to Colorado.

The Writing Process

Edit Your Draft

Review your completed draft. This is the time to put it into finished form. Read it through again, making any changes you want. Then edit carefully, checking for errors.

PURPOSE To apply editing techniques
AUDIENCE Yourself
LENGTH 2–4 paragraphs

WRITING RUBRICS To edit your draft, you should

- make sure forms of verbs and pronouns are correct
- look for mistakes in punctuation, capitalization, and spelling
- look for extra words or words that have been left out
- check for fragments and run-on sentences

Using Computers

Use the grammar checker or spelling checker to check your draft. It's always a good idea to have an extra set of eyes (even electronic ones) looking at your work. Still, the program will not catch everything. Make sure that you edit the draft yourself too.

Grammar Link

Avoid fragments and run-on sentences in your writing.

Edit and rewrite to correct the following sentences. For examples of fragments and run-ons, see Maya's draft on page 71.

1. Lee collects pictures of her favorite singers she has a large collection.
2. She even has some old pictures. Of the Beatles.
3. She goes to many concerts sometimes she gets autographs of the stars.
4. She has lots of pictures in her room it looks great.
5. Lee also has a good collection of tapes. From rock to hip-hop.

See Unit 7 Troubleshooter; and Lessons 8.2, page 299; and 8.6, page 307.

Listening and Speaking

COOPERATIVE LEARNING In a small group, share your ideas about ways that the computer can help you prewrite, draft, revise, edit, and present your work. Use the computer to make a table summarizing your ideas. Post the table in your classroom.

Publishing/Presenting: Sharing Your Work

*T*here are several ways to share your writing. Keep in mind, however, that some writing is private and not meant to be shared.

Maya chose to share her writing in the school newspaper. When she saw her article in print, she was very proud. She ran into her homeroom waving *The Wilson Chronicle*. Her friends were excited to see it, but Maya was the most excited of all.

Plan Your Publishing or Presentation

You can present your writing in many different ways. Each way of presenting requires a different kind of final copy. Your teacher might want your name, the date, and the paper's title in the upper-right corner of your paper. A school newspaper might require that the final copy be typed with your name at the end.

No matter what the specific requirements are, any final copy should be clean and readable. The chart below offers some suggestions about presenting certain types of writing.

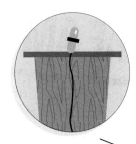

Oral Presentation
Almost anything you write can be shared aloud. Consider holding a group reading or using background music in your presentation.

Class Book
Collect copies of classmates' finished writing in a class book. You can keep it in class to enjoy, or you can donate it to the school library.

Newspaper
Items about local people and events are important parts of newspaper writing.

Literary Magazines
Literary magazines such as *Stone Soup* and *Cricket* publish poems and stories by students.

Journal Writing

In your journal, brainstorm ideas about different ways you might present your finished piece of writing. Which would be the most fun? The most exciting? How would you like to have your piece illustrated?

Prepare the Final Copy

Read this part of Maya's article as it appeared in *The Wilson Chronicle*. You can trace some ideas back to Maya's prewriting notes. Other ideas came up along the way.

THE WILSON CHRONICL

WILDCATS' HOBBIES ARE AMAZI'

by Maya Gonzales

It's time for a Wilson Elementary Wildcats Quiz. Who has attended bike-racing camp in Colorado? Who has boxes of money in his closet? Whose gumbo can make you feel like you're in Louisiana? Whose name do you see in every edition of this paper? They're all fellow Wildcats, students with some amazing hobbies.

Take Jaime Sánchez, for example. He and his sister Marta love biking. They both have been part of a local bike-racing club for two years. This spring Jaime wanted to learn even more about racing. His club sent him to a four-day racing camp sponsored by the United States Cycling Federation. "I never thought racing camp would be so super," Jaime says. "I found some new friends there, and I learned a lot about being a better racer!"

SOS, who draws "Wildcat World" for this newspaper, also likes to learn. SOS stands for Sharon Olivia Sanders. Sharon loves cartooning. She has been drawing pictures since she was three. She can draw animals, spaceships, or anything else you can imagine. Sharon makes cartooning look easy, but she works really hard at it. She has sketchbooks filled with cartoon ideas. Two pages, for example, show a horse running, jumping, sticking its head out a stable door, and winking. Sharon's favorite subjects, however, are people. She says, "I learn by studying people's faces and watching them move. I think that's why my cartoons are realistic as well as funny."

Hector Huang enjoys biking and canoeing, but for h favorite hobby he can stay indoors. You see, Hector i numismatist, a co collector. Hector began his collect three years ago

> Note that Maya stayed with the order of details she considered while prewriting. (See page 52.)

> How has Maya changed this sentence? Why do you think she made this change?

Present Your Work

Now that your writing is complete, decide how you will present it and to whom.

PURPOSE To present a finished piece of writing

AUDIENCE Your choice

LENGTH 2–4 paragraphs

WRITING RUBRICS To present your writing, you should

- find out the requirements for the form of presentation you have chosen
- be sure your work is prepared properly
- present your work in the way you have chosen

Viewing and Representing

COOPERATIVE LEARNING In a small group, think about how you can start your own class book. Would it be illustrated? By whom? What kinds of writing would it have? How many pieces of writing would it include? Who would gather the writing? Who would make sure that it is legible? Pick two or three people to write up the group's ideas and suggestions. Then present them to the class.

Grammar Link

Use commas correctly in your writing.

Sharon's favorite subjects, ***however,*** *are people.*

Revise each sentence below, using commas to set off interrupters.

1. Maya's hobby as you can imagine is writing stories.
2. Not all of her stories however have been published.
3. Her favorite topics of course are people.
4. Several of her stories in fact tell about members of her family.
5. One story as you may know tells about her brother's trip to Chicago.

See Lesson 19.2, page 491.

Using Computers

After completing the Grammar Link, try typing the sentences into the computer. Use the grammar-check feature to check your work.

Writing Process in Action

The Writing Process

In previous lessons you've learned about writers' tasks during each stage of the writing process. Now you will practice more of what you've learned: prewriting, drafting, revising, editing/ proofreading, and publishing/presenting. You will also practice using the techniques used in Maya's article.

Assignment

Context

You are going to send a piece of writing to a student publication called *The Way Things Were,* which publishes stories about pastimes or forgotten activities from earlier times.

Purpose

To remember for others a lost activity

Audience

Student readers of *The Way Things Were*

Length

1 page

WRITING Online

Visit the *Writer's Choice* Web site at **writerschoice.glen-coe.com** for additional writing prompts.

The pages that follow offer step-by-step advice on how to approach this assignment. You don't have to remember it all. Read through the pages before you start. Then refer to each stage if you need help while you work on your assignment.

The Writing Process

Prewriting

What do machines do today that people did by hand a century ago? What was life like before microwave ovens, computers, and video games? Do you know anyone who has milked a cow or made soap?

Use one of the options at the right or an idea of your own to begin exploring a topic. You can develop your topic by freewriting.

Look at pages 46–53 for help with other kinds of prewriting.

Option A
Visit a living-history museum.

Option B
Read old magazines in the library.

Option C
Talk to older people.

Great-grandmother Watkins grew her own vegetables in a garden. Since many vegetables ripened at the same time of year, she had to preserve them so that the family would have vegetables all year.

Drafting

While you review your freewriting notes, think about how you can make the activity you're describing clear and interesting to your readers. Notice how author Betsy Byars uses questions and answers to explain a process.

Drafting Tip

To review ideas for getting "unstuck" when your drafting runs into a snag, see the chart on page 56 of Lesson 2.4.

Literature Model

He moved around the plane. "Look under the cowl. . . . Check the oil—the gas. The gas cap's up here."

"What's that wire sticking out of it?"

Pop unscrewed the cap. "That's the gas gauge. See, there's a cork on the end. The cork floats on the gas, and as the gas goes down, so does the cork and the wire."

Betsy Byars, *Coast to Coast*

You can also use a question-and-answer format as you write your draft. Write out a few important questions that can be asked about your topic. What types of things would student readers of *The Way Things Were* ask about your topic? Respond to the questions with answers that help describe your topic. Use these questions as you complete your draft.

Revising

To begin revising, read over your draft to make sure that what you have written fits your purpose and audience. Then have a **writing conference.** Read your draft to a partner or a small group. Use your audience's reactions to help you evaluate your work.

Question A
Will readers understand what I'm writing about?

Question B
Have I varied the length of my sentences?

Question C
Are my paragraphs well constructed?

> I always thought of pickles as something that came in a jar, but my great-grandmother Watkins used to pickle almost everything in her garden. Whether She pickled watermelon rind, summer squash, onions, cauliflower, carrots, and green beans, as well as cucumbers. The ~~process for all of these was very similar.~~ she used a similar process. First, She had to gather and clean the vegetables. To clean the vegetables, she washed and first examined then each one. Then she removed bruises and spots with a paring knife.

You can also set your writing aside for a day or two before you make revisions. Then you can read your work as a reader would. The questions in the boxes below can help both you and the listeners in your writing conference.

Editing/Proofreading

You've worked hard to decide what you want to say and how to say it well. You want your final draft to be free of errors. During the editing stage, you can get rid of any mistakes that distract readers from your ideas. The editing checklist at the right will help you catch errors. When you find one, mark it with the appropriate **proofreading** symbol. Read your work one time for each type of error. Use a dictionary and the Grammar, Usage, and Mechanics section of this book for additional help.

Publishing/Presenting

Make sure your explanation is legibly written or typed on clean white paper before submitting it to *The Way Things Were*. To help readers understand your subject, draw your own diagrams, or include clipped or photocopied illustrations.

If you have the opportunity to make an oral presentation, think about how you could demonstrate the activity in your writing. Use objects related to your subject, or simply act out the process.

Editing/Proofreading Checklist

- Have I used the proper forms of verbs and pronouns?
- Do I have any sentence fragments or run-on sentences?
- Are my spelling, punctuation, and usage correct?

Proofreading Tip

For proofreading symbols, see page 72 or 267.

Journal Writing

Reflect on your writing process experience. Answer these questions in your journal: What do you like best about your writing? What was the hardest part of writing it? What did you learn in your writing conference? What new thing have you learned as a writer?

Literature Model

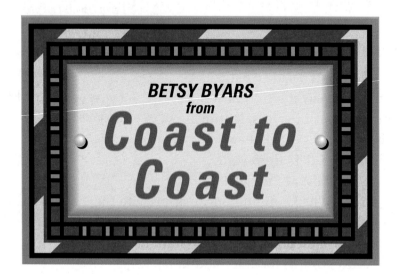

BETSY BYARS
from

Coast to Coast

Coast to Coast tells the story of thirteen-year-old Birch, her retired grandfather, Pop, and what happens when Birch suggests that they fly his 1940 airplane cross-country. As you read, think about how the author gets and keeps her readers' attention. After reading, try the activities in Linking Writing and Literature on page 87.

"I do. I want to do something. I can't explain it. I have to do something. And here is this perfectly good airplane." His jaws moved, chewing on the idea.

"What I meant about getting old, Pop, was that it's not getting pain in your joints or bad teeth. It's, like, not wanting to have fun."

Her grandfather got busy. He emptied the bucket and put the wet towels inside. "Help me push the plane back in the hangar. I'm tired of talking about my age."

"Yes, but it's my turn to pick. Remember? I picked being named for a tree, you picked flying in the war, now I pick this. I want to talk about you."

"Birch, the airplane is sold."

"You haven't got the money yet."

"I don't want to take any chances."

"See? Don't take any chances— that's exactly what getting old is. Don't step on the grass. Don't go out of the yard!"

"That's enough. I mean it."

Birch was silent for a moment. Then in a different voice, as if she were taking up a new topic, she said, "You never have taken me up."

Her grandfather glanced at the sky. Beneath her eyeshade, Birch's eyes narrowed. She knew she had him now.

> **"Birch was silent for a moment. Then in a different voice, as if she were taking up a new topic, she said, 'You never have taken me up.'"**

"I really want to go!" As she said it, she realized it was true. She needed to get away from this world, and this was the way to do it. "What are we waiting for?"

"I don't guess it would hurt to fly to the beach and back."

"Then get in! Let's go!"

"Don't get in too big a hurry." Her

Robert Delaunay, *Homage to Blériot,* c. 1913–1914

grandfather smiled. It was his first real smile of the afternoon.

Birch followed him around the plane. "What are you doing?"

"Well, right now, I'm doing a preflight inspection. I check the tires, the control surfaces, move them for freedom and cable looseness." He raised the aileron[1] and looked at the cable underneath. "I check the tail wheel springs . . . the stabilizer trim . . ."

"Does everybody do this? Or are you just extra careful?"

"There used to be a saying. 'Kick the tire. Twang the wire. Light the fire and let her go.' Nowadays a pilot checks everything—the prop for nicks, the cowling pins for security . . ." He

---

1 **aileron** (ā′ lə ron′) movable part on the back of an airplane wing

Henri Rousseau, *View of the Bridge at Sèvres*, 1908

moved around the plane. "Look under the cowl—birds are very fond of building nests under cowls. Check the oil—the gas. The gas cap's up here."

"What's that wire sticking out of it?"

Pop unscrewed the cap. "That's the gas gauge. See, there's a cork on the end. The cork floats on the gas, and as the gas goes down, so does the cork and the wire."

Pop reached in the cabin and removed a clear plastic tube from the seat pocket. He drained some gas into the tube, checked it and threw it out. "Good! No water got in the gas from our wash job."

"How do you know, Pop?"

"Water's heavier than gas, so it would be on the bottom. And they look different."

"So can I get in now?" He nodded, and Birch stepped to the right side of the plane. "Do I sit in the front or back?"

"The pilot sits in the back."

"But how do you see the instruments?"

"I can see all I have to. Put your foot on the tire, not on the strut and . . ."

Birch pulled herself in and fastened the seat belt. "This is the first time I've been in a little airplane. Pop, your instruments are ancient."

"They're 1940, same as the plane." Her grandfather leaned into the cockpit. "This is the altimeter—it tells you how high you are. I'm setting that to the altitude of the field—it's about sea level so I set it on zero. Carburetor heat—off. Switch—off."

He moved the stick back and forth while looking at the tail, then from side to side while watching the wing. "Put your heels on the brake pedals."

"Oh, we both have brake pedals?"

"Yes, it's dual control."

She looked down at the pedals and positioned her feet so that her heels were on the smaller ones.

"I'm going to swing the prop to start the engine."

"You mean, like, it's going to start and I'm going to be sitting in here by myself with the engine going?"

Pop opened the throttle a half inch.

"Look at my feet, Pop, and make sure they're on the brakes."

"I did."

"Because I do not want to take off by myself. I saw that in an Abbott and Costello movie."

"This is the gas primer." Pop pulled out a knob and slowly pushed it back in. Then he stepped to the front of the plane and gave the prop a few turns. Birch listened to the clicks and watched the tip of the prop over the cowling.

> **" Pop leaned in and pushed the throttle back. The propeller turned slowly at idle, almost invisible against the blue sky. "**

"Now turn that overhead ignition switch on for me."

"This?"

"Right, and yell 'Contact' just before you do."

"Incidentally, I'm terrified. Contact!"

"Brakes?"

"Brakes!" she yelled, pressing her heels harder.

Pop came around and stood by the cabin. He reached forward with his right hand and gave the prop a quick downward pull. The engine caught. Pop leaned in and pushed the throttle back. The propeller turned slowly at idle, almost invisible against the blue sky.

Then he climbed in. "I got the brakes now," he yelled above the noise of the engine.

Birch took her feet off the pedals. "I feel a lot better with you in here."

The plane started forward. Following the yellow line on the pavement, they moved from the ramp down the taxiway and stopped just short of the runway.

"I'm revving up the engine now to check the magnetos² and carburetor heat."

"Check everything!"

He leaned forward. "Belt tight?"

"You bet. Let's go!"

"Birch?"

"What, Pop?"

"Let's don't say anything about this to your mom."

"Of course not! It's a secret mission." She put one hand on the window. "Aren't you going to close this?"

"We can close it later if you get too much wind."

"No, I like it open! Let's go!" And Birch's heart raced as Pop turned the J-3 onto runway nine.

---

2 magnetos (mag nē′ tōz) small machines composed of magnets that provide the electric spark to make an engine start

Linking Writing and Literature

 Collect Your Thoughts

Think about Birch, Pop, and the J-3. What does the airplane represent for Pop? For Birch? Why does Birch want Pop to keep the airplane? Explore your thoughts in your notebook.

 Talk About Reading

Discuss the excerpt from *Coast to Coast* with a group. Choose one student to lead the discussion and another to take notes. Use the following questions to guide your discussion.

1. **Connect to Your Life** Think about a special relationship you have with an elderly person—a relative, perhaps, or a neighbor. What makes the relationship good for both of you? What do the two of you share?

2. **Critical Thinking: Evaluate** Compare and contrast Birch and Pop. How are they similar? In what ways do they differ? Do their personalities complement each other?

3. **6+1 Trait®: Sentence Fluency** During the preflight check, Pop and Birch often speak in brief, clipped sentences—sometimes just a single word. Explain why these types of sentences are appropriate to the action in the story.

4. **Connect to Your Writing** What type of organization does Byars use to describe starting the airplane? Why is this organization appropriate to what's happening in the story?

 Write About Reading

Journal Entry Write an entry in your journal that describes a special relationship you have with a person much older than you. Reflect on how this person became a part of your life and the admirable qualities the person possesses. Also, think about what it is about you that this person appreciates.

Focus on Sentence Fluency A journal entry is informal, personal writing, but it can still contain sentence fluency. Try to vary sentence length and style and use transitional words to connect ideas.

For more information on sentence fluency and the 6+1 Trait® model, see **Writing and Research Handbook,** pp. 682–684.

Reflecting on the Unit

Summarize what you learned in this unit by answering the following questions.

❶ What are the five steps of the writing process?

❷ What are the important elements of each step?

❸ What are some specific strategies you can use as you move through each step?

 ## Adding to Your Portfolio

CHOOSE A SELECTION FOR YOUR PORTFOLIO Look over the writing you did for this unit. Select a favorite piece for your portfolio. The writing you choose should show some or all of the following:

- ideas developed from prewriting
- a sensible organization of ideas
- a clear main idea supported by detail sentences
- interesting and varied sentences
- careful editing and proofreading
- neat, legible handwriting

REFLECT ON YOUR CHOICE Attach a note to the piece you chose, explaining briefly why you chose it and what you learned from writing it.

SET GOALS How can you improve your writing? What skill will you focus on the next time you write?

Writing Across the Curriculum

MAKE A SCIENCE CONNECTION Describe a game or hobby you like. To do that, first use prewriting techniques to come up with an activity that uses technology or requires some up-to-the-minute information.

Draft a paragraph explaining how to do the activity, including your reason for writing about this activity. Revise, edit, and proofread your work. Decide how you would like to present it.

TIME

Facing the Blank Page

Inside the writing process with TIME writers and editors

OCTOBER 18, 1999 $3.50

Writing for TIME

Each week, TIME publishes stories that are the work of experienced professionals who research, write, and edit for a living. The writing is clear; the facts are accurate; and the grammar, spelling, and punctuation are as error-free as possible.

Behind the scenes, however, another story emerges. TIME staffers face many of the same challenges that students do in the messy, trial-and-error process that is writing. Just like you, they must find a topic, conduct research, get organized, write a draft, and then revise, revise, and revise again. In these pages, they tell you how they do it.

Is there a secret to the quality of TIME's writing? Beyond experience and hard work, the key is collaboration. As the chart below illustrates, TIME stories are created through a form of "group journalism" that has become the magazine's hallmark. The writers and editors teach and learn from each other every week. You can do the same. Try out the writing and collaboration strategies in "Facing the Blank Page" to discover what's effective for you.

PREWRITING

| Editor | Writer | Correspondent |

Story idea is born

Writer takes assignment, refines topic, asks researchers and reporters for help

Research begins

Correspondents investigate, conduct interviews

Researchers gather material from reliable sources: "clips" from articles, studies, statistics

DRAFTING

Correspondents send their reporting or "files" to writer

Researchers compile and submit research files

Writer reads and organizes information, drafts the story

REVISING

Editor reads draft, suggests revisions

Correspondents
check interpretation,
make suggestions

<── ·········· ──>

**Writer revises,
sends draft to
members of the
team for comments**

<── ·········· ──>

Researchers
check accuracy,
details

Writer and editor revise again, "green" (edit for length)

EDITING AND PROOFREADING

Checks for conformity to TIME
style and conventions

<── ········· ──>

Copy Desk

<── ········· ──>

Checks and corrects grammar,
mechanics, spelling

PUBLISHING AND PRESENTING

**Managing Editor chooses to
print, hold, or "kill" (omit) story**

Circulation of TIME
rises or falls

<── ·········· ──>

**Readers respond
to published story**

<── ·········· ──>

E-mail and letters
to the editor

Prewriting
Generating Ideas

Martha Pickerill, Assistant Managing Editor of TIME FOR KIDS.

Where do ideas for stories come from? Martha Pickerill explains how it works at TIME FOR KIDS, TIME's "kid-sister" publication:

❝We're fortunate that our first stop is TIME magazine. We have access to all of TIME's reporting and photos, and sometimes their graphics people will help us out, too. It's not always the case that what TIME is doing in any week is appropriate or is the best cover story for kids, who are our readers. So sometimes we'll take a story that's been quite small in TIME and turn it into a cover story. ❞

Pickerill recalls a story idea the TIME FOR KIDS (TFK) staff developed on its own because it was such a good fit for TFK's reading audience:

❝The story was actually suggested by a parent of a boy involved in Boundless Playgrounds, an organization that develops playgrounds for kids who are in wheelchairs or otherwise physically disabled. It started with a short e-mail from the boy's father, who had seen our magazine. So we contacted the organization and did some more legwork.

The interesting thing is that these playgrounds are built so that able-bodied

kids can use them, too. A lot of the ideas came from kids who had tried to use playgrounds and couldn't because of their physical limitations. And so they came up with a better idea, and they convinced somebody to build it. It was a perfect story for us, because kids really made a difference in what was going on in their world. It showed kids being powerful. ❞

LEARNING FROM THE EDITOR

DISCUSSION
What are your sources for writing ideas? (Possibilities include your imagination, brainstorming with friends and family members, newspapers, magazines, TV, and radio.) Make a class list.

TRY IT OUT
1. Start small. Look through a newspaper or magazine to identify a small story that could be expanded for a sixth-grade reading audience. Research and write the story!

2. Brainstorm with the class. Try working with a partner or with a small group to generate ideas for future writing projects.

The Value of Outlining

Jill Smolowe, now an Associate Editor at *People* magazine, was a Senior Writer at TIME from 1994 to 1996. She prepares to write a story by carefully outlining her ideas and supporting information. Her method, she admits, is not for everyone—but it's highly effective in helping her meet deadlines!

MARIO RUIZ FOR TIME

**Jill Smolowe:
Following a road map.**

Jill Smolowe:

❝The way I work is very personal. Since I often write lengthy stories and I often write them on deadline, I really need to know where I'm going before I start. If I just leap in and don't have a road map, then I may veer off and find myself not knowing where the story is going.

So I outline very carefully. I literally take the line count I'm given, and I estimate 20 lines per paragraph. Then I list the number of paragraphs. I literally think through every paragraph: what is the theme I'm going to tackle? Which anecdotes and which information will I be inclined to use? As I actually write the story, that may shift, but at least when I sit down to write, I have a road map. These outlines are very much like the ones I learned to do in school, and they do serve the function of keeping me on a path as I'm writing. With deadlines, that's very, very important. ❞

LEARNING FROM THE WRITER

TALK ABOUT IT
1. Smolowe compares writing to taking a trip and sees a parallel between an outline and a road map. How do you see writing? Explore the comparison further. How can you be creative while following a route? How can you learn along the way? Is there more than one road to a given destination?

2. How do you organize your ideas before you begin a piece of writing? As a class, share and compare styles of outlining or organizing ideas for various writing purposes.

TRY IT OUT
Outline backwards. Take a piece of writing you finished recently and, whether or not you made an outline for it before you began, make an outline *from* it now.

LOOK IT OVER
Does this new outline reflect what you originally wanted to say? If not, how should you revise your writing so that it conveys your message?

Drafting

Getting Organized

Nancy Gibbs, Senior Editor at TIME, shares a way to think about writing that one of her mentors taught her as a young journalist:

Nancy Gibbs: Building the chair.

DIANA WALKER FOR TIME

❝ Organization is the first thing you have to learn, and in some ways, it's the hardest, because everything follows from there. One of the editors who was teaching me the craft a long time ago used to liken writing a story to building a chair. The craftsmanship is basic: the chair has to stand up. It has to support weight. Ideally, it should be comfortable. Even better, it ought to be nice to look at. But at the most basic level, it

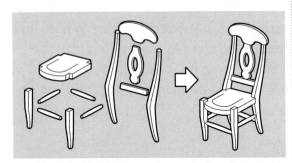

has to be structurally sound. It needs four legs, and a seat that won't fall through, and a back that won't collapse. From there, you can decide what kind of chair it's going to be, and how it might be carved, decorated, and upholstered.

I really believe in collaborative writing. You send a paragraph to someone and say, 'Does this work? Am I making the point?' Words and imagery may be one person's strength, while clarity and structure may be another's. If writing is like building a chair, here at TIME we hand the chair to one another. **❞**

LEARNING FROM THE WRITER

TALK ABOUT IT
1. When Gibbs likens writing a story to building a chair, she uses a *simile,* a figure of speech that points out what is similar about two seemingly unlike things. What does her use of this comparison suggest about the way she writes?

2. In what ways is the comparison of writing a story to building a chair appropriate or inappropriate?

TRY IT OUT
Create your own simile. It can be for writing in general or for one part of the writing process.

LOOK IT OVER
Analyze a piece of your writing. Does it hold up under the "well-built chair test"? Is it structurally sound, with a good beginning, middle, and end? Is it "upholstered" with enough details? What could you revise to make it "a better chair"?

Approaching the First Draft

James Poniewozik, a Staff Writer at TIME, starts a writing project by "thinking" on paper. Writing a first draft shows him what he wants to say in the final piece. He describes his process this way:

Writing as thinking

❝Some people believe that before you begin to write, you should pretty much know exactly what you want to say—and I think the opposite is true. There's a famous quote from the writer E. M. Forster: 'How do I know what I think until I see what I say?' I think that's really true. Writing is not just getting down a completely formed thought that you have in your head. Writing is actually a process of thinking in itself.❞

Starting to write

❝What I'll generally do to start off is to write out sections of a piece: things that I definitely want to get in. I'll write a paragraph here and a paragraph there. As I start writing them, it'll seem to make sense: I see how the paragraphs should be organized, and then I'll sense the flow of the piece.❞

First drafts: Topic sentences

❝It's important that you remember that it is just a first draft, and that you'll need to go back and revise. When you start writing, it's good to concentrate on the idea of having topic sentences for individual paragraphs. It does help focus you. By the time you're done, it may have changed, but at least it gives you a strong focus point to start from.❞

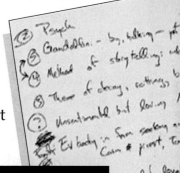

Poniewozik's notes: An order emerges.

TALK ABOUT IT
1. Explore the idea that writing is thinking on paper. What did E. M. Forster mean when he asked, "How do I know what I think until I see what I say?"
2. Summarize the steps that James Poniewozik takes in the process of writing an article. How are your drafting steps like or unlike his?

TRY IT OUT
Think on paper. Select one of the topics for writing that the class listed during the brainstorming session and try working on it the way Poniewozik does. Write down the ideas you want to get in and develop them into paragraphs in any order. Next put the paragraphs in an order that makes sense. Connect them with writing that helps each paragraph's main idea flow smoothly into the next. You now have a first draft!

LOOK IT OVER
How well did Poniewozik's method work for you? Read each paragraph to see that it has a topic sentence with a clearly stated main idea and that all of the other sentences develop that idea. Rewrite paragraphs that need help.

Revising

The Role of the Editor

Janice Simpson, Senior Editor at TIME, describes her role:

❝The biggest trick of editing is to make someone else's words sound their best, not to substitute your own words. It's a collaborative effort, because you're working very intimately. Writing is an act of creation. I don't think what we do is an art form; it's a craft, but it's a very fine craft. When writers create something, they put a piece of themselves into it. So when you're editing, like it or not, you're commenting on that person. And in the editing process, what you're doing is looking at their story and saying, 'Let me figure out what it was you wanted to say. Not what I wanted to say, what you wanted to say.'❞

An editor is the first audience for a piece of writing.
Senior Editor Bill Saporito:

❝The real job of the editor is to be the stand-in for the reader. You've got to decide what you think the reader is

Janice Simpson: Making writers' words sound their best.

most interested in, and you also have to make the story readable if it's not in that shape when it comes in.

You want to make sure that a story is organized properly, that it's not too long or too short. Were all the important questions answered? Did the reporter and the writer do the job that you sent them to do? If not, how do you change it? Do you send it back for a rewrite, do it yourself, or simply ask for more information?

Sometimes you simply ask the writer questions: 'Is this right? Have you asked about this? What about these aspects?'❞

LEARNING FROM THE EDITOR

TALK ABOUT IT
List your hobbies or interests. Which would you classify as crafts? Which do you think of as art forms? What does Simpson mean when she says that the editing process is a craft, not an art form? What is your view of the process?

TRY IT OUT
Define the editor's role. As peer editor for other students, what should your role be? Draft a job description.

LOOK IT OVER
Who edits your writing—classmates, friends, family? Which group's approach works best for you, and why?

Knowing Your Audience

Nelida Cutler is the senior editor at TIME FOR KIDS. "A good editor enhances the work of a good writer by making changes that improve the story," says Cutler. When Cutler edits TFK articles, she asks herself the following:

- ■ **Is the information accurate?**
- ■ **Does the story make sense?**
- ■ **Did the writer choose the best words and phrases for the intended audience?**
- ■ **Are the spelling and grammar correct?**

LEARNING FROM THE EDITOR

Cutler helps adapt stories from the World Report Edition of TFK for the younger News Scoop Edition.

WORLD REPORT EDITION

Fun for All

In elementary school, Hannah Kristan's least favorite part of the day was recess. "I never got to do anything except sit there," she recalls.

Hannah, 12, was born with spina bifida (*spy*-na *biff*-eh-dah), a condition that kept her spine from forming completely. She uses a wheelchair. For kids in wheelchairs, most playgrounds are terrible places to play. Wheelchairs can sink in the parks' soft surfaces, and chairs won't fit on the equipment.

Three years ago, Hannah heard about the Hasbro National Resource Center for Boundless Playgrounds, a group that creates playgrounds for children of all abilities.

NEWS SCOOP EDITION

A Dream Comes True

When Hannah Kristan was in elementary school, her least favorite part of the day was recess. "I never got to do anything except sit there," she recalls.

Hannah, 12, was born with a disease that kept the bones in her back from forming properly. She uses a wheelchair. For kids in wheelchairs, most playground equipment is off limits.

In 1996 Hannah heard about Boundless Playgrounds. The group, formed by a toy company, creates special playgrounds for children of all abilities.

TALK ABOUT IT
Compare the TFK articles. How do their language and their details differ? Which lines did Cutler change?

TRY IT OUT
Revise a section of a piece of your writing. Rewrite it for a younger audience—perhaps a younger friend or sibling. What changes will you have to make? As you draft and revise the new version of your writing, use the TFK articles above as guides.

Editing and Proofreading

Copy Editing

Once a TIME story has been written and edited, it needs to be copy-edited and proofread before the final version is printed in the magazine. Copy editors read a story to make sure every word is correct, using a set of symbols to mark up an article.

Judy Paul is TIME's Deputy Copy Chief:
"Our mandate is plain: we're responsible for checking spelling, basic grammar, and TIME style. TIME style is the way TIME does something differently from the dictionary or other publications."

Judy's department receives letters from TIME readers who pay close attention to the language in the magazine:
"We have always gotten lots of reader mail about style and usage. It's something that interests people, and the letters show that people care. I think the tendency in society is to say that how we speak is not important; you only need to make yourself understood. But people care a lot more than that. They want writing to be elegant and correct."

LEARNING FROM THE EDITOR

TALK ABOUT IT
Like Paul's letter writers, point out some examples of incorrect usage that you have seen and heard. On the board, list each example along with its correct form. What is the importance of following rules of usage in spoken language? In written language?

TRY IT OUT
Use proofreading power.
Trade papers with a partner and use the checklist and the basic proofreading symbols in Lesson 2.8 as you proofread each other's work. How do your marked-up pages compare with this page from TIME's copy desk?

Publishing and Presenting

L ike TIME, TIME FOR KIDS solicits feedback by asking readers to write or e-mail the magazine with comments. Then the editors publish letters in a section called "Kids Talk Back!" Here are some letters received by TFK.

Kids Talk Back!

Dear TFK,
I think that kids' sports ["Sports Overload?", 11/5] are getting too competitive, and some coaches are so worried about winning that they take all the fun out of it for us kids.
—**Kari Bjerke, Waukesha, WI**

Kids Talk Back!

Dear TFK,
In my neighborhood we lost 26 trees because of Hurricane Floyd ["A Monster Hurricane," 9/24]. I covered the hurricane for my science journal, and I found out that some of the trees that died were 90 years old, the same age as my grandmother.
—**Alexander Chris, Baltimore, MD**

Dear TFK,
Maybe if everyone greeted each other like the Maori tribe, with a *hongi* (pressing noses) ["A Warm Welcome," 9/24], we would be a nicer society. What a different way to say hello!
—**Kelsie Alexander, Madison, AL**

Dear TFK,
It's great that people are taking the time to make playgrounds for handicapped kids ["Fun for All," 11/5]. I know someone in a wheelchair, and she hates to go to playgrounds because she can't get up on the swings. There should be more playgrounds like these.
—**Courtney Roche, Enfield, CT**

LEARNING FROM THE WRITERS

TALK ABOUT IT
The writers of the letters above in "Kids Talk Back!" comment on articles in TFK by sharing personal opinions and experiences. For what reasons did these kids decide to "talk back" to TFK? Reread the letters and try to determine each writer's purpose.

TRY IT OUT
1. Write a letter to the editor. Respond to something you have read in a magazine or newspaper or take a stand on a topic that interests you. For suggestions on how to make your point as clearly as possible, read Lesson 6.1, "Taking a Stand," in the unit on persuasive writing. For tips on punctuating letters

correctly, see Lessons 18.1, 19.3, and 19.5.
2. Write a letter to a friend. Lesson 1.3, "Making Personal Connections," offers advice on writing friendly letters. After reading the lesson, write a letter to a friend or a family member with whom you have not been in touch in a while.

"*The wind had carried knives and cut through everything standing in its path.*"

—Julius Lester, "Why Dogs Are Tame"

Descriptive Writing

Writing in the Real World: *John Boulanger*   *102*

Lesson **3.1**   **Painting a Picture with Words**   *106*

Lesson **3.2**   **Observing and Taking Notes**   *110*

Lesson **3.3**   **Elaborating: Focusing on the Details**   *114*

Lesson **3.4**   **Ordering Descriptive Details**   *118*

Lesson **3.5**   **Describing a Place**   *122*

Lesson **3.6**   **Writing About Literature:
                      Getting to Know a New Place**   *126*

Writing Process in Action   *130*

**Literature Model: from *Morning Girl*
by Michael Dorris**   *134*

Unit 3 Review   *141*

Descriptions bring colorful images to many forms of writing—even scientific articles! In the following excerpt, scientist John Boulanger paints pictures for readers of a scene in the far northern Yukon. What was Boulanger doing there? He and six other scientists were investigating life on nunataks (nun' ə taks')—small islands in a sea of ice. The nunataks are home to all kinds of livings things. The scientists were hoping especially to find pikas—stocky little animals reported to live on some of the most remote nunataks. In this excerpt, Boulanger describes the moment he discovered his first one.

from "Attacking the Nunataks," *International Wildlife*

by John Boulanger

I quietly wait for the sun to rise and rouse any pikas from their boulder homes. About 30 minutes later, an animal with a gray coat and white underside peers up at me from a boulder 10 meters (about 11 yds.) away. Yahoo!! Here at last is a collared pika, a member of the rabbit family that more closely resembles a large mouse.

The animal sniffs curiously at me. For the next 20 minutes I watch as it sizes me up. It stares at me for a few seconds at a time, disappearing now and then with a characteristic chirp under a boulder. In between staring bouts, it clips

some grass and scampers back to safety.

Pikas spend the short growing season harvesting grass and other plant material. They stash it in hay piles under the boulders to keep as food for the long winter.

I wonder why these pikas are so jumpy in such an isolated location. My question gets a quick answer when a new visitor appears, a short-tailed weasel, perhaps looking for a pika breakfast. The newcomer moves continuously over and between the boulders like a snake.

A weasel is a formidable predator for a pika. About the same girth as its prey, this hunter can go anywhere a pika can. Unexpectedly, the weasel runs up to me, obviously curious. Then fear overcomes curiosity, and it flees to a nearby meadow.

I observe other activity in this meadow. Insects bounce around in the multicolored array of alpine flowers. Water pipits and snow buntings fly erratically searching for insects in the luxuriant meadows. Golden eagles soar above, looking for inattentive ground squirrels whose chirps fill the air.

A Writer's Process

Prewriting
Observing a World

Boulanger, along with the six other scientists on the mission, would spend two months in the icy Yukon investigating life on the nunataks. All of that time would be part of the prewriting process for Boulanger. Although his main mission there was to gather facts as a scientist, he also was recording information for an article in the magazine *International Wildlife*. Doing these jobs meant carefully observing the strange, cold world. Taking good notes of his observations was an equally important task.

Even as he was taking notes, Boulanger thought about how he could convey the world in front of him to his readers. "I was always trying to figure out ways that I could describe being up there to someone who had never been there before," Boulanger says. "For example, in one area we came to a place where gigantic glacial streams were running on either side of us." How would Boulanger describe the roaring streams? Could he compare them to something familiar? "Finally, it struck me that these streams were like water slides at an amusement park," he says.

Boulanger looked for visual details as he sat on nunataks, watching the animals. When he spotted a pika, for instance, he noted its color, texture, size—details that would help him write a vivid word picture.

He also recorded other sensory details, such as the sounds of the animals and the feel of the ice and slush.

Writing in the Real World **103**

Writing in the Real World

To be sure his notes were safe, Boulanger used a special reporter's notebook. It was made of paper that could get wet and not fall apart. Boulanger wrote with a pencil so his notes wouldn't blur if they fell into snow.

Boulanger wrote whenever something caught his eye. Usually, the team was moving and Boulanger had to dash off impressions. "I didn't pay that much attention to grammar," he says. "I'd just quickly spill my mind out and then use the notes later to remember."

Sometimes, he had time to write a full description. Confronted with the icy, roaring "water slides," Boulanger stopped and wrote. "That moment was so intense, I sat down and took ten or fifteen minutes to really try to describe it," he says.

At 8:00 or 9:00 P.M., after a full day of work, Boulanger often crawled into his sleeping bag and expanded his notes. In the far north at that time of year, the sun doesn't set until midnight. Even at 9:00 P.M., it's still light and often warm enough to write. Some of Boulanger's longest entries were made at these quiet times.

Drafting
Writing the Article

Faced with so many amazing sights, Boulanger wrote more than 200 pages of notes. Rich in detail, they formed the basis of his science article.

Before starting to draft, Boulanger developed a plan for his article. After opening with a description of his thrilling plane ride into the wilds, he explained what the scientific team had set out to do. From there, Boulanger wrote his article like a field journal. He entered a date and then described the day's discoveries and listed his questions. The reader would learn along with the team.

When drafting descriptions, Boulanger continued to search for comparisons that would relate this alien icebound world to something more familiar. Besides conveying information, his comparisons helped readers visualize scenes in a fresh, imaginative way. For example, to describe the intense sunlight, Boulanger wrote: "The sun is intensely bright, and its fiery reflection on the snow makes me feel as if I am in a gigantic frying pan."

One of the hardest parts of writing was choosing what to write about. Boulanger had to boil down two months of notes into a short magazine article. "You have to be very selective," he explains. "I chose things I thought were interesting. That way, readers can live the experience with me, feel like they're there, too."

Examining Writing in the Real World

Analyzing the Media Connection

Discuss these questions about the article excerpt on pages 102–103.

1. To what other animals does Boulanger compare a pika and a weasel? Why do you think he makes these comparisons?
2. What visual details does he provide about various animals' color, size, or appearance?
3. In the second paragraph, what picture of the pika do the details draw?
4. Boulanger says that the pika "peers up at me." Find other examples where he uses vivid verbs.
5. In the last paragraph point out three descriptive adjectives or adverbs and tell how they enhance the word picture.

Analyzing a Writer's Process

Discuss these questions about John Boulanger's writing process.

1. How and when did Boulanger take notes?
2. How does Boulanger's style of notetaking compare to yours?

3. Why did he use familiar comparisons to describe life on the nunataks?
4. Why was turning his notes into an article a challenging task for Boulanger?

Make sure the subject and verb in a sentence agree, even when a phrase comes between them.

> The **variety** of plants and animals **is** amazing.

Write the following sentences. In each one, underline the subject once and the verb twice. If they agree, write *correct.* If they do not agree, correct the verb.

1. The team of scientists skis across glaciers.
2. The nunataks, small islands in a sea of ice, is home to many living things.
3. John Boulanger, with other biologists, travel by plane to Mt. Logan.
4. Gigantic streams of glacial water is on either side of us.
5. A weasel in the pika colony hopes to catch his breakfast.

See Lesson 15.1, page 439.

Painting a Picture with Words

An effective written description is one that presents a clear picture to your reader. An interesting description attracts the reader. Descriptions can present broad views or close-ups.

Good descriptive writing can take a reader anywhere. In the excerpt below, writer Jean Craighead George takes you to the Arctic. She describes the world of Miyax, an Inuit girl.

The writer sets the scene for the action by describing the sky and the landscape first.

Which precise details help you see what Miyax sees?

Literature Model

Miyax pushed back the hood of her sealskin parka and looked at the Arctic sun. It was a yellow disc in a lime-green sky, the colors of six o'clock in the evening and the time when the wolves awoke. Quietly she put down her cooking pot and crept to the top of a dome-shaped frost heave, one of the many earth buckles that rise and fall in the crackling cold of the Arctic winter. Lying on her stomach, she looked across a vast lawn of grass and moss and focused her attention on the wolves she had come upon two sleeps ago.

Jean Craighead George
Julie of the Wolves

Zoom In

Like George, you can use descriptive writing to help your reader see what you see, hear what you hear, and feel what you feel. In the paragraph below, George continues her description. Notice how she zooms in closer to the scene.

Which details help bring you closer to the wolf?

Literature Model

Amaroq [one of the wolves] glanced at his paw and slowly turned his head her way without lifting his eyes. He licked his shoulder. A few matted hairs sprang apart and twinkled individually. Then his eyes sped to each of the three adult wolves that made up his pack and finally to the five pups who were sleeping in a fuzzy mass near the den entrance. The great wolf's eyes softened at the sight of the little wolves, then quickly hardened into brittle yellow jewels as he scanned the flat tundra [plain].

Jean Craighead George
Julie of the Wolves

Compare the two paragraphs from *Julie of the Wolves*. In the first, George sets the overall scene. In the second, she moves in closer. She draws the reader into the wolf's world. She lets the reader see the wolf's emotions through its eyes.

Journal Writing

Having read the two descriptions from *Julie of the Wolves*, make a word picture of the scene. To start, list the descriptive details that made the scene clear to you. If you wish, draw a sketch of the scene.

Vocabulary Tip

When you get ready to describe something, close your eyes and picture it. Then list words and phrases that tell how it looks, feels, smells, sounds, or tastes.

Ideas for Descriptive Writing

Books aren't the only place where descriptions are used. In fact, you probably use descriptions every day. For example, when you tell a friend about a new movie, you probably use description. When you take notes on a field trip, you probably use description for that, too.

Maybe you've taken a trip to the zoo. Did you notice the descriptive writing all around you? Signs at the zoo describe the animals. Posters describe new attractions. Advertisements describe food for sale. What examples of descriptive writing can you find in the illustration below?

Descriptive Writing

New at Zoo **Baby Spotted Owl!**

Fresh Hot Roasted Nuts

From China's Bamboo Forests

The **Giant Panda...**

Zoo Guide

The Polar Bear lives along the frozen shores of the icy Arctic Ocean. Adult Polar Bears weigh about 1,000 pounds.

Write a Description of a Wolf

Write a description of a wolf for a group of younger students. Imagine that your description will prepare them to see this animal at the zoo. Look at the photo on page 107 or at other pictures of wolves. Ask yourself: How big is the wolf? What does it remind me of? What color is its coat? What color are its eyes?

PURPOSE To describe an animal
AUDIENCE Younger students
LENGTH 1–2 paragraphs

WRITING RUBRICS To write a description, you should

- look at or think about what you want to describe
- list details about what you see or remember
- use your list to write your description

Listening and Speaking

COOPERATIVE LEARNING In a small group, take turns orally describing places that are familiar to you. For example, you might describe a specific place in or near your school. Describe these places without naming them. As each person tells about his or her place, other group members should write down the details that provide the best clues about what the place is and then identify it.

Using Computers

Look at your list of descriptive details from the Journal Writing activity on page 107. On the computer, write each descriptive detail in a new way.

Grammar Link

Use possessive pronouns to show ownership of something.

Notice how Jean Craighead George uses possessive pronouns in the models on pages 106 and 107.

Replace each underlined word or group of words with a possessive pronoun.

1. Miyax's attention was focused on the wolves.
2. The wolf's and Miyax's eyes met.
3. The wolf's eyes glittered in the light.
4. Three other adult wolves and five pups made up the wolf's pack.
5. Jean Craighead George's book *Julie of the Wolves* is an award-winner.

See Lesson 11.4, page 367.

Descriptive Writing

Observing and Taking Notes

Sensory details call up realistic images of taste, sound, smell, touch, and sight. These details can add richness to your descriptions of everyday things.

In the model below, Maya Angelou describes a picnic she remembers from her childhood. Notice the sensory details Angelou uses to help readers picture the scene.

Literature Model

The summer picnic gave ladies a chance to show off their baking hands. On the barbecue pit, chickens and spareribs sputtered in their own fat and a sauce whose recipe was guarded in the family. . . . Pound cakes sagged with their buttery weight and small children could no more resist licking the icings than their mothers could avoid slapping the sticky fingers. . . . On one corner of the clearing a gospel group was rehearsing. Their harmony, packed as tight as sardines, floated over the music of the county singers and melted into the songs of the small children's ring games.

Maya Angelou, *I Know Why the Caged Bird Sings*

> The writer uses parallelism to aid her description.

Grammar Tip

For more information on parallelism, see **Writing and Research Handbook,** page 678.

Angelou brings her description of the picnic to life by including details that help you see, hear, feel, taste, and smell the picnic. In your own descriptive writing, you can do the same thing. Just learn to pay attention to your senses.

Notice What's Around You

Whenever you see, hear, smell, taste, or touch, you learn something about the world around you. Look at the picture on this page. Then look at the list of sensory descriptive words alongside the picture. Which things in the picture relate to each sensory word?

Hot

Colorful

Sweet

Smoky

Musical

Journal Writing

Recall one of your favorite places. Which senses do you use most when you're there? Make a list of details that you see, hear, touch, taste, and smell. Then circle the details that best describe your place.

Take Notes

Exploring the world around you can be an adventure. Make careful notes about important experiences. Taking notes can help you remember your experiences and share them with others later.

When you take notes on an experience, don't worry about grammar, spelling, or punctuation. Just ask yourself what you see, hear, touch, taste, and smell. Then jot down whatever details will help you remember the experience.

Later, when you prepare to write a draft, reread your notes. Keep in mind that you don't have to use all the details you gathered. Choose those details that create the strongest impression of the experience. If you're describing a concert, for example, you might focus on sights and sounds. If you're describing a holiday dinner, you might concentrate on smells and tastes.

A hot, sticky day. We played touch football. The ball felt hard and the laces felt like large mountains on a globe. Afterward I got a hamburger well done. The hard, burnt, top layer was crunchy, but the inside was soft. I chewed slowly, closing my eyes. I heard the wind blow through the trees. I smelled hamburger and it reminded me of summer. Then there was a water fight. The water felt so good, my clothing molding to my body like a second layer of skin.

Laura Makinen
St. Clement School
Chicago, IL

BLOCK PARTY

WHEN: Tuesday, July 30
5 p.m.

WHERE: Willow Is...

Descriptive Writing

Write a Description of Living Things

Study the scene in this painting. If it were real, what would you see and smell? What do the flowers, caterpillars, and moths look like? Write a description that other students might use to identify the plant and insects shown.

PURPOSE To make a scene recognizable to others

AUDIENCE Other students

LENGTH 1–2 paragraphs

WRITING RUBRICS To write a strong description, you should

- use sensory details—tell how something looks, sounds, smells, tastes, or feels
- take notes on what you notice
- include the most effective details in your draft

Maria Sibylla Merian, *Coral Bean Tree and Saturniid*, c. 1700

Listening and Speaking

Observe a subject in nature. You might choose a dandelion, a spider, a rock, or whatever interests you. Take field notes—careful notes based on what you observe. Use your five senses to gather details. Afterward, use your notes to describe what you saw to a partner.

Cross-Curricular Activity

SCIENCE The saturniid moth, shown in the picture, is also called the giant silkworm moth. Read about it in the encyclopedia. Then write a descriptive paragraph about it.

Grammar Link

Use action verbs to make your descriptive writing come to life.

Notice the variety of action verbs Angelou uses in the model on page 110. Replace the blank in each sentence below with an action verb.

1. The boys _____ through the woods looking for tracks.
2. The children _____ the fried chicken.
3. Marley _____ her guitar for us.
4. Birds _____ in the surrounding trees.
5. We _____ at the dog's antics.

See Lesson 10.1, page 333.

Elaborating: Focusing on the Details

*W*ith strong descriptions, you can help your readers see what you see. Use details that create that effect.

In the model below, Ian Fleming describes a wonderful car— a magical *Paragon Panther*—that has just been fixed up to look like new. Notice the details Fleming includes.

What details does the writer use to show readers that the car was flashy?

Literature Model

Every detail gleamed and glinted with new paint and polished chrome down to the snarling mouth of the big boa-constrictor horn. . . . from the rows and rows of gleaming knobs on the dashboard to the brand-new, dark-red leather upholstery; from the cream-colored collapsible roof to the fine new tires; from the glistening silver of the huge exhaust pipes snaking away from holes in the bright green hood to the glittering license plates that said GEN II.

Ian Fleming,
Chitty Chitty Bang Bang

Fleming elaborates on his description by focusing only on the details showing that the car looked new. By including these details and leaving out others, he presents a clear picture of the car.

Pay Attention to First Impressions

Even an ordinary car has details that you can put into a description. All you have to do is look closely. Start with your first impressions—your first thoughts upon noticing something. In the notes on the right are the first impressions one writer had of the car shown on this page.

You might try thinking about your own first impressions as you walk down a street. What are the first things you notice? What details stick in your mind after you get home?

shiny

glare of sun's reflection

canary yellow

boxy shape

fat, black tires

loud

Journal Writing

Find three familiar objects in your classroom. Write your first impressions of them. What are your first thoughts on noticing each one? Then elaborate, writing three or four additional details you notice about each object.

Grammar Tip

Details listed in a series of three or more items require commas to separate them. For more information, see Lesson 19.2, page 491.

Take a Closer Look

After noting your first impressions, start gathering details. One way is to identify the small things that help create each impression. For example, your first impression of a car might be "shiny." You might take a closer look and notice the polished chrome, freshly waxed paint, and gleaming hubcaps. All these details create the impression of "shiny."

Another way of gathering details is to reexamine your subject. Check for details you might have overlooked. Try to use all your senses. Maybe you forgot to describe the roar of the engine or the smell of the exhaust. Maybe you didn't notice how warm the hood was in the sun.

Kenny Scharf, *Stellaradiola*, 1985

Write a Description of Art

Above is a photo of a detailed piece of art. Examine the picture carefully. Describe the piece as if you were writing an article for your school newspaper.

PURPOSE To convey an impression by using details

AUDIENCE Readers of your school paper

LENGTH 2–3 paragraphs

WRITING RUBRICS To use details effectively in a description, you should

- start with one of your first impressions
- elaborate, adding specific details
- use details that help the reader visualize what you are describing

Viewing and Representing

COOPERATIVE LEARNING In a small group, discuss the artwork. What does its title, *Stellaradiola,* mean? What is the art piece about? How did the artist show his ideas? What do you think the artist wants you to feel or understand?

Cross-Curricular Activity

GEOGRAPHY Landmarks are natural or man-made objects. They help people know where they are. Pick an object you see on your way to school. Describe the object carefully so that a new student could use it as a landmark for finding the school.

Use commas to separate items in a series.

A comma usually precedes *and* when three separate details are listed. An example is

polished chrome, freshly waxed paint, and gleaming hubcaps.

Add commas in the following sentences. Write *correct* if a sentence needs no commas.

1. The art was humorous colorful and unique.
2. The front grill, headlight trim, and bumper were made of chrome.
3. The book is concise well written and informative.
4. The moth was grey soft and furry.
5. The car tires were old fat and ugly.

See Lesson 19.2, page 491.

Descriptive Writing

LESSON 3.4

Ordering Descriptive Details

If details are presented in a sensible order, readers get a picture in their minds. Transition words help make the picture sharper.

In the model below, Freeman Hubbard orders details in his description of a circus parade in the early 1900s. Notice that Hubbard gives details in the order of their appearance in the parade. This makes it easy for readers to picture the scene.

Literature Model

The street was alive with noise as the first four lovely ladies on horseback, trumpets lifted to their lips, came into sight. They were always lithe and lovely, and the plumes they wore danced as their horses pranced. Then came the band, in red uniforms with gold braid, riding on a gilded band wagon that was sometimes drawn by as many as forty horses. The band never stopped playing: the big bass drum thumped steadily, the trumpets shrilled and blared, the cymbals flashed in the sun. Behind the band came great floats.

Freeman Hubbard, *Great Days of the Circus*

Decide Where to Start

To order your own descriptive details, you might imagine your eye is a video camera lens. First, pick a starting point. Then pick a way to move your eye's camera across your subject. One way is to start at the front and move toward the back. Another way is to start at one side and move toward the other side. The order you use should be one that makes sense to your reader.

Drafting Tip

When you're drafting a description, make a quick sketch of the scene. The sketch can help you decide how to order your details.

Descriptive Writing

Front to Back

At the front of the parade came the women on horseback. After them the band rode in on a wagon. The great floats rolled in behind the band.

Left to Right

On the left a tall blonde rider pranced on horseback. To the right came another rider draped with a banner. Two riders waving at the crowd were at the far right.

Journal Writing

Describe your classroom, using two different ordering methods. Compare the results. Which order makes more sense? Why?

Grammar Tip

Prepositional phrases, such as *in the middle,* can also tell position. For information about using commas with prepositional phrases, see Lesson 19.2, page 491.

Use Transitions

Words and phrases such as *after, on the left,* and *to her right* are called transitions. They show how the details in the descriptions are related. Transitions make the descriptions on page 119 easier to follow. Below is another example. Notice how the description changes when just the transition words are changed.

In back of the floats marched the drum major.

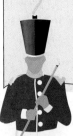

In front of the floats marched the drum major.

Transitions are powerful tools. Without them, you just have a list of details—not a description. Transition words can turn the details into vivid images. The chart below shows some additional transitions you can use.

Transitions		
in back of	beside	first
in front of	above	last
to the left of	below	then
to the right of	next	after

Describe a Scene

The painting on this page shows a farm. How could you describe it? Start by listing the details. Use your list to write your description.

PURPOSE To order details in a description
AUDIENCE Yourself, later
LENGTH 1–2 paragraphs

WRITING RUBRICS To organize the details in a description, you can

- begin with the details that are at the front
- end with the details that are at the back
- use transitions to tell where objects are located

Louisa Matthiasdottir, *Sheep in Blue Landscape,* 1991

Using Computers

Use a drawing software program to create a graphic organizer. In the graphic organizer, list the details that describe the farm scene. Number the details in the order in which you will use them.

Listening and Speaking

COOPERATIVE LEARNING Write a brief description of an object or place. Then read your description aloud to a small group. Group members should draw a picture of what they hear. Discuss whether it was easy or difficult to draw the object or place and tell why.

Grammar Link

Use prepositional phrases to show location.

Add a prepositional phrase to each sentence to show location.

1. The farm _____ belonged to the Kinsmans.
2. The barn _____ was painted red.
3. The cows stood calmly _____.

See Lesson 14.2, page 417.

Describing a Place

By using sensory details, writers are able to share images and experiences with their readers.

In the model below, Eric Garcia describes a place like the one shown in the photo. Notice how the details help you experience the place as if you were there, too.

What details does Eric include to appeal to the senses other than sight?

Details and word choice such as "clean air" and grass "soft like a waterbed" help create the impression of a pleasant and peaceful place.

Student Model

I am up in the Sierra Nevada mountains. I breathe clean air and smell the pine trees. I lie on grass, soft like a waterbed, high green trees around me blocking the sun. The forest animals are all around me making chirping noises. I feed birds and squirrels while I'm on the ground. They seem so peaceful when I am feeding them. When I feed them, they tickle my funny bone.

Eric Garcia, Emperor School
San Gabriel, California

Explore a Place

Choose a special place to write about. When you describe your own special place, include specific details as Eric did. Without details, readers might think your place is like the picture below—dark and uninteresting. To fill in the details, ask yourself questions.

Vocabulary Tip

Specific nouns and adjectives can help make your description more precise. For more information about adjectives, see Lesson 12.1, page 379.

Descriptive Writing

Questions	Answers
Q. What do I see?	**A.** A crane, some wading birds, jungle trees, and rapids
Q. What do they look like?	**A.** The crane is white. The flock of birds is scarlet. The jungle trees are dark green. The rapids make a waterfall.
Q. What sounds do I hear?	**A.** Water roaring over rocks

Journal Writing

Pick a place that you can observe and describe it. Ask yourself questions to generate details. List the details, and then underline the ones that show your place most clearly.

Describe the Scene

Once you've selected your details, use them to write a draft. What order should you use? Questions like the ones shown below can help you decide.

- Which details go together?

- Where are they located?

- Can you link the details with transitions?

- The rapids are on the right, between the rocks.

- The white crane is rising from the rocks.

- The flock of birds is flying through the dark green jungle.

As you draft your description, think about ways to draw your readers in. You might start by choosing one strong impression of your place. Then choose only those details that help create that impression vividly for your readers. In the model below, the writer describes a jungle river valley.

Presenting Tip

Read your description to a friend. What questions does he or she have about it?

What words help you picture the location of the details?

Words like "witch's cauldron," "heavy wings," "scarlet," and "dark green" create a feeling of mystery and drama.

Literature Model

As the jungle valley broadened, the river became an archipelago [group] of islets [small islands]. To the right a gorge opened up, with rapids cascading between sheer walls of rock. The water boiled like a witch's cauldron. . . . From the rocks a white crane rose on heavy wings; a flock of ibis [tall wading birds] fled in a wedge formation, scarlet against a backdrop of dark green.

Armstrong Sperry, *Thunder Country*

Describe a Place

Pick a place that's special, such as a neighborhood basketball court or a quiet corner of the library. Observe your place closely or just think about it. Then write a description of it for a student magazine called *Special Places*.

Try to elaborate by using all the details that make your place special to you. Ask yourself: What colors do I see? What do I smell? What do I hear?

PURPOSE To describe a favorite place accurately

AUDIENCE Readers of a student magazine

LENGTH 2–3 paragraphs

WRITING RUBRICS To use details effectively in a description, you should

- decide which details go together
- order the details to present a clear picture
- use transitions to link ideas

Using Computers

Some word processing programs have a built-in electronic thesaurus. You might use the electronic thesaurus to help you choose interesting nouns and verbs. By carefully choosing your words, you can make your place description more vivid.

Grammar Link

Use adjectives to create clear pictures for readers.

Specific adjectives help to make descriptions vivid and precise. Notice the adjectives Armstrong Sperry uses to modify nouns in the model on page 124.

Add at least one adjective to each sentence below to make the statement clearer and more interesting.

1. The bird flew over the river.
2. The man wrote in his notebook.
3. We hiked on the trails.
4. The air nipped at our noses.
5. The wolf watched over the pups in the den.

See Lesson 12.1, page 379.

Viewing and Representing

In a small group, create a collage of special places. Use pictures from magazines, photographs, or drawings. Each person should tell about the places he or she selected. You may want to choose a picture in the collage as a special place to describe for the writing assignment.

WRITING ABOUT LITERATURE

Getting to Know a New Place

Descriptive writing can create strong feelings in a reader. Specific details help to set a mood.

Descriptive writing can also bring out new feelings. In the model below, a young city girl finds herself in the woods for the first time. Think about your own feelings as you read Nicholasa Mohr's description.

Literature Model

The sun came through the leaves, stems, and petals, streaming down like rows of bright ribbons landing on the dark green earth. . . . Nilda walked over to the flowers and touched them. Inhaling the sweet fragrance, she felt slightly dizzy, almost reeling. She sat down on the dark earth and felt the sun on her face, slipping down her body and over to the shrubs covered with roses. The bright sash of warm sunlight enveloped her and the flowers; she was part of them; they were part of her.

Nicholasa Mohr, *Nilda*

> Details like "sweet fragrance" and "warm sunlight" create a soft, dreamy feeling.

> How does Nilda feel about this place?

Reading Mohr's description, you might have thought about the warm sun. You might have thought about being dizzy or happy. When you read something, there's no right or wrong way to feel. The same piece of writing can bring out different responses in different people.

Respond to a Description

One way to respond to a place description is with a creative project of your own. To begin, you might choose a place that the description makes you think of.

Once you've chosen your place, you might take some photos of it. With photos you can focus on details that create the feeling of your place. Here two students show photos from their trip to Bandelier National Monument in New Mexico.

Another way to describe your place is by making a map of it and drawing in the details. Below, the students show Bandelier National Monument in a homemade map.

Jenny and Katie Bresee,
George Washington Carver School,
San Francisco, California

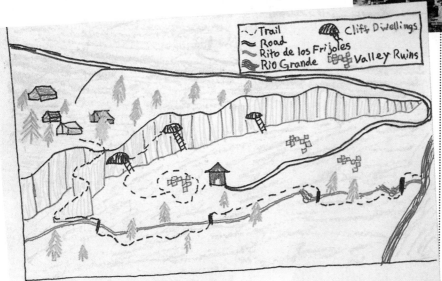

Journal Writing

List the most memorable details in the model on page 126. What did they make you think or feel? Write your response in your journal.

Proofreading Tip

Names of places are proper nouns and always start with capital letters. For more information about proper nouns, see Lesson 9.1, page 319.

Do a Double Take

You can create a travel brochure by adding captions to your photos and map. Travel brochures describe places that people might like to visit. To create your own brochure, concentrate on the details of your place. Which ones might interest other people? Here is Jenny and Katie's travel brochure for Bandelier National Monument.

travel brochure

When you enter Bandelier National Monument it's a whole other world. It's like going back in time. There are cliff dwellings, ruins, rivers, streams, and even a bat cave.

When early humans came to Bandelier, they found that the small caves that dotted the cliff face made excellent homes. Inside the caves, the air is musty and cool like air conditioning.

The creek that runs through Bandelier is the Rito de los Frijoles. Lots of plants and animals depend on the water from the creek. You can see skunks, rabbits, mice, birds, bats, deer, coyotes and mountain lions come to drink at the Rito de los Frijoles.

Trail
Road
Rito de los Frijoles
Río Grande
Cliff Dwellings
Valley Ruins

Write a Travel Brochure

Create your own travel brochure. The purpose of the brochure is to get people to visit the place that is described. Plan to include at least two photos, drawings, or maps in your brochure. Then describe your place in writing.

PURPOSE To create a travel brochure
AUDIENCE Vacationers
LENGTH 3–4 paragraphs

WRITING RUBRICS To write a description of a place for a travel brochure, you should

- freewrite to think of a place to describe
- list details that tell what's special about the place
- include your own feelings about the place
- choose facts that will interest your readers

Using Computers

Some word processing programs offer a page-layout option. Using this option can help make your travel brochure look like the real thing. With page layout, you can design and view your brochure on screen. You can decide where to put text and captions and where to leave space for photos and maps. Then, after you print, you can put the photos and maps in the blank spaces.

Grammar Link

Capitalize proper nouns.

The names of specific people and places are proper nouns, which always begin with a capital letter. Note the proper nouns Jenny and Katie Bresee used in their travel brochure on page 128.

Write the sentences below. Then revise them, adding capital letters as necessary.

1. The island of puerto rico is near Florida.
2. The island's capital city is san juan.
3. The island is part of a group called the west indies.
4. Puerto rico is bounded on the north by the atlantic ocean.
5. To the south lies the caribbean sea.

See Lesson 9.1, page 319.

Listening and Speaking

PRESENTING Take turns reading your travel brochures in a small group. Tell about your map and pictures. Read your captions. Other group members should take notes. They should jot down words that make the place easy to picture and that create images that stay in their minds. After each reading, share ideas about your descriptions.

Writing Process in Action

Descriptive Writing

In the preceding lessons, you've learned how to paint pictures with words. You've also had the chance to use details as you wrote descriptions of places, animals, and things. Now it's time to put together what you learned. In this lesson, you will describe something memorable in your life.

Assignment

Context

An artist friend wants you to write a description of something memorable in your life. Afterward, your friend plans to paint a detailed picture based on your description.

Purpose

To inspire an artist with a memorable description

Audience

An artist

Length

1 page

WRITING Online

Visit the *Writer's Choice* Web site at **writerschoice. glencoe.com** for additional writing prompts.

The following pages can help you plan and write your description. Read through them. Then refer to them as you need to, but don't be tied down by them. Remember that you're in charge of your own writing process.

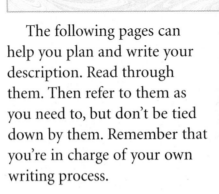

Prewriting

You know so many people, places, and things. How do you choose a subject to describe? You might try exploring the possibilities through prewriting. The options on this page suggests several methods of prewriting. You can freewrite, as the writer has in the example here. You can also build a cluster of details or brainstorm for a list of impressions. You can even try combining approaches.

Option A
Make a cluster of details.

Option B
Brainstorm for a list of impressions.

Option C
Freewrite for ideas.

> My grandmother cooks my favorite spaghetti sauce. It smells of peppers and garlic. Her blue apron gets all stained. She walks in soft shoes that make flopping sounds. The kitchen is hot from the stove.

As you explore through prewriting, remind yourself to use all five senses. Try to discover specific details for each sense. Think about the small details that make things special.

Now that you've chosen a subject, think about what details an artist would need to paint it. What order of details would be easiest to follow? What impressions do you want to give your reader?

Remember that there's no right or wrong prewriting strategy to use. Stick with whatever works best for you.

Drafting

While you draft, think about turning your prewriting into a clear, detailed description. Don't worry about your grammar, spelling, and punctuation at this point. Just let your ideas flow in an order that makes sense to you now. Try to make your reader understand what it's like to be there, up close to your subject. In the following model, Michael Dorris vividly describes a young girl's sense of wonder as she discovers the details of her own face reflected in her father's eyes.

TIME

For more about generating ideas for details, see **TIME Facing the Blank Page,** page 90.

Drafting Tip

For more information about gathering and recording effective details, see Lessons 3.2–3.3, pages 110–117.

Descriptive Writing

Literature Model

I leaned forward, stared into the dark brown circles, and it was like diving into the deepest pools. Suddenly I saw two tiny girls looking back. Their faces were clear, their brows straight as canoes, and their chins as narrow and clean as lemons. As I watched, their mouths grew wide. They were pretty.

Michael Dorris, *Morning Girl*

Revising Tip

For more information about ordering details and using transitions, see Lesson 3.4, pages 118–121.

Revising

To begin revising, read over your draft to make sure that what you've written fits your purpose and audience. Then have a writing conference. Read your draft to a partner or small group. Use your audience's reactions to help you evaluate your work.

Question A
Have I used all my senses?

Question B
Are my details vivid?

Question C
Have I made effective use of transitions?

i like hiding under the kitchen table while
Beneath the table
my grandmother cooks spaghetti. I can smell
simmering
the garlic and green peppers cooking and watch
r
my grandmother stiring the sauce. Her apron
red
always gets covered with these tiny spatters.
She doesn't mind, though. She's too busy testing
padding   soft
the noodles or going to the sink in her house
slippers.

Editing/Proofreading

Now's the time to check for the standard conventions—grammar, spelling, and mechanics. At this stage you'll add the finishing touches to the word picture you've painted.

To go with your description, you might also draw a picture. By sketching the same details you used in your writing, you can make your images even easier to imagine.

Use the checklist at the right to help you during proofreading. It's best to focus on one question at a time.

Publishing/Presenting

This is the moment you've worked toward—sharing the description you wrote for your artist friend. As you've probably discovered, writing can be a very satisfying way to describe the world around you. By writing, you can tell others about all the special details you notice every day.

Editing/Proofreading Checklist

- Have I used descriptive adjectives and action verbs?
- Do my transitions help the reader?
- Do my subjects and verbs agree?
- Have I used proper punctuation and capitalization?
- Is every word spelled correctly?

Proofreading Tip

For proofreading symbols, see page 72 or 267. The computer can help you proofread. Use its spelling checker and grammar checker features.

Journal Writing

Reflect on your writing process experience. Answer these questions in your journal: What do you like best about your description? What was the hardest part of writing it? What did you learn in your writing conference? What new thing have you learned as a writer?

Literature Model

• Michael Dorris •

from

MORNING GIRL

*Award-winning author Michael Dorris describes the world of Morning Girl—
the Bahamas in 1492, shortly before Columbus's arrival. In this excerpt from the novel,
Morning Girl seeks her family's help in learning what her own face looks like.
As you read, pay special attention to Dorris's descriptions and the impressions and
images they create. Then try the activities in Linking Writing and Literature on page 140.*

The water is never still enough. Just when I can almost see my face, when my eyes and my nose and my mouth are about to settle into a picture I can remember, a fish rises for air or a leaf drops to the surface of the pond or Star Boy tosses a pebble into my reflection and I break into shining pieces. It makes no sense to him that I'm curious about what people see when they look at me.

"They see *you*," he said, as if that answered my question. We were searching for ripe fruit on the trees behind our house.

"But what *is* me?" I asked him. "I wouldn't recognize myself unless I

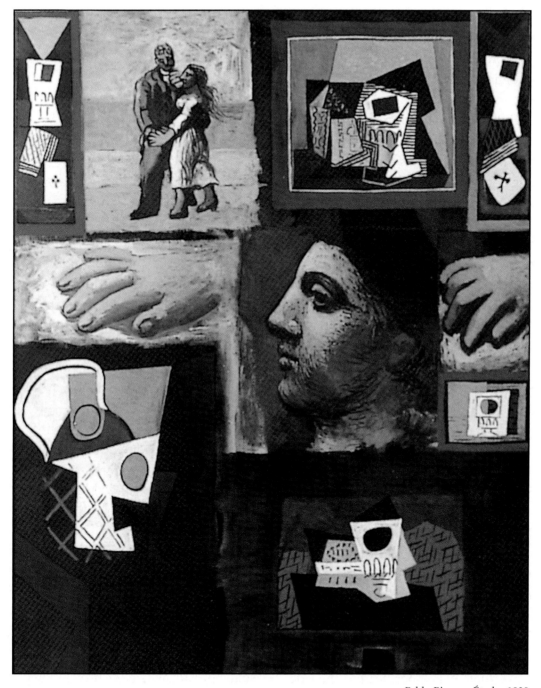

Pablo Picasso, *Études,* 1920

was sitting on the bottom of a quiet pool, looking up at me looking down."

"You are . . . *you.*" He lost his patience and walked away to find his friend Red Feathers.

But what did "you" mean? I knew my hands very well. I study them when I trim my nails with the rough edge of a broken shell, making them smooth and flat. I could spread my fingers and press them into wet sand to see the shape they leave. Once I tried to do that with my head, but all I got was a big shallow hole and dirty hair.

I knew the front of my body, the bottoms of my feet. I knew the color of my arms—tan as the inside of a yam after the air has dried it—and if I stretched my tongue I could see its pink tip.

"Tell me about my face," I asked Mother one day when we were walking along the beach.

She stopped, turned to me in confusion. "What *about* your face?"

"Is it long and wrinkled, like Grandmother's, or round as a coconut, like Star Boy's? Are my eyes wise like yours or ready to laugh like Father's? Are my teeth as crooked as the trunks of palm trees?"

Mother cocked her head to the side and made lines in her forehead. "I don't think I've ever looked at you that way," she said. "To me you've always been yourself, different from anyone else."

"But I want to *know*," I begged her.

> **❝** *'Tell me about my face,' I asked Mother one day . . .* **❞**

Mother nodded. "I remember that feeling. Try this."

She took my hand and guided it to my neck. "Touch," she told me. "Very softly. No, close your eyes and think with your fingers. Now compare." She placed my other hand on her face, the face I know better than any other.

I traced the line of her chin. Mine was smaller, pointier. I followed her lips with one thumb, my own with the other. Hers seemed fuller.

"Your mouth is wider," I cried, unhappy with myself.

"That's because I'm smiling, Morning Girl."

And suddenly my mouth was wide, too, and my cheeks were hills on either side.

Next I found the lashes of our eyes, then moved above them. Even without watching I could see the curved shape of Mother's dark brows. They made her look surprised at everything, surprised and delighted.

"Mine are straight," I said.

Paul Gauguin, *Tahitian Women*, or *On the Beach*, 1891

"Like your grandfather's."

He had always looked tired. I liked surprised better.

"Now, here." Mother cupped my fingers around the tip of my nose. I could feel the breath rush in and out of my nostrils. I could smell the fruit I had picked with Star Boy.

Finally we moved to the ears, and in the dark they were as delicate and complicated as the inside of a spiral[1] shell, but soft.

"Our ears are the same," I told Mother, and she felt with her own hand, testing and probing every part.

"You're right." She sounded as pleased as I was.

I opened my eyes and memorized her ears. At least *that* part I would now recognize.

---

1 spiral (spī′rəl) curving, winding

"Did this help you?" she asked me. "Do you know Morning Girl any better?"

"Oh yes," I said. "She has a chin like a starfish and brows like white clouds on the horizon. Her nose works. Her cheeks swell into mountains when she smiles. The only thing right about her is her ears."

> **" Do you know Morning Girl any better? "**

Mother covered her mouth, the way she does when she laughs and doesn't want anyone to stare. "That's my Morning Girl," she said. "That's her exactly."

The next day, as I was getting up and Star Boy was about to go to sleep on his mat, I leaned close to him.

"What does my chin look like?" I demanded.

He blinked, frowned, made his eyes small while he decided. "A starfish," he finally said.

I was very worried until I saw he was making a joke.

"I heard Mother telling Father," he confessed when I pinched him. "But

---

2 **juts out** (jutz out) sticks out

I don't know." He rubbed his arm, showed me where I had made it turn red. "To me it looks like the end of the rock that juts out[2] into the ocean near the north end of the island. The one they call 'The Giant Digging Stick.'"

"You don't have to be curious about *your* face," I whispered. "All you have to do is wait for a jellyfish to float on shore and get stranded when the tide leaves. Sometimes I see one and I think it's you, buried in the sand up to your neck."

When I went outside, Father was sitting on a log fixing a shark's tooth to use as a hook at the end of his fishing lance.

"Who is this?" he asked the lance. "Who is this with my wife's ears stuck onto the side of her head?"

> **" Why should my own face be a secret from me? "**

"You laugh at me, too," I said. "But why is it so strange to want to know what everyone else already knows? Why should my own face be a secret from me?"

"There *is* a way," Father said kindly, and motioned me to stand beside him. He knelt down so that we would be the same size. "Look into my eyes," he told me. "What do you see?"

I leaned forward, stared into the dark brown circles, and it was like diving into the deepest pools. Suddenly I saw two tiny girls looking back. Their faces were clear, their brows straight as canoes, and their chins as narrow and clean as lemons.

As I watched, their mouths grew wide. They were pretty.

"Who are they?" I couldn't take my eyes off those strange new faces. "Who are these pretty girls who live inside your head?"

"They are the answer to your question," Father said. "And they are always here when you need to find them."

Linking Writing and Literature

 Collect Your Thoughts

Think about Morning Girl's desire to know what she looks like. Do you think she's just being vain, or is she expressing some deeper desire? In your journal, jot down some thoughts about Morning Girl's quest.

 Talk About Reading

Discuss the excerpt from *Morning Girl* with a small group. Ask one person to lead the group's discussion and another to take notes. Use the following question to guide you.

1. **Connect to Your Life** Unlike Morning Girl, you can see yourself in mirrors, photographs, videos, and so on. But is the person you *see* the person you *are?* Why?

2. **Critical Thinking: Interpret** Morning Girl asks, "Who are these pretty girls who live inside your head?" What does her father mean when he replies, "They are the answer to your question, and they are always here when you need to find them."

3. **6+1 Trait®: Voice** How does the author's voice change when Morning Girl's mother or father is speaking? What signals this change?

4. **Connect to Your Writing** Why is Morning Girl's conversation with her father important to the main idea of the excerpt? What lesson does this teach you about your own writing?

 Write About Reading

Personal Essay Like Morning Girl, everyone wonders at some time or another who they really are and how other people see them. In a personal essay, describe who you are. How do you see yourself? How do others—your family, teachers, friends, new acquaintances—see you? Draw a picture of yourself with words.

Focus on Voice. Voice is the authentic self of the writer or a character expressed through words. As you write about who you are, choose language and sentence structures that express your true voice.

For more information on voice and the 6+1 Trait® model, see **Writing and Research Handbook,** pages 682–684.

6+1 Trait® is a registered trademark of Northwest Regional Educational Laboratory, which does not endorse this product.

Reflecting on the Unit

Summarize what you learned in this unit by answering the following questions.

❶ What are some strategies for observing and noting details before you write?

❷ What kinds of details can help give the reader a vivid picture?

❸ How can you organize the details of your writing so that they have a clear order?

❹ How can you draw readers in and help them share your experiences and feelings?

Adding to Your Portfolio

CHOOSE A SELECTION FOR YOUR PORTFOLIO Look over the descriptive writing you did for this unit. Choose one completed piece for your portfolio. The piece you choose should show some or all of the following:

- a general impression, followed by details that create that impression
- descriptive details gathered by using all the senses
- a logical way of ordering of details that is clear to the reader
- transitions that are used to connect details

REFLECT ON YOUR CHOICE Attach a note to the piece you chose, explaining briefly why you chose it and what you learned from writing it.

SET GOALS How can you improve your writing? What skill will you focus on the next time you write?

Writing Across the Curriculum

MAKE AN ART CONNECTION Find a photograph of an outdoor scene in the country, and compare it with the painting on page 121. Study details such as light and shadow, shapes, and color. Then describe both the painting and the photograph, and tell how each one makes you feel.

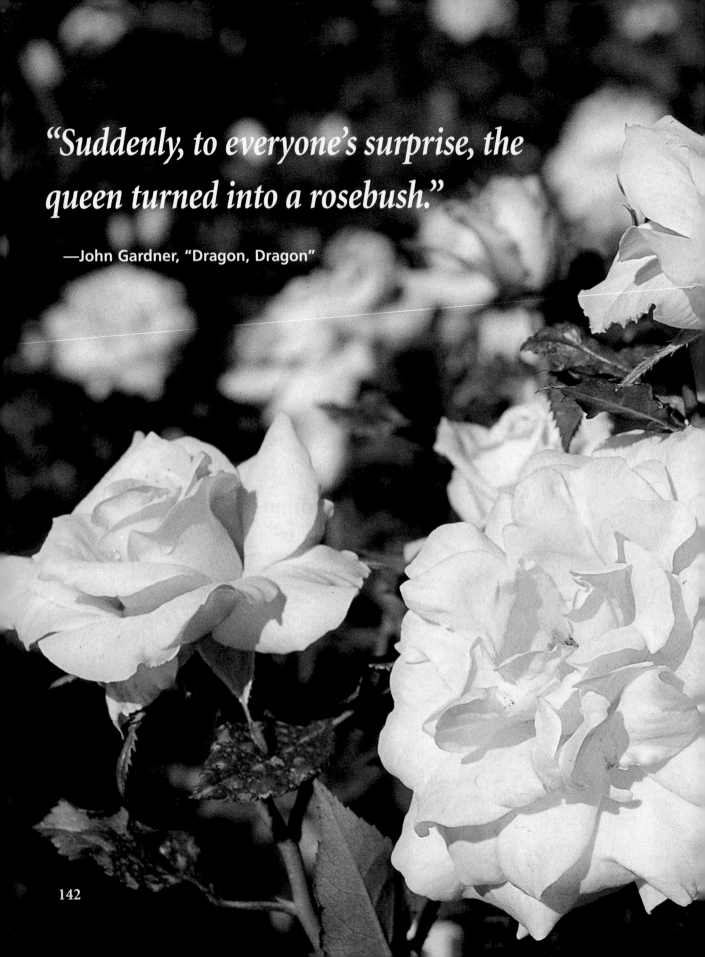

"Suddenly, to everyone's surprise, the queen turned into a rosebush."

—John Gardner, "Dragon, Dragon"

Narrative Writing

Writing in the Real World: *Virginia Hamilton*   144

Lesson **4.1**   **Developing a Real-Life Story**   148

Lesson **4.2**   **Keeping a Story Organized**   152

Lesson **4.3**   **Writing Dialogue**   156

Lesson **4.4**   **Writing About an Event**   160

Lesson **4.5**   **Writing About Literature:
Responding to a Biography**   164

Writing Process in Action   168

Literature Model: "The Jacket" *by Gary Soto*   172

Unit 4 Review   179

Agood biography satisfies our natural curiosity about the lives of other people. A biography may be short, such as a personality profile in a newspaper or a magazine. Or, it may be book-length, such as Virginia Hamilton's biography of W. E. B. Du Bois, a great civil rights leader and educator. The following excerpt opens Hamilton's Du Bois biography.

from W. E. B. Du Bois: A Biography

By Virginia Hamilton

Dr. William Edward Burghardt Du Bois lay dying in the city of Accra, Ghana, on the coast of West Africa. He was the black man who, with obvious love, had called all black people "my people." The age-old fight for equality waged by blacks everywhere had been "his" battle for more than half a century, and winning it would have been the greatest achievement of his life. For years William Du Bois had led "his" people in their protest struggle for liberty; now he lay dying far away from America, the country of his birth.

Life flickered and flamed, then faltered, in the ninety-five-year-old Dr. Du Bois. He had moments of consciousness throughout the solemn evening, and he was told that all was well in America. Back home it was the eve of a monumental gathering. Blacks and whites by the thousands were preparing to march on Washington, D.C., the next day. Every step they took would lead them closer to the freedom of which the Doctor had dreamed. Every song they sang would speak of justice, which he had worked so hard to make a reality.

Twenty minutes before midnight, on August 27, 1963, Dr. W. E. B. Du Bois died. The following day nearly half a million Americans carried out the largest protest demonstration ever seen in the United States. In the songs and slogans of the thousands on the move was the courageous spirit for which the Doctor had strived in the past.

A Writer's Process

Prewriting
Building a Story

Choosing the subject for her biography was not difficult for Virginia Hamilton. Her interest in Dr. Du Bois had sprouted many years earlier. Her father often read stories aloud that were written by Du Bois. Hamilton recalls, "I didn't know the significance of it at the time. I just knew that Du Bois was someone my father greatly admired." Later, as a young woman, Hamilton heard Du Bois speak in her hometown of Yellow Springs, Ohio. His eloquence impressed her, and the interest in her future biographical subject grew.

Hamilton published *W. E. B. Du Bois: A Biography* in 1972. Researching and writing about Du Bois's long life—he lived to be ninety-five—took Hamilton about five years. By the end of the research phase, Hamilton had collected a huge number of facts. Now she needed to "find the story." She recalls, "The material itself began to speak to me for him."

Organizing the information was a big task, but Hamilton tried to keep it simple. She started with the most basic information—what she calls "the bare bones." Hamilton explains, "You've got all this material, all these facts, when you do a biography. All the dates in the world! And you say, 'How am I going to do this?' Well, the way you do it is you start with the beginning. You start with, this man was born, or this man died, and you go from there."

Drafting
Making It Real

A biography is a narrative that makes a real person come alive through words. Like any other narrative, a biography must tell an engaging story. Hamilton is very much aware of this. "I'm strongly plot-oriented," she says. "I try to represent original ideas—and good stories."

To advance the plot, Hamilton quotes her subject as much as possible. She knows that readers want to hear the person's own words. Hamilton believes strongly that biographers should quote their subjects' actual words, not invent their own dialogue.

In addition to using actual quotations, Hamilton uses concrete details about her subject's life. For example, Hamilton found information about young Du Bois's packing for school that she included in the biography. The details seemed real to her, and she hoped they would bring Du Bois alive to her readers as well.

Revising
Shaping the Story

Writing a biography can become complicated. All the facts and quotations can tangle the thread of the narrative. A biographer's task is to shape the material into a clear and understandable story. During the revision process, parts often need to be cut or rearranged. Hamilton explains, "All that information can't go into one, small biography. So you have to pick and choose."

To keep the story interesting, a biographer can present events in a way that creates suspense. For example, Hamilton began her Du Bois biography with his death in Africa rather than chronologically with his birth in America.

She presented events out of sequence because she wanted readers to wonder why Du Bois was dying far from his home. She wanted them to question why huge crowds came the next day to a rally in Washington, D.C. Beginning with the end of her subject's life allowed Hamilton to open the story dramatically and build suspense. In the first three paragraphs, readers can sense the impact of Du Bois's life on others.

Editing
Finishing Touches

As she shaped the story of Du Bois's life, Hamilton focused on her writing style, or voice, including word choice, sentence length, and figures of speech. She kept the narrative simple. The story itself "demanded I write it as simply as I could," she notes, "and introduce to people this person whom they probably would have a hard time believing had existed."

Analyzing the Media Connection

Discuss these questions about the model on page 144.

1. Why do you think Hamilton mentions both Africa and America?

2. Writers use *alliteration*—the repetition of initial consonants—to flavor their language. Find one example of alliteration in Hamilton's writing and explain its effect.

3. What is Hamilton's opinion of Du Bois? What words and phrases helped you identify the author's feelings about her subject?

4. Based on the opening, what do you think the excerpt's theme is?

5. What major events from Du Bois's life does the excerpt present?

Analyzing a Writer's Process

Discuss these questions about Virginia Hamilton's writing process.

1. How did Hamilton choose the subject for her biography?

2. What details did Hamilton include to make her subject come to life?

3. Why does Hamilton believe in quoting the subject's own words?

4. Do you agree with Hamilton's claim that the biographer must identify with the subject in a personal way? Why or why not?

5. What must a biographer do with all the information she or he collects? Explain.

Grammar Link

Virginia Hamilton uses actual quotations to advance the plot and describe the characters.

"I want to go to Harvard," Du Bois said, "because it is the oldest and largest and most widely known college."

Correctly punctuate and capitalize each direct quotation.

1. in 1888, Du Bois graduated from Fisk, said Cass.

2. did you know Marley asked he was the first African American to earn a PhD.?

3. "he believed college-educated African Americans should lead the fight against discrimination, said Ms. Bean.

4. Kate noted, "the narrative begins by describing Dr. Du Bois's death.

5. David added, "what a dramatic beginning!

See Lesson 18.1, page 473.

TIME

For more about story ideas, see **TIME Facing the Blank Page,** page 92.

LESSON 4.1

Developing a Real-Life Story

A real-life story tells about actual events that happen to real people. A well-written real-life narrative, like good fiction, should hold the reader's attention by presenting interesting characters in a carefully thought-out setting and plot.

You can find stories in books, on television, and in films. What about the true stories in your own mind? You also have fascinating real-life stories to tell.

Stories can be as different as the people who tell them. No two storytellers have exactly the same background or outlook. Think of a hundred people having the same experience, such as attending a sporting event or watching a parade. Each of them would probably tell about the experience in a different way.

Capture the Reader's Attention

A narrative is a story that answers the question *What happened?* Before you begin a narrative, decide why someone might read the story. Then think about *who* will read it.

Above all, a good narrative must capture a reader's attention from the very beginning. Strong opening paragraphs make the reader want to continue. Read the beginning of the story below.

Grammar Tip

When you edit your draft of a narrative, make sure that all verb tenses are used correctly. For more information, see Lessons 10.4–10.7, pages 339–346.

Narrative Writing

Literature Model

"Owen! Time to go!"
I was spying down from behind the crest of the sand dune back of the house. Our car looked like an upside-down bug, a bug with spindly legs waving frantically in the air. Fishing rods were sticking out the back window, my bike was hanging off the rear, and the roof rack was piled with more junk than we had brought. It was the end of summer. Labor Day. Two o'clock in the afternoon. Time to go home.

But not me. I was going to stay.

"Owen! *Time to go!*"

My parents stood there, helpless, not knowing where to even begin to look for me.

Avi, A Place Called Ugly

How does the writer grab your attention and make you want to read on?

All well-written stories have the same elements. Good stories tell about characters who are involved in some sort of action in a certain place, and the events are presented in a clear order.

Journal Writing

You have stories to tell about experiences you've had. In your journal, jot down an idea for a story. Note the characters, place, and action for your story.

Find the Right Idea

Real-life stories may come from successes or failures in the lives of real people. They may come from accidents or struggles. Sometimes you'll find that ideas for real-life stories come easily. Other times you may find that you can't come up with an idea at all. When this happens, you may want to try a few different strategies. Reread some of your journal entries, or make a list of places, events, or people you know. Browse through a family scrapbook. Look at the ideas below.

MOVERS

Moving into our new house

Ben comes home from the hospital

Our friend Loo Wang from China

Building the doghouse

Listing

1. Important dates in history

2. People I admire

3. Fun vacations

4. Exciting events I have taken part in

5. Things that make me laugh

Journal Entry
Today Mom and Ben and I went for a ride in a helicopter. At first, Ben was afraid of flying in something so small. Mom and I had to let him sit between us. Then, as soon as we got up in the air, he had to sit by the

4.1 | Writing Activities

Write About the Past

Think of an important event in your life that you could describe to a friend. Think about what you want to tell about it and how. To prepare for writing, list some sentences or phrases with beginnings such as *I saw, I remember,* and *I felt.*

PURPOSE To record a real-life experience
AUDIENCE A friend
LENGTH 3–4 paragraphs

WRITING RUBRICS To write an effective real-life narrative, you should

- use your list to help you compose
- establish characters, a place, and action
- include interesting details
- create interest with your first paragraph

Listening and Speaking

COOPERATIVE LEARNING Think of your favorite school experience from a past year. Write a brief narrative about this experience. Working in a small group, read your narratives to one another. Revise your own narrative based on what the group said was unclear or uninteresting. Assemble all the narratives into a booklet.

Viewing and Representing

MAKE A POSTER Create a poster that illustrates the school experience you

Use consistent verb tenses when you write.

Notice the consistent use of verb tense in this sentence from the model (all refer to a time in the past):

*Fishing rods **were sticking** out the back window, my bike **was hanging** off the rear, and the roof rack **was piled** with more junk. . . .*

Rewrite each sentence below to make the verb tenses consistent.

1. On our vacation last year, my family and I visited Denver, and we see the capitol.
2. At camp I will learn to canoe; it was fun.
3. The game ended in a tie, and everyone in the stands will cheer for the teams.
4. My family move to San Diego at the end of the year, and my mom bought a business.
5. When I got home from school, my dog ran happily and jumped with joy.

See Lessons 10.4–10.7, pages 339–346.

wrote about. Display the posters in your classroom and see whether students can match your poster with your narrative.

Keeping a Story Organized

To tell a story that is clear, the events and details need to be arranged in a logical order. Many stories can even be told without words.

Glen Rabena,
Mosquito Mask (in a
Native American style),
n.d.

Rhythmic drumbeats, beautifully dressed dancers, colorful masks, tall totem poles, carved house fronts—these are the props of the Kwakiutl storytellers. The Kwakiutl peoples of the northwestern coast of North America tell stories as a part of their everyday lives. They may use art, dancing, chanting, or the beating of drums. A new baby or a wedding may call for celebration with stories from nature. Often these storytellers use no words, yet the people understand their tales. The storyteller gives important details and events in an understandable order.

How would you tell a story without using words? Make a list of the ways you would try.

Edward S. Curtis, *Masked Kwakiutl Dancers,* c. 1915

Sort Through the Details

When you write a story, you use words. Like the Kwakiutl storytellers, you should choose your details carefully. You also need to organize the details in a way that's clear to your readers.

When you begin to draft your narrative, you may find that you have too many details to tell. Choose only the details that are essential to your story. If you do this, your readers won't get confused by ideas that don't really matter. Sometimes you may have to cut out some details in order to keep the most important details clear. Look at the following notes, taken by a student preparing to write a short narrative. Which three notes do you think would be the strongest parts of a narrative called "My Paper Route"?

Revising Tip

When you are ready to revise, have a partner read your draft. Ask if you have left out any important details or if the order of the details is confusing.

Narrative Writing

My Paper Route

My paper route was more than 3 miles long.

My sister got a job in a bakery.

I began my paper route the day after my tenth birthday.

The morning edition has better comics than the evening edition.

Every morning I got up at 5:00 A.M.

Journal Writing

Recall a day from last week. List the important events of that day. Highlight the events that were most important.

Organize Events

After you've chosen the important events for your narrative, you need to place them in some particular order. Time order is an effective way to organize your story. When using time order, you tell what happened first, second, and so on. You may use words like *then* or *next*. These words will help your readers follow your story.

The writer of the real-life story below uses three of the statements shown on page 153. Notice the other details the writer adds to fill out the story.

I began my paper route the day after my tenth birthday.

I began my paper route the day after my tenth birthday. The first day was the worst. A man from the newspaper office came with me. He and I walked more than 3 miles and delivered 423 papers. On the third day, I went out all by myself.

Every morning I got up at five o'clock. Then I rode my bike down to the drop-off point to pick up my papers. For the first few weeks, I didn't think I would ever finish. I felt so tired, and my feet hurt. My route, you see, was more than 3 miles long. After a few weeks, though, it didn't seem so bad. Sometimes, especially on nice mornings, I actually liked it.

Every morning I got up at 5:00 A.M.

My paper route was more than 3 miles long.

Write a Real-life Narrative

A magazine called *Challenge* is looking for narratives about exciting experiences. Think about an exciting experience you have had and write a narrative, arranging details to build interest and suspense.

PURPOSE To organize details to write about a real experience

AUDIENCE The editors of *Challenge*

LENGTH 3–4 paragraphs

WRITING RUBRICS To use details effectively in a narrative, you should

- choose the details that are most important to your story
- arrange the details to make your story clear and dramatic
- proofread to check grammar and spelling

Listening and Speaking

TELLING A STORY Turn your narrative about an exciting experience into a story that you tell orally. Deliver it first to a group of three or four classmates. Ask them for comments and suggestions to make your story more interesting and exciting. Rehearse it several times and then present it for the entire class as part of a storytelling series that might be spread over the school term.

Grammar Link

Use the comparative forms of *bad* correctly.

When you compare two things, use *worse*. Use *worst* to compare three or more things.

The first day was the **worst.**

Complete each sentence below with the correct form of *bad.*

1. Is Janice's cold _____ than Bill's?
2. Of all the suggestions, that one is the _____ .
3. Was the accident a _____ one?
4. That is the _____ idea of all.
5. My handwriting is _____ than yours.

See Lesson 12.4, page 385.

Cross-Curricular Activity

MUSIC Find a piece of music on a CD or cassette that tells a story. It might be a version of an old ballad or a modern folk or country song. Write a brief narrative of the story line in the song. Then, meet with a small group and play your musical selections for each other. Discuss what the music adds to the story in terms of the song's meaning and the feelings it evokes.

Writing Dialogue

*D*ialogue is the words spoken by the characters in a story. Well-written dialogue can help bring characters and events to life. What characters say, and how they say it, tells a lot about them.

Dialogue can help make a story lifelike and exciting. Read the passage below. Think about the message the dialogue gives about the characters.

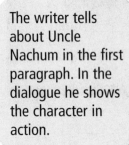

Literature Model

The writer tells about Uncle Nachum in the first paragraph. In the dialogue he shows the character in action.

You don't have to use a short phrase to identify speakers each time they speak if the identity of the speaker is clear.

Uncle Nachum had a joke or witty remark for every occasion, telling them in his hoarse voice and enjoying what he said with a hearty laugh. . . . As I watched him at his tricks, he would throw me one of his clever questions, such as, "How many ends does a stick have?"

"Two!" I answered.

"And half a stick?"

"One!" I loudly declared.

And then Uncle Nachum would rock with great, thundering laughter. How did that short body come by such a tremendous laugh? When he laughed it seemed the walls laughed too.

Benjamin Tene, *In the Shade of the Chestnut Tree*

Identify the Speaker

When you write a dialogue, you need to help your readers keep track of who is speaking. Show which words a character speaks by putting quotation marks around the words. Also, tell who is speaking by using a phrase such as *she said*. When a different character begins to speak, start a new paragraph.

Now look at how this conversation can be written as dialogue.

"Tommy told a funny story at school today. I almost died!" said Calvin.

"Tell it to me," said Hobbes.

"Well, actually the story itself wasn't so funny. It was the *way* he told it."

"How did he tell it?" asked Hobbes.

"He was drinking milk and when he laughed, it came up his nose!"

Tips for Writing Dialogue	
Here's How Use quotation marks before and after the speaker's exact words. Use phrases with a word such as *said*. Start a new line each time a different character speaks.	**Here's Why** To show which words the character actually spoke To let the reader know who is speaking To make the dialogue easier to follow

Journal Writing

Recall a recent conversation you had with a friend. Practice dialogue by recording the conversation in your journal. Be careful to make clear who is saying what.

Listen Carefully

Paying attention to conversations is one of the best ways to get to know people. In your narrative writing, the words your characters say can help readers get to know them, too.

Two short narratives are shown below. The first one does not use dialogue; the second one does. See how dialogue shows the personalities of the two characters in the second narrative. What is one example of how dialogue helps you get to know Meg and Ralph?

Last summer I almost got lost in the woods. My sister Meg and my little brother Ralph were with me. Meg is nine and has a pretty wild imagination. Ralph is just a little kid.

Our family was camping at Lake McGee. The first day we hiked the trail to the overlook. Everything went fine until we came to some big trees that had fallen over the trail. We walked around them. On the other side, though, we couldn't see the trail! We retraced our steps, but we still couldn't find the trail!

"Well, I think we may be lost," I announced.

"L-l-lost?" Ralph said softly, grabbing my hand.

"Well, not _really_ lost, kiddo. Just lost for a minute," I said, trying to reassure him—and myself. "Let me think. What color were those trail blazes?"

"Maybe wolves will find us, and we'll become wolf children and live in the woods forever!" said Meg excitedly. Ralph began to whimper.

"You're not helping, Meg. Now, let's try to think. Which way is the trail?"

The writer uses the adverbs "softly" and "excitedly" in these identifying phrases.

Write a Dialogue

Write a conversation between two characters of different ages, backgrounds, or personalities.

PURPOSE To use dialogue for characterization
AUDIENCE Your class
LENGTH At least 8 lines of dialogue

WRITING RUBRICS To write effective dialogue, you should

- use dialogue that reveals character
- use phrases that identify speakers
- indent and punctuate correctly to indicate clearly who is speaking

Cross-Curricular Activity

ART Study the Edvard Munch painting. What might these women be saying? Describe the painting by writing a short narrative that includes dialogue.

Edvard Munch, *Women on a Bridge*, c. 1903

Grammar Link

Use quotation marks before and after a direct quotation.

To make dialogue clear, use quotation marks around the words a character says.

"It may rain," Sue said.

Write the following sentences, adding quotation marks to mark the beginning and end of dialogue.

1. Maria said, It's pouring. Where did this rain come from?
2. Let's run under that awning! yelled Kiko.
3. Maria yelled back, We may have to swim there!
4. I'm not moving, said Seth as he sat in a puddle.
5. Oh no, said Maria, Seth is soaked to the bone!

See Lesson 19.6, page 499.

Listening and Speaking

DRAMATIC READINGS Working in groups of three or four, look through a literature book for examples of dialogue that reveal information about the characters and their personalities. In your group, develop a dramatic reading of the passage and present it to the class. Have someone in the group provide the appropriate sound effects.

Writing About an Event

Real-life narratives often grow out of special experiences in a writer's life. The writer usually finds a way to tell readers how the experience was special.

Here's how one student wrote about a camping trip. Look for the ways she tells that this was a special event, and notice how she brings her story to a conclusion.

> The writer begins her story by telling you that this was a real experience.

Student Model

It was during our most recent camping trip, in Yellowstone, that I had my first real bear experience. We'd finished dinner so we hung our leftover roast beef in a tree out of reach of any hungry bears, played three rounds of Boggle, and went to sleep.

In the middle of the night I woke up with an urgent need for the bathroom. I had just popped my head out of the tent when I saw someone reaching for our roast beef . . . . He looked a little larger than my father, but who else could it be? I looked back into our tent and there was my father peacefully snoring. . . . I realized what it was—a bear!!! I zipped up the tent flap very, very slowly (all needs for the bathroom instantly cured) and crawled back into my sleeping bag.

Rebecca Bardach, Berkeley, California
First appeared in *Cricket*

Make the Most of an Idea

Rebecca Bardach told her story because it was her first experience with a live bear. She gave some details about the camping trip to set the scene for her readers. Also, she let readers know she was frightened and unfamiliar with bears.

When you write about a real-life experience, think of the specific things that made it special to you. Make some notes about information you have that your audience may not have; these notes will help you realize what background you may need to give your readers. As you plan your story, use the three questions below to help you.

Prewriting Tip

To get started, imagine that you are telling your story to a friend on the telephone. Make a list of things you would tell your friend.

Narrative Writing

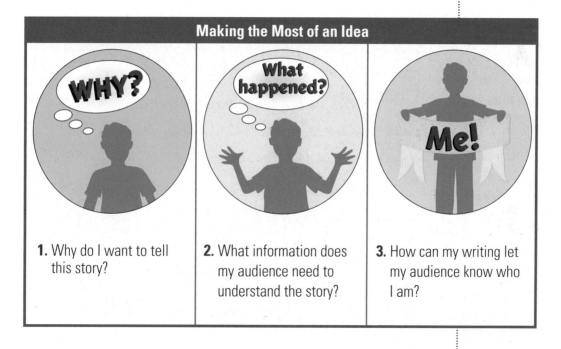

Making the Most of an Idea

WHY?

What happened?

Me!

1. Why do I want to tell this story?

2. What information does my audience need to understand the story?

3. How can my writing let my audience know who I am?

Journal Writing

Write a journal entry about a family event. What made this event special?

Grammar Tip

Proofread your narrative for spelling and punctuation. For information about punctuation of dialogue, see Lesson 19.6, page 499.

Finish the Job

Every well-written narrative has a conclusion. One type of conclusion sums up the story and reflects on what happened.

The conclusion should give your audience the feeling that the story is complete. You might conclude with phrases like these: *I learned that . . .* or *From then on, I knew . . .* or *Ever since this experience, I have felt . . .*

Read this draft of a young writer's story. Notice how the writer revised the draft using the questions on page 161.

> I am really excited about the ways that a computer has changed my life. It even helped me find a lost pet's owner.
>
> When the kitten first showed up at our back door, I wanted to keep it. I knew, though, that it belonged to someone else.
>
> Then I got an idea. I could use the computer at school to find the kitten's owner. I typed up an announcement with a description of the kitten and my address and phone number. Then I added a graphic of a cat at the top. ^
>
> After school I put a copy of the announcement on the porch of every house on my street. At 7:30 that night, I was petting the kitten when the phone rang. "Yes, she's right here, and she's fine," I told the voice on the phone. ^

The writer left out an important detail. Readers need to know that she made many copies of the announcement.

I printed thirty copies of the announcement on orange paper.

When I hung up the phone, I had a good feeling inside.

To complete the story, the writer needs to tell how she felt about finding the kitten's owner.

Write a Narrative About Learning a Skill

Learning a skill often takes hard work. Draft a narrative about a skill, such as swimming or riding a bike, you had difficulty learning. Write your narrative for a younger person who is having trouble mastering the skill.

As you plan your draft, list details about what helped you learn and what you learned about yourself from the experence.

PURPOSE To share a real-life experience
AUDIENCE A younger person
LENGTH 3–4 paragraphs

WRITING RUBRICS To write a narrative about what you learned from mastering a skill, you should

- include essential information
- reveal how you felt
- build to a conclusion
- proofread to avoid run-on sentences

Grammar Link

Avoid run-on sentences.

A run-on sentence is two or more sentences incorrectly written as one.

Correct each run-on below. To do so, you may write separate sentences. You may also combine the sentences with a comma and a conjunction (*and, or,* or *but*) or with a semicolon.

1. Helen Keller's life is an inspiration she worked tirelessly for the visually and hearing impaired.
2. John F. Kennedy was president in the 1960s, he started the Peace Corps.
3. Harriet Tubman was born a slave she escaped and led 300 other enslaved people out of slavery.
4. I didn't think I'd ever be able to do it I finally learned to ski.

See Lesson 8.6, page 307.

Using Computers

The line-spacing function on your word processor can help when you plan to have a peer review your work. Double-space your draft to make it easier to read. Also, leave wide margins around your text. These changes will give your partner plenty of room to write comments.

Listening and Speaking

COOPERATIVE LEARNING With a partner, exchange your skill narratives and have each partner proofread the other's paper. Then have your partner read your paper aloud, while you take notes about ways to make it clearer or more dramatic.

Narrative Writing

WRITING ABOUT LITERATURE

Responding to a Biography

Reading biographies lets you learn about other people. In addition, your personal response to a biography may lead to other discoveries—about yourself and the world around you.

Rosa Parks is often called the mother of the civil rights movement in America. Her years of brave work began on a bus in Montgomery, Alabama. The following passage about the beginning of her 50-year struggle is from *Rosa Parks: The Movement Organizes* by Kai Friese.

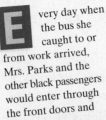

Every day when the bus she caught to or from work arrived, Mrs. Parks and the other black passengers would enter through the front doors and buy a ticket from the driver. Then they would get off the bus, enter through the rear doors, and look for a seat at the back of the vehicle. The front half of the bus was reserved for whites, and blacks couldn't set foot in it. If the white section was filled, blacks were expected to give their seats to white passengers.

Rosa Parks was finding it more and more difficult to accept this kind of treatment. She would argue with bus drivers who told her to give up her seat, and she would march straight through the front section of the bus after paying her fare.

One day in 1943, she was thrown off a bus by a driver named James F. Blake for refusing to use the rear door. Blake told her that if she thought she was too important to go to the back door, she should stay off his bus. Many drivers learned to recognize Rosa Parks, with her hair in a braided bun, and her wire spectacles. If they saw her standing alone at a stop, they would often drive right past her.

22

23

Learn About Others

A biography is one kind of real-life narrative. It's the story of a person's life, written by someone else. The person being written about is the subject of the biography.

When you read a biography, you learn about a person's life and accomplishments. You learn about the events that affected the person's life. You may also learn, as in the story of Rosa Parks, how the subject of a biography affected history. Look at what the student writer of the model below learned from reading *Rosa Parks: The Movement Organizes.*

Prewriting Tip

To help you recall information as you read a biography, jot down notes about the details that impress you.

Narrative Writing

Student Model

Rosa Parks was a brave black woman who believed in herself. When she saw how unfairly blacks were treated by white people in Montgomery, she decided to fight back. She didn't fight with violence but with the "weapon of protest." One day she refused to give up her seat on a bus to a white person, so she was arrested. She had always obeyed this rule before, but this time she was tired of being pushed around.

Even though her arrest was a small matter, it started a big movement. First came the boycott of buses and businesses. Then came the protests and sit-ins. Then came the civil rights movement. Rosa Parks showed everyone how much power you can have if you believe in yourself.

Timmy Baltz, Hufford School, Joliet, Illinois

Journal Writing

Recall a biography you have read in a book, magazine, or newspaper, or one you have seen on film. Write in your journal what you thought about this biography.

Narrative Writing

Grammar Tip

As you revise your writing, make sure not to shift your verb tenses without a reason. For help with verb tenses, see Lessons 10.4–10.9, pages 339–350.

Respond in Different Ways

When you read a biography, you may be surprised. You may laugh. You may even cry. Probably more than anything else, you'll learn things you never expected to learn.

A good biography may prompt you to respond. You might tell a friend about it. You may respond in writing. The list below tells different ways you can respond to a biography.

Ways to Respond to a Biography

1. Write an account of an event as if the subject of the biography is describing it.
2. Write a journal entry for one day in the person's life.
3. Compare the way the person reacted to an event to the way you would have reacted to the same event.
4. Write an imaginary interview with the person, using questions similar to those below.

An Interview with Rosa Parks

Why did you decide not to give up your seat that day?

Do you mean that you had not stood up for your rights before this time?

Were you afraid of what might happen to you?

Mashi Fisher, Evanston, Illinois

Write a Brief Biography

Read a biography or a short biographical article about an athlete, musician, or movie star. Then imagine that you have spent a day with the person. Write an account of what you did with this person. Tell where you went and what you talked about.

PURPOSE To respond to a biography
AUDIENCE Yourself
LENGTH 3–4 paragraphs

WRITING RUBRICS To write an effective biography, you should

- use information you learned from your reading
- relate that information to your own experience
- use appropriate verb tenses

Using Computers

With three or four classmates, choose a public figure who, like Rosa Parks, might be a good role model. Use the Internet to find more information on the figure and then have each person write questions he or she would like to ask the subject.

Listening and Speaking

COOPERATIVE LEARNING In your group, take turns role-playing the subject while the others ask questions. Use the

Don't overuse the present tense of verbs in your writing.

Write the correct form of the verb in parentheses to complete each sentence.

1. Rosa Parks's life has (inspire) many young African Americans.
2. When Parks (refuse) to give up her seat, she made history.
3. I have (learn) how to play the clarinet this year.
4. I (practice) every day.
5. Our top player (pitch) a perfect game last night.
6. He had (pitch) another perfect game earlier this season.
7. It (snow) last night.
8. It has (snow) twice this winter.
9. Last year, it had (snow) more by this date.
10. I have (like) snow since I was a little kid.

See Lessons 10.4, 10.5, and 10.7, pages 339–342 and 345–346.

information from your Internet search to help you answer the questions. Record your questions and answers as a group response to the biography.

Narrative Writing

In the preceding lessons, you've learned about turning real-life experiences into good stories. You've practiced elaborating with details in chronological order and writing dialogue that shows what characters are like. You've also had the chance to learn how to write a brief biography. Now it's time to put together everything you've learned. In this lesson, you will tell the story of how a piece of clothing affected your life.

Assignment

Context

You want to submit a real-life narrative to a make-believe publication called *Wore Stories*. Your story will focus on how a piece of clothing affected your life.

Purpose

To retell a past experience through a narrative

Audience

Student readers of *Wore Stories*

Length

1 page

WRITING *Online*

Visit the *Writer's Choice* Web site at **writerschoice. glencoe.com** for additional writing prompts.

The next few pages can help you plan and write your story. Read through them and then refer to them as you need to. Don't be tied down by them, however. Remember, you're in charge of your own writing process.

Prewriting

Prewrite to explore your thoughts about an old piece of clothing. How did you get it? How did you feel about wearing it? What happened to you while wearing it? The graphic to the right offers options to help you recall your thoughts and feelings.

Option A
Use a cluster diagram.

Option B
Review your journal.

Option C
Freewrite about a topic.

I always felt great in my too-big red shirt. I got it as a gift. It was soft and had white shiny buttons, and I wore it whenever I wanted to feel ready for my day. Why do I remember it so well?

Pages 8–11 offer more tips on freewriting. Your goal is to gather details and experiences to use in your real-life narrative.

Drafting

As you look over the prewriting notes you made, think about how you want to begin your real-life narrative. The opening paragraph should capture and hold readers' attention from the very beginning. For example, notice how Gary Soto begins his narrative.

> **Drafting Tip**
>
> For help with developing your opening, see Lesson 4.1, pages 148–151.

Literature Model

My clothes have failed me. I remember the green coat that I wore in fifth and sixth grades when you either danced like a champ or pressed yourself against a greasy wall, bitter as a penny toward the happy couples.

Gary Soto, "The Jacket"

Soto begins by telling the reader that his clothes have let him down. Then he introduces a specific piece of clothing (his

Grammar Tip

If you need help revising dialogue, see Lesson 4.3, pages 156–159.

jacket) that he wore during a certain period of time (fifth and sixth grade).

How will you begin your narrative? Perhaps you'll start by describing the piece of clothing. The choice is up to you.

Revising

To begin revising, read over your draft to make sure that what you have written fits your purpose and your audience. Then have a **writing conference.** Read your draft to a partner or a small group. Use your audience's reactions to help you evaluate your work so far. The following questions can help you and your listeners.

Question A

Does my first sentence grab readers' attention?

Question B

Have I included all the important information?

Question C

Are the events in an order that makes sense?

My Aunt Jane shouted, "Surprise!" She held out a red shirt. It was a gift that I instantly, loved even though I could tell it was to big. older Just wearing it, though, made me feel bigger. huge That night I wore the shirt to dinner, where my parents let me sit at the head of the table. When I reached for my napkin, my sleeve knocked over a glass of water. The shirt's sleeves puffy hung down almost into my food. A dark area spread across the tablecloth. My shirt was wet, too.

Editing/Proofreading

You've worked hard to write your real-life narrative. You want your readers to focus on what you've written. You don't want to distract them with any mistakes. Pay attention to capitalization, punctuation, and spelling. Make sure your writing is legible and neat. You can find more specific **proofreading** help on pages 70–73.

Publishing/Presenting

Before writing your final copy, you may want to have a family member or friend read your narrative. She or he may have some suggestions that will help. Maybe you'd rather not share your story with anyone except your teacher.

You could include a photograph or a drawing of yourself wearing the piece of clothing. That would help your reader picture the events in your narrative even more clearly.

Editing/Proofreading Checklist

- Have I used correct and varied verb forms?
- Are my sentences complete?
- Is it clear who's talking in my dialogue?
- Have I used quotation marks and other forms of punctuation correctly?

Proofreading Tip

For proofreading symbols, see page 72.

Journal Writing

Reflect on your writing process experience. Answer these questions in your journal. What do you like best about your narrative? What was the hardest part of writing it? What did you learn from your writing conference? What new thing have you learned as a writer?

Literature Model

Gary Soto

THE JACKET

In this narrative, Gary Soto writes about a time when he felt the shame and anger
of an outsider. He blames his experiences on an ugly jacket he had to wear.
As you read the story, note how Soto uses descriptive details to help the reader
understand the importance of this real-life experience. Then try the activities in
Linking Writing and Literature on page 178.

My clothes have failed me. I remember the green coat that I wore in fifth and sixth grades when you either danced like a champ or pressed yourself against a greasy wall, bitter as a penny toward the happy couples.

When I needed a new jacket and my mother asked what kind I wanted, I described something like bikers wear: black leather and silver studs with enough belts to hold down a small town. We were in the kitchen, steam on the windows from her cooking. She listened so long while stirring dinner that I thought she understood for sure the kind I wanted. The next day when I got

Augustín Lazo, *Head*, 1940

home from school, I discovered draped on my bedpost a jacket the color of day-old guacamole. I threw my books on the bed and approached the jacket slowly, as if it were a stranger whose hand I had to shake. I touched the vinyl sleeve, the collar, and peeked at the mustard-colored lining.

Literature Model

Carmen Lomas Garza, *Cakewalk,* 1987

From the kitchen mother yelled that my jacket was in the closet. I closed the door to her voice and pulled at the rack of clothes in the closet, hoping the jacket on the bed-post wasn't for me but my mean brother. No luck. I gave up. From my bed, I stared at the jacket. I wanted to cry because it was so ugly and so big that I knew I'd have to wear it a long time. I was a small kid, thin as a young tree, and it would be years before I'd have a new one. I stared at the jacket, like an enemy, thinking bad things before I took off my old jacket whose sleeves climbed halfway to my elbow.

I put the big jacket on. I zipped it up and down several times, and rolled the cuffs up so they didn't cover my hands. I put my hands in the pockets and flapped the jacket like a bird's wings. I stood in front of the mirror, full face, then profile, and then looked over my shoulder as if someone had called me. I sat on the bed, stood against the bed, and combed my hair to see what I would look like doing something natural. I looked ugly. I threw it on my brother's bed and looked at it for a long time before I slipped it on and went out to the backyard, smiling a "thank you" to my mom as I passed her in the kitchen. With my hands in my pockets I kicked a ball against the fence, and then climbed it to sit looking into the alley. I hurled orange peels at the mouth of an open garbage can and when the peels were gone I watched the white puffs of my breath thin to nothing.

I jumped down, hands in my pockets, and in the backyard on my knees I teased my dog, Brownie, by swooping my arms while making bird calls. He jumped at me and missed. He jumped again and again, until a tooth sunk deep, ripping an L-shaped tear on my left sleeve. I pushed Brownie away to study the tear as I would a cut on my arm. There was no blood, only a few loose pieces of fuzz. [That] dog, I thought, and pushed him away hard when he tried to bite again. I got up from my knees and went to my bedroom to sit with my jacket on my lap, with the lights out.

That was the first afternoon with my new jacket. The next day I wore it to sixth grade and got a D on a math

> **"*I saw their heads bob with laughter, their hands half-covering their mouths.*"**

quiz. During the morning recess Frankie T., the playground terrorist, pushed me to the ground and told me to stay there until recess was over. My best friend, Steve Negrete, ate an apple while looking at me, and the girls turned away to whisper on the monkey bars. The teachers were no help: they looked my way and talked about how foolish I looked in my new jacket. I saw their heads bob with laughter, their hands half-covering their mouths.

Even though it was cold, I took off the jacket during lunch and played kickball in a thin shirt, my arms feeling like braille from goose bumps. But when I returned to class I slipped the jacket on and shivered until I was warm. I sat on my hands, heating them up, while my teeth chattered like a cup of crooked dice. Finally warm, I slid out of the jacket but a few minutes later put it back on when the fire bell rang. We paraded out into the yard where we, the sixth graders, walked past all the other grades to stand against the back fence. Everybody saw me. Although they didn't say out loud, "Man, that's ugly," I heard a buzz-buzz of gossip and even laughter that I knew was meant for me.

And so I went, in my guacamole jacket. So embarrassed, so hurt, I couldn't even do my homework. I received Cs on quizzes, and forgot the state capitals and the rivers of South America, our friendly neighbor. Even the girls who had been friendly blew away like loose flowers to follow the boys in neat jackets.

> **"*And so I went, in my guacamole jacket.*"**

I wore that thing for three years until the sleeves grew short and my forearms stuck out like the necks of turtles. All during that time no love came to me—no little dark girl in a Sunday dress she wore on Monday. At lunchtime I stayed with the ugly boys who leaned against the chain-link fence and looked around with propellers of grass spinning in our mouths. We saw girls walk by alone, saw couples, hand in hand, their heads like bookends pressing air together. We saw them and spun our propellers so fast our faces were blurs.

I blame that jacket for those bad years. I blame my mother for her bad taste and her cheap ways. It was a sad time for the heart. With a friend I spent my sixth-grade year in a tree in the alley waiting for something good to happen to me in that jacket, which had become the ugly brother who tagged along wherever I went. And it was about that time that I began to grow. My chest puffed up with muscle and, strangely, a few more ribs. Even my hands, those fleshy hammers, showed bravely through the cuffs, the fingers already hardening for the coming fights. But that L-shaped rip on the left sleeve got bigger; bits of stuffing coughed out from its wound after a hard day of play. I finally taped it closed, but in rain or cold weather the tape peeled off like a scab and more stuffing fell out until that sleeve shriveled into a palsied arm. That winter the elbows began

> **"*I blame that jacket for those bad years.*"**

to crack and whole chunks of green began to fall off. I showed the cracks to my mother, who always seemed to be at the stove with steamed-up glasses, and she said that there were children in Mexico who would love

Narrative Writing

that jacket. I told her that this was America and yelled that Debbie, my sister, didn't have a jacket like mine. I ran outside, ready to cry, and climbed the tree by the alley to think bad thoughts and watch my breath puff white and disappear.

> **"** . . . *I went outside with my jacket across my arm.* **"**

But whole pieces still casually flew off my jacket when I played hard, read quietly, or took vicious spelling tests at school. When it became so spotted that my brother began to call me "camouflage," I flung it over the fence into the alley. Later, however, I swiped the jacket off the ground and went inside to drape it across my lap and mope.

I was called to dinner: steam silvered my mother's glasses as she said grace; my brother and sister with their heads bowed made ugly faces at their glasses of powdered milk. I gagged too, but eagerly ate big rips of buttered tortilla that held scooped up beans. Finished, I went outside with my jacket across my arm. It was a cold sky. The faces of clouds were piled up, hurting. I climbed the fence, jumping down with a grunt. I started up the alley and soon slipped into my jacket, that green ugly brother who breathed over my shoulder that day and ever since.

Linking Writing and Literature

 ## Collect Your Thoughts

Think about "The Jacket," the excerpt from Gary Soto's memoir *Living Up the Street.* What do you think is the main idea of the excerpt? Make some notes that explain what the story is about.

 ## Talk About Reading

Discuss "The Jacket" with your classmates. Select one person to lead the discussion and another to take notes. Use the following questions to guide the discussion.

1. **Connect to Your Life** Have you ever found yourself in a situation similar to that of the narrator's? How did being in that situation make you feel? Did you experience any of the same emotions as the narrator?

2. **Critical Thinking: Draw Conclusions** Think about what the narrator's mother does and says. How would you describe her?

3. **6+1 Trait®: Word Choice** What words does Soto use to describe the jacket? How does his word choice help you to understand how he feels about it?

4. **Connect to Your Writing** What makes "The Jacket" interesting to read? What makes it seem realistic to you? Make a list of the qualities that make the excerpt enjoyable. Then discuss how you could create those qualities in your own writing.

 ## Write About Reading

Autobiographical Essay Write an auto-biographical essay in which you tell about an experience that affected you, like the new jacket affected the narrator of the excerpt. Explain what happened, how it made you feel, and why you felt that way.

Focus on Word Choice Think carefully about the words you choose to tell your story. Use precise action words, modifiers, and figurative language that paint clear and colorful images for your readers.

For more information on word choice and the 6+1 Trait® model, see **Writing and Research Handbook,** pages 682–684.

6+1 Trait® is a registered trademark of Northwest Regional Educational Laboratory, which does not endorse this product.

UNIT 4 Review

Reflecting on the Unit

Summarize what you learned in this unit by answering the following questions.

1. What are the characteristics of a well-written real-life story?
2. How can you keep a story clearly on track?
3. What are the important things to remember when you write dialogue?
4. How can you help your readers understand what was special about an event?
5. In what ways might you learn from and respond to a biography?

Adding to Your Portfolio

CHOOSE A SELECTION FOR YOUR PORTFOLIO Look over the narrative writing you did during this unit. Select a completed piece of writing to put into your portfolio. The piece you choose should show some or all of the following:

- a beginning that makes the reader want to continue reading
- believable characters in a specific place, involved in clearly explained action
- realistic dialogue that gives details about the characters
- an order that helps the reader follow the action
- a conclusion that winds up the story

REFLECT ON YOUR CHOICE Attach a note to the piece you chose, explaining briefly why you chose it and what you learned from writing it.

SET GOALS How can you improve your writing? What skill will you focus on the next time you write?

Writing Across the Curriculum

MAKE A SOCIAL STUDIES CONNECTION Think about how someone from another culture or part of the world might react to your narrative about a piece of clothing. How might you meet this person? What questions might he or she ask? How might you need to change or add to your narrative? Write brief notes to respond to these questions.

"*Koko is one of an endangered species. The foundation she inspired, The Gorilla Foundation, is dedicated to breeding gorillas in captivity.*"

—Jean Craighead George,
"Koko: Smart Signing Gorilla"

Expository Writing

Writing in the Real World: *Julie Sheer*   182

Lesson **5.1**   **Writing to Help Others
Understand**   186

Lesson **5.2**   **Comparing and Contrasting
Two Things**   190

Lesson **5.3**   **Explaining How to Do Something**   194

Lesson **5.4**   **Writing a Report**   198

Lesson **5.5**   **Writing About Literature:
Writing a Book Report**   202

Writing Process in Action   206

**Literature Model: "Bathing Elephants"
by Peggy Thomson**   210

Unit 5 Review   215

Writing in the Real World

MEDIA
Newspaper Article
Connection

A significant number of articles in the press are expository—they explain what the public is curious about. In the article excerpted below, sports writer Julie Sheer of the *Chicago Tribune* tries to answer a critical question for hoops fans: "How *does* Michael Jordan fly?"

from "How Does Michael Fly?"

by Julie Sheer

No conversation about Michael Jordan is complete without references to hang time. So, what exactly is hang time? The velocity, or speed, a player has when he takes off, combined with the path his center of gravity follows on the way up, plus body manipulations along the way, fool us into thinking he's hanging in the air for an unusually long period of time. . . .

. . . So, how is it he's able to hit the heights he does? Michael's rocket-powered leaps are helped by long legs and a slender torso, which give him a higher center of gravity. However, it's the makeup of his muscles, mainly the quadriceps, calf muscles and gluteus, that gives him the power.

A good jumper will have muscles that store elastic energy and also a larger percentage of fast-twitch than slow-twitch fibers. . .

When it comes to technique, Jordan's flight patterns can't be duplicated. "I just make it up," he admits.

A Writer's Process

Prewriting
Capturing an Idea

A newspaper staff is always on the lookout for good ideas. What are people curious about? What information would they like to have? Steve Cvengros, editor at the *Chicago Tribune*, knew he'd found a good story idea when he saw a headline in *USA Today.* "It only seems [Michael] Jordan floats longer. There's no such thing as defying gravity," the story said.

Cvengros brought the idea to his *Tribune* team—writer Julie Sheer and artist Dennis Odom. The three agreed to do the story as a graphic—drawings and words combined.

Writer Sheer went immediately to work. She had many questions: Why is Chicago Bulls star Michael Jordan able to jump so high? Can he really hang in the air? How does gravity affect his flight?

She found some answers in reference books, such as *Sport Science*, and in books on Jordan. She gathered more information by interviewing coaches and scientists on the phone.

Sheer and Odom also interviewed Jordan to get his point of view.

Little by little, Sheer and Odom started to get the picture.

They learned that Jordan has a great number of fast-twitch fibers in his leg muscles that act as springs to rocket him off the ground. In flight, Jordan's arm and leg movements make him look as if he's floating.

Drafting
Writing and Illustrating

Many expository articles have information that is best explained through graphics—charts, graphs, and pictures. In this case, the *Tribune* team agreed that they wanted a big painting of Jordan in the center of their full-page article.

Odom's first challenge was to do the painting. To find just the right pose, he studied thousands of photographs of Jordan in action. Then Odom went to work on the smaller illustrations.

Meanwhile Sheer began to write. To help organize her draft, Sheer needed to break down the information into topics. "I sat down at a computer and typed up some headlines," she said. These served as subheads that broke down the main topic of "flight" into smaller topics—"the muscle behind the magic" and "stages of a vertical jump."

The writing job was tough, Sheer said. "I had to pick out what was most important and boil it down so I understood it. Then I had to explain it so a reader could understand."

Revising
Designing the Page

When Sheer finished writing her draft, she gave it to Cvengros, the editor. He checked the draft for words used too often, facts without sources, and writing that had become so technical that it had lost its fun.

Odom finished his illustrations and turned his attention to drawing an outline of the finished page. He photocopied his painting of Jordan and pasted it in the center. Now the team was ready to fit the other pieces of art and copy onto the page.

How did the team organize the information to explain Jordan's skill? After several tries, they decided on two columns. The left column would explain the science of "hang time." The column on the right would explain the special features of Jordan's muscular system.

Editing/Proofreading
Fine-Tuning

With the pieces put together, the team was ready to fine-tune the page. They read the headlines and subheads. Were they clear? Were they fun? They saw that some ideas needed more space. Others had to be cut.

During the final checking, they made sure that the facts were printed correctly. Copy editors proofread for errors such as misspelled words and mistakes in grammar. The sports editor reviewed the final page too. "He's a real basketball nut, so he read every word," Sheer said.

Publishing
Going to Press

At last the page went to press. According to Cvengros, the big colorful graphic was a huge success. Jordan himself liked the page. "We had a special copy made for Michael," Cvengros said proudly.

Examining Writing in the Real World

Analyzing the Media Connection

Discuss these questions about the model on page 182.

1. What kinds of things does Sheer assume her audience knows about Michael Jordan? How can you tell?

2. What term does Sheer define in the excerpt? Why do you think she provides this definition?

3. What cause-and-effect explanation does Sheer give? Why is this information important?

4. Whom does Sheer quote in the article? In your opinion, how does the quote add or detract from the article's effect?

5. Would you describe Sheer's writing style as formal or informal? Support your answer with examples.

Analyzing a Writer's Process

Discuss these questions about Julie Sheer's writing process.

1. How did writer Julie Sheer gather information for her story?

2. Why did Sheer find writing the story difficult?

3. Describe Sheer's technique for organizing her draft. How does your organizational technique differ from Sheer's?

4. How did the *Tribune* team work together to design and review the page?

5. What did the team members check before sending the page to press?

Avoid double comparisons when you write.

Never use *more* or *most* with adjectives or adverbs ending in *-er* or *-est*.

A good jumper will have . . . a larger percentage of fast-twitch . . . fibers.

Revise the sentences below, correcting the double comparisons.

1. Michael Jordan jumped more better than any other player.

2. On the court, Jordan was an even more greater performer than Julius Erving.

3. His center of gravity is more higher than that of most people.

4. Jordan had the most longest "hang time" of the Chicago Bulls.

5. Jordan is one of the most greatest players ever.

See Lesson 12.3, page 383, and Lesson 13.3, page 399.

Writing to Help Others Understand

Expository writing is writing that shares knowledge. It informs or explains, sometimes by defining, classifying, or giving directions.

Literature Model

Some 20,000 years ago, people realized that they could get light by burning oil, and the first lamps appeared. These lamps were hollowed-out rocks full of animal fat. Lamps with wicks of vegetable fibers were first made in about 1000 B.C. They had a simple channel to hold the wick; later, the wick was held in a spout.

Lionel Bender, *Invention*

You may never have used an oil lamp. Having read this explanation, though, you know how and when lamps were invented. Bender has shared some knowledge on a subject you may not have known about.

Learn from Expository Writing

Bender's paragraph is a good example of expository writing. It informs. It helps people learn about the world around them.

You can find expository writing in many places: textbooks, cookbooks, encyclopedias, newspapers, instruction manuals. No matter where you find it, expository writing is always meant to help people learn.

If you've ever jotted down directions for someone, you have already done some expository writing. You've helped someone learn how to get somewhere. Look at the following directions. How does the writer share knowledge with the reader?

TOP SECRET

Peter —
- Look out your window. See the mailbox on the corner? At 2:30 p.m. Sunday, go there.

- Next, walk three blocks down West Liberty Street. Then turn right onto Central.

- The third house on the left is my aunt's place. She said we could practice in her basement. I'll be waiting with my guitar, and we'll make that tape for your mom's surprise party.

Journal Writing

List some topics that you could explain to others. Choose one idea and write down three pieces of information about it.

Inform and Explain in Different Ways

Directions, such as those on page 187, are one kind of expository writing. Other kinds of expository writing explain a process, provide a definition, compare and contrast two things, or divide things into groups. Read the two kinds of expository writing shown below.

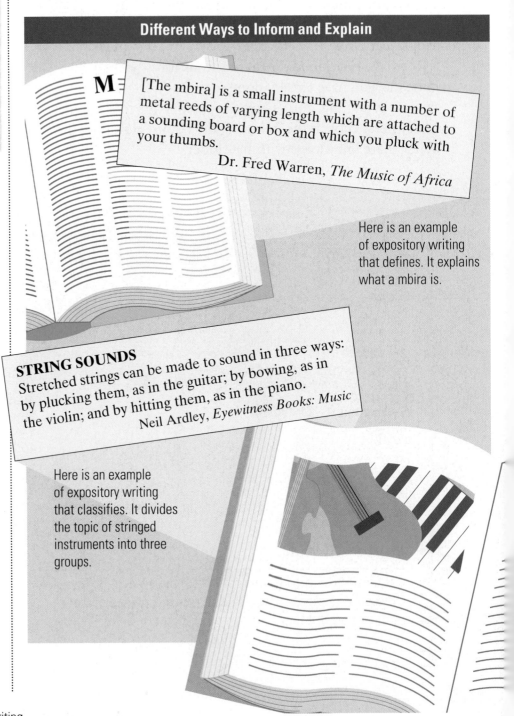

Different Ways to Inform and Explain

M

[The mbira] is a small instrument with a number of metal reeds of varying length which are attached to a sounding board or box and which you pluck with your thumbs.

Dr. Fred Warren, *The Music of Africa*

Here is an example of expository writing that defines. It explains what a mbira is.

STRING SOUNDS
Stretched strings can be made to sound in three ways: by plucking them, as in the guitar; by bowing, as in the violin; and by hitting them, as in the piano.

Neil Ardley, *Eyewitness Books: Music*

Here is an example of expository writing that classifies. It divides the topic of stringed instruments into three groups.

Expository Writing

Write an Explanation of a Game

Think about how to play a simple playground game. List the rules for playing. Then write an explanation of the game for a younger student who has never played it.

PURPOSE To teach a new game
AUDIENCE A younger student
LENGTH 1–2 paragraphs

WRITING RUBRICS To write an effective explanation of a game, you should

- define the game and its goal
- explain the steps in the game, from first to last
- print legibly for a young reader

Cross-Curricular Activity

HISTORY In a history book, find a paragraph that explains something, such as how the Constitution was adopted. Read the paragraph at least twice. Then, in your own words, write a summary of what the paragraph says.

Make a pronoun clearly refer to its antecedent.

. . . **people** realized that **they** could get light. . . .

Rewrite each sentence to make the meaning clear.

1. People have always invented things, and they have helped them learn more about the world.
2. Telescopes help us learn about the stars; they bring them into focus.
3. The inventor has a brother, and he helps him with his experiments.
4. They have many books about inventions in the school library.

See Lesson 11.3, page 365.

Viewing and Representing

ILLUSTRATING AN EXPLANATION To help a younger student understand your game, provide some drawings to explain its rules and action. Draw four or five pictures (stick figures will do) that would help a young student see how the game really works. Compare your writing with your drawings to make sure the drawings send the same message as the writing.

LESSON 5.2

Expository Writing

Comparing and Contrasting Two Things

Comparison-contrast analysis is one kind of expository writing. When you compare two things, you explain how they are similar. When you contrast them, you explain how they differ.

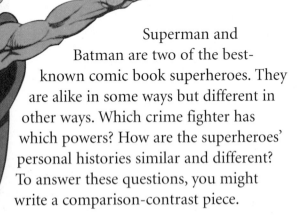

VS.

Superman and Batman are two of the best-known comic book superheroes. They are alike in some ways but different in other ways. Which crime fighter has which powers? How are the superheroes' personal histories similar and different? To answer these questions, you might write a comparison-contrast piece.

Organize the Details

To compare and contrast in writing, you'll need to keep your details organized. The following methods can help you do that.

EXAMINE YOUR SUBJECTS A good way to begin your comparison-contrast piece is with a careful examination. First think about one subject, and list descriptive details that go with that subject. For example, you might note that Batman travels by car and wears a mask and a cape. Then make a list of the same kinds of details for Superman. How does he get around? What does he wear?

SORT WHAT YOU SEE Once you've listed some details, you can sort them for comparison and contrast. At this point, some writers use a Venn diagram like the one below. A Venn diagram is made of two ovals. Each oval contains the details of one of the subjects. Details that the two subjects have in common go where the ovals overlap.

Grammar Tip

When comparing and contrasting two people, use the comparative form of an adjective. When comparing and contrasting two actions, use the comparative form of an adverb. For more about comparative adjectives and adverbs, see Lessons 12.3 and 12.4, pages 383–386, and Lesson 13.3, page 393.

Expository Writing

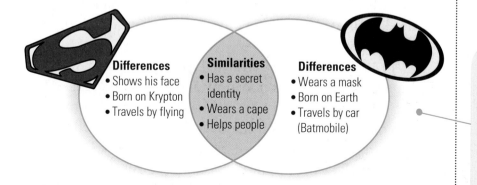

Differences
- Shows his face
- Born on Krypton
- Travels by flying

Similarities
- Has a secret identity
- Wears a cape
- Helps people

Differences
- Wears a mask
- Born on Earth
- Travels by car (Batmobile)

Notice how the details for each superhero come from a look at the same points of concern: costume, method of travel, birthplace, mission, and identity.

Journal Writing

Pick your two favorite activities. List the details of each activity. Then put the details into a Venn diagram. What is similar and different about the two activities?

Revising Tip

When revising a comparison-contrast piece, try making a separate paragraph for each subject you discuss. This will make the piece easier for your readers to follow. For more information about revising paragraphs, see Lesson 2.6, pages 62–65.

Take a look at the similarities and differences covered in this selection. Notice that they are the same ones shown in the Venn diagram on page 191.

TIME

For more about organizing a draft, see **TIME Facing the Blank Page,** page 94.

Write the First Draft

Now that you've made a Venn diagram, you're ready to write your draft. Details you pull from the middle of the Venn diagram are similarities. Details pulled from the outsides are differences. As you think about the order of presenting information, pull details from your diagram.

Notice how the following comparison-contrast piece is organized. First it tells about Superman. Then it tells about Batman. This kind of organization is called subject by subject. It's a way of showing clearly the similarities and differences between two subjects. It helps readers picture the subjects side by side.

Literature Model

The Great Depression was in its final years. World War II waited across the ocean in Europe. Out of this time came two of our earliest comic-book superheroes.

Superman appeared in 1938. When fighting crime, he flew through the air, wearing a caped costume to disguise his true identity. Today we know him as The Man of Steel, dedicated to helping others, an orphan from the planet Krypton.

In 1939 Batman was created. Like Superman, he was a caped hero with a secret identity and a mission to make the world a better place. In some ways, however, Batman was one of a kind. For instance, he was the first Earth-born superhero. He covered his face with a mask. And to get around, he drove a one-of-a-kind car called the Batmobile.

Today, the world is a different place with many different problems. Although times have changed, many of our superheroes have stayed with us. With luck there will always be superheroes to call on whenever we need one.

Write a Comparison-Contrast Piece

Write to a good friend who has moved away. In your letter compare and contrast two things of interest to you both. For example, you might compare two athletes or a movie and a book.

PURPOSE To share information by comparing and contrasting

AUDIENCE A friend

LENGTH 2–3 paragraphs

WRITING RUBRICS To write a good comparison-contrast piece, you should

- list details about each subject
- create a Venn diagram
- organize details subject by subject
- write legibly in cursive or manuscript
- proofread to ensure correct grammar and punctuation

Using Computers

Find two Web sites that provide sports coverage and information. Write a brief report in which you compare and contrast the features of the sites. In your conclusion, you might answer questions such as the following: Which would be better for fans who want recent game results? Which would be better for fans who want background on games? Which covers a greater number of sports?

Grammar Link

Be sure verbs agree with compound subjects.

When two or more subject words are linked by *or* or *nor,* the verb agrees with the subject that is closer to it.

Complete each sentence below by writing the correct form of the verb in parentheses.

1. Neither the superheroes' costumes nor their mission (has, have) changed in fifty years.
2. Either powers or weaknesses (is, are) more important.
3. The Power Rangers or Batman (is, are) the most popular today.
4. Neither Superman nor the Power Rangers (drives, drive) an amazing car.
5. (Is, Are) superheroes or a real-life hero more important to you?

See Lesson 15.3, page 443.

Listening and Speaking

COOPERATIVE LEARNING In a small group, study and talk about two kinds of pets. Each group member should add details to a Venn diagram comparing and contrasting the two animals. Each should use the diagram to draft a short comparison-contrast piece.

Explaining How to Do Something

Expository writing is used to explain a process, step by step. Transition words help make the order of the steps clear for the reader.

Pictured above is French painter Henri Matisse (1869–1954), an important artist of modern times. His painting was known for its bright colors and unusual shapes. Late in his life, Matisse became physically unable to paint as he once had. He then took up a new form—the collage. With the help of an assistant, he pinned paper shapes together to create pictures.

If you were Matisse explaining your method to a new assistant, how would you make your instructions clear? Where would you start?

Break the Process into Steps

If you've ever used a recipe or built a model, you've probably followed a process step by step. Almost any job is easier if you approach it one step at a time.

Explaining how to make a collage is no exception. If you explain the process in steps, your reader will have an easier time understanding it. Be sure to include every step and to present steps in the right order. Explain with extra care any steps that might be confusing.

Expository Writing

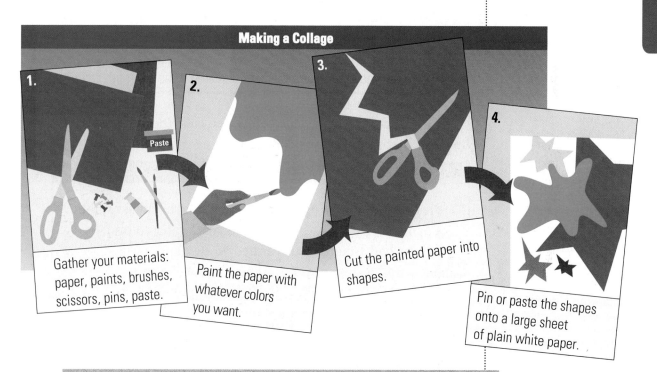

Making a Collage

1. Gather your materials: paper, paints, brushes, scissors, pins, paste.

2. Paint the paper with whatever colors you want.

3. Cut the painted paper into shapes.

4. Pin or paste the shapes onto a large sheet of plain white paper.

Journal Writing

Think of a process you go through every day. List all the steps in the process. Circle any steps that you think are hard to understand. Make notes about ways to explain these steps.

Link the Steps

Once you've broken a process into steps, you're ready to write a draft. As you write, you might want to combine some steps. You might decide to explain others further. Think especially about the transitions between steps. What words will help link one step to another? The chart below shows some transition words that link the steps in making scrambled eggs.

How to Make Scrambled Eggs	
Transitions	
First	gather eggs, butter, a frying pan, a fork, a spoon, and a bowl.
Then	break the eggs into the bowl, and beat them with the fork.
After	beating the eggs, warm some butter in the frying pan on the stove.
Next	pour the eggs into the frying pan, and stir them with the spoon.
Finally	stir the eggs over a medium flame until they're ready to eat.

Now notice, in the passage below, the transition words that help link steps in Matisse's collage-making process.

"Then" is a transition word linking steps in the process.

What does the writer do to make this explanation clear and simple?

If you had never created a collage before, could you use this explanation to make one?

Literature Model

In order to do his paper cut-outs, Matisse had assistants paint sheets of paper with gouaches [water colors]; then he had a piece of unpainted white paper pinned to the wall of his studio. . . . Then he cut the painted papers into the shapes he wanted and pinned them, or, usually, directed an assistant to pin them, into the desired composition.

Jack Cowart, *Henri Matisse: Paper Cut-Outs*

By completing the process explained above, Matisse and his assistants were able to create beautiful collages. Look at the next page and see for yourself.

Write a "How to" Explanation

Pretend you will create a collage like the one shown below. You can use paper, ribbons, buttons, or other small objects. Make a rough sketch of your collage. Then write an explanation of how to create such a collage.

PURPOSE To explain how to make a collage

AUDIENCE Students in your art class

LENGTH 1–2 paragraphs

WRITING RUBRICS To write an effective "how to" explanation, you should

- break the process into steps
- present each step in proper order
- use transitions to link the steps

Henri Matisse, *Madame de Pompadour,* 1951

Grammar Link

Use action verbs to make your explanations clear.

Complete the steps in the recipe below by adding an exact action verb to each.

How to Make a Milkshake

1. _____ 8 ounces of milk into a blender.
2. _____ 1–2 scoops of ice cream into the milk.
3. _____ 2 teaspoons of syrup for extra flavor.
4. _____ together the ingredients in the blender for 30 seconds.
5. For a smoother milkshake, _____ the blender on for another 30 seconds.

See Lesson 10.1, page 333.

Listening and Speaking

Create a design using a few simple, connected shapes. In a small group, give directions to guide group members in drawing your design without showing it to them. Take turns giving and taking directions. Then check the drawings to see how close they come to the originals.

Cross-Curricular Activity

MATH Scan your math textbook and choose a word problem. Write a paragraph explaining the steps in solving the problem.

Writing a Report

To write a report, choose a topic that interests you. Gather information from a variety of sources. Organize what you learn and present it in your own words to inform your readers.

As the diagram below illustrates, you need to choose a topic that is the right size. A topic that is too broad will have too much information for a short report. A narrow topic will not give you enough about which to write.

All About Sharks

The Truth About Shark Myths

Swimming Speed of Pacific Nurse Sharks

Gather Information

When you write a research report, you share what you know—and what you have learned—about your topic. Spend a few minutes jotting notes about what you think you know about your topic. What do you hope to find out? Make a list of questions that you'd like your research to answer. Let your questions guide your research, and write down new questions that come to you as you learn more about your topic.

Begin your research at the library. Encyclopedias and other reference works can give you some basic information about your topic and lead you to other sources. Be sure to look for books and magazine articles on your topic. You may also use CD-ROMs and the Internet to conduct research.

Once you've found a few sources on your topic, begin reading and taking notes. Put quotation marks around any information you copy from your sources word for word. But think about what you're reading and take notes using your own words when you can.

For every note, be sure to jot down a page reference and the title and author of the source as well as publication information. That way, you'll be able to properly give credit to your sources as you write. For information about exploring a variety of sources and giving credit as you write, see the Writing Research Papers section of the **Writing and Research Handbook,** pages 685–690. Study the sample source and note card below.

Editing Tip

Don't throw away your notes before your report is finished. As you edit, if you need to check a fact, you can look back at your notes.

Expository Writing

Shark Behavior
Eugenie Clark, "Sharks: Magnificent and Misunderstood," "National Geographic, August 1981.
When I read that Dr. Eugenie Clark thinks sharks normally don't bother people, it made me think I could go swimming in the ocean without being scared.

SHARKS

No creature on earth has a worse, and perhaps less deserved, reputation than the shark. During 26 years of research on sharks, I have found them to be normally unaggressive and even timid towards man.

Eugenie Clark, "Sharks: Magnificent and Misunderstood"

Journal Writing

Think of a topic that you'd like to write a report about. In your journal, jot down a list of questions about your topic that you'd like your research to answer. Also note some ideas about the types of sources you might use to explore your topic.

Write About What You've Learned

After taking notes, organize them so that you can write. You might begin by asking yourself, "What's the report about?" Your

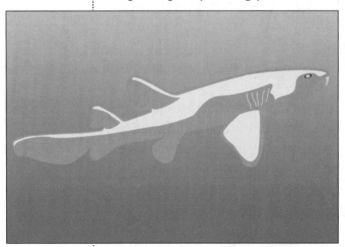

answer can become the introduction to your report. As you write the body of your draft, answer this question: "What did I discover?" Finally, as you tie your paper together in the conclusion, think about what you learned. A good conclusion can include a summary of information

and leave your readers with a better understanding of your topic. Read the model below and notice the three main parts.

Model

In what way does the introduction do what it should do?

Most people are scared of sharks, but Dr. Eugenie Clark, a famous marine biologist, says that they shouldn't be. She and other scientists have done studies to prove that sharks aren't so scary. She published some of her findings in the *National Geographic* article "Sharks: Magnificent and Misunderstood" in August 1981.

The body of the report shows what information the writer discovered.

According to Clark, sharks don't just swim around, eating all the time. Some sharks go for weeks without eating. Basking sharks and whale sharks eat only plankton and small fish. Sharks typically do not bite people unless they feel threatened and need to protect themselves.

What does the conclusion say about what the writer learned?

After reading about Dr. Clark's adventures, I learned that people still have much to learn about sharks. It's good to learn more, though, because the new information lets us understand what's really true about sharks. Now I can swim without being scared.

Write a Report

Review what you wrote for the Journal Writing activity on page 199 and continue working on your report. Find sources on your topic in the library and look for answers to your research questions as you read. Take notes, carefully recording the source of each piece of information. Organize your data in a logical order and write a report.

PURPOSE To present information about a topic of your choice

AUDIENCE Your classmates and teacher

LENGTH 3–5 paragraphs

WRITING RUBRICS To write an effective report, you should

- locate sources of information
- take notes on what you find
- organize the information into an introduction, a body, and a conclusion
- proofread for legibility and grammatical correctness

Using Computers

Desktop publishing software can give your report a professional look. Using desktop publishing, you can put text into columns and make a cover page. You can even provide space for pictures or diagrams to be scanned in or pasted on after printing.

Grammar Link

When you take notes, capitalize the names of authors. Capitalize the first and last words and all other important words in a title.

Note how the writer of the report on sharks wrote the title and author of the source: *Eugenie Clark, "Sharks: Magnificent and Misunderstood."*

Write each name or title below, using capital letters as needed.

1. virginia morrell
2. "The really secret life of plants"
3. *Presidential curiosities: The complete book of U.S. presidents*
4. *the oregon trail*
5. "antarctica, the last continent"
6. esther forbes

See Lesson 18.2, page 475, and Lesson 18.4, page 479.

Listening and Speaking

PRESENTING Take turns reading your reports aloud in a small group. Prepare for your turn by practicing your oral reading. Speak slowly, clearly, and with appropriate expression and body language. Display any maps, graphs, or photos that enhance your report and help communicate your message.

WRITING ABOUT LITERATURE

Writing a Book Report

Reading is a ticket to adventure. By reading, you can travel to exciting places, meet interesting people, and learn about things you never knew existed. When you want to share reading experiences with others, write a book report.

Maybe the next book you read will be Mildred Taylor's *Roll of Thunder, Hear My Cry*. In this book you will meet the Logans, an African American family living in Mississippi. The year is 1933, and Cassie Logan and her brothers experience racial prejudice almost every day. When her parents challenge this prejudice, Cassie faces more danger than ever before.

Include Information About the Book

A book report provides readers with information about a book. The report can also include your feelings about the book. The chart below explains the parts of a typical book report.

Expository Writing

Parts of a Book Report	
Title	Include the title of the book. Be sure to look at the book cover to make certain that you have spelled and punctuated it correctly.
Author	Include the name of the author. Again, you want to give the author all the credit he or she deserves, so double-check the spelling of the name.
Main Characters	Give the names of the main characters and a few words about who they are. That way, people will know whom the book is about.
Setting	Tell about the setting. It includes when and where the story takes place. Telling about the setting helps people imagine the story.
Summary	Briefly explain what happens in the book. Just a few sentences to summarize should do it. But be sure not to give away any surprises.
What I Thought	At the end of a book report, write down how you feel about the book and why. This part of the report gives you a chance to express yourself.

Vocabulary Tip

In prewriting, try listing some words that express how the book made you feel. The list makes a good starting point for thinking about your book.

Presenting Tip

Proofread and refine copies of class members' final book reports and assemble them into a class book. Display the book in class or donate it to the school library.

Journal Writing

Make a list of three or four books you've read. Pick the book you liked most or the book you liked least. Write a few sentences that explain why you feel that way.

Tell Your Feelings

One of the most useful parts of a book report is your feelings about the book. Here's how one student felt after reading *Roll of Thunder, Hear My Cry*.

In this report, the writer gives the title of the book right at the beginning. Why do you think she gives it again near the end?

At the end Natalie gives her opinion of the book—a definite thumbs-up.

Title: *Roll of Thunder, Hear My Cry*

Author: Mildred D. Taylor

Main Characters: The main characters are a black family called the Logans. Cassie is the only girl. Stacey is the older boy. Little Man is the younger boy.

Setting: Rural Mississippi in 1933

Summary: The novel is about the prejudiced way blacks were still being treated after the end of slavery. One example is the first day of school, when Cassie's and Little Man's teacher, Mrs. Crocker, tells them that this year they will have the privilege of using books. Cassie and Little Man are overjoyed—until they receive the tattered books and find out they received them only because they were too ripped up for the white children. When Cassie and Little Man refuse to use the books, they get punished by Mrs. Crocker. Much to Mrs. Crocker's surprise, though, Cassie and Little Man's mother think they did the right thing.

What I Thought: *Roll of Thunder, Hear My Cry* really shows you the unfair way blacks were treated back then, and it's a funny story in some parts and sad in others. It makes you think of the book's title, which comes from a song that slaves once sang. The song tells people not to be defeated by their enemies. That's mostly what the book's about, and I would definitely recommend reading it.

Natalie Bogira, Chute Middle School, Evanston, Illinois

Write a Book Report

Write a short report about a book you like for your school newspaper. Jot down your thoughts about the book. Then write the first draft.

PURPOSE To share your ideas about a book
AUDIENCE Readers of the school newspaper
LENGTH 3–4 paragraphs

WRITING RUBRICS To write an effective book report, you should

- include the title and author
- identify the main characters and the setting
- summarize the story
- explain your personal reactions

Using Computers

Find Web sites that contain book reviews. Find reviews of two or three of the books you've read recently. Compare and contrast your own views with those of the reviewers.

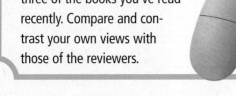

Listening and Speaking

COOPERATIVE LEARNING In a small group, prepare an oral book report. Note the book's title, author, characters, and setting. Agree on a plot summary. Then discuss different opinions of group members about the book to include in the report.

Make subjects and verbs agree.

When two or more subjects are joined by *and,* the verb is usually plural. Note the subject-verb agreement in this sentence.

> ***Cassie Logan and her brother experience*** racial prejudice.

For each sentence write the correct form of the verb in parentheses.

1. Courage and pride (are, is) what the Logan family possesses.
2. Both Cassie's mother and her father (understand, understands) the importance of the land.
3. Farming fields and a vast forest (cover, covers) their 400 acres.
4. Big Ma and Mama also (own, owns) part of the land.
5. The taxes and mortgage on the land (have, has) not been paid.
6. Papa and other farmers (leave, leaves) home looking for work.
7. Big Ma, who is in her sixties, and Mama (run, runs) the farm.
8. Stacey and Little Man (set, sets) off for school in threadbare clothes.
9. First-graders and fourth-graders (share, shares) a classroom.
10. Where (are, is) Miss Crocker and Miss Davis?

See Lesson 15.3, page 443.

Writing Process in Action

Expository Writing

In preceding lessons you learned about ways to share knowledge with others through expository writing. You also had a chance to do your own expository writing—to compare and contrast, give directions, and write a report. Now it is time for you to put together what you know. In this lesson you are invited to write a "how-to" explanation of a process.

Assignment

Context

The editors at *How To,* a magazine written by and for students wanting to share something they know, want you to write about a step-by-step process.

Purpose

To write an explanation of something you've learned to do

Audience

Student readers of *How To*

Length

1 page

Visit the *Writer's Choice* Web site at **writerschoice. glencoe.com** for additional writing prompts.

The following pages can help you plan and write your explanation. Read through them and then refer to them as you need to. Don't feel limited by them. Remember that you're in charge of your own writing process.

Prewriting

Whether telling how to bathe an elephant or make a sandwich, you must explain one step at a time to make it easier for a reader to follow along. These options can help you explore ways to begin your explanation.

You might visit the library to find more information. Remember to make notes about what you discover. If you're still stuck, try reviewing pages 198–200 for more ideas about research.

Option A
Try clustering to discover what steps go together.

Option B
Try drawing a picture of each step.

Option C
List everything you can recall about the process.

1. choose a stone
2. roll the stone
3. other players toss sticks
4. measure to see which stick is closest

Drafting

In your draft, try to include as much information as you can. Don't leave out anything your reader might need to know.

While you draft, think about ways to link the steps you listed in the prewriting stage. Consider combining or expanding steps. Note how much detail Peggy Thomson includes for one step in the process of bathing elephants at the zoo.

> **Vocabulary Tip**
>
> For a list of transition words you can use to link steps in a process, see Lesson 5.3, page 196.

Literature Model

Kathy pours out green oil soap from a bottle, letting it spread across the great gray expanses of skin and foaming it up with streamers from her hose. Now, with her ankus propped against the railings and her hose lying on the floor, she lights into a two-handed scrub job.

Peggy Thomson
Keepers and Creatures at the National Zoo

Writing Process in Action

Revising Tip

When revising a "how-to" explanation, ask another person to follow your explanation. This will help you identify steps that are unclear or missing. For more help see Lesson 5.3, page 195.

Some steps can be explained simply. Others may be so complicated that a diagram or picture will give the clearest explanation. As you draft, try whatever method seems best.

Revising

To begin revising, read over your draft to make sure that what you have written fits the assignment, especially your purpose and your audience. Then have a **writing conference.** Read your draft to a partner or small group. Use your audience's reactions to help you evaluate your work so far. The questions below can help you and your listeners.

Question A
Have I included every step in the proper order?

Question B
Is each step stated clearly?

Question C
Have I linked my steps with transitions?

Chunkey, *is* a game invented by
Mississippians, ~~is fun even today.~~ These were
the ancient Native Americans who lived in the
Mississippi River Valley. To play, you first need
to get a small *round* stone. ~~It should be a rounded~~
~~stone.~~ Then one player rolls the stone. Other
players stand aside and throw sticks at ~~where~~ *the spot where*
they think the stone will stop rolling. ~~After it~~ *When the stone*
stops, you check to see which stick is the closest.
Whoever threw that stick is the winner.

Editing/Proofreading

Following the steps of a process takes concentration. For that reason you'll want to **proofread** your draft for spelling, grammar, and punctuation errors. Such small mistakes might distract your audience.

The questions on the notepad can be your starting point. You also might share your draft with a friend or family member. Another person can often discover mistakes you have overlooked.

Publishing/Presenting

Before presenting your explanation, ask yourself if *How To* readers could complete the process, following only your steps. If the answer is yes, then you're ready to present

your paper. The final copy may include diagrams or pictures that would make your explanation even easier to understand.

Editing/Proofreading Checklist

- Have I used action verbs that make sense?
- Have I used pronouns correctly?
- Do verbs agree with subjects?
- Have I checked the spelling of any words I'm unsure of?

Proofreading Tip

For proofreading symbols, see page 72 or 267.

Grammar Tip

When editing your report, check that you have used pronouns correctly. If you need help with pronouns, refer to Lessons 11.1–11.5, pages 361–370.

Journal Writing

Reflect on your writing-process experience. Answer these questions in your journal: What do you like best about your explanation? What was the hardest part of writing it? What did you learn in your writing conference? What new things have you learned as a writer?

Literature Model

Peggy Thomson

BATHING ELEPHANTS

In Keepers and Creatures at the National Zoo, Peggy Thomson explains how zoo-keepers go about their everyday tasks as well as how they relate to the animals. Giving elephants a daily bath is one way keeper Kathy Wallace has earned the elephants' trust and respect. As you read this chapter from the book, try picturing each step in the bathing process Thomson describes. Then complete the activities in Linking Writing and Literature on page 214.

"Okay, Biki! Okay, Shant! Wiggle your ears!" Kathy commands. "And keep them wiggling." During this wash-behind-the-ears time, the keeper runs her fingers over the thin skin at the back of the ears and pricks a bit at the stick-out veins with the point of her ankus,[1] hoping to prepare the animals for occasional needle pricks during checkups by a veterinarian.

Now she wants her animals down. Lying down is a vulnerable[2] position for them. It's only because of feeling

---

1 **ankus** (ang' kəs) a pointed stick with a hook, that is used for leading an elephant
2 **vulnerable** (vul' nər ə bəl) subject to physical injury

safe with her that Ambika and Shanthi obey. They go to their knees. At commands of "Down!" they flop to one side. And here the scrub up of this pair begins.

Elephants are cursed with dry, old skin on their backs. It builds up in a way that's unsightly and probably itchy. The skin cracks and harbors infections down inside, so keepers have to scrub away day in, day out, to lift the dead stuff off. Today Kathy uses a scrub brush on Ambika and, because of her blisters, a sponge on Shanthi. For Nancy's worse case of dead skin on the back she has tools of a rougher sort—a cement block with a handle and the kind of scraper used to remove rust from car bodies.

At this point Kathy pours out green oil soap from a bottle, letting it spread across the great gray expanses of skin and foaming it up with streamers from her hose. Now, with her ankus propped against the railings and her hose lying on the floor, she lights into a two-handed scrub job. Steam rises all about, shifted by whuffling puffs of air from the elephants' trunks. The keeper works hard, talking to Ambika: "This place is beginning to smell like a beauty parlor," and to Shanthi: "All right, I see you squinching³ up your eyes. It stings on your blisters, I bet it does." Whatever the discomfort, the young elephant lies still, her feet crossed, her trunk up, quietly feeling about her forehead, her ears, her back and on beyond to touch "Auntie" and twine briefly with "Auntie's" trunk.

Midway through the bath, keeper Kathy masterminds the shift of the two large bodies, the rocking back up onto the knees and the flop down again from left to right side. Along the way various scraped patches of skin receive smeary dabs of yellow salve. (Elephant keepers say they never order lemon meringue pie at restaurants. They've lost their appetite for it.) Sometimes, though not today, there's also an oiling for the wiry black bristles at the end of the tail.

Footwork, which comes last, is the most difficult part of the bath and the most crucial,⁴ for feet must be sound to support an elephant's great weight. With the two bathers standing again, admired, praised, patted, hugged about the knees, Kathy asks for a "Foot up! Way up! Thank you!" A foot is presented, and she begins her careful look through all the cracks and fissures⁵ of its pad for the presence of pebbles and other foreign matter.

---

3 squinching (skwinch' ing) looking with the eyes partly closed
4 crucial (kroo' shəl) very important
5 fissures (fish' ərz) long, narrow, deep cracks

Over the microphone the narrator describes the foot, how its callousy pads wear down in the wild with the long hikes each day in search of food, but how in a zoo the pads, which grow quickly, need to be rasped[6] down or even carved away in slices; and how keepers then check the fresh, smooth surface for tiny holes, which tell them a pebble has entered and may be working its way upward with each step, to cripple the elephant painfully once it touches bone.

Watchers from the railing can't see the foot up close. They see the probings with the pick or with the point of the ankus. They see Kathy using both hands on a drawknife[7] to cut away a slice of leathery, rubbery pad and then another. (It doesn't hurt the elephant.) And they hear the thunk of the slice into her bucket.

This morning Kathy does only one of Shanthi's front feet. At that, it takes almost half an hour, for she has to work around tender bruises and to wind up with a nicely rounded shape to the pad. Her knife will need a sharpening before she next uses it on the other feet, this afternoon and tomorrow. She must also rasp down the nails, which get too little scuffing in zoo life to wear down properly.

Bath and foot-care time now flows into demonstration time directed by the keeper team of Kathy and Morna out in the yard. Here people clap to see the elephants maneuver[8] on command, present a foot, balance on tiny stools, and move huge logs with their trunks. By the time Ambika and Shanthi take their bows, the keepers are beginning to wilt. There's an element of tension in the playful-looking baths they give and in the training shows—in just dealing with animals who could so easily pulverize[9] them if they chose to.

In the office, keepers Kathy and Morna speak of the awe they feel in the animals' trust of them and in the animals' forbearance,[10] *not* to hurt the keepers. They also speak of a kind of communication that goes on among the elephants, sometimes during bath time, more often first thing in the morning. "We're aware of it when we enter the building," says Morna. "We feel something. We feel it before we hear it, a kind of vibrating in the air,

---

6 **rasped** (raspt) scraped or rubbed

7 **drawknife** (drô′ nīf′) a knife with a handle at each end, used to shave surfaces

8 **maneuver** (mə nōō′ vər) to move or proceed skillfully toward a desired goal

9 **pulverize** (pul′ və rīz′) to break down or crush completely

10 **forbearance** (fôr bār′ əns) patience

like a cat's purring, only just beyond
our hearing. Sometimes that rum-
bling seems to be a message to us.
Like: It's good to see you. We're glad
you're here."

Andy Warhol, *Endangered Species: African Elephant,* 1983

Linking Writing and Literature

 Collect Your Thoughts

Think about what Peggy Thomson is describing in this chapter from her book. Make some notes that explain what she is describing *generally* and what she is describing *specifically*.

 Talk About Reading

Discuss the selection "Bathing Elephants" with your classmates. Select one person to lead the discussion and another to take notes. Use the following questions to guide the discussion.

1. **Connect to Your Life** What did you learn about the health requirements of elephants in a zoo?

2. **Critical Thinking: Draw Conclusions** After reading this excerpt, what conclusions can you draw about the temperament of elephants?

3. **6+1 Trait®: Organization** How does Thomson signal new steps in the process she is describing? What words and phrases does she use?

4. **Connect to Your Writing** When you write to describe a process, what are some things you can do to ensure that your description will be clear to the reader?

 Write About Reading

Expository Essay Write an expository essay in which you describe a process as Peggy Thomson did in "Bathing Elephants." Include your description as part of an interesting story, such as how you bathed your dog after she encountered a skunk or how you repaired a flat tire on your bike when you were a long way from home.

Focus on Organization Be sure to organize the steps in the process in correct order. Use appropriate words and phrases to signal new steps. If other people were involved in the process, use dialogue to make the story more interesting to your readers.

For more information on organization and the 6+1 Trait® model, see **Writing and Research Handbook,** pages 682–684.

6+1 Trait® is a registered trademark of Northwest Regional Educational Laboratory, which does not endorse this product.

Expository Writing

Reflecting on the Unit

Summarize what you learned in this unit by answering the following questions.

❶ What are the different kinds of expository writing and the purpose of each?

❷ What prewriting methods can you use to organize information for a comparison-contrast essay?

❸ What strategies can help you write a clear explanation of a process?

❹ How do you gather information for a research report?

❺ What are the six main parts of a book report?

Adding to Your Portfolio

CHOOSE A SELECTION FOR YOUR PORTFOLIO Look over the expository writing you did for this unit. Choose a completed piece for your portfolio. The piece you select should show some or all of the following:

• for a comparison-contrast essay, details organized from a prewriting list, chart, drawings, or Venn diagram

• for a process explanation, steps presented in a clear order and with transitions to link them

• for a report, information gathered through research

• a clear introduction, body, and conclusion

REFLECT ON YOUR CHOICE Attach a note to the piece you chose, explaining briefly why you chose it and what you learned from writing it.

SET GOALS How can you improve your writing? What skill will you focus on the next time you write?

Writing Across the Curriculum

MAKE A HISTORY CONNECTION Scan your history textbook and identify two people to compare and contrast—perhaps two political leaders or two explorers. List details about each person and create a Venn diagram showing the similarities and differences. Organize your findings, and then draft a short comparison-contrast essay.

"Can wolves and humans coexist? The answer is clear: We can. The deeper truth is even clearer: We must."

—Sigurd Olson, *The Singing Wilderness*

UNIT 6

Persuasive Writing

Writing in the Real World: *Douglas Anderson*   218

Lesson 6.1   **Taking a Stand**   222

Lesson 6.2   **Stating a Position**   226

Lesson 6.3   **Using Facts and Opinions**   230

Lesson 6.4   **Writing About Literature:
Writing a TV Review**   234

Writing Process in Action   238

**Literature Model: from *Thanking the Birds*
by Joseph Bruchac**   242

Unit 6 Review   247

Writing in the Real World

MEDIA Screenplay Connection

When producers at Children's Television Workshop (CTW) decided to do a program on the way people devour the world's resources, they asked Douglas Anderson to write the script. Anderson set out to create a program that would persuade viewers of the need to save vital resources on the planet Earth. How many resources do people consume? In the excerpt that follows, Anderson finds a creative way to answer that question.

from "A Popular Little Planet"
by Douglas Anderson

A baby is born. One person more! That's wonderful. But now we'll need a lot more stuff, because the average American, over a lifetime, is gonna use resources, like:

• one hundred million gallons of water;

• three hundred bushels of apples;

• seven best friends;

• shirts;

• oil;

• underwear;

• paper;

• and 147 pairs of shoelaces.

And, if this person is anything like me, then he's gonna want even *more* stuff, like:

• three library cards;

• 35 hats;

• 4,000 comic books;

• two cats;

• three skateboards;

• a mountain of fries;

• seven cars;

• and a lifetime of stuff I can't even think of right now!

```
    And that's just for        about 250,000 people
one person! Remember,          born every day!
172 people are born on            Do we have enough
this planet every              stuff?
minute. And that's
```

A Writer's Process

Prewriting
Researching and Outlining

Work on the program began with careful research. As Anderson said, "You don't necessarily know your position on an issue before you start researching."

The staff at CTW helped Anderson learn more about the earth's resources and how people use them. Researcher Vivian Trakinski received information from the National Science Foundation. Scientist Edward Atkins suggested books and articles on resources for Anderson to read.

Anderson and the CTW staff learned that the human population has reached five billion and that it is using vital resources at an alarming rate. Gathering reliable information was important to Anderson. "In any kind of writing you have a responsibility to get the facts right. All the neat ideas for the show come out of this work."

Their research completed, the group then stated the program's position: To avoid running out of resources, people need to conserve and share.

Using this position and the facts uncovered in research, Anderson drafted an outline for the program.

"This is where you define the ideas you want to convey and the order in which you want to say them," he said. He shared the outline with Trakinski, Atkins, and the producer.

The group discussed the outline for "A Popular Little Planet," as the show would be called. They decided that the program would emphasize three major points: First, five billion people now live on the planet. Second, people gobble up resources. Sometimes they fight over resources because there aren't enough to go around. Third, there are ways people can help solve this problem. By sharing and conserving resources, people can make sure there is enough for everyone.

Writing in the Real World

Drafting
Writing the Script

Anderson now had to figure out how to use the resources of television to make his points. He said, "I knew I could use everything from music to cartoons and graphics."

Anderson had to think of ways to dramatize each point. How, for example, could he show the alarming amount of resources people use? Anderson wrote a scene in which Z, one of the actors, lists the things that belong to just one person. That scene, excerpted on page 218, ends with "Do we *have* enough stuff?"

To answer that question, in one scene Z and his partner, Stephanie, decide to make cookies and brownies. The problem? They each have only half the ingredients they need.

In the scene Stephanie and Z fight over the ingredients. "Then," Anderson said, "they realize that by sharing resources each person can have what he wants."

Anderson ended the segment with a real-life example of people and resources. He showed a film about water shortages in California, where 30 million people live. The point was clear: People must conserve water so that everyone will have enough.

Anderson thinks these scenes were persuasive for several reasons. First, they were energetic and entertaining. Just as important, ideas drew viewers in step by step. "Using fun examples, we built up to the point we wanted to make," he said.

Anderson believes that building a strong case is the way to convince people. He explains, "Rule number one in persuasive writing is that you have to know what you're talking about. Number two, telling people what to think doesn't work. Very often the most persuasive thing you can do is to set out the facts and let people develop their own ideas."

Revising/Presenting
Rewriting the Script

Anderson's draft went through many reviews and revisions at CTW. First, the producer checked to be sure the show would both entertain and persuade. Then the science adviser checked it for accuracy. CTW executives and students also reviewed the script. Anderson used everyone's comments to write a second draft, and after that he prepared a third version. Finally, several months later, after taping and editing were complete, "A Popular Little Planet" went on the air.

"There's no way of knowing for sure whether people started behaving differently," Anderson said. "But we did get a lot of mail, and the mail was wonderful."

Examining Writing in the Real World

Analyzing the Media Connection

Discuss these questions about the script excerpt on page 218.

1. What is the main point that scriptwriter Douglas Anderson makes in the excerpt?

2. Why do you think Anderson lists the resources that just one person might use, instead of giving facts about global use of resources?

3. Why do you think Anderson includes such items as comic books and fries in his list?

4. Does Anderson write in a formal or informal tone? Support your answer with examples.

5. Why do you think Anderson ends by posing a question, not a statement about the planet's limited resources?

Analyzing a Writer's Process

Discuss these questions about Douglas Anderson's writing process.

1. What was the main goal of the program that Anderson wrote for CTW?

2. How did Anderson gather his information? How important does Anderson think research is to the final script?

3. What purpose did writing an outline serve for Anderson and his co-workers?

4. At what point did the group determine the program's position? What three points would the program emphasize?

5. After Anderson drafted the script, what kinds of review and revision did it go through?

Grammar Link

Use commas to set off direct quotations.

"Then," Anderson said, "they realize that by sharing resources each person can have what he wants."

Write the following sentences, adding commas to set off the quotations.

1. "Our trash disposal is a big problem" said the mayor.

2. "We hope" she continued "that the recycling program will help."

3. A reporter asked "Will the recycling include magazines?"

4. "Not until next year" a council member answered.

5. "For details" the mayor added "read the brochure we are mailing to each home."

See Lesson 19.4, page 495.

LESSON
6.1

Taking a Stand

One purpose of persuasive writing is to make readers think or feel a certain way about an idea or a product. Another purpose is to make readers take action. Sometimes it does both. What is the writer's goal in the model below?

Literature Model

Most dogs are very friendly once they get to know you. But, like people, dogs don't always want to be friends right away. They need time to get acquainted and decide that you're okay.

Don't make the mistake of trying to pet or hug a strange dog. You wouldn't like it if someone you didn't know ran up and hugged you. Most dogs don't like it either.

Dr. Ann Squire
101 Questions and Answers About Pets and People

What does the writer tell you that might lead you to approach dogs carefully?

What Does It Take to Convince You?

Often persuasive writing begins by stating the writer's goal. Then evidence—information to support that goal—follows. Some support statements will make you think ("The rain forest is disappearing at the rate of . . ."). Some support statements will make you feel a certain way ("You won't fit in unless you wear . . ."). Finally, there is usually a reminder of what the writer wants you to think or do.

As a reader, you need to think carefully about the support presented in persuasive writing. After all, the writer is trying to change your thoughts or actions. From the excerpt on page 222, do you agree with the support statement in the chart below?

Drafting Tip

When drafting, make sure your main idea, or position, comes across in a sharp, clear statement. A single, carefully worded sentence usually works best.

Persuasive Writing

Goal	Support
Do not hug or pet a strange dog.	Dogs don't always want to be friends right away.

Journal Writing

List in your journal three examples of persuasive writing you have read recently. Have any persuaded you to change your thoughts or actions? Write a brief paragraph explaining why or why not.

How Often Do You Persuade?

Persuasive writing can take many forms, from a 500-page book to a few words on a billboard. It can even exist in friendly letters or cards.

Suppose that you want to persuade a friend who lives out of town to visit you during the summer. You might make up a package including posters, brochures, and articles about the attractions of your home town. You could present your best persuasive ideas in a letter like the one at the left. Read it to see where Rachel put her main idea and her support.

Dear Jenna,

Hi! How's life? I'm fine. I was just hit by a killer idea. Why don't you come to Iowa City for the July Fourth week? Doesn't that sound great?! Not only could we see fab fireworks, but the jazz festival is that weekend. You would love it. Tons of music and great people. They block off the streets and different kinds of food shops set up stands. From frozen yogurt to bar-be-que. It's great.

When we're not listening to music, there is a wonderful bead shop in this little row of second-story shops called the Hall Mall. Every kind of bead you could imagine. Of course we would have to get the world's best chocolate malts at this quaint little drug store.

I don't know if this sounds fun, but it is. Well, gotta motor. Think about my offer.

Love ya,
Rachel

Rachel Hardesty
Willowwind School
Iowa City, Iowa

Create a Poster

Make a poster to convince students to wear safety equipment when biking or skateboarding. Use photos or drawings to reinforce your words.

PURPOSE To persuade others to use safety equipment

AUDIENCE Other students

LENGTH 1 page

WRITING RUBRICS To write a persuasive essay, you should

- state clearly your main goal
- give at least two support statements
- end with a reminder of what you want people to think or do

Jasper Johns. *Numbers in Color.* 1958–1959

Avoid sentence fragments in your writing.

A *fragment* is a group of words that does not present a complete thought and may lack a subject, a predicate, or both.

Revise each sentence fragment below to make a complete sentence. Write clearly and legibly, and check your spelling.

1. Tons of music and great people.
2. From frozen yogurt to barbeque.
3. Every kind of bead you could imagine.

See Lesson 8.2, page 299.

Cross-Curricular Activity

ART Study the reproduction of *Numbers in Color* on this page, and then state your opinion of it. Supply at least two support statements to back up your opinion.

Listening and Speaking

PRESENT A DEBATE Stage a debate about *Numbers in Color.* Take turns presenting your opinions and support statements to the class. Then encourage the class to evaluate the persuasiveness of the arguments presented.

Stating a Position

When you have a goal you really care about, the challenge is winning over your audience.

As you choose a goal for your persuasive piece, answer the questions in the chart below. If you can answer yes to each question, you've found a good topic.

Finding a Persuasive Writing Topic

- Do I know enough about this topic?
- Do I care about this topic?
- Do people disagree about this topic?

The students at one school have several ideas for projects. Some want to put in a juice machine to raise money for new computers. Some want to start a garden to grow vegetables for a food pantry. Some want to organize an ethnic festival to celebrate different cultures. If you were the student council representative to the school board, it would be your job to persuade the school board to adopt one of the ideas.

Do I know enough about this topic?

Do I care about this topic?

Do people disagree on this topic?

Give Reasons

Why should people adopt your ideas? You need to provide convincing reasons.

The proposal written by last year's representative to the school board appears below. Notice the clear organization and persuasive sound of the letter.

Grammar Tip

When you write a letter that speaks for a group or an organization, be sure to use the right pronouns. For more information on pronouns, see Lessons 11.1–11.5, pages 361–370.

Literature Model

Dear Ms. Perez and the school board:

For this year's student project, we would like to set up paper-recycling bins at key places around the school. This project will benefit the school in several ways. It will give students a chance to improve the environment by cutting down on waste. It will encourage students from all grades to work together to set up and run the recycling project. It will also help raise money we can use for future projects.

We would like to put a recycling bin in each classroom. A group of students will be chosen each week to collect the bins and set them out for pickup. A permanent group will oversee the project with Mr. Hansen, the science teacher. With your support, this project will be a success.

Note that the first sentence is a statement of the main goal.

What reasons does the student provide in support of the proposal? Are they convincing?

Journal Writing

Take two minutes to list as many persuasive-writing topics as you can. Circle those topics to which you can answer yes for all three of the questions on page 226. Why are some topics not circled? Change these enough so that you can circle them. Keep these topics for use in future projects.

Presenting Tip

Choose the form that best presents your argument. Will you send a letter or face your audience in person? The form of presentation may affect how you state your ideas.

Consider Your Audience

Whenever you try to convince someone of something, you need to keep your audience in mind. For example, imagine that you're trying to get your family to plan a day of activities in the city. You might spark your sister's interest by telling her about the great restaurants. Your mom might take more interest in the museums. The street performers might appeal more to your brother.

Different people have different interests and different levels of knowledge. Choose reasons that appeal to your audience. One student's goal was to argue for the ethnic festival. She sent a letter to the school board and another letter to the students. Her goal was the same in both letters, but at least one of her reasons was different. Why?

An ethnic festival will build pride and help students understand cultures different from their own.

The reason presented to the school board focuses on what the festival will teach students. The reason statement for students focuses on how much fun the festival will be.

An ethnic festival will give us a chance to enjoy sharing many different foods and customs.

Write a Proposal

Choose a project that your sixth-grade class might do in the school or in the community. Explain your idea in a written proposal to your teacher or the school principal.

PURPOSE To practice persuading an adult audience

AUDIENCE Your teacher or principal

LENGTH 2–4 paragraphs

WRITING RUBRICS To write a persuasive proposal, you should

- state your goal clearly
- follow it with supporting reasons that will appeal to your audience

Using Computers

E-mail Using an attachment function, e-mail your proposal to a friend or relative for his or her evaluation. Use the comments you get back to help you revise your work.

Grammar Link

Capitalize proper nouns and adjectives.

Capitalize the names of languages, countries, and nationalities in the list. You will need to capitalize 10 words.

1. haitian, chinese, and italian food
2. art from mexico
3. tapes of irish, israeli, and russian music
4. jewelry from india and greece
5. a cuban band

See Lesson 18.4, page 479.

Viewing and Representing

TRAVEL DISPLAY Find some attractive pictures of your town or neighborhood in a magazine, book, or brochure. With a partner, make a display on a poster or a bulletin board and write a few paragraphs telling other students your age why you think they would enjoy coming to visit your area. Invite classmates to comment on your display.

Using Facts and Opinions

What kinds of evidence will you use to support your goal and your reasons?

Each year Mrs. Van's class chooses a class pet. Her students write persuasive papers, arguing for their choice. What pet would you argue for? What evidence could you present to prove your point?

Literature Model

Ever since a snake tempted Eve with an apple in the Garden of Eden, snakes have been considered evil, hateful, and repulsive creatures. However, most snakes are harmless and helpful. They kill rats and other rodents that destroy crops and invade our homes. Many kinds make fascinating, even beautiful pets. They are not slimy. Their scaly skin feels like dry leather. They don't make a sound, they are odorless, and you don't have to feed them every day.

Leda and Rhoda Blumberg
Lovebirds, Lizards, and Llamas: Strange and Exotic Pets

What evidence do the writers use to suggest that snakes can make good pets?

Gather the Evidence

You believe that a snake would be the perfect class pet. How can you persuade your classmates and your teacher? Persuading people to change their attitudes or to take action requires evidence. Evidence comes in two forms: facts and opinions.

FACTS Facts are statements that can be proved. For example, the statement "They are not slimy" is a fact. You could prove it by touching a snake or by reading about snakes.

Revising Tip

As you gather evidence, write down the source of each fact or opinion you intend to use.

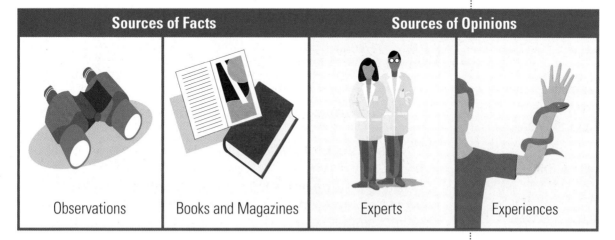

Sources of Facts		Sources of Opinions	
Observations	Books and Magazines	Experts	Experiences

OPINIONS An opinion is a personal belief or feeling. It can't be proved. The authors of the excerpt on page 230 think that snakes make fascinating pets. Because the authors are experts, you would probably believe them. The opinions of experts can be powerful evidence. Personal experience can also be good evidence. A person who has a lot of experience is often considered an expert.

Journal Writing

Select a persuasive article from a newspaper or magazine, and identify the goal. Save the article in your journal. Make notes in your journal about how facts and opinions support the goal. Make sure your writing is legible.

Organize Your Argument

After you gather your evidence, review it piece by piece. Which evidence is the strongest or most convincing? Sometimes you might want to put the strongest piece of evidence first in your paper. Other times you might want to save it until the end. Decide which order of evidence best supports your goal.

Make a list of your evidence in the order that seems most persuasive. Use this list to draft your persuasive argument. Of course, you may change the order of the evidence during revision. Notice the revisions of this draft about pet snakes.

What evidence does the writer use to support the goal statement? Are word choices precise?

Because this was written for Ms. Van, the writer decided to start with what the students would learn from a snake.

In choosing a class pet, we could pick no
finer
~~better~~ animal than a snake. Experts point out that snakes are quiet, clean, and easy to care for. They aren't slimy, and they make fascinating pets.

The smaller kinds, which we are most likely
eat
to get, ~~feed on~~ worms. So they would be easy and inexpensive to feed. Also, people don't have allergies to snakes as they do to dogs, cats, and birds.

Snakes behave very differently from more common pets. We would learn more about the animal world by adopting a snake than we would by choosing a pet we know well.

Write a Persuasive Letter

Television shows are canceled all the time. Sometimes even a popular TV show goes off the air. If many people write or call the network, sometimes the show returns. What if your favorite show had just been canceled? Write a letter to the president of the network to persuade him or her to bring back the show.

PURPOSE To keep your favorite TV program from being canceled

AUDIENCE A network executive

LENGTH 2–3 paragraphs

WRITING RUBRICS To write a persuasive letter, you should

- make your point clear in a goal statement
- use facts or opinions as evidence
- organize your evidence to appeal to your audience

Cross-Curricular Activity

COOPERATIVE LEARNING In a small group, plan a campaign to persuade fellow students to support a community project. For example, you could suggest setting up donation boxes for homeless people or forming an after-school club to work on community environmental issues. Agree on the goal you wish to pursue. List evidence—facts and opinions—to support your position. Have two people

Use commas to separate three or more items in a series.

Snakes have been considered evil, hateful, and repulsive.

Add commas as needed in the sentences below.

1. Let's find a good project for the fourth fifth and sixth graders.
2. We could plant flowers shrubs and trees around the building.
3. Students could sweep rake and trim on a regular schedule.

See Lesson 19.2, page 491.

plan ways to present your proposal while others think of slogans and attention-getting phrases that present your evidence.

Listening and Speaking

DISCUSSING PETS Together with students from various cultural backgrounds, make a presentation to the class in which each of you talks about the most common pets in your own culture. Where appropriate, give the names for these pets in languages other than English. Take part in a class discussion of differences and similarities regarding the importance of pets within cultures.

WRITING ABOUT LITERATURE
Writing a TV Review

Do you ever find yourself trying to convince a friend to watch a rerun of a TV show? Try writing a review and reaching a larger audience.

All week you have looked forward to the National Geographic television special about the North Pole. What's it like at the top of the world? What animals live there, and how do they survive? What would it be like there in the summer when the sun never sets?

The program not only answers your questions, but it does more. It tells you about brave explorers who faced many dangers as they mapped the frozen lands. It makes you feel as if you're taking part in a month-long dog-sled journey. The beautiful photography and the haunting music fascinate you. To share what you've learned from this show, you could write a review of the program and try to persuade people to watch it in a rerun or on videotape.

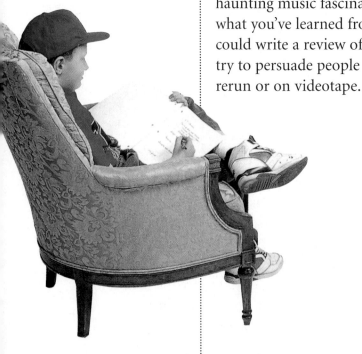

Gather Information

The best way to gather information for a TV review is to take notes while you watch the program. Jot down notes about facts or images that grab your attention.

You can use other methods, too, to help you review a TV program. If you have a videocassette recorder, tape the program and watch it again. The tape can help you strengthen your ideas about the program and add to your notes. You might watch the show with a friend. Afterward, discuss what each of you thought of the show. You can also make a chart like the one below to collect and organize information about a TV program.

Gathering Information for a TV Review	
Name of show and network	*National Geographic Explorer,* "North to the Pole," WTBS
Subject of the show	Dog-sled expedition to the North Pole
Characters (if appropriate)	Six-member team that takes part in the expedition
Strengths	Fast-paced, exciting
Weaknesses	Not enough information on the history of such expeditions
My responses	Makes me want to travel north and learn about winter camping

Journal Writing

Make a chart like the one above, and fill it in as you watch a television program. How does the chart help you gather information about the program? What questions could you add to make the chart a better prewriting tool? How else could you improve it?

Grammar Tip

When you edit a review, make sure you've used tenses correctly. Most reviews discuss programs in present tense. For more information see Lesson 10.4, page 339.

TIME

For more about the drafting process, see **TIME Facing the Blank Page,** page 94.

Drafting the Review

Writing a review of a TV program is fairly straightforward. The best way to persuade people to watch a television show is to tell them what you like most about the program. Your enthusiasm can persuade your friends, teachers, parents, and anyone else who reads your review to give the show a try.

In the model below, Jack Costello's excitement about an episode of *The New Explorers* comes through in his review. How might his thumbs-up review make you want to watch the program?

Student Model

The name of the program I watched is *The New Explorers* and it is on WTTW. The subject of the program is computer art and how it is used in entertainment and medicine.

The program's strengths are that it is educational and fun to watch. I like the examples of computer graphics like *Tin Toy. Tin Toy* is an award-winning short cartoon about a toy soldier that comes to life. It is both funny and realistic. The weakness of this show is that it mentions only a few of the many people involved in making computer graphics.

Overall, I feel that the show is cool and really taught me a lot. Computer graphics can be used just about everywhere, including TV, movies, and commercials. It can also be used to help surgeons in the operating room. I think I might want to do something like this when I grow up.

Jack Costello, St. James School,
Arlington Heights, Illinois

Write a TV Review

Imagine that the most popular segments of your favorite television program have just come out on videotape. Write a two- or three-paragraph review of the videotape that will appear on the package or on posters. The review, aimed at people who have never seen the program, should encourage people to buy the videotape.

PURPOSE To persuade someone to buy a videotape

AUDIENCE Customers of a video store

LENGTH 2–3 paragraphs

WRITING RUBRICS To write an effective review, you should

- tell what you like about the program
- give reasons that other people would enjoy it
- explain why someone would want to own a copy of the tape

Using Computers

Graphics Some computer programs allow the user to create charts. You can choose the number of columns and rows. You can even put a special border around your chart or shade certain areas. Create your own chart for reviewing TV programs. Use the chart on page 235 as a guide. Add any sections you think would be useful.

Grammar Link

Use apostrophes to form possessive nouns.

Use an apostrophe and an *–s* to form the possessive of a singular noun.

the **program's** strengths.

Where you place the apostrophe in a plural noun depends on whether or not the plural ends in *–s*:

people's   *adults'*

Write the sentences below, adding apostrophes to show possession.

1. The TV news show was about our towns plan to build a bike path.
2. The shows purpose was to include opinions from all age groups.
3. I liked the boys suggestions.

See Lesson 19.7, page 501.

Viewing and Representing

PUBLISH YOUR REVIEW Videotape your review, either alone or with a partner, or use the computer to print it out and then post it on the bulletin board. Be sure to check your spelling and punctuation if you print your review. Invite classmates to view your video or read your printed review and then evaluate your arguments in a class discussion.

Persuasive Writing

Writing Process in Action

Persuasive Writing

In preceding lessons you've learned about persuasive writing—about the importance of strong reasons, about using facts and opinions as evidence, about appealing to your audience. You've had the opportunity to do some persuasive writing, including a TV review. Now it's time to put together all that you've learned. In this lesson you're invited to write a persuasive newspaper article. You will try to convince your readers to take some action on an environmental issue.

Assignment

Context

Write an article for a local newspaper to persuade readers to make (or support) some change that will protect the environment.

Purpose

To convince people to think about or take action on an environmental issue

Audience

Readers of all types and ages

Length

1 page

WRITING Online

Visit the *Writer's Choice* Web site at **writerschoice.glencoe.com** for additional writing prompts.

The following pages can help you plan and write your newspaper article. Read through them and then refer to them as you need to. Don't be limited by them. You are in charge of your own writing process.

Prewriting

What environmental issue do you think is especially important? Saving rain forests? Cleaning up air and water pollution? What issues have had a direct effect on your community?

Once you've selected a topic, explore your ideas by listing, clustering, or freewriting. Then use one of the options at the right, or an idea of your own, to select supporting evidence.

Before you draft, write your goal statement. Then list reasons that will persuade your audience.

Option A
Read a daily newspaper for new information.

Option B
Check a library magazine index or online resource for helpful articles.

Option C
Read other materials on your topic at the library.

Electric cars—very soon we will be able to buy cars that use less than $100 worth of electricity to travel 10,000 miles. They run on batteries. Without engines, they don't need as many repairs.

Drafting

As you draft, keep your audience constantly in mind, and use language that will be persuasive. Joseph Bruchac tells how a Native American named Swift Eagle persuaded some boys to change their behavior. Read Swift Eagle's words:

Literature Model

"You know, our Creator gave the gift of life to everything that is alive. Life is a very sacred thing. But our Creator knows that we have to eat to stay alive. That is why it is permitted to hunt to feed ourselves and our people. So I understand that you boys must have been very, very hungry to kill those little birds."

Joseph Bruchac, "Thanking the Birds"

Writing Process in Action

Drafting Tip

For help with organizing your information, see Lesson 6.2, pages 226–229.

Revising Tip

For ideas about reviewing and improving your draft, see Lesson 6.3, page 232.

Do Swift Eagle's words persuade you? Do they help you feel responsibility for treating nature with respect?

Remember, in the drafting stage you need to express your ideas in sentences and paragraphs. Don't worry about grammar and spelling now. You can make changes later. This is the time to get your ideas on paper.

Revising

To begin revising, read over your draft to make sure that what you've written fits your purpose and audience. Then have a **writing conference.** Read your draft to a partner or small group. Use your audience's reactions to help you evaluate your work. The following questions can help you and your listeners.

Question A

Have I made my position clear?

Question B

Does my evidence support my position?

Question C

Have I directed my writing toward my audience?

Exhaust from cars is called auto emissions.
~~Electric cars should be built and sold in the~~
Auto emissions are a leading cause of
~~United States because car smoke causes~~ air

pollution. Car exhaust is hard on buildings,
Some cities in Europe
too. ~~I've heard about cities that~~ have banned

downtown traffic to protect old buildings and

works of art. We may not have to go that far,

however, if we let auto makers know that we
them to build and sell
want electric cars in the United States.

Editing/Proofreading

As you prepare your article, **proofread** it to eliminate distracting errors. A newspaper editor is more likely to publish your writing if it is free of mistakes in spelling, grammar, and usage.

The checklist at the right will help you catch errors you might otherwise overlook. Read and reread your work with care. Use a dictionary and the Grammar, Usage, and Mechanics section of this book to help you.

Publishing/Presenting

Make sure your article is neatly written in cursive or manuscript writing or typed on clean white paper before you submit it to your local newspaper. You might want to include a photo or drawing that illustrates the environmental issue you're writing about. Also, include any visual aids such as charts or graphs that make the evidence easier to understand.

Another way to present your writing is for you and your classmates to produce a school newsletter. The purpose of the newsletter would be to keep students up to date on issues that affect the environment.

Editing/Proofreading Checklist

- Have I used commas correctly in series and with quotations?
- Are all my sentences clear and complete?
- Have I capitalized proper nouns and adjectives?
- Have I used possessive nouns and pronouns correctly?
- Have I used standard punctuation and correct spelling?

Proofreading Tip

For proofreading symbols see page 72 or 267.

Journal Writing

Reflect on your writing process experience. Answer these questions in your journal: What do you like best about your article? What was the hardest part of writing it? What did you learn in your writing conference? What new thing have you learned as a writer?

Literature Model

Joseph Bruchac

THANKING THE BIRDS

The following essay is taken from Keepers of the Earth, *a book created to help people understand the delicate relationship between humans and the natural world. Joseph Bruchac is an award-winning novelist and poet who was born in the Adirondack Mountain region. As you read, pay special attention to the ways he tries to change people's attitudes and behaviors. Then try the activities in Linking Writing and Literature on page 246.*

One day 30 years ago, Swift Eagle, an Apache man, visited some friends on the Onondaga Indian Reservation in central New York. While he was out walking, he heard sounds of boys playing in the bushes.

"There's another one. Shoot it!" said one of the boys.

When he pushed through the brush to see what was happening, he found that they had been shooting small birds with a BB gun. They had already killed a chickadee, a robin and several blackbirds. The boys looked up at him, uncertain what he was going to do or say.

There are several things that a non-Indian bird lover might have done:

given a stern lecture on the evil of killing birds; threatened to tell the boys' parents on them for doing something they had been told not to do; or even spanked them. Swift Eagle, however, did something else.

Amy Cordova, *The Red Dress*, 1989

"Ah," he said, "I see you have been hunting. Pick up your game and come with me."

He led the boys to a place where they could make a fire and cook the birds. He made sure they said a 'thank you' to the spirits of the birds before eating them, and as they ate he told stories. It was important, he said, to be thankful to the birds for the gifts of their songs, their feathers, and their bodies as food. The last thing he said to them they never forgot—for it was one of those boys who told me this story many years later: "You know, our Creator gave the gift of life to everything that is alive. Life is a very sacred thing. But our Creator knows that we have to eat to stay alive. That is why it is permitted to hunt to feed ourselves and our people. So I understand that you boys must have been very, very hungry to kill those little birds."

I have always liked that story, for it illustrates several things. Although there was a wide range of customs, lifeways and languages—in pre-Columbian[1] times more than 400 different languages were spoken on the North American continent— many close similarities existed between virtually all of the Native American peoples. Thus ideas held by an Apache from the Southwest fitted into the lives and traditions of Onondagas in the Northeast.

> **❝** . . . He told stories that pointed out the value of those birds as living beings . . . .**❞**

One of these ideas, expressed in Swift Eagle's words to the boys, was the continent-wide belief that mankind depended on the natural world for survival, on the one hand, and had to respect it and remain in right relationship with it, on the other. . . .

As the anecdote[2] about Swift Eagle also shows, the children were taught the values of their culture through example and stories. Instead of scolding or lecturing them, Swift Eagle showed the boys how to build a fire and cook the game they had shot, giving the songbirds the same respect he would have given a rabbit or deer.

---

1 **pre-Columbian** before Columbus's arrival in 1492
2 **anecdote** (an'ik dōt') a brief retelling of an actual event

He told stories that pointed out the value of those birds as living beings. The ritual[3] activity of making the fire, thanking the spirit of the birds, hearing the stories and then eating the game they had killed taught the boys more than a hundred stern lectures would have done, and the lesson stayed with them all their lives.

---

3 **ritual** (rich′ oo əl) a system of special ceremonies

Linking Writing and Literature

 Collect Your Thoughts

Think about what Joseph Bruchac is saying in "Thanking the Birds." In your journal, make some notes about the main idea of this excerpt from *Keepers of the Earth*.

 Talk About Reading

Discuss "Thanking the Birds" with your classmates. Select one person to lead the discussion and another to take notes. Use the following questions to guide the discussion.

1. **Connect to Your Life** Why is it important for people to respect nature? In what ways do you respect nature in your own life?

2. **Critical Thinking: Draw Conclusions** After reading the excerpt, what conclusions can you draw about the relationship between Native Americans and nature?

3. **6+1 Trait®: Ideas** What lesson do the boys learn from Swift Eagle? What lesson might they have learned if he had simply scolded them or told their parents what they had done?

4. **Connect to Your Writing** How does Bruchac's anecdote make his theme easier for the reader to understand? When can you use anecdotes in your own writing?

 Write About Reading

Editorial Write an editorial for your community newspaper that considers the following questions.
- Why it is important for everyone to develop a personal relationship with the natural world?
- How can people develop such a relationship?
- What will be the benefits for people and nature?

If appropriate, include a brief anecdote in your editorial to help readers understand your point.

Focus on Ideas Before you begin writing, spend some time thinking about the main idea of your editorial. Be sure the main idea is clear in your own mind so that you can explain it well to your readers.

For more information on ideas and the 6+1 Trait® model, see **Writing and Research Handbook,** pages 682–684.

Reflecting on the Unit

Summarize what you learned in this unit by answering the following questions.

1 When you write to persuade, why is it important to keep your audience in mind?

2 What are some good ways to use opinions as supporting evidence?

3 How can you use the revising stage to improve a piece of persuasive writing?

4 What techniques can help you gather information to review a television program?

Adding to Your Portfolio

CHOOSE A SELECTION FOR YOUR PORTFOLIO Look over the persuasive writing you did in this unit. Select a completed piece of writing to put into your portfolio. The writing you choose should show some or all of the following:

- an attempt to get readers to believe or do something
- a clear goal statement
- reasons that support the goal statement
- evidence ordered in a way that is persuasive to the intended audience
- accurate spelling and legible cursive or manuscript writing

REFLECT ON YOUR CHOICE Attach a note to the piece you chose, explaining briefly why you chose it and what you learned from writing it.

SET GOALS How can you improve your writing? What skill will you focus on the next time you write?

Writing Across the Curriculum

MAKE A GEOGRAPHY CONNECTION Think about a weather condition or natural phenomenon that might threaten your community (a tornado, flood, electrical storm, or earthquake). Write a persuasive argument to convince people to protect themselves or their property. Put your argument in any form you wish—perhaps a newspaper article, poster, or radio announcement.

"*Arithmetic is where the answer is right and everything is nice and you can look out of the window and see the blue sky . . .*"

—Carl Sandburg, *Arithmetic*

Troubleshooter

Use Troubleshooter to help you correct common errors that you might make in your writing. You can indicate the errors on your paper, using the handwritten codes in the left-hand column. Then the Table of Contents below will help you locate solutions to correct errors.

frag	Lesson **7.1**	**Sentence Fragment**	*250*
run-on	Lesson **7.2**	**Run-on Sentence**	*252*
agr	Lesson **7.3**	**Lack of Subject-Verb Agreement**	*254*
tense	Lesson **7.4**	**Incorrect Verb Tense or Form**	*256*
pro	Lesson **7.5**	**Incorrect Use of Pronouns**	*258*
adj	Lesson **7.6**	**Incorrect Use of Adjectives**	*260*
com	Lesson **7.7**	**Incorrect Use of Commas**	*262*
apo	Lesson **7.8**	**Incorrect Use of Apostrophes**	*264*
cap	Lesson **7.9**	**Incorrect Capitalization**	*266*

7.1 Sentence Fragment

Problem 1

Fragment that lacks a subject

frag   Tess left town. (Went to Maine.)
frag   The horse trotted home. (Ate some hay.)
frag   Hasina teaches school. (Teaches English literature.)

SOLUTION   Add a subject to the fragment to make a complete sentence.

Tess left town. She went to Maine.
The horse trotted home. It ate some hay.
Hasina teaches school. She teaches English literature.

Problem 2

Fragment that lacks a predicate

frag   The woman was singing. (The beautiful song.)
frag   A noise woke me up. (The dog next door again.)
frag   Joyce bought a skirt. (That blue linen skirt.)

SOLUTION   Add a predicate to make the sentence complete.

The woman was singing. The song was beautiful.

A noise woke me up. The dog next door was barking again.

Joyce bought a skirt. That skirt was blue linen.

Problem 3

Fragment that lacks both a subject and a predicate

frag   Miriam left work late. (With her friend.)

frag   The store closed. (At two o'clock.)

SOLUTION   Combine the fragment with another sentence.

Miriam left work late with her friend.

The store closed at two o'clock.

If you need more help avoiding sentence fragments, see Lesson 8.2, page 299.

7.2 Run-on Sentence

Two main clauses separated by only a comma

run-on (*I like to play volleyball, Luis prefers hockey.*)

SOLUTION A   Replace the comma with a period or other end mark. Begin the new sentence with a capital letter.

I like to play volleyball. Luis prefers hockey.

SOLUTION B   Replace the comma between the main clauses with a semicolon.

I like to play volleyball; Luis prefers hockey.

SOLUTION C   Insert a coordinating conjunction after the comma.

I like to play volleyball, but Luis prefers hockey.

Two main clauses with no punctuation between them

run-on (*Ada writes poetry she dances, too.*)

SOLUTION A   Separate the main clauses with a period or other end mark.

Ada writes poetry. She dances, too.

SOLUTION B   Place a semicolon between the main clauses.

Ada writes poetry; she dances, too.

SOLUTION C   Insert a comma and a conjunction between the main clauses.

Ada writes poetry, and she dances, too.

Problem 3

Two main clauses with no comma before the coordinating conjunction

run-on   *I climbed the mountains and I explored the forests.*

SOLUTION   Insert a comma before the coordinating conjunction.

I climbed the mountains, and I explored the forests.

If you need more help avoiding run-on sentences, see Lesson 8.6, page 307.

7.3 Lack of Subject-Verb Agreement

A subject that is separated from the verb by an intervening prepositional phrase

agr   One of the jars (are) broken.

SOLUTION   Ignore a prepositional phrase that comes between a subject and a verb. Make sure that the verb agrees with the subject of the sentence. The subject is never the object of the preposition.

One of the jars is broken.

A sentence that begins with *here* or *there*

agr   There (is) private beaches all over that tropical island.

SOLUTION   The subject is never *here* or *there*. The subject comes after the verb. The verb must agree with this subject.

There are private beaches all over that tropical island.

Problem 3

A compound subject that is joined by *and*

> *agr*   *Music and dance (is) taught at school.*

SOLUTION   If the parts of the compound subject refer to more than one person or thing, use a plural verb.

Music and dance are taught at school.

Problem 4

A compound subject that is joined by *or* or *nor*

> *agr*   *Neither the bat nor the mitts (belongs) to me.*
>
> *agr*   *Either cookies or ice cream (are) a good dessert.*

SOLUTION   Make the verb agree with the subject that is closer to it.

Neither the bat nor the mitts belong to me.
Either cookies or ice cream is a good dessert.

If you need more help with subject-verb agreement, see Lessons 15.1 through 15.3, pages 439–444.

7.4 Incorrect Verb Tense or Form

Problem 1

An incorrect or missing verb ending

tense   *I have (learn) how to play the violin in the past year.*

SOLUTION   Add *-ed* to a regular verb to form the past tense and the past participle.

I have learned how to play the violin in the past year.

Problem 2

An improperly formed irregular verb

tense   *Jan (builded) a greenhouse in the yard.*

The past and past participle forms of irregular verbs vary. Memorize these forms, or look them up.

SOLUTION   Use the correct past or past participle form of an irregular verb.

Jan built a greenhouse in the yard.

Problem 3

Confusion between the past form and the past participle

tense   *Carlos (has began) to play the guitar.*

SOLUTION   Use the past participle form of an irregular verb, not the past form, when you use the auxiliary verb *have*.

Carlos has begun to play the guitar.

Problem 4

Improper use of the past participle

tense   *I (seen) two plays this month.*

SOLUTION   Insert the auxiliary verb *have* before the past participle of an irregular verb to form a complete verb.

I have seen two plays this month.

If you need more help with correct verb forms, see Lessons 10.3 through 10.9, pages 337–350.

7.5 Incorrect Use of Pronouns

Problem 1

A pronoun that could refer to more than one antecedent

> pro Carla went to the concert with Ana, but (she) didn't stay long.
>
> pro When the neighbors accused my brothers, (they) were angry.

SOLUTION Rewrite the sentence, substituting a noun for the pronoun.

Carla went to the concert with Ana, but Carla didn't stay long.

When the neighbors accused my brothers, my brothers were angry.

Problem 2

Object pronouns as subjects

> pro Kyoko and (me) left for summer camp.
>
> pro (Her) and Satchel had an argument today.
>
> pro Nita and (them) are in the school play.

SOLUTION Use a subject pronoun as the subject of a sentence.

Kyoko and I left for summer camp.

She and Satchel had an argument today.

Nita and they are in the school play.

Problem 3

Subject pronouns as objects

pro   *Please help Amos and ⃝I with the groceries.*

pro   *Sonia left her books with Alan and ⃝I.*

pro   *Megan bought tickets for ⃝she and Ian.*

SOLUTION Use an object pronoun as the object of a verb or a preposition.

Please help Amos and me with the groceries.

Sonia left her books with Alan and me.

Megan bought tickets for her and Ian.

If you need more help with the correct use of pronouns, see Lessons 11.1 through 11.5, pages 361–370.

7.6 Incorrect Use of Adjectives

Problem 1

Incorrect use of *good, better, best*

> adj Selma felt (more good) after her nap.
>
> adj Harry is the (most good) artist in the class.
>
> adj Vinnie is a (more) better writer than Jenny.

SOLUTION The comparative and superlative forms of *good* are *better* and *best*. Do not use *more* or *most* before irregular forms of comparative and superlative adjectives.

Selma felt better after her nap.

Harry is the best artist in the class.

Vinnie is a better writer than Jenny.

Problem 2

Incorrect use of *bad, worse, worst*

> adj This painting is (more bad) than the one in the den.
>
> adj This is the (baddest) book I've ever read.
>
> adj That was the (most) worst speech of the day.

SOLUTION The comparative and superlative forms of *bad* are *worse* and *worst*. Do not use *more* or *most* before irregular forms of comparative and superlative adjectives.

This painting is worse than the one in the den.

This is the worst book I've ever read.

That was the worst speech of the day.

Problem 3

Incorrect use of other comparative and superlative adjectives

frag   Greta is (more) younger than her sister.

frag   Samuel drove the (most fastest) car in the race.

SOLUTION Do not use both *-er* and *more* or *-est* and *most* at the same time.

Greta is younger than her sister.

Samuel drove the fastest car in the race.

If you need more help with the correct use of adjectives, see Lessons 12.3 and 12.4, pages 383–386.

Troubleshooter

7.7 Incorrect Use of Commas

Problem 1

Missing commas in a series of three or more items

com   *Today we studied history, science, and mathematics.*

com   *Orson Welles wrote, directed, and starred in many classic films.*

SOLUTION   Use commas to separate three or more items in a series.

Today we studied history, science, and mathematics.

Orson Welles wrote, directed, and starred in many classic films.

Problem 2

Missing commas with direct quotations

com   *"This movie," Marcia said, "is really exciting."*

com   *"I want to leave," Dorie said, "before the storm begins."*

SOLUTION   The first part of an interrupted quotation ends with a comma followed by quotation marks. The interrupting words are also followed by a comma.

"This movie," Marcia said, "is really exciting."

"I want to leave," Dorie said, "before the storm begins."

If you need more help with commas, see Lessons 19.2 through 19.4, pages 491–496.

Unit 7.7 Incorrect Use of Commas   **263**

7.8 Incorrect Use of Apostrophes

Omission of apostrophe and -s with singular possessive nouns

apos   We found James calculator lying on Martas desk.

SOLUTION   Use an apostrophe and an -*s* to form the possessive of a singular noun, even one that ends in -*s*.

We found James's calculator lying on Marta's desk.

Omission of apostrophe with plural possessive nouns ending in -s

apos   The acrobats stunts thrilled their audience.

apos   The horses bridles are in the stable.

SOLUTION   Use an apostrophe alone to form the possessive of a plural noun that ends in -*s*.

The acrobats' stunts thrilled their audience.
The horses' bridles are in the stable.

Problem 3

Omission of apostrophe with plural possessive nouns not ending in -s

apos   The childrens paints are on the table.

SOLUTION Use an apostrophe and an -s to form the posses-sive of a plural noun that does not end in -s.

The children's paints are on the table.

Problem 4

Incorrect use of apostrophe with possessive personal pronouns

apos   This seat is her's, and the one over there is your's.

SOLUTION Do not use an apostrophe with any of the possessive personal pronouns.

This seat is hers, and the one over there is yours.

If you need more help with apostrophes, see Lesson 19.7, page 501.

Problem 1

Failure to capitalize words referring to ethnic groups, nationalities, and languages

cap — A *brazilian* student is studying *french.*

SOLUTION Capitalize proper nouns and adjectives that refer to ethnic groups, nationalities, and languages.

A Brazilian student is studying French.

Problem 2

Failure to capitalize the first word of a direct quotation

cap — Duane said, "*school* will begin soon."

SOLUTION Capitalize the first word in a direct quotation.

Duane said, "School will begin soon."

If you need more help with capitalization, see Lessons 18.1 through 18.4, pages 473–480.

	Proofreading Symbols	
⊙	Lieut‿Brown	Insert a period.
∧	No one came⌃the party.	Insert a letter or a word.
⌃;	The bell rang⌃the students left for home.	Insert a semicolon.
≡	I enjoyed paris.	Capitalize a letter.
/	The Ølass ran a bake sale.	Make a capital letter lowercase.
‿	The campers are home⌒sick.	Close up a space.
⊘	They visited (N.Y.) ⊘	Spell out.
⌃	Sue⌃please help.	Insert a comma.
∩	He enjoyed feild day.	Transpose the position of letters or words.
#	all⌃together	Insert a space.
℘	We went to to Boston.	Delete letters or words.
❝ ❞	She asked⌄Who's coming?⌄	Insert quotation marks.
/ = /	mid⌃January	Insert a hyphen.
¶	"Where?" asked Karl.¶"Over there," said Ray.	Begin a new paragraph.
⌄	She liked Sarah⌄s glasses.	Insert an apostrophe.

Business and Technical Writing

Contents

Business Letters	269
Memos	274
Application Forms	278
Instructions	282
Incident Reports	286
Multimedia Presentations	290

Business Letters

A business letter serves a variety of purposes. Business letters are formal and are usually written to unknown people. A neat, brief, well-organized letter makes a good first impression and encourages a prompt and positive response.

The following sample business letter makes a request. The letter is written in block form. Notice how the writer follows the tips in the chart on the following page and notice also how the business letter differs from the personal letter on page 270.

4716 Edgewood Rd.
Canton, MI 48187
September 6, 2005

Mr. Joseph Leright, Manager
State of Michigan Bureau of Tourism
2000 Lake St.
Lansing, MI 48273

Dear Mr. Leright:

I am writing to request information on winter camping in state campgrounds in Michigan's Upper Peninsula.

My scout troop is planning a campout for Friday and Saturday nights, December 2 and 3. Which campgrounds are open on those dates, and what accommodations are offered? I am interested in knowing which campgrounds have cabins with heaters and how many persons they will accommodate.

Please include information on rates, campground rules, how to make reservations, a map showing campground locations, and any other information you think will be helpful to my troop in making our plans.

Thank you for your help in planning our trip.

Sincerely,

Marietta Murphy

Marietta Murphy

> The letter is addressed to a specific person.

> The writer tells the purpose of the letter.

> The writer makes specific requests.

> The writer requests additional information.

> The writer thanks the person for his or her help.

Business Letters

Friendly Letters

A friendly letter is a form of writing that is used to communicate with someone you know well. Notice how a friendly letter differs from a business letter.

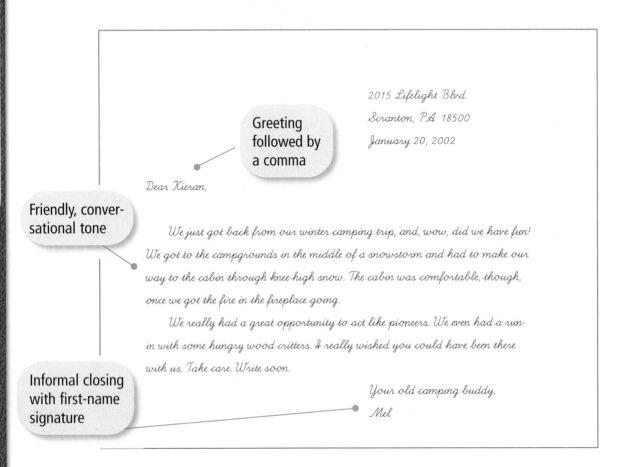

Greeting followed by a comma

2015 Lifelight Blvd.
Scranton, PA 18500
January 20, 2002

Dear Kieran,

Friendly, conversational tone

We just got back from our winter camping trip, and, wow, did we have fun! We got to the campgrounds in the middle of a snowstorm and had to make our way to the cabin through knee-high snow. The cabin was comfortable, though, once we got the fire in the fireplace going.

We really had a great opportunity to act like pioneers. We even had a run-in with some hungry wood critters. I really wished you could have been there with us. Take care. Write soon.

Informal closing with first-name signature

Your old camping buddy,
Mel

Types of Business Letters

A business letter gives information or asks for action. Knowing how to write a good business letter is a skill you will use many times throughout your life.

Use the business letter to inquire about something; order a product; make a complaint or request; express your views or apply for a job, a scholarship, or acceptance into a special program.

When you write a business letter, keep your purpose in mind. Don't include details or information not needed to achieve your purpose. Limit your letter to one page or less in length, if possible. The people you are writing to are likely to be very busy, so the shorter and neater your letter looks, the more likely it is to be read. Make the tone of your business letter formal: avoid slang and use polite language.

Types of Business Letters

REQUEST LETTER	COMPLAINT LETTER	OPINION LETTER	APPLICATION LETTER
Be brief.	Be polite.	State the issue briefly.	Write to a specific person.
State your request clearly. Include all necessary information.	Identify the product or service clearly.	State your opinion in the first sentence or two.	Describe the job or program for which you're applying.
Make your request specific and reasonable.	Describe the problem accurately.	Support your opinion with reasons, facts, and examples.	List your qualifications.
Include your phone number or a self-addressed, stamped envelope.	Request a specific solution.	Summarize your main points and offer a solution, if possible.	Explain why you're the best person for the position or award.
	Keep a copy of your letter until your complaint has been resolved.		Request an application form or an interview.

Style

Business letters are usually written in one of two forms: block style or modified block style.

Block Style In block style, all lines begin at the left margin. Paragraphs are not indented but are separated by a line space. The letter on page 269 is typed in block style.

Modified Block Style In modified block style, the heading, the closing, your signature, and your typed name begin at the center of the paper. The paragraphs may be indented—five spaces on a typewriter or half an inch on a computer—or not indented. The following letter is in modified block style with paragraphs indented. There is no need to leave a line space between indented paragraphs.

Business Letters

2234 Platt St. • — Heading
Northville, KY 00293
January 15, 2005

Bryce Benton, Manager
Spotless Dry Cleaners • — Inside Address
304 S. Main St.
Northville, KY 00293

Dear Mr. Benton: • — Salutation

Now is the time to show your support for Northville Middle School and promote your business by reserving an ad in our yearbook, *The Legend.*

Last year, Northville Middle School sold more than five hundred copies of *The Legend,* and this year advance orders already exceed that number. The yearbook is read not only by students but also by their • — Body parents and other family members. When people see your ad, they will learn more about your business and will recognize that you are a supporter of our school. All profits from yearbook ads are used to support the school's football team and marching band.

The enclosed reservation form lists ad sizes and prices. I've also included a self-addressed envelope for your reply. All ads and payments must be received by the yearbook committee by February 15.

I look forward to hearing from you,

Name and Signature — •

Juan Garcia

Juan Garcia,
Yearbook Chairman

Activity

Think of a place you would like to visit, such as a zoo, museum, or factory. Write a business letter requesting the information that you need to plan your trip.

- Make a list of questions to ask.
- Use the models on pages 269 and 272 to help you plan and revise your letter.
- Use polite language and correct spelling, grammar, capitalization, and punctuation.
- For your final draft, type, use a computer, or write neatly.

PURPOSE To write a business letter

AUDIENCE Director of a recreational institution or business

LENGTH One page

WRITING RUBRICS To write an effective letter requesting information, you should
- be clear and brief
- state your request in the first paragraph
- use business-letter format
- check your letter for grammar, spelling, and mechanics.

The Parts of a Business Letter

A business letter has six parts.

Heading There are three lines in the heading:
- your street address
- your city, state, and ZIP code
- the date

Inside Address The inside address has three or more lines:
- the name of the person to whom you're writing (with or without a courtesy title such as *Ms., Mr.,* or *Dr.*)
- the title of the person to whom you're writing (A short title, such as *Manager* or *Vice President,* may be placed on the same line with the person's name. A long title requires a separate line.)
- the name of the business or organization
- the street address of the business or organization
- the city, state, and ZIP code

Salutation or Greeting When you know the name of the person to whom you're writing, the salutation should include a courtesy title: *Dear Mr. Marconi* or *Dear Dr. Lewsky.* If you don't know the name of the person, you can begin with *Dear* and the person's title: *Dear Editor* or *Dear Director of Human Resources.* A colon follows the salutation of a business letter.

Body The body is the most important part of your letter. It states your message.

Closing The closing is a final word or phrase, such as *Sincerely* or *Respectfully yours.* A comma follows the closing.

Name and Signature Type your name four lines below the closing. Then sign your name in the space between the closing and your typed name. If your first name could belong to either a male or a female, include *Miss, Ms.,* or *Mr.* in parentheses before your typed name.

Neatness Counts

Your letter is more likely to get a serious reading if you follow closely the formal rules for business letters:

- Type your letter or create it on a computer.
- Use unlined white $8\frac{1}{2}$-by-11-inch paper.
- Leave a two-inch margin at the top of the page and margins of at least one inch at the left, right, and bottom.

- Single-space the heading. Allow one or more blank lines between the heading and the inside address, depending on the length of your letter.
- Single-space the remaining parts of the letter, leaving an extra line between the parts and between the paragraphs in the body if they are not indented.

Memos

A memo (the short form of *memorandum*) is a brief note that communicates important information. Memos use polite language and have a friendly tone.

The following model is a memo sent by the building supervisor of a school to teachers. Notice how the writer follows the tips in the chart on the following page.

TO: All Teachers

FROM: Joseph Macady, Building Supervisor

SUBJECT: New Desks Are Coming

DATE: February 28, 2005

New student and teacher desks will be placed in your classrooms over the weekend of October 2 and 3.

During the last period on Friday, March 2, please have your students remove any personal belongings left in or on their desks. I suggest that they store their things in their assigned lockers.

You will also need to empty your desk. Store the contents in the classroom closet or pile them in a corner.

Thanks for your help. When you come to school on Monday morning, your new desks will be in place.

The writer states the subject in a very few words.

The writer begins with specific information.

The writer gives instructions.

The writer thanks the readers for their help.

Types of Memos

Memos can be used to communicate on a wide variety of topics. A memo can make an announcement or request, ask or answer a question, or assign a task. In a business office, a memo can remind all employees of the date of the company picnic or ask people for suggestions on how to improve the company newsletter.

You can use a memo when you want to communicate in a brief and formal way. You might remind club members about a meeting or let teammates know about changes in the practice schedule.

One thing that all memos have in common is that they are short and to the point—ideally no longer than one page. When you write a memo, do not include any unnecessary details or information. Make the tone of your memo friendly but avoid slang. Use plain language and don't be wordy. "Please remember to sign in every morning" is better than "It's important that our records be accurate, so please try to remember to sign in each and every morning." If you are writing a memo to request something, tell your readers exactly what you want them to do. Use directions such as "Please send me the information by Monday" or "Please see me at 4 o'clock."

Types of Memos			
ANNOUNCEMENT	**REMINDER**	**REQUEST**	**ASSIGN A TASK**
Sum up your announcement in a very few words on the subject line.	Begin your message with a phrase such as "Remember to . . ." or "This is to remind you . . ."	Use the subject line to show that the memo is a request by using a phrase such as "Your help needed" or "Please help."	Name the assignment in the subject line.
Make the announcement in one or two short sentences in the first paragraph.	Give the most important information in the first sentence or two.	Make your request clearly in the first sentence.	Use words such as "Your job is to . . ." or "This assignment includes . . ." in the first sentence.
Give details in a second paragraph or in a bulleted list. Include necessary information such as dates and phone numbers.	Give other important information in the second paragraph.	Tell how the person can respond to your request.	Briefly describe the task.
	Include necessary dates, times, addresses, and phone numbers.	Thank the person for his or her help.	Give more details if necessary.
			Tell when the assignment must be finished.

Style

Memos are written in block style. Headings and paragraphs start at the left margin. Each heading is printed in capital letters (often in boldface type) and followed by a colon. The main words following the colons are capitalized because they form the subtitles for the memo.

Sometimes memos include bulleted or numbered lists, as in the model below. Unlike a letter, a memo does not end with a closing or signature. The last line of the message acts as a final word.

Technology Tip

If your word processing software includes a memo template, open a new document in the program. (Select **New** from the **File** menu.) You will then see a dialogue box that offers such options as letters, memos, and reports. Select the **Memo** option and open the memo template. You can then replace the filled-in copy on the template with your own message.

TO: All Scouts — *Headings*

FROM: Jason Jakola

SUBJECT: May 30 Meeting in the School Gym

DATE: May 23, 2005 — *Date*

At a meeting in the school gym on May 30 at 3:00 P.M., we will be making and decorating leather vests. Vest kits will be provided. — *Message*

To decorate your vest, please bring materials such as the following.
- colored pens
- award patches
- feathers
- permanent markers
- beads
- fringe
- braid

Bulleted list

Glue guns will be available for attaching decorations to vests. See you at the meeting!

The Parts of a Memo

Memos have two basic parts.

The Headings Each memo heading consists of a title word in capital letters, followed by a colon and a subtitle. Most memos have at least four headings:

- the person(s) to whom the memo is addressed (Memos can be addressed to individuals or groups.)
- the sender of the memo
- the subject of the memo, a very brief description—no more than six words
- the date

The Message The message of a memo is written in one or more paragraphs. Sentences are usually short. Some memos include a bulleted or numbered list. Most memo messages end with a concluding thought, such as thanking the person if a request was made or giving an instruction on how to respond to the memo. A reminder memo might end with a friendly remark.

Neatness Counts

Write a memo on a computer or a word processor. If neither is available, use a pen to print headings in capital letters. Then fill in the heading information and the message in neat handwriting.

- Use white $8\frac{1}{2}$-by-11-inch paper.
- Leave a two-inch margin at the top of the page and margins of at least one inch at the left, right, and bottom.

- Use a line space between the heading lines, between the headings and the message, and between paragraphs.
- Single-space lines in the message.

Activity

Write a Memo. Pretend that you are organizing a class picnic. Write a memo announcing the picnic. Include details about the date, the time, and the location. With a partner, read each other's memos and look for unnecessary information or wordiness. Check to make sure that information appears in order of importance. Revise the memos and post them in the classroom.

- Before writing your memo, make a list of details and rank them in order of importance.
- End your message on a friendly note.

PURPOSE To write a memo announcing an event

AUDIENCE A classmate

LENGTH Less than one page

WRITING RUBRICS To write an effective memo, you should

- use correct memo format
- convey your message clearly and briefly
- include all necessary details
- end on a friendly note
- proofread your message carefully

Application Forms

An application is a formal request for something—a job, membership in a group, an award. The information helps the reader decide whether to accept or deny the request.

Application forms can be created for many purposes, as shown on the chart on page 279. Following the instructions on a form and filling in information neatly makes a positive impression. Below is an example of a filled-out application form.

Fifth Annual Young Writer's Workshop
November 12, 2005, at Central Middle School
1827 Windy Drive, Greenleaf, Montana 98763

To be considered as a participant in the Writer's Workshop, you must complete this application form and provide a writing sample. Applications must be received by October 12, 2005.

Participant's name: _Kim Chan_

Address: _11263 Aspen Drive_

City: _Greenleaf_   State: _MT_   ZIP CODE: _98763_

Phone: _(206) 555-2863_

Birth date: _June 6, 1995_   Grade in school: _6_

Parent name: _Jae Chan_

Parent's daytime phone: _(206) 555-6827_

Please check the workshop you are most interested in attending:
- ❏ Poetry
- ☑ Writing Mystery Stories
- ❏ Writing Science Fiction Stories
- ❏ Creating Realistic Characters

Tell us why you want to participate in the Young Writer's Workshop:
I like to write and want to learn more about how to write mystery stories.

Writing Sample
Use the back of this form or attach a separate sheet of paper. The length of the sample should be 150–200 words. Please type or write neatly.
Please see attached page.

Applicant's signature: _Kim Chan_   Date: _Sept. 10, 2005_

Mail completed application and writing sample to
    Fifth Annual Young Writer's Workshop
    P.O. Box 3948
    Greenleaf, Montana, 98763-9876

Applicants will be notified by mail within two weeks of receipt of application.

This application is for a specific event.

The application includes the rules for applying and a deadline.

This application has space for filling in information.

The applicant writes or prints neatly.

The applicant indicates that he or she is attaching a separate piece of paper for this answer.

This application requires a signature and a date.

Types of Application Form

Application forms are used in many different situations. You may be required to fill out an application form for a job; for membership in a club or other group; to attend a camp, conference, or other event; or to join a team.

When filling out an application form, read all instructions carefully and follow them exactly. Include information that will help persuade the person reading the application to consider you or grant your request.

When mailing an application form, make sure you reply to the address that appears in the instructions. Sometimes you must send a fee or other materials along with your application—for example, a writing sample, an essay, or letters of recommendation.

When you need to *create* an application form, you should include any information the applicant needs and instructions for filling out the form. If there is a date by which applicants need to reply, include it on the form. You should also include space in which the applicant can provide information.

The kinds of information you request will depend on what the application is for. If you are making an application form for admission to a backpacking group, you might ask how long the person applying has been backpacking, the length of previous backpack trips, and the person's level of physical fitness. If you are making up an application form for membership in a softball team, you might ask for the applicant's playing experience, favored position, and jersey size.

Types of Applications			
MEMBERSHIP OR SCHOOL APPLICATION	**EVENT APPLICATION**	**AWARD APPLICATION**	**JOB APPLICATION**
States the requirements for membership or acceptance	States the name of the event	Describes the award	Asks for personal information about the applicant
Includes instructions on how to apply	Includes information about the time and place that the event will be held	Asks for the applicant's qualifications	Asks about the applicant's qualifications and ability to do the job
Includes room for required information from the applicant	Specifies a deadline for returning the application	May ask the applicant to write an essay or answer essay questions	Sometimes includes space for listing references
Sometimes includes essay questions			May require a cover letter and a résumé
Sometimes requests a fee for applying			

Application Forms

Style

An application form begins with a heading at the top of the page. The heading can be centered or aligned with the left margin. The body of an application form is created for a specific purpose. Usually all questions begin at the left margin, but certain questions may be indented. The body of an application form may be divided into sections, as in the following model.

A colon is used after each question prompt (applicant's name: _____) and write-on lines are provided for answers.

The Northwood Observer
Application for Newspaper Carrier — Heading

To apply for the position of newspaper carrier, you must be at least twelve years old and able to deliver the *Northwood Observer* every Monday and Thursday afternoon.

Required Information — Body of application, divided into sections. Section 1

Carrier's Name: _____

Address: _____

City: _____ State: _____ ZIP CODE: _____

Telephone: _____ Age: _____ Grade: _____

Social Security Number: _____

School: _____

Use this space to tell us why you want to be a *Northwood Observer* carrier. — Answer to essay question here

_____

_____

_____

Route Preferences — Body of application, Section 2
Circle route areas for which you want to be considered.

Downtown   East Side   Kerry Town
West Side   North suburbs   Clearport

References — Body of application, Section 3
Please include as references the names and phone numbers of two adults who are not family members.

Reference 1: _____

Reference 2: _____

Applicant's signature: _____ Date: _____ — Section for signature of applicant

Parent's or Guardian's Signature: _____

Please submit your application to
Carrier Coordinator: Ms. Susan Brautmeyer — Information on where to send application
   The Northwood Observer
   29388 E. State St.
   Northwood, MN 49387-9845

The Parts of an Application Form

Most application forms include the following parts:

The Heading The heading can be the title of a contest, the name of a group or company, or simply the word *Application.*

Instructions An application form may include such instructions as

- how to fill out the form
- date by which to submit the application form
- where to send the application form

Questionnaire Section Part of the application form requests information about the applicant. Most application forms require certain basic information, such as the name, address, and phone number or e-mail address of the applicant.

Signature and Date The application form is signed and dated by the applicant.

Neatness Counts

Your application is more likely to be given favorable consideration if you follow directions exactly and fill the form in neatly. You can type your answers. Neat handwritten answers in black or blue ink are also acceptable.

When completing an application form, first write your answers on a separate sheet of paper so that you can edit them if you think changes are necessary. Then fill out the actual application form. Some companies and organizations have forms that you can fill out online while you are visiting their Web sites.

Activity

Imagine that you want to form a sports team or a hobby club. Create a membership application form for your group. Then trade application forms with a classmate and fill out the form you received, following its instructions. Collaborate with your partner to revise your applications.

- List the information you will require from applicants, such as name, address, experience, or answers to essay questions.
- Think about how to organize your application form into sections, and use clusters to list the information asked for in each section.
- Use a computer and word processing software to create and revise your application form.

PURPOSE To create and fill out an application form

AUDIENCE A classmate

LENGTH One page

WRITING RUBRICS To successfully create and fill out an application form, you should

- include instructions and request all the necessary information in your form
- organize the form into logical sections and clusters
- use computer software to create the form
- fill out all parts of the form neatly
- proofread your application and responses

Business and Technical Writing

Instructions

Instructions are a set of step-by-step directions for how to do something. You can write instructions for many specific tasks. A clear and complete set of instructions will help your reader understand exactly what to do.

Here is an example of instructions on how to give a dog a bath. Notice how the writer follows some of the tips in the chart on the following page.

How to Give Your Dog a Bath

Materials
- sink (for small dogs) or bath tub or shower (for large dogs)
- non-slip surface such as a shower mat
- short hose that attaches to the faucet or small plastic bucket
- dog shampoo or baby shampoo
- soft towels

Procedure
1. Make sure the sink or tub drain is open.
2. Place a small dog on a mat in the sink. Lead a large dog into the tub or shower. (If using a shower, you can put on your swimming suit and get in with your pet.)
3. Turn on the water and test it with your hand until it is warm but not hot.
4. Use the hose or bucket to get the dog wet.
5. Put small amounts of shampoo all over the dog's wet coat. Be careful not to get shampoo in its eyes. (You can wash the dog's face by gently wiping it with a wet washcloth.)
6. Use your hands to work the shampoo into a lather.
7. Use the hose or bucket to rinse all the shampoo out of the coat.
8. Allow the dog to shake while it's still in the sink or tub.
9. Rub the dog with towels to absorb all the loose moisture.
10. Lift a small dog out of the sink onto a towel on the floor; lead a big dog out of the tub onto a towel.
11. Use a hair dryer on a low setting to dry the dog completely or let the air complete the drying.
12. Comb the dog's coat while it is still damp.

CAUTION: Be sure the dog is fairly dry before you turn it loose. Sometimes a just-washed dog likes to run through the house and shake or rub itself against the walls or furniture. *Never* put a wet dog outside in cold weather. Beware! Sometimes a wet dog likes to roll in the dirt!

> The writer tells what the instructions are for.

> The writer lists everything the reader needs to do the job.

> The writer gives clear instructions in a set of numbered steps.

> The writer lists steps in the proper order.

> The writer includes a note about possible problems.

Types of Instructions

You can write instructions to describe a process—for example, tying a shoe, making a paper airplane, filling out an application, installing a software program, or planting a tree.

You can also use instructions to tell how to assemble something from parts, such as a bicycle, toy, model car, or doghouse.

Before you write instructions, you need to understand the process completely. Every detail must be included in your instructions, and details must appear in the correct order.

Make your instructions as simple as possible. Don't include unneeded information or details. Use plain English, and keep each step brief. Take extra care in explaining any step that might be confusing, or divide a complicated step into smaller steps. Choose words that express exactly what you mean. For example, instead of saying "Bend the pipe cleaner into a series of circles," say, "Twist the pipe cleaner into a long, slim spiral."

Style

Instructions usually begin with some form of heading or title that is centered on the page. Instructions can be written in paragraph form or in a list of numbered steps. Begin all paragraphs and numbered steps at the left margin. Leave a line space between each paragraph or between the steps of a procedure.

List each item in a materials list (if needed) on a separate line or use bullets.

If your instructions include just one illustration, it may appear before or after the numbered steps. If your instructions include a series of illustrations, you can write the steps below the illustrations as captions.

Two Types of Instructions

INSTRUCTIONS FOR A PROCESS	INSTRUCTIONS FOR ASSEMBLING AN ITEM
• List the materials needed in the order in which they will be used.	• Instruct readers to put parts together in logical order.
• Number your steps in the order in which they should be completed.	• Do the assembly yourself as you write the steps so that you don't leave anything out.
• Be sure you don't leave out a step.	• Use a labeled illustration to show the different parts.
• Be brief when describing a step.	• Tell your readers everything they need to know and nothing extra.
• If instructions are complicated, use a series of illustrations to show the steps.	

Instructions

The Parts of a Set of Instructions

Instructions are usually divided into the following parts.

Heading or Title The heading or title tells what the instructions are for.

Materials List If materials are needed for a procedure, list them under a heading, which can be the single word *Materials*. List materials in the order in which they will be used. Describe materials exactly.

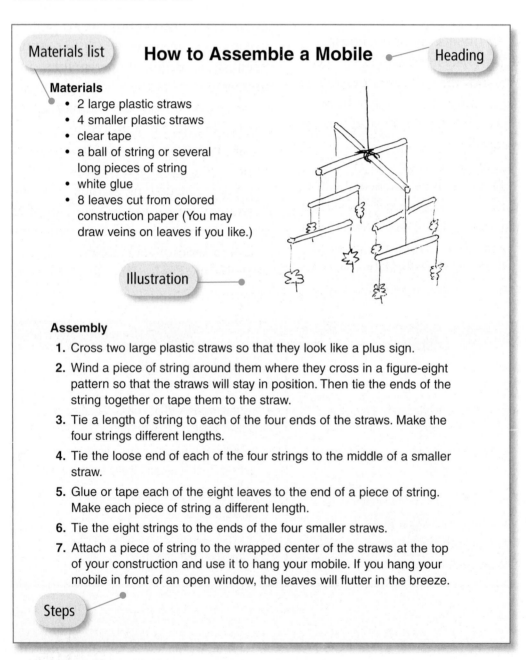

Materials list

How to Assemble a Mobile — **Heading**

Materials
- 2 large plastic straws
- 4 smaller plastic straws
- clear tape
- a ball of string or several long pieces of string
- white glue
- 8 leaves cut from colored construction paper (You may draw veins on leaves if you like.)

Illustration

Assembly
1. Cross two large plastic straws so that they look like a plus sign.
2. Wind a piece of string around them where they cross in a figure-eight pattern so that the straws will stay in position. Then tie the ends of the string together or tape them to the straw.
3. Tie a length of string to each of the four ends of the straws. Make the four strings different lengths.
4. Tie the loose end of each of the four strings to the middle of a smaller straw.
5. Glue or tape each of the eight leaves to the end of a piece of string. Make each piece of string a different length.
6. Tie the eight strings to the ends of the four smaller straws.
7. Attach a piece of string to the wrapped center of the straws at the top of your construction and use it to hang your mobile. If you hang your mobile in front of an open window, the leaves will flutter in the breeze.

Steps

Steps List steps in the order in which they are to be done. Numbering steps is a great way to keep your readers from getting lost.

Illustrations Some simple instructions may be clear without an illustration, but often illustrations can make your meaning clearer.

Technology Tip

Some word processing programs have an automatic numbering and bulleting feature that can organize your instructions automatically. If your software lacks this feature, you can use the indention markers on the ruler to set up lists or steps so that the lines indent uniformly after the bullets or numbers.

Activity

Write a set of instructions for how to do something or assemble something.

- Do the process or think it through carefully, noting the materials and steps needed as you go along.
- Arrange your steps in logical order.
- Use exact language to be clear.
- Draw an illustration if it will help you to be more concise.

Then trade instructions with a classmate. Follow the classmate's instructions, if possible, or imagine the process as you read. Discuss how the instructions could be made clearer.

PURPOSE To write instructions

AUDIENCE A classmate

LENGTH One page

WRITING RUBRICS To write a set of clear instructions, you should

- list any needed materials
- divide the process into clear and logical steps
- use exact language
- include an illustration if necessary
- carefully proofread your work

Incident Reports

An incident report uses a specific form to record information about something that has interrupted normal activity or caused a crisis. Incident reports are written by a witness or by a person gathering information.

The following model is an incident report completed by a student bus-stop monitor. Such a report would be turned in at the principal's office.

March Middle School Incident Report

Submitter of Report

Name: _Tamika Brown_

Phone: _(622) 555-3820_

Grade and homeroom: _6th_   _Mr. Penniman's Room_

Check one:
❑ teacher   ☑ student   ❑ staff member   ❑ other _____

> The reporter gives information on how to contact her.

Incident Information

Date of Incident: _February 12, 2005_   Time of Incident: _3:15 p.m._

Location of Incident: _Front of school — bus zone_

Type of Incident (accident, vandalism, safety violation, other):

safety violation

> The reporter answers the questions *when? where?* and *what?*

Details

(Use space below and/or additional pages if necessary.)

A red Ford pickup truck, license plate #MTS206, was parked at the curb in the bus loading zone. The buses could not pull up to the curb, so students had to walk into the street, which was icy, in order to board the bus. Some students slid on the ice, but none were injured.

> The reporter describes the incident in detail.

Date Reported: _February 13, 2005_

Signature: _Tamika Brown, Monitor_

> The reporter signs her name.

Types of Incident Report

Businesses, institutions, and schools use incident reports for recording many different kinds of situations, such as accidents, thefts, damage to property, safety violations, fights, and threats.

You may be asked to fill out a report if you witness an incident at your school. When filling out an incident report, give all the information that is asked for on the report form. Supply exact details. "On the sidewalk at the northeast corner of Brush and Fifth Avenue" is more precise than "It happened at the corner." Include the answers to the questions *who? what? where?* and *when?* Provide all you *know* about the incident but not opinions or guesses, such as why you *think* somebody did something.

You yourself could create an incident report form on which could be reported incidents in your classroom. If you make up such a form, you will want to ask for information on the person filling out the form and detailed information on the incident.

Three Types of Incident Reports		
ACCIDENT	**THEFT**	**SAFETY VIOLATION**
Label blanks for listing details, including date, time, and location.	Ask for the date and time that the theft was discovered and contact information for the person who discovered it.	Make a section for information on the person reporting the incident so that he or she can be reached if needed.
Provide space for the names, addresses, and phone numbers of witnesses.	Include a fill-in section with space for listing stolen items, their descriptions, and their estimated values.	Provide a section for recording specific details, such as the date, time, and location.
Provide space or give a direction to use the back of the paper to sketch the scene.	Label a space that can be used for a description of the details of the incident.	
Give a direction to attach a photograph if available.		

Incident Reports

Style

Most incident reports are in block style. All of their lines begin at the left margin. A heading (title) at the top of the page may be centered. Some incident reports may have headings centered at the beginnings of sections.

The words that prompt a fill-in response are followed by a colon; for example, *Name:* _____ .

Incident Report — Heading

Contact Information — Information about the person filling out the form

Name: _____

Address: _____

City: _____ State: _____ ZIP CODE: _____

Phone: _____

Incident Information — Information on the incident

Date of incident: _____ Time of incident: _____

Location of incident: _____

Type of incident: _____

Details
(Give complete details, including quotations from people involved in the incident. Continue on the back of this form or an attached sheet if necessary.) — Space for writing in details

_____

_____

_____

_____

_____

_____

Date reported: _____ — Date of report

Signature: _____ — Signature

The Parts of an Incident Report

Most incident reports have four basic parts.

Heading The heading or title can be simply *Incident Report* or it can include the name of the business or institution. The title can also refer to the kind of incident being reported, such as *Safety Incident Report.*

Contact Information Basic contact information includes four or more lines:
- name of person filling out report
- street address
- city, state, and ZIP code
- phone number

Incident Information Information about the incident usually includes the following:
- date
- time
- location
- type of incident

The report may also provide space for writing a more detailed description and may include an instruction to attach another sheet of paper if needed.

Signature and Date The report usually ends with the reporter's signature and the date the report was written.

Activity

Create an incident-report form on a computer. Then trade forms with a classmate. Fill out the form on any recent incident at your school. If necessary, interview witnesses to gather information. If you can't think of any recent incidents to describe, create a fictional one.

- Think about the kinds of information needed on an incident report form to be used at your school.
- Use a cluster organizer to sort the information into categories.
- Create your form on a computer.
- Exchange forms with a classmate and fill out his or her form by typing, printing, or writing neatly.

PURPOSE To create and fill out an incident report

AUDIENCE Your classmates

LENGTH 1 page

WRITING RUBRICS To create and fill out incident report, you should
- use a computer to create a form
- organize information into categories
- include all necessary information
- describe the incident clearly
- type or print your responses clearly

Multimedia Presentations

A multimedia presentation is a report that uses several media, or means of communication. When you speak to an audience and show visuals (slides or pictures), you are giving a multimedia presentation that has both sound and graphics.

The photograph on this page shows some parts of one student's multimedia presentation. Its purpose is to persuade the audience that whale hunting should be stopped.

The writer creates a persuasive poster.

The writer uses a slide to add visual interest.

Save the Whales!

Blue Whale Facts
- World's largest living animal
- Length of 75 to 80 feet
- Weight of up to 100 tons
- Heart the size of a small car

Endangered Status
estimated number before whaling:
200,000
estimated number today:
5,000-10,000

The writer shows facts that support the argument.

The writer adds sound effects.

Types of Media

You can add a combination of videos, photos, slides, music, and other media to an oral presentation. Multimedia presentations can be used to report on a wide variety of topics. They can also be used to persuade an audience to agree with an opinion or to take some kind of action. The following chart shows examples of different kinds of media.

Many multimedia presentations are persuasive, which means that their purpose is to convince others of a point of view or to prompt them to take a certain action. You can do research at the library and on the Internet to find facts, statistics, and expert opinions and use the information to support your point of view.

To persuade others to change their opinions, you must address their concerns. If you are trying to convince the school board to keep the marching band when budget cuts have to be made, you might offer a plan to raise money to pay for uniforms and instruments. If you want to convince people to write letters to support a cause, make a handout with an address to which they can write and include suggestions concerning what they might include in the letter.

Types of Media		
VISUALS	**SOUND**	**OTHER OPTIONS**
Use a video or slide show to make your subject clear.	Use a cassette recorder to help your audience hear your subject (for example, a wolf's howl or a train's whistle).	Appeal to your audience's sense of touch by passing around an object related to your topic.
Use video animation or a series of photographs, drawings, or transparencies to show a process.	Choose a CD to play in the background that will help put your audience in the right mood.	Don't neglect appeals to other senses. A food topic, for example, lends itself to appeals to smell and taste. The more senses your presentation appeals to, the more memorable it will be.
Make handouts of information you want your audience to take with them.	Add sound effects to a slide show.	
Create a poster to help convince your audience of your viewpoint.	Play a short recorded interview with an expert on your topic.	

Style

A multimedia presentation can be given orally or narrated on tape, with other sounds and visuals used to enrich the message. It's up to you to use the various media in the most effective way. For example, if your purpose were to convince people to support keeping the school marching band, you might introduce your topic by playing a recording of the band's most popular piece. Perhaps you might stop the music abruptly in mid-number to suggest the idea that the band may be dropped.

Technology Tip

Some computer software programs can be used to create multimedia presentations that combine text with images and sounds. These programs allow you to produce "slide shows" or a series of hypertext "cards" that can be shown on a computer monitor. Investigate the use of such software if your school has access to it. Use it to create your multimedia presentation.

A transparency is used for the introduction.

Slides are used as part of the body of the presentation.

A handout with further information is used for the conclusion.

Music introduces the topic and sets the mood.

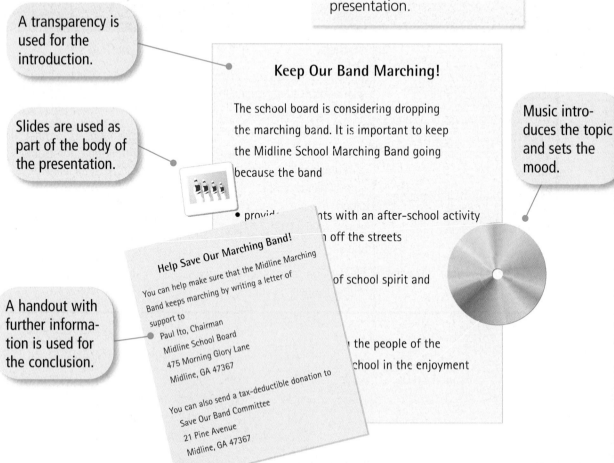

Keep Our Band Marching!

The school board is considering dropping the marching band. It is important to keep the Midline School Marching Band going because the band

• provid___ ___ ___nts with an after-school activity
___ ___ off the streets

___ of school spirit and

___ the people of the
___chool in the enjoyment

Help Save Our Marching Band!

You can help make sure that the Midline Marching Band keeps marching by writing a letter of support to

Paul Ito, Chairman
Midline School Board
475 Morning Glory Lane
Midline, GA 47367

You can also send a tax-deductible donation to
Save Our Band Committee
21 Pine Avenue
Midline, GA 47367

The Parts of a Multimedia Presentation

A multimedia presentation has three parts.

Introduction Begin your presentation by introducing your topic. Your introduction can also list the major points of your argument.

- Introduce yourself and your topic.
- Use a transparency or a slide to show your topic in headline form, while you introduce yourself orally.
- Use music to set the mood; then introduce yourself and your topic.

Body The body is the most important part of your presentation. In the body, you will give support for your opinion and convince your audience to agree with you.

Appeal to your listeners' sense of reason. Support your opinion with facts. For example, you could quote newspaper clippings showing that teen crime rose in a community where the school band was cut. Appeal visually to your readers' emotions. You could show a slide of happy band members in uniforms and then follow it with a slide of troubled teens on the streets. Anticipate your audience's objections and address their concerns.

Conclusion Sum up your thesis in a few sentences that are a logical conclusion of your argument.

Activity

Create a multimedia presentation to convince an audience to share your opinion on a subject or to take action. Choose the form of your presentation and the kinds of media you will use. Make your presentation to the class.

- Choose a topic you're interested in and know well or would like to learn more about.
- Research multiple resources on your topic and think of new questions for further investigation.
- Summarize and organize ideas gained from research by making outlines, maps, organizers, diagrams, graphs, or other illustrations.
- Document your sources in a bibliography.
- Include visuals and sound that will support your ideas.

PURPOSE Create a persuasive multimedia presentation

AUDIENCE Classmates and teacher

LENGTH 3–6 minutes

WRITING RUBRICS To create a successful multimedia presentation, you should

- research your topic
- present persuasive arguments to support your opinions
- include graphic organizers, other visuals, and sounds
- organize your presentation carefully
- list the sources of information you used

"Then the volcano, which was named Mount St. Helens, began to stir."

—Patricia Lauber, *Volcano*

PART 2

Grammar, Usage, and Mechanics

Unit 8   **Subjects, Predicates, and Sentences**   *296*

Unit 9   **Nouns**   *318*

Unit 10   **Verbs**   *332*

Unit 11   **Pronouns**   *360*

Unit 12   **Adjectives**   *378*

Unit 13   **Adverbs**   *394*

Unit 14   **Prepositions, Conjunctions, and Interjections**   *414*

Unit 15   **Subject-Verb Agreement**   *438*

Unit 16   **Glossary of Special Usage Problems**   *454*

Unit 17   **Diagraming Sentences**   *464*

Unit 18   **Capitalization**   *472*

Unit 19   **Punctuation**   *488*

Unit 20   **Sentence Combining**   *516*

Fuji in Clear Weather *by Katsushika Hokusai. British Museum, London.*

295

UNIT 8

Subjects, Predicates, and Sentences

Lesson 8.1   **Kinds of Sentences**   297

Lesson 8.2   **Sentences and Sentence Fragments**   299

Lesson 8.3   **Subjects and Predicates**   301

Lesson 8.4   **Finding Subjects**   303

Lesson 8.5   **Compound Subjects and Compound Predicates**   305

Lesson 8.6   **Simple, Compound, and Complex Sentences**   307

Grammar Review   309

Writing Application   317

8.1   Kinds of Sentences

- A **sentence** is a group of words that expresses a complete thought.

    Different kinds of sentences have different purposes. A sentence can make a statement, ask a question, give a command, or express strong feeling. All sentences begin with a capital letter and end with a punctuation mark.

- A **declarative sentence** makes a statement or tells something. It ends with a period.

    James M. Barrie lived in England**.**

- An **interrogative sentence** asks something. It ends with a question mark.

    Have you read the book *Peter Pan***?**

- An **exclamatory sentence** shows strong feeling. It ends with an exclamation point.

    What fun Peter had**!**

- An **imperative sentence** commands someone to do something. It usually ends with a period.

    Tell me about the movie**.**

The movie *Hook* was based on the book *Peter Pan*.

What amazing special effects the movie has**!**

Have you seen the movie yet**?**

Describe Captain Hook.

Exercise 1   Identifying Kinds of Sentences

Write *declarative, interrogative, exclamatory,* or *imperative* to identify each sentence.

1. Peter Pan protected a group of young orphans.
2. Did he protect them?
3. How mean Captain Hook and his pirates were!
4. Watch carefully for pirate ships on the horizon.
5. How did Peter Pan learn to fly?

Exercise 2   Punctuating Different Kinds of Sentences

Write the following sentences, beginning and ending each correctly.

1. my favorite character in the story is Tinker Bell
2. how I love fantasy stories
3. why did Peter hide outside the window
4. peter lost his shadow in Wendy's home
5. please sew my shadow back onto my feet
6. come to Never-Never Land with me
7. how excited Wendy must have been
8. the pirates kidnapped Wendy and the children
9. what will the wicked pirates do to the poor children
10. explain how Peter rescued his friends
11. who walked off the end of the plank
12. the story has been a play on Broadway, a television show, and an animated movie
13. do you know when the play was first produced
14. believe it or not, it was about one hundred years ago
15. a woman played the role of Peter in the Broadway play
16. how excited audiences were to see her fly through the air
17. the fairy Tinker Bell helps Peter
18. tell me the story again
19. do you think adults believe in Tinker Bell
20. what a great story this is

8.2 Sentences and Sentence Fragments

Every sentence has two parts: a subject and a predicate.

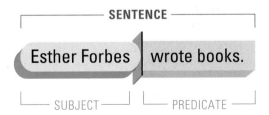

- The **subject part** of a sentence names whom or what the sentence is about.
- The **predicate part** of the sentence tells what the subject does or has. It can also describe what the subject is or is like.

A sentence must have both a subject and a predicate. It must also express a complete thought.

- A **sentence fragment** does not express a complete thought. It may be missing a subject, a predicate, or both.

You often use sentence fragments when you speak. You should avoid using them when you write, however.

Correcting Sentence Fragments		
Fragment	**Problem**	**Sentence**
Paul Revere.	The fragment lacks a predicate. *What did Paul Revere do?*	Paul Revere warned the people.
Worked for Paul Revere.	The fragment lacks a subject. *Who worked for Paul Revere?*	Johnny Tremain worked for Paul Revere.
About history.	The fragment lacks both a subject and a predicate.	Esther Forbes wrote books about history.

Exercise 3   Identifying Sentences and Fragments

Write *sentence* or *fragment* for each item. If an item is a fragment, explain what is missing.

1. The book *Johnny Tremain* is historical fiction.
2. A Newbery Medal winner.
3. Esther Forbes's nonfiction book on Paul Revere won a Pulitzer Prize.
4. The silversmith Paul Revere.
5. Offered Johnny a job.
6. Johnny liked his work.
7. Made things of silver.
8. Johnny burned his hand.
9. A terrible accident.
10. An operation made his hand well again.

Exercise 4   Identifying Subjects and Predicates

Write each sentence, underlining each subject part once and each predicate part twice. If the item is not a complete sentence, write *fragment*.

1. The setting is the American Revolution.
2. Sam Adams, John Hancock, and Paul Revere.
3. Real historical characters fill the book.
4. Americans wanted independence from England.
5. Fought for freedom of speech and other rights.
6. Johnny participated in the Boston Tea Party.
7. The Americans disliked the British tax on tea.
8. The townspeople disguised themselves.
9. As Mohawk Indians.
10. The Sons of Liberty planned the Boston Tea Party.
11. The rebels threw the tea into the harbor waters.
12. British officials decided to close Boston harbor.
13. Starved into submission.
14. The other colonies came to Boston's rescue.
15. Johnny's injured hand prevented him from being a soldier.

8.3 Subjects and Predicates

A sentence consists of a subject and a predicate, which together express a complete thought. Both a subject and a predicate may consist of more than one word.

Complete Subject	Complete Predicate
The main character	is Kit Tyler.
Kit	travels from the tropics to Connecticut.

■ The **complete subject** includes all of the words in the subject of a sentence.

■ The **complete predicate** includes all of the words in the predicate of a sentence.

Not all of the words in the subject or the predicate are of equal importance.

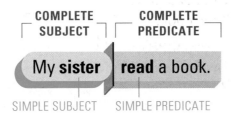

COMPLETE SUBJECT   COMPLETE PREDICATE

My **sister** | **read** a book.

SIMPLE SUBJECT   SIMPLE PREDICATE

■ The **simple subject** is the main word or group of words in the complete subject.

The simple subject is usually a noun or a pronoun. A **noun** is a word that names a person, a place, a thing, or an idea. A **pronoun** is a word that takes the place of one or more nouns.

■ The **simple predicate** is the main word or group of words in the complete predicate.

The simple predicate is always a verb. A **verb** is a word that expresses an action or a state of being.

Sometimes the simple subject is also the complete subject. Similarly, the simple predicate may also be the complete predicate.

Exercise 5   Identifying Complete Subjects and Predicates

Write each sentence. Underline each complete subject once and each complete predicate twice.

1. My sister read *The Witch of Blackbird Pond*.
2. The book was written by Elizabeth George Speare.
3. It describes island life in the 1680s.
4. A young girl is the main character.
5. Kit lived a life of luxury.
6. She loved the island life.
7. This girl of the islands enjoyed the sun and the sea.
8. Her grandfather gave many parties.
9. Many friends attended her festive dance parties.
10. Kit's happiness ended with her grandfather's death.
11. Young Kit lost all her money.
12. Her life of luxury was over.
13. Kit had no family left in the islands.
14. Her aunt lived in the Connecticut Colony in America.
15. Kit went there to live.
16. She traveled to America by ship.
17. She was very lonely aboard ship.
18. A storm blew Kit's ship about for four days.
19. The ship approached land after many days.
20. The Connecticut Colony shore looked gray and bleak.

Exercise 6   Identifying Simple Subjects and Simple Predicates

Write the simple subject and simple predicate from each sentence.

1. Kit traveled far to meet her new family.
2. They were very different from Kit.
3. Kit's new family worked very hard.
4. The colonists wore plain clothing.
5. Kit's bright, colorful dresses shocked them.
6. These serious people discouraged parties.
7. Kit's strange island customs made her unpopular.
8. Snow was a surprise for Kit.
9. Kit's past winters were balmy.
10. Kit longed for her island home.

8.4   Finding Subjects

Most statements begin with the subject.

Other kinds of sentences, such as questions, may begin with part or all of the predicate. The subject comes next, followed by the rest of the predicate.

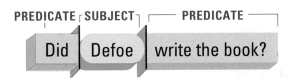

To locate the subject of a question, rearrange the words to form a statement.

Predicate	Subject	Predicate
Have	all of the students	finished reading the book?
	All of the students	have finished reading the book.

Sometimes statements may have inverted word order. In these sentences, the predicate comes before the subject.

In requests and commands, the subject is usually not stated. The word *you* is understood to be the subject.

Subjects, Predicates, and Sentences

Rewrite each question as a statement. Underline each complete subject.

1. Did Robinson build a house?
2. Did the goats on the island provide fresh milk?
3. Did Robinson plant corn on the island?
4. Did the stranded man carve a canoe out of a tree?
5. Was the weather favorable?

Exercise 8 **Finding Subjects**

Write each sentence. Underline each subject. Write *(You)* before any sentence with an understood subject.

1. Did a parrot learn English from Robinson?
2. Many years passed before Robinson's rescue.
3. Did the time pass slowly without a clock?
4. Robinson explored every part of the island.
5. Read the last chapter for homework.
6. Do animal skins make good clothing?
7. He sent smoke signals from the top of a hill.
8. On the beach sat a man.
9. Tell me the ending of the story.
10. On the island waited the unfortunate man.
11. Describe how Robinson returns to London.
12. Did Robinson find his own footprint in the sand?
13. Defoe wrote the adventure almost three hundred years ago.
14. He based his story on a real person, Alexander Selkirk.
15. Selkirk survived four years on a deserted island.
16. Imagine having to survive by your wits.
17. Was Robinson Crusoe on the island twenty-four years?
18. England changed greatly in that time.
19. Defoe wrote his book for adults.
20. Many young people like the book too!

8.5 Compound Subjects and Compound Predicates

Some sentences have more than one subject.

■ A **compound subject** has two or more subjects that have the same predicate. The subjects are joined by *and, or,* or *but.*

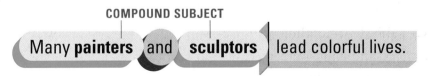

COMPOUND SUBJECT

Many **painters** and **sculptors** lead colorful lives.

Other sentences have more than one predicate.

■ A **compound predicate** has two or more verbs that have the same subject. The verbs are joined by *and, or,* or *but.*

COMPOUND PREDICATE

Juan **lived** in Spain and **studied** painting.

Some sentences have both a compound subject and a compound predicate.

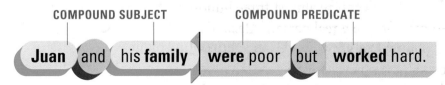

COMPOUND SUBJECT   COMPOUND PREDICATE

Juan and his **family** **were** poor but **worked** hard.

When a sentence has three or more subjects or three or more predicates, the word that joins the compound parts usually comes before only the last subject or predicate. Notice the position of *and* in the sentence below.

> **Velázquez, El Greco, *and* Picasso** are three famous Spanish painters.

Subjects, Predicates, and Sentences

Exercise 9 — Identifying Compound Subjects and Predicates

For each sentence below, write the compound subject and compound predicate. Underline the compound subjects and circle the compound predicates.

1. Many authors and artists have varied interests.
2. Elizabeth Borton de Treviño researched and wrote the book *I, Juan de Pareja.*
3. She studied violin and worked at a newspaper.
4. She and Juan knew and valued hard work.
5. Illness and poverty made Juan very weak.
6. A monk and a dog nursed him back to health.
7. Young Juan and his father loved art but lacked money for art supplies.
8. Brushes, canvas, and paint were available but cost too much money for the family.
9. Juan left his hometown and looked for a job.
10. He missed his home but longed to be an artist.
11. A baker hired him but paid him very little.
12. Did Juan work in the bakery and sleep there too?
13. The boy left the bakery and traveled to Madrid.
14. Juan met an artist in Madrid and worked for him.
15. The king or his family often posed for the artist.
16. The painter and his helper worked well together.
17. Juan cured the king's sick dog and won a reward.
18. Juan and Velázquez traveled and studied together.
19. Have you read this book or heard about it?
20. King Philip IV of Spain liked Velázquez and made him the official court painter.
21. Velázquez painted people skillfully and showed the dignity and worth of each subject.
22. Sensitive portraits of ordinary people and a great portrait of Pope Innocent X are among Velázquez's well-known works.
23. The Infanta Margarita, her two maids, and the artist appear in Velázquez's famous painting *Las Meninas.*
24. The painting's subject, its composition, and its size were unique for the time.
25. Most paintings at that time showed people in formal poses and depicted important events.

Simple, Compound, and Complex Sentences

A **compound sentence** is a sentence that contains two or more simple sentences. Each simple sentence in a compound sentence is called a **main clause.** A clause is a group of words containing a subject and a predicate.

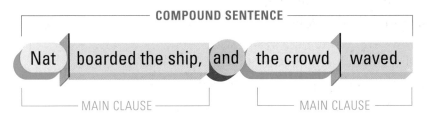

COMPOUND SENTENCE

Nat | boarded the ship, (and) the crowd | waved.

MAIN CLAUSE   MAIN CLAUSE

Besides a main clause, some sentences have a **subordinate clause,** one that cannot stand alone as a sentence.

■ A **complex sentence** is a sentence that has one main clause and one or more subordinate clauses.

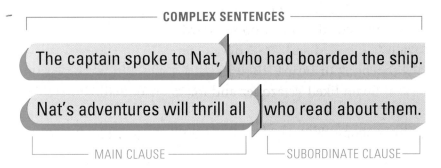

COMPLEX SENTENCES

The captain spoke to Nat, | who had boarded the ship.

Nat's adventures will thrill all | who read about them.

MAIN CLAUSE   SUBORDINATE CLAUSE

When a subordinate clause is not necessary for the sentence to make sense, it is separated from the main clause by commas.

■ A **run-on sentence** is two or more sentences incorrectly written as one sentence. Notice the way run-on sentences may be corrected.

Correcting Run-on Sentences	
Run-on Sentences	**Corrected Sentences**
Nat boarded the ship the crowd waved.	Nat boarded the ship. **T**he crowd waved.
Nat boarded the ship, the crowd waved.	Nat boarded the ship; the crowd waved.
	Nat boarded the ship, **and** the crowd waved.

Write whether each of the following sentences is *simple* or *compound*.

1. Nat and his family valued a good education.
2. His family had little money; he frequently worried about them.
3. The boy found a job and worked in a supply store for a while.
4. Nat read about sailing, or he studied mathematics.
5. Will Nat read about the stars, study navigation, and go to sea?
6. No teacher taught him, but Nat learned Spanish.
7. The boy sailed on a ship and worked as a navigator.
8. Sailors used charts of the stars, but Nat found errors in some of the measurements.
9. Nat taught the sailors mathematics, and the crew learned quickly.
10. He gathered information and wrote a book about navigation.

Exercise 11   Identifying Simple, Compound, Complex, and Run-on Sentences

Write whether each of the following sentences is *simple, compound, complex,* or *run-on.*

1. *The True Confessions of Charlotte Doyle* describes an adventure that takes place at sea.
2. Charlotte was brought up as a proper young lady she attended boarding school in England.
3. She returned to America her voyage to her home would not be an easy one.
4. Crew members wanted revenge on Captain Jaggery who had treated them cruelly.
5. Charlotte spoke to the captain; she told him about the planned mutiny.
6. Charlotte took responsibility and offered to help the crew.
7. The ship pitched and rolled in an awful storm, and the captain sent Charlotte aloft to fix a sail.
8. The captain who had killed his first mate accused Charlotte of the murder.
9. The crew thought Charlotte was guilty; they didn't lift a finger to save her.
10. How did Charlotte escape being hanged, and what did she do upon reaching America?

SUBJECTS, PREDICATES, AND SENTENCES

In this passage from *A Tree Grows in Brooklyn*, it is 1912, and eleven-year-old Francie Nolan plans to read every book in her local library. The passage has been annotated to show some of the sentence elements and sentence structures covered in this unit.

Literature Model

from A Tree Grows in Brooklyn
by Betty Smith

Francie thought that all the books in the world were in that library and she had a plan about reading all the books in the world. She was reading a book a day in alphabetical order and not skipping the dry ones. She remembered that the first author had been Abbott. She had been reading a book a day for a long time now and she was still in the B's. Already she had read about bees and buffaloes, Bermuda vacations and Byzantine architecture. For all of her enthusiasm, she had to admit that some of the B's had been hard going. But Francie was a reader. She read everything she could find: trash, classics, time tables and the grocer's price list. Some of the reading had been wonderful; the Louisa Alcott books for example. She planned to read all the books over again when she had finished with the Z's.

Saturdays were different. She treated herself by reading a book not in the alphabetical sequence. On that day she asked the librarian to recommend a book.

- Compound predicate
- Simple subject
- Simple predicate
- Complete subject
- Simple sentence
- Complete predicate

Grammar Review

Review: Exercise 1 Writing Sentences from Fragments

The following sentences and sentence fragments are based on the passage from *A Tree Grows in Brooklyn* on the preceding page. Rewrite each fragment as a complete sentence.

SAMPLE   Francie loved to read. Planned to read all the books in the world.
ANSWER   She planned to read all the books in the world.

1. She hoped to read a book a day. The first author.
2. Some of the books interested Francie more than others. Those by Louisa Alcott.
3. Francie read the books in alphabetical order. Was working her way through the B's.
4. One day a week she allowed herself a treat. Were special.
5. Francie asked the librarian to recommend a book. Didn't have to be in alphabetical order.

Review: Exercise 2 Identifying Subjects and Predicates in Questions

Rewrite each question to form a statement. Then underline each complete subject once and each complete predicate twice.

SAMPLE   Does the librarian recommend a book?
ANSWER   The librarian recommends a book.

1. Has Francie read the book before?
2. Do Francie and the librarian like the book?
3. Does the girl choose a book for Sunday?
4. Can Francie read the book quickly?
5. Have the girl's parents encouraged her?
6. Can Francie read more than one book a day?
7. Does Francie read many books a day?
8. Are those books the most interesting?
9. Does Francie prefer adventure?
10. Is she in the library this afternoon?

Review: Exercise 3 **Identifying Kinds of Sentences**

The following paragraph gives some information about the author Avi, who wrote *The True Confessions of Charlotte Doyle*. Write whether each sentence is *declarative, interrogative, exclamatory,* or *imperative*.

SAMPLE   Learn more about the writer Avi.
ANSWER   imperative

¹Why do parents, teachers, and students all praise Avi's novels? ²As Avi himself said, "Most of all I want them to enjoy a good read." ³His notably readable, award-winning novels include mystery, adventure, historical, and comic novels. ⁴Imaginative, fast-paced plots capture the reader quickly. ⁵How exciting the books are! ⁶Readers would be misled, however, if that is all they expected. ⁷What are Avi's other goals as a writer for young people? ⁸Avi writes about complex issues that are full of contradiction and irony. ⁹He wants readers to think about these issues. ¹⁰Check out an Avi book today.

Review: Exercise 4 **Identifying the Subject of a Sentence**

Write the simple subject from each sentence. Write *(You)* for any sentence with the subject understood.

SAMPLE   A vivid imagination is one of Avi's gifts.
ANSWER   imagination

1. Avi was born in Manhattan in 1937.
2. His great-grandparents were writers.
3. In school Avi had difficulty with writing.
4. A learning disability caused him to misspell many words.
5. His teachers thought he was sloppy and inattentive.
6. In spite of constant criticism, Avi succeeded.
7. Was Avi's first published book a collection of short stories for very young readers?
8. Avi based the book on his stories for his young sons.
9. Avi's writing for his growing sons became more sophisticated.
10. Read Avi's Newbery Honor books, *The True Confessions of Charlotte Doyle* and *Nothing but the Truth*.

Grammar Review

Turn the following sentence fragments into complete sentences by adding a complete subject or a complete predicate. Include at least two examples of each sentence type: declarative, interrogative, imperative, and exclamatory.

SAMPLE   My favorite books
ANSWER   My favorite books have lots of action.

1. Adventure books for young readers.
2. Faces great danger.
3. Life on the high seas.
4. Climbs the rigging.
5. Tells of strange lands.
6. The courageous captain.
7. Loved ships and the sea.
8. Explored the harbor.
9. Listened to the storytellers.
10. Spent her childhood near the water.
11. Some of the best adventure stories.
12. The whole plot.
13. Portrays fires and shipwrecks.
14. Another author of adventure stories.
15. Ran away to live on a mountain.
16. Have been made into movies and plays.
17. A buried treasure.
18. Floated down the river on a raft.
19. An adventure on the river.
20. Survived in the wilderness.
21. Almost drowned in the rapids.
22. Saved the boy's life.
23. A leaky boat.
24. My two favorite heroes.
25. Held the captain hostage.
26. Followed the map's directions.
27. An action-packed movie.
28. Bobbed down the Delaware in an inner tube.
29. Always finds a good solution.
30. My next adventure story.

Grammar Review

Review: Exercise 6 Identifying Simple and Complete Subjects and Predicates

The following sentences tell about the author Louisa May Alcott. Write each sentence. Underline the complete subject once and the complete predicate twice. Then circle the simple subject and the simple predicate.

SAMPLE   Alcott's family influenced her writing.
ANSWER   Alcott's (family)(influenced) her writing.

1. Louisa May Alcott's father ran schools unlike most others of the time.
2. Mr. Alcott used his liberal ideas in teaching his four daughters.
3. Louisa May Alcott wrote "rubbishy novels" under the name A. N. Barnard.
4. She published her famous novel *Little Women* in 1869.
5. Alcott based the story of the March girls on her own family.

Review: Exercise 7 Identifying Compound Subjects and Predicates

Write each sentence. If the sentence has a compound subject, draw a line under each subject. If the sentence has a compound predicate, draw two lines under each predicate.

SAMPLE   France and Impressionism are closely identified.
ANSWER   France and Impressionism are closely identified.

1. Painters in Paris in the late-nineteenth century experimented with color and developed new techniques.
2. Rapid brushstrokes and dabs of color created the style of painting called Impressionism.
3. Light and color give Impressionist paintings their brilliance.
4. Impressionist artists escaped from the studio and captured the life of the streets and open air.
5. Monet, Degas, Pissarro, and Renoir were all important Impressionist painters.

Subjects, Predicates, and Sentences

Review: Exercise 8 **Writing Compound and Complex Sentences**

The following pairs of related simple sentences are about Francie and her family in *A Tree Grows in Brooklyn*. Combine each pair to form a compound or complex sentence.

SAMPLE   Francie buys bread for her family. Her brother Neeley helps her carry it home.

ANSWER   Francie buys bread for her family, and her brother Neeley helps her carry it home.

1. Francie's father works as a singing waiter. He can't always find work.
2. Her mother cleans houses for a living. She also cooks the family's meals.
3. On Saturdays the family eats a big dinner. They even have dessert.
4. Francie's parents don't have very much money. They work very hard to provide for their children.
5. The family must save every spare penny. They won't have enough money for their daily food.

Review: Exercise 9 **Correcting Run-on Sentences**

Correct the following run-on sentences by rewriting them as separate sentences or combining them, using a semicolon or a comma and the word *and*, *or*, or *but*.

SAMPLE   Writing for children of any age is not an easy task writing for very young children is the most difficult.

ANSWER   Writing for children of any age is not an easy task, but writing for very young children is the most difficult.

1. Beatrix Potter wrote in the early twentieth century, her books for young children are now considered classics.
2. She spent her summers in the country, she spent winters in London.
3. Potter's summer experiences sparked her imagination she found life in the country exciting and vital.
4. *The Tale of Peter Rabbit* was originally written as a letter to a child who was ill Potter added to the letter and sent it to a publisher.
5. The Beatrix Potter books are strong because of their common sense and humor they are exciting because of their action and adventure.

Review: Exercise 10

Proofreading

The following passage is about the artist Pierre-Auguste Renoir, whose work appears on this page. Rewrite the passage, correcting errors in spelling, capitalization, grammar, and usage. Add any missing punctuation. There are ten errors.

Pierre-Auguste Renoir

[1]Best known for his cheerful scenes of everyday life, french artist Pierre-Auguste Renoir (1841–1919) was an Impressionist painter [2]The

Pierre-Auguste Renoir, *The Reading*, 1892

(continued)

Subjects, Predicates, and Sentences

Impressionists tried to represent what they saw at one particular moment in time ³They preferred to paint outdoors there subjects could sit in natural light. ⁴Renoir frequently painted people outdoors, women and children were his favorite subjects. ⁵In *The Reading,* for example, two young girls reads a book in a pretty, sunlit setting. ⁶Like the passage from *A Tree Grows in Brooklyn,* the painting show a childs' love of reading. ⁷Can you imagine yourself in this picture

Review: Exercise 11

Mixed Review

Revise each example, following the directions in parentheses.

1. Monet spent the summer of 1869 at Bougival. Renoir spent that summer at Bougival, also. (Write one simple sentence with a compound subject.)
2. Did Renoir and Monet develop the broken-color technique that became known as Impressionism? (Rewrite the sentence as a declarative sentence.)
3. Renoir traveled to Italy in 1880. He studied Renaissance painters there. (Write one simple sentence with a compound predicate.)
4. Concentrated on drawing for several years after this trip. (Make the fragment into a sentence.)
5. He studied at Charles Gleyre's studio. He was influenced by Edouard Manet. (Rewrite the pair as a compound sentence using *and, but,* or *or.*)
6. Light color and atmospheric effects are important elements of Impressionist paintings (Punctuate the sentence.)
7. Monet used muted colors to paint landscapes Renoir was more interested in painting figures and using rich color. (Correct the run-on sentence.)
8. Painters before the Impressionists painted in studios and used north light. The Impressionists painted outdoors and used natural light. (Rewrite the pair as a compound sentence.)
9. Who were some important Impressionist painters (Punctuate the sentence.)
10. What a marvelous sense of color and form Renoir had (Punctuate the sentence.)

Subjects, Predicates, and Sentences

Writing Application

TIME

For more about the importance of using verbs correctly, see **TIME Facing the Blank Page,** page 98.

Compound Predicates and Compound Sentences in Writing

To give her writing interest and texture, Nicholasa Mohr varies her sentences in this passage from *Nilda*. Some sentences have compound predicates. The last sentence is a compound sentence. As you read the passage, focus on the italicized parts.

> The sun came through the leaves, stems, and petals, streaming down like rows of bright ribbons landing on the dark green earth. . . . Nilda *walked* over to the flowers and *touched* them. Inhaling the sweet fragrance, she felt slightly dizzy, almost reeling. She *sat* down on the dark earth and *felt* the sun on her face, slipping down her body and over to the shrubs covered with roses. *The bright sash of warm sunlight enveloped her and the flowers; she was part of them; they were part of her.*

Techniques with Sentences

Try to apply Nicholasa Mohr's writing techniques when you write and revise your work.

❶ Use a compound predicate to make two simple sentences into one.

TWO SENTENCES Nilda *walked* over to the flowers. She *touched* them.

MOHR'S VERSION Nilda *walked* over to the flowers and *touched* them.

❷ Combine simple sentences into compound sentences.

SEPARATE SENTENCES The bright sash of warm sunlight enveloped her and the flowers. She was part of them. They were part of her.

MOHR'S VERSION The bright sash of warm sunlight enveloped her and the flowers; she was part of them; they were part of her.

Practice Practice the techniques with sentences by revising the following passage on a separate sheet of paper. Use compound and complex sentences.

Children's Book Week has a long history. In the early twentieth century, Frederic Melcher headed the American Booksellers Association. Melcher wanted children to read more good books. He suggested that a medal be given for outstanding children's books. He organized a special committee. The committee decided to celebrate Children's Book Week each year. The first Children's Book Week was held in 1919. The idea was a success. The event still occurs each year. It attracts people from all over.

Subjects, Predicates, and Sentences

UNIT 9 Nouns

Lesson 9.1   **Common and Proper Nouns**   *319*

Lesson 9.2   **Singular and Plural Nouns**   *321*

Lesson 9.3   **Possessive Nouns**   *323*

Grammar Review   *325*

Writing Application   *331*

9.1 Common and Proper Nouns

■ A **noun** is a word that names a person, a place, a thing, or an idea.

Nouns	
Persons	brother, judge, athlete, teacher, mother-in-law
Places	neighborhood, county, city
Things	book, shoe, flower, pencil
Ideas	pride, skill, truth, democracy, success

There are two basic kinds of nouns: common nouns and proper nouns.

■ A **common noun** names *any* person, place, thing, or idea.

■ A **proper noun** names a *specific* person, place, thing, or idea.

A proper noun may consist of one or more words. You should always begin a proper noun with a capital letter. For proper nouns of more than one word, capitalize the first word and all other important words. Some examples of proper nouns are listed below.

	Common Noun	Proper Noun
People	actor	Chris O'Donnell
	singer	Mariah Carey
	athlete	Mia Hamm
Places	building	Tower of London
	city	Tucson
	river	Nile
Things	book	*Johnny Tremain*
	movie	*Peter Pan*
	song	"This Land Is Your Land"

Exercise 1   Identifying Nouns

Write every noun that each sentence contains.

1. Historians trace the origin of the game of tennis to France.
2. The modern outdoor game of tennis probably evolved from an indoor game.
3. In the past, people hit the ball with their hands instead of rackets.
4. Walter Wingfield improved the game.
5. Mr. Wingfield patented his form of tennis more than a century ago.
6. Eventually the game became known as lawn tennis.
7. The first rackets were made of wood.
8. Later, people used aluminum or fiberglass.
9. Now some rackets are made of titanium.
10. Many players have a favorite racket they always use during important games.

Exercise 2   Identifying Common and Proper Nouns

Write each noun in the following sentences. Label the common nouns *C* and the proper nouns *P*.

1. Both youngsters and older people play in tournaments.
2. The United States Tennis Association sponsors contests for amateurs.
3. Matches for players also take place in Great Britain, France, and Australia.
4. The games at Wimbledon in England are very popular.
5. International teams compete for a special trophy, the Davis Cup.

Exercise 3   Using Proper Nouns

Write the proper nouns in each sentence. Use capital letters.

1. Many thousands of people attend the U.S. Open tournament in flushing meadows, new york, each year.
2. The u.s. open is one of four tournaments that are called the Grand Slam.
3. Players from all over the world also compete in the french open, the british open, and the australian open.
4. Martina navratilova was a top player for twenty years.
5. Before martina retired in 1994, she won many tournaments, in singles and doubles, but winning at Wimbledon was the most special.

9.2 | Singular and Plural Nouns

A **singular noun** names one person, place, thing, or idea. A **plural noun** names more than one. To form the plural of most nouns, you simply add -s. Other plural nouns are formed in different ways.

Forming Plural Nouns		
Nouns Ending With	**To Form Plural**	**Examples**
-s, -ss, -zz, -ch, -sh, -x	Add *-es*.	bus buzz box bus**es** buzz**es** box**es**
-o, preceded by a vowel	Add *-s*.	cameo studio stereo cameo**s** studio**s** stereo**s**
-o, preceded by a consonant	Usually add *-es*.	hero potato echo hero**es** potato**es** echo**es**
	Sometimes add *-s*.	zero photo piano zero**s** photo**s** piano**s**
-y, preceded by a vowel	Add *-s*.	day donkey turkey day**s** donkey**s** turkey**s**
-y, preceded by a consonant	Usually change *-y* to *-i*, and add *-es*.	city dairy penny cit**ies** dair**ies** penn**ies**
-f or *-fe*	Usually change *-f* to *-v*, and add *-es*.	leaf life half lea**ves** li**ves** hal**ves**
	Sometimes add *-s*.	roof chief belief roof**s** chief**s** belief**s**

Words such as *family* and *team* are called collective nouns.

■ A **collective noun** names a group of people or things.

A collective noun can take either a singular or a plural verb, depending on how it is used. The noun is singular when all the members of the group act as a single unit. It is plural when each member of the group acts separately.

The **team shares** the field with its opponent. [singular]

The **team share** their jokes with each other. [plural]

Nouns

Exercise 4 — Identifying Plural Noun Forms

Write the correct form of the noun in parentheses.

1. My father loves to tell funny baseball (stories, storys).
2. He said that at one game the first four (benchs, benches) in the stadium collapsed.
3. The (spectatores, spectators) crashed to the ground and were covered with mud, but no one was hurt!
4. The umpires were the (heros, heroes) at that game.
5. They interrupted the game so that the fans could clean (themselves, themselfs) off.

Exercise 5 — Forming Plural Nouns

Write the plural form of each singular noun.

1. radish
2. box
3. cherry
4. watch
5. country
6. ant
7. banana
8. horseshoe
9. loaf
10. valley
11. bush
12. bus
13. baby
14. piano
15. echo
16. volcano
17. radio
18. self
19. mosquito
20. knife

Exercise 6 — Identifying Collective Nouns

Write each collective noun and label it *S* for *singular* or *P* for *plural*. Pay close attention to the verb.

1. The volleyball club meets after school.
2. Each volleyball team has six players.
3. The group take their individual positions.
4. The committee discuss their reactions.
5. Our class watches the volleyball match.
6. The school band plays at every game.
7. Our family arrive at the stadium at different times.
8. The crowd is always friendly at the games.
9. The team share their feelings about each game at the end.
10. The coaching staff also meet after each game to discuss their strategies.

9.3 Possessive Nouns

A noun that shows ownership or possession is called a **possessive noun.** Possessive nouns, like all nouns, can be singular or plural.

■ A possessive noun names who or what has something.

Notice the possessive nouns in the following sentences.

The World Cup is the amateur **skiers'** competition.
A prize is awarded for the outstanding **men's** achievement.
The **women's** division also awards a prize.

The following chart shows how to form possessives from singular and plural nouns.

Forming Possessive Nouns		
Nouns	**To Form Possessive**	**Examples**
Most singular nouns	Add an apostrophe and -*s* (*'s*).	Karen has new skis. Karen**'s** skis are new.
Singular nouns ending in -*s*	Add an apostrophe and -*s* (*'s*).	Chris got new skis last year. Chris**'s** skis are in the attic.
Plural nouns ending in -*s*	Add an apostrophe (*'*).	Many skiers wear goggles. The skiers**'** goggles are sturdy.
Plural nouns not ending in -*s*	Add an apostrophe and -*s* (*'s*).	The men have warm sweaters. The men**'s** sweaters are warm.

When you are writing, remember that possessive nouns always contain apostrophes. Plural nouns do not.

Distinguishing Between Possessive Nouns and Plural Nouns	
Singular possessive noun	Where is the **athlete's** school?
Plural possessive noun	Where is the **athletes'** school?
Plural noun	Where are the **athletes**?

Identifying Possessive Nouns

Write each possessive noun and label it *S* for *singular* or *P* for *plural.*

1. The *Fédération Internationale du Ski* is an amateurs' organization.
2. The World Ski Championships are a skier's goal.
3. A committee reviews all entrants' applications.
4. It considers skiers' qualifications for the races.
5. The committee's guidelines for amateur status are very strict.

Using Singular and Plural Possessives

Write the possessive form of the noun in parentheses.

1. The (sport) history began thousands of years ago.
2. Each (person) skis were made of animal bone.
3. Leather straps held the (skier) boots to the skis.
4. Many (skiers) toe straps came loose.
5. One (historian) discoveries include skis from Sweden.
6. The (skis) ages ranged from 2,500 to 5,000 years.
7. In Norway a (soldier) means of travel was skiing.
8. A (Norwegian) skis were for both cross-country and downhill skiing.
9. The (men) cross-country speed record was broken by Bill Koch.
10. (Koch) average speed was 15.57 miles per hour.

Forming Possessive Nouns

Copy and complete the chart, adding the possessive forms.

SINGULAR NOUN	SINGULAR POSSESSIVE	PLURAL NOUN	PLURAL POSSESSIVE
1. woman		women	
2. Ms. Smith		the Smiths	
3. child		children	
4. senior		seniors	
5. family		families	

Nouns

Grammar Review

NOUNS

Black Star, Bright Dawn by Scott O'Dell is about a young Inuit woman named Bright Dawn who enters the Iditarod, a sled dog race. The race covers more than a thousand snow-covered miles between Anchorage and Nome, Alaska. The passage below shows some of the kinds of nouns covered in this unit.

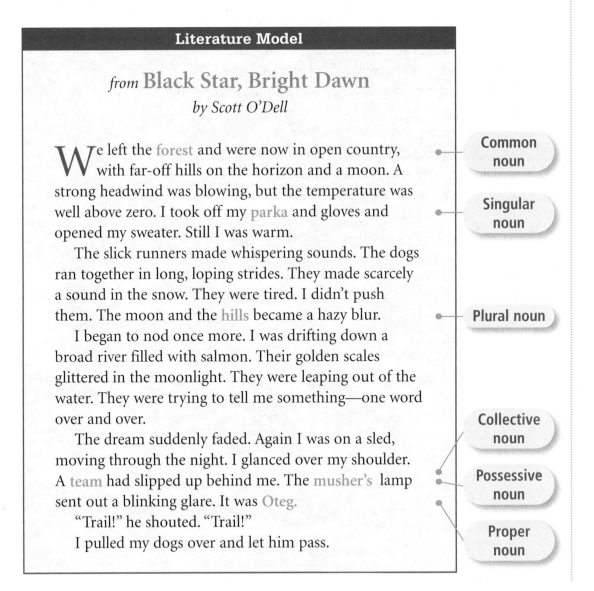

Literature Model

from Black Star, Bright Dawn
by Scott O'Dell

We left the forest and were now in open country, with far-off hills on the horizon and a moon. A strong headwind was blowing, but the temperature was well above zero. I took off my parka and gloves and opened my sweater. Still I was warm.

The slick runners made whispering sounds. The dogs ran together in long, loping strides. They made scarcely a sound in the snow. They were tired. I didn't push them. The moon and the hills became a hazy blur.

I began to nod once more. I was drifting down a broad river filled with salmon. Their golden scales glittered in the moonlight. They were leaping out of the water. They were trying to tell me something—one word over and over.

The dream suddenly faded. Again I was on a sled, moving through the night. I glanced over my shoulder. A team had slipped up behind me. The musher's lamp sent out a blinking glare. It was Oteg.

"Trail!" he shouted. "Trail!"

I pulled my dogs over and let him pass.

- Common noun
- Singular noun
- Plural noun
- Collective noun
- Possessive noun
- Proper noun

Nouns

Grammar Review

Review: Exercise 1 **Using Common Nouns**

Rewrite each sentence, correcting the capitalization of common and proper nouns.

SAMPLE   Bright Dawn chose her dog black star to lead her Team of dogs in the iditarod.

ANSWER   Bright Dawn chose her dog Black Star to lead her team of dogs in the Iditarod.

1. The team raced from anchorage on the gulf of alaska to nome on the bering sea.
2. The temperature rose as the inuit woman mushed across alaska's lonely, open Wilderness.
3. As bright dawn raced over the moonlit Landscape, she became sleepy.
4. Bright Dawn dreamed of golden Salmon leaping from a broad River.
5. A Racer named oteg, who had befriended the young woman, woke her.

Review: Exercise 2 **Using Proper Nouns**

Replace the underlined words with proper nouns. Use the information and the literature model on page 325 to help you.

SAMPLE   An author wrote *Black Star, Bright Dawn*.

ANSWER   Scott O'Dell wrote *Black Star, Bright Dawn*.

1. The state is cold for much of the year.
2. The race was between Anchorage and another city.
3. The race is one of the most dangerous races in the world.
4. The girl was in danger of freezing to death.
5. Her dog led the team.

Review: Exercise 3 Forming Plural Nouns

Write the plural form of the noun in parentheses.

SAMPLE   The real (hero) of the Iditarod are the dogs.
ANSWER   The real heroes of the Iditarod are the dogs.

1. (Husky) are the dogs most often used to pull sleds.
2. The (life) of these animals are devoted to the sport.
3. Their (reflex) are quick, and their strength is amazing.
4. They usually race over flat ground rather than hills or (valley).
5. During the Iditarod, newspapers run many (photo) of these dogs and the sleds they pull.

Review: Exercise 4 Using Collective Nouns

Write the correct form of the verb in parentheses.

SAMPLE   Bright Dawn's family (lives, live) in its home in the small village of Womengo.
ANSWER   lives

1. Her family (perform, performs) their daily activities.
2. At school Bright Dawn's class (studies, study) its English lesson.
3. A team of dogs (helps, help) its owner, Bright Dawn's father, hunt for food.
4. The team (scatters, scatter) in different directions when he drifts toward the sea on an ice floe.
5. A group of men (does, do) its best to save him.
6. Bright Dawn's family (are, is) supportive of one another.
7. Because of the difficult journey, the team (was, were) tired.
8. The team of dogs (struggle, struggles) on, listening for Bright Dawn's words of support.
9. Another group (pull, pulls) its sled in front of Bright Dawn.
10. The crowd (was, were) surprised when it saw the winner was Bright Dawn.

Grammar Review

Review: Exercise 5 Forming Possessive Nouns

Write each possessive noun correctly.

SAMPLE   Bright Dawns father encouraged her to enter the race.
ANSWER   Bright Dawn's

1. The mens faces looked doubtful when the young woman announced she would compete.
2. Bright Dawn depended on her one lead dogs guidance.
3. Otegs advice also helped her during the race.
4. The young womans lead was erased when she stopped to help other mushers.
5. Her parents eyes teared when Bright Dawn won.

Review: Exercise 6 Using Singular and Plural Possessive Nouns

Write a sentence using each of the following nouns in the possessive form shown in parentheses.

SAMPLE   team (singular possessive)
ANSWER   The team's owner is Bright Dawn.

1. dog (singular possessive)
2. woman (plural possessive)
3. class (singular possessive)
4. group (plural possessive)
5. man (singular possessive)
6. skier (plural possessive)
7. snow (singular possessive)
8. crowd (singular possessive)
9. team (plural possessive)
10. sled (plural possessive)
11. Alaska (singular possessive)
12. winner (plural possessive)
13. sport (singular possessive)
14. wilderness (singular possessive)
15. race (singular possessive)
16. bear (singular possessive)
17. village (singular possessive)
18. doctor (plural possessive)
19. family (plural possessive)
20. journey (singular possessive)
21. newspaper (plural possessive)
22. river (singular possessive)
23. hill (plural possessive)
24. moonlight (singular possessive)
25. wolf (plural possessive)

Nouns

Proofreading

The following passage is about artist Rockwell Kent, whose work appears on this page. Rewrite the passage, correcting the errors in spelling, capitalization, grammar, and usage. Add any missing punctuation marks. There are ten errors.

Rockwell Kent

¹Rockwell Kent (1882–1971) was an important american book illustrator and landscape painter. ²Many of his paintings depicts the open sea rugged mountains, and coastlines'. ³Kent used these scenes to convey peoples lonelyness.

Rockwell Kent, *The Expedition*

(continued)

Nouns

⁴The artist visited alaska in 1918 and was inspired by the vast spaces near the Arctic Circle. ⁵Kents' experiences resulted in *The Expedition.* ⁶The painting, which depicts figures guiding their dogs' and sleds, could be an illustration for *Black Star, Bright Dawn.* ⁷It's easy to imagine the lifes of these people.

Review: Exercise 8

Mixed Review

Write all the underlined nouns. Label each one *common* or *proper*, *singular* or *plural*, and *possessive* if it shows ownership.

SAMPLE   Hikers respect natural resources.
ANSWER   Hikers – common, plural

1. <u>People</u> hike on paths and trails across America.
2. The <u>Appalachian Trail</u> goes through fourteen states.
3. The <u>campers'</u> gear must be light enough to be carried on their backs.
4. Storms are the <u>camper's</u> worst fear.
5. My family hikes in the <u>Berkshire Mountains</u> in Massachusetts.
6. Sleeping bags help provide a good <u>night's</u> sleep for a camper.
7. Many camping <u>stores'</u> supplies are limited.
8. <u>Tents</u> protect campers from rain and wind.
9. A <u>tent's</u> usefulness depends on many factors.
10. Next year my <u>class</u> is going on a trip to the Rocky Mountains.
11. We plan to travel by bus across the <u>Midwest</u>.
12. The seventh <u>grade</u> will go too.
13. The <u>buses'</u> seats will be filled with suitcases.
14. The <u>classes</u> are looking forward to the trip.
15. To raise money, we have established <u>West Middle School's</u> Dog and Car Wash.

Writing Application

TIME

For more about making good word choices, see **TIME Facing the Blank Page**, pages 96–97.

Nouns in Writing

In her book *Keepers and Creatures at the National Zoo*, Peggy Thomson describes zookeeper Kathy Wallace's daily routine. In the passage below, the author describes the care of an elephant's feet. Examine the passage, paying special attention to the italicized nouns.

> *Watchers* from the *railing* can't see the foot up close. They see the *probings* with the *pick* or with the point of the *ankus*. They see *Kathy* using both *hands* on a *drawknife* to cut away a *slice* of leathery, rubbery pad and then another. (It doesn't hurt the elephant.) And they hear the *thunk* of the slice into her *bucket*.

Techniques with Nouns

When you write and revise your own work, try to use nouns in some of the ways Peggy Thomson does.

❶ Whenever possible, replace general words with precise concrete nouns.

GENERAL WORDS thing, tool

THOMSON'S VERSION pick, ankus, drawknife

❷ To identify people clearly in your writing, use proper nouns or specific common nouns.

GENERAL WORDS woman, people

THOMSON'S VERSION Kathy, watchers

❸ Whenever possible, expand single common nouns into longer word groups that create images of details.

SINGLE NOUNS noise, sound

THOMSON'S VERSION the thunk of the slice into her bucket

Practice Practice the techniques with nouns by revising the following passage. Use a separate sheet of paper. Pay particular attention to the underlined words.

On one <u>day</u>, <u>our teacher</u> took <u>our class</u> to a <u>zoo</u>. We took our school <u>things</u> and our <u>food</u>. The purpose of the <u>visit</u> was to study and compare the eating habits of different <u>animals</u>. A <u>person</u> from the <u>place</u> first led us to the monkey <u>place</u>. A <u>man</u> fed the <u>animals</u>. They peeled the <u>food</u> and ate as they swayed from one <u>place</u> to another. Then we went to observe the big <u>cats</u>. Lunchtime in their <u>place</u> was quite different. They were serious as they tore apart their <u>food</u>. These <u>animals</u> were not thinking about play. Later we ate our own <u>food</u>.

Nouns

UNIT 10 Verbs

Lesson 10.1   **Action Verbs and Direct Objects**   *333*

Lesson 10.2   **Indirect Objects**   *335*

Lesson 10.3   **Linking Verbs and Predicate Words**   *337*

Lesson 10.4   **Present, Past, and Future Tenses**   *339*

Lesson 10.5   **Main Verbs and Helping Verbs**   *341*

Lesson 10.6   **Present and Past Progressive Forms**   *343*

Lesson 10.7   **Perfect Tenses**   *345*

Lesson 10.8   **Irregular Verbs**   *347*

Lesson 10.9   **More Irregular Verbs**   *349*

Grammar Review   *351*

Writing Application   *359*

Action Verbs and Direct Objects

There are two main kinds of verbs: action verbs and linking verbs. Action verbs tell what the subject does.

- An **action verb** names an action. It may contain more than one word.

Jay **has visited** Africa.

ACTION VERB

ACTION VERB

An action verb is often followed by a noun that receives the action of the verb. This noun is called the direct object. In the sentence above, the noun *Africa* is the direct object of the verb *has visited*.

- A **direct object** receives the action of a verb. It answers the question *whom?* or *what?* after an action verb.

Sightseers paid the **fees.**

DIRECT OBJECT

Not all action verbs take direct objects.

- A **transitive** verb has a direct object.
- An **intransitive** verb does not have a direct object.

You must examine how an action verb is used in a sentence to determine whether it is transitive or intransitive. Some verbs can be used both ways.

Sheila **read** a book about Africa. [transitive]
Sheila **read** in a great hurry. [intransitive]

Verbs

Exercise 1   Identifying Action Verbs and Direct Objects

For the sentences below, write each action verb. If the verb has a direct object, write it and underline it.

1. The equator divides Africa in two.
2. Streams and wells create oases in the desert.
3. Camels can travel in the desert for days without water.
4. Not even cars cross the sand dunes.
5. In the eastern Sahara, the sun shines for thousands of hours every year.
6. Boats transport goods down the Nile River.
7. In flat regions the Nile River flows slowly.
8. Many people build their homes in the Nile Valley.
9. Grasslands border the Sahara on the south.
10. Bushes and small trees grow in the grasslands.
11. Wild animals roam the grasslands of Central Africa.
12. Large herds of cattle graze on the grasslands.
13. Herders tend the cattle.
14. African farmers grow coffee.
15. Much rain falls in the tropical forests.
16. Many tourists visit the jungles.
17. Europeans established colonies in Africa.
18. Explorers crossed the Mediterranean Sea for riches.
19. Others hunted elephants for their ivory tusks.
20. Miners sought gold under the ground.
21. African ethnic groups later won their independence.
22. Anthropologists explore for evidence of early peoples.
23. Scientists study gorillas in remote forests.
24. Game parks protect wildlife.
25. Northern Africans raise livestock.

Exercise 2   Writing Action Verbs

Write five brief sentences about yourself. Use an action verb in each sentence. Underline the action verb. If the verb has a direct object, circle the direct object.

SAMPLE ANSWER   I <u>eat</u> a big (breakfast.)

Indirect Objects

A direct object answers the question *whom?* or *what?* after an action verb. In the sentence below, the direct object is *Egypt. Egypt* answers the question *what?* after the action verb *visited.*

Rachel visited **Egypt** last year.

An action verb may also have an indirect object.

■ An **indirect object** answers the question *to whom?* or *for whom?* the action was done.

Sightseers paid the **guides** fees.

INDIRECT OBJECT

The direct object in the sentence above is *fees.* It answers the question *what?* after the action verb *paid.* The indirect object is *guides. Guides* answers the question *to whom?* after the action verb.

Indirect objects appear only in sentences that have a direct object. Two clues will help you identify indirect objects. First, the indirect object always comes before the direct object. Second, if you add the word *to* or *for* in front of the indirect object, the sentence still makes sense.

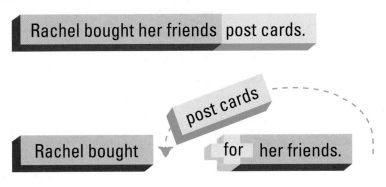

Rachel bought her friends post cards.

post cards

Rachel bought for her friends.

Distinguishing Between Direct and Indirect Objects

Write whether the underlined word is a *direct object* or an *indirect object*.

1. Egypt gives <u>tourists</u> lessons in history.
2. The pyramids show <u>visitors</u> life in the past.
3. Sculptors produced <u>statues</u> for tombs and temples.
4. Artists made decorative <u>objects</u> of pottery.
5. Archaeologists study the ancient <u>tombs</u>.
6. The tombs contain valuable historic <u>scrolls</u>.
7. The guide read the <u>tourists</u> the scrolls' messages.
8. Send <u>us</u> a map of Egypt.
9. We gave my parents a <u>cruise</u> on the Nile.
10. Artists gave the <u>pharaohs</u> beautiful golden objects.
11. The ruins offer <u>historians</u> facts about a culture of long ago.
12. Ancient Egyptians built <u>pyramids</u> for their pharaohs.
13. Government leaders gave the <u>people</u> guidance.
14. Instructors taught students <u>mathematics</u>.
15. Scribes taught composition <u>skills</u> to the boys.
16. Festivals gave <u>Egyptians</u> relaxation from work.
17. Musicians offered the <u>families</u> entertainment.
18. Governors sent the pharaoh <u>taxes</u>.
19. The people gave the priests their <u>obedience</u>.
20. People sail <u>barges</u> down the Nile.

Exercise 4 **Identifying Direct and Indirect Objects**

For each sentence, write the direct object. Then write and underline each indirect object.

1. The floodwaters of the Nile gave farmers rich soil.
2. Wealthy Egyptians built themselves beautiful homes.
3. Parents fed their children bread.
4. Some Egyptians wrote relatives letters.
5. Gardens and rivers gave the Egyptians food.

Verbs

10.3 Linking Verbs and Predicate Words

■ A **linking verb** connects the subject of a sentence with a noun or an adjective in the predicate.

Africa **is** a continent.

LINKING VERB

LINKING
VERB

In the sentence above, the linking verb *is* connects *Africa*, the subject, with *continent*, a noun in the predicate. *Continent* is called a *predicate noun.*

■ A **predicate noun** is a noun that follows a linking verb and tells what the subject is.

■ A **predicate adjective** is an adjective that follows a linking verb and tells what the subject is like.

Predicate Nouns and Adjectives	
Predicate Noun	Zambia is a **country.**
Predicate Adjective	Zambia is **scenic.**

In the first sentence above, the predicate noun *country* renames the subject. In the second sentence, the predicate adjective *scenic* describes the same subject. Predicate nouns and predicate adjectives follow only linking verbs.

Some linking verbs can also be used as action verbs.

The farmer **grows** tired. [linking verb]

The farmer **grows** corn. [action verb]

Common Linking Verbs			
be	seem	feel	grow
become	appear	taste	look

Exercise 5 · Identifying Action and Linking Verbs and Predicate Words

For each sentence, write the verb. Then write whether it is an *action* verb or a *linking* verb. If it is a linking verb, write whether it is followed by a *predicate noun* or a *predicate adjective.*

1. Village life changes slowly in Zambia.
2. Many people live in grass-roofed houses.
3. Villagers raise food crops on the land.
4. Some farmers appear content with their lives.
5. Other people move to the mining towns.
6. The country is rich in copper.
7. The copper industry grows successful.
8. A common food in Zambia is corn porridge.
9. Many Zambians respect the old customs.
10. They seem happy with their traditions.
11. Zambia is a land of farmers and miners.
12. Each family group developed its own culture.
13. Traditions became important for each group.
14. No individual owned land.
15. The family group was responsible for its members.
16. Most Zambians speak a native Bantu language.
17. Sometimes communication between groups is a problem.
18. The English language is common among businesspeople.
19. Some languages seem unfamiliar to a nearby group.
20. Zambia's population grows quickly.

Exercise 6 · Using Predicate Nouns and Adjectives

To complete each sentence, write a predicate noun or predicate adjective as indicated in parentheses. You may need to write more than one word.

1. I feel *(predicate adjective).*
2. My family is *(predicate adjective).*
3. I am *(predicate noun).*
4. My favorite food is *(predicate noun).*
5. I think basketball is *(predicate adjective).*

10.4 Present, Past, and Future Tenses

A verb changes its form to show tense and to agree with its subject. The **tense** of a verb tells when an action takes place.

■ The **present tense** of a verb names an action that happens regularly. It can also express a general truth.

The present tense is usually the same as the base form of the verb. When the subject is a singular noun or *he, she,* or *it,* however, you usually form the present tense by adding **-s** to the base form. The chart below shows the present tense forms of the verb *visit.*

Present Tense Forms	
Singular	**Plural**
I **visit.**	We **visit.**
You **visit.**	You **visit.**
He, she, *or* it **visits.**	They **visit.**

Present Tense
Thousands of tourists **visit** the pyramids each year.

The present tense of the verb *be* differs from the base form *be: am, are, is.*

■ The **past tense** of a verb names an action that already happened.

Form the past tense of most verbs by adding *-ed* to the base form of the verb.

■ The **future tense** of a verb names an action that will take place in the future.

Form the future tense by adding the helping verb *will* or *shall* to the base form of the verb.

Past Tense
The people of ancient Egypt constructed the pyramids.

Future Tense
Many more tourists **will go** to Egypt next year.

Distinguishing Present, Past, and Future Tenses

For each sentence write the verb. Then write whether it is in the *present*, *past*, or *future* tense.

1. Larry learns about archaeology in the library.
2. Someday he and his parents will travel to Egypt.
3. Larry and his friend Ann watched a film about the Sahara.
4. This vast desert extends into Egypt.
5. The survival of the ancient Egyptians depended on the Nile River.
6. The Nile still provides the country's water.
7. Silt from the Nile fertilized farmland.
8. The Nile flows into the Mediterranean Sea.
9. Silt protected land near the Mediterranean from erosion.
10. The Aswan High Dam harnesses the water of the Nile.
11. Water from the dam will increase Egypt's agricultural production.
12. The dam traps the silt from floodwaters in Lake Nasser.
13. Instead of silt, farmers will use chemical fertilizers.
14. The dam will damage the environment.
15. A Greek historian called Egypt the "gift of the Nile."
16. Like other ancient civilizations, Egypt developed on fertile land near a river.
17. Egyptian monuments will puzzle people far into the future.
18. The Nile's floods help the crops.
19. Farmlands cover less than 4 percent of the land of Egypt.
20. Today Egypt exports cotton.

Exercise 8 **Using Present, Past, and Future Tenses**

For each sentence write the present, past, and future forms of the verb in parentheses.

1. The capital, Cairo, (prosper) near the base of the Nile delta.
2. This part of the country (collect) the most rain.
3. The Western Desert (contain) few oases.
4. Oases (support) small villages and farms.
5. The sands of the Eastern Desert (extend) from the Nile River almost to the Red Sea.

Main Verbs and Helping Verbs

Verbs have four principal parts. The chart below shows the principal parts of the verb *learn*.

Principal Parts of the Verb *Learn*			
Base Form	**Present Participle**	**Past Form**	**Past Participle**
learn	learning	learned	learned

The principal parts of a verb can be combined with helping verbs to form verb phrases.

- A **helping verb** is a verb that helps the main verb tell about an action or make a statement.
- A **verb phrase** consists of one or more helping verbs followed by a main verb.

The most common helping verbs are *be* and *have*. The helping verb *be* makes a verb phrase with the present participle of a main verb.

Be and the Present Participle			
Present		**Past**	
Singular	**Plural**	**Singular**	**Plural**
I **am** learning.	We **are** learning.	I **was** learning.	We **were** learning.
You **are** learning.	You **are** learning.	You **were** learning.	You **were** learning.
She **is** learning.	They **are** learning.	He **was** learning.	They **were** learning.

The helping verb *have* makes a verb phrase with the past participle of a main verb.

Have and the Past Participle			
Present		**Past**	
Singular	**Plural**	**Singular**	**Plural**
I **have** learned.	We **have** learned.	We **have** learned.	We **had** learned.
You **have** learned.	You **have** learned.	You **had** learned.	You **had** learned.
She **has** learned.	They **have** learned.	He **had** learned.	They **had** learned.

Verbs

Identifying Helping Verbs in Verb Phrases

Write each verb phrase. Then underline the helping verb.

1. Some African societies have changed greatly.
2. The people of Malawi were living in family groups.
3. They have looked to chiefs for leadership.
4. They have formed one nation from many different family groups.
5. Many children in Malawi are working at jobs.
6. Malawi workers have produced beautiful items for export.
7. The country's name has changed along with its society.
8. Today it has become Malawi, "land of flame."
9. Before 1964 people had called the country Nyasaland.
10. For almost thirty years, Hastings Banda had ruled the country.

Identifying Past and Present Participles

Write each verb phrase and label its main verb as a *present participle* or *past participle*.

1. Malawi had acquired independence in 1964.
2. Bakili Muluzi has now assumed leadership.
3. The people have named Mr. Muluzi president.
4. The president has appointed a cabinet.
5. The cabinet is helping the president.
6. Malawi is developing into a stable nation.
7. The government has improved agriculture.
8. Malawi's economy has strengthened.
9. Young people are training for leadership roles.
10. The people of Malawi have learned valuable skills.
11. Farmers are tending cattle, goats, and sheep.
12. Malawi is depending on other nations for access to the sea.
13. Men with jobs in cities have mailed money home.
14. Most farmers are growing enough food for themselves and their families.
15. Half of the people in Malawi are living in small villages.
16. In Malawi women historically have raised the crops.
17. The economy is based on agriculture.
18. Malawi has received money from the United States for its schools.
19. Europeans have planted tea in the highlands.
20. The Bantu people had arrived in the region of Malawi in the 1500s.

10.6 Present and Past Progressive Forms

The present tense of a verb names an action that occurs regularly. To describe an action that is continuing, use the present progressive form of the verb.

■ The **present progressive form** of a verb tells about an action that is continuing right now.

The children **are listening** to a story.

The present progressive form of a verb consists of the present participle of the main verb and the helping verb *am*, *are*, or *is*.

Present Progressive Form	
Singular	**Plural**
I **am singing.**	We **are singing.**
You **are singing.**	You **are singing.**
He, she, *or* it **is singing.**	They **are singing.**

The past tense describes an action that was started and completed in the past. To describe an action going on some time in the past, use the past progressive form.

■ The **past progressive form** of a verb names an action that continued for some time in the past.

The women **were singing** a folk song.

The past progressive form of a verb consists of the present participle and the helping verb *was* or *were*.

Past Progressive Form	
Singular	**Plural**
I **was singing.**	We **were singing.**
You **were singing.**	You **were singing.**
He, she, *or* it **was singing.**	They **were singing.**

Using Present and Past Progressive Forms

For each sentence, write the present progressive or past progressive form of the verb in parentheses. Be sure your sentences make sense.

1. Students today (learn) about African nations.
2. For years a few European countries (rule) some parts of Africa.
3. Many Africans (grow) eager for independence in the 1950s.
4. Today most African countries (govern) themselves.
5. Now changes (take) place in African governments.
6. Many countries now (hold) elections.
7. More Americans (visit) Africa nowadays.
8. They (find) the scenery spectacular.
9. The Mali Empire (flourish) in West Africa for about two hundred years.
10. People still (visit) Timbuktu in Mali.

Exercise 12 **Using the Progressive Forms**

For each sentence, write the progressive form of the verb. If the verb is in the present tense, change it to the present progressive form. If the verb is in the past tense, change it to the past progressive form.

1. Visitors see great differences across the continent.
2. Temperatures average more than 100° in the Sahara.
3. Oases become dry.
4. Nomadic herders roam across northern Africa.
5. A family constructed a house with hard mud walls.
6. Architects design modern houses or apartments.
7. Technology replaces some traditions.
8. Families cooked food over an open fire.
9. Modern stoves reduce wood use by 500 percent.
10. Textile mills in Cairo make cloth from cotton.
11. Tourists shop in Cairo.
12. Visitors explore the old parts of many cities.
13. The economy of Egypt improves.
14. In the nineteenth century, tourists visited Egypt in large numbers.
15. Each year tourism becomes more important to the economy.

10.7 | Perfect Tenses

■ The **present perfect tense** of a verb tells about something that happened at an indefinite time in the past. It also tells about an action that happened in the past and is still happening now.

> Sheila **has collected** African jewelry for years.

In the sentence above, Sheila began to collect African jewelry at some time in the past and still collects it.

The present perfect tense of a verb consists of the helping verb *have* or *has* followed by the past participle of the main verb.

Present Perfect Tense	
Singular	**Plural**
I **have collected.**	We **have collected.**
You **have collected.**	You **have collected.**
He, she, *or* it **has collected.**	They **have collected.**

■ The **past perfect tense** of a verb names an action that happened before another action or event in the past.

> Before her last birthday, Sheila **had collected** only coins.

In the sentence above, Sheila started and finished collecting coins before another event that also occurred in the past, her last birthday.

The past perfect tense of a verb consists of the helping verb *had* and the past participle of the main verb.

Past Perfect Tense	
Singular	**Plural**
I **had** started.	We **had** started.
You **had** started.	You **had** started.
He, she, *or* it **had started.**	They **had** started.

Review: Identifying Tenses

For each sentence, write the verb. Then write whether the verb is in the *present*, *past*, *present perfect*, or *past perfect* tense.

1. Moroccan ships pass through the Strait of Gibraltar.
2. Morocco has exported fish and minerals.
3. In the year 711, Moroccans invaded Spain.
4. For some time, they ruled most of Spain.
5. The Moroccans had left many influences in Spain.
6. Most Moroccans speak Arabic.
7. Farmers had raised dates, olives, and citrus fruit.
8. Craft workers have handed down their skills.
9. Craft workers have often learned their skills from earlier generations.
10. Tourists value Moroccan leather.

Exercise 14   **Using the Perfect Tenses**

For each sentence, write the perfect tense of the verb. If the verb is in the present tense, change it to the present perfect tense. If the verb is in the past tense, change it to the past perfect tense.

1. Before modern times, Moroccan artisans created intricate silver jewelry.
2. They pounded metal into delicate shapes.
3. In the recent past, craftspeople constructed products from leather.
4. They also work on carpets for export.
5. Farmers raise barley, wheat, fruits, and vegetables.
6. Shepherds tend their flocks in green meadows.
7. Morocco trades with many other countries.
8. Long ago, ships from many countries docked in Casablanca.
9. Tourists visited the old section of the city.
10. Merchants crowded the narrow streets.
11. Marrakesh's hospitality charmed many travelers in the nineteenth century.
12. Fat bears dance in the public square.
13. Visitors watch talented jugglers and acrobats.
14. The Berbers lived in the mountains for centuries.
15. Centuries ago, the Moroccan Berbers helped the Arabs conquer Spain.

10.8   Irregular Verbs

Irregular verbs do not form their past forms and past participle by adding the ending -ed. The irregular verbs below are grouped according to how their past forms and past participle are formed.

	Irregular Verbs		
Pattern	**Base Form**	**Past Form**	**Past Participle**
One vowel changes to form the past form and the past participle.	begin	began	begun
	drink	drank	drunk
	ring	rang	rung
	shrink	shrank *or* shrunk	shrunk
	sing	sang	sung
	spring	sprang *or* sprung	sprung
	swim	swam	swum
The past form and the past participle are the same.	bring	brought	brought
	buy	bought	bought
	catch	caught	caught
	feel	felt	felt
	get	got	got *or* gotten
	keep	kept	kept
	lay	laid	laid
	lead	led	led
	leave	left	left
	lend	lent	lent
	lose	lost	lost
	make	made	made
	pay	paid	paid
	say	said	said
	seek	sought	sought
	sell	sold	sold
	sit	sat	sat
	sleep	slept	slept
	swing	swung	swung
	teach	taught	taught
	think	thought	thought
	win	won	won

Verbs

Exercise 15   Using the Past Tense of Irregular Verbs

For each sentence, write the past tense form of the verb in parentheses.

1. African merchants (begin) work before dawn.
2. Peddlers (bring) their goods to market.
3. They (lay) out their wares in attractive displays.
4. The sun (feel) hot in the open marketplace.
5. Children (seek) the shade of date trees.
6. Infants (sleep) in spite of the chaos.
7. People (make) requests about animals for sale.
8. Some traders (sing) songs about their goods.
9. Some people (buy) gourds of all sizes.
10. A tailor (win) some new customers.

Exercise 16   Using the Past Participle of Irregular Verbs

For each sentence, write the past participle of the verb in parentheses.

1. Some women have (sell) bracelets and necklaces.
2. Traders had (bring) gorgeous robes and veils.
3. The material has not (shrink).
4. Herders have (leave) cattle in the stalls.
5. Herders had (lead) livestock to market.
6. The herder has (catch) the stray.
7. Some people have (keep) pots of stew warm.
8. Craft workers have (teach) their children their craft.
9. Some merchants have (sleep) in the sun.
10. The market has (lose) business to other villages.
11. The merchants had (think) competition might be good.
12. One merchant has (say) the market needs competition.
13. People have (pay) by trading.
14. How much fruit have people (buy)?
15. A mother has (lend) her child money to buy a trinket.
16. The child had (get) some candy.
17. The candy had (begin) to stick to the child's fingers.
18. Merchants have (sit) on beautiful rugs.
19. By evening a cool breeze has (spring) up.
20. Wind chimes have (ring) in the breeze.

10.9 More Irregular Verbs

Irregular Verbs			
Pattern	**Base Form**	**Past Form**	**Past Participle**
The base form and the past participle are the same.	become	became	become
	come	came	come
	run	ran	run
The past form ends in *-ew,* and the past participle ends in *-wn.*	blow	blew	blown
	draw	drew	drawn
	fly	flew	flown
	grow	grew	grown
	know	knew	known
	throw	threw	thrown
The past participle ends in *-en.*	bite	bit	bitten *or* bit
	break	broke	broken
	choose	chose	chosen
	drive	drove	driven
	eat	ate	eaten
	fall	fell	fallen
	give	gave	given
	ride	rode	ridden
	rise	rose	risen
	see	saw	seen
	speak	spoke	spoken
	steal	stole	stolen
	take	took	taken
	write	wrote	written
The past form and the past participle do not follow any pattern.	be (am, are, is)	was, were	been
	do	did	done
	go	went	gone
	tear	tore	torn
	wear	wore	worn
The base form, past form, and past participle are all the same.	burst	burst	burst
	cut	cut	cut
	let	let	let
	put	put	put

Verbs

Exercise 17   Using the Past Tense of Irregular Verbs

For each sentence, write the past tense form of the verb in parentheses.

1. Crystal (do) research for her project.
2. She (go) to the library for books about Nigeria.
3. Some of her information (come) from magazines.
4. Fulani people (eat) well in the rainy season.
5. Children (ride) on cattle from camp to camp.
6. Their camps (are) temporary homes.
7. The Hausa (become) skilled potters and weavers.
8. The men (wear) long robes and loose-fitting trousers.
9. Teachers (run) schools for Nigerian children.
10. In 1954 the government (take) control of all the schools.

Exercise 18   Using the Past Participle of Irregular Verbs

For each sentence, write the past participle form of the verb in parentheses.

1. In Kenya's dry season, no rain had (fall).
2. A dry wind has (blow) over the land.
3. The families had (eat) beans and potatoes.
4. By March the farmers had (go) to the fields.
5. People have (do) the farm work by hand.
6. Pumps had (draw) water from wells.
7. Farmers had (grow) gardens close to the house.
8. By noon the sun had (rise) high in the sky.
9. Travelers have (go) to Kenya for years.
10. Tourists have (see) herders with cattle sticks.
11. The herders had (choose) each new camp carefully.
12. A fire had (drive) away mosquitoes and flies.
13. Kenyans have (grow) tea and coffee in the highlands.
14. Tourists have (fly) over Kenya's Tsavo National Park.
15. They have (ride) in trucks deep into the countryside.
16. Have you (speak) to any of them?
17. My parents had (take) many pictures on a photo safari.
18. One camera had (break).
19. They had (knew) the tour guide.
20. The tour guide has not (let) tourists off the paths.

Grammar Review

VERBS

The excerpt below is from a traditional Ashanti folktale. The Ashanti are the largest and most powerful ethnic group in the West African country of Ghana. The passage has been annotated to show some of the kinds of verbs covered in this unit.

Literature Model

from All Stories Are Anansi's
an Ashanti folktale by Harold Courlander

In the beginning, all tales and stories belonged to Nyame, the Sky God. But Kwaku Anansi, the spider, yearned to be the owner of all the stories known in the world, and he went to Nyame and offered to buy them.

The Sky God said: "I am willing to sell the stories, but the price is high. Many people have come to me offering to buy, but the price was too high for them. Rich and powerful families have not been able to pay. Do you think you can do it?"

Anansi replied to the Sky God: "I can do it. What is the price?"

"My price is three things," the Sky God said. "I must first have Mmoboro, the hornets. I must then have Onini, the great python. I must then have Osebo, the leopard. For these things I will sell you the right to tell all stories."

Anansi said: "I will bring them."

- Past tense
- Present progressive form
- Present perfect tense
- Linking verb followed by a predicate noun
- Action verb followed by a direct object

Verbs

Grammar Review

Review: Exercise 1   Identifying Action Verbs and Direct Objects

For the sentences below, write each action verb and direct object. Underline the direct objects. If a sentence has no direct object, write *none*.

1. We boarded the ship for Africa.
2. Our ship entered the harbor after a long wait.
3. We photographed the animals.
4. We visited several African plateaus.
5. Boaters rode the river rapids.
6. Hikers walked through the jungles.
7. Our guide traveled with us.
8. She selected the best places for overnight camps.
9. We traced our trip on a large map.
10. The tourists gave the guide a generous tip.

Review: Exercise 2   Identifying Direct and Indirect Objects

For each sentence, write the verb plus any direct object and indirect object. Then circle the verb and underline each *direct object* once and each *indirect object* twice. (Not all sentences will have both kinds of object. One sentence has neither.)

SAMPLE   Storytellers tell children fascinating stories.
ANSWER   tell <u>stories</u>, <u>children</u>

1. Joel Chandler Harris adapted African American folk legends.
2. He collected the stories in the book *Uncle Remus, His Songs and Sayings.*
3. Uncle Remus tells a boy stories about a fox, a rabbit, and a bear.
4. Brer Rabbit is the American version of the African character Zomo.
5. Brer Rabbit told Brer Fox his terms.
6. Harris used humor in his stories.
7. The *Atlanta Constitution* published the stories.
8. As a boy, Harris visited a plantation near his home.
9. African Americans told Harris stories.
10. The stories influenced modern authors.

Verbs

Review: Exercise 3 Distinguishing Linking Verbs from Action Verbs

For each sentence, write the verb and whether it is an *action verb* or a *linking verb*. If it is a linking verb, write whether it is followed by a *predicate noun* or a *predicate adjective*.

1. The Nile River is the world's longest river.
2. The Nile flows from Lake Victoria.
3. Bright blue and orange birds seem exotic.
4. Africa is a land of geographical wonders.
5. Its plateaus appear flat.
6. Wild animals graze on the plains.
7. The weather in the high plateaus and mountains is mild.
8. The mountain looks beautiful.
9. Community ceremonies are an important rural tradition.
10. Everyone gathers for celebrations of births and marriages.

Review: Exercise 4 Writing Predicate Nouns and Predicate Adjectives

Write a predicate noun or a predicate adjective as indicated to complete each sentence below. You may need to add other words. (Use the Literature Model on page 351 to help you.)

1. The Sky God was _____. (predicate noun)
2. Nyame was _____. (predicate noun)
3. Anansi was _____. (predicate adjective)
4. Anansi is a _____. (predicate noun)
5. Onini is a _____. (predicate noun)
6. Hornets are _____. (predicate noun)
7. Anansi stories are _____. (predicate noun)
8. The python is _____. (predicate adjective)
9. Osebo is _____. (predicate noun)
10. The price of the stories is _____. (predicate adjective)

Grammar Review

Review: Exercise 5 Using Present, Past, and Future Tenses

For each sentence, write the verb form indicated in parentheses.

1. Folklorists (present tense of *collect*) stories from all parts of Africa.
2. Many stories (future tense of *tell*) about the past.
3. Animals (present tense of *act*) like humans in some stories.
4. Folklorists (past tense of *record*) many "Why" stories.
5. One story (present tense of *explain*) why there are rainbows.
6. Many stories' endings (past tense of *surprise*) listeners.
7. Children (present tense of *enjoy*) the surprises.
8. Folklorists (past tense of *discover*) versions of an Ethiopian tale in Turkey.
9. A Congolese fable (future tense of *teach*) children that families stick together.
10. These stories (future tense of *help*) children understand other cultures.

Review: Exercise 6 Using Present, Past, and Progressive Forms

For each sentence, write the verb form indicated in parentheses.

SAMPLE   Most Ashanti people (present progressive form of *live*) in Ghana.
ANSWER   are living

1. Desert (present tense of *cover*) most of northern Africa.
2. In parts of western Africa, rain (present tense of *fall*) all year long.
3. Nomads (past progressive form of *travel*) to grazing areas.
4. Animals (present progressive form of *roam*) the lands by the lake.
5. Berber families (past progressive form of *end*) their meal with tea and pastries.
6. The Ashanti (present tense of *remain*) a very powerful ethnic group.
7. Many Ashanti people (present progressive form of *work*) as farmers.
8. For years the Ashanti (past tense of *speak*) English as a second language.
9. The British (past tense of *rule*) several colonies in West Africa.
10. In the 1950s, the Ashanti and other African peoples (past progressive form of *struggle*) for their independence.

Review: Exercise 7 **Using Present Perfect and Past Perfect Tenses**

For each sentence, write the verb form indicated in parentheses.

SAMPLE   Young people (present perfect tense of *learn*) crafts from their elders.

ANSWER   have learned

1. Many people (past perfect tense of *plant*) crops.
2. Others (past perfect tense of *raise*) livestock.
3. Some people (present perfect tense of *migrate*) to the cities.
4. Many rural families (past perfect tense of *live*) in mud houses.
5. Village life (past perfect tense of *stay*) the same for generations.
6. Some farmers (past perfect tense of *use*) the same methods as their ancestors did.
7. Some people (present perfect tense of *try*) new methods.
8. The architecture in cities (past perfect tense of *reflect*) traditional styles.
9. Some city families (present perfect tense of *rent*) modern apartments.
10. Outdoor markets (present perfect tense of *open*) on city streets.

Review: Exercise 8 **Using Past and Past Participle Forms of Irregular Verbs**

For each sentence, write the past or past participle form of the verb in parentheses. Be sure your sentences make sense.

1. Explorers (seek) prehistoric paintings in the Sahara.
2. Early peoples (draw) pictures of animals.
3. Figures and masks of wood have (come) from many African sculptors.
4. Some early Africans (make) bronze or ivory sculptures.
5. Until the 1900s, few people outside Africa had (know) about African arts.
6. Western art has (grow) from the influence of African sculpture.
7. African Americans (sing) songs incorporating African musical rhythms.
8. Africans have (sing) complicated rhythms.
9. Only in a few areas had Africans (write) their stories down.
10. In the past, many Egyptians (write) in Coptic letters.

Verbs

Review: Exercise 9 Writing Present Perfect and
Past Perfect Tenses of Irregular Verbs

Write each sentence, using the verb and tense indicated in the parentheses.

SAMPLE Some Africans (present perfect tense of *leave*) their rural homes.
ANSWER Some Africans have left their rural homes.

1. Many African cities that were once poor (present perfect tense of *become*)
   prosperous.
2. Before people began moving into cities, many (past perfect tense of *grow*)
   corn or maize on farms in the countryside.
3. Now city attractions (present perfect tense of *lead*) many rural people to
   move.
4. Many African countries (past perfect tense of *make*) progress in agriculture.
5. Periods of drought (present perfect tense of *be*) a problem.
6. Elders (past perfect tense of *teach*) traditional skills and values before
   university-trained teachers set up schools.
7. Foreign rulers (past perfect tense of *pay*) little attention to education.
8. They (past perfect tense of *give*) no thought to independence for their
   African colonies.
9. Now most African peoples (present perfect tense of *win*) their independence.
10. Black South Africans (past perfect tense of *seek*) and attained the right to
    vote and to rule themselves.

Review: Exercise 10 Identifying Verb Tenses and Forms

Write the italicized verbs in the following sentences. For each verb, write
whether it is in the *present, past, future, present perfect,* or *past perfect* tense.
Underline all the verbs that are in the progressive form.

[1]I *am leaving* next week on a trip to Africa. [2]I *have saved* my money
for two years. [3]My whole family *is going*. [4]We *have gotten* all the tourist
brochures. [5]The travel agent *helped* us plan our route. [6]We *will go* to
Morocco, Egypt, and Kenya. [7]I *had hoped* for a stop in Ghana, too. [8]My
parents *chose* a different tour. [9]We *were studying* the maps last night.
[10]The trip *looks* terrific!

Proofreading

The following passage is about Nancy Schutt's painting *Vanishing*, which appears on this page. Rewrite the passage, correcting the errors in spelling, capitalization, grammar, and usage. Add any missing punctuation. There are ten errors.

Nancy Schutt

¹The artist has took an endangered species as the subject for this painting, the animal she has chose is the leopard. ²The size and strength of these cats have gave them a feirce reputation. ³Will their reputation

Nancy Schutt, *Vanishing*, 1992

(continued)

saved them from extinction? ⁴That is the question Nancy Schutt addressing in her painting *Vanishing.* ⁵Many of Schutts' paintings deals with the theme of interaction among humans animals, and the natural world.

Review: Exercise 12

Mixed Review

For each sentence, write the verb and tell whether it is an *action verb* or a *linking verb.* Then write and label any *direct object, indirect object, predicate noun,* or *predicate adjective.*

SAMPLE   We left home last month for our trip.
ANSWER   left, action verb; home, direct object

1. We boarded the ship for Africa.
2. The ship seemed large and modern.
3. It was a freighter.
4. We photographed the animals.
5. We sent our friends pictures.

For each sentence, write the form of the verb indicated in parentheses.

6. Herds of elephants (past perfect tense of *live*) on many parts of the African continent.
7. People (present perfect tense of *cause*) animals' habitats to shrink.
8. The white rhinoceros and the gorilla (present progressive form of *become*) extinct.
9. Animal parks (future tense of *protect*) some endangered species.
10. Governments (present progressive form of *outlaw*) hunting in these areas.

Writing Application

TIME

For more about the importance of using interesting verbs, see **TIME Facing the Blank Page**, page 98.

Action Verbs in Writing

Jean Craighead George uses precise action verbs in this passage from *Julie of the Wolves* to make her writing lively and vivid. Examine the passage, focusing especially on the italicized verbs.

> Amaroq [one of the wolves] *glanced* at his paw and slowly *turned* his head her way without *lifting* his eyes. He *licked* his shoulder. A few matted hairs *sprang* apart and *twinkled* individually. Then his eyes *sped* to each of the three adult wolves that made up his pack and finally to the five pups who were sleeping in a fuzzy mass near the den entrance. The great wolf's eyes *softened* at the sight of the little wolves, then quickly *hardened* into brittle yellow jewels as he *scanned* the flat tundra [ground].

Techniques with Action Verbs

Try to apply some of Jean Craighead George's writing techniques when you write and revise your own work.

❶ Whenever possible, replace general words with precise verbs. Compare the following:

GENERAL WORD looked

GEORGE'S VERSION glanced, scanned

❷ Expand a single verb into longer groups of words with more than one specific verb:

SINGLE VERB A few matted hairs *separated*.

GEORGE'S VERSION A few matted hairs *sprang* apart and *twinkled* individually.

Verbs

Practice Practice the Techniques with Action Verbs by revising the following passage. Use a separate sheet of paper.

The lioness lay lazily in the hot sun. Her two cubs played nearby. She occasionally moved her head to look around her. She was suddenly alert. A herd of zebra was nearby. The lioness watched her prey. Partially hidden in the tall grass, she moved close to the zebra herd. She suddenly came out of the grass. The zebras walked away, but one was small and weak. The huntress moved again and caught the zebra. She brought the dead zebra back to the cubs. They all ate their fill. Afterward they cleaned themselves, and then they rested.

Lesson **11.1**   **Personal Pronouns**   *361*

Lesson **11.2**   **Using Pronouns Correctly**   *363*

Lesson **11.3**   **Pronouns and Antecedents**   *365*

Lesson **11.4**   **Possessive Pronouns**   *367*

Lesson **11.5**   **Indefinite Pronouns**   *369*

Grammar Review   *371*

Writing Application   *377*

Personal Pronouns

■ A **pronoun** is a word that takes the place of one or more nouns and the words that describe those nouns.

The most frequently used pronouns are called personal pronouns. The words *she* and *it* in the sentence below are personal pronouns.

Dana has a favorite folktale, and **she** tells **it** often.

■ Pronouns that are used to refer to people or things are called **personal pronouns.**

Personal pronouns perform different functions in sentences. Some personal pronouns are used as the simple subject. Others are used as the direct or indirect object of a verb. In the example above, the pronoun *she* replaces the noun *Dana*, which is used as the subject. The pronoun *it* replaces the noun *folktale* and is the direct object.

■ A **subject pronoun** is a personal pronoun in the nominative case. It is used as a subject.

■ An **object pronoun** is a personal pronoun in the objective case. It is used as the direct or indirect object of a verb.

I will read that fable. [subject pronoun]

Jesse told **me** about the story. [object pronoun]

Personal Pronouns		
	Singular	**Plural**
Used as Subjects	I	we
	you	you
	he, she, it	they
Used as Objects	me	us
	you	you
	him, her, it	them

Pronouns

Exercise 1 | Identifying Personal Pronouns

Write each pronoun and label it *subject* or *object*.

1. I read "The Bundle of Sticks," a fable by Aesop.
2. It taught me the value of cooperation.
3. A man had four sons, and they always fought.
4. They started an argument in the morning and continued it all day.
5. He became impatient and scolded them.
6. They ignored him and continued to argue.
7. He decided to teach the sons a lesson.
8. They needed it.
9. The father was sure this plan would help them.
10. Now I will tell you the end of the fable.

Exercise 2 | Using Pronouns in Nominative and Objective Cases

Write a personal pronoun to replace the underlined words.

1. The father asked the sons for a bundle of sticks.
2. The father tied the bundle up with string.
3. The father gave the bundle to the sons.
4. The father said, "Break the bundle."
5. The boys tried, but the boys were too weak to break the bundle.
6. Then the father untied the bundle.
7. The brothers easily broke the sticks one by one.
8. United, the brothers were strong.
9. The father said, "This lesson has taught my sons."
10. The sons also realized the importance of cooperation.

Exercise 3 | Using Pronouns in Nominative and Objective Cases

For each numbered item, write the correct pronoun in parentheses.

[1]George and Maria love stories. (They, Them) especially like fables. [2]Maria wanted to go to the library with George. Could (he, him) go after school?

[3]"We can borrow some books of stories by Aesop," (she, her) said.

[4]George said, "Our friends may have checked (they, them) out already. [5](We, Us) should go to the used bookstore."

11.2 Using Pronouns Correctly

People sometimes confuse pronouns in the nominative and objective cases. They write or say *me* when they should use *I*. They use *we* when they should use *us*. Remember to use a subject pronoun as the subject. Use an object pronoun as the object of a verb.

> **She** owns a collection of fables. [subject]
> He told **her** an amusing fable. [indirect object]
> The fable entertained **us**. [direct object]

Be sure to use a subject pronoun in a compound subject and an object pronoun in a compound object.

> Richard and **I** recited the fable. [not *Richard and me*]
> Jennifer helped Richard and **me**. [not *Richard and I*]

In the first sentence above, *Richard and I* is the compound subject. In the second sentence, *Richard and me* is the compound object of the verb *helped*.

If you're having trouble deciding which form of the pronoun to use in a compound subject or compound object, try saying the sentence without the noun. *Me recited the fable* does not sound correct. *I recited the fable* sounds—and is—correct.

Whenever the pronoun *I* or *me* is joined with a noun or another pronoun to form a compound subject or object, *I* or *me* should come last.

Richard and I visited a storyteller.

> Jennifer and **I** enjoy folktales. [not *I and Jennifer*]

In formal writing and speaking, always use a subject pronoun—not an object pronoun—after a linking verb. If the sentence sounds awkward, rearrange the words.

> The winner is **she**. [not *The winner is her*]
> **She** is the winner.

She told Richard and me a fascinating story.

Exercise 4   Using Pronouns in Nominative and Objective Cases

Read the following dialogue between the North Wind and the Sun.
Write the correct pronoun for each item.

1. North Wind: (I, me) am the strongest power.
2. Sun: How will you show (I, me)?
3. North Wind: You and (I, me) will have a contest.
4. Sun: A traveler is approaching (we, us).
5. North Wind: I see his dog and (he, him).
6. Sun: You or (I, me) must steal his cloak from him.
7. North Wind: The winner will be you or (I, me).
8. Sun: No, (I, me) cannot lose this contest.
9. North Wind: Watch (I, me) closely as I blow the cloak from the traveler.
10. Sun: I will watch (him, he), but I know you will fail.

Exercise 5   Using Pronoun Cases Correctly

Write a personal pronoun to replace each underlined group of words. Label
each pronoun *subject* or *object*.

1. The North Wind blew fiercely. (He, Him)
2. The traveler resisted the North Wind. (he, him)
3. The North Wind watched the Sun work. (she, her)
4. The man felt the rays of the Sun on his back. (they, them)
5. Before long the man was glad to remove the cloak. (he, him)
6. "Now North Wind and the Sun know who's more powerful," said the Sun.
   (you and I, you and me)
7. The North Wind could not overpower the Sun. (He, Him)
8. However, the Sun and North Wind realized that they both had powers.
   (she and he, her and him)
9. "This world needs both North Wind and the Sun," said the Sun.
   (you and me, you and I)
10. From that point on, the world respected the Sun and North Wind equally.
    (they, them)

Exercise 6   Writing with Personal Pronouns

Write five sentences. Use at least one of these pronouns in each sentence:
I, she, he, we, they, me, her, him, us, them. Use both subject and object
pronouns.

Pronouns and Antecedents

■ The noun or a group of words that a pronoun refers to is called its **antecedent.**

> Albert read "Sleeping Beauty." **He** found **it** exciting.

Here, the noun *Albert* is the antecedent of the pronoun *He.* *"Sleeping Beauty"* is the antecedent of the pronoun *it.*

The pronoun must agree with its antecedent in **number** (singular or plural) and **gender.** The gender of a noun may be masculine (male), feminine (female), or neuter (referring to things).

> The king and queen were proud of the baby girl, and **they** loved **her** dearly.

In the sentence above, the pronoun *they* agrees with its antecedent, *The king and queen.* The pronoun *her* agrees with its antecedent, *the baby girl.*

The antecedent of a pronoun should be clear.

> The parents showed the baby to friends. **They** admired **her.**

In the second sentence above, does the pronoun *they* refer to *parents* or *friends?* If the antecedent is not clear, it is best to avoid using a pronoun altogether.

> **The friends** admired the baby.

Be especially careful when you use the pronoun *they.*

> They have many books of folktales at the library. [unclear]
> The library has many books of folktales. [clear]

Exercise 7　Identifying Antecedents

The sentences below are about "The White Bear," a Russian folktale. Write the antecedent of each underlined pronoun.

1. A man lived in the forest. <u>He</u> was very poor.
2. He had many children. He could not feed <u>them</u>.
3. One night the wind blew hard. <u>It</u> shook the walls.
4. The house stood firm. <u>It</u> was well built.
5. The children heard a noise outside. <u>They</u> were afraid.
6. A white bear appeared. The man approached <u>it</u>.
7. The bear asked the man, "Will you give <u>me</u> your youngest daughter?"
8. This was a strange request. The man had never heard anything like <u>it</u>.
9. His daughter was dear to the man. What could he tell <u>her</u>?
10. The man listened to the bear. <u>He</u> wanted to learn what it would offer.

Exercise 8　Using Personal Pronouns

Write the correct pronoun to complete each sentence below. Then write and circle its antecedent.

1. The bear made a promise. _____ promised the family great wealth.
2. The man spoke with his children. He told _____ about the bear's request.
3. The youngest daughter became worried. The bear's request frightened _____ .
4. The girl listened to her family. They said, "If _____ go, the bear promises _____ will be rich."
5. Finally the girl told her father and her brothers and sisters, "_____ will go because I love _____ ."

Exercise 9　Writing with Personal Pronouns

Read each sentence. Rewrite the sentence, replacing the underlined antecedent with a personal pronoun.

1. <u>Many stories</u> have a wolf as a main character.
2. In one story, <u>three pigs</u> outsmart a wolf.
3. <u>Little Red Riding Hood</u> meets a wolf in another story.
4. Instead of a wolf, <u>Goldilocks</u> meets three bears.
5. Goldilocks ate <u>the porridge</u> before the bears returned.

11.4 Possessive Pronouns

Some personal pronouns indicate ownership or possession. These pronouns are called possessive pronouns, and they replace the possessive forms of nouns.

■ A **possessive pronoun** is a pronoun in the possessive case. It shows who or what has something.

Some possessive pronouns are used before nouns. They replace the name of the person or thing that has something.

> **Aesop's** fables are famous. **His** fables are famous.
>
> **A fable** is a brief tale. **Its** characters are often animals.

Other possessive pronouns stand alone in a sentence.

> This book is **yours.**
>
> **Aesop's Fables** is a favorite of **mine.**

The chart below shows the singular and plural forms of the two different kinds of possessive pronouns.

Possessive Pronouns		
	Singular	**Plural**
Used Before Nouns	my your her, his, its	our your their
Used Alone	mine yours hers, his, its	ours yours theirs

Possessive pronouns do not contain an apostrophe. Do not confuse the possessive pronoun *its* with the word *it's. It's* is a contraction, or shortened form, of the words *it is: It's a humorous tale.*

Exercise 10　Identifying Kinds of Possessive Pronouns

The sentences below are about a fable. List each possessive pronoun and write whether it *stands alone* or is used *before a noun*.

1. A miller, his son, and a mule walked to market.
2. "Ride on its back," a stranger suggested.
3. The boy got on, and his father walked.
4. A man they knew saw them and said, "You will spoil that son of yours."
5. The man said, "Will you follow a stranger's advice or mine?"

Exercise 11　Using Pronouns in the Possessive Case

Write a possessive pronoun to replace each underlined word or phrase.

1. The miller talked to a friend and followed <u>the friend's</u> advice.
2. The boy walked beside the mule; the man rode on <u>the mule's</u> back.
3. Next a woman gave <u>the woman's</u> opinion, and they followed that advice and rode together.
4. <u>The man and the boy's</u> weight was too great.
5. The mule collapsed, and the man and boy worried about <u>the mule's</u> health.
6. They carried the mule on <u>the man's and the boy's</u> shoulders.
7. The man's shoulders were tired. He asked the boy, "How do <u>your shoulders</u> feel?"
8. "<u>My shoulders</u> are tired as well," the boy answered.
9. The man saw that only fools think other people's opinions are better than <u>the fools'</u> own.
10. If the miller had followed <u>the miller's</u> own instincts, the mule would not have collapsed.

Exercise 12　Writing Sentences with Possessive Pronouns

Write a pair of sentences using each phrase. In one sentence of each pair, replace part of the phrase with a possessive pronoun.

SAMPLE　the boy's bike
ANSWER　The boy's bike was new. His bike was new.

1. the woman's idea
2. the friends' words
3. the mule's back
4. a girl's opinion
5. people's thoughts

11.5 | Indefinite Pronouns

■ An **indefinite pronoun** does not refer to a particular person, place, thing, or idea.

Like possessive pronouns, indefinite pronouns can be used alone or with nouns.

> Has **any student** read this Native American folktale?
>
> Have **any** read "The Voice of the River"?

When used alone, indefinite pronouns may be singular or plural.

INDEFINITE PRONOUNS			
ALWAYS SINGULAR			**ALWAYS PLURAL**
another	everybody	no one	both
anybody	everyone	nothing	few
anyone	everything	one	many
anything	much	somebody	others
each	neither	someone	several
either	nobody	something	

When an indefinite pronoun is used as the subject of a sentence, the indefinite pronoun may be singular or plural, depending on the noun that follows. Indefinite pronouns that change their number include *all, any, most, none,* and *some.*

> **Some** of the people **are** familiar with this folktale. [plural]
>
> **Most** of this tale **takes** place in Africa. [singular]
>
> **Most** of the characters **are** animals. [plural]

Possessive pronouns often have indefinite pronouns as their antecedents. In such cases, the pronouns must agree in number.

> **Many** are happy to share **their** folktales. [plural]
>
> **Each** must be willing to wait **his** or **her** turn. [singular]

Exercise 13   Using Indefinite Pronouns

For each sentence, write the correct singular or plural indefinite pronoun in parentheses.

1. (Everyone, Many) likes to read an exciting myth.
2. (Each, Many) are originally from Greece.
3. (One, Others) from Greece is about a father and a son.
4. (Anyone, Few) were able to guess the myth's ending.
5. (All, Anybody) enjoy the myth of Daedalus and Icarus.
6. (Both, One) of the mythical characters live on the island of Crete.
7. Daedalus has artistic talents; (none, nobody) can deny that.
8. (Few, Somebody) match Daedalus's skill in design.
9. (Some, Each) of these students model their work on his art.
10. (Each, Both) of the characters is interesting.

Exercise 14   Using Indefinite Pronouns

Write the word or words in parentheses that correctly complete each sentence.

1. Most of the people (praises, praise) Daedalus's ideas for the huge palace.
2. Few know (his, their) craft as well as Daedalus.
3. No one (is, are) more pleased than King Minos.
4. Although many try, no one (escapes, escape) the king's maze.
5. Everything (changes, change) when Daedalus tells the secret.
6. At last someone finds (his or her, their) way out.
7. Some of the readers (knows, know) the rest of the story: the kind forbids Daedalus to leave.
8. Something (takes, take) shape in Daedalus's skilled hands—wax wings for himself and Icarus.
9. Both (plans, plan) an escape across the sea.
10. Each puts on (his, their) pair of waxy wings.
11. At first everything (goes, go) well for the pair.
12. Several (sees, see) them flying in the sky.
13. One (flies, fly) too close to the sun; the wax melts, and he plunges to his death.
14. Which one (lands, land) safely in Sicily?
15. When someone tries to do the impossible, disaster can strike (him or her, them.)

PRONOUNS

In "The Wise Old Woman," a Japanese folktale, a young lord banishes everyone over seventy-one years of age from his village. A farmer disobeys the ruler and hides his mother. In the following passage, the ruler discovers that the old woman has saved the village. The passage has been annotated to show some of the pronouns covered in this unit.

Literature Model

from The Wise Old Woman

Japanese Folktale

Retold by Yoshiko Uchida

The young farmer was amazed at **his** mother's wisdom. "You are far wiser than **any** of the wise men of the village," he said, and he hurried to tell the young lord how to complete Lord Higa's third demand.

When the lord heard the answer, he was greatly impressed. "Surely a young man like you cannot be wiser than all my wise men," he said. "Tell **me** honestly, who has helped you solve all these difficult problems?"

The young farmer could not lie. "My lord," he began slowly, "for the past two years I have broken the law of the land. **I** have kept my aged mother hidden beneath the floor of my house, and it is she who solved each of your problems and saved the village from Lord Higa."

He trembled as he spoke, for he feared the lord's displeasure and rage. Surely now the soldiers would be called to throw him into the dark dungeon.

> Possessive pronoun

> Indefinite pronoun

> Object personal pronoun

> Subject personal pronoun

Pronouns

(continued)

Grammar Review

> But when he glanced fearfully at the lord, he saw that the young ruler was not angry at all. Instead, the lord was silent and thoughtful. At last **he** realized how much wisdom and knowledge old people possess.

Review: Exercise 1 Using Personal Pronouns as Subjects and Objects

Read the following dialogue. For each item, write the correct pronoun.

1. The Ruler: (I, Me) declare that all old people are useless.
2. Farmer: The other villagers and (I, me) do not agree with you.
3. The Ruler: What can you tell (I, me) to change my mind?
4. Farmer: It is my old mother who saved this village. You do not know (she, her), but (her, she) is wise.
5. The Ruler: Perhaps I was wrong. Let it be known to all old people. (Me, I) declare (they, them) are welcome in the land.

Review: Exercise 2 Making Pronouns and Antecedents Agree

Write the correct pronoun to complete the second sentence in each pair.

SAMPLE The young farmer's mother was not troubled by Lord Higa's tasks._____ knew how to complete them.

ANSWER She

1. The problems hadn't been solved by the wise men. _____ were bewildered.
2. The farmer told the lord that he had hidden his mother. "It is _____ who saved the village," he said.
3. The young farmer was frightened. He thought the soldiers would throw _____ into the dungeon.
4. The young lord looked thoughtful. He said, "_____ have been wrong."
5. The ruler had thought that old people were useless. At last _____ realized that they should be honored.

Grammar Review

Review: Exercise 3 Identifying Personal Pronouns as Subjects or Objects

Write each pronoun and label it *subject* or *object*.

1. Aesop is famous. He wrote many fables.
2. He was a Greek writer who lived in the sixth century B.C.
3. People admire him.
4. A girl told me that Aesop's fables are fun to read.
5. I asked her to name a favorite fable.
6. She named "The Fox and the Mouse."
7. Because Aesop's stories are often about animals, children especially enjoy them.
8. Roman and medieval writers collected them.
9. We read Aesop's fables that were collected by Phaedrus.
10. You can find them in many anthologies.

Review: Exercise 4 Using Personal Pronouns as Compound Subjects and Objects

Write pronouns to replace the underlined words.

SAMPLE   Kate and Martin read the story.
ANSWER   She and he
SAMPLE   Kate and Martin liked it.
ANSWER   They

1. Amy and John wrote a fable.
2. They read Mr. Jackson and Ms. Diaz the tale.
3. Gina and I saw Amy and John after school.
4. Amy and John asked us to watch them act out their fable.
5. Gina and I applauded Amy and John after their great performance.
6. Amy and John thanked Gina and me.
7. They told Gina and me that they appreciated our applause.
8. Mr. Jackson and Ms. Diaz applauded too.
9. Ms. Diaz gave Amy and John a flower.
10. Mr. Jackson saluted Amy and John.

Pronouns

Grammar Review

Review: Exercise 5 Using Possessive Pronouns with Nouns

The following sentences based on passages in "The Wise Old Woman" do not appear in this textbook. Write a possessive pronoun to replace the underlined words in each sentence.

SAMPLE   <u>The villagers'</u> leader issued a cruel decree.
ANSWER   Their

1. The ruler wanted all of <u>the ruler's</u> people to be young and strong.
2. The lord said, "I have no use for old people in <u>the lord's</u> village."
3. No one guessed that the woman was hiding in <u>the young farmer's</u> house.
4. The ruler was amazed by <u>the old woman's</u> wisdom.
5. The farmer told the ruler, "It was the farmer's aged mother who solved <u>the ruler's</u> problems."
6. The villagers were no longer forced to abandon <u>the villagers'</u> parents in the mountains.
7. Lord Higa left the village alone, declaring that <u>the village's</u> people be allowed to live in peace.
8. The young farmer now had <u>the farmer's</u> worry lifted from the farmer's mind.
9. <u>The ruler's</u> new understanding would allow the villagers to live full lives.
10. The people would always remember how the farmer's courage had saved <u>the people's</u> village.

Review: Exercise 6 Writing Sentences with Indefinite Pronouns

Write a sentence for each item below. Use the pronoun as the subject and the correct word from each pair as the verb.

1. Someone   listens, listen   4. Everybody   plays, play
2. All   makes, make   5. Many   enjoys, enjoy
3. Several   talks, talk

Review: Exercise 7

Proofreading

The following passage is about African American artist Jacob Lawrence. Rewrite the passage, correcting the errors in spelling, capitalization, grammar, and usage. Add any missing punctuation. There are ten errors.

Jacob Lawrence

[1]Jacob Lawrence, who was born in 1917, growed up in Harlem. [2]This thriving artistic center influenced he. [3]Lawrence chose to become a painter in his teens and him was encouraged by artists in his community. [4]Lawrence was twenty-four years old when his' work was exhibited in a New york art gallery.

Jacob Lawrence, *Men Exist for the Sake of One Another,* 1958

(continued)

Pronouns

⁵Lawrence's paintings portrays the lives and struggles of African Americans. ⁶Most people finds his work apealing. ⁷In the painting on the previous page, Lawrence shows a man talking to some children. ⁸The painting reminds us that everyone learn from others.

Review: Exercise 8

Mixed Review

Number a sheet of paper from 1 to 20. Then choose a pronoun from the list below to fill in each blank. You will not need to use all the pronouns, but you may need to use some pronouns more than once. Use correct capitalization.

everyone	its	she
her	me	them
him	mine	they
his	my	us
I	nobody	we
it	our	yours

¹_____ class read a fable written by Aesop. ²_____ was the story of a very hungry fox. Some grapes tempted ³_____. However, ⁴_____ were out of ⁵_____ reach. The fox knew other animals could probably reach the grapes. The fox thought of a way to reach ⁶_____ too. If you want to know how this story ends, you will have to read ⁷_____.

Almost ⁸_____ enjoys a good folktale. Our teacher told ⁹_____ class a story based on a Native American folktale. Mae and I found ¹⁰_____ wise. The story taught ¹¹_____ about life in a village. It amused and surprised both her and ¹²_____. Later Mae read the tale again to ¹³_____ sister, Ann.

Yesterday my brother and ¹⁴_____ went to the library. ¹⁵_____ were both looking for a book of fables. ¹⁶_____ brother found a book of Aesop's fables. ¹⁷_____ is better known for fables than Aesop. The book is now a favorite of ¹⁸_____. ¹⁹_____ has a story has about a vixen. In it, she talks about ²⁰_____ cubs.

Writing Application

TIME

For more about usage rules, see **TIME Facing the Blank Page**, page 98.

Pronouns in Writing

Michael Dorris uses pronouns in this passage from *Morning Girl* to make his writing clear and concise. Read the passage, paying particular attention to the pronouns that are italicized.

> I knew *my* hands very well. *I* study *them* when *I* trim *my* nails with the rough edge of a broken shell, making *them* smooth and flat. *I* could spread *my* fingers and press *them* into wet sand to see the shape *they* leave. Once *I* tried to do that with *my* head, but *all* I got was a big shallow hole and dirty hair.
>
> *I* knew the front of *my* body, the bottoms of *my* feet. *I* knew the color of *my* arms—tan as the inside of a yam after the air has dried *it*— and if *I* stretched *my* tongue *I* could see *its* pink tip.

Techniques with Pronouns

Use pronouns in your writing as does Michael Dorris.

❶ Always check that a pronoun agrees with its antecedent.

INCORRECT USE I knew my *hands* very well. I study *it* . . .

DORRIS'S VERSION I knew my *hands* very well. I study *them* . . .

❷ To make your writing smooth, replace repeated nouns and their modifiers with pronouns.

REPEATED WORDS I could spread *my fingers* and press my fingers into wet sand to see the shape *my fingers* leave.

DORRIS'S VERSION I could spread *my fingers* and press *them into* wet sand to see the shape they leave.

Pronouns

Practice Practice the techniques with pronouns by revising the following passage on a separate sheet of paper.

Morning Girl spends every day with Morning Girl's brother Star Boy. Morning Girl and Star Boy go to the beach. The brother and sister walk along the shore. Star Boy finds smooth pebbles. Star Boy finds unbroken shells and gives them to Morning Girl. The boy and girl wade in the shallow water and find tiny crabs and starfish. Morning Girl and Star Boy take Morning Girl's and Star Boy's treasures home. They put their treasures in a shaded pool next to the house where they live with their parents. Morning Girl and Star Boy will watch the crabs and starfish for several hours. Then the children will return the live creatures to the sea.

UNIT 12 Adjectives

Lesson **12.1**   **Adjectives and Proper Adjectives**   *379*

Lesson **12.2**   **Articles and Demonstratives**   *381*

Lesson **12.3**   **Adjectives That Compare**   *383*

Lesson **12.4**   **Special Adjectives That Compare**   *385*

Grammar Review   *387*

Writing Application   *393*

12.1 Adjectives and Proper Adjectives

The words that we use to describe people, places, and things are called adjectives.

■ An **adjective** is a word that describes a noun or a pronoun.

Adjectives describe, or modify, nouns in three ways.

How Adjectives Describe Nouns	
What kind?	We studied **modern** history.
How many?	I read **four** volumes.
Which one?	**That** invention changed the world.

Most adjectives come before the nouns they modify. Sometimes adjectives follow linking verbs and modify the subject, as in the example below. These adjectives are called **predicate adjectives.**

These inventions are important.

Some adjectives are formed from proper nouns and begin with a capital letter. These are called **proper adjectives.**

■ **Proper adjectives** are adjectives formed from proper nouns.

Proper adjectives often have the same form as the noun. Others are formed by adding an ending to the noun form.

FORMING PROPER ADJECTIVES

PROPER NOUN	PROPER ADJECTIVE
Oranges from **Florida**	**Florida** oranges
A symphony by **Mozart**	A **Mozart** symphony
Food from **Italy**	**Italian** food

Exercise 1   Identifying Adjectives

Write each adjective. Beside it, write the noun or pronoun it describes. If it is a predicate adjective, label it *P.A.*

1. Young Gandhi studied at a small school in India.
2. He later lived for a while in busy London.
3. Sometimes Gandhi was homesick.
4. Gandhi heard the truth of an inner voice.
5. He was courageous and purposeful.
6. Gandhi often fasted for many days.
7. After fasting, Gandhi grew weak, but he remained determined.
8. The mature Gandhi returned to India and led the nationalist movement.
9. He used nonviolent resistance as a protest against foreign rule.
10. He spent seven years in prison for that resistance.
11. The long struggle against foreign rule ended in 1947.
12. Two separate nations—India and Pakistan—were formed.
13. Most Hindus remained in independent India.
14. Large numbers of Muslims settled in Pakistan.
15. In 1971 the eastern portion of Pakistan became the new nation of Bangladesh.

Exercise 2   Identifying Proper Adjectives

Write each adjective. Beside it, write the noun it describes. Capitalize each proper adjective.

1. Victoria was a famous ruler in english history.
2. She was the energetic granddaughter of George III.
3. Victoria was the english queen from 1837 to 1901.
4. Victoria was also the queen of the scottish and welsh people.
5. During that time, Britain built a colonial empire.
6. The vast empire included indian plantations.
7. Victoria established asian and african colonies.
8. The colonial empire made Britain a rich country.
9. Victoria was wise and capable.
10. She became the symbol of british greatness.
11.. The diamond jubilee was celebrated by immense crowds.
12. The Royal Princess Victoria married a german prince.
13. Prince Edward was crowned the next british monarch.
14. Students of english history are knowledgeable about the victorian era.
15. The elizabethan and edwardian eras are famous too.

12.2 Articles and Demonstratives

The words *a, an,* and *the* are special kinds of adjectives. They are called **articles.**

The points to a specific item or items. *A* and *an* refer to any one item of a group. Use *a* before words that begin with a consonant sound. Use *an* before words that begin with a vowel sound.

> William Shakespeare is **the** most famous English playwright.
>
> Getting a lead role in **a** Shakespeare play is **an** honor.

The words *this, that, these,* and *those* are called **demonstrative adjectives.** They are used to point out something.

> Take **this** umbrella with you.   **That** store is closed.
>
> Take **these** boots also.   **Those** clouds are lovely.

Use *this* and *that* with singular nouns. Use *these* and *those* with plural nouns. Use *this* and *these* to point out something that is close to you. Use *that* and *those* to point out something that is far from you.

Demonstratives		
	Singular	**Plural**
Near	this	these
Far	that	those

Demonstratives can be used with nouns or without them. When used alone, they are called **demonstrative pronouns.**

> **This** is mine.   **These** are for you.

Exercise 3   Using Articles

For each sentence, write the correct article.

1. William Shakespeare was (an, the) English playwright.
2. Was he (a, the) greatest writer of all time?
3. (A, The) town of Stratford-on-Avon was his birthplace.
4. Shakespeare was (a, an) country boy.
5. He was (a, an) poet and (a, an) actor.
6. His plays caused (a, an) sensation in London.
7. Shakespeare had one of (a, the) largest vocabularies of any English writer.
8. Many of his plays were performed at (a, the) Globe Theatre.
9. *Romeo and Juliet* is (a, an) popular play.
10. (An, The) annual celebration of Shakespeare's birth takes place on April 23.

Exercise 4   Using Demonstratives

For each sentence, write the correct demonstrative word.

1. (This, That) biography I'm holding is about Florence Nightingale.
2. (This, These) woman dreamed of being a nurse.
3. Her friends encouraged (that, those) dream.
4. (That, Those) sick soldiers lacked expert care.
5. (This, These) injustice created great concern.
6. (This, These) concern brought about reforms.
7. Florence Nightingale led (that, those) nurses.
8. Nightingale could organize and take care of details, and (that, those) abilities made her successful.
9. (This, These) behavior was unusual for a rich woman of her time.
10. Florence Nightingale's achievements remain famous to (this, that) day.

Exercise 5   Writing Sentences with Demonstratives

Write a pair of sentences for each of these words: *this, that, these,* and *those.*
In one sentence of each pair, use the word as a demonstrative adjective. In
the other, use it as a demonstrative pronoun.

 ❧ SAMPLE ANSWER   <u>These</u> boots are too small. (demonstrative adjective)
<u>These</u> will fit you. (demonstrative pronoun)

12.3 Adjectives That Compare

You can use adjectives to compare two or more nouns.

■ The **comparative form** of an adjective compares two things or people.

For most adjectives of one syllable, form the comparative by adding *-er*. For most adjectives of two or more syllables, form the comparative by using *more* before the adjective.

> Is Venezuela **larger** than Peru?
>
> Is Argentina **more beautiful** than Ecuador?

■ The **superlative form** of an adjective compares more than two things or people.

For most adjectives of one syllable, form the superlative by adding *-est*. For most adjectives of two or more syllables, form the superlative by using *most* before the adjective.

> Is Brazil the **richest** country in South America?
>
> Simón Bolívar was one of South America's **most successful** generals.

Do not use *more* or *most* before adjectives that already are in the comparative or superlative form.

Comparative and Superlative Forms		
Adjective	**Comparative**	**Superlative**
small	small**er**	small**est**
dark	dark**er**	dark**est**
active	**more** active	**most** active
intelligent	**more** intelligent	**most** intelligent

Using the Comparative and Superlative Forms

Write the correct comparative or superlative form of the adjective in parentheses.

1. Simón Bolívar is one of the (great) heroes of South America.
2. He was (successful) as an older man than as a younger man.
3. The general was (wise) than before about the struggle.
4. Simón Bolívar was one of the (loyal) of patriots.
5. The general cherished the (important) dream of all.
6. He is (famous) in Europe than in the United States.
7. Maria Tallchief was one of the (noted) dancers in the world.
8. Her Canadian tour was the (challenging) of all the tours.
9. Away from home, Tallchief was (homesick) this time than ever before.
10. Maria received the (marvelous) opportunity of all.
11. The Russian composer Igor Stravinsky thought she was the (suitable) dancer for some of his ballets.
12. Tallchief is perhaps (memorable) for her role in *The Firebird.*
13. George Balanchine gave her the (prominent) roles of all.
14. George Balanchine may be the (famous) ballet choreographer of this century.
15. Some of his ballets are (inventive) than others.
16. Balanchine choreographed ballets to music that was (romantic) than Stravinsky's music.
17. Dancing requires (hard) work than some other professions.
18. Only the (dedicated) dancers become professionals.
19. Although ballets have music, scenery, and costumes, the (important) part is the dancing.
20. American ballet is often (energetic) than Russian ballet.

Exercise 7   **Writing Sentences to Show Comparison**

Write five sentences that make comparisons. After each sentence, write whether the comparison is in the *comparative* or *superlative* form.

SAMPLE ANSWER   The dancers needed longer rehearsals. (comparative)

12.4 Special Adjectives That Compare

Many **More** **Most**

The comparative and superlative forms of some adjectives are not formed in the regular manner.

> Harriet Tubman believed in a **good** cause.
> She knew that freedom was **better** than slavery.
> The Underground Railroad was the **best** route to freedom.

In the sentences above, *better* is the comparative form of the adjective *good*. *Best* is the superlative form of *good*.

Irregular Comparative and Superlative Forms		
Adjective	**Comparative**	**Superlative**
good	better	best
bad	worse	worst
much, many	more	most
little	less	least

Do not use *more* or *most* before irregular adjectives that are already in the comparative or superlative form.

> Tubman felt **better** at the end of the day. [not *more better*]

Adjectives

Identifying the Comparative and Superlative Forms

Identify the form of each underlined adjective as *comparative* or *superlative.* Then write the adjective from which it was formed.

1. Martin Luther King Jr. wanted a <u>better</u> life for all Americans.
2. His <u>best</u> speeches inspired people.
3. He worked hard on his <u>better</u> speeches.
4. There were <u>more</u> people in his audience near the end of his life than there had been in the beginning.
5. King paid <u>less</u> attention to his critics than to his supporters.
6. King believed that nonviolent protest was the <u>best</u> way to achieve equality for everyone.
7. Other people believed in the use of <u>more</u> force.
8. Some of the <u>worst</u> conditions in housing were in northern cities, rather than in the South.
9. Many hoped for a <u>better</u> education for their children.
10. <u>Most</u> listeners were inspired by King's "I Have a Dream" speech.

Exercise 9   **Using the Comparative and Superlative Forms**

Write the correct comparative or superlative form of the adjectives in parentheses.

1. After her husband's death, Eleanor Roosevelt did even (much) work than before.
2. Mrs. Roosevelt's newspaper column was (good) than many other newspaper columns.
3. She gave her (good) efforts to the United Nations.
4. Perhaps she did her (good) work of all in the cause of peace.
5. Which of her speeches is the (good)?
6. She had (many) projects than the previous first ladies.
7. She may have been the (good) writer of them all.
8. When Franklin was alive, Eleanor made (many) trips than he did.
9. Being affected by polio was one of the (bad) personal problems Franklin faced.
10. Eleanor worked to help people who had (little) power and influence than she had.

Grammar Review

ADJECTIVES

In the following selection, Chicago writer Studs Terkel looks at the early years of famed jazz musician Louis Armstrong. The passage has been annotated to show some of the kinds of adjectives covered in this unit.

Literature Model

from Giants of Jazz
by Studs Terkel

Kid Ory's Band was the most popular one in New Orleans. They played just about everywhere, for fancy parties as well as for rough-and-tumble get-togethers. Louis was the most sought-after jazzman. He had no days off. When the Ory group was resting, he'd be playing at some dance or funeral. Often he blew second cornet with the Papa Celestin's Tuxedo Brass Band. In later years he recalled, "I thought I was in heaven, playing with that band. They had funeral marches that would touch your heart, they were so beautiful."

One day he was approached by a red-headed band leader. It was Fate Marable, the riverboat king. Excellent jazz was being played on the excursion boats that glided up and down the Mississippi. Easily the best of these boat bands was Marable's, of the steamer *Sydney*. His repertoire was far more varied than that of any New Orleans band. His men could *read* music!

"Come on, Louis," urged Fate. "Join us and see what the rest of the country looks like." Armstrong, eager for new adventures and new learning, readily accepted.

Annotations:
- Superlative form of *popular*
- Demonstrative adjective
- Predicate adjective
- Comparative form of *varied*
- Proper adjective
- Article

Adjectives

Grammar Review

Review: Exercise 1 **Using Articles**

Write the correct article for each blank.

SAMPLE   Jazz is truly _____ American style of music.
ANSWER   an

1. While it is impossible to say when and where jazz was first played, many people call New Orleans _____ one and only "cradle of jazz."
2. Improvisation and syncopation made jazz _____ unusual form of folk music.
3. In the late nineteenth century, creative musicians combined _____ rhythms of West Africa with European harmony and American folk music.
4. Jazz historians say that before _____ turn of _____ century, this type of music was not as popular as it is today.
5. In the South, many bands played _____ new music in street parades and funeral processions.

Review: Exercise 2 **Identifying Adjectives and Proper Adjectives**

The following sentences are about jazz. Write each adjective. (Do not include articles.) Beside it, write the noun it describes. Capitalize any proper adjectives you find.

SAMPLE   Jazz is an american style of music.
ANSWER   American style

1. The rhythm section of a jazz band usually includes a piano and drums.
2. Scott Joplin was a good pianist and a noted composer of ragtime music.
3. Joplin received a special Pulitzer award in 1976.
4. The popular Gene Krupa drew attention for skill on the drums.
5. The famous drummer started a new band.
6. The mournful sound of "blues" characterized early jazz.
7. Bessie Smith was a blues singer.
8. The legendary Buddy Boldon was a new orleans musician.
9. Musicians on mississippi riverboats brought the new sound to Chicago.
10. Benny Goodman, a clarinet player, started a dance band in Chicago.

Adjectives

Grammar Review

Review: Exercise 3 Distinguishing Kinds of Adjectives

Number your paper from 1 to 5. Identify each underlined word as a *proper adjective*, a *predicate adjective*, an *article*, or a *demonstrative adjective*.

¹<u>American</u> musicians often serve as goodwill ambassadors to other countries. ²Jazz is <u>popular</u> all over the world. ³Audiences everywhere respond enthusiastically to <u>this</u> music. ⁴<u>A</u> musician may be as well known overseas as at home. ⁵Music seems to be <u>an</u> international language.

Review: Exercise 4 Using Demonstratives

Write the best demonstrative—*that, this, those,* or *these*—for each sentence.

SAMPLE   A truly unique style of music is _____ music called jazz.
ANSWER   this

1. Many people living in New Orleans have said, "_____ city is the cradle of jazz."
2. When players make up some of the music they are playing, _____ players are improvising.
3. In syncopation, _____ beats that are normally unaccented are accented.
4. Improvisation and syncopation— _____ give jazz its unusual form.
5. Louis Armstrong was one of _____ early jazz musicians who became famous throughout the United States.
6. Armstrong also traveled to many foreign countries; he was very popular with fans in _____ countries.
7. In 1955 Armstrong toured Western Europe; _____ trip was a smashing success.
8. Armstrong was the first to use scat; in _____ kind of singing, meaningless syllables replace words.
9. Many other jazz singers have copied _____ style.
10. Armstrong's great trumpet playing and his famous scratchy voice are still admired _____ days.

Adjectives

Grammar Review

Review: Exercise 5 — Identifying Comparative and Superlative Forms

Write whether each underlined adjective is in the *comparative* or *superlative* form. Then write the adjective from which it is formed.

SAMPLE Some of the <u>liveliest</u> jazz was once played on a cornet.
ANSWER superlative, lively

1. The cornet and the trumpet are very similar brass instruments, but the cornet is the <u>shorter</u> of the two.
2. Duke Ellington had some of the <u>greatest</u> musical ideas of his time.
3. Many people think Ellington's band was the <u>finest</u> band of the swing era.
4. Was Benny Goodman a <u>better</u> clarinet player than any other clarinet player of his time?
5. Bebop was perhaps the <u>best</u> jazz style developed in the decade of the 1940s.

Review: Exercise 6 — Using Adjectives That Compare

Write the correct comparative or superlative form of the adjective in parentheses.

SAMPLE Louis Armstrong received his (early) formal music instruction at a children's home in New Orleans.
ANSWER earliest

1. Being (persistent) than other teenage spectators, Armstrong borrowed clothes and went to the jazz clubs almost every evening.
2. Fate Marable's group had the (great) repertoire of any New Orleans band.
3. Was Joe "King" Oliver the (good) cornet player in Kid Ory's orchestra?
4. Many critics feel that of these two great musicians, Armstrong was the (talented).
5. Armstrong ranks high among the world's (popular) jazz musicians of all time.

Review: Exercise 7

Proofreading

The following passage discusses the art of Lois Mailou Jones, an African American artist, whose work appears below. Rewrite the passage, correcting the errors in spelling, capitalization, grammar, and usage. Add any missing punctuation. There are ten errors in all.

Lois Mailou Jones

¹This painting by Lois Mailou Jones combines images from a age of Egypts greatness with images from African American art drama, and music. ²The climbing figures are bathed in golden light and gold is used

Lois Mailou Jones, *The Ascent of Ethiopia*, 1932

(continued)

again on the pyramids and the circle that represents music. ³The entire painting consists of shades of gold, green, blue, and violet; blue is the more prominent color of all, however.

⁴The artist was born in Boston and studied at two boston art schools. ⁵Later she gone to other american cities and to Paris to learn more about painting, she has won many awards for her work.

Review: Exercise 8

Mixed Review

For each sentence write the correct choices from the words in parentheses. When you find a proper adjective that is not capitalized, write it with the correct capitalization.

1. Boogie-woogie was (a, an) popular jazz style that used eight beats to a bar instead of (a, the) usual four beats to a bar.
2. Boogie-woogie, which developed in (a, the) 1930s, was (more intense, most intense) than other jazz styles.
3. Two of the (more important, most important) boogie-woogie artists of all were Pinetop Smith and Meade Lux Lewis.
4. Cool jazz emphasized (a, an) lagging beat and (more unusual, unusualler) orchestrations.
5. A belgian guitarist and (a, an) english pianist influenced american jazz artists.
6. The newport festival, first held in 1954, and other (big, biggest) jazz festivals introduced the new music to ever (larger, largest) audiences.
7. Since the 1950s, small combos have become (more prominent, most prominent) than before.
8. Jazz musicians continue to incorporate influences from (many, most) sources; the (better, best) among them constantly try new sounds and new combinations of instruments.
9. The american jazz musicians of the modern era that are (better, best) known include guitarist George Benson, trumpeter Wynton Marsalis, and pianist Herbie Hancock.
10. Wynton Marsalis, known for his excellent tone and flawless technique, was perhaps the (better, best) new jazz musician of the 1980s.

Writing Application

TIME

For more about using adjectives, see **TIME Facing the Blank Page,** page 98.

Adjectives in Writing

Yoshika Uchida uses specific words and adjectives in this passage from *The Invisible Thread* to convey her feelings about a visit to the country. Examine the passage, focusing especially on the italicized adjectives.

> They [the stars] seemed *brighter* and *closer* than they were in Berkeley. It was as though the *entire* sky had dropped closer to earth to spread out its *full* glory right there in front of me.
>
> I listened to the *slow* clop-clop of the mules as they plodded through the fields, probably wondering why they were pulling a wagonload of people in the dark, instead of hauling boxes of grapes to the shed under the *hot, dry* sun.

Techniques with Adjectives

Try to apply some of Yoshiko Uchida's writing techniques when you write and revise your own work.

❶ Whenever possible, use specific adjectives to make your descriptions more precise.

WITHOUT ADJECTIVES under the sun

UCHIDA'S VERSION under the *hot, dry* sun

❷ Use comparisons for clarity and brevity.

WITHOUT COMPARISONS [the stars] seemed bright and close

UCHIDA'S VERSION They seemed *brighter* and *closer* than they were in Berkeley.

Practice Practice these techniques by revising the following passage, using a separate sheet of paper. Add adjectives to enhance the description. Use comparisons where appropriate.

At dusk we were one of the groups of people enjoying a picnic on the grass. We were clustered on blankets on the hill in front of the band shell. The smells of foods floated in the air around us. The dark descended as the musicians gathered on stage and tuned their instruments. They began the concert with several jazz standards. Some people in the audience stood and began to sway to the music. Soloists took turns showing their skills. Soon everyone was standing, moving, and swaying.

UNIT 13 Adverbs

Lesson 13.1   **Adverbs Modifying Verbs**   *395*

Lesson 13.2   **Adverbs Modifying Adjectives and Adverbs**   *397*

Lesson 13.3   **Adverbs That Compare**   *399*

Lesson 13.4   **Telling Adjectives and Adverbs Apart**   *401*

Lesson 13.5   **Avoiding Double Negatives**   *403*

Grammar Review   *405*

Writing Application   *413*

13.1 Adverbs Modifying Verbs

Adjectives are words that modify, or describe, nouns and pronouns. Adverbs are another type of modifier. They modify verbs, adjectives, and other adverbs.

■ An **adverb** is a word that describes a verb, an adjective, or another adverb.

In the example below, the adverb *grandly* describes the action verb *entertained*.

Thomas Jefferson entertained **grandly** at the White House.

An adverb supplies one of three types of information.

Ways Adverbs Modify Verbs	
Adverbs Tell	**Examples**
How	grandly, royally, quickly
When	rarely, later, immediately, often, usually
Where	downstairs, below, here

When modifying an adjective or another adverb, an adverb usually comes before the word. When modifying a verb, an adverb can occupy different positions in a sentence.

Positioning of Adverbs	
Position	**Examples**
Before the Verb	Guests **often** dined in the State Dining Room.
After the Verb	Guests dined **often** in the State Dining Room.
At the Beginning	**Often** guests dined in the State Dining Room.
At the End	Guests dined in the State Dining Room **often.**

Most adverbs are formed by adding *-ly* to an adjective, as in *actively, fondly,* and *quietly.* Some adverbs are exceptions, however. These include *after, often, now,* and *later.*

Exercise 1 — Identifying Adverbs

On your paper, write the adverb to complete each sentence.

1. The federal government looked _____ for an architect. (build, eager, everywhere, official)
2. A committee _____ chose James Hoban. (decide, finally, happy, enthusiastic)
3. Hoban's White House stood _____ on a large plot of land. (proud, sit, majestically, to)
4. The Adams family _____ moved into the unfinished house. (eagerly, quick, had, grand)
5. They _____ gave visitors tours of their new home. (glad, proudly, want, famous)

Exercise 2 — Identifying Adverbs

Write each sentence. Underline the adverb and draw an arrow to the word the adverb describes.

1. Thomas Jefferson lived happily in the White House.
2. Jefferson quickly sought the aid of another architect.
3. Fire nearly destroyed the mansion during the War of 1812.
4. Theodore Roosevelt had it rebuilt completely.
5. Franklin Roosevelt further expanded it.
6. Workers built a swimming pool indoors.
7. One president thoughtfully added a bowling alley.
8. Eager tourists often come to the White House.
9. They proudly tour their nation's capital.
10. Our school always sends the seventh graders on a trip to Washington, D.C.

Exercise 3 — Writing Adverbs to Complete Sentences

On your paper, write an adverb that describes the verb in each sentence.

1. Our class _____ goes to the White House when visiting Washington, D.C.
2. We _____ visit the other attractions.
3. We _____ travel by bus to our nation's capital.
4. Last year the seventh graders waited _____ in line to see Congress in session.
5. The tour guide spoke _____ to us.

13.2 Adverbs Modifying Adjectives and Adverbs

Adverbs are often used to modify adjectives and other adverbs. Notice how adverbs intensify the meaning of the adjectives in the following sentences. Most often they tell **how.**

Harry Truman used **extremely** direct language.

He became a **very** popular president.

In the first sentence, the adverb *extremely* modifies the adjective *direct*. The adverb tells how direct Truman's language was. In the second sentence, the adverb *very* modifies the adjective *popular*. The adverb tells how popular Truman was.

In the sentences below, adverbs modify other adverbs.

Truman entered politics **unusually** late in life.

He moved through the political ranks **quite** quickly.

In the first sentence above, the adverb *unusually* modifies the adverb *late. Unusually* tells how late Truman entered politics. In the second sentence, the adverb *quite* describes the adverb *quickly. Quite* tells how quickly Truman moved through the ranks.

When modifying adjectives and other adverbs, adverbs almost always come directly before the word they describe. Below is a list of some adverbs that are often used to describe adjectives and other adverbs.

ADVERBS OFTEN USED TO DESCRIBE ADJECTIVES AND OTHER ADVERBS

very	really	rather	just
too	so	nearly	somewhat
almost	partly	barely	totally
quite	extremely	unusually	hardly

Exercise 4   Identifying Adverbs

Write each sentence. Underline each adverb and draw an arrow to the word the adverb modifies. Then write whether that modified word is a *verb*, an *adjective*, or an *adverb*.

1. Truman's career as vice president was unusually brief.
2. The extremely tragic death of Franklin D. Roosevelt left the presidency in Truman's hands.
3. Truman established a new procedure almost immediately.
4. He arose quite early each morning for a walk.
5. News reporters nearly always followed him.
6. Very important events took place during Truman's term.
7. World War II finally ended.
8. It ended almost immediately after Truman became president.
9. Truman very often played the piano for guests.
10. He found music particularly soothing.
11. Truman regularly spent his evenings at home.
12. Rather serious problems were discovered in the White House.
13. The Trumans moved somewhat abruptly into Blair House.
14. They felt reasonably secure in that place.
15. They lived in Blair House for nearly four years.
16. Dwight Eisenhower was elected president next.
17. Eisenhower was greatly admired as a general during World War II.
18. His wife, Mamie, was quite popular throughout the country.
19. In the newspapers, Dwight Eisenhower was most often referred to as Ike.
20. Ike's vice president, Richard Nixon, was eventually elected president.

Exercise 5   Writing Adverbs to Modify Adjectives and Adverbs

Choose an adverb from the box to modify each word below. On your paper, write a sentence for each pair of words you form.

nearly	hardly	just	extremely	somewhat
very	unusually	too	rather	so

1. _____ ever
2. _____ enough
3. _____ quiet
4. _____ late
5. _____ popular
6. _____ hungry
7. _____ difficult
8. _____ quickly
9. _____ angrily
10. _____ finished

13.3 Adverbs That Compare

■ The **comparative** form of an adverb compares two actions or things. The **superlative** form of an adverb compares more than two actions or things.

For most adverbs of only one syllable, add *-er* to make the comparative form and *-est* to make the superlative form.

Comparing One-Syllable Adverbs	
Comparative	Ronald Reagan served **longer** as president than Jimmy Carter.
Superlative	Franklin Roosevelt served **longest** of any president.

For adverbs that end in *-ly* or that have more than one syllable, use the word *more* to form the comparative and *most* to form the superlative.

Comparing Two-Syllable Adverbs	
Comparative	Our class studied Roosevelt **more thoroughly** than Reagan.
Superlative	We studied Abraham Lincoln **most thoroughly** of all.

If an adverb already is comparative or superlative, do not add *more* or *most*. Never say, for example, *more harder* or *most hardest*.

Some adverbs do not form the comparative and superlative in the regular manner. Study the irregular forms below.

IRREGULAR COMPARATIVE FORMS

ADVERB	COMPARATIVE	SUPERLATIVE
well	better	best
badly	worse	worst
little (amount)	less	least
far (distance)	farther	farthest
far (degree)	further	furthest

Exercise 6   Using the Comparative and Superlative Forms

For each sentence, choose the correct form of the adverb in parentheses.
Write the adverb on your paper.

1. Of all Theodore Roosevelt's nieces, Eleanor Roosevelt came (close, closest) to the presidency.
2. Many liked Mrs. Roosevelt (better, best) than they had liked any of the previous first ladies.
3. Mrs. Roosevelt worked (more actively, most actively) for human rights than for any other cause.
4. She fought (harder, hardest) of all for minorities.
5. She appeared at human-rights rallies (more frequently, most frequently) than her husband.

Exercise 7   Writing Comparative and Superlative Forms

Write each sentence. Use *-er, -est, more,* or *most* to make the needed form of the adverb in parentheses. Write the adverb on your paper.

1. Of all the first ladies, Eleanor Roosevelt gave (freely) of her time.
2. She traveled (readily) than any other president's wife to distant parts of the globe.
3. She journeyed (far) in her later years than in her youth.
4. She was (sympathetic) than many other people to the plight of the poor.
5. Eleanor Roosevelt lived (long) than her husband.
6. As Franklin Roosevelt became weaker, Eleanor took on some of his duties and worked (busily) than ever.
7. She (often) attended meetings in place of the president than many people realize.
8. Mrs. Roosevelt seemed to care (deeply) of all about the problems of ordinary people.
9. Eleanor Roosevelt was even (widely) recognized for her work with the United Nations than she had been for her devotion to duty as first lady.
10. Her humanitarian reputation surely will extend years (long) than her life.

13.4 Telling Adjectives and Adverbs Apart

It can be hard to tell whether a word in a sentence is an adjective or an adverb. Look carefully at how the word is used.

Martha Washington was **happy** at Mount Vernon.

Martha Washington lived **happily** at Mount Vernon.

In the first sentence, *happy* is a predicate adjective. It follows the linking verb *was* and modifies the subject. In the second sentence, *happily* is an adverb. It modifies the action verb *lived*.

People sometimes confuse the words *bad, badly, good,* and *well. Bad* and *good* are both adjectives. They are used after linking verbs. *Badly* and *well* are adverbs. They are used after action verbs. *Well* can also be used after linking verbs to describe a person's health or appearance. At these times, *well* is an adjective—for example, *He looks well.*

DISTINGUISHING ADJECTIVES FROM ADVERBS

ADJECTIVE	ADVERB
The sound is **bad.**	The actor sang **badly.**
The band sounds **good.**	The band played **well.**

Three pairs of modifiers often confuse people: *real, really; sure, surely;* and *most, almost. Real* and *sure* are adjectives. *Really, surely,* and *almost* are adverbs. *Most* can be an adjective or an adverb.

DISTINGUISHING ADJECTIVES FROM ADVERBS

ADJECTIVE	ADVERB
Music is a **real** art.	Music is **really** popular.
A pianist needs **sure** hands.	Piano music is **surely** popular.
Most pianos have eighty-eight keys.	Piano strings **almost** never break.

Adverbs

Exercise 8   Telling Adjectives and Adverbs Apart

On your paper, write each sentence, using the correct adjective or adverb.

1. Martha Washington lived (courageous, courageously).
2. She managed the position of first lady (good, well).
3. She supported her husband (active, actively).
4. President Washington must have felt (good, well) about his wife's support.
5. (Sure, Surely) he was appreciative.
6. Martha Washington was known as a (real, really) gracious hostess.
7. During the war, Mrs. Washington had (able, ably) organized a sewing circle.
8. The group was (quick, quickly) in mending clothes for the troops.
9. In those days, it was important to be able to sew (good, well).
10. If a woman sewed (bad, badly), she would rip her work out.
11. People (most, almost) always took notice of Mrs. Washington's common sense and charm.
12. It is also said that she was (real, really) beautiful.
13. She and her husband lived (good, well).
14. Their life together at Mount Vernon remained (cheerful, cheerfully).
15. Martha Washington had been married (previous, previously) to Daniel Parke Custis.
16. After his death, she became (popular, popularly) known as one of the richest widows in Virginia.
17. When she married George Washington, she added (substantial, substantially) to his property.
18. Martha was known as an (amiable, amiably) hostess at the many formal dinners Washington held as president.
19. She outlived her husband by a (short, shortly) time.
20. Two years after his death, Martha died (peaceful, peacefully) at Mount Vernon.

Exercise 9   Identifying and Using Adjectives and Adverbs

On your paper, identify each word as an *adjective* or an *adverb*. Then write a sentence using the word correctly.

1. good
2. really
3. sure
4. almost
5. real
6. surely
7. well
8. badly
9. bad
10. most

13.5 | Avoiding Double Negatives

The adverb *not* is a **negative word,** expressing the idea of "no" in a sentence. The word *not* often appears in its shortened form, the contraction *-n't*.

CONTRACTIONS WITH *NOT*

is not = isn't	cannot = can't	have not = haven't
was not = wasn't	could not = couldn't	had not = hadn't
were not = weren't	do not = don't	would not = wouldn't
will not = won't	did not = didn't	should not = shouldn't

Other words besides *not* may be used to express the negative. Each negative word has several opposites, or affirmative words, that show the idea of "yes." Study the following list of negative and affirmative words.

NEGATIVE AND AFFIRMATIVE WORDS

NEGATIVE	AFFIRMATIVE
never	ever, always
nobody	anybody, somebody
none	one, all, some, any
no one	everyone, someone
nothing	something, anything
nowhere	somewhere, anywhere

People sometimes mistakenly use two negative words together, as in the sentence *Lincoln hadn't never gone to college.* Avoid using a **double negative** such as this. You need only one negative word to express a negative idea.

You can correct a double negative by removing one of the negative words or by replacing it with an affirmative word, as in the following sentences.

Lincoln had **never** gone to college.

Lincoln had **not ever** gone to college.

Exercise 10   Expressing Negative Ideas

On your paper, write each sentence so that it correctly expresses a negative idea.

1. Lincoln didn't (never, ever) have a speech writer.
2. Nothing (didn't make, made) him bitter during the war.
3. Lincoln wasn't dishonest with (no one, anyone).
4. The president didn't (never, ever) become discouraged.
5. A strong leader, Lincoln wasn't afraid of (nobody, anyone).
6. Honest Abe didn't (never, ever) try to trick the public.
7. He tried not to show favoritism to (anybody, nobody).
8. Nothing (meant, didn't mean) more to Lincoln than justice.
9. Nobody (ever, never) cared more about saving the Union than Lincoln.
10. There wasn't (nobody, anybody) more loyal to the cause of the Civil War.
11. I can't find Carl Sandburg's biography of Lincoln (nowhere, anywhere).
12. Some feared the country wouldn't (ever, never) get over the shock of Lincoln's death.
13. You can't tell me (nothing, anything) about Lincoln that I don't know.
14. I never met (nobody, anybody) who found Lincoln's life uninteresting.
15. Some people might think he didn't (never, ever) make a mistake.
16. A humble man, Lincoln wouldn't (ever, never) believe he was perfect.
17. You couldn't find a more concerned president (nowhere, anywhere).
18. The local libary hasn't got (any, no) books about Lincoln's children.
19. As a volunteer in the Black Hawk War, Lincoln didn't see (any, no) fighting.
20. There aren't (no, any) other presidents that were born in Kentucky.

Exercise 11   Writing Sentences to Express Negative Ideas

On your paper, write five sentences to express negative ideas. In each sentence, use the word from Column A and one of the words from Column B.

Column A	Column B
1. couldn't	ever, never
2. has	anything, nothing
3. doesn't	any, no
4. can	anywhere, nowhere
5. nothing	anybody, nobody

ADVERBS

The action in Irene Hunt's *Across Five Aprils* takes place during the Civil War, which began in April 1861 and ended in April 1865. The following excerpt from the book focuses on a letter sent by a character named Shadrach Yale to a younger boy named Jethro. The passage has been annotated to show some of the adverb uses covered in this unit.

Literature Model

from Across Five Aprils

by Irene Hunt

Shadrach wrote that he and Jenny had seen the President and General Grant as they drove through the Washington streets *together*.

"... *The President's face is* deeply *lined, and his cheeks are gaunt. I have seen* so *many soldiers whose cheeks have had that sunken look, even though they were young faces. ... The President looks at least twenty years older than the pictures you and I used to study together in the early days of the war. But his face was full of light as the crowds cheered; I think he knew they were cheering Grant and that pleased him, for I'd guess that he, too, wanted to cheer the little man who sat beside him.*

Grant does **not** *have the appearance of a great general; he looks awkward, ill at ease, and carelessly dressed. But we have had enough of charm and polish; this commander who doesn't even walk like a military man is the one who will, I believe, restore the Union.*"

> Adverb modifying the verb *drove*

> Adverb modifying the adjective *lined*

> Adverb modifying the adjective *many*

> Negative adverb modifying the verb *does have*

Adverbs

Grammar Review

Review: Exercise 1 Writing Adverbs to Modify Verbs

On your paper, write an adverb to complete each sentence correctly.

SAMPLE Students _____ read *Across Five Aprils* in sixth grade.
ANSWER sometimes

1. Librarians _____ order new copies of *Across Five Aprils* because of the book's popularity.
2. _____ our teacher assigns a group book report to the class.
3. My friends and I _____ volunteered to write about *Across Five Aprils*.
4. I thought I left my copy of *Across Five Aprils* _____.
5. Irene Hunt was _____ honored when she received the Newbery Award for her book.

Review: Exercise 2 Identifying Adverbs That Modify Verbs

On your paper, identify the adverb in each sentence and write whether it tells *how, when,* or *where.*

SAMPLE I read the book quickly.
ANSWER quickly—how

1. Soon Shadrach would write to his friend Jethro.
2. He proudly described his experience.
3. War can age a president rapidly.
4. Shadrach saw President Lincoln there.
5. Grant was often criticized.
6. Sometimes Grant felt uncomfortable around people.
7. Lincoln privately admired Grant.
8. Lincoln sat outside with Grant.
9. They drove together through Washington, D.C.
10. Shadrach firmly believed in Grant's ability as a leader.

Review: Exercise 3   Identifying Adverbs and the Words They Modify

On your paper, write each sentence. Underline each adverb. Then write the word that the adverb describes and write whether the word is a *verb, adjective,* or *adverb.* (Some sentences have more than one adverb.)

SAMPLE   President Lincoln and General Grant rode through the streets together.

ANSWER   President Lincoln and General Grant rode through the streets <u>together</u>. (rode—verb)

1. Jethro read the letter, and he placed it carefully in a big envelope.
2. Shadrach wrote thoughtfully; he described events in Washington.
3. The large crowd cheered loudly for the popular General Grant.
4. Lincoln was very pleased that the crowd reacted enthusiastically.
5. Union troops fought extremely well under General Grant.
6. Eventually Grant would be elected president.
7. He triumphed quite easily over his Democratic opponent.
8. Grant carefully organized his presidency as he had organized the army.
9. Grant was unanimously renominated by his party to run for a second term as president.
10. Scandals were quite widespread during his second term.

Review: Exercise 4   Writing Adverbs in Sentences

On your paper write each sentence, replacing the blank with an adverb that describes the underlined word.

SAMPLE   Being a large-boned man, Lincoln was _____ <u>suited</u> for hard work.

ANSWER   Being a large-boned man, Lincoln was **quite** suited for hard work.

1. As a boy, Lincoln was a _____ <u>gifted</u> speaker.
2. He worked _____ <u>hard</u> as a clerk in a store.
3. In 1832 Lincoln _____ <u>bought</u> a grocery store with a partner.
4. _____ the grocery store <u>failed</u>.
5. Even though his partner died, Lincoln _____ <u>paid off</u> the debts from the store.

Adverbs

Grammar Review

Review: Exercise 5   **Using the Comparative and Superlative Forms**

On your paper, rewrite each sentence, using the correct comparative or superlative form in parentheses.

SAMPLE   The troops fought (harder, more harder) under General Grant.
ANSWER   The troops fought harder under General Grant.

1. The crowd applauded (more loudly, loudlier) than they had for any other Union general.
2. The North fared (worse, worst) than the South until Grant took command.
3. Grant drove his armies (farther, farthest) into the South than they had gone before.
4. Grant commanded (better, best) than the other Union generals.
5. Crops in the North suffered (less, lesser) from the war than crops in the South did.
6. The divisions caused by the war lasted far (longer, more longer) than anyone expected.
7. Grant was (more careless, more carelessly) dressed than Shadrach had expected.
8. President Lincoln's face was (more deeper, more deeply) lined than it had been in the days before the war.
9. Of all his generals, Lincoln admired Grant (more, most).
10. The Civil War lasted years (longer, longest) than people had thought it would.

Review: Exercise 6   **Using Comparative and Superlative Adverbs**

On your paper, write each sentence, using the comparative or superlative adverb form of the word in parentheses.

1. Which is the (frequently) visited building in the city?
2. Who entertained (grandly), Dolley Madison or Elizabeth Monroe?
3. Of the two, who guarded her privacy (carefully)?
4. Of all the presidents, who enjoyed the White House the (little)?
5. Who lived there (long) of all?

Review: Exercise 7 **Telling Adjectives and Adverbs Apart**

On your paper, write the correct word from parentheses. Then write whether the word is an *adverb* or *adjective*.

1. Dolley Madison gave (lavish, lavishly) parties.
2. She entertained (good, well).
3. She (proud, proudly) wore rich silks.
4. She was (great, greatly) admired.
5. Her parties were (most, almost) always a success.
6. From 1801 to 1817, Dolley was an (elegant, elegantly) Washington hostess.
7. While the White House was being rebuilt, she lived with President Madison in a (private, privately) mansion.
8. Wherever she lived, Dolley entertained (extravagant, extravagantly).
9. She (real, really) enjoyed her role as hostess.
10. After her husband's death, Dolley (surprising, surprisingly) returned to live in Washington.

Review: Exercise 8 **Using Adverbs and Adjectives Correctly**

On your paper, write the following paragraph. Choose an adjective or adverb from the list below to go in each blank. Write *adjective* or *adverb* to identify each word you add.

difficult	good	least	best
very	less	better	easily
easy	quite	great	eventually

Elizabeth Blackwell had a(n) ¹_____ desire for a medical education. Her goal was not a(n) ²_____ one. She faced a(n) ³_____ struggle to become a doctor. Blackwell began by writing letters to doctors all over the country. ⁴_____ few answered her. Most people thought it was ⁵_____ foolish for a woman to think of becoming a doctor, but Blackwell was not ⁶_____ discouraged. She wrote to the ⁷_____ medical schools in the country, hoping they would admit her. She then wrote to schools that were ⁸_____ famous than the others. She was accepted by one school in Geneva, New York, and ⁹_____ became the first American woman to receive a medical degree. Elizabeth Blackwell's example remains a ¹⁰_____ model for young women today.

Adverbs

Grammar Review

Review: Exercise 9 Avoiding Double Negatives

On your paper, complete each sentence so that it correctly expresses a negative idea.

1. No one (ever, never) forgets our twenty-sixth president.
2. I can't find (anyone, no one) else in history like Theodore Roosevelt.
3. I didn't know (nothing, anything) about him until recently.
4. I wasn't (ever, never) expecting to be so impressed.
5. I didn't expect to find (any, no) books about Teddy Roosevelt at the library.
6. I couldn't have learned more about him (anywhere, nowhere) else.
7. You might think there isn't (nobody, anybody) else as interested in him as I am.
8. There wasn't (no, any) other president who worked harder.
9. It seemed he didn't do (anything, nothing) else.
10. There isn't (anyone, no one) I admire more.

Review: Exercise 10 Expressing Negative Ideas

On your paper, rewrite each sentence to express a negative idea correctly. (There is more than one correct way to write most sentences.)

SAMPLE   The Browns didn't never expect to visit Washington, D.C.
ANSWER   The Browns didn't ever expect to visit Washington, D.C.

1. The Browns weren't never planning to go to the capital.
2. Margie Brown had never met no one who had been there.
3. They hadn't gone nowhere near Washington before last summer.
4. Little Billy hadn't known nothing about the surprise trip.
5. The family hadn't never seen nothing as impressive as the White House.
6. Nobody in their family had never seen the Cherry Blossom Festival.
7. They couldn't never have imagined the beauty of the mall in springtime.
8. They hadn't never before visited the Senate Office Building.
9. Never before hadn't they imagined the thrill of the Air and Space Museum.
10. They concluded that no one shouldn't turn down an opportunity to visit the nation's capital.

Review: Exercise 11

Proofreading

The following passage is about American artist Roger Brown, whose painting *Lost America* appears below. Rewrite the passage, correcting the errors in spelling, capitalization, grammar, and usage. Add any missing punctuation. There are ten errors.

Roger Brown

¹Born in 1941, Roger Brown a painter who lives in Chicago. ²His works, such as *Lost America,* have sure made him influential in the art world. ³Brown has develop a highly individualized style over the past

Roger Brown, *Lost America*, 1989

(continued)

Adverbs

twenty years. ⁴*Lost America* clear exhibits many of the characteristics of his work.

⁵The painting is immediate recognizable as a portrait of Abraham Lincoln. ⁶It's not nothing as simple as that. ⁷Lincoln is silouetted agenst a sky full of threatening clouds lined up in tightly packed rows. ⁸At the bottom of the painting is vegetation that resembles the kind of fence that soldiers' erect in battle.

⁹Except for the dark purple of his face, the figure of Lincoln is entire in black and white. ¹⁰Lincoln appears real gloomy and thoughtful; perhaps, as the title *Lost America* suggests, he is thinking about the war and the possible division of the United States into two separate countries."

Review: Exercise 12

Mixed Review

Rewrite each sentence, replacing the underlined word with an adverb that makes sense. Underline your adverb.

SAMPLE   An eccentric *usual* behaves in an unexpected way.
ANSWER   An eccentric *usually* behaves in an unexpected way.

1. Claiming to be emperor of the United States would <u>certain</u> be considered eccentric behavior.
2. In the middle of the nineteenth century, Joshua Norton <u>actual</u> claimed to be Norton I, Emperor of the United States.
3. The people of San Francisco <u>willing</u> accepted his claim.
4. Emperor Norton took his job quite <u>serious</u>.
5. The best clothing store in the entire city made clothing <u>special</u> for him.
6. Their "emperor" was <u>real</u> loved by the people of San Francisco.
7. The people of San Francisco haven't <u>never</u> forgotten Norton.
8. Perhaps Norton's ideas were inspired <u>part</u> by Napoleon.
9. Napoleon conquered <u>most</u> all of Europe.
10. Norton <u>sure</u> would have heard about Napoleon.

Writing Application

TIME

For more about usage rules, see **TIME Facing the Blank Page,** page 98.

Adverbs in Writing

In this excerpt from Betsy Byars's novel *Coast to Coast*, 13-year-old Birch tries to convince her grandfather to take her up in his 1940 airplane. As you read, pay special attention to the underlined words.

"I <u>really</u> want to go!" As she said it, she realized it was true. She needed to get <u>away</u> from this world, and this was the way to do it. "What are we waiting for?"

"I don't guess it would hurt to fly to the beach and back."

"Then get <u>in</u>! Let's go!"

"Don't get in <u>too</u> big a hurry." Her grandfather smiled. It was his first real smile of the afternoon.

Birch followed him around the plane. "What are you doing?"

"Well, <u>right now</u>, I'm doing a preflight inspection. I check the tires, the control surfaces, move them for freedom and cable looseness."

Examine the passage, focusing on the underlined words.

Techniques with Adverbs

Try to apply some of Betsy Byars's writing techniques when you write and revise your own work.

❶ To make your writing more vivid, add adverbs to tell exactly when the action is occurring. Compare the following:

GENERAL WORDS Well, I'm doing a preflight inspection.

BYARS'S VERSION Well, *right now* I'm doing a preflight inspection.

❷ Use adverbs to reinforce the mood and tone of your writing.

UNSPECIFIED TONE I want to go.

BYARS'S VERSION I *really* want to go.

Practice Practice these techniques by revising the following passage on a separate sheet of paper. Remember that adverbs can modify verbs, adjectives, and other adverbs.

Many people read Betsy Byars's books. She is one of the popular young adult authors of our time. In her book *Coast to Coast,* Ms. Byars's love of flying comes across to her readers. Thirteen-year-old Birch does not want her grandfather to sell his plane. She is sure the plane can keep him young at heart. Birch talks her grandfather into letting her get into the plane. He shows her how to operate it. He gets into the plane with her. Will Birch and her grandfather fly the old airplane? You'll have to read this exciting book to find out.

Adverbs

UNIT
14

Prepositions, Conjunctions, and Interjections

Lesson 14.1	**Prepositions**	415
Lesson 14.2	**Prepositional Phrases**	417
Lesson 14.3	**Pronouns After Prepositions**	419
Lesson 14.4	**Prepositional Phrases as Adjectives and Adverbs**	421
Lesson 14.5	**Telling Prepositions and Adverbs Apart**	423
Lesson 14.6	**Conjunctions**	425
Lesson 14.7	**Interjections**	427
Grammar Review		429
Writing Application		437

■ A **preposition** is a word that relates a noun or a pronoun to some other word in a sentence.

The dictionary **on** the desk was open.

An almanac was **under** the dictionary.

Meet me **at** three o'clock tomorrow.

COMMONLY USED PREPOSITIONS

aboard	as	despite	near	since
about	at	down	of	through
above	before	during	off	to
across	behind	except	on	toward
after	below	for	onto	under
against	beneath	from	opposite	until
along	beside	in	out	up
amid	between	inside	outside	upon
among	beyond	into	over	with
around	by	like	past	without

A preposition can consist of more than one word.

I borrowed the almanac **along with** some other reference books.

PREPOSITIONS OF MORE THAN ONE WORD

according to	along with	because of	in spite of	on top of
across from	aside from	in front of	instead of	out of

Read each sentence below. Any word that fits in the blank is a preposition.

Use the almanac that is _____ the table.

I took the atlas _____ your room.

Exercise 1   Identifying Prepositions

Write each preposition from the following sentences.

1. Many famous libraries around the world are tourist attractions.
2. The New York Public Library on Fifth Avenue serves the New York metropolitan community.
3. Two marble lions in front of the library greet visitors.
4. The library houses a large number of books on a vast range of topics.
5. The library also holds several exhibitions during the year.
6. Its branches hold millions of volumes.
7. The New York Public Library is one of the largest library systems in the world.
8. The first public library in America was built in the year 1833.
9. Many important library developments occurred during the nineteenth century.
10. Melvil Dewey established a system for the classification of books.

Exercise 2   Identifying Prepositions of More Than One Word

Write the preposition or prepositions from each sentence. Circle each preposition of more than one word.

1. The classification number of a library book is found upon the spine of the book, usually below the title.
2. Along with the Dewey Decimal Classification system, Melvil Dewey also established the American Library Association and the *Library Journal.*
3. The Dewey system organizes books into ten main categories.
4. The research library in front of the administration building uses a different system of classifying books.
5. The Library of Congress classification system categorizes books into twenty-one major areas of knowledge.
6. This system was developed in the early twentieth century because of the large number of books in this library.
7. Aside from being one of the largest research libraries in the world, the Library of Congress has the largest collection of books printed before 1501.
8. Among the books in its collection is a perfect copy of the Gutenberg Bible.
9. According to the guide, the library provides reference assistance along with research for the United States Congress.
10. On the back of a book's title page, you will find cataloging data.

14.2 Prepositional Phrases

■ A prepositional phrase is a group of words that begins with a preposition and ends with a noun or pronoun, which is called the object of the preposition.

> Dr. Chin has an almanac **from the nineteenth century.**
> The almanac has a special meaning **for him.**

A preposition can have a compound object.

> Almanacs contain lists **of facts and figures.**
> Grace showed one **to her sisters and her classmates.**

A sentence can have more than one prepositional phrase.

> We left our notes **under the almanac on the shelf.**

A prepositional phrase can appear anywhere in a sentence—at the beginning, in the middle, or at the end.

> **At the library** students examined the almanac.
> Students **at the library** examined the almanac.
> Students examined the almanac **at the library.**

Sometimes you can use a prepositional phrase to combine sentences.

> Gary wrote a newspaper article.
> He wrote about old almanacs.
> Gary wrote a newspaper article **about old almanacs.**

In the second sentence above, the prepositional phrase *about old almanacs* tells more about the newspaper article. You can combine the sentences by adding the phrase to the first sentence.

Write each prepositional phrase. Underline each object of the preposition. Some sentences have more than one prepositional phrase.

1. Calendars are often included in almanacs.
2. Many almanacs predict the weather through a certain year and give information on population.
3. Some newspapers and organizations publish almanacs with special information.
4. *Poor Richard's Almanac* is a well-known almanac from the American colonial period.
5. Benjamin Franklin published the book in 1733.
6. It is filled with facts and lists of various sorts.
7. Many other kinds of reference books are found in the library.
8. The library is open from nine o'clock in the morning to nine o'clock at night.
9. Encyclopedias are located in the reference section of most school and public libraries.
10. International cookbooks contain information about foods from various countries.
11. The pages of a dictionary list many different kinds of words.
12. Almanacs are useful for the study of many kinds of information.
13. An atlas can help you learn about the location of all the countries in the world.
14. In most libraries the reference material cannot be taken out of the building.
15. Many libraries today have collections of phonograph records, CDs, and videotapes.
16. Many large cities have branch libraries in various neighborhoods.
17. School libraries and public libraries are funded by taxes and contributions.
18. Because of the rising cost of material and equipment, library budgets have been under pressure.
19. One-third of the public libraries in the United States are branch libraries.
20. A library should have a good collection of reference materials, current magazines, and technical reports.

14.3 Pronouns After Prepositions

When a pronoun is the object of a preposition, remember to use an object pronoun and not a subject pronoun.

> Yoshi handed the dictionary to Akilah.
> Yoshi handed the dictionary to **her.**

In the example above, the object pronoun *her* replaces *Akilah* as the object of the preposition *to*.

Sometimes a preposition will have a compound object consisting of a noun and pronoun. Remember to use an object pronoun in a compound object.

> I borrowed the almanac from Jorge and Lisa.
> I borrowed the almanac from Jorge and **her.**

An object pronoun is used in the sentence above. *Jorge and her* is the compound object of the preposition *from*.

If you are unsure about whether to use a subject pronoun or an object pronoun, try saying the sentence aloud with only the pronoun following the preposition.

The pronouns *who* and *whom* are often confused. *Who* is a subject pronoun, and *whom* is an object pronoun. Note how the pronouns are used in the following sentences.

> **Who** told you about it?
> To **whom** did you lend the almanac?

Exercise 4   Choosing Pronouns After Prepositions

For each sentence, write the correct pronoun.

1. Jorge and Lisa told you about (who, whom)?
2. Vanessa spoke to Lisa and (he, him) at the game.
3. What did Vanessa show to (them, they)?
4. Mr. Valdes bumped into Vanessa and (she, her) in the corridor.
5. Lisa had still not given her homework assignment to (him, he).
6. He walked with Lisa and (her, she) to the door.
7. Who knows what he said to (they, them)?
8. After class they had lunch with Jorge and (he, him).
9. Lisa is going to the library with (he, him).
10. She picked a topic that would interest both of (they, them).

Exercise 5   Using Pronouns After Prepositions

In each item, a proper noun is underlined. Replace the proper noun with the correct object pronoun.

1. Mr. Valdes handed an almanac to <u>Alice</u>.
2. Alice learned about Ukraine from <u>Mr. Valdes</u>.
3. Ukraine had been one of <u>the Soviet republics</u>.
4. Alice wanted information for <u>Uncle Oscar</u>.
5. Uncle Oscar often speaks of <u>Greta</u>, his sister.
6. Greta lives with <u>Victor</u>, her husband.
7. Alice mailed a package to <u>Greta</u>.
8. Faraway places are exciting to <u>Alice</u>.
9. Alice wants to learn much more about <u>Greta</u>.
10. She plans a visit to <u>Greta</u> and <u>Victor</u> next year.

Exercise 6   Writing Sentences with Prepositions and Object Pronouns

Write a sentence for each item. Use the pronouns listed as objects of a preposition. Underline the preposition and its object pronoun.

SAMPLE   them

ANSWER   We wrote a letter <u>to them</u>.

1. me
2. her
3. her and him
4. them
5. him

Prepositional Phrases as Adjectives and Adverbs

Prepositional phrases function as adjectives and adverbs in sentences.

■ A prepositional phrase functioning as an **adjective** describes a noun or a pronoun.

These phrases can describe subjects, direct and indirect objects, predicate nouns, or objects in other prepositional phrases. An adjective phrase usually comes directly after the noun or pronoun it describes.

Africa is a continent **with many natural resources.**

One **of the articles** describes Africa vividly.

The wildlife **of Africa** is varied and abundant.

■ A prepositional phrase functioning as an **adverb** describes a verb, an adjective, or another adverb.

Adverb Phrases	
Function	**Examples**
Describes a Verb	Wildlife abounds **in Africa.** Dry savannas extend **over many acres.**
Describes an Adjective	Birds are exotic **in color.**
Describes an Adverb	The Nile River flows west **of Cairo.**

Exercise 7 Identifying Adjective and Adverb Phrases

Write each prepositional phrase and whether it is used as an *adjective* or an *adverb*.

1. The Congo Basin lies on the equator.
2. The grass grows quickly near the rain forests.
3. The Red Sea borders Africa on the northeast.
4. What is the climate of Cairo?
5. There is little vegetation in the Sahara.
6. I read a brief article about new African nations.
7. The people of Somalia are suffering a great deal of hardship.
8. Burkina Faso is a small country that lies between Mali and Ghana.
9. The waters of the Atlantic Ocean wash the shores of the Ivory Coast.
10. Southern African nations have recently emerged from years of conflict.
11. Much of this kind of information can be found in an atlas.
12. Bill gave an atlas to Cheryl for her birthday.
13. Cheryl left it beside the globe.
14. An atlas tells about geography.
15. Facts and figures are shown on maps and in tables.
16. An index is an important part of an atlas.
17. It is the guide to the riches of an atlas.
18. Information in an atlas is useful for research.
19. Several governments publish national atlases about their countries.
20. Early atlases had maps that were hand-drawn by cartographers.

Exercise 8 Writing Adjective and Adverb Phrases

On your paper, expand each sentence below by adding at least one adjective or adverb phrase to the sentence. Draw a line from each phrase to the word it describes.

1. An atlas gives information.
2. The birds are colorful.
3. The zebras gather.
4. The monkeys are calling.
5. The lion dozes.
6. The climate is humid.
7. The desert seems endless.
8. The plants bloom.
9. A traveler needs water.
10. The sunset glows.

14.5 Telling Prepositions and Adverbs Apart

Sometimes it is difficult to tell whether a word is a preposition or an adverb. Both types of words can answer the questions *where?* and *when?* In addition, some words can be used as either prepositions or adverbs.

We ate our lunch **outside.**

We ate our lunch **outside** the **library.**

WORDS THAT CAN BE USED AS PREPOSITIONS OR ADVERBS

about	below	out
above	down	outside
around	in	over
before	inside	through
behind	near	up

If you're having trouble deciding whether a word is used as a preposition or as an adverb, look at the other words in the sentence. If the word is followed closely by a noun, the word is probably a preposition, and the noun is the object of the preposition.

> We ate our lunch **outside** the **library.**

In the sentence above, the word *outside* is followed closely by the noun *library. Outside* is a preposition, and *library* is the object of the preposition.

If the word is not followed closely by a noun, then the word is probably an adverb.

> We ate our lunch **outside.**

In this sentence, the word *outside* answers the question *where?* but is not followed by a noun. In this sentence, *outside* is an adverb.

Prepositions, Conjunctions, and Interjections

14.5 Telling Prepositions and Adverbs Apart **423**

Exercise 9   Distinguishing Between Adverbs and Prepositions

Write whether each underlined word is used as a *preposition* or as an *adverb*.

1. Who left this book of quotations <u>behind</u>?
2. Gene found the book <u>behind</u> the lockers.
3. We searched <u>through</u> the biographical dictionary.
4. I had read the same article <u>before</u>.
5. I will report on the article <u>before</u> Friday.
6. Please look <u>inside</u> the almanac.
7. Jeff will bring the encyclopedia <u>inside</u>.
8. Kim pointed to the important notes <u>below</u>.
9. My note cards lie <u>below</u> the top shelf.
10. Did you read the article <u>about</u> Gandhi?
11. It was <u>about</u> his early life.
12. <u>Outside</u> class I shall have a chance to read the article <u>carefully</u>.
13. I can think my impressions <u>over</u> while taking a walk <u>outside</u>.
14. I enjoy a walk <u>in</u> the park.
15. Kim carried the atlas <u>around</u>.
16. She walked hastily <u>around</u> the library.
17. Lee carried his article <u>up</u> the stairs but came <u>down</u> without it.
18. Bob's dictionary was found <u>near</u> his desk.
19. Kim reads <u>down</u> the pages of the almanac.
20. Her conversation goes <u>over</u> my head.
21. A map of the United States hangs <u>near</u> the front door.
22. A portrait of the president hangs <u>above</u>.
23. Mr. Cleese brought <u>in</u> an overdue video about India.
24. Did I leave my card <u>in</u> that book?
25. The librarians searched <u>around</u> for my card.

Exercise 10   Using Words as Prepositions or Adverbs

Write each word below in a sentence. If you use the word as a preposition, underline the prepositional phrase.

1. above	6. out	
2. in	7. through	
3. around	8. before	
4. near	9. over	
5. up	10. down	

14.6 Conjunctions

■ A **conjunction** is a word that joins words or groups of words in a sentence.

The most common conjunctions are *and, but,* and *or.* They are called **coordinating conjunctions**. *And* and *or* are used to form compound subjects. *And, but,* and *or* are used to form compound predicates and compound sentences.

Using Conjunctions to Form Compounds	
Compound Subject	Mexico **and** Canada are both on a map of North America.
Compound Predicate	Students can check the map **or** use the globe.
Compound Sentence	I would lend you my atlas, **but** Felicia already borrowed it.

A comma should be placed before the conjunction in a compound sentence. Do not, however, place a comma between the two parts of a compound subject or a compound predicate.

Although the conjunctions are used in a similar fashion, they are not interchangeable. Each has a different meaning.

Coordinating Conjunctions		
Conjunction	Meaning	Example
And	Introduces an additional idea	The map **and** the globe are in the classroom.
But	Introduces a contrasting idea	The map is old, **but** the globe is new.
Or	Introduces a choice or second possibility	Students check the map **or** use the globe.

Pairs of conjunctions such as *either, or; neither, nor;* and *both, and* are called **correlative conjunctions**. They join the same kinds of words as do the conjunctions *and, but,* and *or.*

Either Lucy **or** I will use the atlas.

Exercise 11   Identifying Conjunctions and Compounds

Write each conjunction. Then write whether it forms a *compound subject,* *compound predicate,* or *compound sentence.*

1. Ramón and Sal are using the class atlas.
2. They are studying rivers and comparing figures.
3. The Mississippi River flows southward and increases in width along the way.
4. The Amazon is long, but it is not the longest river.
5. Who has studied or visited mountains in Europe?
6. The Chaco and the Serengeti are vast plains.
7. Sal has been to Argentina, or he is planning to go there.
8. Either the Himalayas or the Urals are the world's highest mountains.
9. Bolivia contains some of the highest mountains in South America but also has some very hot, humid lowlands.
10. Denver is called the mile-high city, but Leadville is at an even higher altitude.

Exercise 12   Using Conjunctions

Write the conjunctions that best fit in the sentences.

1. Judy wrote a report _____ drew a map of the Himalayas.
2. Tibet _____ Nepal lie north of India.
3. Is the Upper Nile in north _____ south Egypt?
4. Australia _____ New Zealand is easy to reach from North America.
5. Is Mount Everest in Asia, _____ is it in Europe?
6. I have a map of India, _____ I do not have one of Japan.
7. _____ Tokyo _____ Hiroshima are in Japan.
8. Her ambition was to climb the highest mountain on each continent, _____ she planned to start with Mt. McKinley in Alaska.
9. Mt. Everest is the highest at 29,028 feet, _____ two other Himalayan peaks are more than 28,000 feet high.
10. _____ Mt. Fuji in Japan _____ Mt. Etna in Italy is nearly as high.

14.7   Interjections

© Watterson. 1987 Universal Press S.

■ An **interjection** is a word or group of words that expresses strong feeling.

COMMON INTERJECTIONS

aha	great	oh	phew
alas	ha	oh, no	well
eek	hey	oops	wow
goodness	hooray	ouch	yes

An interjection that expresses a very strong feeling may stand alone, either before or after a sentence. Such interjections are followed by an exclamation mark.

Oh, no! I wrote *horse* instead of *hoarse*.

When an interjection expresses a milder feeling, it appears as part of the sentence. In that case, it is separated from the rest of the sentence by a comma.

Oh, I thought I knew the definition of that word.

Use interjections sparingly. Overuse ruins the effect.

Write each interjection. Include any punctuation mark that goes with it.

1. Phew, this dictionary is heavy.
2. Jack will carry it for me. Hooray!
3. Great! I made no mistakes on my spelling test.
4. Oh, no! I forgot the double *b* in *hobble.*
5. Oops, I think I forgot to sign my name.
6. Hey! Studying the English language is fun!
7. Simon has the answer to our problem. Aha!
8. Well, I would like to know more about Old English.
9. Ouch! Spelling rules can be complicated.
10. I am going to the state spelling bee. Yes!
11. Mr. Robinson just showed me the unabridged dictionary. Awesome!
12. Oh, no! Do I need that to prepare for the spelling bee?
13. So this is Middle English. Well!
14. Ha! I recognize a few words.
15. Oh, I didn't hear you, Mr. Lyons.
16. Oops, I lost my English book.
17. Mr. Lyons found it on the floor. Great!
18. Aha! I dropped it in the reference room.
19. Mr. Lyons, you saved the day. Phew!
20. Ouch! It's time to get back to that dictionary.
21. Hey, spellers! Watch out for me.
22. Oh, no! I think I spelled *accommodate* with one *m* and two *d*'s.
23. Hey, do you know how to spell *embarrass*?
24. Well, if *alto* is from an Italian word meaning "high," why does it refer to low female singing voices?
25. I had no idea so many common expressions were originally written by Shakespeare. Wow!

Exercise 14 Writing Sentences with Interjections

Write ten sentences, using a different interjection in each. Take care to punctuate each sentence correctly.

Grammar Review

PREPOSITIONS, CONJUNCTIONS, AND INTERJECTIONS

Eudora Welty is an American short story author and novelist who writes about small-town life in the South. In her book *One Writer's Beginnings,* published in 1984, she describes the influence of her family and surroundings on her writing. The following passage has been annotated to show some uses of prepositions and conjunctions.

Literature Model

from One Writer's Beginnings
by Eudora Welty

Mrs. Calloway made her own rules **about** books. You could not take back a book to the Library on the same day you'd taken it out; it made no difference to **her** that you'd read every word in it **and** needed another to start. You could take out two books at a time and two only; this applied as long as you were a child and also for the rest of your **life,** to my mother as severely as to me. So two by two, I read library books as fast as I could go, rushing them home in the basket **of my bicycle.** From the minute I reached our house, I started to read. Every book I seized on, from *Bunny Brown and His Sister Sue at Camp Rest-a-While* to *Twenty Thousand Leagues Under the Sea,* stood for the devouring wish to read being instantly granted. I knew this was bliss, knew it **at the time.** Taste isn't nearly so important; it comes in its own time. I wanted to read *immediately.* The only fear was that of books coming to an end.

- Preposition
- Pronoun as object of the preposition
- Conjunction connecting compound predicate
- Noun as object of the preposition
- Prepositional phrase (adjective phrase)
- Prepositional phrase (adverb phrase)

Grammar Review

Review: Exercise 1 **Identifying Prepositions**

Write each preposition in the sentences below.

SAMPLE Eudora Welty writes about the beginning of her love for books.
ANSWER about, of, for

1. Mrs. Calloway was an important part of Welty's early reading life.
2. The rules made by Mrs. Calloway seemed ridiculous to a young reader.
3. The library's rules were the same for all.
4. The important thing for Eudora Welty was having books available.
5. Welty read books by any author about any topic.

Review: Exercise 2 **Using Prepositions**

Write an appropriate preposition to replace each blank. Try to use a different preposition in each sentence.

SAMPLE Libraries _____ very large communities often have several branches.
ANSWER in

1. People _____ library cards can take home any of the books on the shelves.
2. All _____ the branches are available to anyone with a library card in the city.
3. There are library rules _____ children and adults.
4. A librarian is usually available to help you find your way _____ the library.
5. Short story collections are _____ the fiction section.
6. _____ this library is a wonderful section of young-adult fiction.
7. The section is _____ the back wall.
8. You can find it _____ the librarian's desk.
9. The librarian's desk is _____ the reference section.
10. The reference section is _____ the rare-book room and the fiction section.

Review: Exercise 3 Identifying Prepositional Phrases and Their Objects

Write the prepositional phrases from each sentence. Underline the object of each preposition.

SAMPLE Scholars often go to specialized libraries for information.
ANSWER to specialized <u>libraries</u> for <u>information</u>

1. Researchers needing information about fine arts or early printed books may go to the Morgan Library in New York City.
2. Near the Capitol in Washington, D.C., is the Folger Shakespeare Library.
3. Opposite the Folger, across the street, sits the huge Library of Congress.
4. The Beinecke Rare Book and Manuscript Library at Yale University is housed inside a six-story glass enclosure on campus.
5. Because of the excellent collections within these libraries, scholars can study any subject along with you and me.

Review: Exercise 4 Choosing Object Pronouns

Write the correct pronoun for each sentence.

1. Books were Mrs. Calloway's subject, and she made rules about (they, them).
2. To (who, whom) did Mrs. Calloway's rules apply?
3. The rules applied equally to the two of (they, them), Eudora and her mother.
4. Eudora read so many books that she seemed to race through (they, them).
5. According to (she, her), she started to read as soon as she returned from the library.
6. Although Eudora may not have liked Mrs. Calloway, despite (she, her), the girl certainly enjoyed reading.
7. Although Eudora does not mention her father in this passage, her love of books may have been influenced by (he, him).
8. I, too, have always loved having books around (I, me).
9. My family and I always keep stacks of unread books near (we, us).
10. Without (they, them) we feel lost.

Grammar Review

Review: Exercise 5   Telling Prepositions from Adverbs

The following sentences are about Eudora Welty's life. Identify each underlined word as a *preposition* or an *adverb*. If the word is a preposition, write its object or objects.

1. *One Writer's Beginnings* is Eudora Welty's book <u>about</u> her own life.
2. The book discusses how the effects of her early years in the South come <u>through</u> in her stories.
3. Eudora Welty is an important Southern writer known <u>for</u> both her short stories and her novels.
4. <u>In</u> a library drawer, Welty's father kept musical instruments of all kinds.
5. Welty often looked <u>inside</u> to see the wonderful instruments.

Review: Exercise 6   Identifying Adjective and Adverb Phrases

Write each sentence. Underline each prepositional phrase and draw an arrow to the word it describes. Write whether the phrase functions as an *adjective* or an *adverb*.

SAMPLE   Eudora Welty writes about her love of books.

ANSWER   Eudora Welty writes <u>about her love</u> <u>of books</u>.
                        adverb phrase   adjective phrase

1. Mrs. Calloway was an important part of Welty's early reading life.
2. Mrs. Calloway's rules were tiresome for an ardent reader.
3. Welty said everyone except her mother was afraid of Mrs. Calloway.
4. Mrs. Calloway asked everyone for silence.
5. The library's rules applied to adults and children.
6. Eudora rode her bike to the library.
7. Because of her love of books, she obeyed Mrs. Calloway's rules.
8. Eudora read books by any author.
9. A critic said parts of *One Writer's Beginnings* are a gift from Welty to her readers.
10. The Weltys had five encyclopedias in the bookcase in the living room.

Review: Exercise 7 Using Conjunctions to Combine Sentences

Combine each pair of sentences below by using the conjunction in parentheses to form a compound sentence, compound subject, or compound object. Write whether your sentence is a *compound sentence* or a sentence with a *compound subject* or a *compound predicate*.

SAMPLE   Public libraries provide useful services. Budget problems are forcing some public libraries to cut back the services they provide. (but)

ANSWER   Public libraries provide useful services, but budget problems are forcing some public libraries to cut back the services they provide. compound sentence

1. What do you think of your local library? How do you use your library? (and)
2. Consider the function of the library. Also think about the ways in which it serves the community. (and)
3. Our library is in a municipal building. The same building houses the town government. (and)
4. Some libraries provide a place for community meetings. Other libraries are just for reading and research. (or)
5. Small towns have limited funds for a library. Small towns may join with other nearby communities to form a regional library. (but)
6. Large cities have more than one library. Each of those libraries may house a specialized collection, such as business or health and medicine. (and)
7. No library can contain all the books its users need. Interlibrary loans allow readers to borrow books from other libraries. (but)
8. At the library, people can exchange community information and post notices. People can pick up tax forms and other printed material. (either, or)
9. A library exhibit can highlight special events and seasonal activities. The exhibit can suggest reading related to the topic. (or)
10. Libraries often have special collections of books for children. Libraries may provide story hours, films, and workshops for children. (and)

Grammar Review

Review: Exercise 8   **Writing Sentences**

Write fifteen sentences, following the directions given below.

SAMPLE   Write a sentence that begins with an interjection and contains a compound predicate.

ANSWER   Oh, I fell and skinned my knee!

1. Write a sentence with a compound subject.
2. Write a compound sentence joined by the conjunction *and*.
3. Write a sentence that begins with an interjection followed by a comma.
4. Write a sentence with a compound predicate.
5. Write a sentence that uses the correlative conjunction *either, or*.
6. Write a sentence that is preceded by an interjection followed by an exclamation mark.
7. Write a compound sentence joined by the conjunction *but*.
8. Write a sentence that includes a prepositional phrase with a compound object.
9. Write a sentence that uses the conjunctions *both* and *and*.
10. Write a compound sentence that is joined by the conjunction *or* and contains an interjection.
11. Write a sentence that begins with a prepositional phrase in which the object is a pronoun.
12. Write a sentence that ends with a prepositional phrase in which the object is made up of two pronouns.
13. Write a sentence in which one part of the compound object of a preposition is a pronoun.
14. Write a compound sentence that contains a preposition of more than one word.
15. Write a sentence that contains two prepositional phrases, one used as an adjective and one as an adverb.

Review: Exercise 9

Proofreading

The following passage is about Janet Fish, whose painting *Toby and Claire Reading* appears on this page. Rewrite the passage, correcting the errors in spelling, capitalization, grammar, and usage. Add any missing punctuation. There are ten errors.

Janet Fish

¹Janet Fish' early interest in art is similar to Eudora Welty's love of books ²Her ambiton from early childhood was to be a sculptor. ³Fish's mother was a sculptor and her grandfather was a painter. ⁴Fish studied sculpture, printmaking and abstract painting in college, but painting was to become her lifes work. ⁵The effects of light on various surfaces are especially interesting to she. ⁶The painting *Toby and Claire Reading* show the importance of light and color for her. ⁷Although Fish's paintings are realistic, her art is strongly influence by she training in abstract painting. ⁸The painting *Toby and Claire Reading* mirror Eudora Welty's early love of books.

Janet Fish, *Toby and Claire Reading*, 1984

Review: Exercise 10

Mixed Review

Rewrite each item, following the directions in parentheses.

SAMPLE   The Maya wrote their history _____ stone monuments. (Add a preposition.)

ANSWER   on

1. Information was written _____ clay tablets in Mesopotamia and on papyrus in Egypt. (Add a preposition. Write whether the prepositional phrase is used as an *adjective* or an *adverb*.)

2. Papyrus was a writing material made _____ the fibers of water reeds. (Add a preposition. Draw an arrow from the prepositional phrase to the word it describes.)

3. _____ the fragile nature of papyrus, many ancient writings have not survived. (Begin with a preposition of more than one word.)

4. Ptolemy I made the Alexandrian Library the greatest in the ancient world. Ptolemy II made the Alexandrian Library the greatest in the ancient world. (Use a conjunction to form one sentence with a compound subject.)

5. It is amazing that not a trace of such a great library has ever been found. (Add an interjection.)

6. In 1859 British archaeologists found thousands of clay tablets. Scholars have not been able to understand the writing on them. (Use a conjunction to form a compound sentence.)

7. To _____, the cuneiform script on the tablets has been an unbreakable code. (Add an object pronoun to replace the words *the archaeologists*.)

8. Monks in monasteries copied religious works such as the Bible. They preserved the works of ancient scholars. (Use a conjunction to write one sentence with a compound predicate.)

9. Paper made books easier to produce. Movable type made books easier to produce. (Use a pair of correlative conjunctions to write one sentence with a compound subject.)

10. _____ the invention of the printing press, it took many hours of hand-copying to produce a Bible. (Add a preposition.)

Writing Application

TIME

For more about the importance of using language effectively, see **TIME Facing the Blank Page,** page 98.

Prepositions and Conjunctions in Writing

Freeman Hubbard uses prepositions and conjunctions in this passage from *The Great Days of the Circus* to help him convey the excitement of the circus's arrival. Examine the passage, focusing especially on the italicized words.

> The street was alive *with noise* as the first four lovely ladies on horseback, trumpets lifted to their lips, came into sight. They were always lithe and lovely, *and* the plumes they wore danced as their horses pranced. Then came the band, *in red uniforms with gold braid,* riding *on a gilded band wagon* that was sometimes drawn by as many as forty horses. The band never stopped playing: the big bass drum thumped steadily, the trumpets *shrilled and blared,* the cymbals flashed *in the sun.* Behind the band came great floats.

Techniques with Prepositions and Conjunctions

Try to apply some of Hubbard's writing techniques when you write and revise your own work.

❶ Use prepositional phrases as adjectives and adverbs to add specific details to your writing.

WITHOUT PREPOSITIONAL PHRASES Then came the band.

HUBBARD'S VERSION Then came the band, in red uniforms with gold braid, riding on a gilded band wagon.

❷ To vary your writing, use conjunctions to form compound subjects, predicates, and sentences.

WITHOUT CONJUNCTIONS The trumpets shrilled. The trumpets blared.

HUBBARD'S VERSION The trumpets shrilled and blared.

Practice Practice these techniques by revising the following passage on your own paper. Use prepositional phrases to add details and conjunctions to vary your sentences.

Marty and Josh had some free time. They decided to go to the library. It was a favorite place. The reading corner was surrounded by shelves. There were chairs and a couch. Marty chose a best-seller. Josh picked out a magazine. They settled down for a good read. They had an hour before Josh's mother was to pick them up. The room was quiet. The light was soft. No one disturbed them. It was so restful that both boys forgot the time.

Prepositions, Conjunctions, and Interjections

UNIT

15

Subject-Verb Agreement

Lesson **15.1** **Making Subjects and Verbs Agree** *439*

Lesson **15.2** **Problems with Locating the Subject** *441*

Lesson **15.3** **Agreement with Compound Subjects** *443*

Grammar Review *445*

Writing Application *453*

15.1 Making Subjects and Verbs Agree

A subject and its verb are the basic parts of a sentence. The subject and its verb must *agree in number*. A singular noun subject takes a singular form of the verb. A plural noun subject takes a plural form of the verb. In the present tense, the singular form of the verb usually ends in *-s* or *-es*.

Read the sentences in the chart below. You can see that the subjects and verbs agree in number.

Subject Noun and Verb Agreement	
Singular	**Plural**
A **mountain rises** sharply to the sky.	**Mountains rise** sharply to the sky.
A **naturalist teaches** us about nature.	**Naturalists teach** us about nature.

Verbs and subject pronouns must also agree in number. In the present tense, the *-s* ending is used with the subject pronouns *it, he,* and *she.*

Subject Pronoun and Verb Agreement	
Singular	**Plural**
He, she, or it **travels.**	We **travel.**
You **travel.**	You **travel.**
I **travel.**	They **travel.**

The irregular verbs *be, do,* and *have* can be main verbs or helping verbs. They must agree with the subject, whether they are main verbs or helping verbs.

I **am** fine. He **is** ready. [main verb]
They **are** questioning a ranger. [helping verb]

She **does** well. [main verb]
She **does** work hard. They **do** sing. [helping verb]

He **has** a boat. [main verb]
He **has** visited Utah. They **have** eaten. [helping verb]

Exercise 1   Using Subject and Verb Agreement

For each sentence, write the correct form of the verb in parentheses.

1. Acadia National Park (lies, lie) along Maine's coast.
2. Several islands (is, are) in the park.
3. Acadia (features, feature) a rocky coastline.
4. Mount Desert Island (is, are) very beautiful.
5. Many people (travels, travel) to Acadia every year.
6. They (photographs, photograph) the wildlife.
7. Mammoth Cave (is, are) in Kentucky.
8. The passageways (winds, wind) for nearly two hundred miles.
9. An underground river (flows, flow) through the caves.
10. Tour guides (leads, lead) people through the chambers.
11. Many visitors (enjoys, enjoy) the sense of adventure.
12. For example, my mother (does, do).
13. Yellowstone National Park (has, have) some of the few surviving grizzly bears.
14. Campers (does, do) enjoy the wilderness.
15. Large bears sometimes (approaches, approach).
16. Park visitors (does, do) require protection.
17. A camper (carries, carry) bedding and supplies.
18. Yellowstone (has, have) a beautiful waterfall.
19. Our national parks (contains, contain) natural wonders.
20. Wind Cave (has, have) unusual crystals.
21. Tiny white crystals (lines, line) the cave walls and ceiling.
22. Ancient animal fossils (lies, lie) in the Agate Fossil Beds.
23. The park (includes, include) the remains of two-horned rhinoceroses.
24. Unusual rock formations (fills, fill) Death Valley.
25. The National Park Service (protects, protect) Death Valley and other national monuments.

Exercise 2   Writing Sentences with Subject and Verb Agreement

Write ten original sentences. Use singular subjects in some sentences and plural subjects in others. Be sure each verb agrees with its subject. In each sentence, underline the subject once and the verb twice. Write whether the subject is *singular* or *plural.*

SAMPLE ANSWER: My <u>friends</u> <u>are packing</u> for a camping trip. (plural)

Problems with Locating the Subject

You know how to make a subject and a verb agree when the verb directly follows the subject. However, sometimes a prepositional phrase comes between the subject and the verb. When that happens, make sure that the verb agrees with the subject of the sentence and not with the object of the preposition.

A **park** in the islands **contains** a volcano.

The **parks** of Hawaii **contain** volcanoes.

In the first sentence, *in the islands* is a prepositional phrase. The singular verb *contains* agrees with the subject of the sentence, *park*, not with the plural noun *islands*, which is the object of the preposition.

In the second sentence, *of Hawaii* is a prepositional phrase. The plural verb *contain* agrees with the plural subject *parks,* not with the singular noun *Hawaii,* which is the object of the preposition.

Some sentences begin with *here* or *there. Here* or *there* is never the subject of a sentence. Look for the subject after the verb in this type of sentence.

There **is** a **park** on Maui.

Here in the park **are** tropical **forests.**

To make it easier to find the subject, try rearranging these sentences and placing the subject and verb in their usual positions. This rearrangement makes clear how the subject and the verb agree in number.

A **park is** there on Maui.

Tropical **forests are** here in the park.

Exercise 3   **Choosing the Correct Verb Form**

For each sentence, write the correct form of the verb in parentheses.

1. The island of Oahu (has, have) a mild climate.
2. Islands of volcanic origin (rises, rise) in the Pacific.
3. Travelers to Haleakala (sees, see) a huge crater.
4. A hike along the cliffs (is, are) exciting.
5. There (is, are) lush green trees everywhere.
6. Our trip to the islands (delights, delight) us.
7. A busload of tourists (arrives, arrive) in the park.
8. Parts of Kauai (has, have) served as movie locations.
9. The rain forests of Hawaii (needs, need) protection.
10. There (is, are) many visitors to the Hawaii Volcanoes National Park.

Exercise 4   **Making Subjects and Verbs Agree**

Write each sentence. Underline the simple subject once and its verb twice. If they agree, write *correct*. If they do not agree, correct the verb.

1. Protection of rare plants are vital.
2. Our system of parks include forests.
3. The islands of Hawaii contain two national parks.
4. A student of volcanoes prepare an exhibit.
5. Studies of plant life occurs in the parks.
6. Protectors of the environment works there.
7. There are many opportunities for research.
8. Here is a list of the national parks.
9. Our system of national parks have protected natural wonders.
10. The oldest park in the system is Yellowstone.
11. The National Park Service oversees our parks and monuments.
12. There are many activities throughout the park system.
13. Tour guides from the service describes points of interest to guests.
14. Visitors to the Appalachian National Scenic Trail hike from Maine to Georgia.
15. There is rafting adventures at the Delaware Scenic River Park.

Exercise 5   **Using Subject-Verb Agreement in Sentences**

Write five original sentences. Begin each sentence with *Here is, Here are, There is,* or *There are.* Underline the subject of each sentence.

15.3 Agreement with Compound Subjects

A subject and its verb must agree in number. A singular noun subject takes a singular form of the verb. A plural noun subject takes a plural form of the verb. In the present tense, the singular form of the verb usually ends in -s or -es.

A **hawk** soars.
SINGULAR SUBJECT

Two **hawks** soar.
PLURAL SUBJECT

A **compound subject** contains two or more subjects that have the same verb. You can tell whether the compound subject takes a singular or a plural verb form by looking at the way the subjects are joined. When two or more subjects are joined by *and* or by *both . . . and,* the verb is plural.

> **Both** a grizzly bear **and** a bobcat **live** near here.

This sentence refers to more than one thing, so the form of the verb is plural. When two or more subjects are joined by *or, nor,* or *either . . . or* or *neither . . . nor,* the verb must agree in number with the subject that is closest to it.

> An eagle **or** a hawk **soars** in the sky.
> **Either** the loon **or** its chicks **swim** nearby.
> **Neither** the bears **nor** the bobcat **crosses** our path.

In the first sentence, the verb *soars* agrees in number with *hawk,* which is the subject closer to the verb. The verb is singular in form because *hawk* is a singular subject. In the second sentence, the verb *swim* agrees with *chicks,* which is the closer subject. The verb is plural in form because *chicks* is a plural subject. In the third sentence, the verb *crosses* agrees with *bobcat,* which is the closer subject. The verb is singular in form because *bobcat* is a singular subject.

Exercise 6　Identifying the Correct Verb Form

For each sentence, write the correct form of the verb in parentheses.

1. A deer and a heron (wades, wade) in the lake.
2. Both a coyote and an antelope (outruns, outrun) a bear.
3. Neither hunting nor mining (is, are) allowed in protected areas.
4. An alligator and an egret (hunts, hunt) for food in the swamp.
5. Both Bryce Canyon Park and Yellowstone Park (has, have) wonderful hiking trails.
6. Birds and insect life (thrives, thrive) in the swamp.
7. Either experienced campers or the ranger (leads, lead) the evening talks.
8. Neither heat nor mosquitoes (disturbs, disturb) us.
9. Dams and pollution (is, are) destroying the swamp.
10. Newspapers and television (reports, report) on this problem.

Exercise 7　Making Verbs Agree with Compound Sentences

Write each sentence, correcting the verb if necessary. Underline the subject once and its verb twice. Remember to underline the complete compound subjects.

1. Either the factories or the swamp are in danger.
2. Both bears and frogs hibernate in winter.
3. Neither alligators nor crocodiles likes the cold.
4. The blue heron and the egret lives in the Everglades.
5. Our national seashores and parks are a great resource.
6. The grizzly bear and the polar bear is carnivorous.
7. Both Florida and Hawaii have underwater parks.
8. There is breeding sea lions and nesting birds at Channel Islands National Park in California.
9. A rare orchid or brilliantly colored birds attracts many photographers.
10. Wolves and a large moose herd roams the Isle Royale National Park.

Exercise 8　Using Compound Subjects in Sentences

Write five original sentences with compound subjects. Join the subjects in each sentence by using the word or words indicated.

1. and
2. or
3. both . . . and
4. either . . . or
5. neither . . . nor

Subject-Verb Agreement

Grammar Review

SUBJECT-VERB AGREEMENT

John Muir by Eden Force is a biography of the naturalist and explorer whose efforts influenced Congress to pass the Yosemite National Park Bill in 1890. The bill established both Yosemite and Sequoia National Parks. Both of these parks are justly famous for their variety of breathtaking natural wonders. In the following excerpt from the book, the writer describes the beautiful scenery of Yosemite Valley, which Muir explored for six years. The passage has been annotated to show some examples of subject-verb agreement covered in this unit.

Literature Model

from John Muir
by Eden Force

Yosemite Valley includes some of the world's most awe-inspiring natural wonders. El Capitan, a block of stone more than 600 times Muir's height, faces Bridalveil Fall. Bridalveil tumbles 620 feet from high rocks into the valley. Farther up the Merced River is Yosemite Falls, rushing down in two sections to Yosemite Valley. North of the river is North Dome, a dome-shaped peak about as high as El Capitan. It towers above the landscape. South of North Dome and east of Tenaga Creek stands a strange peak even taller than North Dome. It is Half Dome. As the name suggests, Half Dome looks like a dome that a giant has sliced down the middle from top to bottom. Only one half of the rock dome remains.

> **Agreement between a singular noun subject and a singular verb**

> **Agreement between a singular pronoun subject and a singular verb**

> **Agreement between a singular subject and verb that have a prepositional phrase between them**

Grammar Review

Review: Exercise 1 Making Subjects and Verbs Agree

Write the correct form of the verb in parentheses.

SAMPLE   Merced River (forms, form) a white ribbon through the valley.
ANSWER   forms

1. Sometimes a family of bears (stops, stop) to swim and play in the river.
2. El Capitan (rises, rise) high above Yosemite Valley.
3. In shape it (resembles, resemble) a boot.
4. Yosemite's natural wonders (is, are) awe-inspiring.
5. They (attracts, attract) thousands of visitors.
6. The visitors (hike, hikes) seven hundred miles of trails.
7. The most spectacular scenery (is, are) in Yosemite Valley.
8. The peaks of California's Sierra Nevada (is, are) millions of years old.
9. Deep gorges (creates, create) beautiful views.
10. The National Park Service (has, have) begun a public transportation system to reduce traffic in the park.

Review: Exercise 2 Making Subjects and Verbs Agree

Write each sentence, correcting the verb if necessary. Write whether the subject is *singular* or *plural*.

1. Yosemite National Park lies in the mountains two hundred miles east of San Francisco.
2. Giant sequoias graces three groves in the park.
3. The Grizzly Giant Tree measure thirty-four feet in diameter, more than most roads.
4. This huge tree stands in the famous Mariposa Grove.
5. The sequoias are some of the oldest living things on earth.
6. The wood of the sequoias resists fire.
7. Sequoia National Park feature some giant trees with the names of Civil War generals.
8. Redwoods are related to giant sequoias.
9. The redwood grow even taller than the giant sequoia.
10. These enormous trees grows from tiny seeds.

Review: Exercise 3 Identifying Subjects and Making Verbs Agree

Write the correct form of the verb in parentheses.

SAMPLE There (is, are) books written by John Muir.
ANSWER are

1. The Sierra Club, with branches throughout the United States, (owes, owe) its existence to Muir.
2. Muir's campaign for preserving forests (continues, continue) to inspire environmentalists.
3. In California there (is, are) a redwood forest called Muir Woods.
4. The forest near San Francisco (honors, honor) the achievements of John Muir.
5. A glacier in Alaska also (bears, bear) his name.
6. *The Yosemite* by John Muir (is, are) a classic.
7. Copies (is, are) available at my local library.
8. Muir, in his journals, (describes, describe) the natural wonders of Yosemite.
9. The governor of California (declares, declare) each April 21 "John Muir Day."
10. Admirers of Muir and his causes (celebrates, celebrate) at the John Muir National Historic Site.

Review: Exercise 4 Locating Subjects and Making Verbs Agree

Locate and write the subject of each sentence. If the verb in the sentence is correct, write *correct*. If the verb is not correct, rewrite the sentence, correcting the verb.

1. There is the Merced River in Yosemite Valley.
2. There are rough terrain in some Yosemite wilderness areas.
3. There is lovely landscapes in the valley.
4. Here in Yosemite Valley are effects of volcanoes and glaciers.
5. There is a book about Muir's glacial theory.

Subject-Verb Agreement

Grammar Review

Review: Exercise 5 **Making Verbs Agree with Compound Subjects**

For each sentence, write the correct form of the verb in parentheses.

1. Both Glacier Point and Taft Point (provides, provide) a great view.
2. Neither Half Dome nor El Capitan (is, are) the highest point in the valley.
3. Both Vernal Falls and Nevada Falls (pours, pour) over giant rocks formed by glaciers.
4. Neither cold weather nor drenching rains (discourages, discourage) backpackers.
5. Bears or other animals sometimes (steals, steal) the backpackers' food.
6. A student and a backpacker (walks, walk) toward the glacier.
7. A van and a camper (waits, wait) at the entrance to the park.
8. Snow or ice (lies, lie) in many of the ravines of the Sierra Nevada.
9. Both a robin and a yellow warbler (sings, sing) near the campsite.
10. Either a dome or spires (crowns, crown) the granite mountains forming the valley.

Review: Exercise 6 **Writing the Correct Verb Form for Compound Subjects**

For each sentence, write the correct present-tense form of the verb in parentheses. Make sure your verb agrees with the subject of the sentence.

SAMPLE   Parks and other areas (be) part of the National Park System.
ANSWER   are

1. A noteworthy landscape or a historic site (form) the basis of most national parks.
2. Both Indiana and Wisconsin (boast) national lakeshores.
3. The Blue Ridge and the Natchez Trace (be) national parkways.
4. National battlefields and a national scenic trail (be) part of the National Park System.
5. Air and water pollution and overcrowding (pose) threats to the most popular parks.

Subject-Verb Agreement

Review: Exercise 7 Choosing Verbs

Write the subject of each sentence and the correct present tense of the verb in parentheses.

1. Geysers (attract) visitors to Yellowstone National Park.
2. We (photograph) the geysers and hot springs at the park.
3. Yellowstone, in the northwest corner of Wyoming, (be) the oldest national park in the United States.
4. Pools of hot mud (bubble) in the Lower Geyser Basin section of the park.
5. Steam (change) the hard surrounding rock into soft clay.
6. Yellowstone Lake, with geysers and hot springs along its shores, (be) the largest high-altitude lake in North America.
7. Evergreen forests of fir, spruce, and pine (cover) much of the park.
8. The feeding of bears within the park's boundaries (defy) park regulations.
9. Park regulations about fishing in the lakes and rivers (be) also strict.
10. The variety of landscapes in the region (surprise) new visitors to the park.
11. Memorials to past events (exist) in every state.
12. Some of these memorials (become) national historical parks.
13. The junction of two rivers (form) one such park.
14. The Potomac River (meet) the Shenandoah River at Harpers Ferry, West Virginia.
15. The park by the rivers (be) Harpers Ferry National Historical Park.
16. Students of the Civil War (visit) this park.
17. They (learn) about John Brown's attack on the arsenal at Harpers Ferry in 1859.
18. A museum at the park (record) how John Brown worked for the end of slavery.
19. John Brown's actions at his trial for treason (become) an inspiration to some writers.
20. John Brown (be) the subject of an epic poem by Stephen Vincent Benét.

Subject-Verb Agreement

Grammar Review

Review: Exercise 8   Making Verbs Agree

For each sentence, write the correct present-tense form of the verb in parentheses.

1. Acts of Congress (designate) areas as part of the National Park System.
2. Unique natural landscapes or historic sites (form) the basis of the majority of national parks.
3. The Edgar Allan Poe National Historic Site and the Georgia O'Keeffe National Historic Site (honor) famous Americans.
4. Prehistoric dwellings (be) preserved at a number of different sites.
5. Some people (be) surprised to learn that the White House is part of the National Park System.
6. The largest of the national parks (be) the Wrangell-St. Elias system in Alaska.
7. National parks (range) in area from 8 million acres to about 6 thousand acres.
8. The John F. Kennedy birthplace and some other national historic sites (occupy) less than an acre.
9. National battlefield parks and national battlefield sites (include) Civil War and Revolutionary War sites.
10. There (be) other areas primarily for recreational use.
11. There (be) national parklands along rivers in eleven states.
12. The Alganak Wild River Park and New River Gorge Park (have) exciting stretches of white water.
13. There (exist) national recreation areas in states across the country from New York to California.
14. Alaska or Texas (contain) most of the national preserves.
15. Blue Ridge and Natchez Trace (be) the only national parkways.
16. The John D. Rockefeller Jr. Memorial Parkway (connect) two beautiful national parks, Yellowstone and Grand Teton.
17. The Appalachian National Scenic Trail (extend) for two thousand miles from Maine to Georgia.
18. The Glen Canyon Dam and the Hoover Dam (create) the largest national recreation areas.
19. Sand dunes in both Colorado and Indiana (form) part of the National Park System.
20. Arizona (have) many national monuments and two national parks.

Review: Exercise 9

Proofreading

The following passage is about artist Thomas Moran, whose work appears below. Rewrite the passage, correcting the errors in spelling, capitalization, grammar, and usage. Add any missing punctuation. There are eleven errors.

Thomas Moran

¹When he were an art student, Thomas Moran (1837–1926) admirred European landscape painters. ²However, Moran wanted to "paint as an american." ³His paintings, such as *Cliffs of the Upper Colorado River, Wyoming Territory,* captures the beauty of the American West.

Thomas Moran, *Cliffs of the Upper Colorado River, Wyoming Territory,* **1882**

(continued)

⁴The painting on page 451 show a scene in the West. ⁵Two seperate rocks appears in the distance. ⁶The sun bathe the rocks in light and shadow. ⁷Tones of rust, brown, tan orange, and sand are used by the artist. ⁸The riders and horses pauses near the river to view natures majesty.

Review: Exercise 10

Mixed Review

Rewrite each sentence, correcting the verb if necessary. Write whether the subject is *singular, plural,* or *compound.*

1. The sculptures and paintings of Frederic Remington records the changing West of the nineteenth century.
2. Action and drama characterizes the best of Remington's art.
3. Other recorders of the land and life of the Old West includes Albert Bierstadt, Charles M. Russell, and George Catlin.
4. Russell's experience as a cowboy and trapper show in his detailed artwork.
5. George Catlin's paintings records the life of Native Americans along the Missouri River and the Western Plains.
6. Catlin's portrait of a Blackfeet chief hangs in The Smithsonian Institution.
7. Albert Bierstadt is one of the great American Romantic landscape painters.
8. Drama and grandeur sometimes overtakes realism in his huge canvases.
9. Both Bierstadt and Thomas Moran has large paintings on display in the U.S. Capitol.
10. George Caleb Bingham are remembered for his scenes of frontier life.
11. The Metropolitan Museum of Art and the National Gallery house his colorful work.
12. Events from the Wild West springs to life through these works.
13. What forms of art depict today's events?
14. A great twentieth-century photographer of the American West is Ansel Adams.
15. The granite domes of Yosemite are the subjects of many of Adams's photos.

Subject-Verb Agreement

Writing Application

TIME

For more about the importance of using verbs correctly, see **TIME Facing the Blank Page,** page 98.

Subject-Verb Agreement in Writing

Peggy Thomson uses singular, plural, and compound subjects in this passage from "Bathing Elephants." Examine the passage, noting how subjects and verbs agree in number.

Bath and foot-care time now flows into demonstration time directed by the keeper team of Kathy and Morna out in the yard. Here people clap to see the elephants maneuver on command, present a foot, balance on tiny stools, and move huge logs with their trunks. By the time Ambika and Shanthi take their bows, the keepers are beginning to wilt. There's an element of tension in the playful-looking baths they give and in the training shows—in just dealing with animals who could so easily pulverize them if they chose to.

Techniques with Subjects and Their Verbs

Try to use singular, plural, and compound subjects when you write and revise your own work. Be sure your subjects and their verbs agree in number. Look at these examples from "Bathing Elephants."

❶ With a singular subject, be sure you use the singular form of the verb. With a plural subject, be sure you use the plural form of the verb.

THOMSON'S EXAMPLES Bath and foot-care <u>time</u> now <u>flows</u>; <u>people</u> <u>clap</u>; <u>keepers</u> <u>are</u>

❷ With a compound subject using *and*, be sure to use the plural form of the verb.

THOMSON'S EXAMPLES <u>Kathy and Morna</u> <u>speak</u>; <u>Ambika and Shanthi</u> <u>take</u>

Practice Revise the following passage. Be sure all the subjects and their verbs agree in number.

¹My family and I am going on a car trip through Colorado and Wyoming this summer. ²We plan stops at a number of different national parks and historic sites. ³The first stop on our journey are Yellowstone, the oldest park in the national park system. ⁴We have reservations at Old Faithful Inn. ⁵The beautiful open lobby of the inn rise more than ninety feet.

Glossary of Special Usage Problems

Lesson **16.1**   **Using Troublesome Words I**   *455*

Lesson **16.2**   **Using Troublesome Words II**   *457*

Grammar Review   *459*

Writing Application   *463*

Using Troublesome Words I

Like all languages, English contains a number of confusing words. The following glossary will help you understand some of the more troublesome ones.

Word	Meaning	Example
accept	"to receive"	Ships **accept** most cargo.
except	"other than"	Ships move at a rapid speed **except** in storms.
all ready	"completely prepared"	The flight crew is **all ready.**
already	"before" or "by this time"	The plane had **already** left when I arrived at the airport.
all together	"in a group"	The wagons traveled **all together** for protection.
altogether	"completely"	Wagons are **altogether** too slow.
a lot	"very much" *A lot* is two words. Its meaning is vague; avoid using it.	Sailors travel **a lot.** [vague] Sailors travel frequently. [more precise]
beside	"next to"	Railroad tracks often run **beside** roads.
besides	"in addition to"	**Besides** trains we ride buses.
between	Use *between* when referring to two people or things.	Ships sail **between** ports.
among	Use *among* when talking about groups of three or more.	Trains are **among** the best ways to travel.
choose	"to select"	Many people **choose** a window seat when they fly.
chose	"selected"	I **chose** an aisle seat the last time I flew to New York.
in	"inside"	Freight is stored **in** cargo bays.
into	indicates movement from outside to a point within	The pilot guided the ship **into** port.
its	the possessive form of *it*	The ship is moving to **its** pier.
it's	the contraction of *it is*	**It's** hard to dock a ship.

Glossary of Special Usage Problems

Exercise 1   Choosing the Correct Word

Write each sentence, choosing the correct word or words in parentheses.

1. We are traveling (altogether, all together).
2. The conductor will (accept, except) our tickets.
3. Every railroad car (accept, except) ours is going all the way to Chicago.
4. Did we (choose, chose) the wrong one?
5. (Its, It's) difficult to choose without checking the schedule.
6. The train that is (beside, besides) ours at the station is headed for Omaha.
7. The conductor says we are (all ready, already) to leave.
8. Before you know it, the train has (all ready, already) left the station.
9. We settle (in, into) our seats and look out the window.
10. My friend let me (choose, chose) the seat closest to the window.
11. The train is moving along (its, it's) track at a steady speed.
12. We talk (between, among) ourselves about the passing scenery.
13. There are many people on this train (besides, beside) my family.
14. Freight trains are (between, among) the busiest carriers.
15. Elevators load grain (in, into) railroad hoppers.

Exercise 2   Using the Correct Word

Write each sentence, using the correct word or words from the lesson as defined in parentheses.

1. Truckers stop _____ highways to rest. (next to)
2. Truckers can drive _____ the city. (from outside to a point within)
3. Heavy trucks can cause _____ too much damage to highways. (completely)
4. Our moving van is _____. (completely prepared)
5. The circus trucks have _____ left. (by this time)
6. Of all the trucks on this lot, which one would you _____ to drive? (select)
7. Does this parkway _____ trucks? (receive)
8. This highway runs _____ Baltimore, Maryland, and Washington, D.C. (referring to two places)
9. _____ truck traffic, the highway gets much commuter traffic. (in addition to)
10. The highway is crowded _____ on weekends. (other than)

16.2 Using Troublesome Words II

Like all languages, English contains a number of confusing words. The following glossary will help you understand some of the more troublesome ones.

Word	Meaning	Example
lay	"to put" or "to place"	Sailors **lay** the ropes in coils.
lie	"to recline" or "to be positioned"	Passengers **lie** in bunks.
learn	"to receive knowledge"	Crews **learn** rescue tactics.
teach	"to give knowledge"	Some pilots **teach** flying.
leave	"to go away"	Most buses **leave** on time.
let	"to allow"	**Let** the children board.
loose	"not firmly attached"	**Loose** cargo is dangerous.
lose	"to misplace" or "to fail to win"	You could **lose** your luggage.
raise	"to cause to move upward"	The sailors **raise** the anchors before the ships depart.
rise	"to move upward"	The anchors **rise** slowly.
set	"to place" or "to put"	Cranes **set** cargo in the hold.
sit	"to place oneself in a seated position"	I will **sit** by you.
than	*Than* introduces the second part of a comparison.	Ships are larger **than** boats.
then	"at that time" or "soon after"	Raise the anchor and **then** sail.
their	*Their* is the possessive form of *they*.	We like **their** fast trains.
they're	*They're* is the contraction of *they are*.	**They're** designed for speed.
to	"in the direction of"	Trains carry coal **to** ports.
too	"in addition to" or "excessively"	Coal is **too** bulky for planes.
two	the number after one	The supertanker is as long as **two** football fields.
who's	*Who's* is the contraction of *who is*.	I have a friend **who's** a pilot.
whose	*Whose* is the possessive form of *who*.	**Whose** flight leaves first?

| Exercise 3 | Choosing the Correct Word |

Write each sentence, choosing the correct word in parentheses.

1. (Who's, Whose) instructions will the pilot follow?
2. The pilot will (learn, teach) you to use radar.
3. The pilot will help you with math (to, too).
4. The best pilots (set, sit) their planes down gently.
5. Planes are faster (than, then) trains.
6. Once in flight, passengers may (lay, lie) back in their seats.
7. Planes almost never (loose, lose) their way.
8. After taking off, planes (raise, rise) to a suitable flying height.
9. During this time, the plane's pilot (raises, rises) the landing gear.
10. The plane reaches its cruising altitude; (than, then) the crew can relax more.
11. They may (set, sit) and chat.
12. They may study the navigational charts that (their, they're) using.
13. They understand (who's, whose) responsible for what duties.
14. (Their, They're) well trained, and all crew members know their jobs.
15. (Who's, Whose) job is it to fly the plane?
16. (Raise, Rise) your hand if you know the answer.
17. I sometimes wonder whether flying the plane is more difficult (than, then) tending the passengers.
18. Flight attendants see that all (loose, lose) luggage is safely secured.
19. (Their, They're) primary responsibility is the safety and comfort of the passengers.
20. They (leave, let) the flying to the pilot and copilot.

| Exercise 4 | Using the Correct Word |

Write each sentence, using the correct word or words from the lesson as defined in parentheses.

1. _____ near the bow so that we can see the harbor. (place yourself in a seated position)
2. Ships will not _____ port until high tide. (go away)
3. _____ me help you down the gangplank. (allow)
4. The crew saw the playful whale _____ from the water. (move upward)
5. Vessels _____ flags as signals. (cause to move upward)

Grammar Review

GLOSSARY OF SPECIAL USAGE PROBLEMS

In *Exploring the* Titanic, Robert D. Ballard writes about his explorations of the largest ship of its time, the *Titanic,* which sank after hitting an iceberg in the North Atlantic Ocean on April 15, 1912. More than 1,500 passengers and crew died; fewer than half that number survived.

Literature Model

from Exploring the *Titanic*
by Robert D. Ballard

It looked as though the metal hull was slowly melting away. What seemed like frozen rivers of rust covered the ship's side and spread out over the ocean bottom. It was almost as if the blood of the great ship **lay** in pools on the ocean floor.

> Past tense of the verb *lie,* meaning "to be positioned"

As *Alvin* rose in slow motion up the ghostly side of the ship, I could see our lights reflecting off the still-unbroken glass of the *Titanic*'s portholes. They made me think of cats' eyes gleaming in the dark. In places the rust formations over the portholes looked like eyelashes with tears, as though the *Titanic* were crying. I could also see **a lot** of reddish-brown stalactites of rust over the wreck, like long icicles. I decided to call them "rusticles." This rust turned out to be very fragile. If touched by our sub, it disappeared like a cloud of smoke.

> *A lot* spelled as two words

As we **rose** further and began to move across the mighty forward deck, I was amazed at the sheer size of everything: giant bollards and shiny bronze capstans that were used for winding ropes and cables; the huge links of the anchor chains. When you were there on the spot, the ship was truly titanic.

> Past tense of the verb *rise,* meaning "to move upward"

Grammar Review

Review: Exercise 1 Making Usage Choices

Write each sentence, choosing the correct word or words in parentheses.

SAMPLE   The *Titanic* hit an iceberg (in, into) the North Atlantic.
ANSWER   The *Titanic* hit an iceberg in the North Atlantic.

1. The *Titanic* was on its way (to, too, two) New York when it hit an iceberg.
2. Passengers hurriedly crowded (in, into) the lifeboats.
3. Crew members sat (between, among) the passengers in the crowded boats.
4. The *Titanic* had (all ready, already) sunk by the time other ships got to the area.
5. More passengers died (than, then) survived.

Review: Exercise 2 Making Usage Choices

Write each sentence, choosing the correct word or words in parentheses.

SAMPLE   The explorers could see the *Titanic*'s (to, too, two) anchors.
ANSWER   The explorers could see the *Titanic*'s two anchors.

1. The *Titanic* (lays, lies) on the ocean floor nearly two and a half miles below the surface.
2. The sub *Alvin* rose slowly (beside, besides) the ship.
3. By exploring the wreck up close, Ballard was able to (learn, teach) what he wanted to know about the *Titanic*.
4. The entire ship was visible (accept, except) for the bow.
5. The *Titanic*'s bow was (all together, altogether) buried in the mud.

Proofreading

The following passage is about American artist Richard Shaw, whose work appears on this page. Rewrite the passage, correcting the errors in spelling, capitalization, grammar, and usage. Add any missing punctuation. There are ten errors.

Richard Shaw

[1]Richard Shaw was born in 1941 he was risen in Hollywood, California. [2]His father worked as a cartoonist for Walt Disney Studio and his mother was an artist two. [3]They're friends were all artists, cartoonists, and writers. [4]Shaw remembers spending much time as a child drawing train wrecks, battles and maritime disasters.

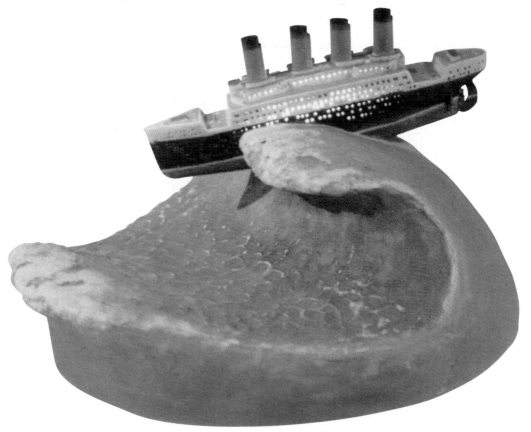

Richard Shaw, *Rough Seas*, 1991

(continued)

Glossary of Special Usage Problems

⁵Beside his interest in painting, Shaw also became interested in filmmaking and ceramic sculpture. ⁶In the work on the previous page, he uses ceramic to show the immense power of the see. ⁷The ocean liner sets precariously on the top of a huge wave. ⁸The *Titanic*, of course, met it's fate in the form of an iceberg, not a wave.

Review: Exercise 4

Mixed Review

The following sentences provide information about icebergs. For each sentence, write the correct word in parentheses.

1. An iceberg is a large drifting piece of ice that has broken off (altogether, all together) from a freshwater glacier.
2. It is really a (loose, lose) piece of ice floating in the sea.
3. In the Northern Hemisphere, the main source of icebergs (lays, lies) along the southwestern coast of Greenland.
4. In the south, the glacial flow from Antarctica releases large icebergs, some of which (raise, rise) hundreds of feet into the air.
5. Moving (among, between) a large number of icebergs is dangerous for ships, since only a small portion of each iceberg is visible above the water.
6. Most of the iceberg (lays, lies) under the water.
7. The biggest of the icebergs are (to, too) large to be easily recognized as icebergs.
8. They are much larger (than, then) the largest supertankers.
9. Sometimes (their, they're) over sixty miles long.
10. If you were on a big ship (beside, besides) one of these giant icebergs, you might think you were next to an island.
11. Would you (choose, chose) to live in such an icy place?
12. (Its, It's) hard to imagine, but some animals do!
13. Emperor penguins swim (between, among) ice and land.
14. Seals (set, sit) on the frigid surfaces.
15. (Leave, Let) me bask on a sunny, sand-filled beach!

Writing Application

TIME

For more about usage rules, see **TIME Facing the Blank Page,** page 98.

Usage of Glossary Words in Writing

In this passage from *The Jacket*, Gary Soto uses several of the words you have studied to describe the boy's reactions to his new jacket. As you read, concentrate on the italized words.

"I threw my books on the bed and approached the jacket slowly, as if it were a stranger *whose* hand I had to shake. I touched the vinyl sleeve, the collar, and pecked at the mustard-colored lining.

From the kitchen Mother yelled that my jacket was *in* the closet. I closed the door *to* her voice and pulled at the rack of clothes *in* the closet, hoping the jacket on the bedpost wasn't for me but my mean brother."

Techniques with Correct Usage

Gary Soto was careful to use the correct word of a pair that could easily be confused. When you draft and revise your writing, try to be as careful.

❶ Remember the difference between the use of *who's* and *whose.*

INCORRECT . . . as if it were a stranger *who's* hand I had to shake.

CORRECT . . . as if it were a stranger *whose* hand I had to shake.

❷ Learn the difference between *in* and *into.*

INCORRECT My jacket was *into* the closet.

CORRECT My jacket was *in* the closet.

❸ Don't confuse *to, too,* and *two.*

INCORRECT I closed the door *too* her voice . . .

CORRECT I closed the door *to* her voice . . .

Glossary of Special Usage Problems

Practice Practice these techniques by rewriting the following paragraph, making the correct choice from each word pair.

What was (in, into) the back of the closet? I tiptoed nervously (to, too) the closet door. Gingerly, I opened the door and reached (in, into). Slowly, I edged my hand further (in, into) the closet. My hand slid between (too, two) coats that seemed almost (to, too) silky to the touch. (Who's, Whose) could they be? A sudden screech sent me crashing sideways (in, into) the door. "(Who's, Whose) that?" I managed to whisper. The answer launched itself (in, into) me, knocking me backwards. My dog!

UNIT 17

Diagraming Sentences

Lesson **17.1** **Diagraming Simple Subjects and Simple Predicates** 465

Lesson **17.2** **Diagraming the Four Kinds of Sentences** 466

Lesson **17.3** **Diagraming Direct and Indirect Objects** 467

Lesson **17.4** **Diagraming Adjectives and Adverbs** 468

Lesson **17.5** **Diagraming Predicate Nouns and Predicate Adjectives** 469

Lesson **17.6** **Diagraming Prepositional Phrases** 470

Lesson **17.7** **Diagraming Compound Sentence Parts** 471

17.1 Diagraming Simple Subjects and Simple Predicates

Every sentence contains a subject and a predicate. To diagram a sentence, first draw a horizontal line. Then draw a vertical line that crosses the horizontal line.

To the left of the vertical line, write the simple subject. To the right of the vertical line, write the simple predicate. Use capital letters as they appear in the sentence, but do not use punctuation.

Waves crash.

| Waves | crash |

Be sure to write only the simple subject and the simple predicate in this part of the diagram. Remember that the simple predicate can include a helping verb.

The **breakers are pounding** the rocks.

| breakers | are pounding |

Exercise 1   Diagraming Simple Subjects and Simple Predicates

Diagram the simple subject and simple predicate of each sentence.

1. Families arrive.
2. They began the day early.
3. Some people are swimming.
4. A child has found a shell.
5. Gwen has built a sand castle.

17.2 Diagraming the Four Kinds of Sentences

The simple subject and the simple predicate of the four kinds of sentences are diagramed below. Note that the location of the simple subject and the simple predicate in a sentence diagram is always the same, regardless of word order in the sentence.

DECLARATIVE

Fishers depend upon the sea.

Fishers	depend

INTERROGATIVE

Do you live near the ocean?

you	Do live

IMPERATIVE

Read this book about the sea.

(you)	Read

EXCLAMATORY

How majestic the **oceans are!**

oceans	are

In an interrogative sentence, the simple subject often comes between the two parts of a verb phrase. In an imperative sentence, the word *you* is understood to be the simple subject.

Exercise 2   Diagraming Simple Subjects and Simple Predicates

Diagram the simple subject and simple predicate of each sentence.

1. Have you seen an ocean?
2. Oceans cover about seventy percent of the earth's surface.
3. Does our planet look like one large ocean?
4. Think about that.
5. How small the continents seem!
6. The largest ocean on earth is the Pacific Ocean.
7. Look at the map in this atlas.
8. Does the Pacific Ocean extend to Japan?
9. Is the Indian Ocean the smallest one?
10. Find it on the globe.

Diagraming Sentences

17.3 Diagraming Direct and Indirect Objects

The predicate of a sentence often contains an action verb and a direct object. In a sentence diagram, place the direct object to the right of the action verb. Draw a vertical line to separate the action verb from the direct object. This vertical line, however, does *not* cross the horizontal line.

The sea contains many **creatures.**

| sea | contains | creatures |

In some sentences, an indirect object comes between the action verb and the direct object. In a diagram, place the indirect object on a line below and to the right of the verb. Draw a slanted line to connect the indirect object to the verb.

Coral reefs give some **animals** a home.

| reefs | give | home |
  \animals

Exercise 3 **Diagraming Sentences**

Diagram the simple subject, simple predicate, and direct object of each sentence. If the sentence contains an indirect object, diagram it too.

1. Sea plants get minerals from the water.
2. Seaweeds include the long, thin kelp.
3. Scientists have found animal life at impressive depths.
4. Many sea animals show us their picturesque behavior.
5. Some anemones make homes in crab shells.
6. They attach their bodies to the shells of hermit crabs.
7. Hermit crabs use the shells of sea snails for homes.
8. They must protect their soft abdomens.
9. The crabs twist their bodies into the snail shells.
10. The Atlantic hermit crab makes itself a home in a whelk shell.

17.4 Diagraming Adjectives and Adverbs

An adjective modifies a noun or pronoun. In a diagram, write the adjective on a slanted line beneath the noun or pronoun it modifies. Diagram possessive nouns and pronouns and the articles *a, an,* and *the* just as you would diagram other kinds of adjectives.

Our new boat encountered **a stormy** sea.

An adverb can modify a verb, an adjective, or another adverb. Note how adverbs are diagramed.

We have **almost never** seen **such** violent weather.

Exercise 4 **Diagraming Sentences**

Diagram each sentence.

1. Winds cause most waves.
2. Gravity causes the tides.
3. Earthquakes sometimes create dangerous waves.
4. Enormous waves move quite rapidly.
5. Ocean storms frequently cause coastal floods.
6. A very severe flood damaged a seaside town.
7. It rapidly leveled several wooden houses.
8. The inhabitants fortunately escaped.
9. Their supplies had been washed away.
10. Most people had never seen a worse flood.

17.5 Diagraming Predicate Nouns and Predicate Adjectives

In a sentence diagram, the direct object is placed to the right of a vertical line after the action verb.

Ancient peoples sailed the oceans.

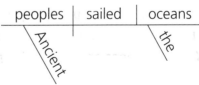

Similarly, in a sentence diagram, place the predicate noun to the right of the linking verb. Draw a slanted line to separate the linking verb from the predicate noun.

The Phoenicians were **explorers.**

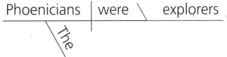

Diagram a predicate adjective just as you would diagram a predicate noun.

These ships were quite **seaworthy.**

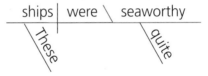

Exercise 5   Diagraming Sentences

Diagram each sentence.

1. The ancient Greeks were seafarers.
2. Roman ships looked graceful.
3. Viking vessels were numerous.
4. Historical exploration is a recent development.
5. Jacques Cousteau became a famous explorer.

17.6 Diagraming Prepositional Phrases

To diagram a sentence with a prepositional phrase used as an adjective, follow the model below.

The waves **along the rocky shore** crashed loudly.

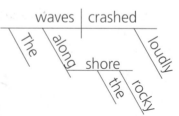

The prepositional phrase, *along the rocky shore,* is connected to the word that it modifies, the noun *waves.*

The following example shows the same prepositional phrase used as an adverb.

Enormous waves crashed **along the rocky shore.**

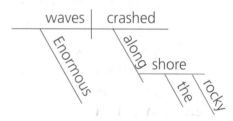

The prepositional phrase, *along the rocky shore,* is connected to the word that it modifies, the verb *crashed.*

Exercise 6   Diagraming Sentences

Diagram each sentence.

1. The floor of the ocean has remarkable features.
2. Many mountains exist beneath the surface.
3. These mountains below the waves include active volcanoes.
4. Many Pacific islands are really mountains on the ocean floor.
5. Deep trenches cut into the South Pacific floor.

17.7 Diagraming Compound Sentence Parts

Conjunctions such as *and, but,* and *or* are used to join words, phrases, and sentences, creating compound constructions. When you diagram compound parts of a sentence, place the second part of the compound below the first.

COMPOUND SUBJECT

The sea and its products benefit people.

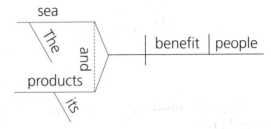

COMPOUND PREDICATE

Sea creatures **eat and sleep.**

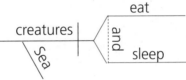

COMPOUND SENTENCE

Some sea creatures are plentiful, but others are scarce.

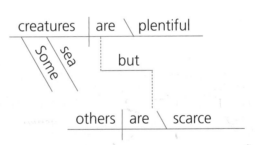

Exercise 7   **Diagraming Sentences**

Diagram each sentence.

1. Fish and shellfish are plentiful ocean products.
2. The undersea world lives and grows.
3. Herring and cod are good food.
4. The ocean is unpredictable, but it lures many travelers.
5. The water wears many faces, and it shows different moods.

UNIT
18
Capitalization

Lesson **18.1** **Capitalizing Sentences,
Quotations, and Salutations**   *473*

Lesson **18.2** **Capitalizing Names and Titles
of People**   *475*

Lesson **18.3** **Capitalizing Names of Places**   *477*

Lesson **18.4** **Capitalizing Other Proper Nouns
and Adjectives**   *479*

Grammar Review   *481*

Writing Application   *487*

18.1 Capitalizing Sentences, Quotations, and Salutations

A capital letter appears at the beginning of a sentence. A capital letter also marks the beginning of a direct quotation and the salutation and closing of a letter.

RULE 1: Capitalize the first word of every sentence.

The country of Canada extends across North America.

RULE 2: Capitalize the first word of a direct quotation that is a complete sentence. A direct quotation gives a speaker's exact words.

Duane said, "**A**bout twenty-nine million people live in Canada."

"**M**any Canadians live near the southern border," Regina said.

RULE 3: When a quoted sentence is interrupted by explanatory words, such as *she said*, do not begin the second part of the sentence with a capital letter.

"Most Canadians," said Minh, "**l**ive in cities or towns."

"Canada's largest city," Lois added, "**i**s Toronto."

When the second part of a quotation is a new sentence, put a period after the interrupting expression and begin the second part of the quotation with a capital letter.

"I've been to Toronto," said Paul. "**M**y mother was born there."

RULE 4: Do not capitalize an indirect quotation. An indirect quotation does not repeat a person's exact words and does not appear in quotation marks. It is often introduced by the word *that*.

Paul said **that h**is mother was born in Toronto.

RULE 5: Capitalize the first word in the salutation and closing of a letter. Capitalize the title and name of the person addressed.

Dear **M**rs. **M**oulin,   **Y**ours truly,

To whom it may concern,   **S**incerely yours,

Exercise 1   Capitalizing Sentences, Quotations, and Salutations

Write each sentence. Use capital letters where needed. If a sentence contains no errors, write *correct*.

1. we were talking about our summer vacations.
2. Renée said, "last summer I visited Canada."
3. "you were lucky," said Paul, "because you went in the summer."
4. "Canada has cold winters," Jim remarked.
5. Paul said that summer winds from the Gulf of Mexico often bring hot weather to Canada.
6. "does that mean that on some days it's as hot in Canada as it is in Mexico?" asked Jim.
7. Jim said that in the Northwest Territories the summers are very short.
8. "I'm not surprised," said Renée, "for the Northwest Territories reach up to the North Pole."
9. "anyway," she said, "we visited only Quebec."
10. Paul said that he'd go to Quebec next year.

Exercise 2   Using Capitalization in a Letter

Rewrite the letter, using correct capitalization. The letter contains ten errors.

January 2, 2000

dear Jack,

   my family and I are having a great vacation here in the New Hampshire mountains. Dad says that We may come back again next year. The snow is perfect, and we love the town where we are staying.

   believe it or not, your cousin is also here on vacation. She told me today that you were not feeling well. "perhaps a letter," I said, "Will cheer him up." So I sat down after lunch and wrote you this letter. I hope You are feeling better. Next week I will be returning home. then I can visit you in person.

your good Friend,

Pete

18.2 Capitalizing Names and Titles of People

A common noun is the general name of a person, place, or thing. A common noun is not capitalized. A proper noun names a particular person, place, or thing and is capitalized.

RULE 1: Capitalize the names of people and the initials that stand for their names.

Louis **H**. **L**afontaine   **S**. **D**. **T**hompson   John **C**abot

RULE 2: Capitalize a title or an abbreviation of a title when it comes before a person's name or when it is used in direct address.

General James Wolfe   **D**r. Michelle Turner   **M**s. Chavez
In 1610 **C**aptain Hudson searched for a passage to Asia.
Later people asked him, "Did you find it, **C**aptain?"

Do not capitalize a title that follows or stands for a person's name.

Henry Hudson was captain of a ship.

RULE 3: Capitalize the names and abbreviations of academic degrees that follow a person's name. Capitalize *Jr.* and *Sr.*

Tina Ibarra, **Ph**.**D**.   Linda Tsang, **M**.**D**.   David Melo, **J**r.

RULE 4: Capitalize words that show family relationships when used as titles or as substitutes for a person's name.

Last year **F**ather and **A**unt Beth retraced Cartier's journey.

Do not capitalize words that show family relationships when they follow a possessive noun or pronoun.

Jody's **u**ncle took photographs of the voyage.

RULE 5: Always capitalize the pronoun *I*.

Champlain is the explorer **I** admire most.

Exercise 3 Capitalizing Names and Titles

Write each item. Use capital letters where needed.

1. ms. lucy jojola
2. dr. claude c. islas
3. captain richards
4. aunt anna
5. richard bennett jr.
6. daniel roget, ph.d.
7. uncle louis
8. jeanette canales, m.d.
9. judge jean luc
10. w. r. mackenzie
11. president jefferson
12. sir james smith
13. mr. robert townsend sr.
14. queen victoria
15. madame marie curie
16. lord roy nesbett
17. warren g. malloy jr.
18. professor talmon
19. mr. and mrs. ortiz
20. general davidson

Exercise 4 Using Capital Letters in Names and Titles

Write each sentence. Use capital letters where needed for names and titles.

1. In 1497 king henry VII of England hired a navigator.
2. This navigator, john cabot, landed in what is now Canada.
3. The Italian navigator verrazano probably reached Canada in 1524.
4. In 1534 king francis I of France, i believe, sent jacques cartier to the New World.
5. In 1608 another French explorer, champlain, founded Quebec.
6. In 1673 joliet and marquette sailed down the Mississippi River.
7. Nine years later, the explorer la salle claimed for France all the land drained by the Mississippi River.
8. In 1789 sir alexander mackenzie followed a river to the Arctic Ocean.
9. Last year dad and Uncle bill traveled down this river.
10. Pike's Peak was first sighted by mr. zebulon Pike in 1806.

The **d**octor will see you now.

This is **D**r. Gonzales.

18.3 Capitalizing Names of Places

The names of specific places are proper nouns and are capitalized. Do not, however, capitalize articles and prepositions that are part of geographical names.

RULE 1:	Capitalize the names of cities, counties, states, countries, and continents.

Toronto	Mexico	Europe
New Hampshire	Cook County	Hong Kong

RULE 2:	Capitalize the names of bodies of water and other geographical features.

Atlantic Ocean	Hudson Bay	Cape Cod
Mojave Desert	the Great Lakes	Monument Valley

RULE 3:	Capitalize the names of sections of the country.

the Southwest	New England	Midwest

RULE 4:	Capitalize compass points when they refer to a specific section of the country.

the East Coast	the South	the Northeast

Do not capitalize compass points when they are used to indicate direction.

Mexico is south of San Diego.

Do not capitalize adjectives formed from words showing direction.

northerly wind	eastern Texas

RULE 5:	Capitalize the names of streets and highways.

Hyde Street	Hollywood Freeway

RULE 6:	Capitalize the names of specific buildings, bridges, and monuments.

Washington Monument	Empire State Building

Exercise 5   Capitalizing Place Names

Write each word or group of words. Use capital letters where needed.

1. new mexico
2. acapulco
3. asia
4. peru
5. brooklyn bridge
6. yucatán peninsula
7. the pacific northwest
8. amarillo avenue
9. northern texas
10. san diego freeway
11. interstate 80
12. chrysler building
13. the southeast
14. indian ocean
15. alaska
16. portola valley
17. southern oregon
18. washington monument
19. rocky mountains
20. the united states

Exercise 6   Using Capital Letters for Place Names

Write each sentence. Use capital letters where needed for geographical names.

1. The country of mexico is south of the united states of america.
2. Mexico is the most northern country in latin america.
3. Its capital and largest city is mexico city.
4. This city of 19 million people has the largest population of any city in north america and south america.
5. The largest cities in mexico exist in the region known as the plateau of mexico.
6. The large peninsula located west of the gulf of california is known as baja california.
7. The sierra madre is part of the rockies.
8. The highest mountain in north america is mount mcKinley.
9. Mount mcKinley is in central alaska.
10. hawaii is surrounded by the pacific ocean, and puerto rico has the atlantic to the north and the caribbean sea to the south.

Exercise 7   Writing Place Names in a Paragraph

Write at least five sentences telling about the state you live in. Include the names of cities, rivers, and other specific places. Name the states that border your state.

Capitalizing Other Proper Nouns and Adjectives

Many nouns besides the names of people and places are proper nouns and, therefore, are always capitalized. The adjectives that are formed from proper nouns are called proper adjectives and are also always capitalized.

RULE 1: Capitalize all important words in the names of clubs, organizations, businesses, institutions, and political parties.

Fraternal Order of Police   Girl Scouts

RULE 2: Capitalize brand names but not the nouns following them.

Downhome cookies   Cruncho crackers

RULE 3: Capitalize all important words in the names of important historical events, periods of time, and documents.

War of 1812   Bronze Age   Constitution

RULE 4: Capitalize the names of days of the week, months of the year, and holidays. Do not capitalize names of the seasons.

Monday   August   New Year's Day   spring

RULE 5: Always capitalize the first and last words of the titles of literary works, songs, films, television series, magazines, and newspapers. Capitalize all other words except articles, coordinating conjunctions, and prepositions of fewer than five letters.

Julie of the Wolves   *Time* magazine

RULE 6: Capitalize the names of ethnic groups, nationalities, and languages.

Native American   Canadian   Italian

RULE 7: Capitalize all proper adjectives, including those formed from names of ethnic groups and nationalities.

Native American crafts   Mexican art   Victorian era

popcorn

Capitalization

Exercise 8   Capitalizing Proper Nouns and Adjectives

Write the following items. Use capital letters where needed.

1. madison school
2. december
3. world war I
4. native american poetry
5. "casey at the bat"
6. *oliver twist*
7. input corporation
8. mello yogurt
9. french
10. japanese
11. "we are the world"
12. *chicago tribune*
13. international workers union
14. "my life and difficult times"
15. african american stories
16. valentine's day
17. girl scouts of the united states of america
18. *popular mechanics* magazine
19. spanish dances
20. declaration of independence

Exercise 9   Using Capital Letters for Proper Nouns and Adjectives

Write each sentence. Use capital letters where needed for proper nouns and adjectives.

1. Mexico is a latin american country rich in art and tradition.
2. For centuries the arts have played a very important part in mexican life.
3. Long before Columbus discovered america, the maya and toltec peoples built beautiful temples.
4. The aztec people composed music and poetry.
5. The mexican revolution of 1910 changed the course of Mexico's art and literature.
6. Have you read the poem "wind and water and stone," by the famous mexican writer Octavio Paz?
7. In Mexico independence day is in september.
8. Holidays in mexico are colorfully celebrated.
9. We learned that mexico is the most southern part of the continent of north america.
10. The names of many cities in the southwestern united states originated from mexican and spanish words.

Grammar Review

CAPITALIZATION

A Secret for Two, by Quentin Reynolds, tells the story of a visually impaired milk deliverer, Pierre Dupin, and Joseph, the horse that drew his wagon. The passage has been annotated to show some of the rules of capitalization covered in this unit.

Literature Model

from A Secret for Two
by Quentin Reynolds

Montreal is a very large city, but, like all large cities, it has some very small streets. Streets, for instance, like **P**rince **E**dward **S**treet, which is only four blocks long, ending in a cul-de-sac. No one knew Prince Edward Street as well as did **P**ierre **D**upin, for Pierre had delivered milk to the families on the street for thirty years now.

   During the past fifteen years the horse which drew the milk wagon used by Pierre was a large white horse named Joseph. In **M**ontreal, especially in that part of Montreal which is very **F**rench, the animals, like children, are often given the names of saints. When the big, white horse first came to the **P**rovincale **M**ilk **C**ompany, he didn't have a name. They told Pierre that he could use the white horse henceforth. Pierre stroked the softness of the horse's neck; he stroked the sheen of its splendid belly, and he looked into the eyes of the horse.

   "**T**hat is a kind horse, a gentle and a faithful horse," Pierre said. . . .

> Name of a street

> Name of a person

> First word of a sentence

> Name of a city

> Proper adjective

> Name of a company

> First word of a direct quotation

Grammar Review

Review: Exercise 1   Capitalizing Sentences and Quotations

Rewrite each sentence, correcting any errors in capitalization. If a sentence has no errors, write *correct*.

SAMPLE   Pierre Dupin said, "no one loves Joseph as much as I do."
ANSWER   Pierre Dupin said, "No one loves Joseph as much as I do."

1. for most of his adult life, Pierre Dupin delivered milk to the families on Prince Edward Street.
2. after fifteen years of delivering milk, Pierre got his horse, Joseph.
3. the horse would lead his master to each house on the street.
4. Pierre thought, "what would I do without my loyal Friend, Joseph?"
5. Pierre and Joseph spent many years together in Montreal, Canada.
6. all the families on the street recognized Pierre and Joseph.
7. Pierre said, "fifteen years ago my supervisor gave me a horse to pull my milk wagon."
8. "Look into his eyes," said the supervisor. "this horse will be your faithful friend."
9. Pierre thought His new horse was kind and gentle.
10. "I think," said Pierre, "That I will name him Joseph."

Review: Exercise 2   Using Capitalization in a Letter

Rewrite the following letter, using correct capitalization. The letter contains ten errors.

March 19, 2001

dear Sara,

    Today we read a story about a milk deliverer. My teacher said, "class, I know you will like this story. it is one of my favorites." I can see why my teacher says He likes the story so much.

    last summer you said to me, "someday I hope I can have my own horse." you might like to read this story. It's called "A Secret for Two." tell me What you think of it.

your friend,
Chris

Review: Exercise 3   Capitalizing Names and Titles of People

Rewrite the following names and titles, using correct capitalization. If an item contains no errors, write *correct*.

1. mr. robert chang
2. uncle john
3. the club's president
4. professor r. d. diego
5. my aunt and uncle
6. queen elizabeth
7. margaret lee, m.d.
8. lieutenant juarez
9. the captain of the ship
10. ms. evert
11. governor whitman
12. dr. chris cross
13. president lincoln
14. emily cox, ph.d.
15. e. b. white
16. mrs. doubtfire
17. sir edmund hillary
18. aunt maria and i
19. ken griffey jr.
20. lady jane grey

Review: Exercise 4   Capitalizing Titles and Names of People and Places

Write each sentence. Use capital letters where needed.

SAMPLE   Our art teacher, ms. whitney, showed us paintings from mexico.
ANSWER   Our art teacher, Ms. Whitney, showed us paintings from Mexico.

1. The brilliant Mexican artist diego rivera painted murals.
2. Born in 1886, rivera became famous for his murals of mexico.
3. Last summer aunt sharice saw the murals in the national palace in mexico city.
4. My aunt then visited the yucatán peninsula.
5. That peninsula is surrounded by the gulf of mexico and the caribbean sea.
6. Her tour guide was juan perez, ph.d.
7. One evening dr. perez discussed general santa anna.
8. In 1833 the general became president of mexico.
9. Santa anna led the fight against the American colonists who wanted to take texas from mexico.
10. He was captured in a famous battle fought on the banks of the san jacinto river in 1836.

Grammar Review

Review: Exercise 5   Capitalizing Proper Nouns

Rewrite each sentence, correcting any errors in capitalization.

SAMPLE   Within a year joseph knew the milk route as well as Pierre.
ANSWER   Within a year Joseph knew the milk route as well as Pierre.

1. Pierre began his work for the provincale milk company every morning at five o'clock.
2. Without any direction from pierre, Joseph stopped at each house on prince edward street.
3. Jacques, the Supervisor of the company, thought that Pierre should retire after thirty years of work.
4. Jacques didn't know that pierre was visually impaired.
5. Only Joseph, i believe, knew Pierre couldn't see.

Review: Exercise 6   Capitalizing Proper Nouns and Proper Adjectives

Rewrite each sentence, correcting any errors in capitalization.

SAMPLE   Montreal is in the canadian province of quebec.
ANSWER   Montreal is in the Canadian province of Quebec.

1. The city is located in Southern Quebec, the province's most fertile region.
2. In 1535 Jacques Cartier of france became the first european explorer to reach present-day montreal.
3. The British captured the city in 1760 during the french and indian war.
4. Today french is the official language of Montreal.
5. Montreal is the largest french-speaking city in the world after Paris.
6. In addition to french, english is spoken in Montreal.
7. The St. lawrence river runs Northeast through quebec, a province of Canada.
8. Two states in new england and two canadian provinces border Quebec on the East.
9. Quebec shares its Southern border with New york and vermont.
10. The National capital of canada is ottawa.

Proofreading

The following passage is about the artist John Kane, whose work appears below. Rewrite the passage, correcting the errors in spelling, capitalization, grammar, and usage. Add any missing punctuation. There are ten errors.

John Kane

¹Born in scotland, John Kane (1860–1934) immigrated to Pennsylvania with his family when he was nineteen. ²Kane began sketching as a youth, but he couldn't afford to go to Art school.

John Kane, *Across the Strip*, 1929

(continued)

Capitalization

Grammar Review

³The self-taught Artist finally achieved reckognition at the age of sixty-seven with the exhibition of one of his paintings in Pittsburgh.

⁴Many of Kanes' paintings present detailed images of everyday life in Pittsburgh, where the artist spent much of his life. ⁵In *Across the Strip*, for example, mills and warehouses risen up behind apartment buildings, where clothes are hung out to dry. ⁶A man in a horse-drawn wagon delivers bread on a route similar to that in "A Secret for two." ⁷like Pierre and Joseph, the man and horse is a familiar part of their City's daily life.

Review: Exercise 8

Mixed Review

Rewrite the following letter, capitalizing all necessary words. You will need to capitalize twenty-five letters.

april 21, 2001

dear lenny,

Since you were absent last week, I thought I would tell you what we did in our history class. we are learning about pyramids. ms. nelson said that great civilizations thrived in Mexico a thousand years ago.

Barry asked, "is it true that some native americans built pyramids?"

Anna answered, "at the town of teotihuacán, people built pyramids dedicated to the sun."

Our teacher added, "in the religious centers of southern Mexico, the mayan people built pyramids with temples on top. In addition," she continued, "there are other ancient pyramids."

Ms. Nelson then told us about the pyramids in egypt. The Great Pyramid stands near the nile river. It is believed to have been built about 2700 B.C. when pharaoh khufu reigned. some pyramids were actually the tombs of egyptian pharaohs.

Maybe we will still be studying pyramids when you return next week. All of us at west middle school miss you.

your pal,
stan

Capitalization

Writing Application

TIME

For more about proofreading for capitalization errors, see **TIME Facing the Blank Page,** page 98.

Capitalization in Writing

Study the italicized examples of capitalization in this excerpt from Joseph Bruchac's essay "Thanking the Birds." Think about why each is capitalized.

> *One* day 30 years ago, *Swift Eagle,* an *Apache* man, visited some friends on the *Onondaga Indian Reservation* in central *New York. While* he was out walking, he heard sounds of boys playing in the bushes.
>
> *"There's* another one. Shoot it!" said one of the boys.
>
> *When* he pushed through the brush to see what was happening, he found that they had been shooting small birds with a BB gun.

Techniques with Capitalization

Try to apply the rules of capitalization in your own writing, just as Joseph Bruchac has done in his.

❶ Capitalize adjectives that are formed from proper nouns.

INCORRECT VERSION an apache man
BRUCHAC'S VERSION an Apache man

❷ Capitalize the names of specific geographical places.

INCORRECT VERSION the onondaga indian reservation
BRUCHAC'S VERSION the Onondaga Indian Reservation

❸ Do not capitalize adjectives formed from words showing direction or location.

INCORRECT VERSION
Central New York
BRUCHAC'S VERSION
central New York

Practice   Practice using correct capitalization by revising the following passage on a separate sheet of paper.

today the official languages of canada are english and French. however, most of the people of quebec are French-speaking canadians. Although it was the french explorer champlain who founded quebec, the english captured Quebec City during the french and indian war. They acquired quebec by the Treaty of Paris in 1763. Over the next few decades thousands of british colonists came to canada from the british Isles and the american colonies.

Capitalization

UNIT 19 Punctuation

Lesson **19.1**   **Using the Period and Other End Marks**   *489*

Lesson **19.2**   **Using Commas I**   *491*

Lesson **19.3**   **Using Commas II**   *493*

Lesson **19.4**   **Using Commas III**   *495*

Lesson **19.5**   **Using Semicolons and Colons**   *497*

Lesson **19.6**   **Using Quotation Marks and Italics**   *499*

Lesson **19.7**   **Using Apostrophes and Hyphens**   *501*

Lesson **19.8**   **Using Abbreviations**   *503*

Lesson **19.9**   **Writing Numbers**   *505*

Grammar Review   *507*

Writing Application   *515*

Different end marks are used with the different types of sentences. The period is used for declarative and imperative sentences. The question mark is used for interrogative sentences. And the exclamation point is used for exclamatory sentences.

RULE 1: Use a period at the end of a declarative sentence. A declarative sentence makes a statement.

The Wright brothers built the first successful airplane.

They built this pioneering machine at a cost of about $1,000.

RULE 2: Use a period at the end of an imperative sentence. An imperative sentence gives a command or makes a request.

Open your book to the chapter on airplanes. [command]

Please read about the first successful flight. [request]

RULE 3: Use a question mark at the end of an interrogative sentence. An interrogative sentence asks a question.

When did jet planes first begin flying?

Do most jet planes have space for more than a hundred passengers?

RULE 4: Use an exclamation point at the end of an exclamatory sentence. An exclamatory sentence expresses strong feeling.

What a wonderful invention the jet engine was!

How fast jet planes fly!

RULE 5: Use an exclamation point at the end of an interjection. An interjection is a word or group of words that expresses strong emotion.

Wow!   Whew!

My goodness!   Ouch!

Write the correct end mark for each sentence. Then write whether the sentence is *declarative, imperative, interrogative,* or *exclamatory.*

1. Leonardo da Vinci drew a design of an airplane more than four hundred years ago
2. How imaginative da Vinci was
3. Did the Wright brothers make the first successful airplane flight
4. On December 17, 1903, Orville Wright made the first successful piloted flight in a power-driven airplane
5. What an important day in history it was
6. Please tell me the name of Orville's brother
7. On that day Wilbur Wright also made a successful flight
8. The Wright brothers did not believe airplanes would ever be able to fly at night
9. How wrong they were
10. The Wright brothers were from Dayton, Ohio
11. Why did the brothers begin flying
12. The Wright brothers read about the death of a glider pilot named Otto Lilienthal
13. How that man's work affected them
14. Why did they make their flights in Kitty Hawk, North Carolina
15. Did the Weather Bureau in Washington advise them
16. In 1900 they tested their own glider
17. Did that early glider have good lifting power
18. They received a patent on a glider they made in 1902
19. Describe that machine
20. Later the two brothers built a motor-powered airplane
21. They took experimental flights for several years
22. In 1905 they made 105 flights, totaling only forty-five minutes in the air
23. Imagine that
24. Newspapers began giving longer reports on their flights after that time
25. Don't forget the Wright brothers' important role in history

19.2 Using Commas I

Commas can make sentences easier to understand because the commas signal a pause or separation between sentence parts.

RULE 1: Use commas to separate three or more items in a series.

Mary McLeod Bethune served as a teacher, adviser, and administrator.

Bethune lived, studied, and worked in the South.

RULE 2: Use a comma to show a pause after an introductory word.

Yes, she became the first African American woman to head an agency in the United States government.

No, her family had very little money.

RULE 3: Use a comma after two or more prepositional phrases at the beginning of a sentence.

For a number of years, she served as director of the National Youth Administration's Division of Negro Affairs. [two prepositional phrases—*For a number* and *of years*]

You need not use a comma after a single prepositional phrase, but it is not incorrect to do so.

For years she served as President Roosevelt's special adviser on minority affairs. [one prepositional phrase—*For years*]

RULE 4: Use commas to set off words that interrupt the flow of thought in a sentence.

Bethune, as you might imagine, spent her life improving educational opportunities for African Americans.

Mary McLeod Bethune, of course, served as president of the famous Bethune-Cookman College.

RULE 5: Use commas to set off names used in direct address.

Clarisse, did you know that Ms. Bethune opened a school for girls?

Pardon me, Ms. Moeti, when did she open this school?

Read about Bethune-Cookman College in Florida, Derek.

Exercise 2   Using Commas

Write the following sentences, adding commas where needed. Write *correct* if a sentence needs no commas.

1. Mary McLeod Bethune we have learned was the daughter of enslaved persons.
2. Bethune attended a mission school a seminary and the Moody Bible Institute.
3. In the early part of the twentieth century she opened a girls' school.
4. Bethune served in various capacities for presidents Coolidge Hoover Roosevelt and Truman.
5. From 1935 to 1944 she served as President Franklin Roosevelt's special adviser on minority affairs.
6. Mr. Fenster is it true Bethune was the first African American woman to head a federal agency?
7. Yes she was and she also was awarded the Spingarn Medal.
8. Joel E. Spingarn was a leader of the National Association for the Advancement of Colored People and I think an American literary critic.
9. From 1913 to the present the Spingarn Medal has been awarded to African Americans for outstanding achievement.
10. In 1958 the Spingarn Medal was given to the eight young people who were the first African Americans to attend Little Rock Central High School.

Exercise 3   Identifying Comma Rules

Write the following sentences, adding commas where needed. Write whether the commas are needed because of Rule 1, 2, 3, 4, or 5 on page 491.

SAMPLE   Ms. Lamm is it true that Bethune became a friend of Eleanor Roosevelt?

ANSWER   Ms. Lamm, is it true that Bethune became a friend of Eleanor Roosevelt? (Rule 5)

1. Yes Mrs. Roosevelt was a great admirer of Bethune.
2. Both women or so I've read worked hard during World War II.
3. Bethune and Roosevelt worked with people who were young poor and illiterate.
4. After her husband's illness in 1921 Eleanor became active on his behalf.
5. Both Bethune and Roosevelt are famous Mr. Branwell for their noble work.

19.3 Using Commas II

You need to use commas correctly in compound sentences, after salutations and closings in letters, and to prevent misreading.

RULE 6: Use a comma before *and, or,* or *but* when it joins simple sentences into a compound sentence.

Phillis Wheatley began to write poetry at the age of fourteen, and she became the first important African American poet.

She was born in Africa, but she was enslaved and taken to Boston.

Phillis Wheatley's poems discuss the question of religion, or they treat the issue of slavery.

RULE 7: Use a comma after the salutation of a friendly letter and after the closing of both a friendly letter and a business letter.

Dear Dad,   Your friend,   Yours truly,

RULE 8: Use a comma to prevent misreading.

Instead of one, two friends visited Phillis.

Dear General Washington,

Dear George,

Dear Mr. President,

Exercise 4   Using Commas

Write the following sentences, adding commas where needed. Write *correct* if a sentence needs no commas.

1. Phillis Wheatley was taken to Boston on a slave ship and there she was sold at a slave auction.
2. She was sold to a wealthy family and this family gave her their name and their religion.
3. The Wheatleys recognized Phillis's great talents and they taught her to read and write.
4. They encouraged her to study geography history and Latin.
5. Phillis read the great English poets and she studied the famous Latin writers.
6. She began writing poetry when she was a teenager and many of her poems were published.
7. A book of her poems was published in London in 1773.
8. The title of the book was I believe *Poems on Various Subjects, Religious and Moral.*
9. Ms. Schofield have you read any of her poems?
10. Wheatley traveled to London but she returned to Boston.

Exercise 5   Using Commas

Write each numbered item or sentence. Add a comma or commas where needed.

¹Dear Phillis

²I read your poem today and I thought it showed great promise. ³You should send it to the local newspaper or maybe a magazine would publish it. ⁴You'll be able to travel to London but I know you'll want to return to Boston. ⁵Instead of one two people will go to London with you. ⁶I suggest that you see Westminster Abbey and Mr. Garns thinks you should visit the Tower of London while you are there. ⁷These buildings escaped damage thank goodness during London's Great Fire of 1666. ⁸Mr. Garns says that most of the city has been rebuilt and the new buildings are of brick and stone. ⁹Of course we all hope that you have a wonderful trip.

¹⁰Your friend

Hannah

Using Commas III

Several rules for using commas, including those for punctuating dates, addresses, and titles, are a matter of standard usage.

RULE 9: Use commas before and after the year when it is used with both the month and the day. Do not use a comma if only the month and the year or the month and the day are given.

The flight began on June 18, 1983, and lasted six days.

The flight ended in June 1983 and lasted six days.

RULE 10: Use commas before and after the name of a state or a country when it is used with the name of a city. Do not use a comma after the state postal abbreviation followed by a ZIP code.

People came from as far away as Albany, New York, and Guatemala City, Guatemala, to watch the launch.

The address on the envelope was 42 Campus Drive, Stanford, CA 94305.

RULE 11: Use a comma or pair of commas to set off an abbreviated title or degree following a person's name.

The first American woman to participate in a space mission was Sally Ride, Ph.D.

Norman E. Thagard, M.D., accompanied Sally Ride on that memorable mission.

RULE 12: Use a comma or pair of commas to set off *too* when *too* means "also."

Kathy Sullivan, too, is a famous astronaut.

RULE 13: Use a comma or pair of commas to set off a direct quotation.

Claude said, "Sally Ride received her doctor's degree from Stanford University in 1978."

"I think," said Lotoya, "that Kathy Sullivan became the first woman spacewalker in history."

Exercise 6   Using Commas

Write the following sentences, adding commas where needed. Write *correct* if a sentence needs no commas.

1. A letter from a friend in Houston Texas arrived in the mail yesterday.
2. The letter was postmarked March 19 1995.
3. It focused attention on Sally Ride Ph.D.
4. On the June 1983 space mission the other astronauts with Ride were Hauck Fabian and Crippen.
5. Ride and Fabian conducted experiments and they tested the shuttle's remote manipulator arm.
6. They launched a communications satellite for the Indonesian government and one for the Canadian government too.
7. Sally Ride became an astronaut candidate the same year she got her Ph.D. in physics.
8. Yes I think Sally Ride should inspire young women to learn everything they can about math and science.
9. Before her mission in 1983 Sally Ride married a fellow astronaut.
10. "It's true" Lee said in the letter "that Sally Ride is a pioneer and is very brave."

Exercise 7   Using Commas

Write each numbered item or sentence in the following letter. Add a comma or commas where needed.

[1]16 Wallace Avenue
[2]Richmond VA 23203
[3]October 4 2000

[4]Dear Monica,

[5]On April 6 2000 my class held auditions for a play. [6]Alice Perri M.A. was our director. [7]"With two students for each part" she said "we can perform the play twice." [8]I won a major role, and my friend Sonia got a part too. [9]We performed the play on May 1 2000 and on May 8 2000.

[10]Your friend
Deling

19.5 Using Semicolons and Colons

The semicolon and the colon are punctuation marks that separate parts of a sentence that might otherwise be confused.

RULE 1: Use a semicolon to join parts of a compound sentence when a conjunction such as *and, but,* or *or* is not used. Remember that a compound sentence has two or more simple sentences that are joined by a conjunction.

Albert Einstein made many discoveries in science; his theory of relativity changed scientific thought.

Einstein was born in Germany in 1879; he moved to the United States in 1933.

Einstein liked classical music; he played the violin.

RULE 2: Use a colon to introduce a list of items that ends a sentence. Use a phrase such as *these, the following,* or *as follows* before the list.

A list of the greatest scientists in history usually begins with **these** names: Newton and Einstein.

Einstein's relativity theory advanced new ideas about **the following:** time, space, mass, and motion.

Einstein wrote his famous equation **as follows:** $E = mc^2$.

Do not use a colon immediately after a verb or a preposition. Either leave out the colon, or reword the sentence.

Einstein **studied** mathematics, physics, and English.

During his lifetime he lived **in** Germany, Switzerland, and the United States.

RULE 3: Use a colon to separate the hour from the minute when you write the time of day.

Einstein's train left Princeton at 10:15 A.M. and arrived at New York City at 12:33 P.M.

RULE 4: Use a colon after the salutation of a business letter.

Dear Sir or Madam: Dear Mrs. Santiago:

Exercise 8   Using Semicolons and Colons

Write each sentence. Add any needed semicolons or colons. Write *correct* if the sentence needs no semicolon or colon added.

1. Albert Einstein was an original thinker he changed our view of the universe.
2. His relativity theory contained new ideas about time, space, mass, motion, and gravitation.
3. Einstein speculated about speeds faster than light no object has yet moved that fast.
4. Einstein worked for seven years at the Swiss Patent Office this job gave him the free time to carry out his scientific investigations.
5. Einstein summarized his relativity theory as follows we can never talk about space without talking about time.
6. Einstein's quantum theory led to the development of these inventions motion pictures with sound, television, and sophisticated security devices.
7. Einstein also thought about the problems of his day he wrote a letter to Franklin Roosevelt about developing the atomic bomb.
8. An atomic bomb was dropped on Hiroshima, Japan, at 645 A.M. on August 6, 1945.
9. In the 1950s Einstein was offered the presidency of the state of Israel he insisted he was not right for this position.
10. Einstein lived the last part of his life in Princeton, New Jersey he considered himself a citizen of the world.

Exercise 9   Using Semicolons and Colons

Write each numbered item in the business letter below. Add semicolons or colons where needed.

¹Dear Ms. Ntinga

²I am sorry that I missed your talk on Albert Einstein. ³I have Glee Club practice at 130 P.M. and could not be at the talk. ⁴I am planning to write about Einstein's life I hope you can suggest some good books. ⁵I bought these books *The Theory of Relativity* and *Einstein, Profile of the Man.*

Sincerely,

Jerome

19.6 Using Quotation Marks and Italics

RULE 1: Use quotation marks before and after a direct quotation.

"Sojourner Truth was born enslaved," said Graciela.

RULE 2: Use quotation marks around each part of an interrupted quotation.

"She was," explained Kazuko, "a great fighter against slavery."

RULE 3: Use a comma or commas to separate a phrase such as *he said* from the quotation itself. Place the comma outside opening quotation marks but inside closing quotation marks.

Victoria said, "Sojourner Truth became free in 1828."

"She finally received her freedom under a New York law," Manny added.

RULE 4: Place a period inside closing quotation marks.

Ms. Yu said, "Sojourner Truth preached concern for the welfare of others."

RULE 5: Place a question mark or an exclamation mark inside the quotation marks when it is part of the quotation.

Chi asked, "Did she find jobs for enslaved persons who escaped?"

RULE 6: Place a question mark or an exclamation mark outside the quotation marks when it is part of the entire sentence but not part of the quotation.

Did Ms. Yu say, "Sojourner Truth visited President Lincoln"?

RULE 7: Use quotation marks for the title of a short story, essay, poem, song, magazine or newspaper article, or book chapter.

"The Open Boat" [short story]   "Shenandoah" [song]

RULE 8: Use italics (underlining) to identify the title of a book, play, film, television series, magazine, or newspaper.

The Grapes of Wrath [book]   *National Geographic* [magazine]

Exercise 10 Using Quotation Marks and Italics

Write each of the following titles. Add the necessary quotation marks or underlining for italics.

1. The Necklace (short story)
2. By the Sea (poem)
3. Newsweek (magazine)
4. A Midsummer Night's Dream (play)
5. Women in Sports (newspaper article)
6. Back to the Future (film)
7. Ivanhoe (book)
8. Treasures of Lascaux Cave (magazine article)
9. Home Improvement (television series)
10. Self-Reliance (essay)
11. Hoop Dreams (film)
12. Amazing Grace (song)
13. New York Times (newspaper)
14. Casey at the Bat (poem)
15. The Morning (book chapter)

Exercise 11 Using Quotation Marks with Other Punctuation

Write each sentence. Add quotation marks and other punctuation marks where needed.

1. Sojourner Truth's real name was Isabella Baumfree said Winona
2. Sojourner Truth changed her name said Winona when she decided to preach.
3. Don't you think her talks and lectures have the ring of truth asked Maya
4. That helped make her one of the best-known American abolitionists of her day said Mr. Scruggs.
5. Abolitionists worked to end slavery said Ms. Yu.
6. Bertha asked What is a sojourner
7. Ms. Yu replied A sojourner is a traveler
8. Did Ms. Yu say Sojourner Truth worked to improve the lives of African Americans living in Washington
9. Bertha exclaimed What a brave woman she was
10. Go to the library Ms. Yu said and find a book about Sojourner Truth

19.7 Using Apostrophes and Hyphens

An apostrophe shows possession and points out the missing letters in a contraction. A hyphen divides a word between syllables and joins the parts of compound words.

RULE 1: Use an apostrophe and an *-s ('s)* to form the possessive of a singular noun.

girl + **'s** = girl**'s**   Charles + **'s** = Charles**'s**

RULE 2: Use an apostrophe and an *-s ('s)* to form the possessive of a plural noun that does not end in *-s.*

women + **'s** = women**'s**   mice + **'s** = mice**'s**

RULE 3: Use an apostrophe alone to form the possessive of a plural noun that ends in *-s.*

girls + **'s** = girl**s'**   cities + **'s** = citie**s'**

Do not use an apostrophe in a possessive pronoun.

These skates are **hers.**   **Theirs** are in the car.

RULE 4: Use an apostrophe to replace letters that have been omitted in a contraction. A contraction is a word that is made by combining two words into one and leaving out one or more letters.

it is = it**'s**   you + are = you**'re**

RULE 5: Use a hyphen to show the division of a word at the end of a line. Always divide a word between its syllables.

With her husband, Pierre, Marie Sklodowska Curie discovered radium and polonium.

RULE 6: Use a hyphen in compound numbers.

sixty-five pianos   forty-two experiments

RULE 7: Use a hyphen or hyphens in certain compound nouns. Consult a dictionary to be sure.

great-uncle   brother-in-law
attorney-at-law   editor in chief

Using the Possessive Form

Write the possessive form of each word or group of words that follows.
Remember to use an apostrophe and an *s* (*'s*) or an apostrophe alone (*'*).

1. men	6. horses	11. Mrs. Jacobs	16. Mr. Sanchez
2. child	7. countries	12. wolves	17. reefs
3. Lois	8. babies	13. day	18. girls
4. Ms. Marie Rossi	9. pig	14. President Ford	19. his
5. oxen	10. house	15. sheep	20. teams

Exercise 13   **Using Apostrophes and Hyphens**

Write each sentence. Add apostrophes and hyphens where needed.
Write *correct* if a sentence needs no changes.

1. Marie and Pierre Curie discovered radium in 1898.
2. The daughter of teachers, Marie studied chemistry and physics in Paris.
3. In 1895 Pierre Curie became her husband.
4. The Curies interest in the discovery of radioactivity led to their discovery of radium.
5. The Curies, however, didnt discover radium until two years later.
6. From more than twenty five tons of uranium ore, they isolated radium and polonium.
7. For their work with radium and polonium, the Curies were awarded the Nobel Prize for physics in 1903.
8. Marie Curies work with the chemical properties of radium and polonium won her a second Nobel Prize in 1911.
9. Madame Curies daughter Irene and son in law Frederic Joliot also won a Nobel Prize for chemistry.
10. In 1934 Marie Curie died of leukemia, the same disease that took her daughters life twenty years later.
11. Eve Curies biography of her famous mother has been published in more than twenty languages.
12. Its amazing to think of how much the Curies accomplished.
13. In 1963 Maria Goeppert Mayer became the second woman ever to win a Nobel Prize in physics.
14. Her award followed Marie Curies second Nobel Prize by fifty two years.
15. Goeppert Mayers husband, Joseph E. Mayer, was a chemist.

RULE 1: Abbreviate the titles *Mr., Mrs., Ms.,* and *Dr.* before a person's name. Also abbreviate the professional or academic degrees that follow a person's name, as well as the titles *Jr.* and *Sr.*

Mr. Ed Hall **Jr.**   Henry Wong, **M.D.**   **Dr.** Ann Chu

Juan Diaz, **Ph.D.**   **Ms.** Ava Danko, **M.F.A.**

RULE 2: Use all capital letters and no periods for abbreviations that are pronounced letter by letter or as words. Exceptions are *U.S.* and *Washington, D.C.*, which do use periods.

NASA National Aeronautics and Space Administration

MVP most valuable player

RULE 3: Use the abbreviations A.M. (*ante meridiem*, "before noon") and P.M. (*post meridiem*, "after noon") for exact times. For dates use B.C. (before Christ) and, sometimes, A.D. (*anno Domini*, "in the year of the Lord," after Christ).

6:15 A.M.   5:30 P.M.   20 B.C.   A.D. 476

RULE 4: Abbreviate calendar items only in charts and lists.

Mon.   Wed.   Thurs.   Jan.   Apr.   Aug.   Nov.

RULE 5: In scientific writing, abbreviate units of measure. Use periods with abbreviations of English units but not of metric units.

inch(es) **in.**   foot (feet) **ft.**   gram(s) **g**   liter(s) **l**

RULE 6: On envelopes abbreviate the words that refer to streets in street names. Spell them out everywhere else.

Street **St.**   Avenue **Ave.**   Road **Rd.**   Court **Ct.**

We live at the corner of Polaris **Avenue** and Maple **Court.**

RULE 7: On envelopes use state postal service abbreviations for the names of states. Everywhere else, spell out state names.

Indiana **IN**   Arizona **AZ**   Alabama **AL**   Delaware **DE**

Maryland **MD**   Georgia **GA**   Florida **FL**   California **CA**

Exercise 14   Using Abbreviations

Write the correct abbreviation for each underlined item.

1. <u>Mister</u> Dean Paxton
2. 4000 <u>before Christ</u>
3. <u>March</u> 2, 1988
4. Hugh Hunt <u>Junior</u>
5. 43 Palm <u>Court</u>
6. <u>Sunday</u>
7. <u>anno Domini</u> 63
8. 456 Laguna <u>Street</u>
9. 8 <u>liters</u>
10. <u>Federal Bureau of Investigation</u>
11. <u>Friday</u>
12. 16 <u>inches</u>
13. Tampa, <u>Florida</u>
14. <u>Mister</u> Harold Wong
15. <u>September</u>
16. San Francisco, <u>California</u>
17. <u>Internal Revenue Service</u>
18. 6 <u>feet</u>
19. 109 Van Dyke <u>Road</u>
20. <u>January</u>

Exercise 15   Using Abbreviations

Write the correct abbreviation for each underlined item in the following sentences.

1. <u>Representative</u> Mari Ramos plans to speak about Elizabeth Blackwell.
2. <u>Doctor</u> Blackwell received her medical degree in 1849 from a college in Geneva, New York.
3. My <u>National Organization for Women</u> chapter will honor another Blackwell; Antoinette Brown Blackwell was the first ordained woman minister.
4. The first woman elected to the United States Senate was <u>Senator</u> Margaret Chase Smith from Maine.
5. The museum director presented a seminar on ancient Rome from 11:45 <u>in the morning</u> until 1:30 <u>in the afternoon</u>.
6. Juan Bosch <u>Junior</u> is known for giving interesting and lively seminars on various topics.
7. The museum is located at 1680 Sequoia <u>Drive</u>.
8. We learned that the first Roman emperor, Augustus, ruled from 27 <u>before Christ</u> to <u>anno Domini</u> 14.
9. Write to the Organization of American Historians at 112 North Bryan Street, Bloomington, <u>Indiana</u> 47401.
10. If you call, ask for <u>Mister</u> Bosch.

19.9 Writing Numbers

In charts and tables, you always write numbers as figures. However, in ordinary sentences, you sometimes spell out numbers and sometimes write them as numerals.

RULE 1: Spell out numbers that you can write in one or two words.

Jackie Robinson helped the Dodgers win **six** pennants.

RULE 2: Use numerals for numbers of more than two words.

The field at Dodger Stadium is **330** feet down the left-field line.

RULE 3: Spell out any number that begins a sentence or reword the sentence so that it does not begin with a number.

Fifty-five thousand fans turned out on opening day.

RULE 4: Write a very large number in numerals followed by the word *million* or *billion*.

In 1991 major league baseball attracted more than **56 million** fans.

RULE 5: If related numbers appear in the same sentence, use all numerals even though you might spell out one of the numbers if it appeared alone.

In 1953 the Dodgers won **105** games and lost **49.**

RULE 6: Spell out ordinal numbers (such as *first, second,* and *third*).

Jackie Robinson was the **first** African American to play in the majors.

RULE 7: Use words to express the time of day unless you are writing the exact time with the abbreviation A.M. or P.M.

Today's baseball game began at **two o'clock.**
Work ended at **5:15 P.M.**

RULE 8: Use numerals to express dates, house and street numbers, apartment and room numbers, telephone numbers, page numbers, amounts of money of more than two words, and percentages. Write out the word *percent*.

May **16, 1865**   **241** Bryant St.   Apartment **3**G   **50 percent**

Use the correct form for writing numbers in the following sentences. Write *correct* if the sentence needs no changes.

1. In the 1930s, many baseball games began at three o'clock in the afternoon.
2. Some World Series games began at twelve thirty P.M.
3. A good batter hits safely thirty percent of the time.
4. Jackie Robinson entered major league baseball in nineteen hundred forty-seven.
5. Robinson was born at the end of the 1st World War.
6. Later he gained fame as an all-star 2nd baseman for the Brooklyn Dodgers.
7. Robinson helped the Dodgers win the World Series for the first time in 1955.
8. In that World Series, each team won 3 times before the Dodgers won an exciting 7th game.
9. Robinson retired from baseball after his 10th season.
10. In his career, Robinson hit 273 doubles, 137 home runs, and fifty-four triples.
11. In Robinson's 1st season in the majors, the average salary was eleven thousand two hundred dollars.
12. In 1992 the average salary for major leaguers was more than 1,000,000 dollars.
13. Satchel Paige was a star pitcher in the Negro baseball leagues for more than 20 years.
14. Paige entered the major leagues in nineteen hundred forty-eight and was elected to the National Baseball Hall of Fame in nineteen hundred seventy-one.
15. Hank Aaron broke Babe Ruth's home-run record and hit a total of seven hundred fifty-five home runs in his career.
16. During the 2nd World War, many people attended women's-league baseball games.
17. A film about the women's leagues, titled *A League of Their Own,* was made in 1992.
18. Willie Mays led the National League in stolen bases 4 times and in home runs 4 times.
19. In 1961 the New York Yankees hit a record two hundred forty home runs.
20. 23 teams played in the National League between 1876 and 1900.

Grammar Review

PUNCTUATION

Harriet Tubman: The Moses of Her People by Langston Hughes tells about the African American woman who escaped from slavery and then helped free hundreds of other enslaved people. The following excerpt from the biographical sketch describes Tubman's activities during the Civil War. The passage is annotated to show some of the rules of punctuation covered in this unit.

Literature Model

from Harriet Tubman: The Moses of Her People
by Langston Hughes

Harriet Tubman's war activities were amazing. She served under General Stevens at Beaufort, South Carolina. She was sent to Florida to nurse those ill of dysentery, small pox, and yellow fever. She was with Colonel Robert Gould Shaw at Fort Wagner. She organized a group of nine Negro scouts and river pilots and, with Colonel Montgomery, led a Union raiding contingent of three gunboats and about 150 Negro troops up the Combahee River. As reported by the Boston *Commonwealth*, for July 10, 1863, they "under the guidance of a black woman, dashed into the enemy's country, struck a bold and effective blow, destroying millions of dollars worth of commissary stores, cotton and lordly dwellings, and striking terror into the heart of rebeldom, brought off near 800 slaves and thousands of dollars worth of property."

> Apostrophe to show possession

> Comma before a state name when used with a city name

> Comma to separate items in a series

> Italics for the title of a newspaper

> Period inside closing quotation marks

Grammar Review

Review: Exercise 1 **Using End Marks**

Write the correct end mark for each sentence, and then write whether the sentence is *declarative, imperative, interrogative,* or *exclamatory.*

1. Harriet Tubman was born enslaved in Maryland
2. Why did she serve in the Union Army
3. What an amazing woman she was
4. Read about her heroic actions in Hughes's book
5. Tubman worked in the fields before escaping to freedom in 1849

Review: Exercise 2 **Using Commas**

Rewrite each sentence, inserting commas as needed.

SAMPLE   During the Civil War Harriet Tubman served as a nurse a scout and a spy.

ANSWER   During the Civil War, Harriet Tubman served as a nurse, a scout, and a spy.

1. Tubman served with Colonel Montgomery and she helped him lead a raid on enemy territory.
2. With the help of an African American woman the troops made a successful raid.
3. During the raid Tubman helped destroy houses provisions and cotton.
4. The *Commonwealth* reported her heroic actions on July 10 1863.
5. Yes Tubman was seen as an extraordinary woman even while she was alive.
6. Harriet's husband discouraged her you may be surprised to learn when she wanted to escape to freedom.
7. Harriet settled in Auburn New York and she brought her parents to live there too.
8. Ms. Buchman do you know how many enslaved persons she helped escape?
9. During one military campaign in the war Tubman helped free more than 750 enslaved people.
10. After the war, Tubman helped African Americans by establishing a home for the elderly and needy in Auburn New York and by raising money for schools.

Review: Exercise 3 **Using Semicolons and Colons**

Rewrite each sentence, inserting semicolons and colons as needed. Write *correct* if the sentence needs no semicolons or colons.

1. Alexander Graham Bell invented the telephone he received the patent for his invention in 1876.
2. I admire Henry Fonda's performance in the following film *The Story of Alexander Graham Bell.*
3. Thomas Edison was a great inventor some of his inventions include the phonograph, the electric lightbulb, the carbon telephone transmitter, and a duplicating machine.
4. I'll pick you up at 315 P.M. to visit Edison's research laboratory in West Orange.
5. Tourists can see Bell's home in Nova Scotia and tour Edison's home in Florida.

Review: Exercise 4 **Using Quotation Marks and Italics**

Rewrite each sentence, inserting quotation marks and underlining for italics as needed.

1. Rachel Carson was an artist, a poet, a scientist, an author, and a reformer, replied Ms. Erlich.
2. The journalist Eric Sevareid compared her to Harriet Beecher Stowe, Mr. Santiago added.
3. Sevareid said that Carson's book Silent Spring sparked a war against pesticides just as Stowe's book Uncle Tom's Cabin helped start the Civil War.
4. A New York Times article called Silent Spring Is Now Noisy Summer stirred great interest across the country, and other newspapers picked up the story.
5. In response to the excitement, Rachel Carson said, As you listen to the present controversy about pesticides, I recommend that you ask yourself who speaks and why.

Punctuation

Grammar Review

Review: Exercise 5 **Using Apostrophes and Hyphens**

Rewrite each sentence, inserting apostrophes and hyphens as needed.
Write *correct* if a sentence needs no apostrophes or hyphens.

1. Probably Booker T. Washingtons greatest contribution was founding the
   Tuskegee Institute, a vocational school for African Americans.
2. Washington opened the school when he was twenty five years old.
3. Washington advised President Theodore Roosevelt and President William H.
   Taft on their racial policies.
4. Its not surprising that W. E. B. Du Bois disagreed with some of Washingtons
   views on civil rights.
5. Theirs was a disagreement about different ways to achieve a similar end: the
   improvement of African Americans lives.

Review: Exercise 6 **Using Abbreviations and Numbers**

Rewrite each sentence, correcting the errors in abbreviations and numbers.

1. In 1872, when he was sixteen, Washington traveled 300 miles to enter an
   industrial school for African Americans—Hampton Institute.
2. 6 years after he graduated from Hampton, Washington founded Tuskegee
   Institute in Tuskegee, AL.
3. Washington told about his rise from slavery to national prominence
   in *Up from Slavery*, published in nineteen hundred one.
4. The autobiography was reprinted 56 years after Washington died.
5. On September eighteenth, 1895, Washington made a speech before a large
   crowd at the Cotton Exposition in Atlanta, GA.
6. He spoke for less than 20 minutes, explaining his theory that African
   Americans could accept segregation in exchange for economic advancement.
7. The speech was widely quoted and was the 1st event to make
   Washington a national figure and adviser to presidents.
8. Today fifty-four percent of the students at Tuskegee are female.
9. The school 1st looks for students with outstanding records.
10. Applications received by March thirty-one are given priority.

Review: Exercise 7 Using End Marks, Commas, Semicolons, and Colons

Rewrite each sentence, inserting end marks, commas, semicolons, and colons as needed.

SAMPLE By overplanting cotton year after year southern plantation owners ruined their land George Washington Carver helped bring the land back to life

ANSWER By overplanting cotton year after year, southern plantation owners ruined their land; George Washington Carver helped bring the land back to life.

1. Carver's radical ideas included rotating these crops peanuts soybeans and sweet potatoes
2. Carver's innovations helped restore the land they also helped diversify the South's economy
3. Did you know that he discovered more than three hundred uses for the peanut
4. These uses included the following a milk substitute printer's ink and face powder
5. Yes he discovered more than one hundred uses for the sweet potato too
6. Carver was born enslaved in 1861 on a farm near Diamond Missouri
7. Carver faced many obstacles to getting an education but he finally graduated from Iowa State Agricultural College in 1894
8. In 1896 with his master's degree behind him Carver joined the faculty at Tuskegee Institute in Alabama
9. Carver put his laboratory onto a mule-driven wagon and his traveling exhibit helped farmers in Alabama and other states
10. Carolyn do you plan to visit the George Washington Carver National Monument after you graduate on June 6 2001

Review: Exercise 8 Using Correct Punctuation in a Letter

To request information about what Tuskegee Institute is like today, write a sample business letter to Suite 101, Old Administration Building, Tuskegee, AL 36088. Punctuate your letter with end marks, commas, semicolons, and colons as needed. For a model letter, turn to pages 496 and 498.

Grammar Review

Review: Exercise 9 Using Commas, Quotation Marks, Italics, and Apostrophes

Rewrite each sentence, inserting commas, quotation marks, italics (underlining), and apostrophes as needed.

SAMPLE Mr. Garns answered Du Bois wrote about his disagreements with Booker T. Washington in his book The Souls of Black Folk.

ANSWER Mr. Garns answered, "Du Bois wrote about his disagreements with Booker T. Washington in his book *The Souls of Black Folk.*"

1. Du Boiss other books include Black Reconstruction in America and The Autobiography of W. E. B. Du Bois.
2. I heard he was the first African American to receive a doctorate from Harvard University said Jarell.
3. Du Bois was dissatisfied with the progress of race relations and he moved to Ghana in Africa as a result said the history professor.
4. Du Bois helped found the National Association for the Advancement of Colored People in 1909 and he was editor of its magazine The Crisis.
5. For information on current activities Amanda suggested that we write to the NAACPs national headquarters at this address: 4805 Mt. Hope Drive Baltimore MD 21215

Review: Exercise 10 Using Apostrophes, Hyphens, Abbreviations, and Numbers

Rewrite each sentence, inserting apostrophes and hyphens as needed and correcting errors in abbreviations and numbers.

1. Thurgood Marshall was chief counsel for the NAACP for twenty three years.
2. As counsel he presented the argument that resulted in the Supreme Courts 1954 decision to end segregation in public schools.
3. For 4 years, he was a United States Appeals Court judge.
4. In 1967 he became the 1st African American to sit on the Supreme Court of the United States.
5. Marshall was born in Baltimore, MD, in 1908.

Review: Exercise 11

Proofreading

The following passage is about African American artist Aaron Douglas, whose work appears below. Rewrite the passage, correcting the errors in spelling, capitalization, grammar, and usage. Add any missing punctuation. There are 10 errors.

Aaron Douglas

[1]Aaron Douglas (1899–1979) is 1 of the best-known artists of the Harlem Renaissance movement of the 1920s. [2]Many African american

Aaron Douglas, *Aspiration*, 1936

(continued)

Punctuation

writers and artist's gathered in Harlem during this period to explore and celebrate African American culture. ³Many of them believed that Douglas' paintings expresed the positive mood of the Harlem Renaissance.

⁴The artist was strongly influenced by the simple forms represented in West African sculpture ⁵Douglas used this style in *Aspiration* to reprezent all African American men and women. ⁶With their backs to the past the figures in the painting looks toward the future. ⁷They envision the following freedom, equality, opportunity.

Review: Exercise 12

Mixed Review

Rewrite each sentence, using correct punctuation. Correct the errors in abbreviations and numbers.

1. Civil rights include the following freedom of speech freedom of the press and freedom of religion

2. During the 12 years after the Civil War Congress passed laws to protect African Americans civil rights

3. In 1883 the Supreme Court ruled that some of these laws were unconstitutional two years later the court upheld a law requiring "separate but equal" accommodations for African Americans

4. Did you know that the "separate but equal" rule remained in effect for more than fifty years

5. The Supreme Court finally ruled segregation unconstitutional in 1954 and 10 years later Congress passed the strongest civil rights bill in its history

6. The Equal Employment Opportunities Commission was established by the Civil Rights Act of nineteen sixty four said Ms Higgins

7. Poll taxes as you may know kept African Americans from voting in many southern states

8. You can learn more about the history of civil right's in the book We Will Be Heard

9. Check it out at the library on Wed.

10. What a fascinating story it is

Writing Application

TIME

For more about checking for punctuation errors, see **TIME Facing the Blank Page,** page 98.

Punctuation in Writing

Punctuation helps readers understand what they are reading. Note Yoshiko Uchida's use of punctuation in this passage from *The Invisible Thread*.

> "Honk the horn to let them know we're here," Papa said.
>
> At which point Keiko not only honked the horn, but simultaneously crashed into Jick's dog house, knocked it over on its side, and stopped just inches short of the walnut tree.
>
> "Look out, for heaven's sake," we all shouted. "Look out!"
>
> Jick barked furiously at the sudden assault on his territory, and the chickens scrambled in every direction, screeching and cackling as though the end of the world had come.

Techniques with Punctuation

Try to apply the rules of punctuation when you write and revise your own work.

❶ Use a comma after items in a series.

WITHOUT COMMAS crashed into Jick's dog house knocked it over and stopped

UCHIDA'S VERSION crashed into Jick's dog house, knocked it over on its side, and stopped

❷ Use direct quotations set off by quotation marks and commas.

WITHOUT QUOTATION We all shouted to look out.

UCHIDA'S VERSION "Look out, for heaven's sake," we all shouted.

Punctuation

Practice On your paper, revise and rewrite the following passage about Richard Wright, an African American author. Add punctuation to make the passage easier to read.

Richard Wright was born near Natchez Mississippi. Wright moved to Chicago Illinois when he was nineteen His second book is a novel about a young African American in the Chicago slums This book, *Native Son,* gained Wright immediate fame Speaking of the book's main character, a reviewer said We get inside Bigger Thomas's head so we can feel the terror and despair of the life of a man who is young poor and black Wright's other books include *The Outsider The Long Dream* and his autobiography *Black Boy* Much of his writing deals with the life of African Americans in the United States Wright moved to New York in 1937 and he lived the last years of his life in Paris

UNIT 20

Sentence Combining

Lesson **20.1** **Compound Sentences** *517*

Lesson **20.2** **Compound Elements** *519*

Lesson **20.3** **Prepositional Phrases** *521*

20.1 Compound Sentences

When you have written a few simple sentences that are closely related in meaning, try combining them to form compound sentences. A compound sentence often states your meaning more clearly than a group of simple sentences does. Also, by using compound sentences, you can vary the lengths of your sentences.

EXAMPLE
    a. The boy wanted a black leather jacket.
    b. His mother bought a green vinyl one instead.
       [, but]

The boy wanted a black leather jacket**, but** his mother bought a green vinyl one instead.

In this example, simple sentence *a* is joined to simple sentence *b* with the coordinating conjunction *but*. Note that a comma is used before the conjunction.

■ A **compound sentence** contains two or more simple sentences. You can combine two or more related simple sentences into a compound sentence by using the conjunctions *and, but,* or *or*.

Exercise 1   **Combining Simple Sentences**

The sentences below are based on the story "The Jacket" by Gary Soto, which you can find on pages 172–177. Combine the sentences in each numbered item into one new sentence by using a comma plus a coordinating conjunction. In the first few items, the coordinating conjunction you should use is in brackets.

1. **a.** The boy had outgrown his old jacket.
   b. His mother wanted to buy him a new one. **[, and]**
2. **a.** The boy thanked his mother for the jacket.
   b. He actually hated it. **[, but]**
3. **a.** His mother did not understand her son's feelings.
   b. Perhaps she simply could not afford a leather jacket. **[, or]**

4. **a.** The boy teased his dog, Brownie.

   b. The animal tore a gash in the jacket's sleeve. [**, and**]

   c. The boy wore his jacket anyway. [**, but**]

5. **a.** The next day the boy wore his jacket to school.

   b. His best friend seemed rude to him.

6. **a.** He got lower grades in school.

   b. Girls seemed to lose interest in him.

7. **a.** One day he decided to throw the jacket away.

   b. He pitched it over a fence.

   c. Something made him pick it up again.

8. **a.** The boy finished dinner.

   b. He went outside with his jacket over his arm.

9. **a.** The night was cold.

   b. The boy soon slipped into his jacket.

10. **a.** He never liked the ugly green jacket.

    b. He had to wear it for three long years.

Exercise 2   Combining Simple Sentences

Rewrite the following paragraphs, combining sentences as you think necessary.

The boy wore the jacket for three long years. He was unhappy for most of that time. He wished for a jacket of a different color. His family could not afford a black leather jacket. This was America. Children in America did not wear jackets like this. He wanted another jacket badly. He wore the ugly one.

The boy began to develop muscles. His arms stuck out of the jacket. He repaired the old rip in the sleeve. The gash widened. Stuffing came out of it. Still he kept the jacket. Perhaps he could not afford another one. Perhaps he had grown attached to his guacamole jacket. The jacket cast a shadow over his life. He would not get rid of it. He called it his "ugly brother." In a sense, the jacket had become part of him.

20.2 Compound Elements

Sometimes several sentences contain the same information—for example, the same subject or verb. By combining such sentences and using compound elements, you can avoid repetition and make your writing more concise. Sentences with compound elements also add variety to your writing.

EXAMPLE   **a.** Morning Girl looked in the water.

            b. Morning Girl **tried to see her own face clearly.** [**and**]

Morning Girl looked in the water **and tried to see her own face clearly.**

Sentences *a* and *b* share information about Morning Girl. The combined version takes the new information from sentence *b, tried to see her own face clearly,* and joins it to sentence *a,* using the coordinating conjunction *and.* The balanced, parallel structure of the verbs *looked* and *tried* makes this sentence effective.

■ You can avoid repeating shared information by combining and using **compound elements.** Join compound elements with the conjunctions *and, but,* or *or.* A comma is not needed after the conjunction.

Exercise 3   Combining Sentences with Compound Elements

The sentences below are based on a passage from *Morning Girl* by Michael Dorris, which you can find on pages 134–139. Combine the sentences in each numbered item, using compound elements joined by the conjunctions *and, but,* and *or.* As you build on the first sentence in each item, include only the new information from the following sentence(s). In the first few items, the new information is in dark type and the conjunctions you should use are in brackets.

1. **a.** Morning Girl could not see her ears in the water.
   b. She could not see **her mouth.** [**or**]
2. **a.** Morning Girl knew the color of her arms.
   b. She did **not** know **the color of her eyes.** [**but**]

3. **a.** Morning Girl asked her mother about her eyes.
   b. She asked about her **teeth. [and]**
4. **a.** Under her mother's direction, Morning Girl touched her own chin.
   b. She touched her own mouth.
5. **a.** Morning Girl and her mother had different eyebrows.
   b. Morning Girl and her mother had the same ears.
6. **a.** Morning Girl's brother laughed at her.
   b. Her brother teased her.
   c. He compared her face to a pointed rock.
7. **a.** She looked into her father's eyes.
   b. She saw two tiny girls looking back.
8. **a.** Each girl had a clear face.
   b. Each girl had a face with a narrow chin.
   c. Each had a face with a wide mouth.
9. **a.** Her father stood up.
   b. Her father went back to his work.
10. **a.** The girl's mother taught her something about her appearance.
    b. The girl's father taught her something about her appearance.

Exercise 4   Combining Sentences with Compound Elements

Rewrite the following paragraphs by combining elements. Make any other changes in wording you think necessary.

Morning Girl found her father outside. She asked him about her face. He was playful. He was also sympathetic. He told her to look into his eyes. Morning Girl stood still. She gazed deep into her father's eyes. She saw two very small girls. They had straight brows. They had pointed chins. They had smiling mouths. Morning Girl found the two strangers fascinating. She found them pretty. Morning Girl was actually looking at herself. She did not know it.

Her father showed her the answer to her question. Her father said the answer would always be there. Afterwards she always remembered the two girls in her father's eyes. Afterwards she always remembered the pretty girls. Afterwards she always remembered the friendly girls.

Prepositional Phrases

Prepositional phrases are effective tools for sentence combining. They help you present more information about a noun or verb just as adjectives and adverbs do.

EXAMPLE
    a. The elephants are being bathed.

    b. They live **at the zoo.**

    c. They are bathed **by keepers.**

The elephants **at the zoo** are being bathed **by keepers.**

New information from sentences *b* and *c* is added to sentence *a* in the form of prepositional phrases. In the new sentence, the prepositional phrase *at the zoo* describes the noun *elephants.* The phrase *by keepers* describes the verb *are being bathed.* Notice that prepositional phrases that describe nouns follow the nouns they describe. Prepositional phrases that describe verbs can occupy different places in the sentence.

■ A **prepositional phrase** is a group of words that begins with a preposition and ends with a noun or pronoun. Prepositional phrases describe nouns and verbs. (For a list of common prepositions, see page 415.)

Exercise 5   Combining Sentences with Prepositional Phrases

The following sentences are based on "Bathing Elephants" by Peggy Thomson, which you can find on pages 210–213. Combine each numbered group of sentences by adding the new information as prepositional phrases in the first sentence. For the first few items, the new information is in dark type.

1. **a.** Elephants in the wild normally bathe themselves.
   b. They bathe **in rivers.**
2. **a.** Elephant baths at the zoo are fun.
   b. They are fun **for the keepers and the elephants.**
3. **a.** Elephants live in herds, or social groups.
   b. These elephants are **in the wild.**

4. **a.** Hay protects the elephants.
   b. It protects them **from sunburn.**
5. **a.** The veterinarians check the elephants' backs.
   b. They check the elephants' backs before the baths.
6. **a.** The keeper sprays water.
   b. She sprays water on the elephants' foreheads and feet.
7. **a.** The elephants' backs are soaked and carefully scrubbed.
   b. They are soaked with green oil soap.
   c. They are scrubbed with brushes.
8. **a.** Scrapes are treated.
   b. The scrapes are on the elephants' backs.
   c. The scrapes are treated with soothing salve.
9. **a.** The elephants' feet are examined.
   b. Their feet are examined in the last part of the bath.
   c. Their feet are examined for pebbles and other irritants.
10. **a.** The keeper has the special ankus stick nearby at all times.
    b. The keeper has the ankus as a sign of authority.
    c. The ankus is a sign of authority to the elephants.

Exercise 6   **Combining Sentences with Prepositional Phrases**

Rewrite the following paragraphs, combining sentences with prepositional phrases. Make any other changes in wording that you feel are necessary.

One of the Washington Zoo's most colorful elephants is named Shanthi. Shanthi was rescued and raised in an elephant orphanage. She was raised with twenty-one other elephants. At the age of one, she was sent from Sri Lanka. She was sent to Washington. She was a gift. The gift was to the children of the United States. Her keeper, Sam, came with Shanthi. He came to the United States. Sam slept near his young charge. He slept in the Elephant House. He slept on a cot.

Before going back to Sri Lanka, Sam gave a tape recording to the zoo. The recording was of his special commands. If the zoo-keepers used the commands, they would have no trouble with Shanthi. This was according to Sam. However, the young elephant turned out to be quite a handful. This is in spite of Sam's assurances. She probably misbehaves to get special attention. She wants attention from her keepers.

Mixed Review

The sentences below are based on a passage from *Coast to Coast* by Betsy Byars, which you can find on pages 82–86. Combine the sentences from each numbered item into one new sentence. Combine sentences and compound elements by using a coordinating conjunction; add new information as prepositional phrases.

1. **a.** Birch wanted to take a ride in the plane.
   b. She knew this was her last chance.
2. **a.** Her grandfather seemed to have lost his desire for fun.
   b. Perhaps he did not want to take any chances.
3. **a.** Her grandfather glanced at the sky.
   b. Her grandfather decided to fly.
4. **a.** Birch grinned with delight.
   b. Her grandfather smiled for the first time that afternoon.
5. **a.** It was a beautiful day for a flight.
   b. Birch knew it.
   c. Her grandfather knew it.
6. **a.** Birch wanted to go right away.
   b. Her grandfather needed to perform a preflight inspection.
7. **a.** Her grandfather found no problems with the tires.
   b. Her grandfather found no problems with the gas.
   c. Her grandfather found no problems with the oil.
8. **a.** The old plane sat on the pavement.
   b. The pavement was in front of the hangar.
9. **a.** Pop steered the plane off the ramp.
   b. He steered it down the taxiway.
   c. He steered the plane onto the runway.
10. **a.** The wind rushed through the open window.
    b. The wind blew on Birch's face.

"*The scientists were saying . . . that the sun, the global problem, would begin to get better. Perhaps for her grandchildren's children . . . Perhaps they would feel the delicious warmth of the sun.*"

—Alma Luz Villanueva, "The Sand Castle"

Breton Women with Umbrellas, by Emile Bernard. 1892

PART 3

Resources and Skills

Unit 21 **Library and Reference Resources** *526*

Unit 22 **Vocabulary and Spelling** *541*

Unit 23 **Study Skills** *568*

Unit 24 **Taking Tests** *583*

Unit 25 **Listening and Speaking** *616*

Unit 26 **Viewing and Representing** *628*

Unit 27 **Electronic Resources** *644*

UNIT 21

Library and Reference Resources

Lesson 21.1   **Using a Library**   *527*

Lesson 21.2   **How Books Are Organized**   *530*

Lesson 21.3   **How to Find a Book**   *532*

Lesson 21.4   **Using References**   *534*

Lesson 21.5   **Using a Dictionary**   *536*

Lesson 21.6   **Understanding a Dictionary Entry**   *539*

21.1 Using a Library

The first free public library in the United States was opened in 1833. Libraries have changed since then.

Today's libraries contain books of all sorts. They also offer magazines, newspapers, audio recordings, videos, and many other resources. In fact, some libraries are now called media centers or resource centers. You can find information about anything from skateboards to Shakespeare, from Persian poetry to pickles.

No two libraries are exactly alike, but all libraries group similar things together. Stories and novels (fiction) are separate from information books (nonfiction). Magazines and audio-visual materials have their own sections. Turn the page to explore the different parts of a library.

Librarian A librarian can help you use the library wisely by directing you to different resources, showing you how to use them, and giving you advice when needed.

Young Adult and Children's Section Find books written for young readers in a separate area of the library. Sometimes reference materials for students, along with periodicals and audiovisual materials, are also shelved here.

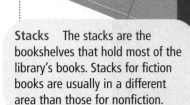

Stacks The stacks are the bookshelves that hold most of the library's books. Stacks for fiction books are usually in a different area than those for nonfiction.

Circulation At the circulation desk you can use your library card to check out materials you want to take home.

No two libraries are alike, but most of them share the same characteristics and have similar resources.

Library and Reference Resources

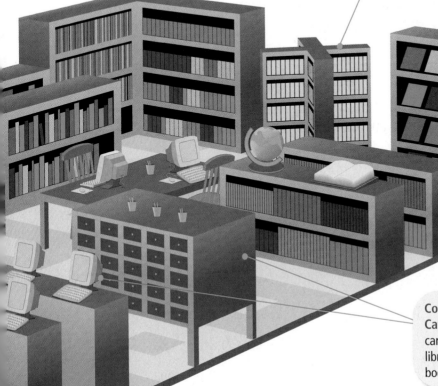

Reference The reference area holds dictionaries, encyclopedias, atlases, and other reference works. Computer database systems in the reference area allow you to search for facts or articles from periodicals and newspapers.

Audiovisual Materials Audiocassettes, compact discs (CDs), videotapes, and computer software are in the audiovisual section. Some libraries have listening and viewing areas to allow you to review materials before checking them out.

Newspapers and Periodicals Find current issues of newspapers and periodicals in the general reading area. Periodicals are arranged alphabetically and by date. Older issues of periodicals may be available. Use the computer catalog to locate them or ask a librarian to help you.

Computer Card Catalog or Card Catalog A card catalog contains a card or listing for each book in the library. Each card or listing describes the book and tells its location in the library.

Exercise 1

In which section of the library would you find each of the following items? Share your results with the class.

1. The monthly magazine *National Geographic*
2. *Atlas of the American Revolution*
3. The novel *My Side of the Mountain*
4. A video of the movie *Old Yeller*
5. *Encyclopedia of Black America*

21.2 How Books Are Organized

A large library may have hundreds of thousands of books. How can you find what you want among all those books? In 1876 librarian Melvil Dewey set up a system for organizing books. His system, the Dewey decimal system, is still used in libraries today.

In this system, all nonfiction books are given numbers. Dewey divided the numbers into groups by topic. Books about science, for example, make up the 500s group. A book about magnets would be placed in the science group. One about the English language would go into the language group—the 400s. The chart shows how the Dewey groups are broken into smaller subgroups. As you search for a book, begin by asking yourself what group it might be classified in.

Dewey Decimal System		
Numbers	**Major Groups**	**Examples of Subgroups**
000–099	General works	Encyclopedias, library science
100–199	Philosophy	Dreams, the senses
200–299	Religion	World religions, mythology
300–399	Social sciences	Law, education, money
400–499	Language	Grammar, foreign languages
500–599	Science	Animals, math, astronomy
600–699	Technology	Tools, medicine, farming
700–799	The arts	Music, painting, sports
800–899	Literature	Poetry, plays
900–999	Geography, history	Travel, biography, U.S. history

Each nonfiction book has a call number on its spine. In most libraries, this is a Dewey decimal number. It's a short code telling the subject of the book. Each digit in the number narrows down the topic. For example, look at the call number for a book called *The Great American Baseball Scrapbook.*

Library and Reference Resources

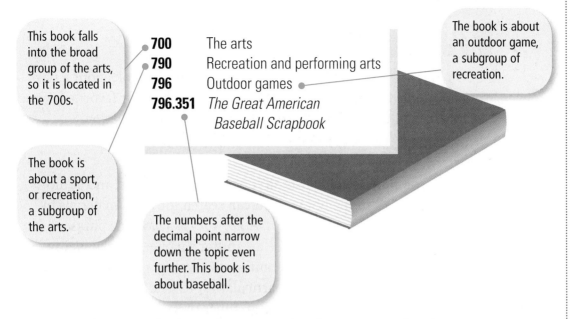

This book falls into the broad group of the arts, so it is located in the 700s.

The book is about a sport, or recreation, a subgroup of the arts.

The numbers after the decimal point narrow down the topic even further. This book is about baseball.

The book is about an outdoor game, a subgroup of recreation.

700	The arts
790	Recreation and performing arts
796	Outdoor games
796.351	*The Great American Baseball Scrapbook*

As a student, you don't need to memorize the Dewey code. It's a good idea, however, to learn the main groups in the Dewey decimal system. Knowing them will make it easier to find the books you need.

Books are shelved by Dewey decimal number and then alphabetically by the author's last name. You might find six books about whales, each book with the number 599.5 on its spine. Within this group a book by Dorothy Hinshaw Patent would appear before a book by John F. Waters.

Fiction works usually don't have Dewey decimal numbers. They are shelved in alphabetical order by the author's last name. The call number may have *F* or *FIC*, for *fiction*, on the first line. The second line has the first three letters of the author's last name. Different books by the same author are shelved alphabetically by title.

Exercise 2

In what Dewey group would you expect each of the following books to be shelved? Give the main group name and the number in hundreds.

1. A book about the solar system
2. A book with the title *A History of the Ancient World*
3. A book about Greek gods and goddesses
4. A book about the origins of jazz
5. A book of poems by Shel Silverstein

21.3 How to Find a Book

While writing a report, you may need to find a book about a particular topic or you may want to locate a book by your favorite writer. How do you find the books you need? Start with the catalog.

Using a Computer Catalog

The computer catalog lists all the books, periodicals, and audiovisual materials in the library. You can search for these materials by title, author, subject, or keyword. A *keyword* is a word or phrase that describes your topic. If you type an author's name, you can view a list of all the books written by that author. By typing a subject, you can view all the books about that particular topic. The computer catalog tells you the title, author, and call number of each book, and whether it is available to check out.

For example, suppose you are looking for books by the writer Milton Meltzer. Your computer search might proceed as follows:

1. **Enter A for Author-Name. A prompt will then ask you for the author's name. Key in Meltzer, Milton.**
2. **The computer will show a list of all the books in the library by this author. Each item will have a call number. These are two of the books you will see by Milton Meltzer.**

```
1. Title:      All Times, All Peoples: A
               World History of Slavery
   Author:     Meltzer, Milton
   Published:  1980
   Media:      Book
   Call No:    326 M528a

2. Title:      American Politics: How It
               Really Works
   Author:     Meltzer, Milton
   Published:  1989
   Media:      Book
   Call No:    320.473 M528a
```

3. **You can also type the call number of the book that interests you. Information about the book will appear, including the book's location and availability.**

Information on Cards

Some libraries use an older method of organizing books called a card catalog. A card catalog is a cabinet of long narrow drawers that holds cards arranged alphabetically. Each card contains the description of a book and has that book's call number in the upper left-hand corner. Fiction books have an author card and a title card. Nonfiction books have a subject card as well. Because each book has two or three cards, it can be found by searching under its title, its author, or sometimes its subject.

Finding a Book

After you look up an author's name, a book title, or any subject in the catalog, carefully copy down the call number of the book you want. Then go to the shelves to see if the book is available.

Nonfiction books are arranged in numerical order by call number. You can look at the signs at the end of each row of shelves to see which call numbers are in that row.

Exercise 3

At your school or neighborhood library, use the catalog to find a book about each of the following topics. List the author, title, and call number of each book.

1. Endangered animals
2. How to build kites
3. South Africa
4. A book by Jean Craighead George
5. The ocean
6. The American Civil War
7. Musical instruments
8. Women in sports

Using References

If you are curious about a topic and want to know more about it, or if you need information for a report, look first in a reference work. Reference books (or on-line reference sources) make it easy to locate information about a person, a place, or almost any other topic. Encyclopedias and atlases are two examples of useful reference works.

Encyclopedias

You can find information on many different topics in an encyclopedia. Major encyclopedias contain a number of volumes. *The World Book Encyclopedia*, for example, is divided into twenty-two volumes.

TIME

For more about the importance of using accurate information in your writing, see **TIME Facing the Blank Page,** page 97.

Guide words at the top of each two-page spread show the first and last entries on that spread.

Articles may contain a list of books you can turn to for more information on the topic.

Encyclopedia entries appear in alphabetical order.

The article or an entry word may refer you to another entry in the encyclopedia.

Nylon 637

How does careful cooking preserve nutritional values?
What is *kwashiorkor? Marasmus?*
What are the seven groups in the Basic Seven?
Who identified beriberi?
What was the first international agency to study nutrition?

Additional resources

Level I
Fodor, Ronald V. *What to Eat and Why: The Science of Nutrition.* Morrow, 1979.
Jones, Jeanne. *Jet Fuel: The New Food Strategy for the High-Performance Person.* Villard, 1984.
Peavy, Linda, and Smith, Ursula. *Food, Nutrition, & You.* Scribner, 1982.
Simon, Seymour. *About the Food You Eat.* McGraw, 1979.

Level II
Brody, Jane. *Jane Brody's Nutrition Book: A Lifetime Guide to Good Eating for Better Health.* Norton, 1981.
Calloway, Doris H., and Carpenter, K. O. *Nutrition & Health.* Holt, 1981.
Time-Life Books Editors. *Wholesome Diet.* Time-Life Books, 1981.
Wenck, Dorothy A., and others. *Nutrition: The Challenge of Being Well Nourished.* 2nd ed. Reston, 1983.

Nutritionist See **Nutrition; Food** (Food research).
Nutting, Mary Adelaide (1858-1948), was a Canadian-born leader in the development of professional nursing in the United States. She worked to establish professional standards in both the education of nurses and the practice of nursing. She developed several training programs that supplemented practical experience in a hospital with classroom instruction in nursing principles.

Nutting was born in Waterloo, Que. She received a nursing certificate from Johns Hopkins Hospital Training School for Nurses in 1891. She then served as a head nurse at the school until 1894, when she became its principal. Nutting held this position until 1907. That year, when she joined the faculty of Teachers College at Columbia University, Nutting became the world's first professor of nursing. Nutting headed the Department of Nursing and Health at the college from 1910 until she retired in 1925.   Ronald G. Keen

Nyasa, Lake See **Lake Nyasa.**
Nyasaland See **Malawi.**
Nye, Bill (1850-1896), was a popular American humorist. He became famous for his clever essays and *anecdotes* (brief stories) on a variety of subjects ranging from the American West to journalism. Nye was also a successful comic lecturer.

Nye was born in Shirley, Me. His full name was Edgar Wilson Nye. In 1876, Nye moved to Wyoming. He first gained national fame as a columnist for the Laramie *Boomerang,* a newspaper he founded in 1881. In 1886, Nye moved to New York City and wrote humorous columns for the New York *World* newspaper. His books include *Bill Nye's History of the United States* (1894) and *Bill Nye's History of England* (1896). Both were widely popular for their satirical treatment of the past. Nye and the American poet James Whitcomb Riley wrote *Nye and Riley's Railway Guide* (1888), a book of poems and witty prose sketches.   David B. Kesterson

Nyerere, nih RAIR ee, Julius Kambarage kahm BAH rah guh (1922-   ), served as president of Tanzania from 1964 until he retired in 1985. Tanzania consists of Tanganyika, a region on the African mainland; and Zanzibar, a nearby offshore island group. Both Tanganyika and Zanzibar were formerly ruled by Great Britain.

Nyerere led the movement that resulted in Tanganyika's independence from Britain in 1961. He became the president of Tanganyika in 1962. He also helped unite Tanganyika and Zanzibar to form Tanzania in 1964, and he became the new country's president. He was first elected as president in 1965 and was re elected in 1970, 1975, and 1980.

As Tanzania's president, Nyerere became a leading spokesman for cooperation among black African nations. He helped unite Tanzania's many ethnic groups and adopted policies that brought economic progress to the nation. In 1979, Nyerere sent Tanzanian troops to Uganda, after Uganda had invaded Tanzania. The Tanzanian troops helped overthrow the dictatorship of Idi Amin Dada in Uganda.

Nyerere was born near what is now Musoma, Tanzania. He was educated at various schools in what are now Tanzania and Uganda, and at the University of Edinburgh in Scotland.   Robert I. Rotberg

See also **Tanzania** (History).

Nylon is the general term for a group of synthetic products. These products are made from chemicals derived from coal, water, air, petroleum, agricultural by-products, and natural gas. Nylon is one of the most important chemical discoveries. It is a tough elastic substance that can be formed into fibers, bristles, sheets, rods, and tubes. It also can be made in powdered form for use in molding operations.

Nylon fibers and fabrics are noted for their strength, ability to be dyed, low shrinkage, silklike appearance, and resistance to abrasion, mildew, and insects. They are not harmed by most kinds of oil and grease or by household cleaning fluids. Nylon fabrics dry rapidly because nylon absorbs little water.

Uses. Nylon is used primarily in fibers and fabrics. Nylon was first made into hosiery, which became available in 1940. It was the first synthetic fabric thought to be superior to natural fabrics. Since then, many uses have been found for nylon. Carpets, tires, upholstery, dresses, underwear, bathing suits, lace, and parachutes are among the many nylon products. Single threads of nylon are used for fishing line and for bristles in brushes. Surgeons use nylon thread to sew up wounds.

Nylon is also important in the plastics industry. Nylon plastics are noted for their electrical properties, toughness, and resistance to chemicals, fire, and wear. They are used in such products as electrical equipment, gears, tubing, and sporting equipment. Plastic nylon body panels have replaced steel on some automobiles.

How nylon is made. Most nylon produced in the United States is made from two chemical compounds—*hexamethylenediamine* and *adipic acid.* Both of these compounds contain carbon and hydrogen. Manufacturers combine the compounds to form *hexamethylenediammonium-adipate,* commonly called *nylon salt.*

Most nylon factories make the substance by placing a

Julius K. Nyerere
Bill Campbell, Sygma

An encyclopedia is a good place to check dates and specific facts, such as when Texas became a state or whether a fungus is a plant. You can also use an encyclopedia to get basic information on a topic quickly.

Atlases

An atlas is a collection of maps. A general atlas contains maps of all parts of the world. It may also have special maps that give information about climate or population. You might use a general atlas when you are writing a report about a particular country.

Other atlases deal with one part of the world, such as Asia, Republic of the Congo, or Oklahoma. Still others cover special topics—for example, an atlas of wildlife. Historical atlases contain maps that show changes over time. Some historical atlases cover lengthy periods of time. Others cover shorter periods, perhaps only a few years. Similarly, they may deal with world history or the history of a single country or region.

Exercise 4

Tell which reference work—an encyclopedia or an atlas—would best answer each question below. Then choose one of the questions to answer. Give the answer and the title of the reference work you used to find it.

1. What countries border the country of Iraq?
2. Which planet has the most moons?
3. How many bones are in a human hand?
4. What sea is between Saudi Arabia and India?
5. How large is the Sahara?

Using a Dictionary

The Dictionary

People often speak of dictionaries as though they were all alike. In fact, people often say that they've looked up a word in *the* dictionary. After all, every dictionary is an alphabetically arranged collection of words and their definitions. However, dictionaries come in different sizes and have different uses. They are meant for different users. The chart below shows some of the ways in which dictionaries differ.

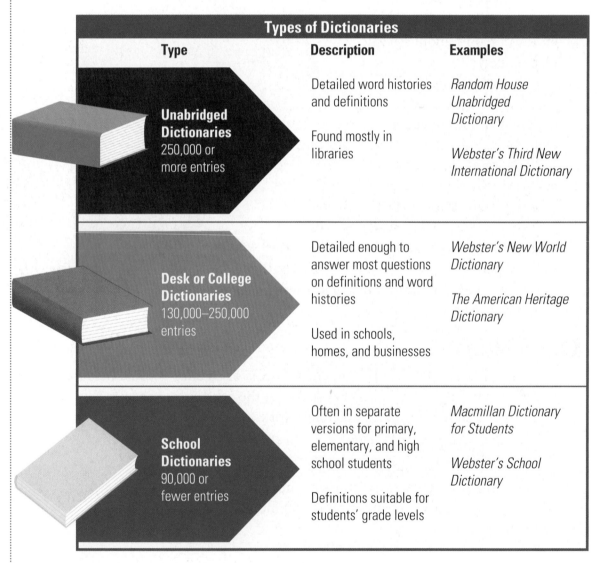

Types of Dictionaries		
Type	**Description**	**Examples**
Unabridged Dictionaries 250,000 or more entries	Detailed word histories and definitions Found mostly in libraries	*Random House Unabridged Dictionary* *Webster's Third New International Dictionary*
Desk or College Dictionaries 130,000–250,000 entries	Detailed enough to answer most questions on definitions and word histories Used in schools, homes, and businesses	*Webster's New World Dictionary* *The American Heritage Dictionary*
School Dictionaries 90,000 or fewer entries	Often in separate versions for primary, elementary, and high school students Definitions suitable for students' grade levels	*Macmillan Dictionary for Students* *Webster's School Dictionary*

The sample dictionary page shows how the entries on a page are arranged. An entry includes the word, its definitions, and other information about the word. The bold type used for each entry term helps you see what words are defined on each page. The entries are in alphabetical order.

specifically to one held under arrest in a prison or under guard while on trial or serving a prison sentence: *The prisoner was released on parole.* **Captive** is restricted to prisoners captured and held by an enemy during war or for ransom and suggests a state of complete subjugation rather than imprisonment: *The downed airman was held as a captive by the enemy for six months.*

prisoner of war, person captured or held by the enemy in war.

pris·sy (pris′ē) **-si·er, -si·est.** *adj.* very prim, fussy, or prudish. [Blend of PRIM and SISSY.]

pris·tine (pris′tēn) *adj.* **1.** of or relating to the earliest time, period, or condition; original; primitive. **2.** pure; uncorrupted; unspoiled: *the pristine beauty of freshly fallen snow.* [Latin *pristīnus* former, primitive.]

prith·ee (priṯẖ′ē) *interj. Archaic.* I pray thee; please.

pri·va·cy (prī′və sē) *pl.,* **-cies.** *n.* **1.** state or condition of being private, secluded, or isolated: *The writer needed privacy to finish his novel.* **2.** right to be free from interference with one's private affairs: *Opening someone else's mail is an invasion of privacy.* **3.** secrecy. —**Syn. 1.** see solitude.

pri·vate (prī′vit) *adj.* **1.** belonging or restricted to or reserved for a particular person or persons: *a private driveway, private property.* **2.** personal; individual. **3.** not intended for general or public knowledge; confidential: *a private conversation.* **4.** not holding public office or having an official position: *a private citizen.* **5.** not supported or managed by or connected with the government: *an agency under private control.* **6.** secluded; isolated. —*n.* **1.** in the U.S. Army and Marine Corps, an enlisted man of the lowest rank. **2.** **privates.** external sex organs; genitals. Also, **private parts. 3. in proposal.** confidentially or secretly; privately. [Latin *prīvātus* apart from the state, belonging to an individual. Doublet of PRIVY.] —**pri′vate·ly,** *adv.* —**pri′vate·ness,** *n.*

private detective, detective who is employed by a private person or group rather than a police force or government agency. Also, **private investigator.**

private enterprise, free enterprise.

pri·va·teer (prī′və tēr′) *n.* **1.** privately owned armed ship commissioned by a government to attack enemy ships, esp. merchant ships. **2.** commander or a member of the crew of such a ship. —*v.i.* to sail on or as a privateer.

private eye *Informal.* private detective.

private first class 1. in the U.S. Army, an enlisted man ranking below a corporal and above a private. **2.** in the U.S. Marine Corps, an enlisted man ranking below a lance corporal and above a private.

private school, school that is supported and managed by a private group rather than by the government.

pri·va·tion (prī vā′shən) *n.* **1.** lack of the comforts or necessities of life or the condition resulting from such a lack. **2.** act of depriving; being deprived. [Latin *prīvātiō* a taking away.]

priv·a·tive (priv′ə tiv) *adj.* **1.** causing deprivation or loss. **2.** *Grammar.* altering the meaning of a word from positive to negative, as by means of a prefix. —*n. Grammar.* privative prefix or suffix. [Latin *prī·vātīvus* denoting privation, negative, from *prīvāre* to deprive, rob.]

priv·et (priv′it) *n.* any of a group of evergreen shrubs or small trees, genus *Ligustrum,* widely used for hedges, usually having white flowers and black berries. [Of uncertain origin.]

priv·i·lege (priv′ə lij, priv′lij) *n.* special right, advantage, benefit, or immunity granted to or enjoyed by a certain person, group, or class. —*v.t.,* **-leged, -leg·ing.** to grant a privilege to. [Latin *prīvilēgium* law for or against an individual, from *prīvus* one's own, individual + *lēx* law.]

priv·i·leged (priv′ə lijd, priv′lijd) *adj.* **1.** having or enjoying a privilege or privileges. **2.** confidential; restricted: *privileged information.*

priv·i·ly (priv′ə lē) *adv.* privately; secretly.

priv·y (priv′ē) *adj.* **1.** participating in the knowledge of something secret or private (with *to*): *Only three people were privy to the plot.* **2.** *Archaic.* secret; concealed. **3.** *Archaic.* private; personal. —*n. pl.,* **priv·ies.** outhouse (*def. 1*). [Old French *prive* intimate, private, from Latin *prīvātus* belonging to an individual. Doublet of PRIVATE.]

Privy Council, honorary body appointed by the British sovereign, having about 300 members.

privy seal, in Great Britain, seal affixed to certain documents.

prize¹ (prīz) *n.* **1.** that which is offered or won as a reward, esp. for winning in a competition or in a game of chance. **2.** anything worth striving for. —*adj.* **1.** that has won or is likely to win a prize. **2.** offered or given as a prize. **3.** worthy of a prize; outstanding.

[Old French *pris* value, honor, from Latin *pretium* value, reward.] **Syn.** *n.* **1. Prize, award, reward** mean an honor, as a payment, medal, or citation, bestowed on a person in recognition of an achievement. **Prize** is applied to what is bestowed on a victor in a competitive contest: *Frank won the first prize in the chess tournament.* **Award** usually suggests that the honor is bestowed by a judge or panel of judges and that the performers have fulfilled certain conditions: *The publishers have offered an award for the best novel of the year.* **Reward** is restricted to a form of payment earned by someone for his effort: *Jack received a reward for returning the lost dog to its owner.*

prize² (prīz) *n.* something seized or captured, esp. an enemy ship captured at sea during wartime. [Old French *prise* seizure, booty, from *prendre* to take, from Latin *prehendere* to seize.]

prize³ (prīz) **prized, priz·ing.** *v.t.* **1.** to value or esteem highly: *to prize a friend's advice.* **2.** to estimate the value of; appraise: *a man who prizes his honor above his life.* [Old French *pr(e)isier* to value, esteem, from Late Latin *pretiāre* to value, from Latin *pretium* value.]

prize⁴ (prīz) **prized, priz·ing.** *also,* **prise.** *v.t.* to raise or force with a lever; pry. —*n.* **1.** instrument used for prying; lever. **2.** leverage. [From PRIZE².]

prize·fight (prīz′fīt′) *n.* boxing match between professional boxers. —**prize′fight′er,** *n.*

prize ring, rope-enclosed area, usually on a raised platform, in which boxers fight.

pro¹ (prō) *adv.* in favor of; for. —*n. pl.,* **pros.** reason, argument, or person in favor of something: *The chairman listed all the pros and cons of the proposal.* [Latin *prō* in favor of, for.]

pro² (prō) *pl.,* **pros.** *Informal. n.* professional; expert. —*adj.* professional. [Short for PROFESSIONAL.]

pro-¹ *prefix* **1.** in favor of; supporting; in behalf of: *proslavery.* **2.** forward; forth; out: *progress, project.* **3.** in place of; acting as; substituting for: *pronoun.* [Latin *prō* in favor of, for, before, instead of.]

pro-² *prefix* before in time or place: *prognosis.* [Greek *pro.*]

pro·a (prō′ə) *n.* swift Malay boat having a triangular sail and a single outrigger. [Malay *prāū.*]

prob. 1. problem. **2.** probable; probably.

prob·a·bil·i·ty (prob′ə bil′ə tē) *pl.,* **-ties.** *n.* **1.** quality or state of being probable; likelihood: *A willingness to negotiate increased the probability of an early settlement.* **2.** something probable or likely. **3.** *Mathematics.* ratio of the number of chances favoring the occurrence of an event to the total number of possible occurrences. **4. in all probability** most probably; very likely.

prob·a·ble (prob′ə bəl) *adj.* **1.** likely to occur or to be true but not certain; that can reasonably be expected or believed: *The experts all agreed on the probable outcome of the boxing match.* **2.** rendering something likely but not certain. [Latin *probābilis* provable, likely, from *probāre* to try, test, approve, demonstrate.]

prob·a·bly (prob′ə blē) *adv.* most likely; in all likelihood.

pro·bate (prō′bāt) *n.* act or process of legally proving a will. —*adj.* of or relating to a probate court or to probate. —*v.t.,* **-bat·ed, -bat·ing.** to establish the authenticity or validity of (a will). [Latin *probātum* thing proved or approved, from *probāre* to test, demonstrate, approve.]

probate court, court having jurisdiction over the probate of wills and over the administration of the property of deceased persons.

pro·ba·tion (prō bā′shən) *n.* **1.** testing or trial of the ability, qualifications, or suitability of a person, as a new employee, usually for a specified period of time. **2.** *Law.* action or practice of allowing a person convicted of a minor or first offense to go free under close supervision and on the condition that his behavior be exemplary. **3.** period of being on probation or the status of one on probation. [Latin *probātiō* a proving, approval.] —**pro·ba′tion·al, pro·ba′tion·ar′y,** *adj.*

pro·ba·tion·er (prō bā′shə nər) *n.* one who is on probation.

probation officer, officer appointed to supervise a probationer.

pro·ba·tive (prō′bə tiv) *adj.* **1.** affording proof or evidence. **2.** serving or designed to test. Also, **pro′ba·to′ry.**

probe (prōb) *n.* **1.** thorough investigation or examination: *The court case led to a Senate probe into prison conditions.* **2.** slender surgical instrument for exploring a body cavity, wound, or similar opening. **3.** device, mechanism, or object used for investigation or exploration, esp. a space probe. —*v.t.,* **probed, prob·ing. 1.** to investigate, examine, or explore thoroughly: *The psychiatrist probed the patient's subconscious in discussing the dream.* **2.** to examine or explore with a surgical probe. —*v.i.* to conduct a thorough investigation or examination: *Scientists probed into the nature of the phenomenon.* [Medieval Latin *proba* ex-

Flowers

Fruit

Leaves

Privet

Proa

at; āpe; cär; end; mē; it; īce; hot; ōld; fôrk; wood; fōōl; oil; out; up; ūse; turn; sing; thin; this; zh in treasure; ə in ago, taken, pencil, lemon, circus.   797

Guide words at the top of each page show the first and last entries on the page. These guide words help you locate an entry.

Illustrations help you understand some definitions. How does the picture of a privet help you understand that word's definition?

A **pronunciation key** appears at the bottom of each page or each pair of facing pages. The pronunciation key gives examples of each pronunciation symbol by using familiar words such as at, āpe, and cär.

Library and Reference Resources

The Thesaurus

A thesaurus is a dictionary of synonyms, or words with similar meanings. A thesaurus is a helpful tool when you're revising your writing. In fact, if you use word processing software, you may even have a thesaurus as part of your software package. You can use a thesaurus to find a more exact or more colorful word to replace a vague or overused word.

In a dictionary-style thesaurus, entries are arranged alphabetically, as in a dictionary. Several synonyms may be listed for a single definition. A cross-reference to another entry or entries may follow the definition.

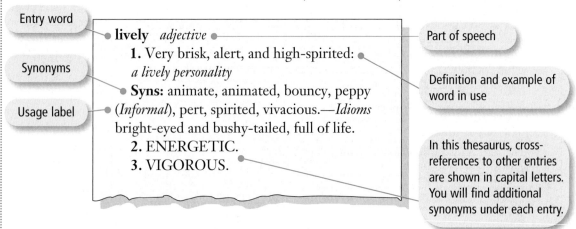

Entry word

Synonyms

Usage label

lively *adjective*
    1. Very brisk, alert, and high-spirited:
a lively personality
    Syns: animate, animated, bouncy, peppy
(*Informal*), pert, spirited, vivacious.—*Idioms*
bright-eyed and bushy-tailed, full of life.
      2. ENERGETIC.
      3. VIGOROUS.

Part of speech

Definition and example of word in use

In this thesaurus, cross-references to other entries are shown in capital letters. You will find additional synonyms under each entry.

Exercise 5

Use a dictionary or a thesaurus to complete each item.

1. What guide words are on the dictionary page on which *gimmick* appears?
2. Which of the following words would you find on a page with the guide words *plagiarism* and *planetoid*?

   plane   plantation   placid
   plank   planetarium   plaid

3. Does the word *skein* rhyme with *green, shine,* or *grain*?
4. List three synonyms for the following:
  a. the verb *shake*
  b. the adjective *rich*

21.6 Understanding a Dictionary Entry

Which is the right spelling: *life style, life-style,* or *lifestyle?* How do you divide *environment* into syllables? Is *domestic* a noun, an adjective, or both? These are just a few of the types of questions you can answer with a dictionary.

The Entry Word and Definition

The entry word begins the entry. If the word has more than one syllable, the entry word shows how it is divided, or hyphenated. Notice how *ba•sin* is divided by the dot. A dictionary will show you that some entries are two words, as in *high school.* Other words are hyphenated, as in *runner-up.* Still others are spelled as one word: *lifeboat.*

Most of the time, you probably look up a word to find a definition. Words usually have more than one definition. Some words, in fact, have many definitions. Your dictionary probably includes more than a dozen different meanings for the word *set.* School dictionaries generally list the most common definition first, as in the entry below.

Entry word

ba•sin (bā′sin) *n.* **1.a.** container that is usually round with a wide, flat bottom and sloping sides; shallow bowl, esp. for holding liquids. **b.** bathroom sink. **2.** contents or capacity of a basin. **3.** the entire region drained by a river and its tributaries. **4.** depression in the earth usually holding water, like a pond, but sometimes dry.

Numbered definitions

Other Information in Entries

How do you say *reign?* Where does the word *caribou* come from? Are there any good synonyms for *slow?* What is the plural of *calf?* Dictionary entries can also answer questions like these. Look at the entry on the next page to locate some of the important parts of a dictionary entry.

Pronunciation The pronunciation follows the entry word. Refer to the key at the bottom of the page if you are not sure what the pronunciation symbols mean. Notice that the second syllable of *fragile* can be pronounced two ways.

Part of Speech An abbreviation shows how the word is used as a part of speech. In this entry, *adj.* stands for *adjective* and *adv.* for *adverb*.

Word Origin Many entries include information about the word's origin, or a history of the word.

frag·ile (fraj´əl,-ĭl) *adj.* easily broken, damaged, or destroyed; delicate. [Latin *fragilis*. Doublet of FRAIL.] —**frag·ile·ly**, *adv.* —**fra·gil·i·ty** (frə jil ə̄ tē), n.
Syn. **Fragile, frail, brittle** mean tending to break easily. **Fragile** suggests that the substance of which a thing is made may result in its breaking if it is not handled with care: *The movers carefully packed the fragile china into cartons.* **Frail** implies that a thing is of weak construction and that it will tend to collapse under strain: *The frail wooden bridge cracked and swayed in the heavy winds.* **Brittle** suggests hardness of such rigidity that the thing may easily break if pressure is applied unwisely: *The bones of an aged person are often quite brittle.*

Synonyms Some entries list synonyms, words with similar meanings. Explanations and examples are often included to help you understand the different meanings. For more information on synonyms, turn to page 552.

Exercise 6

Use a school dictionary to answer the following questions.

1. How is the word *quadrangle* divided into syllables?
2. What is the origin of the word *patio*?
3. What synonyms are given for *journey*?
4. Is *bramble* a noun or a verb?
5. What is the plural of *ox*? Of *loaf*? Of *brother-in-law*?

Vocabulary and Spelling

Lesson **22.1** **Borrowed Words** 542

Lesson **22.2** **Clues to Word Meanings** 544

Lesson **22.3** **Using Word Parts** 547

Lesson **22.4** **Synonyms and Antonyms** 552

Lesson **22.5** **Words That Sound Alike** 555

Lesson **22.6** **Spelling Rules I** 557

Lesson **22.7** **Spelling Rules II** 561

Lesson **22.8** **Problem Words** 565

22.1 Borrowed Words

The English language contains more than 600,000 words, more than any other language. Many of these words have been borrowed from other languages.

Many of the foods you eat originally came from other lands. The names of those foods came from other languages. Think about pizza (Italian), hamburger (German), chili (Spanish), taco (Mexican Spanish), and gumbo (West African). You can probably add more examples of your own. Every time you ask for these foods, you use a borrowed word.

English has also borrowed words for clothing, sports, cars, and hundreds of other items in daily use. Parts of words have also been borrowed. Our word *television*, for example, comes from the Greek *tele*, "far off," and the Latin *visio*, "to see."

Often a word passes from one language to another before becoming a part of English. Our word *theater*, for example, was first used in ancient Greece, where the idea of theater itself began. The word was borrowed by the Romans, who spoke Latin. French speakers later borrowed it from Latin. English speakers then borrowed it from the French.

The map below shows just a few examples of borrowed words. You have probably used many of them without knowing that they came from another language.

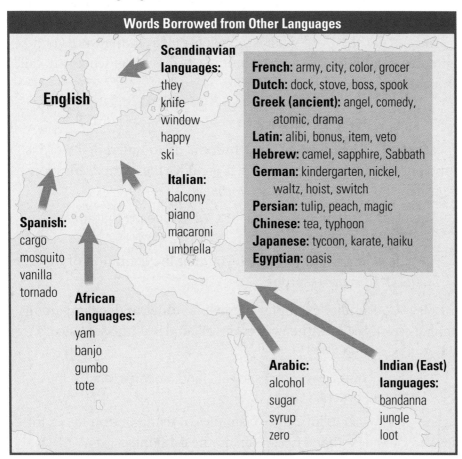

Words Borrowed from Other Languages

Scandinavian languages:
they
knife
window
happy
ski

English

Italian:
balcony
piano
macaroni
umbrella

French: army, city, color, grocer
Dutch: dock, stove, boss, spook
Greek (ancient): angel, comedy, atomic, drama
Latin: alibi, bonus, item, veto
Hebrew: camel, sapphire, Sabbath
German: kindergarten, nickel, waltz, hoist, switch
Persian: tulip, peach, magic
Chinese: tea, typhoon
Japanese: tycoon, karate, haiku
Egyptian: oasis

Spanish:
cargo
mosquito
vanilla
tornado

African languages:
yam
banjo
gumbo
tote

Arabic:
alcohol
sugar
syrup
zero

Indian (East) languages:
bandanna
jungle
loot

Exercise 1

Working in a group, choose one foreign language. See how many words you can find that came into English from that language. Use what group members already know, interviews, and library resources. Present your list to the class.

One way to learn the meaning of a new word is to use a dictionary. However, you won't always have a dictionary handy. Try to figure out the meaning of the word yourself. Look for clues in the words and sentences around it. These surrounding words and sentences are called the context.

Specific Context Clues

DEFINITION The meaning, or definition, of an unfamiliar word is sometimes given in the sentence that includes the word. Definitions are usually introduced with clue words.

> The plant has begun to germinate, which means that it is starting to sprout.

The clue words *which means* tell you that the definition of the word *germinate* is "to start to sprout."

EXAMPLE Familiar examples can help a reader understand an unfamiliar word. See how the writer uses examples in the sentence below.

> Felines, such as lions, domestic cats, and leopards, are natural hunters.

The words *such as* introduce examples of felines. From the examples you can guess that *felines* refers to the cat family.

Interpreting Clue Words		
Type of Context Clue	**Clue Words**	**Example**
Definition: The meaning of the unfamiliar word is given in the sentence.	that is in other words which means	Jerry *inscribed* his name; that is, he wrote his name in the book.
Example: The meaning of the unfamiliar word is explained by familiar examples.	like such as for example including	Some people are afraid of *arachnids,* such as spiders and ticks.

General Context

Sometimes there are no special clue words to help you understand a new word. However, you can still use the general context. That is, you can use the details in the words or sentences around the new word. Look at the following sentences:

> Andrea carefully mixed several pigments with an oil base to produce just the right colors. Then she began her painting.

The sentences tell you that pigments have something to do with painting. They also tell you that pigments can be mixed to produce various colors. From those clues, you can figure out that pigments are a kind of dye or color used to make paint.

Exercise 2

Use context clues to figure out the meaning of the underlined word in each sentence. Write the meaning of the word. Then tell what type of context clue you used to figure out each meaning. The types of context clues will be definition, example, or general context.

1. Brian used a <u>template</u>, or pattern, for cutting the wood he used to build a birdhouse.
2. <u>Vipers</u>, such as rattlesnakes, cobras, and copperheads, can be very dangerous, even deadly.
3. Birds, mammals, and even plants can be <u>insectivores</u>. For example, flycatchers and anteaters are insectivores. So is the Venus's flytrap, a plant that traps flies and then digests them.
4. The scene by the lake was <u>tranquil</u>. There was only a slight breeze, and the surface of the lake was as smooth as glass. Even the birds and insects seemed hushed.
5. Margot is studying <u>calligraphy</u>, which is the art of fine handwriting.

Vocabulary and Spelling

Wordworks

Oui! French Is Spoken Here

Which do you think would smell better, a perfume called Eau de Cochon or one called Happiness? If you guessed Eau de Cochon, you're not alone. Many Americans associate French names with something fancier or more fashionable. Actually, Eau de Cochon means "aroma of pig."

Admiration of the French language began more than 900 years ago. In A.D. 1066 French-speaking Normans conquered England. The people living there spoke a language we now call Old English. The Normans became England's rulers. They controlled the government, the land, the laws, the military, and most of the wealth. Everybody who was anybody spoke French! And people who wanted to be somebody soon began using French words. While English peasants ate the meat of *cows* and *pigs* (words from Old English), ladies and gentlemen of the court dined on *beef* and *pork* (words from French).

> **Challenge**
>
> Based on your reading of this page, under what circumstances do you think one language might borrow words from another?

Shall we visit the *boutique*?

Do you mean the "small shop"?

ACTIVITY

Parlez-vous français?

Write the word or phrase that completes each sentence.

document	matinee	petite
salon	R.S.V.P.	

1. I had my hair cut at the beauty _____.
2. The _____ begins at 2:00 P.M.
3. Angela is very _____.
4. _____ by next Tuesday.
5. The _____ is on my desk.

22.3 Using Word Parts

You often can figure out the meaning of an unfamiliar word by dividing it into parts. The main part of the word is called the **root,** and it carries the word's basic meaning. A root is often a simple word in itself. For example, *read* is a word. When a prefix or a suffix is added to it, *read* becomes a root.

Prefixes and suffixes can be attached to a root to change its meaning. A **prefix** is added to the beginning of a root. A **suffix** is added to the end. A word can have both a prefix and a suffix.

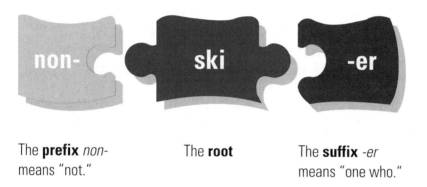

The **prefix** *non-* means "not."   The **root**   The **suffix** *-er* means "one who."

You know what *ski* means. Look at the meanings of the prefix *non-* and the suffix *-er.* You can easily see that a nonskier is "one who does not ski."

The prefix *non-* and the suffix *-er* can be attached to other roots as well. In each case they will produce the meaning "one who does not [do whatever the word root says]." For example, a *nonobserver* is someone who does not observe. A *nonvoter* is a person who does not vote. Try to think of some other root words that would fit between *non-* and *-er.*

Words usually have only one prefix, but may have several suffixes. For example, you can start with *nation,* add *-al* to get *national,* and add *-ity* to get *nationality.* You can see how learning about prefixes and suffixes can help increase your vocabulary. Knowing the meanings of these word parts can also help you understand unfamiliar words.

Prefixes

The following chart shows some prefixes and their meanings. Notice that some prefixes have more than one meaning. Sometimes two or more prefixes have the same or a similar meaning.

pre-

Prefixes		
Prefixes	**Words**	**Meanings**
in- means "not"	inactive incomplete indirect	not active not complete not direct
non- means "without" or "not"	nonfat nonstop nonreturnable	without fat without stopping not able to be returned
dis- means "opposite of" or "not"	disadvantage disagree disarm	an unfavorable condition to not agree to take away arms (weapons)
un- means "opposite of" or "to reverse"	unable unclean untie unset	not able not clean to loosen not yet firm or set
pre- means "before"	prejudge prepay preview	to judge in advance to pay in advance to view in advance
re- means "again" or "back"	rewrite repay reappear	to write again to pay back to appear again

Suffixes

A suffix added to a word can change the word's part of speech as well as its meaning. For example, adding the suffix *-er* to *read* (a verb) makes *reader* (a noun). Adding *-less* to *rain* (a noun) makes *rainless* (an adjective).

Vocabulary and Spelling

The following chart shows some common suffixes and their meanings. As the examples show, sometimes a suffix has more than one meaning. In addition, two or more suffixes may have the same meaning. For example, the suffixes -er, -or, and -ist can all mean "one who."

See if you can identify the part of speech of each example word with and without its suffix. You can review parts of speech in Part 2 of this book.

Suffixes		
Suffixes	**Words**	**Meanings**
-er means "one who," "that which," or "more"	runner baker toaster weaker	one who runs one who bakes that which makes toast more weak
-or means "one who"	actor conductor demonstrator	one who acts one who conducts one who demonstrates
-ist means "one who"	typist violinist scientist	one who types one who plays the violin one who works at science
-less means "without"	hairless spineless merciless	without hair without a spine without mercy
-able means "can be" or "having the quality of"	believable washable valuable	can be believed can be washed having value
-ible means "can be" or "having the quality of"	deductible digestible sensible	can be deducted can be digested having sense
-ness means "quality of" or "state of being"	darkness mildness kindness	being dark quality of being mild state of being kind

Vocabulary and Spelling

Adding a suffix sometimes changes the spelling of a word. As the chart shows, when adding *-er* to *run,* you also must add another *n* to make *runner.* To learn more about spelling changes when adding suffixes, see pages 557-560.

Exercise 3

Divide the following words. Write their parts in three columns headed *prefix, word root,* and *suffix.* (Note that not all the words have both a prefix and a suffix.) In a fourth column, write another word that uses the same prefix or the same suffix (or both if you can). Check your words in a dictionary to make sure the prefixes and suffixes are correctly used.

1. preteen
2. nondriver
3. unforgivable
4. nonprofit
5. deforest
6. collectible
7. disapprove
8. incompleteness

Exercise 4

To name each person described below, use a word that ends in the suffix *-er, -or,* or *-ist.* You should be able to list more than one word for some of the descriptions. Remember that sometimes the addition of a suffix changes the spelling of the root word. Check your answers in a dictionary to be sure you have the correct spelling and suffix.

1. A person who serves food in a restaurant
2. A person who plays a keyboard instrument
3. A person who instructs others
4. A person who appears in plays
5. A person who rides a bicycle

Wordworks

Sounds Like . . .

"How much wood would a woodchuck chuck if a woodchuck could chuck wood?" But if a woodchuck can't chuck wood, how did it get the name *woodchuck*?

When people hear an unfamiliar word, they often try to understand the word by relating it to words they know. The process of inventing an origin for a word is called folk etymology (et′ ə mol′ ə jē).

As to *woodchuck*—English speakers new to North America heard the Cree word for the animal, which is *otchek*. They changed its unfamiliar sounds to the familiar sounds of *wood* and *chuck*. People would later guess that a woodchuck had something to do with wood simply because of its name.

Challenge

Look up the origin of the word *shamefaced* in a college dictionary. How did this word get its spelling and pronunciation?

Sometimes people change the pronunciation of a word because the word not only sounds like one they know but also seems to be related. During the Middle Ages, the French word for "young woman," *femelle*, was borrowed into English. Because *femelle* sounded like *male* and seemed related to *male, femelle* eventually was pronounced and spelled *female*.

ACTIVITY

In Other Words

Figure out the English words related to the following word origins.

1. from the Natick word *musquash* (a North American rodent)
2. from the Middle English word *berfrey* (tower)
3. from the Old English words *brȳd* (bride) and *guma* (man)

Vocabulary and Spelling

22.4 | Synonyms and Antonyms

Suppose that you were describing a rainy day. Imagine how dull your writing would be if you could use only the word *rain*. Fortunately, the English language has many words with meanings similar to *rain*. In describing the rain, you might use the word *downpour*. You could also choose *flood, cloudburst, shower, sprinkle,* or *drizzle.*

English also contains many pairs of words that have opposite meanings. On a rainy day the streets are *wet*. On a sunny day the streets are *dry*.

Synonyms

Words that have similar meanings are called **synonyms.** Knowing synonyms can improve your vocabulary and your writing. It can also help you understand the meanings of unfamiliar words. For example, you may not know what the word *obstinate* means. However, suppose that you knew that its synonyms included *hardheaded* and *stubborn.* Then you'd probably have a pretty good idea of what *obstinate* means.

Synonyms can help you be more precise in your speaking and writing. Synonyms have similar meanings, but they hardly ever have exactly the same meaning. The words *cloudburst* and *downpour* both refer to heavy rain. *Drizzle* and *shower* bring to mind a different, more gentle rain. There's a big difference between a *sprinkle* and a *deluge,* even though both words can mean "rain." When you write about rain—or about anything at all—synonyms help you say exactly what you mean.

You'll find synonyms listed in some dictionary entries. Another place to look for them is in a dictionary of synonyms. Such a dictionary is called a thesaurus. See page 538 for more information on how to use a thesaurus.

The mouse was **small**

or was it...

petite *little*

diminutive *tiny*

Vocabulary and Spelling

Antonyms

Antonyms are words that have opposite or nearly opposite meanings. Knowing antonyms can help you build your vocabulary and help you understand the meanings of other words. Perhaps you don't know the meaning of the word *taciturn*. Knowing that an antonym of the word is *talkative*, you could guess that *taciturn* describes someone who is silent, or untalkative.

You probably know such common antonyms as *hot—cold, love—hate,* and *short—tall.* One common way to form antonyms is to add a prefix meaning "not" or "the opposite of" to a word. (Page 548 has a list of some prefixes with those meanings.) For example, you can make an antonym of *believable* by adding the prefix *un-.*

Exercise 5

In each pair of synonyms below, the first word may be unknown to you. The second word, however, is probably familiar. Use your knowledge of each familiar word to figure out the meaning of its synonym. Then write a sentence using the first word in each pair.

1. benevolent, good
2. apparition, ghost
3. malevolent, evil
4. fatigued, tired
5. nourish, feed

Exercise 6

Write an antonym for each word below by adding the proper prefix to it. Review the list of such prefixes on page 548 if you need to. Check each word in a dictionary to make sure you used the correct prefix.

1. appear
2. sense
3. true
4. equal
5. direct

Vocabulary and Spelling

22.4 Synonyms and Antonyms   **553**

Wordworks

Word Twins

Some English words, called *homographs,* look identical. Homographs are sometimes pronounced differently, but they always have identical spellings. However, homographs have different origins.

Meal (ground grain) and *meal* (eating time) are homographs. Since both refer to food, you might think they have the same origin. Actually, the two words are not related.

The meal used in bread comes from the Old English word *melu,* meaning "to grind." During the Middle Ages (from about A.D. 476 to about A.D. 1450), the word *melu* developed into *meele. Meele* was used as a noun referring to ground grain. By the eighteenth century, the spelling had changed to *meal.*

The meal that refers to an eating time, such as breakfast or lunch, comes from the Old English word *mael,* meaning "appointed time." By the Middle Ages, *mael* had developed into *meel.* In modern English, this word began to be spelled as *meal* and referred to the regular eating times in a day.

Challenge

Using a college dictionary, trace the origins of the homographs *bale* (sorrow) and *bale* (a large bundle of goods). List each form and its meaning.

ACTIVITY

Reading Double

Write the homographs for each pair of definitions below and for the pair of illustrations at right.

1. inner surface of the hand; a tropical tree
2. to shut; nearby
3. able to; a metal container
4. to move or slide out of place; a small piece of paper

Vocabulary and Spelling

Words That Sound Alike

How are a pair and a pear alike? How about a rein and a rain and a reign? The answer, of course, is that these groups of words sound alike. You probably noticed that the words have different meanings and different spellings.

Understanding Homonyms

Words that sound alike but have different meanings are called homonyms. Some homonyms not only sound alike but are spelled alike as well. Such words usually don't cause too many problems. Whether you *ring* a bell or wear a *ring* on your finger, it's still spelled *ring*. You can *file* your nails or *file* some papers. You can even *file* for a job or *file* down the hall with your friends. The spelling of the word *file* remains the same even though its meaning changes.

Homonyms that sound alike but are spelled differently can be tricky. These are the ones you need to be careful with. You don't want to write *new* instead of *knew* in a written report. Imagine writing *threw* on a spelling test when you meant to write *through*. The chart on this page has some more examples of such homonyms. Maybe you can think of other examples.

Homonyms
break to crack, split, or smash
brake to stop a movement
piece a part of something
peace the opposite of war
holey having holes
holy sacred
wholly completely

knight

Using Homonyms

Have you ever been confused about whether to use *their* or *there* in a sentence? Does the difference between *your* and *you're* confuse you sometimes? Because homonyms sound alike, people occasionally don't remember which spelling to use. The chart on the following page shows some common homonyms.

night

Common Homonyms	
Words	**Meanings**
their	belonging to them
there	in that place
they're	contraction for *they are*
its	belonging to it
it's	contraction for *it is* or *it has*
to	in the direction of
too	also
two	the number
your	belonging to you
you're	contraction for *you are*
hear	listen
here	this place
principal	the head of a school; most important
principle	a rule, law, or truth
who's	contraction for *who is* or *who has*
whose	the possessive form of *who*

Exercise 7

Write the correct homonym to fit each sentence.

1. The children are concentrating on what (their, there, they're) doing.
2. Be sure to let me know when (your, you're) going to arrive.
3. (Who's, Whose) responsible for this mess?
4. Coffee is one of the (principle, principal) exports of Colombia.
5. I think (it's, its) going to rain today.
6. Mandy heard the noise; John said that he heard it (to, too, two).

22.6 Spelling Rules I

Improving your spelling can improve your writing. You can improve your spelling skills by noticing common spelling patterns in words with similar sounds and by learning some basic spelling rules.

Suffixes and the Silent *e*

Words that end in a silent *e* can be a spelling problem. They're especially troublesome when you have to add a suffix to them. The rules in the following chart will help you.

Adding Suffixes to Words that End With Silent *e*	
Rules	**Examples**
When adding a suffix that begins with a consonant to a word that ends with a silent *e*, keep the *e*.	pure + -ly = purely grace + -ful = graceful **Common exceptions** awe + -ful = awful argue + -ment = argument
When adding -*ly* to a word that ends with an *l* plus a silent *e*, always drop the *e*.	terrible + -ly = terribly whole + -ly = wholly
When adding a suffix that begins with a vowel or *y* to a word that ends with a silent *e*, usually drop the *e*.	write + -ing = writing shine + -y = shiny **Common exceptions** dye + -ing = dyeing mile + -age = mileage
When adding a suffix that begins with *a* or *o* to a word that ends with *ce* or *ge*, keep the *e* so the word will still have the soft *c* or *g* sound.	change + -able = changeable courage + -ous = courageous
When adding a suffix that begins with a vowel to a word that ends in *ee* or *oe*, keep the *e*.	agree + -able = agreeable hoe + -ing = hoeing

Suffixes and the Final *y*

Adding suffixes to words that end in *y* can cause spelling problems. The chart below shows the rules for changing the *y* to *i* when adding suffixes.

Adding Suffixes to Words That End In *y*	
When a word ends in a consonant + *y*, change the *y* to *i*.	cry + -ed = cried deny + -es = denies
When the suffix begins with an *i*, do not change the *y* to *i*.	cry + -ing = crying deny + -ing = denying
When a word ends in a vowel + *y*, keep the *y*.	joy + -ful = joyful also stay + -ing = staying

Spelling *ie* and *ei*

Some writers get confused when spelling words containing *ie* or *ei*. One way to help with these letter combinations is to memorize a simple rhyming rule.

Rhyming Rule	Examples
Put *i* before *e*	believe, chief, grieve
except after *c*	receive, deceit, receipt
and when sounded like *a*, as in *neighbor* and *weigh*.	eight, weight, veil, freight

Fortunately, there are very few exceptions to the *ie* and *ei* rule. The box below lists the only exceptions you need to remember.

Exceptions to the *ie* and *ei* Rule
species, seize, leisure, weird, either, neither, height

Doubling the Final Consonant

When a word ends in a consonant, you may need to double the final consonant when adding a suffix.

DOUBLE THE FINAL CONSONANT WHEN a word ends in a single consonant following one vowel AND

- the word is one syllable

  sit + -ing = sitting   run + -er = runner

- the word has an accent on the last syllable and the accent stays there after the suffix is added

  prefer + -ed = preferred   reset + -ing = resetting

DO *NOT* DOUBLE THE FINAL CONSONANT WHEN

- the suffix begins with a consonant

  forget + -ful = forgetful   pain + -less = painless

- the accent is not on the last syllable

  develop + -ing = developing   offer + -ed = offered

- the accent moves when the suffix is added

  prefer + -ence = preference   refer + -ence = reference

- two vowels come before the final consonant

  train + -ing = training   moan + -ed = moaned

- the word ends in two consonants

  remind + -er = reminder   bang + -ed = banged

SPECIAL CASE: When a word ends in *ll* and the suffix *-ly* is added, drop one *l*.

  dull + -ly = dully   full + -ly = fully

Using Syllable Boundaries

Some students like to use the syllables or beats in a word to help them with pronunciation as they read or with spelling as they write. Each **syllable** in a word should have one, and only one, vowel sound. Try clapping out the word *wel-come.* You should get two beats. It is easy to find each syllable in two syllable words that contain two consonants in the middle of two vowels (VCCV). Divide the word between the two consonants. How would you separate the following words into syllables?

basket   lantern   dollar   mustard   funny

An **open syllable** is one where a vowel is not followed by a consonant. Sometimes open syllables can be words themselves, such as *a* or *I*. Usually, open syllables are parts of a word, such as in *pro-vide* or *fla-vor.* A **closed syllable** contains consonants on either side of the vowel, such as in the words *champ* and *blast.*

Here are some guidelines to help you divide words into syllables.

- Prefixes form separate syllables, such as in the words *un-hap-py* or *re-pay.*

- Suffixes also form separate syllables, because they, too, contain a vowel. Consider the words *kind-ness* or *help-ful.*

- Endings that form plurals may or may not create a new syllable. If you add *-s* to make a plural, such as in the word *plants,* you won't add a syllable, but if you add *-es,* as in *wishes,* you will add a syllable.

- Compound words divide into syllables according to their word boundaries, such as in *black-bird* or *out-side.*

- A final *-le* picks up the preceding consonant to form a syllable, such as in *ta-ble, sam-ple,* or *un-cle.*

Exercise 8

Carefully examine each set of words below. Find the one word that is misspelled in each set and write the word correctly.

1. blackness, roundness, sterness
2. recieve, achieve, veil
3. dullly, purely, rarely
4. stating, shineing, mileage
5. commited, stopped, regretting

Exercise 9

Correctly complete each of the following word + suffix problems.

1. big + -er =
2. supply + -ing =
3. explain + -able =
4. label + -ed =
5. expel + -ing =

6. choose + -ing =
7. occur + -ed =
8. hoe + -ing =
9. differ + -ence =
10. use + -able =

22.7 | Spelling Rules II

A handful of spelling rules can help you spell thousands of words. For example, the few rules that follow deal with the spelling of plurals. These rules will help you spell the plurals of nearly every English noun.

Forming Plurals

Most nouns in English form plurals by adding an *-s* or *-es*. However, there are other ways to form plurals. The charts that follow show some general and special rules for plurals.

General Rules for Plurals		
If the Noun Ends in	**The Rule is**	**Example**
s, *ch,* *sh,* *x,* or *z*	add *-es*	loss → losses watch → watches bush → bushes box → boxes fizz → fizzes
a consonant + *y*	change *y* to *i* and add *-es*	berry → berries body → bodies baby → babies
a vowel + *y*	add *-s*	key → keys day → days boy → boys
a vowel + *o*	add *-s*	stereo → stereos studio → studios rodeo → rodeos
a consonant + *o*	usually add *-s*	piano → pianos photo → photos solo → solos
	Common exceptions but sometimes add *-es*	potato → potatoes hero → heroes echo → echoes

General Rules for Plurals

If the Noun Ends in	The Rule is	Example
f or *ff*	add -*s*	reef → reefs cuff → cuffs
	Common exceptions change *f* to *v* and add -*es*	leaf → leaves loaf → loaves
lf	change *f* to *v* and add -*es*	half → halves wolf → wolves
fe	change *f* to *v* and add -*s*	life → lives knife → knives

Special Rules for Plurals

Special Case	Examples
To form the plurals of most proper names, add -*s*. But add -*es* if the name ends in *s, ch, sh, x,* or *z.*	Krey → Kreys Jones → Joneses Hatch → Hatches Bush → Bushes Marx → Marxes Sanchez → Sanchezes
To form the plural of one-word compound nouns, follow the general rules for plurals.	textbook → textbooks icebox → iceboxes penknife → penknives blackberry → blackberries
To form the plural of hyphenated compound nouns or compound nouns of more than one word, make the most important word plural.	brother-in-law → brothers-in-law ice cream → ice creams chief of staff → chiefs of staff
Some nouns have irregular plural forms and do not follow any rules.	woman → women ox → oxen foot → feet
Some nouns have the same singular and plural forms.	series → series deer → deer sheep → sheep

Becoming a Better Speller

By following a few simple steps, you can learn to spell new words. Pay attention to unfamiliar words or hard-to-spell words in your reading. Notice and remember spelling patterns in words. As you write, note words that you have trouble spelling. Then use the steps below to learn to spell those difficult words.

Say It
Look at the word on the page, and say it aloud. Say it a second time, pronouncing each syllable clearly.

See It
Close your eyes, and picture the printed word in your mind's eye. Picture how the word is spelled.

Write It
Look at the word again, and write it two or three times. Then write it again without looking at the word.

Check It
Check what you have written. Did you spell it correctly? If not, go through each step again until you can spell the word correctly.

Get into the habit of using your dictionary to find the correct spelling of a word. How do you find it in a dictionary if you can't spell it? Jot down letters and letter combinations that could stand for the sound you hear at the beginning of the word. Try each of these possible spellings as you look for the word in the dictionary. Then *Say It, See It, Write It, Check It,* and learn to spell the word.

Exercise 10

Write the plural form of each of the following words.

1. fox
2. fly
3. elf
4. echo
5. radio
6. dairy
7. bench
8. trouble
9. Juarez
10. mosquito
11. strawberry
12. zebra

Wordworks

Secret Codes

Suppose that you want to send a secret note to a friend but need to make sure no one else can read it. Do what the ancient Greeks did—code it!

People have sent coded messages, or cryptograms, for thousands of years. Messengers first used codes during wartime to carry secret messages across enemy lines.

One common code system substitutes letters. Julius Caesar, a Roman general, used such a system. In his system, you replace each letter in the message with a letter three spaces to the right in the regular alphabet. For example, the message FIGHT would be written as ILJKW in code. Anyone who knows the code can easily figure out the message. To decode the message, you replace each letter with a letter three spaces to the left in the alphabet.

Challenge

Working with a friend, experiment with coded messages. Use a system discussed here, or create your own. What fact about language can you learn from your experiments?

Another code system reverses the order of letters. Suppose that you want to code the message SUE WILL NOT GO WITH JACK. First, divide the letters of the message into groups of five: SUEWI LLNOT GOWIT HJACK. Then reverse the letters in each group: IWEUS TONLL TIWOG KCAJH. This message would be pretty hard to figure out—unless you knew the code.

1 - 20 - 20 - 1 - 3 - 11

3 - 1 - 5 - 19 - 1 - 18

1 - 20 - 4 - 1 - 23 - 14

ACTIVITY

Crack the Code

Suppose that you are one of Caesar's messengers. You have just intercepted this coded message from one of Caesar's enemies. All you know is that the numbers in the code stand for letters in the alphabet. Can you crack the code?

Vocabulary and Spelling

22.8   Problem Words

Like most people, you probably have trouble spelling certain words. Some words are harder to spell than others. Some words don't follow basic spelling rules, but there are some ways you can learn to spell even the most difficult words.

Make a personal word list. List the words that you find especially difficult or that you often misspell. Keep your list up-to-date, adding new words as you come across them. Study them by using the steps shown on page 563. When you're sure you can spell a word, you can remove it from your list.

Difficult Words

The following is a list of words that people often misspell. Are any of your problem words on this list? What other words would you add to the list?

Often Misspelled Words			
absence	definite	leisure	recommend
accidentally	descend	library	restaurant
adviser	disease	license	rhythm
all right	embarrass	misspell	schedule
answer	environment	molasses	sense
athlete	February	muscle	separate
attendant	foreign	necessary	similar
ballet	forty	neighborhood	sincerely
beautiful	funeral	niece	succeed
beginning	genius	ninety	technology
believe	government	occasion	theory
business	grammar	original	traffic
cafeteria	guarantee	parallel	truly
canceled	height	permanent	usually
canoe	humorous	physical	vacuum
cemetery	immediate	probably	variety
choir	jewelry	receipt	various
colonel	laboratory	recognize	Wednesday

Easily Confused Words

Did you ever get confused over the spelling of *through* and *threw?* How about *hour* and *our?* Would you describe a smell as a *sent*, a *cent*, or a *scent?*

Some words are often confused because they sound alike but have different spellings and meanings. You can review many of these troublesome words on pages 455–458. Following are a few more. You may want to add some of these words to your personal word list.

Words That Are Often Confused	
to	toward, in the direction of; as far as *Go **to** the corner, and then turn **to** the left.*
too	also; as well as; more than enough *Mario was **too** tired to dance. His sister was tired **too**.*
two	the number 2 *The **two** of us were the last pair to arrive.*
principle	a basic rule, truth, or law *The **principle** of free speech is important in a democracy.*
principal	first in rank; the head of a school *The **principal** announced that school would close early.*
desert (dez' ərt)	a dry, barren region *They hoped to cross the **desert** before their water ran out.*
desert (di zurt')	to abandon; to leave without permission *The soldier was warned not to **desert** his post.*
dessert (di zurt')	a sweet course served at the end of a meal *I'll have the chocolate cake for **dessert**.*
passed	to have moved on or ahead; completed satisfactorily *Donna **passed** the test with only one error.*
past	time gone by; existed earlier *Jake learned from his **past** mistakes.*
weather	the daily conditions of temperature, moisture, wind, etc. *The northern wind brought a sudden change in the **weather**.*
whether	conjunction used in indirect questions *Everyone wondered **whether** the plane would leave on time.*

Another way to learn problem words is to use memory devices, or tricks for remembering. For example, do you have trouble remembering the difference between *principal* and *principle?* You might memorize: *Your princi**pal** is a **pal**. A princip**le** is a ru**le**.* Do you confuse *to, too,* and *two?* Perhaps you could remember: *__Two__ horses are one __too__ many for me __to__ tend.* Sometimes these memory devices are little rhymes, such as the following:

> *Poor little* Emma,
> *Caught in a di*lemma.

Think of other sentences or rhymes that will help you remember how to spell troublesome words. Do you know any?

Exercise 11

On a separate sheet of paper, write the word in the parentheses that correctly completes each sentence.

1. There were only (to, too, two) of us at breakfast this morning.
2. Camels can travel in the (desert, dessert) better than most other animals.
3. We all wondered (weather, whether) the test would be as hard as the last one was.
4. My parents think I spend (to, too, two) much money on CDs.
5. The helicopter (passed, past) overhead, frightening the animals.
6. My favorite teacher will be the new (principle, principal) next year.
7. I ate so much that I hardly had room for (desert, dessert).
8. Isn't this rainy (weather, whether) ever going to end?
9. I like studying history. The (past, passed) has always interested me.
10. The (principle, principal) purpose of our club is to raise money to help feed the homeless.

UNIT 23

Study Skills

Lesson 23.1	Exploring a Book	569
Lesson 23.2	Planning Your Study	571
Lesson 23.3	Using a Study Method	573
Lesson 23.4	Notes and Outlines	576
Lesson 23.5	Using Graphic Aids	579

Imagine that you are researching a report for science class. In the library you find a book that may help you. Can you find out if the book has what you need without reading all of it?

The pictures on this page show some helpful parts of a book. Learning to use these parts will make it easier for you to find the information you need. The chart on page 570 answers some questions you might ask about a book.

The **table of contents** shows the name and the opening page number for each major section of a book.

The **index** is an alphabetical list of the important topics covered in a book. Page numbers are given for each entry.

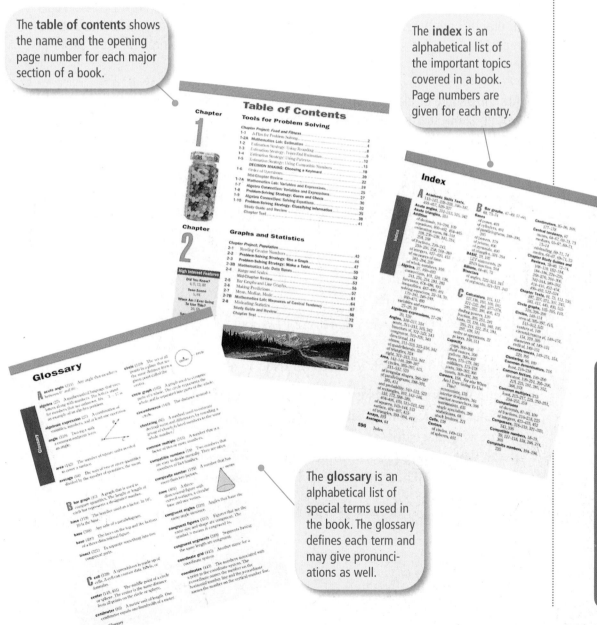

The **glossary** is an alphabetical list of special terms used in the book. The glossary defines each term and may give pronunciations as well.

Study Skills

Questions	Where to Look for the Answers
Can I find information on my particular topic in this book?	The **table of contents** lists the title of each chapter, lesson, or section. It tells you what topics are covered and shows you how the book is organized.
I may need to find particular words or ideas. Does this book have an index and a glossary?	Look in the **table of contents.** If a book contains an index and a glossary, their page numbers will be given there. You can also look in the back part of the book. That's where those features are located.
Does this book have any maps or graphs I might use in my report?	Some books, especially textbooks, contain lists of maps, graphs, and other special illustrations. Such lists usually appear right after the **table of contents.**
Are the people or places I am writing about mentioned in this book?	The **index** gives the number of each page on which a person or place is mentioned. Events and other important topics are also in an index. You can check the index and quickly find the information you need.
Will I be able to understand the terms used in this book?	Textbooks and other books that contain difficult or technical terms often have **glossaries.** A glossary defines such terms.

Exercise 1

Use the table of contents and index of *this* book to answer the following questions. Tell which feature you used to answer each question.

1. Into how many parts is the book divided? Name them.
2. What unit deals with verbs?
3. On what page does the index begin?
4. On what page or pages would you find information about graphs?
5. Who wrote "The Jacket"? On what page does it begin?

Planning Your Study

Some days you may feel that there isn't enough time to learn about all the subjects and skills that interest you. Making a study plan can help you get the most out of the study time you have.

Setting Study Goals

First, you need to set study goals. Some study goals can be met in one study session. For example, you could memorize ten spelling words or read four pages of a textbook in one session. Other study goals require more time. Writing a research report would probably take several weeks.

When setting your study goals, decide how long it should take to meet each one. Be realistic about what you can do in one study session. If you have a long assignment, divide it into smaller tasks. If you're planning a report, for example, one goal will be to find library resources. Another goal will be to skim the books or articles for information you can use.

Study Skills

Using a Calendar

One important tool for making a study plan is a calendar. As you set your goals, write each one on the calendar. For longer tasks, first write the final due date. Then work backward from there, filling in each task. For example, say that a report is due on the fifteenth. Mark the fourteenth on your calendar for proofreading the final report. Then set aside the twelfth and the thirteenth to revise your first draft and write the final draft. Continue working backward in this manner through all the needed tasks.

As you schedule your study time, try to keep all your class assignments balanced. Suppose that an English report is due on Friday—the same day you have a social studies test. You'll need to set aside study time for both goals. Also, keep in mind other important activities. You don't want to schedule writing a report on the day you have a track meet.

Exercise 2

Draw a thirty-day calendar with the first day falling on a Wednesday. Then set study goals, and schedule the following assignments:

- You must read four chapters (about eighty pages) of your social studies text by the end of the month. You must also review an earlier unit (eighty pages) for a test on Friday the tenth.
- A written report for English is due the seventeenth.
- In science a unit test covering five chapters will be given Friday the twenty-fourth.
- You need to review for a short quiz your math teacher gives every Monday.
- You are on the basketball team and have practice every Thursday from 3:30 to 5:00.

23.3 Using a Study Method

When you study, your most important job is to understand and remember information and ideas. You might say that, in order to study well, you need to monitor how well you are thinking. If you don't understand something you've read, stop. Go back and reread the passage more slowly, focusing on finding main ideas and on understanding important vocabulary. Jot down questions and comments. Whatever study strategy or method you use, be sure you find one that works for you—one that helps you learn and remember information.

Look at the diagram below. Can you guess why this study strategy is called SQ3R?

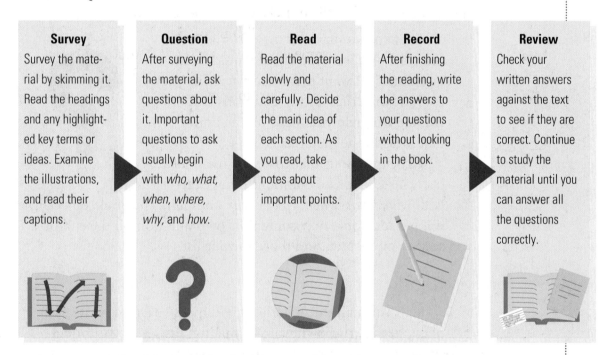

Survey
Survey the material by skimming it. Read the headings and any highlighted key terms or ideas. Examine the illustrations, and read their captions.

Question
After surveying the material, ask questions about it. Important questions to ask usually begin with *who, what, when, where, why,* and *how.*

Read
Read the material slowly and carefully. Decide the main idea of each section. As you read, take notes about important points.

Record
After finishing the reading, write the answers to your questions without looking in the book.

Review
Check your written answers against the text to see if they are correct. Continue to study the material until you can answer all the questions correctly.

You can use the SQ3R method with any subject. Once you've learned the method and use it regularly, it will become a habit. Effective studying will save you time. In addition, it will help you become better prepared in all your classes.

Survey

To survey means to look something over to get a general view of it. You can do that by looking for the main ideas of the material. Read all the headings that divide the material into smaller sections. These headings may help you find the main ideas. They also will show you

how the material is organized. Skim the material to find the main idea of each paragraph. In skimming, you look over the material rapidly to find its main ideas. You will find a paragraph's main idea stated in the topic sentence. The first sentence of a paragraph is often its topic sentence.

Sometimes important material in the text is highlighted or presented in bold type. Read all such sentences or terms. Look at all the pictures, graphs, charts, and other graphic aids. Read the title and caption for each graphic aid, and examine the illustration itself. Think about what each graphic aid tells you about the written material.

Question

After you've surveyed the material, write out a list of questions. These should be the questions you want to have answered as you read the material. Listing questions before reading will help you focus on the important ideas in the material.

Write questions that cover the main idea of each section. Use questions that begin with *who, what, when, where, why,* and *how.* The book, especially if it is a textbook, may contain its own questions at the end of a section or chapter. Add those to your list.

Read

Read through the material carefully. As you read, write each main idea in your own words. Look for answers to your questions. You may also add additional questions to your list as you

read. Make sure you understand each paragraph or passage. If the ideas are complicated, you may need to read passages more than once. Make sure you understand each idea before you move on to the next one.

Record

After you've read the material carefully, write the answers to your list of questions. If the material you're studying is long, divide your reading into smaller sections. Stop after each section to record the answers to your questions about it. Rely only on your memory of what you've read when you write your answers. In this way, you'll test whether you've really learned the material.

Review

After you finish answering the questions, check your answers against the material. If you answered any questions incorrectly, review the section covering that material again. Write new questions that cover the same material. After reviewing the material again, answer the new questions and check your answers. Continue to question,

read, record, and review until you can answer all questions correctly. Keep your review questions and answers in your notebook for later study and review.

Exercise 3

Choose a short chapter or section from one of your textbooks. You can also select a short article from a magazine. Study the material, using the SQ3R method. After you have studied the material, answer the following questions.

1. Where can you find clues about the main ideas of the selection?
2. What are the main ideas of the selection?
3. List your review questions and your answers to them.

23.4 | Notes and Outlines

While working on a report, you'll find many facts and ideas. Most people can't count on memory alone to keep track of everything they read. You need to make notes of the facts and ideas you might use in your report.

Taking Notes

Use a separate note card for each piece of information. The cards will allow you to organize your notes easily. Write the name of your source on the card. (Use the sample note card below as a model.) Then, in your own words, summarize the information from your research.

Write only the details and ideas that relate to your topic. Use a quotation if a sentence or phrase is especially interesting. You may also need to use the words of an authority to strengthen your report. When you do quote something from a source, copy it word for word. Enclose it in quotation marks. The quotation marks will make it clear that you have used another person's thoughts.

History of Surfing Surf ridi[ng]
pastime of the ancient Polyn[esians]
the islands in the Pacific Oc[ean]
land to Tahiti and who are
brought the sport to Haw[aii]
explorer James Cook wit[h]
he discovered the Sandw[ich]
in 1778. He wrote in th[e]
surf broke in Kealakek[ua]
board "place themselv[es]
largest surge by whic[h]
amazing rapidity toward u[...]

Encyclopedia Americana Vol. 26, p. 54.
Capt. James T. Cook saw surfers in
Hawaii in 1778. Wrote that they "place
themselves on the summit of the largest
surge by which they are driven along with
amazing rapidity toward the shore."

Study Skills

Outlining

After completing your research, you're ready to organize the information in an outline. Look through your note cards and write down the main ideas you want to cover. Then decide on the right order for presenting them. For example, suppose that you're writing about the history of ballooning. You'll probably use time order—from earliest event to latest event. For other kinds of topics, think about how you can best group your ideas.

Write your outline. Begin by listing main ideas. Then fill in the supporting details. Look at the outline below.

TIME

For more about the value of using outlines, see **TIME Facing the Blank Page,** page 93.

Each main topic is one of the big ideas of your subject. Suppose that your subject is surfing. The first main topic could be the history of surfing.

I. Main topic
 A. First subtopic
  1. Division of a subtopic
  2. Division of a subtopic
 B. Second subtopic

If you have subtopics under a main topic, there must be at least two. They must relate directly to the main topic.

If you wish to divide a subtopic, you must have at least two divisions. Each division must relate to the subtopic above it.

Study Skills

Put your note cards in order according to your outline. You may not need all the information you've found. Don't try to include ideas that don't fit your outline. An example of a completed outline follows. Notice that you don't have to use complete sentences in an outline.

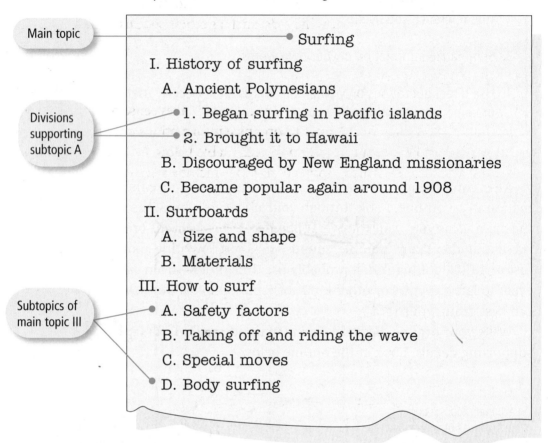

Main topic

Surfing

I. History of surfing

A. Ancient Polynesians

Divisions supporting subtopic A

1. Began surfing in Pacific islands

2. Brought it to Hawaii

B. Discouraged by New England missionaries

C. Became popular again around 1908

II. Surfboards

A. Size and shape

B. Materials

III. How to surf

Subtopics of main topic III

A. Safety factors

B. Taking off and riding the wave

C. Special moves

D. Body surfing

Exercise 4

Choose a historical figure who interests you. Read an encyclopedia article about that person. Make at least five note cards from the article. Be sure to use quotation marks if you use someone else's words.

23.5 Using Graphic Aids

Sometimes you need to present complicated information. You'll find that words don't always provide the best way to do it. Certain kinds of information call for graphic aids, such as tables, graphs, time lines, and maps.

Tables

Tables show pieces of information in a way that makes sense of them. Tables use columns and rows to organize information, which often includes groups of numbers. Look at the table below. Notice how easily you can tell which groups of animals include the most endangered species.

The title identifies the table's topic.

The left column names the groups of animals that are endangered.

Numbers of Endangered Species in the United States and the Rest of the World		
Group	**U.S.**	**Rest of World**
Mammals	61	251
Birds	75	178
Reptiles	14	65
Amphibians	9	8
Fishes	69	11
Insects	28	4

Source: Fish and Wildlife Service, U.S. Department of Interior, 1999

Columns 2 and 3 divide the world into two areas. One column shows figures for the United States. The other gives figures for the rest of the world.

Each row gives the numbers of endangered species for one group.

You can read this table from left to right or from top to bottom. Suppose that you want to know how many species of birds in the United States are endangered. To find out, you don't have to read the whole table. First find the row that shows birds. Then move your eye across the row to the column for the United States. The table also makes it easy to compare numbers for the United States with those for the rest of the world. The numbers for each group of animals are side by side in columns 2 and 3.

Graphs

Graphs always deal with numbers of some kind. They can show the same kinds of information that tables show. However, graphs organize information differently.

BAR GRAPHS   Numbers in a bar graph appear as bars. The bar graph below shows the number of hours young people spend watching television. Notice how easily you can see the highest bar and find the group that watches the most television. You also can easily compare the viewing times of all the groups.

The left side contains a scale divided into hours.

The height of each bar shows the amount of time one group watches television.

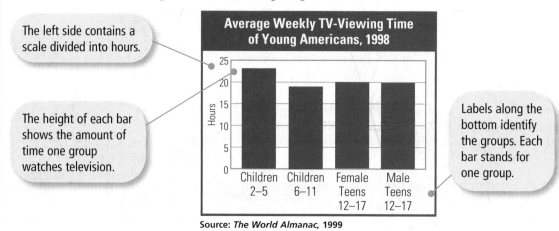

Labels along the bottom identify the groups. Each bar stands for one group.

Source: *The World Almanac,* 1999

To find the number a bar represents, use the scale along the left side. You can see that three of the groups watch close to twenty hours of television per week. Which group watches more than twenty hours per week?

LINE GRAPHS   A line graph shows changes in numbers or amounts over a period of time. For example, a line graph can show the rise and fall of daily temperatures. A line graph can also show any other numbers that change over time. Read the title of the line graph below. What does it show?

The **graph scale** is along the left side. Since the numbers are in millions, 250 stands for 250 million people.

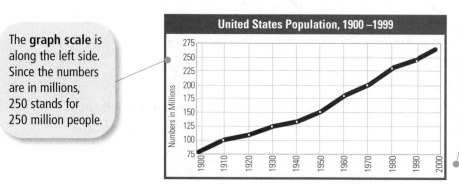

The years are shown along the bottom of the graph. In what year did the U.S. population go over 200 million?

Source: *Statistical Abstract of the United States,* 2000

Study Skills

Time Lines

A time line shows events that happened over a period of time. Time is shown along a line or sometimes a bar. The amount of time shown on a time line can be anything from seconds to eons. A time line allows you to see easily the order in which the events occurred. You can also see how much time passed between certain events. On the time line below, for example, which two events occurred closest in time?

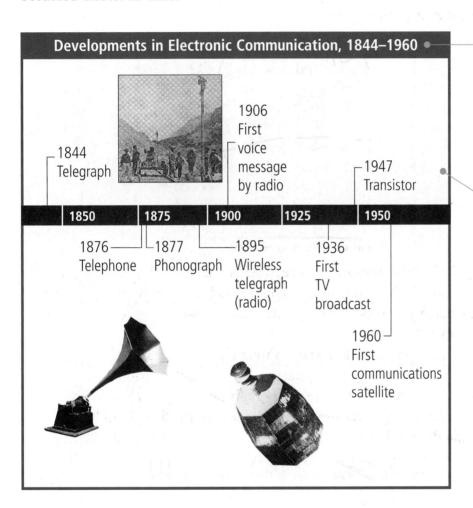

Developments in Electronic Communication, 1844–1960

1844 Telegraph

1906 First voice message by radio

1947 Transistor

1850   1875   1900   1925   1950

1876 Telephone   1877 Phonograph   1895 Wireless telegraph (radio)   1936 First TV broadcast

1960 First communications satellite

The title shows the subject of the time line. It also may include the dates covered.

Space between events shows the amount of time that passed between them. Which two events came closest together?

Maps

Maps show some part of the earth's surface. The area shown can be as small as a playground or as large as the entire world.

Maps are drawn to scale. That is, a certain distance on the map stands for a certain distance on the earth. Maps usually contain a line or bar scale that you can use to measure distances. Use the scale on the map to see if you can tell the distance between New York City and Chicago.

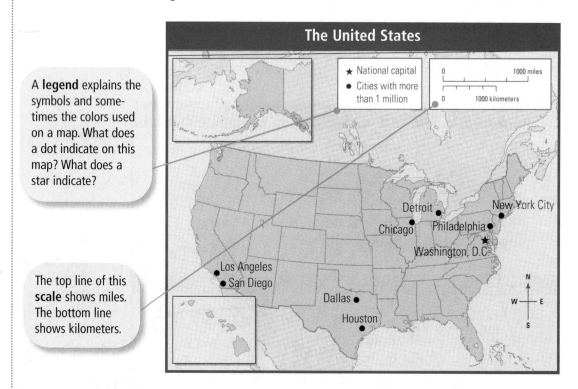

The United States

A **legend** explains the symbols and sometimes the colors used on a map. What does a dot indicate on this map? What does a star indicate?

The top line of this **scale** shows miles. The bottom line shows kilometers.

Exercise 5

Make a graphic aid of your own. Some possibilities include the following:

- a map of your room, your schoolyard, or your neighborhood
- a bar graph that compares the heights or weights of four or five classmates
- a line graph showing the batting averages of your favorite baseball player over several years
- a time line of your life or the life of a historical figure you admire

Study Skills

UNIT 24 Taking Tests

Lesson **24.1**   **Tips for Test Taking**   584

Lesson **24.2**   **Test Items**   586

Lesson **24.3**   **Standardized Tests**   588

Lesson **24.4**   **Standardized Test Practice**   591

24.1 | Tips for Test Taking

"There will be a test on Friday." Do those words throw you into a panic or are you usually well prepared? Either way, you can improve your test-taking skills. This lesson will help you learn a few strategies for taking tests.

Preparing for a Test

Preparing for a test can get you off to a good start. Here are some simple but effective strategies:

- Allow plenty of time to study. Don't wait until the day before the test. Several short review sessions are better than one long one.
- Gather information about the test. When will it be given? How long will it take? Exactly what material will it cover? What types of test items will be used (multiple choice, true or false, essay)?
- Review material from your textbook, class notes, homework, quizzes, and handouts.
- Make up some sample test questions, and answer them.
- Study with a partner or a small group. Quiz one another on topics you think the test will cover.

Taking Tests

Planning Your Time

You normally have a limited amount of time to take a test. Using your time wisely will help you do your best work. Before you begin, plan a general amount of time for each section of the test.

Tips for Using Time Well

- Read all test directions carefully. Understanding the directions will keep you from making mistakes.

- Answer the easier items first. By skipping the hard items, you give yourself time to answer all the easy ones.

- In whatever time is left, return to the items you skipped. Answer them as best you can. If you won't be penalized for doing so, guess.

- Save some time to check your answers before you turn in your test.

Exercise 1

The following statements give advice on taking a test. Which statements give *bad* advice? Write their numbers. Then rewrite each statement so that it gives *good* advice.

1. Do all your studying for the test the night before you take the test.
2. Always study alone for a test.
3. Review your homework and quizzes.
4. Try to learn what the test will cover.
5. Try to study without using your textbook.
6. Always avoid answering any of the difficult test questions.
7. Read the test directions carefully.
8. Answer every test question in order.
9. Never guess at an answer.
10. Check your answers carefully before turning in your test.

24.2 Test Items

The best way to prepare for a test, of course, is to learn the material that will be tested. You can also help yourself by mastering the different types of test items.

True-False Items

A true-false item gives only two choices, true or false. An answer is true only if the *entire* statement is true. If any part of the statement is false, you must mark it *false.* Look at the statement below.

> The earth circles the sun once each day.

The earth does circle the sun. However, it does so once each *year*, not each *day.* The statement is false.

Multiple-Choice Items

In a multiple-choice item you must answer a question or complete a sentence. You do so by picking the *best* response out of the three or four given.

> What is included in our solar system?
> a. the earth and the sun
> b. all the sun's planets
> c. asteroids and moons
> d. all of the above

Item *a* seems true, but be sure to read all the choices before answering.

Reading all responses is especially important when one choice is "all of the above" or "none of the above." The answer is *d.*

Matching Items

In the matching test format, you have two groups or lists of items. You must match each item from the first group with an item in the second group. Complete the easy matches first. That will leave fewer items to choose from when you get to the difficult ones.

Match each river with its continent.
1. Rhine River   a. North America
2. Nile River   b. South America
3. Mississippi River c. Africa
4. Amazon River   d. Asia
                      e. Europe

Exercise 2

Read the passage below. Then use your test-taking skills to answer the questions.

Kilauea is one of the most active volcanoes in the Hawaiian Islands. Since 1983 it has erupted dozens of times. When Kilauea erupts, it rarely explodes. Instead, fast-running lava pours out from cracks and vents. Sometimes it shoots up in fountains hundreds of feet high. Usually the lava runs down the sides of the mountain and cools. These layers of lava have formed Mt. Kilauea's long, gentle slopes. When the lava reaches the ocean, it quickly cools into rugged black rock.

1. Kilauea is an explosive volcano. True or false?
2. The lava from Kilauea
    a. forms mile-high fountains.
    b. has created the mountain's gentle slopes.
    c. is driven back by the ocean.
    d. none of the above
3. Match the terms in column 1 with the descriptions in column 2.
    1. Kilauea   a. a sudden release of lava
    2. eruption   b. a volcano
    3. lava   c. melted rock

Standardized Tests

In addition to classroom tests, you will sometimes take standardized tests. Students all over the country take these tests.

Taking Standardized Tests

Some standardized tests measure your abilities or how well you think. Others measure your knowledge in such subjects as English, math, and science. The following tips can help you do well on standardized tests.

Tips for Taking Standardized Tests

1. Sleep well the night before the test. Eat well in the morning. Try to arrive early for the test. Relax.

2. Listen carefully as directions are given before the test. Ask questions if you don't understand the directions.

3. Complete all the easy items first. Leave hard items until the end.

4. Compare the numbers for test items with the numbers on your answer sheet. Be sure your answers are in the right place.

5. If you can, find out whether points are subtracted for wrong answers. If they are not, you should guess at questions you aren't sure of.

Analogies

Analogy items test how well you can compare the meanings of words. For example, *stop* and *go* have opposite meanings.

A typical analogy item shows one relationship and asks you to complete another. They are often written as follows.

First figure out the relationship in the first pair of words. Eyes are used for seeing.

```
eyes: seeing:: ears:_____

a. smelling     b. hearing     c. touching
```

Then complete the second pair with the same kind of relationship. You use eyes to see and ears to hear. The correct answer is *b*.

The single colon (:) stands for "are to" or "is to." The double colon (::) stands for "as." So you would read the top line as "eyes are to seeing as ears are to ___."

COMMON TYPES OF ANALOGIES		
Antonyms	One word means the opposite of the other	light : dark
Synonyms	Two words have the same general meaning	tired : sleepy
Use	The thing named by one word uses or is used by the other.	rider : horse
Cause and effect	One item causes or results from the other.	cold : shiver

Grammar, Usage, and Mechanics

Standardized tests often will ask you to identify errors in grammar, usage, and mechanics. These errors might include incorrect capitalization, punctuation, or spellings, as well as errors in the use of pronouns, verb tenses, and subject-verb agreement.

Most sentence correction test items will ask you to identify an error in underlined text. Study the item below. Identify the underlined section that contains an error. If the sentence is correct as is, choose d to indicate no error.

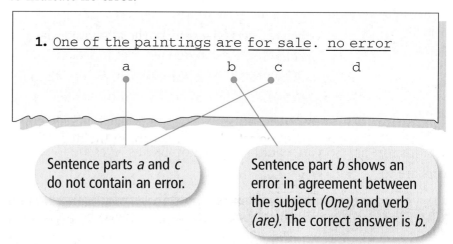

1. One of the paintings are for sale. no error
       a   b   c   d

Sentence parts *a* and *c* do not contain an error.

Sentence part *b* shows an error in agreement between the subject *(One)* and verb *(are)*. The correct answer is *b.*

Exercise 3

Write the letter of the answer that correctly completes each analogy.

1. down : up :: short : ____
   a. heavy   **b.** tall   **c.** far   **d.** tiny
2. calm : still :: brave : ____
   a. peaceful   **b.** daring   **c.** hurt   **d.** cowardly
3. sweeper : broom :: writer : ____
   a. artist   **b.** reader   **c.** pen   **d.** book

Choose the letter of the section containing an error. To indicate no error, choose *e.*

4. Our parents bought a puppy for my brother and I. no error
        a   b   c   d   e

Standardized Test Practice

INTRODUCTION

The following pages of exercises have been designed to familiarize you with the standardized writing tests that you may take during the school year. These exercises are very similar to the actual tests in how they look and what they ask you to do. Completing these exercises will not only provide you with practice, but also will make you aware of areas you might need to work on.

These writing exercises—just like the actual standardized writing tests—are divided into three sections.

SENTENCE STRUCTURE In this section, pages 592 to 599, you will be given a short passage in which some of the sentences are underlined. Each underlined sentence is numbered. After you finish reading the passage, you will be asked questions about the underlined sections. The underlined sections will be either incomplete sentences, run-on sentences, correctly written sentences that should be combined, or correctly written sentences that do not need to be rewritten. You will need to select which is best from the four choices provided.

USAGE In this section, pages 600 to 607, you will also be asked to read a short passage. However, in these exercises, a word or words in the passage will be omitted and a numbered blank space will be in their place. After reading the passage, you will need to determine which of the four provided words or groups of words best belongs in each numbered space.

MECHANICS Finally, in the third section, pages 608 to 615, the short passages will have parts that are underlined. You will need to determine if, in the underlined sections, there is a spelling error, capitalization error, punctuation error, or no error at all.

Writing well is a skill that you will use the rest of your life. You will be able to write more accurate letters to your friends and family, better papers in school, and more interesting stories. You will be able to express yourself and your ideas more clearly and in a way that is interesting and engaging. These exercises should help to improve your writing and to make you comfortable with the format and types of questions you will see on standardized writing tests.

Standardized Test Practice

Read each passage. Some sections are underlined. The underlined sections may be one of the following:

- Incomplete sentences
- Run-on sentences
- Correctly written sentences that should be combined
- Correctly written sentences that do not need to be rewritten

Choose the best way to write each underlined section and mark the letter for your answer on your paper. If the underlined section needs no change, mark the choice "Correct as is."

> Elizabeth Cady Stanton was one of the first Americans to push for women's voting rights, or suffrage. <u>One of her earliest contributions was to help organize the Seneca Falls Convention it was the first women's rights assembly in the U.S.</u>⁽¹⁾ There, in 1848, she unveiled her Declaration of Sentiments. <u>In wording similar to that of the Declaration of Independence. This document called for full voting rights for women.</u>⁽²⁾
>
> The Seneca Falls convention and the Declaration of Sentiments established women's rights as a movement in the U.S. <u>They were the first major steps towards the 19th Amendment to the Constitution. The 19th Amendment finally gave women the right to vote in 1920.</u>⁽³⁾

1 A One of her earliest contributions was to help organize. The Seneca Falls Convention was the first women's rights assembly in the U.S.

B One of her earliest contributions was to help organize the Seneca Falls Convention, the first women's rights assembly in the U.S.

C One of her earliest contributions she helped organize the Seneca Falls Convention, the first women's rights assembly in the U.S.

D Correct as is

2 F In wording similar to that of the Declaration of Independence, calling for full voting rights for women.

G In wording it was similar to that of the Declaration of Independence, it called for full voting rights for women.

H In wording similar to that of the Declaration of Independence, this document called for full voting rights for women.

J Correct as is

3 A They were the first major steps towards the 19th Amendment to the Constitution, which finally gave women the right to vote in 1920.

B They were the first major steps towards the 19th Amendment to the Constitution, or the 19th Amendment finally gave women the right to vote in 1920.

C They were the first major steps towards the 19th Amendment to the Constitution, and the right to vote in 1920 finally gave women.

D They were the first major steps towards the 19th Amendment to the Constitution because finally giving women the right to vote in 1920.

Gardeners struggle to keep insects away from their gardens. Some plants, however, need insects to survive. A jungle plant called a Dischidia, for instance, needs ants. The ants live inside its large, hollow leaves.
(1)
Ants drag dead insects and other materials back to their nest to eat. What the ants are unable to finish, the Dischidia soaks up into its leaves. Scientists call this kind of relationship symbiosis because both sides get
(2)
something from the situation. The ants get a place to build a safe, dry nest, and the Dischidia plant gets a constant source of nutrients. Scientists believe the Dischidia does this. Because there are so few natural
(3)
nutrients in the soil where it grows.

1 A A jungle plant called a Dischidia, for instance, needs the ants that live inside its large, hollow leaves.
  B A jungle plant called a Dischidia, for instance needs, and the ants live inside its large, hollow leaves.
  C A jungle plant called a Dischidia, for instance, that needs the ants that live inside its large, hollow leaves.
  D A jungle plant called a Dischidia, for instance, that needs and lives inside its large, hollow leaves, the ants.

2 F Scientists call this kind of relationship symbiosis. Because both sides get something from the situation.
  G Scientists call this kind of relationship symbiosis, they get something from the situation.
  H Scientists calling this kind of relationship symbiosis and both sides getting something from the situation.
  J Correct as is

3 A Scientists believe the Dischidia does this, this is because there are so few natural nutrients in the soil where it grows.
  B Scientists, believing the Dischidia does this, and so few natural nutrients in the soil where it grows.
  C Scientists believe the Dischidia does this because there are so few natural nutrients in the soil where it grows.
  D Correct as is

Standardized Test Practice

Read each passage. Some sections are underlined. The underlined sections may be one of the following:

- Incomplete sentences
- Run-on sentences
- Correctly written sentences that should be combined
- Correctly written sentences that do not need to be rewritten

Choose the best way to write each underlined section and mark the letter for your answer on your paper. If the underlined section needs no change, mark the choice "Correct as is."

<u>It might seem strange that all clock hands revolve in the same direction there is actually a very good</u>
<u>reason.</u> It started with ancient clocks called sundials. Sundials use the angle of the shadow made by a central
(1)
pole to tell the time. <u>As the sun moves from east to west. The shadow crosses numbers that represent the</u>
(2)
<u>time.</u>

Throughout the day, the shadow moves from left to right across the face of the sundial, crossing the 12
in the middle at noon. The first mechanical clocks imitated this. Their hour hands swept from left to right
across the top of the face. <u>This direction became known as clockwise. It is still used today.</u>
(3)

---

1 A It might seem strange that all clock hands revolve in the same direction, but there is actually a very good reason.

B It might seem strange that all clock hands revolve in the same direction. There being actually a very good reason.

C It might seem strange that all clock hands. It revolves in the same direction, but there is actually a very good reason.

D Correct as is

2 F As the sun moves from east to west, the shadow crosses numbers. That represent the time.

G As the sun moves from east to west, the shadow crosses numbers that represent the time.

H As the sun moving from east to west, the shadow it crosses numbers that represent the time.

J Correct as is

3 A This direction became known as clockwise and is still used today.

B This direction became known as clockwise, that is still used today.

C This direction became known and is still clockwise today.

D This direction became known and used as clockwise today.

Tracy was thinking of tying knots. She was thinking it as she fell asleep. The next day would be the first

(1)

day of sailing camp. Tracy got up early and left for the harbor. At eight o'clock, she got off the bus at the

(2)

pier the sailboats were kept there. She smelled the salty wind and saw boats of all sizes moored to the docks.

It looked like it had on other mornings since Tracy had started sailing six years ago. Only one thing was

(3)

different —when she got to her classroom, she did not sit at the back. She went right up to the front, she sat

(4)

facing the class. This year Tracy was an assistant instructor!

1 A Tracy was thinking of tying knots, and
thinking it as she fell asleep.
  B Tracy was thinking of tying knots when it
was asleep.
  C Tracy was thinking of tying knots as she
fell asleep.
  D Tracy was thinking of tying knots but she
was falling asleep.

2 F At eight o'clock, she got off the bus at the
pier. The sailboats kept there.
  G At eight o'clock, she got off the bus at the
pier. Where the sailboats were kept.
  H At eight o'clock, she got off the bus at the
pier, where the sailboats were kept.
  J Correct as is

3 A It looked like it had on other mornings.
Since Tracy had started sailing six years
ago.
  B It looked like it on other mornings since
Tracy had started sailing six years ago.
  C It looked like it had. On other mornings
since Tracy had started sailing six years
ago.
  D Correct as is

4 F She went right up to the front. And sat
facing the class.
  G Going right up to the front. She sat facing
the class.
  H She went right up to the front and sat
facing the class.
  J Correct as is

STOP

Standardized Test Practice

Read each passage. Some sections are underlined. The underlined sections may be one of the following:

- Incomplete sentences
- Run-on sentences
- Correctly written sentences that should be combined
- Correctly written sentences that do not need to be rewritten

Choose the best way to write each underlined section and mark the letter for your answer on your paper. If the underlined section needs no change, mark the choice "Correct as is."

<u>Mrs. Chen, the sixth-grade science teacher, smiled brightly at her students she was beside the large gray</u>
(1)
<u>machine.</u> She had brought the class on a field trip to the university microscopy laboratory.

A university technician was wearing a white lab coat. <u>She switched on the machine. She turned to the</u>
(2)
<u>class.</u> "This is called a Nomarski interference microscope," she said. "It uses polarized light to make objects more distinct. Today we are going to look at a drop of ordinary pond water."

The first student looked through the microscope eyepiece and let out a gasp. <u>The water had been</u>
(3)
<u>transformed into a land. Of brightly colored amoeba twisting slowly across the plane of view.</u> The other students waited for their turn to look.

---

1 A Mrs. Chen, the sixth-grade science teacher. She smiled brightly at her students from beside the large gray machine.
   B Mrs. Chen, the sixth-grade science teacher, smiled brightly at her students. Beside the large gray machine.
   C Mrs. Chen, the sixth-grade science teacher, smiled brightly at her students from beside the large gray machine.
   D Correct as is

2 F She switched the class on the machine.
   G She switched on the machine and turned to the class.
   H She switched on the machine because she turned to the class.
   J She switched on the machine, and she turned, and it was to the class.

3 A The water had been transformed into a land of brightly colored amoeba twisting slowly across the plane of view.
   B The water transformed into a land of brightly colored amoeba twisting slowly across the plane of view.
   C The water had been transformed into a land, brightly colored amoeba twisted slowly across the plane of view.
   D Correct as is

Do you know what an elephant really uses its trunk for? Just about everything. <u>You have probably seen (1) elephants using their trunks at the zoo. To pick up peanuts or straw for food.</u> In the wild, these powerful appendages help elephants strip branches and leaves from trees to eat and dig minerals out of the earth. <u>An (2) elephant can swim underwater for up to six hours straight. It breathes by keeping the end of its trunk out of the water like a snorkel.</u>

Elephants also have very poor eyesight and use their trunks to recognize each other and communicate. <u>When young elephants wrestle by entwining their trunks, it strengthens the trunks, they learn how to (3) recognize others in their herd.</u>

1 A You have probably seen elephants using their trunks at the zoo to pick up peanuts. Or straw for food.

B You have probably seen elephants using their trunks at the zoo, they use them to pick up peanuts or straw for food.

C You have probably seen elephants using their trunks at the zoo to pick up peanuts or straw for food.

D Correct as is

2 F An elephant can swim underwater for up to six hours straight, or it breathes by keeping the end of its trunk out of the water like a snorkel.

G An elephant can swim underwater for up to six hours straight, by keeping the end of its trunk out of the water like a snorkel.

H An elephant can swim underwater for up to six hours straight, keeping the end of its trunk out of the water like a snorkel.

J An elephant can swim underwater for up to six hours straight because it is like a snorkel with its trunk out of the water.

3 A When young elephants wrestle by entwining their trunks, it strengthens the trunks, and they learn how to recognize others in their herd.

B When young elephants, entwining their trunks it strengthens the trunks. They learn how to recognize others in their herd.

C When young elephants wrestle by entwining their trunks it strengthens the trunks. And they learn how to recognize others in their herd.

D Correct as is

Standardized Test Practice

Read each passage. Some sections are underlined. The underlined sections may be one of the following:

- Incomplete sentences
- Run-on sentences
- Correctly written sentences that should be combined
- Correctly written sentences that do not need to be rewritten

Choose the best way to write each underlined section and mark the letter for your answer on your paper. If the underlined section needs no change, mark the choice "Correct as is."

In 1884, Sarah Winchester began building one of the strangest homes in the world, it is in San Jose, California. (1) The enormous mansion, which took thirty years to complete, later became known as the "Winchester Mystery House." When Sarah bought the house, it was a modest six-room dwelling. When she was finally done with it. The house contained 160 rooms and stood five stories. (2)

The mansion has stairways that lead nowhere, rooms within rooms, and skylights in the floor. It is difficult to understand what could have driven Sarah to build such a bizarre home. In fact, no one really knows.

---

1 **A** In 1884. Sarah Winchester began building one of the strangest homes in the world in San Jose, California.

   B In 1884, Sarah Winchester began building one of the strangest homes in the world in San Jose, California.

   C In 1884, Sarah Winchester began building one of the strangest homes in the world. In San Jose, California.

   D Correct as is

2 **F** When she was finally done with it, the house contained 160 rooms, it stood five stories.

   G When she was finally done with it, the house contained 160 rooms. And it stood five stories.

   H When she was finally done with it, the house contained 160 rooms and stood five stories.

   J Correct as is

Sam was visiting his Aunt Theresa in San Francisco for Thanksgiving. When they were on the Bay Area
(1)
Rapid Transit Train travelling to a museum, Sam noticed something odd.

"Aunt Theresa," Sam said with astonishment, "there was nobody driving that train!"

Aunt Theresa smiled and explained that the trains were electronically controlled. When they were first
(2)
built in 1972, there were frequent equipment malfunctions. There were also frequent control malfunctions.
However, for the past twenty years, they had run quite well, carrying more than 200,000 passengers per day.

The train stopped it dropped Sam and his aunt at the museum.
(3)
"Instead of going to the museum, let's ride the train again!" exclaimed Sam. Aunt Theresa laughed and
they boarded the train again.

1 A Sam, visiting his Aunt Theresa in San
Francisco for Thanksgiving.
B Sam was visiting his Aunt Theresa. He was
in San Francisco for Thanksgiving.
C Sam was visiting his Aunt Theresa in San
Francisco, it was also for Thanksgiving.
D Correct as is

2 F When they were control malfunctions
first built in 1972, there were frequent
equipment.
G When they, which were frequent equipment and control malfunctions, were first
built in 1972.
H When they were first built in 1972, there
were frequent equipment malfunctions,
and there were also frequent control
malfunctions.

J When they were first built which was in
1972, frequent equipment and control
malfunctions.

3 A The train stopped and dropped Sam and
his aunt at the museum.
B The train stopping. The train dropped Sam
and his aunt at the museum.
C The train stopped. And dropped Sam and
his aunt at the museum.
D Correct as is

STOP

Standardized Test Practice

Read each passage and choose the word or group of words that belongs in each space. Mark the letter for your answer on your paper.

The students crowded around Jorry's locker. They were clearly ___(1)___ about the trip to the amusement park that Saturday. Suddenly, Jorry saw Will walking out the door. "Will, are you ___(2)___ without making plans for Saturday?"

"I can't come," Will replied. "I need to use the extra day to paint my parents' garage. It ___(3)___ for weeks."

Later that afternoon, Will was watching TV at home when he heard a noise from out in the backyard. He looked out the window and saw his friends. They had brought ladders, paint, and brushes, and were busy scraping the old paint from the garage.

"If we all help, the garage will be painted by the weekend," called Jorry when she saw Will. "You'll have to try ___(4)___ than that to get away from us!"

---

1 A excitement
   B excite
   C exciting
   D excited

2 F leaving
   G have left
   H left
   J had been leaving

3 A had been planned
   B will be planned
   C has been planned
   D is being planned

4 F more hard
   G hardly
   H most hardly
   J harder

Most people ___(1)___ of finding a pirate's treasure. Barry Clifford actually found one. Using a map from the year 1717, Mr. Clifford spent fifteen years searching the coast off Massachusetts for the sunken remains of a ship called the *Whydah*. Mr. Clifford has found more than 100,000 items from the ship already, but says he ___(2)___ find everything. The sea has spread the treasures far and wide.

Some preservationists feel that the *Whydah* should be ___(3)___ property. They ___(4)___ historic artifacts such as the sunken ship should be kept in museums. However, Massachusetts law says that the ship and everything Mr. Clifford finds belong to him.

1 A has dreamed
   B have dreamed
   C is dreaming
   D were dreaming

2 F will barely never
   G will not never
   H will hardly never
   J will probably never

3 A publicly
   B publicize
   C publics
   D public

4 F think
   G thought
   H had thought
   J was thinking

STOP

Standardized Test Practice

Read each passage and choose the word or group of words that belongs in each space. Mark the letter for your answer on your paper.

Karl was playing in his backyard when a puppy strolled in through a hole in the fence. "Can I keep him?" Karl asked his father hopefully.

"Maybe he already __(1)__ to somebody," said Karl's father.

Karl's father called the puppy over to him and patted him on the head. Then he showed Karl the bright metal tag on the puppy's collar. Karl read the tag: "This puppy's name is Hugo. His owner is Carlos Vasquez, 234 Cedar Road."

"That's next door," Karl's father exclaimed.

Karl and his father __(2)__ the puppy over to their neighbors' house. Mr. Vasquez was grateful to __(3)__ for returning Hugo. His son Carlos picked up the puppy and asked Karl if he wanted to come play with Hugo in __(4)__ backyard. "Sure," said Karl. Hugo wagged his tail and barked.

---

1 A belonged
  B was belonging
  C belongs
  D is belonging

2 F bring
  G has brought
  H had brought
  J brought

3 A they
  B them
  C their
  D theirs

4 F it
  G you
  H their
  J he

In the early 1960s, the area of Costa Rica that is now the Guanacaste Conservation Reserve was rich ranchland and wild forests. By the 1980s, just two percent of the forests remained, and the ranches no longer ____(1)____ enough to stay in business. Ecologist Dan Janzen wanted to help. He decided to buy the useless ranchland and turn ____(2)____ back into forest.

Costa Rica is proud of ____(3)____ environmental policies. The Costa Rican government and other institutions gave Janzen funding for their project. With this money, the reserve ____(4)____ a large organization in itself. It now employs 120 people and covers more than 323,000 acres of ocean and recovering forest. The forest is returning to the original ranchland, but many hundreds of years will have to pass before it regains the majesty it once had.

1 A is producing
   B produced
   C has produced
   D produce

2 F it
   G him
   H us
   J you

3 A them
   B they
   C my
   D its

4 F becomed
   G becoming
   H has become
   J become

STOP

Standardized Test Practice

Read each passage and choose the word or group of words that belongs in each space. Mark the letter for your answer on your paper.

Have you ever eaten caviar? Not many people have. Caviar is a very expensive preparation of fish eggs and salt. It only ___(1)___ from certain kinds of fish, in certain regions of the world. The finest caviar sells for more than $1,000 per pound.

A less expensive caviar, which ___(2)___ for $630 per pound, comes from a fish called a chalbash. The chalbash can easily grow to be five feet long, and weigh more than thirty-five pounds. A master caviar artisan adds a ___(3)___ amount of salt to the chalbash's eggs, then rubs them with his fingers, tasting them from time to time, until he ___(4)___ they are ready. It is a very difficult thing to learn, and that may be one reason why caviar is so expensive.

---

1 A had come
  B came
  C have come
  D comes

2 F selling
  G have sold
  H sells
  J sold

3 A precise
  B precisely
  C more precisely
  D most precise

4 F knew
  G knows
  H has known
  J know

Latorry's class was playing volleyball in physical education. The ball came down towards Latorry, but it was too far away for him to reach. Without thinking, he ___(1)___ out his foot and kicked it. The ball sailed over the net and bounced inside the lines.

When Latorry ___(2)___ off the court, Mr. Russel, the PE instructor, came over to him. "That was a nice move, Latorry," he said.

"But Mr. Russel, ___(3)___ was illegal," Latorry said. "The other team got the point."

"That's true, Latorry, but maybe you'll invent a new game," Mr. Russel replied. "Once a young English soccer player named William Webb Ellis picked up the ball and ran. The move was against soccer's rules, but people enjoyed playing that way. Without William Webb Ellis we ___(4)___ of the sport of rugby."

1 A sticked
  B has stuck
  C sticks
  D stuck

2 F will rotate
  G rotated
  H rotating
  J rotates

3 A I
  B we
  C it
  D you

4 F would never have heard
  G wouldn't never have heard
  H wouldn't barely have heard
  J would never hardly hear

STOP

Standardized Test Practice

Read each passage and choose the word or group of words that belongs in each space. Mark the letter for your answer on your paper.

At any time, there may be 2,000 thunderstorms in activity on earth. Scientists believe that lightning ___(1)___ an average of 100 times per second. Some lightning flashes occur inside a cloud, but the ___(2)___ type of lightning flashes from a cloud down to the ground. This type ___(3)___ when the bottom of the cloud develops a negative charge. As the negatively charged cloud moves over the ground, a positive charge builds below ___(4)___. The positive and negative charges get stronger until they balance themselves in what we call lightning.

---

1 A was flashing
   B had flashed
   C flashes
   D flashed

2 F frequent
   G more frequently
   H frequentest
   J most frequent

3 A is caused
   B has caused
   C was causing
   D have caused

4 F me
   G you
   H it
   J they

When bicycles were first invented, ___(1)___ did not have pedals. Pedals ___(2)___ in 1839 by the Scottish black-smith, Kirkpatrick Macmillan.

The first pedals ___(3)___ to the rear wheel of the bicycle. The wheel turned once with each rotation of the pedals. Speed depended upon how big the front wheel was. The pennyfarthing bicycles of the time had front wheels that were five feet high. The back wheels were ___(4)___ than the wheels of modern bicycles.

1 A they
  B our
  C your
  D their

2 F was inventing
  G invented
  H had invented
  J were invented

3 A has been attached
  B were attached
  C is attached
  D are attached

4 F much smaller
  G more smaller
  H smallest
  J small

STOP

Standardized Test Practice

Read each passage and decide which type of error, if any, appears in each underlined section. Mark the letter for your answer on your paper.

Carlos looked suspiciously at his little brother, Ry. <u>Ry was only seven, after all and Carlos wasn't sure a</u>
(1)

seven-year-old would be able to sustain an interest in <u>playing Music long enough to get it right. Carlos</u>
(2)

carefully explained that all Ry had to do was beat on the drum. He showed him the rhythm he needed.

"As long as you keep it <u>steady, everything will be fine, said Carlos encouragingly.</u>
(3)

Ry <u>started beeting on the drum. "Is that okay?"</u> he asked.
(4)

Carlos <u>answered by picking up his clarinet and playing</u> the melody he had invented that morning. The
(5)

notes mixed in with the drum's beat and became a song.

"It's music!" cried Ry, and missed a beat.

"It sure was," said Carlos. "We'll call ourselves <u>the Carter brothers Band. Let's</u> take it again from the top!"
(6)

---

1 A Spelling error
B Capitalization error
C Punctuation error
D No error

2 F Spelling error
G Capitalization error
H Punctuation error
J No error

3 A Spelling error
B Capitalization error
C Punctuation error
D No error

4 F Spelling error
G Capitalization error
H Punctuation error
J No error

5 A Spelling error
B Capitalization error
C Punctuation error
D No error

6 F Spelling error
G Capitalization error
H Punctuation error
J No error

One day in 1992 Iwan Stössel, <u>a swiss geology student, was</u> walking along the coast of Ireland. He came
(1)
across a <u>strange set of imppressions in a stone that</u> looked like footprints. There were 150 of these fossilized
(2)
<u>footprints, each about the size of a dogs foot.</u> Paleontologists believe that the tracks were left 365 <u>million</u>
(3)
<u>years ago by a tetrapod one of the first creatures ever to walk</u> rather than swim. <u>The tetrapod waded</u>
(4) (5)
through shallow water, Scientists believe, at a time when Ireland was south of the equator. Just how its

ancestors' fins became legs, and <u>how it moved from the shallos up onto dry land, is still a mystery.</u>
(6)

1 A Spelling error
  B Capitalization error
  C Punctuation error
  D No error

2 F Spelling error
  G Capitalization error
  H Punctuation error
  J No error

3 A Spelling error
  B Capitalization error
  C Punctuation error
  D No error

4 F Spelling error
  G Capitalization error
  H Punctuation error
  J No error

5 A Spelling error
  B Capitalization error
  C Punctuation error
  D No error

6 F Spelling error
  G Capitalization error
  H Punctuation error
  J No error

STOP

Standardized Test Practice

Read each passage and decide which type of error, if any, appears in each underlined section. Mark the letter for your answer on your paper.

Jodie looked carefuly across the checkerboard at her opponent. She was playing with her mother. Jodie
(1)
and her mother played checkers every saturday. Sometimes Jodie won and sometimes her mother won.
(2)
Hoping that she would win this time Jodie concentrated very hard. She had worked out a strategy and she
(3)
was feeling confident.

Today, Jodie had the Red pieces and her mother had the black. Her mother hopped over two of Jodie's
(4)
pieces.

"I might just win this time," Jodie's mother said.
(5)
"Don't be so sure!" Jodie said and jumped over four of her mothers pieces. She had won the game!
(6)
"I'll get you next time!" laughed Jodie's mother. As was their tradition, they went into the kitchen and

had some milk and cookies after their game.

1 A Spelling error
   B Capitalization error
   C Punctuation error
   D No error

2 F Spelling error
   G Capitalization error
   H Punctuation error
   J No error

3 A Spelling error
   B Capitalization error
   C Punctuation error
   D No error

4 F Spelling error
   G Capitalization error
   H Punctuation error
   J No error

5 A Spelling error
   B Capitalization error
   C Punctuation error
   D No error

6 F Spelling error
   G Capitalization error
   H Punctuation error
   J No error

In the last half of 1998, a number of scientists mounted <u>donkeys in Dana Jordan. They</u> set out into the
(1)
desert with hand-mined copper ore. They wanted to reduce the ore to metal the way people in that region
did <u>6,500 years ago. Tom levy, an archeologist</u> from California, was one of the leaders of the group.
(2)
After a ten-day <u>trek accross the desert, the team</u> arrived at the site of the ancient village of Shiqmim,
(3)
whose ruins lie in modern day Israel. They used <u>the towns original firepits to try</u> to heat the copper ore and
(4)
reduce it to metal. When they had <u>kept the ore at temperatures of nearly 2000 degrees for a</u> whole hour,
(5)
they were left with only a few pea-sized lumps of copper. They <u>left with a new apreciation of what hard</u>
(6)
<u>work the ancient</u> metalworkers had been faced with!

1 A Spelling error
   B Capitalization error
   C Punctuation error
   D No error

2 F Spelling error
   G Capitalization error
   H Punctuation error
   J No error

3 A Spelling error
   B Capitalization error
   C Punctuation error
   D No error

4 F Spelling error
   G Capitalization error
   H Punctuation error
   J No error

5 A Spelling error
   B Capitalization error
   C Punctuation error
   D No error

6 F Spelling error
   G Capitalization error
   H Punctuation error
   J No error

STOP

Standardized Test Practice

Read each passage and decide which type of error, if any, appears in each underlined section. Mark the letter for your answer on your paper.

Ms. Julie Burke

Koch Laboratories

1800 Abrams Parkway

Dallas, TX 75214

Dear Ms. Burke:

<u>I am the president of the science Club at Roosevelt High School.</u> I read an article recently about your
(1)
company in the newspaper. The <u>tests that you are conducting sound very intresting to me</u>. Would you be
(2)
willing to speak to our club about the work that you do? It would be <u>very informative to hear about your</u>
(3)
<u>studies your background, and your thoughts</u> about the profession.

    <u>The Science Club meets every Tuesday at 4 p.m., but we would be willing to work</u> around your schedule
(4)
if necessary. You can contact <u>our faculty advisor, dr. Harold Ripley, at the school's main office. Thank you</u> in
(5)
advance for your time. I hope we will have the opportunity to meet soon.

    Sincerely,

    Zachary Dunham

---

1 A Spelling error
  B Capitalization error
  C Punctuation error
  D No error

2 F Spelling error
  G Capitalization error
  H Punctuation error
  J No error

3 A Spelling error
  B Capitalization error
  C Punctuation error
  D No error

4 F Spelling error
  G Capitalization error
  H Punctuation error
  J No error

5 A Spelling error
  B Capitalization error
  C Punctuation error
  D No error

Crocodiles first emerged in the pre-historical record 200 million years <u>ago. More than eighty million</u>
<u>years later there</u> were crocodiles forty feet long that may have preyed on dinosaurs. <u>Today, crocodiles vary in</u>
(1)   (2)
<u>size. Dwarf crocodiles</u> are as short as five feet long, while saltwater <u>crocodiles from southeastern asia, can</u>
(3)
<u>grow</u> up to twenty feet in length, and weigh one ton or more.

The female crocodile <u>burries her eggs in a bed of vegetation near</u> the water. Heat from <u>the Sun and the</u>
(4)   (5)
<u>rotting plants</u> incubate the eggs, which hatch about three months later. When the <u>baby crocodiles hatch they</u>
(6)
<u>are still buried.</u> They must call to their mother to dig them out. She then brings them down to the water.

1 A Spelling error
  B Capitalization error
  C Punctuation error
  D No error

2 F Spelling error
  G Capitalization error
  H Punctuation error
  J No error

3 A Spelling error
  B Capitalization error
  C Punctuation error
  D No error

4 F Spelling error
  G Capitalization error
  H Punctuation error
  J No error

5 A Spelling error
  B Capitalization error
  C Punctuation error
  D No error

6 F Spelling error
  G Capitalization error
  H Punctuation error
  J No error

STOP

Standardized Test Practice

Read each passage and decide which type of error, if any, appears in each underlined section. Mark the letter for your answer on your paper.

The bar is a legal term for the body of <u>lawyers who have been qualified to practise at trials.</u> Myra Colby
(1)
Bradwell was one of the first American women to be admitted to the bar. <u>Bradwell was the editor of the</u>
(2)
<u>*chicago Legal News,* and was</u> very influential through <u>editorials she wrote on womens rights.</u> She herself was
(3)
the object of substantial discrimination. <u>Her first aplication to the Illinois bar, in 1869, was rejected because</u>
(4)
<u>she was a woman, even though Illinois law prohibited the</u> barring of persons from any occupation on the
basis of gender. It took eleven years for <u>the Illinois bar to admit her and finally in 1892 she was admitted to</u>
(5)
<u>practice</u> before the U.S. Supreme Court.

---

1 **A** Spelling error
  B Capitalization error
  C Punctuation error
  D No error

2 **F** Spelling error
  G Capitalization error
  H Punctuation error
  J No error

3 **A** Spelling error
  B Capitalization error
  C Punctuation error
  D No error

4 **F** Spelling error
  G Capitalization error
  H Punctuation error
  J No error

5 **A** Spelling error
  B Capitalization error
  C Punctuation error
  D No error

Earthquakes are more <u>common occurences than you might expect. During</u> the 1980s, 15,436 earth-
(1)
quakes with a magnitude of five or greater on the Richter scale were recorded. The vast majority of earthquakes are very <u>small and cause little damage but the largest can be among the most</u> destructive of natural
(2)
catastrophes.

The largest earthquakes occur at subduction <u>zones, where one part of the earths crust</u> is forced beneath
(3)
another. <u>For example, in 1960, an earthquake in chile had a</u> magnitude of 8.5. <u>Another earthquake in kobe,</u>
(4)   (5)
<u>Japan in 1995 was also very destructive.</u>

However, smaller earthquakes can be just as intense. Poor construction and certain soil types can make
even a <u>medium-sized earthquake highly destructive.</u>
(6)

1 A Spelling error
   B Capitalization error
   C Punctuation error
   D No error

2 F Spelling error
   G Capitalization error
   H Punctuation error
   J No error

3 A Spelling error
   B Capitalization error
   C Punctuation error
   D No error

4 F Spelling error
   G Capitalization error
   H Punctuation error
   J No error

5 A Spelling error
   B Capitalization error
   C Punctuation error
   D No error

6 F Spelling error
   G Capitalization error
   H Punctuation error
   J No error

STOP

UNIT 25 Listening and Speaking

Lesson 25.1   **Listening**   *617*

Lesson 25.2   **Informal Speaking**   *621*

Lesson 25.3   **How to Give an Oral Report**   *624*

616

Imagine yourself taking a trip and using a map for directions. How would you know where to go if a part of your map were missing? Traveling without a complete set of directions can be difficult. The same is true in listening. You must listen for *all* the important "road signs." Miss one, and you may not understand what you hear.

Following Instructions

Understanding exactly what your teacher expects of you begins with listening to instructions. The following suggestions can help you improve your listening skills.

Listening to Instructions in Class

1. First try to eliminate any distractions that may make it difficult to listen.
2. Make sure you understand what you are listening for. Are you receiving instructions for homework or for a test? What you listen for depends upon the type of instructions being given.
3. Think about what you are hearing, and keep your eyes on the speaker. This will help you stay focused on the important points.
4. Listen for word clues the speaker is using. Examples of word clues are expressions such as *above all, the most important,* and *the three basic parts.* These clues can help you identify important points you should remember.
5. Take notes on what you hear. Write down only the most important parts of the instructions.
6. If you don't understand something, ask questions. Then, if you're still unsure about the instructions, repeat them aloud to your teacher to receive correction on any key points you've missed.

Taking Notes

Taking notes as you listen is a good way to sort out main ideas and supporting details. The process of taking notes also helps you remember what you've heard. You may already have your own way of taking notes. Here are a few useful note-taking tips you may want to keep in mind:

- **Have a purpose for listening.** Are you trying to gain information or solve a problem? Asking these questions will give you a focus when you are taking notes.
- **Key ideas** are the ones you want to remember. Listen for them.
- **Don't be in a hurry** to start writing. It can take time to complete an idea. Make sure the speaker has completed a key idea before you write it down.
- **Keep listening** as you take notes. Stay alert so that you don't miss important information as you write.
- **Keep your notes brief.** Don't try to take down everything the speaker says. You don't need to write complete sentences. A few words are usually enough to help you remember a key idea. Remember, your notes are for you.
- **Use graphic aids** to organize information clearly. Charts, pictures, tables, or even arrows and lines can help you understand and remember how points are related. You can review the information about graphic aids on pages 579–582.
- **Review your notes.** Read over your notes a few hours after you have written them. Reviewing what you have written will help you remember the information.

Listening to Persuasive Speech

Have you ever listened to a politician speak or to an editorial on the news? Do you listen to radio or television commercials? If you said *yes*, you have heard persuasive speech. All of these speakers have one thing in common—they are trying to convince you of something. They may want to get your vote, to sell you a certain product, or to change your mind about an issue that is important to them.

Listening to Commercials

Nowhere is persuasive speech more obvious than in commercials. Commercials provide information, but they also try to sell you products. Advertisers use many different techniques to convince you to buy their products. They know you often decide what to buy based on your feelings rather than on the facts.

- **Endorsement.** In an endorsement, a famous person or an expert, such as a doctor, tells you that he or she uses a certain product. For example, a famous basketball player may be shown wearing a certain brand of shoes. The advertiser hopes that if you see someone you know or respect with a product, you will be more likely to buy it. Or, you may think that if you buy that product, it will make you as successful or even as good-looking as the person who is endorsing the product.
- **Exaggeration.** Some advertisers use exaggeration to persuade you to buy their products. Commercials are sprinkled with words and slogans such as "new and improved," "the greatest," "perfect," and so on. If a spot remover product promises "amazing" results, what exactly does that mean? What is amazing to one person may not be to another. Exaggerations in advertising are often just statements of opinion that are not based on facts.

- **Hidden Fears.** Some commercials appeal to your fears. They suggest that by using a certain product you will be protected from something unpleasant or even dangerous. For instance, some soap manufacturers try to convince buyers that their special "germ-killing formula" will protect you from all kinds of illness. Other advertisers might suggest that if you don't use their perfume or their mouthwash, other people won't want to be around you.
- **Bandwagon.** Some advertisers encourage buyers to "jump on the bandwagon" and buy their product because it is the most popular of its kind. A blue jean commercial might claim that everyone at school will be wearing a certain brand of blue jean this year. Advertisers who use the bandwagon technique often try to convince consumers that if they don't buy the most popular brand, then they will not be popular themselves.

Exercise 1

Working with a small group, pick several programs to watch on television. Choose different types of programs, such as news, comedy, drama, science, and sports. Each group member should watch one program and take notes on it. Afterward, share with the group your notes on the program you watched. Try to help the group members "see" the program you describe for them.

Exercise 2

Listen carefully to several radio or television commercials. If possible, tape record them. Then choose one that uses one or more of the techniques listed above. Create a chart to list a sample of how each technique is used in the commercial you chose. Then use your chart as a graphic aid to prepare and present a short oral report on your findings.

25.2 Informal Speaking

Did you know that you're already an expert in at least one type of public speaking—informal speaking? Most of your talking with other people is informal. There are many ways to speak informally. Examples include talking with friends, speaking in small groups in class, and communicating on the telephone.

Using the Telephone

When you call someone on the telephone, always identify yourself right away. Don't make the person on the other end try to guess who you are. You might say, "Is Gabriel there? This is Maria calling."

Here are some more tips for using the telephone:

- Speak clearly. Make sure the person on the other end can understand you easily. If a listener keeps asking you to repeat what you're saying, you may be mumbling.
- If the person you called is not there, try to leave a message. First ask if you can do so. Then give the person who answered time to get a pencil and paper.
- Speaking clearly becomes especially important if you must leave a recorded message. Remember, the recording can't ask you to repeat something.
- Deliver your message clearly. Give your name and your phone number. Then tell what information you'd like to leave for the person you've called. Try to make your message short and to the point.
- Be polite. Good telephone communication depends on how willing the other person is to listen to you. Good manners can help keep the other person interested.

Listening and Speaking

Giving Directions

When someone asks you for directions, it's important to give detailed and exact information. You want to be sure that the person listening understands exactly what you're saying. The examples in the following chart will help you understand how to give clear directions.

Giving Directions		
Unclear	**Clear**	**Remember to**
Go a few blocks, then turn, and go two more blocks.	Go straight ahead for three blocks. Then turn left, and go on for two more blocks.	**Be precise.**
Mix the eggs and milk and the flour.	First mix the eggs and milk. Next sift the flour, and then combine it with the eggs and milk.	**Use proper ordering.**
Graham stopped by. He wants you to meet him later.	Graham stopped by at noon. He wants you to meet him in the library at about seven tonight.	**Give complete information.**
That's how you do it. Now you try it.	Before you try it yourself, do you have any questions about what I've said?	**Make sure you've been understood.**

Taking Part in an Informal Discussion

A small-group meeting in class is one example of an informal discussion. Other examples include planning a party with friends or discussing vacation plans with your family. Informal discussions should be relaxed. You usually don't have to prepare for what you'll say. You should, however, be ready to talk about the topic the group wishes to discuss.

Group members should express their own opinions and argue in favor of them. Members should feel free to disagree with one another, but in a polite way. The chart on the following page presents some useful tips on taking part in an informal discussion.

Tips For Informal Discussions

1. Be sure you've listened carefully to what other people have said. To respond well, you should have considered your classmates' points and perspectives.
2. Decide what ideas you want to get across when you speak. You need not have the wording completely planned ahead of time.
3. Help the discussion move forward. Make sure each comment adds something important to the topic.
4. Take turns listening and speaking without interrupting other speakers.
5. Speak in a normal tone of voice. Feel free to use gestures to stress a point you want to make strongly. The idea in informal speaking is to express yourself as naturally as you can.
6. Accept and evaluate criticism of your ideas.

Exercise 3

Working in pairs, take turns pretending to speak to each other on the telephone. Each caller should leave a short, clear message after asking for someone who is not available. The person receiving the call should write an accurate, complete message. Calls might be made to the dentist, to a friend, to a grandparent or other relative, or to a teacher or instructor.

Exercise 4

Work with a small group. Use a topic from the list below or one of your own choosing and hold a ten-minute discussion on it.
- Using cellular phones in public places
- Eliminating the long summer vacation in schools
- Watching television versus reading a book

25.3 How to Give an Oral Report

Speaking in front of an audience can be exciting. You can make sure your talk goes smoothly by taking care as you prepare it. Good planning also will help your audience gain the most from what you say.

TIME

For more about using the writing process, see **TIME Facing the Blank Page,** page 90.

Preparing an Oral Report

The following five-step plan can help you prepare and deliver an oral report. You'll find the plan familiar. It's very much like the one you use to do a written report.

1. **Prewriting**   Decide on your topic. Make sure it's narrow enough to cover in a short oral report. Do research, take notes, and outline as you would for a written report.
2. **Drafting**   Write out your report just as you'd like to deliver it orally. Let your thoughts flow, but keep to your outline. Make sure all the details help support your main ideas.
3. **Revising**   Review what you've written. Do your ideas flow from one to another? Is there a better way to organize your material? Is it the right length? Does it need revision for style? Rework your draft as needed. Keep reworking it until you're satisfied it's right.

Listening and Speaking

4. **Practicing**   Practice giving your report in front of a mirror. Try not to read from your written copy. Use it only as notes for your talk. You might ask a friend or relative to listen to you and offer suggestions. You can also tape-record your talk.

5. **Presenting**   Relax! If you've prepared well, you can trust that your oral report will go smoothly.

Presenting an Oral Report

Actually, it's not unusual to feel a bit nervous when speaking before an audience. Even well-known actors feel nervous, no matter how often they've performed. Here are some suggestions for giving an oral report.

Tips For Effective Speaking
1. Speak slowly, clearly, and in a normal tone of voice. Raise your voice a bit or use gestures to stress important points.
2. Pause a few seconds after making an important point. This lets your audience think about what you've said.
3. Use words that will help your audience picture what you're talking about. Visual aids such as pictures, graphs, charts, and maps can also help make your information clear to the audience.
4. Stay in contact with your audience. Make sure your eyes move from person to person in the group you're addressing.

Storytelling

For thousands of years, people from many different cultures used storytelling as a way to pass on their history, to teach the young, to explain why things happen in nature, and to entertain. Today, in the United States, storytelling has become an art and is mostly used to entertain and delight audiences of all ages. Good storytellers rely on their voices and words to create pictures in the minds of their listeners. use the plan on the following page to help you sharpen your storytelling skills and prepare a storytelling performance that your audience won't soon forget.

Listening and Speaking

1. **Finding the right story to tell.** Check at your library for books of folktales. You will want to visit the young people's section as well as the adult section. You might wish to choose a story that is from your own culture, or a culture that is similar to yours. The story should be short and interesting. It should capture the audience's attention with a surprise twist, a remarkable moment, or a satisfying ending.

2. **Familiarize yourself with the story.** Read the story several times. First read it for pleasure. Then read the story over and over again to become familiar with the style and structure of the story. Are there any unusual words and phrases, or ones that are repeated? What happens in the beginning and at the end?

   Think about what the story's characters are like. How does each one speak? What is the setting? What does it look like? What is it about the story that you would like to share with your listener? its humor? its sense of wonder?

3. **Practice telling the story.** Be yourself as you practice retelling your story in your own words. First tell it to your family, friends, or stand in front of a mirror. The following tips will help you as you practice.

   a. Don't memorize. Just remember the main details of the plot and go from there. Your story will probably be a little different every time you tell it, and that's fine. The more you let your own words and imagination flow, the more interesting the story will be.

   b. Make sure that you pace the story correctly. Each story has its own pace. Some stories, like "The Gingerbread Man," have a brisk pace, while others have a slow and steady pace. Some stories are made up of both slow and fast parts. Study your story to determine how you should pace it. Limit your first story to a length of five to ten minutes.

   c. Take time to come up with vivid descriptions of sounds, colors, smells, and other details in the story. If you forget what you want to say for a moment, use these descriptions to fill in the space. No one will know, because it's your story.

   d. Use your voice to make your storytelling interesting. Use a pleasant, low-pitched voice, and speak loudly enough so that all of your listeners can easily hear. Try to give each character a distinct voice. You don't need to give a shy character a high, squeaky voice and a pushy character a low, growling voice; you may simply have one character speak more softly. Whichever voice you choose for your characters, make sure it suits the character and that you use the same voice for each one throughout.

e. Don't be afraid to pause to allow an idea to sink in or to create a feeling of suspense. Stress important words by saying them more loudly, or even by whispering them. Sometimes a whisper captures your audience's attention more than a shout.

f. Look directly at your audience, moving your eyes from face to face. Your gestures and facial expressions should be natural—don't try to act out every action in the story. Remember that you are telling a story, not putting on a play.

4. **Limit distractions as much as possible.**   Make sure that your audience is comfortable and ready to give you their full attention.

Exercise 5

Work with a small group. Each member should select a topic and write a two- to three-minute oral report about it. Be sure to narrow your topic before you begin. Practice giving your talk before your group. Allow group members to suggest improvements. Group members may give their oral reports later before the entire class.

Exercise 6

Work with a partner. Each of you should select a story and prepare to tell it to a group of people. Your story should be no longer than ten minutes and no less than five. Practice telling your story to your partner first. Have your partner time your story, evaluate your presentation, and make suggestions for improvement. Then tell each of your stories to the class.

Viewing and Representing

Lesson **26.1**   **Interpreting Visual Messages**   *629*

Lesson **26.2**   **Analyzing Media Messages**   *635*

Lesson **26.3**   **Producing Media Messages**   *640*

26.1 Interpreting Visual Messages

Statistics show that nearly one out of every five nine-year-olds watches six or more hours of television every day. By the time many of those nine-year-olds graduate from high school, they will have spent more time experiencing television and other forms of **mass media** than they will have spent going to school!

The term *mass media* means "a form of communication that is widely available to many people." Examples include newspapers, magazines, television, radio, movies, videos, and the Internet. Television and other forms of mass media have a great influence on your life. The influences can be both positive and negative.

You can enjoy the benefits of the media and still protect yourself from its problems. The best way to do this is to learn how to interpret, analyze, and evaluate the many messages that are sent to you—by the press, over the airwaves, and through the Web. This unit will help.

Understanding Visual Design

You know that written and spoken words contain verbal messages. Pictures, however, carry *visual messages.* You have learned to read verbal messages carefully and to evaluate them. You can do the same thing when you "read" visual messages. Like written messages, some visual messages are valuable and truthful, but others are not.

Photographs, paintings, cartoons, and drawings are all created very carefully to send messages to you, the viewer. So are advertisements, television programs, videos, movies, Internet graphics, and video games. Understanding how pictures send messages will help you to "read" each message and then decide whether the message is valuable.

Photographers and artists carefully plan the design of their pictures. They think about how they want to arrange the people and objects so that you, the viewer, will "read" their message and then respond in a certain way. The arrangement of features in a picture is called **composition**. The chart on the following page lists some basic elements of a picture's composition. It also describes how the artist or photographer can work with these elements to send visual messages.

Elements of Picture Design and Composition

What to Look For	Possible Effect
Lines	
Heavy, thick lines	Suggest boldness or power
Thin or broken lines	Suggest weakness or lightness
Straight lines	Point in a direction, or lead the eye, to something else
Curved lines	Suggest motion
Vertical lines	Suggest power
Horizontal lines	Suggest peace or stillness
Diagonal lines	Suggest tension, action, energy
Colors	
Cool colors (blue, green, gray)	Can suggest either calmness or coldness
Warm colors (orange, yellow, red)	Often suggest energy and pep
Bright colors	Often suggest joy, action, or excitement
Subdued or pastel colors	Suggest innocence or softness
Position of subjects	
Center of picture	Suggests strength, dominance; draws attention to the subject
Top of picture	Suggests power, importance
Bottom of picture	Suggests weakness, lack of power
Space	
Large space around subject	Draws attention to subject; can suggest loneliness, vastness
Small amount of space around subject	Makes subject seem very powerful

Viewing and Representing

Study this drawing that illustrator Lynn Munsinger created for the children's book *Listen Buddy,* by Helen Lester. The bear is in the center of the picture. As the chart shows, the bear's central position makes him dominate the picture. The reader's eyes are drawn to him first. Also, the curved lines in the bear's body suggest motion. The diagonal line created by his position suggests tension, action, and energy. How do the colors of the bear's clothing and his facial expression work together with these design elements?

Exercise 1

Use the Elements of Picture Design and Composition chart and the interpretation of the bear to interpret what visual message the artist aims to send through the rabbit. Explain how lines and position, as well as colors and facial expression, work together to send that message. Include reasons that the artist might have chosen to use thick, heavy lines to outline the bear and thin or broken lines to outline the rabbit.

Many artists and photographers work in black and white rather than in color. Some choose to do so because the absence of color lets them emphasize dark, light, and shadows. Others, like many newspaper cartoonists, must work in black and white because their medium, the newspaper, is in black and white.

Paul Szep, the *Boston Globe* political cartoonist, drew this cartoon. The local NHL hockey team, the Boston Bruins (*bruins* means "bears"), had just lost an important game, and many people felt that the team had played poorly.

THE MIGHTY BRUINS KNOCKED OUT OF STANLEY CUP

MEE YOW!

Exercise 2

Think about the cartoonist's use of lines, position, and space in this cartoon. Then note the facial expression and the words that the character is speaking. Summarize in your own words the message that the cartoonist wanted to send to viewers of this cartoon. Then compare the bear in this cartoon with the bear in the first drawing you examined. How are they alike and different? What different visual messages did each artist aim to send to the viewer?

Understanding Film Techniques

Think of a time you have seen a movie based on a book you have read. How did the two versions compare? Did seeing the film or reading the book help you better understand characters, themes, or twists in the plot? Or did seeing one version after the other change your first opinion of the entire story?

Creators of movies and videos use the same elements of picture design and composition that artists and photographers use. In addition to those elements, they use many different camera and lighting techniques to tell stories and send visual messages. This chart shows some of these techniques and the effects they can have.

Film and Video Techniques for Sending Visual Messages	
Technique	**Possible Effects**
Camera angle	
High (looking down on subjects)	Often makes subject seem smaller, less important, or more at risk
Low (looking up at subject)	Emphasizes subject's importance
Straight on (eye level)	Puts viewer on equal level with subject; can make viewer identify with subject
Camera shots	
Close-up (picture of subject's face)	Emphasizes character's facial expressions; leads viewer to identify with him or her
Long shot (wide view, showing character within larger setting)	Shows relationship between character and setting
Lighting	
High, bright lighting	Creates cheerful tone
Low, shadowy lighting	Creates gloomy or scary tone
Lighting from above	Makes subject seem to glow with power or strength
Lighting from below	Often creates tension or fear
Background music	
Loud, strong music	Creates tone of action or power
Soft melodies	Create tone of sadness or sweetness
Music that builds from slow to fast or from soft to loud	Often creates suspense or fear

Examine the elements of visual design and film techniques used in this still from the movie *E.T. The Extra Terrestrial.* The movie director wants us to identify with E.T. and Elliott. Therefore, the camera angle is straight on, and viewers are at eye level with both characters. Note also that this shot is a close-up. Our attention is drawn to the facial expressions of both characters. How do you think each character feels? What clues help you to read that verbal message?

Note also in this movie still that E.T. and Elliott are lit from above, in high, bright lights. Such lighting gives the characters a positive glow and gives the still a cheerful tone.

If you were on the creative staff of this movie, what type of background music would you choose for this scene?

Exercise 3

Study this movie still from *The Empire Strikes Back.* It shows the giant camel-like "Imperial Walkers" shooting laser weapons at the rebel heroes of the film. What visual message does this scene send you? Explain how the movie director used lines, color, lighting, camera angle, and camera shot to create that message. Then describe the type of background music you imagine in this scene. Explain your choice.

Viewing and Representing

26.2 Analyzing Media Messages

Drawings, cartoons, photographs, movies, and television programs often seem realistic. However, every medium is made with one goal—to send the viewer a message that carries a particular point of view and to use such techniques as color, line, and camera angles to persuade the viewer to accept that point of view.

In a documentary film about endangered animals, for example, the director makes decisions about pictures and information to include, what camera angles will prove most effective, and what information should *not* be included. Every time you view an example of mass communications, analyze it carefully. Begin by using these steps.

KEY QUESTIONS

To analyze a media message, ask yourself these Key Questions:

- What message is this visual medium trying to send to readers or viewers? (The visual might be a photo, drawing, cartoon, television program, movie, video, or commercial.)
- What techniques were used to try to persuade readers or viewers to agree with that message?
- What do I already know about this subject?
- How can I use what I already know to judge whether this message is
    - fair or unfair?
    - based on reality or fantasy?
    - based on facts or opinions?
- What additional sources might I use to find other viewpoints that I can trust on this subject?
    - parent, teacher, or other trustworthy adult
    - reliable books or other reference sources

On the basis of your answers and of viewpoints you can trust, make a decision about the message. Make sure you can support that decision.
- I agree with the visual message because . . . .
- I disagree with the visual message because . . . .

You can practice using the Key Questions by examining again the Paul Szep cartoon on page 632.

- **What the message is:** During the big game, the Boston Bruins hockey players acted more like gentle little cats than fierce bears.

- **What techniques were used:** All cartoonists use humor and exaggeration to get their messages across. In this cartoon, Paul Szep made the bear look very big and tough. Also, he added the bandage and the missing tooth to suggest that the bear had been injured during the game. However, he then showed the bear meowing like a little cat instead of growling like a big, tough bear.

- **What you know:** You might have watched the game. You might have followed the team during the season and have observed that the players are usually good.

- **How you can use what you know:** If you watched the game, you can form your own opinion about how well the team played. You can also look back on the season and decide that although the team may not have played a great game this time, it's unfair to picture the players as weak or gentle. Maybe they just had a bad day!

- **Other sources you might use to find other viewpoints that you can trust:** You might seek viewpoints from hockey fans in your family or at school. You might also read *factual* newspaper or magazine articles about the game and weigh these new points of view against your own feelings and the visual message in the cartoon.

Decision time! You could then make a well thought-out decision, based on your analysis, about agreeing or disagreeing with the cartoon's visual message. Your decision would be valuable because *it would be backed up by careful analysis.*

Exercise 4

Working with a partner, find a cartoon in a current newspaper or newsmagazine. With your partner, use the Key Questions on page 635 to help you analyze the visual message of the cartoon. Present your findings to the class.

Analyzing Movies, Music Videos, Television Shows, and Video Games

You can use the Key Questions to help you identify and judge a variety of types of mass-media messages. In this section, use the Key Questions to help you analyze the messages that the producers of movies, music videos, television shows, and video games send viewers.

Most people have fictional characters, movies, television shows, and games that they particularly like. Sometimes, however, the actors and performers in these forms of media, or the forms of media themselves, seem more "real" than they actually are. Actors in movies and television shows play fictional characters. Characters in video games are fictional characters living only in fantasy settings. What visual messages do such characters and settings send viewers, and are these messages valuable and fair? Use the Key Questions on page 635 to help you decide.

Exercise 5

Watch carefully as your teacher plays a scene or two from a popular movie or television show. Then work together as a class to use the Key Questions on page 635 to help you analyze and evaluate the visual messages you received.

Exercise 6

Choose a favorite movie, television show, music video, or video game. Use the Key Questions to analyze and evaluate its visual messages. Write a brief report on your findings and conclusions.

Analyzing Advertisements and Commercials

You can also use the Key Questions to help you identify and judge the value of the media messages appearing in newspaper and magazine advertisements and on television commercials.

More than any other form of media, advertisements and commercials have one main goal: *to persuade the viewer to buy the product being advertised.* Along with the Elements of Picture Design and Composition listed on page 630, and the Film and Video Techniques for Sending Visual Messages listed on page 633, advertisers often use one or more of the following advertising techniques to accomplish that goal.

Leading Advertising Techniques		
Technique	**Description**	**Example**
Bandwagon: "Jump on the bandwagon and join in the fun!"	showing images or using words implying that popular, attractive, well-liked people use this product	an advertisement for jeans, showing attractive people having fun
Testimonial: "Be like your favorite celebrity!"	showing a popular star, athlete, or musical performer using the product	an advertisement for running shoes, showing a leading basketball player
Partial truth: "Use this for incredible results!"	using oils, dyes, and other substances to make the results of using the product look "too good to be true"	an advertisement for shampoo, in which a model's hair shows a terrific, but unrealistic, silkiness and shine
Card stacking: "Leading experts are convinced that you should use this product."	using actors that pretend they are experts to present the advertiser's message	an advertisement for a toothbrush; an actor portrays a dentist
Name calling or appeal to guilt: "You mean you don't know how nutritious this product is?"	manipulating data to convince viewers that another product would be foolish or wasteful	an advertisement for breakfast cereal, suggesting to parents that it is the most healthful

How can viewers "cut through" the nonsense and hard-sell tactics of advertisements and commercials to make informed, wise decisions about which products to buy? The Key Questions can help!

Examine the following model of an advertisement.

Food for Champions

When CHAMPION

tennis player **Marie Ziegler's** pups tell her it's time for a treat, they scramble for **PUPPY FOOD**!

Her tennis game isn't the only thing that Marie has perfected! She has learned that leading veterinarians and animal nutrition experts agree that **PUPPY FOOD** is the best food for healthy young dogs. It delivers all the essential nutrients, including calcium and protein, that her puppies need for strong bones and muscles!

Terrific tennis player, terrific dogs! Shouldn't you feed your puppies PUPPY FOOD too?

Puppy Approved! ✓

Exercise 7

Use the Key Questions on page 635 to help you analyze and evaluate this advertisement. Discuss your findings with classmates.

Exercise 8

Watch carefully as your teacher plays a video clip of one or more television commercials. Then work as a class to use the Key Questions to identify, analyze, and evaluate the messages that the commercials convey.

Producing Media Messages

There is another great way in which you can increase your knowledge about the techniques that mass media producers use to send visual messages. Practice those techniques yourself by creating your own media messages! This section will help you to create two forms of media messages: cartoons and advertisements.

Creating a Cartoon

The artist often uses one or more of the following elements of humor in cartoons.

ELEMENTS OF HUMOR OFTEN USED BY CARTOONISTS

- **Exaggeration:** Making something bigger or greater than it really is

  Examples: Paul Szep gave his bear an enormous face and a fiercer-than-normal expression. Similarly, a cartoon about the problem of having too much homework might show a student buried under a mile-high stack of books and papers.

- **Surprise:** Providing an outcome that is completely unexpected or unusual

  Examples: Paul Szep's fierce-looking bear "meows" in the gentle voice of a cat. Similarly, a cartoon about the importance of avoiding accidents might show someone smiling confidently while stepping carefully over a banana peel—straight into an open manhole.

- **Puns:** Making a play on words

  Examples: A "fly swatter" might be portrayed as a fly dressed up as a baseball batter "swatting" (hitting) a baseball. Similarly, a "baseball batter" might be portrayed as a bowl of pancake batter into which someone is stirring several baseballs.

- **Satire:** Poking fun at a person, event, or situation

  Examples: Each day, political cartoonists publish satirical cartoons in newspapers to poke fun at politicians, news events, or situations that they find amusing. This type of cartoon often carries the strongest visual message, because its purpose is not only to create humor but to carry a message of criticism about a person, event, or situation.

TIPS FOR CREATING A CARTOON

1. **Begin by brainstorming.** Think about situations that you find funny or that you would like to poke fun at. It might be a rule that you think is unnecessary, a part of human behavior that you think is silly, a famous person that you'd enjoy poking fun at, or a personal experience that made you laugh. Jot down several ideas and then pick one to develop into a cartoon.

2. **Identify your purpose and message.** What underlying message do you want your cartoon to send to your readers? Is your purpose merely to make your readers laugh at your humor, or do you also want them to agree with your point of view? On notebook paper, write a sentence that states your purpose. Then write another sentence that states your message. Keep both in mind as you draw.

3. **Make sketches.** On scrap paper, draw several versions of the cartoon. Refer to the Elements of Picture Design and Composition chart on page 630 for ideas about use of lines, colors, and positions of your subjects. Experiment with different elements and techniques, always keeping in mind the techniques that will be most effective in getting your message across.

4. **Decide whether to use words.** Will your message be clear from your picture alone, or do you need a caption to make your message precisely clear? Experiment with using and omitting a caption. In addition, consider whether any characters in your cartoon should speak. If you feel that their words will help to make your message clear, write the words in speech balloons.

5. **Make your final copy.** When you are satisfied with your sketches and your decision about whether to include words in your cartoon, make a final copy.

6. **Publish your cartoon.** Share your cartoon with viewers—friends, classmates, and family members who share your sense of humor or who might particularly understand and enjoy the message you want to send. Ask for comments and suggestions. Find out whether your viewers "read" and agreed with your message.

Exercise 9

Use the tips to create a cartoon that uses one or more elements of humor to send a media message.

Creating an Advertisement

What product would you like to convince viewers to buy? It might be a realistic product, such as jeans, running shoes, or in-line skates. Or, you might dream up a fantastic product, such as a robot that does a student's homework, a hat that allows the wearer to fly, or a dog food that enables a dog to sing rap songs.

You can write an ad with a strong, persuasive message for any product you choose. The following tips will help.

TIPS FOR CREATING AN ADVERTISEMENT

1. **Begin by looking at published advertisements.** Look at several different types of advertisements in newspapers and magazines. What techniques did the advertisers use? Which of these techniques do you think are most effective at getting the message across? Clip out samples to look at as you think about your topic.

2. **Brainstorm.** Jot down the names of several realistic products that you particularly enjoy using. Your own enthusiasm for the product will help you to write a convincing ad. Then make a second list of "fantastic" products that might be fun to advertise, such as the examples listed in the first paragraph of this section. Review your lists carefully. Select one product for your ad.

3. **Mold your message.** As you begin to draft the words and visual images you'll use in your ad, keep in mind that you have one and only one purpose: to convince the viewer to buy your product. Think carefully about how you can most effectively get your message across. Refer to the Leading Advertising Techniques chart on page 638 for ideas. Jot down phrases and sentences that you think work well.

4. **Make layout sketches.** On scrap paper, draw several layout sketches for your ad, showing what visual images you will use, where they will appear in the ad, and how you might use lines, colors, and space to enhance your message. Refer to the Elements of Picture Design and Composition chart on page 630 for ideas. Then, once you have decided on the placement of your images, add the words. Looking once again at the published ads you gathered earlier may give you additional ideas about the placement of visual images and words.

TIME

For more about brainstorming and generating ideas for writing, see **TIME Facing the Blank Page,** page 92.

Viewing and Representing

5. **Make your final copy.** Once you are satisfied with your layout sketches, make a final copy of your ad, using color and lines in a way that seems most effective.

6. **Publish your advertisement.** Think carefully about where to display your ad. An ad for in-line skates would probably not appear in a magazine geared toward senior citizens. Nor would an ad for baby clothes appear in a magazine geared toward people your age. Where in the school would the people most interested in your product be most likely to see and respond to your ad? Place a response box next to your ad, asking people for comments. Find out whether your viewers "read" and accepted your message.

Exercise 10

Use the tips to create an advertisement that uses elements of picture design and composition, as well as leading advertising techniques. Convince your viewers to buy your product!

Electronic Resources

Lesson **27.1**   **The Internet**   645

Lesson **27.2**   **Getting on the Internet**   647

Lesson **27.3**   **Evaluating Internet Sources**   651

Lesson **27.4**   **Using E-Mail**   654

Lesson **27.5**   **Other Electronic Resources**   656

27.1 The Internet

The Internet is like a giant storehouse of information that you can tap into by using a computer. It uses telephone lines, cable lines, and satellites to link your computer to computers all over the world. As recently as the 1980s, few people even knew about the Internet. Today, the computer terms *cyberspace, information superhighway,* and *surfing the Web* have become part of our vocabulary.

History

The Internet was developed in 1969 to connect computers at four different universities. This early version of the Internet, called ARPANET, was all words, or text, and very unorganized. It was used for research, educational, and government purposes. Most of the users were computer experts, scientists, and engineers. Commands had to be given in computer language. As the demand for information grew, so did the Internet. By the early 1990s, the Internet had become popular with home computer users.

Today, what most people generally refer to as the Internet is actually only a part of the Internet called the **World Wide Web.** Using the World Wide Web is one of the best ways to explore the Internet. It is designed to make it easy to connect to millions of different Web sites. Web sites may include video, graphics, animation, and sound as well as text.

The Internet has changed the way we live, think, and communicate. In the years since the Internet was developed, the number of users has skyrocketed. Today, the Internet reaches over 200 million people worldwide. Eighty million of these people live in the United States. Americans spend an average of 8.8 hours a week online viewing news, information, travel, weather, music, shopping, and technology Web sites. In the next five years, more than 500 million people will be surfing the Web.

Affordable computers, easy-to-use software, and speedy Internet connections have boosted the Internet's popularity. With the click of a mouse button, a person using the Internet can search through millions of documents without leaving home. Students can use the Internet for help with their homework, families can use it to plan vacations, and doctors can use it for medical research.

Exercise 1

Work with a small group to make a glossary that lists and defines words related to using the Internet. Combine your group's glossary with the glossaries of other groups to create a classroom "Internet Dictionary." The **boldfaced** terms in this unit will give you a good start.

Electronic Resources

Getting on the Internet

The three basic things you need to access the Internet are a computer, a modem, and an Internet service provider. A **modem** is a device that allows a computer to communicate and share information with other computers over telephone or cable lines. Most computers now come with a modem built in. An **Internet service provider,** or ISP, provides a service (for a fee) that allows your computer to dial into the Internet. You can also get onto the Internet by using an online service, such as America Online or Microsoft Network. These services let you access the Internet as well as their own private services. For example, America Online users can use private chat rooms and message boards. **Message boards** are places where you can read or write messages about subjects that interest you.

To display the contents of a Web site, your computer must have a browser. A **browser** is a software program that displays Web pages as text, graphics, pictures, and video on your computer. The best-known browsers are Netscape Navigator and Microsoft Internet Explorer. Once you have a browser, you'll be able to navigate, or get around, the Web. You don't have to own a computer to get on the Internet. Many public libraries now have Internet terminals that their patrons can use, and most schools have some that their students can use.

Net Addresses

The World Wide Web is made up of millions of Web sites. A **Web site** is a page, or collections of pages, created by a person, a company, or an organization such as a university. A **Webmaster** is the person who is in charge of building and maintaining a Web site. Some Web sites consist only of text, while others include photos, artwork, sound, and video.

To get to a particular Web site, you need to know its address. Every Web site on the Internet has a unique address or URL. **URL** stands for Uniform Resource Locator. No two Web sites can have the same URL.

Each part of its URL provides information about a site.

Following is the address for the Web site that lists the six pillars of character supported by the AYSO (American Youth Soccer Organization).

http://www.soccer.org/abc/c_pillar.htm#sixpillars

1. The http:// at the beginning of an address stands for **hypertext transfer protocol.** These are the rules by which your computer gets information from any other computer hooked to the Web. All computers on the Web use this protocol and this four-letter prefix.

2. The *www* in an address refers to the World Wide Web, the part of the Internet in which this site is located.

3. The second part of a Web site address, called the **domain name,** tells your Web browser about the computer (or server) that stores the Web files. The domain name is usually the name (sometimes shortened) of the company or organization that maintains the site.

4. A suffix usually follows the domain head, separated from it by a period, or "dot." The suffix tells what type of organization the domain belongs to. The most common suffixes are *.com* (a business), *.gov* (a government agency), and *.edu* (an educational organization, such as a school).

5. The **path** identifies the route followed to get to a particular part or page of a site.

6. The **file name** follows the path; it leads you to the specific file that you're looking for on a Web site.

Write down the addresses of some of your favorite Web sites and see if you can identify the parts of the addresses. Remember that some URLs do not have paths or file names. When that's the case, the URL will take you to the site's **home page,** or opening page.

As an Internet user, you may want to keep track of some Web sites that you visit. You can keep a record of them by using your browser's **Bookmark** or **Favorites** option. This option lets you keep a list of the addresses of your favorite sites so that you do not have to type an address each time you want to view a Web site. Instead, simply go to the Bookmark or Favorites menu of your browser and click on the site's name.

Hyperlinks

You may notice as you begin to investigate various Web sites that some words or phrases are underlined or are in a color that is different from the rest of the text. These words or phrases are called hyperlinks. **Hyperlinks** are text or graphics that, when clicked on, take you to a new page or a related Web site. Sometimes it may be difficult to find the hyperlinks on a Web page. If you are not sure whether the text or graphics contain a hyperlink, drag the cursor arrow over the possible hyperlink. If the arrow changes to a pointing finger, you've found a hyperlink.

Searching the Internet

When writing a report, doing research, or using the Internet for pleasure, you may want to find specific information. How do you find the Web sites you are looking for? The fastest way is start with a search engine. A **search engine** helps you look for information on the Web by searching for keywords. A keyword is a word or phrase that describes your topic.

If you haven't narrowed your search to a specific topic, you can start with a subject directory. A **subject directory** lists general topics, such as arts and humanities, science, education, entertainment, sports, and health. After you select a broad topic, the directory will offer a list of possible subtopics from which to choose. Each subtopic may lead to topics that are even more specific. Various search engines and subject directories, such as those in the chart on the following page, are available for your use on the Internet.

Some Popular Search Tools		
Search Tool	**Type**	**URL**
Alta Vista	search engine	http://www.altavista.com
Excite	search engine	http://www.excite.com
Galaxy	subject directory	http://www.galaxy.com
Yahoo!	subject directory	http://www.yahoo.com

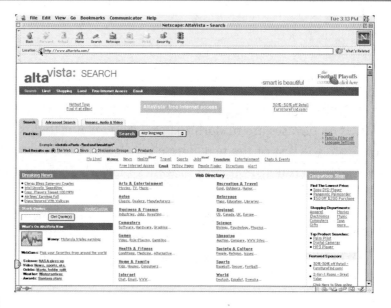

Exercise 2

Use a search engine to find Web sites about the following subjects. Write down the URL of one Web site for each subject. Briefly describe each of the Web sites and compare your findings with those of other students.

1. *New York Times*
2. Will Smith
3. The Toledo Mudhens
4. Princeton University
5. Hammerhead sharks

Exercise 3

Find a Web site that has hyperlinks to other Web sites. Select one of the links and follow it to the next Web site. (If you find a site with no links, try another site.) Find the links on that Web site and choose one to follow. Continue doing this until you have been to five different Web sites. Write down in order the URL and the name of each Web site that you visit. Share information about the sites with your class.

Evaluating Internet Sources

As you search the Internet and discover new Web sites, remember that anyone can create a Web site. As a result, you cannot always be sure that the Web site information is correct. It is your responsibility to determine what information is useful to you, whether that information is accurate, and how current the information is.

You'll want to make sure the sources you use in a presentation or research paper are reliable. How can you be sure? One way is to find out who owns the Web site or who created it. For instance, if you are looking for the batting average of a baseball player, www.majorleaguebaseball.com, the official site of major league baseball, should be accurate. A reputable sports news organization, such as ESPN, should also be useful. However, if the site was created by a baseball fan, you may want to find a second source to back up the information.

How to Evaluate the Usefulness of a Web Site

When evaluating a Web site, ask these questions:
1. What person, organization, or company created the Web site? Generally, you can expect a government or university site to be more accurate than an individual's site.
2. Does the site provide information on where the information was gathered or for what purpose?
3. Is there a way to check the information by contacting the person or organization that created the site?
4. Was the site recommended by a reliable person or reference book?

Exercise 4

Choose a famous person from the past and find a Web site that provides information about that person. Write down the URL and five to ten facts that you find about the person on the Web site. Check the accuracy of the facts in another source, such as an encyclopedia. Then report on the accuracy of the Web site.

Troubleshooting Guide

As you work on the Web, you may need help in dealing with possible problems.

Here are some error messages that you might see as you spend time on the Web. They are followed by their possible causes and some suggestions for eliminating the errors.

Message: Unable to connect to server. The server may be down. Try connecting again later.

Possible Causes: The server is having technical problems. The site is being updated or is not communicating properly with your browser.

Suggestion: It usually helps if you try again in a few minutes; however, it could be a few days before the server is working properly.

Message: Unable to locate the server: www.server.com. The server does not have a DNS (Domain Name System) entry. Check the server name in the URL and try again.

Possible Causes: You have typed in the URL incorrectly, or the site no longer exists.

Suggestion: Be sure you have entered the URL correctly—check for proper capitalization and punctuation. If you have entered it correctly, try using a search engine to find the site. Keep in mind, though, the possibility that the site may have been abandoned.

Message: File Not Found: The requested URL was not found on this server.

Possible Causes: You have reached the server, but that particular file no longer exists or you have entered the path or file name incorrectly.

Suggestion: Check the URL again. If you have entered it correctly, try searching for the page from the server's home page.

Message: Network connection refused by the server. There was no response.

Possible Causes: You have reached the server, but it is too busy (too many other people are trying to access it) or temporarily shut down.

Suggestion: Try to access the site later.

Message: Connection timed out.

Possible Causes: Your browser attempted to contact the host, but the host took too long to reply.

Suggestion: Try to access the site later.

Message: Access denied. You do not have permission to open this item.

Possible Causes: The URL has moved, the Webmaster no longer allows public access to the site, or you have been denied access to the site.

Suggestion: Contact the Webmaster to verify the URL or try the site again in a few days. Sometimes there is nothing you can do if access has been denied. Many colleges, for example, allow access to parts of their sites only to faculty and registered students.

Electronic Resources

27.4 Using E-Mail

Electronic mail, or **e-mail,** is a popular feature of the Internet. Millions of Americans send or receive e-mail every day. With the click of a button, e-mail lets you send messages to anyone in the world. You can also add computer files of text or graphics as **attachments** to an e-mail message. You can send pictures of yourself to an e-mail pen pal, send a sound clip of your favorite song to a friend, or send a report you have written to one of your teachers.

To send e-mail, you need an e-mail address. Like Web site addresses, e-mail addresses are unique. No two people can have the same e-mail address. Your Internet service provider should provide you with an e-mail address. You can also use a service, such as Yahoo!, to provide you with an e-mail account.

A typical e-mail address has four parts. The first part is the **user name.** This is the name you have chosen for yourself or that is assigned to you by your Internet service provider. The second part is the @ symbol, which stands for "at." This symbol separates the user name from the rest of the e-mail address. The third part is the **domain name,** which is the name of your ISP's server or the service that hosts your e-mail account. The last part of an e-mail address is the suffix. The **suffix** indicates the type of organization that provides your e-mail service.

Just as you can send an e-mail message to any address in the world, anyone in the world can send an e-mail message to you. Sometimes you will receive junk e-mail, or **spam.** It is similar to the junk mail you receive at home. Advertisements are the main form of spam, and sometimes this kind of e-mail can be offensive. If you receive e-mail from someone whose e-mail address you do not recognize, show it to an adult. Do not write back unless the adult gives you permission. Some people send links to Web sites through e-mail. If you receive a message with a link to a Web site, show it to an adult before clicking on the link. When you send e-mail, be sure to extend courtesy to those you are addressing.

E-Mail Etiquette

When sending e-mail, you should follow the Internet rules etiquette, which are usually referred to as **Netiquette.** Here are some of the important Netiquette rules.

- Use the subject line wisely. Be as brief as you can, but let the person to whom you are sending e-mail know what your message is about.
- Keep messages short and to the point.
- Use appropriate capitalization. Using all capital letters is considered SHOUTING.
- Avoid sending unfriendly e-mail. Sending an unfriendly e-mail message is called "flaming."
- Always check your spelling before sending an e-mail message. Your e-mail software may have a spelling-check function you can use.
- Always include your e-mail address at the bottom of any message you send.
- Be careful when using humor or sarcasm. It can be difficult to indicate emotion in print. Use "smileys" if you want to show emotion. Smileys are also called *emoticons,* a term made up of the words *emotion* and *icons.* They are little faces made by the characters on a keyboard. Tilt your head to the left to see them.

    :-)   (a smile)   ;-)   (a wink)
    :-((frown)   :-D   (laughing)

- Remember that good behavior on the Internet is no different from good behavior in face-to-face situations. Treat others as you would like them to treat you.

Exercise 5

If at some time you want to set up your own e-mail account, with your parents' approval, you can do so by accessing one of the free e-mail providers on the Web. Your teacher can explain how to establish your account. You will need to create a name for your e-mail address and to share addresses with friends, classmates, and relatives with whom you want to correspond.

Discuss in a small group the reasons you might have for wanting e-mail access. Discuss the rules of etiquette listed above and be sure you understand the meaning of each rule and the reason for its inclusion on this list.

Other Electronic Resources

In your search for information, you may use sources of electronic information other than the Internet. CD-ROMs, DVDs, and diskettes all store information electronically.

CD-ROMs

A **CD-ROM,** or Compact Disc–Read-Only Memory, looks like an audio compact disc, but it stores more than just audio information. **Read-only memory** is computer memory on which data has been prerecorded. Once data has been written onto a CD-ROM, it cannot be removed or changed. It can only be read. A CD-ROM can store text, graphics, and video files. Because a CD-ROM can store large amounts of information, many dictionaries, encyclopedias, and other reference works are stored on CD-ROMs. In fact, one CD-ROM can store as much information as hundreds of floppy diskettes. You can use CD-ROMs to read text and look at pictures. You can also use them to view video and audio files.

To use a CD-ROM, your computer must have a CD-ROM drive. A CD-ROM drive is standard on most new computers. Some CD-ROM drives are "read only"—that is, they can only use the information put on the disc. Other drives are able to record information on the disc just as you might record music on an audiocassette. Once recorded, that information cannot be changed. The newest CD-ROM drives, however, can record over and over on the same disc, just as you can do with a tape.

DVDs

A **DVD,** or Digital Video Disc, can store up to six times the data of a CD-ROM on the same surface area. Similar in size and shape to a CD-ROM, a DVD can hold enough information for a full-length movie. A DVD player can be used like a VCR to watch movies. Like a CD-ROM, a DVD requires a special drive on a computer. Although a DVD drive can play CD-ROMs, a CD-ROM drive cannot play DVDs.

Removable Storage

Diskettes, also called floppy disks, are commonly used to store text documents. The average computer still uses diskettes to store information, although most software is now distributed on CD-ROMs rather than diskettes. Some newer computers no longer contain diskette drives. Instead, they have a Zip drive, which uses a small disc that can store about seventy times as much information as a diskette. Other types of removable discs can hold even more information. The greater capacity of such discs has become necessary, now that users deal with large graphic files. A file for a single large color photo, for example, simply won't fit on a diskette.

Digital magnetic tape for a computer is similar to tape for an audiocassette player. The tape stores information on a magnetically coated strip of plastic. The tape can store large amounts of information, but it is not as convenient to use as a CD-ROM or a removable disc. It is more difficult to access information from a magnetic tape. If you need to view information that is at the end of a tape, you must sort through all of the information on the tape until you find it. CD-ROMs and removable discs let you choose the information you wish to view with the click of a button. Magnetic tape is used mainly for backing up information or storing large quantities of information that do not have to be accessed quickly.

Exercise 6

At your local library, check out a CD-ROM on any subject that interests you. Before viewing it, make a list of five questions that you have about the subject. Then look for the answers to your questions as you view the CD-ROM. Draw a diagram that shows each step you have to take to find each answer.

WRITING AND LANGUAGE GLOSSARY

This glossary will help you quickly find definitions used in writing and grammar.

A

Adjective. A word that modifies, or describes, a noun or a pronoun. An adjective may tell *what kind, which one, how many,* or *how much.*

    The **comparative degree** of an adjective compares two people, places, things, or ideas. (*worse, sadder*)

    The **superlative degree** of an adjective compares more than two people, places, things, or ideas. (*worst, saddest*)

    A **possessive adjective** is a possessive pronoun used before a noun.

    A **predicate adjective** always follows a linking verb. It modifies the subject of the sentence.

    A **proper adjective** is formed from a proper noun. It always begins with a capital letter.

    A **demonstrative adjective** is the word *this, that, these,* or *those* used before a noun.

Adverb. A word that modifies a verb, an adjective, or another adverb. Adverbs may tell *how, when, where, in what manner,* and *how often.* Some adverbs have different forms to indicate **comparative** and **superlative degrees.** (*loud, louder, loudest; sweetly, more sweetly, most sweetly*)

Allusion. A reference in a piece of writing to a well-known character, place, or situation from a work of literature, music, or art or from history.

Analysis. The act of breaking down a subject into its separate parts to determine its meaning.

Anecdote. A short story or incident usually presented as part of a longer narrative.

Antecedent. *See* Pronoun.

Appositive. A noun placed next to another noun to identify it or add information about it. (My basketball coach, *Ms. Lopes,* called for a time out.)

Argument. A statement, reason, or fact for or against a point; a piece of writing intended to persuade.

Article. The adjectives *a, an,* and *the. A* and *an* are **indefinite articles.** They refer to any one item of a group. *The* is a **definite article.** It indicates that the noun it precedes is a specific person, place or thing.

Audience. The person(s) who reads or listens to what the writer or speaker says.

Auxiliary verb. *See* Phrase.

B

Base form. *See* Verb tense.

Bias. A tendency to think a certain way. Bias may affect the way a writer or speaker presents his or her ideas.

Bibliography. A list of the books, articles, and other sources used as reference sources in a research paper.

Body. The central part of a composition that communicates the main idea identified in the introduction.

Bookmarks/favorites. The feature on many Web browsers that allows the user to save addresses of Internet sites so that sites can be accessed quickly.

Brainstorming. A group activity in which people generate as many ideas as possible without stopping to judge them.

C

Case. The form of a noun or pronoun that is determined by its use in a sentence. A noun or pronoun is in the **nominative** case when it is used as a subject, in the **objective** case when it is used as an object, and in the **possessive** case when it is used to show possession.

Cause-and-effect chain. A series of events in which one cause leads to an effect that in turn leads to another effect, and so on.

Characterization. The methods a writer uses to develop the personality of the character. A writer may make direct statements about a character's personality or reveal it through the character's words and actions or through what other characters think and say about the character.

Chronological order. The arrangement of details according to when events or actions take place.

Clarity. The quality of a piece of writing that makes it easy to understand.

Clause. A group of words that has a subject and a predicate and that is used as part of a sentence.
> An **independent clause,** also called a **main clause,** has a subject and a predicate and can stand alone as a sentence.
> A **dependent clause,** also called a **subordinate clause,** has a subject and a predicate, but it makes sense only when attached to a main clause.

Cliché. An overused expression. *(white as snow)*

Clustering. The grouping together of related items as a way of organizing information.

Coherence. A quality of logical connection between the parts of a paragraph or composition.

Cohesive writing. A type of writing in which sentences and paragraphs are logically connected to one another.

Collaboration. The process of working with others on writing or other projects.

Colloquialism. A casual, colorful expression used in everyday conversation.

Comparative degree. *See* Adjective; Adverb.

Comparison-and-contrast. A way of organizing ideas by illustrating their similarities and differences.

Complement. A word or phrase that completes the meaning of a verb. Three kinds of complements are **direct objects, indirect objects,** and **subject complements.**

Conceptual map. A graphic device that develops a central concept by surrounding it with examples or related ideas in a weblike arrangement.

Conclusion. A restatement or summing up of the ideas in a composition that brings it to a definite close.

Conflict. The struggle between two opposing forces that lies at the center of the plot in a story or drama.

Conjunction. A word that joins single words or groups of words.
> A **coordinating conjunction** (*and, but, or, nor, for, yet*) joins words or groups of words that are equal in grammatical importance.
> **Correlative conjunctions** (*both . . . and, just as . . . so, not only . . . but also, either . . . or, neither . . . nor*) are pairs of words used to connect words or phrases in a sentence.

Connotation. The thoughts and feelings associated with a word, rather than its dictionary definition.

Constructive criticism. Comments on another person's writing made with the intention of helping the writer improve a particular draft.

Context. The words and sentences that come before and after a specific word and help to explain its meaning.

Coordinating conjunction. *See* Conjunction.

Conventions. Correct spelling, grammar, usage, and mechanics.

Correlative conjunction. *See* Conjunction.

Credibility. The quality of a speaker or writer that makes that person's words believable.

D

Declarative sentence. A sentence that makes a statement.

Deductive reasoning. A way of thinking or explaining that begins with a general statement or principle and applies that principle to specific instances.

Definite article. *See* Article.

Demonstrative adjective. *See* Adjective.

Denotation. The dictionary definition of a word.

Dependent clause. *See* Clause.

Descriptive writing. Writing that uses sensory detail to convey an impression of a setting, a person, an animal, and so on.

Desktop publishing. The use of computer programs to format and produce a document that may include written text, graphics, and/or images.

Dialect. A variety of a language spoken by a particular group of people. A dialect may be regional (based on location) or ethnic (based on cultural heritage).

Dialogue. The conversation between characters in a written work.

Diction. A writer's choice of words and the arrangement of those words in phrases, sentences, or lines of a poem.

Direct object. *See* Complement.

Documentation. Identification of the sources used in writing research or other informative papers; usually in the form of endnotes or footnotes, or using parenthetical documentation.

Drafting. One of the steps in the writing process; the transforming of thoughts, words, and phrases into sentences and paragraphs.

E

Editing. One of the steps of the writing process in which a revised draft is checked for standard usage, varied sentence structure, and appropriate word choice.

Editorial. An article in a newspaper or other form of media that expresses an opinion about a topic of general interest.

Elaboration. The support or development of a main idea with facts, statistics, sensory details, incidents, anecdotes, examples, or quotations.

Ellipsis. A mark of punctuation consisting of three spaced periods, that shows the omission of a word or words.

E-mail. Short for electronic mail. Messages, usually text, sent from one person to another by way of computer.

Evaluating. Making a judgment about the strengths and weaknesses of a draft in content, organization, and style.

Evidence. Facts or examples from reliable sources that can be used to support statements made in speaking or writing.

Exclamatory sentence. A sentence that expresses strong or sudden emotion.

Explanatory writing. *See* Expository writing.

Expository writing. A kind of writing that aims at informing and explaining. Examples of expository writing are news articles, how-to instructions, and research papers.

Expressive writing. Writing that emphasizes and conveys the writer's feelings.

Fact. A piece of information that can be verified.

Feedback. The response a listener or reader gives to a speaker or writer about his or her work.

Figurative language. Words used for descriptive effect that express some truth beyond the literal level. Figures of speech such as similes, metaphors, or personification are examples of figurative language.

Formal language. Language that uses correct grammar and omits slang expressions and contractions. It is especially common in non-fiction writing that is not personal.

Fragment. An incomplete sentence punctuated as if it were complete.

Freewriting. A way of finding ideas by writing freely, without stopping or limiting the flow of ideas, for a specific length of time.

Future tense. *See* Verb tense.

Generalization. A statement that presents a conclusion about a subject without going into details or specifics.

Genre. A division of literature or some other medium. The main literary genres are prose, poetry, and drama. Each of these is further divided into subgenres.

Graphic organizer. A visual way of organizing information; types of graphic organizers are charts, graphs, clusters, and idea trees.

Home page. The location on a Web site by which a user normally enters the site. A typical home page may explain the site, summarize the content, and provide links to other sites.

Hyperlink. Highlighted or underlined phrases or words on a Web page that, when clicked, move the user to another part of the page or to another Web page.

Hypertext. Links in some electronic text that take the user to another document or to a different section in the same document.

Ideas. In writing, the message or theme and the details that elaborate upon that message or theme.

Idiom. A word or phrase that has a special meaning different from its standard or dictionary meaning. (*Burning the midnight oil* is an idiom that means "staying up late.")

Imagery. Language that emphasizes sensory impressions that can help the reader of a literary work to see, hear, feel, smell, and taste the scenes described in the work.

Imperative sentence. A sentence that makes a request or gives a command.

Indefinite article. *See* Article.

Independent clause. *See* Clause.

Inductive reasoning. A way of thinking or explaining that begins with a series of examples and uses them to arrive at a general statement.

Informative writing. A kind of writing that explains something, such as a process or an idea. *See also* Expository writing.

Intensifier. An adverb that emphasizes an adjective or another adverb. (*very* important; *quite* easily)

Interjection. A word or phrase that expresses strong feeling. An interjection has no grammatical connection to other words in the sentence.

Internet. A worldwide computer network that allows users to link to any computer on the network electronically for social, commercial, research, and other purposes.

Interpretation. An explanation of the meaning of a piece of writing, a visual representation, or any other type of communication.

Interview. A question-and-answer dialogue that has the specific purpose of gathering up-to-date or expert information.

Introduction. The beginning part of a piece of writing in which a writer identifies the subject and gives a general idea of what the body of the composition will contain.

Inverted order. The placement of a predicate before the subject in a sentence. In most sentences in English, the subject comes before the predicate.

Irregular verb. *See* Verb tense.

Jargon. Special words and phrases used by a particular group of people.

Journal. A personal notebook in which a person can freewrite, collect ideas, and record thoughts and experiences.

L

Learning log. A journal used for clarifying ideas about concepts covered in various classes.

Listing. A technique used for finding ideas for writing.

Literary analysis. The act of examining the different elements of a piece of literature in order to evaluate it.

Logical fallacy. An error in reasoning often found in advertising or persuasive writing. Either-or reasoning and glittering generalities are types of logical fallacies.

M

Main clause. *See* Clause.

Main idea. *See* Thesis statement.

Main verb. The most important word in a verb phrase.

Media. The forms of communication used to reach an audience; forms such as newspapers, radio, TV, and the Internet reach large audiences and so are known as mass media.

Memoir. A type of narrative nonfiction that presents an account of an event or period in history, emphasizing the narrator's personal experience.

Metaphor. A figure of speech that compares seemingly unlike things without using words such as *like* or *as*. (*He is a rock.*)

Mood. The feeling or atmosphere of a piece of writing.

Multimedia presentation. The use of a variety of media, such as video, sound, written text, and visual art to present ideas or information.

N

Narrative writing. A type of writing that tells about events or actions as they change over a period of time and often includes story elements such as character, setting, and plot.

Nonfiction. Prose writing about real people, places, and events.

Noun. A word that names a person, a place, a thing, an idea, a quality, or a characteristic.

Number. The form of a noun, pronoun, or verb that indicates whether it refers to one (**singular**) or more than one (**plural**).

Object. *See* Complement.

Onomatopoeia. The use of a word or phrase that imitates or suggests the sound of what it describes. (*rattle, boom*)

Opinion. A belief or attitude that cannot be proven true or false.

Oral tradition. Literature that passes by word of mouth from one generation to the next. The tradition of a culture may reflect the cultural values of the people.

Order of importance. A way of arranging details in a paragraph or other piece of writing according to their importance.

Organization. The arrangement of main points and supporting details in a piece of writing.

Outline. A systematic arrangement of main and supporting ideas, using Roman numerals, letters, and numbers, for a written or an oral presentation.

Paragraph. A unit of writing that consists of related sentences.

Parallelism. The use of a series of words, phrases, or sentences that have similar grammatical form.

Paraphrase. A restatement of someone's ideas in words that are different from the original passage but retain its ideas, tone, and general length.

Parenthetical documentation. A specific reference to the source of a piece of information; placed in parentheses directly after the information appears in a piece of writing.

Peer response. Suggestions and comments provided by peers, or classmates, about a piece of writing or another type of presentation.

Personal pronoun. *See* Pronoun.

Personal writing. Writing that expresses the writer's own thoughts and feelings.

Personification. A figure of speech that gives human qualities to an animal, object, or idea.

Perspective. *See* Point of view.

Persuasion. A type of writing that aims at convincing people to think or act in a certain way.

Phrase. A group of words that acts in a sentence as a single part of speech.
   A **prepositional phrase** begins with a preposition and ends with a noun or a pronoun. A **verb phrase** consists of one or more **auxiliary verbs** followed by a main verb.

Plagiarism. The dishonest presentation of another's words or ideas as one's own.

Plot. The series of events that follow one another in a story, novel, or play.

Plural. *See* Number.

Poetry. A form of literary expression that emphasizes the line as the unit of composition. Traditional poetry contains emotional, imaginative language and a regular rhythm.

Point of view. The angle, or perspective, from which a story is told, such as first- or third-person.

Portfolio. A collection of various pieces of writing, which may include finished pieces and works in progress.

Predicate. The verb or verb phrase and any modifiers that make an essential statement about the subject of a sentence.

Predicate adjective. *See* Adjective.

Preposition. A word that shows the relationship of a noun or pronoun to some other word in the sentence.

Prepositional phrase. *See* Phrase.

Presentation. The way words and design elements look on the page.

Presenting/Publishing. The last step in the writing process; involves sharing the final writing product with others in some way.

Prewriting. The first stage in the writing process; includes deciding what to write about, collecting ideas and details, and making an outline or a plan. Prewriting strategies include brainstorming, and using graphic organizers, notes, and logs.

Prior knowledge. The facts, ideas, and experiences that a writer, reader, or viewer brings to a new activity.

Progressive form. *See* Verb tense.

Pronoun. A word that takes the place of a noun, a group of words acting as a noun, or another pronoun. The word or group of words that a pronoun refers to is called its **antecedent**.
  A **personal pronoun** refers to a specific person or thing.

Pronoun case. *See* Case.

Proofreading. The final part of the editing process that involves checking work to discover typographical and other errors.

Propaganda. Information aimed at influencing thoughts and actions; it is usually of a political nature and may contain distortions of truth.

Proper adjective. *See* Adjective.

Prose. Writing that is similar to everyday speech and written language, as opposed to poetry and drama.

Publishing. The preparation of a finished piece of writing, often involving available technology, so that it can be presented to a larger audience.

Purpose. The aim of writing, which may be to express, discover, record, develop, reflect on ideas, problem solve, entertain, influence, inform, or describe.

R

Regular verb. *See* Verb tense.

Representation. A way in which information or ideas are presented to an audience.

Research. The search for information on a topic.

Review. The analysis and interpretation of a subject, often presented through the mass media.

Revising. The stage of the writing process in which a writer goes over a draft, making changes in its content, organization, and style in order to improve it. Revision techniques include adding, elaborating, deleting, combining, and rearranging text.

Root. The part of a word that carries the main meaning.

Run-on sentence. Two or more sentences or clauses run together without appropriate punctuation.

S

Sensory details. Language that appeals to the senses; sensory details are important elements of descriptive writing, especially of poetry.

Sentence. A group of words expressing a complete thought. Every sentence has a **subject** and a **predicate**. *See also* Subject; Predicate; Clause.

A **simple sentence** has only one main clause and no subordinate clauses.

A **compound sentence** has two or more main clauses. Each main clause of a compound sentence has its own subject and predicate, and these main clauses are usually joined by a comma and a coordinating conjunction. A semicolon can also be used to join the main clauses in a compound sentence. A **complex sentence** has one main clause and one or more subordinate clauses.

Sentence fluency. The smooth rhythm and flow of sentences that vary in length and style.

Sentence variety. The use of different types of sentences to add interest to writing.

Setting. The time and place in which the events of a story, novel, or play takes place.

Simile. A figure of speech that compares two basically unlike things, using words such as *like* or *as.* (*Her hair was like fine wire.*)

Simple predicate. *See* Predicate; Sentence; Subject.

Simple sentence. *See* Sentence.

Spatial order. A way of presenting the details of a setting according to their location—from left to right or from top to bottom.

Standard English. The most widely used and accepted form of the English language.

Style. The writer's choice and arrangement of words and sentences.

Subject. The noun or pronoun that tells who or what the sentence is about.

Subordinate clause. *See* Clause.

Summary. A brief statement of the main idea of a composition.

Supporting evidence. *See* Evidence.

Suspense. A literary device that creates growing interest and excitement leading up to the climax and resolution of a story. A writer creates suspense by providing clues to the resolution without revealing too much information.

Symbol. An object, a person, a place, or an experience that represents something else, usually something abstract.

T

Tense. *See* Verb tense.

Theme. The main idea or message of a piece of writing.

Thesis statement. A one- or two-sentence statement of the **main idea** or purpose of a piece of writing.

Time order. The arrangement of details in a piece of writing based on when they occurred.

Tone. A reflection of a writer's or speaker's attitude toward a subject.

Topic sentence. A sentence that expresses the main idea of a paragraph.

Transition. A connecting word or phrase that clarifies relationships between details, sentences, or paragraphs.

U–V

Unity. A quality of oneness in a paragraph or composition that exists when all the sentences or paragraphs work together to express or support one main idea.

URL. The standard form of an Internet address; Stands for Uniform Resource Locator.

Venn diagram. A graphic organizer consisting of two overlapping circles; used to compare two items that have both similar and different traits.

Verb. A word that expresses an action or a state of being and is necessary to make a statement.

Verb phrase. *See* Phrase.

Verb tense. The form a verb takes to show when an action takes place. The **present tense** names an action that happens regularly. The **past tense** names an action that has happened, and the **future tense** names an action that will take place in the future. All the verb tenses are formed from the four principal parts of a verb: a **base form** (*freeze*), a **present participle** (*freezing*), a **simple past form** (*froze*), and a **past participle** (*frozen*).

    A **regular verb** forms its simple past and past participle by adding *-ed* to the base form. Verbs that form their past and past participle in some other way are called **irregular verbs.**

    In addition to present, past, and future tenses, there are three perfect tenses—**present perfect, past perfect,** and **future perfect.**

    Each of the six tenses has a **progressive** form that expresses a continuing action.

Voice. A writer's unique way of using tone and style to communicate with the audience.

Web site. A location on the World Wide Web that can be reached through links or by accessing a Web address, or URL. *See also* URL; World Wide Web.

Word choice. The vocabulary a writer chooses to convey meaning.

Word processing. The use of a computer for the writing and editing of written text.

World Wide Web. A global system that uses the Internet and allows users to create, link, and access fields of information. *See also* Internet.

Writing process. The series of stages or steps that a writer goes through to develop ideas and to communicate them.

GLOSARIO
DE ESCRITURA Y LENGUAJE

Este glosario te ayudará a encontrar fácilmente las definiciones utilizadas en escritura y en la gramática del inglés.

Adjective/Adjetivo. Palabra que modifica, o describe, un nombre (*noun*) o pronombre (*pronoun*). Un adjetivo *indica qué tipo, cuál, cuántos o cuánto.*

> **Comparative degree/Grado comparativo.** Adjetivo que compara a dos personas, lugares, cosas o ideas (*worse, sadder;* en español: *peor, más triste*).
>
> **Superlative degree/Grado superlativo.** Adjetivo que compara más de dos personas, lugares, cosas o ideas (*worst, saddest;* en español: *el peor, la más triste*).
>
> **Possessive adjective/Adjetivo posesivo.** Pronombre posesivo que va antes del nombre.
>
> **Predicative adjective/Adjetivo predicativo.** Siempre va después de un verbo copulativo y modifica al sujeto de la oración.
>
> **Proper adjective/Adjetivo propio*.** Adjetivo que se deriva de un nombre propio; en inglés siempre se escribe con mayúscula.
>
> **Demonstrative adjective/Adjetivo demostrativo.** Se usa antes del nombre: *this, that, these, those (este, ese, aquel, estos, esos, aquellos).*

Adverb/Adverbio. Palabra que modifica a un verbo, adjetivo u otro adverbio. Los adverbios indican *cómo, cuándo, dónde, de qué manera* y *qué tan seguido* sucede algo.

Algunos adverbios tienen diferentes formas para indicar los grados **comparativo** (*comparative*) y **superlativo** (*superlative*) (*loud, louder, loudest; sweetly, more sweetly, most sweetly;* en español: *fuerte, más fuerte, lo más fuerte; dulcemente, más dulcemente, lo más dulcemente*).

Allusion/Alusión. Referencia en un texto escrito a un personaje, lugar o situación muy conocidos de una obra literaria, musical, artística o histórica.

Analysis/Análisis. Acción de descomponer un tema o escrito en distintas partes para encontrar su significado.

Anecdote/Anécdota. Narración breve o incidente que se presenta como parte de una narrativa más larga.

Antecedent/Antecedente. *Ver Pronoun.*

Appositive/Apositivo. Nombre colocado junto a otro para identificarlo o agregar información sobre él. (Mi entrenadora de baloncesto, *Ms. Lopes*, pidió tiempo fuera.)

Argument/Argumento. Afirmación, razón o hecho en favor o en contra de algún comentario; texto escrito que trata de persuadir.

Article/Artículo. Nombre dado a las palabras *a, an* y *the* (en español: *un, uno/a, el, la*). *A* y *an* son artículos **indefinidos** (*indefinite articles*), que se refieren a cualquier cosa de un grupo. *The* es un artículo **definido** (*definite article*);

indica que el nombre al que precede es una persona, lugar o cosa específicos.

Audience/Público. Persona (o personas) que lee o escucha lo que dicen un escritor o un hablante.

Auxiliary verb/Verbo auxiliar. *Ver Phrase.*

B

Base form/Base derivativa. *Ver Verb tense.*

Bias/Tendencia. Inclinación a pensar de cierta manera. La tendencia influye en la manera en que un escritor o hablante presenta sus ideas.

Bibliography/Bibliografía. Lista de los libros, artículos y otras fuentes que se utilizan como referencia en una investigación.

Body/Cuerpo. Parte central de una composición que comunica la idea principal identificada en la introducción.

Bookmarks/favorites/Marcadores/favoritos. Característica de muchos buscadores de red que permiten guardar direcciones de Internet para entrar a ellas rápidamente.

Brainstorming/Lluvia de ideas. Actividad de grupo en que se generan tantas ideas como sea posible sin detenerse a analizarlas.

C

Case/Caso. Forma de un nombre o pronombre que está determinado por su uso en la oración. El nombre o pronombre está en caso **nominativo** (*nominative case*) cuando se utiliza como sujeto; en caso **acusativo** y **dativo** (*objective case*) cuando recibe la acción del verbo, y en caso **posesivo*** (*possessive case*) cuando se utiliza para indicar posesión o propiedad.

Cause-and-effect chain/Cadena de causa y efecto. Serie de acontecimientos en que una causa lleva a un efecto que, a su vez, lleva a otro efecto, y así sucesivamente.

Characterization/Caracterización. Métodos que utiliza un escritor para crear sus personajes. Puede ser describiendo directamente su personalidad, o revelándola con sus palabras y acciones, o bien a partir de lo que otros personajes piensan y dicen de él.

Chronological order/Orden cronológico. Organización de detalles de acuerdo con el tiempo en que sucedieron los acontecimientos o acciones.

Clarity/Claridad. Cualidad de un escrito que lo hace fácil de entender.

Clause/Proposición. Grupo de palabras que consta de sujeto y predicado, y que se usa como parte de una oración compuesta.

> **Independent clause/Proposición independiente.** También llamada **proposición principal** (*main clause*); tiene sujeto y predicado y hace sentido por sí misma.
> **Dependent clause/Proposición dependiente.** También llamada **proposición subordinada** (*subordinate clause*); tiene sujeto y predicado pero depende de la proposición principal.

Cliché/Cliché. Expresión usada con demasiada frecuencia (*blanco como la nieve*).

Clustering/Agrupamiento. Reunión de temas relacionados para organizar la información.

Coherence/Coherencia. Relación lógica entre las partes de un párrafo o composición.

Cohesive writing/Escritura coherente. Tipo de escritura en que las oraciones y párrafos están lógicamente relacionados entre sí.

Collaboration/Colaboración. Proceso de trabajar en equipo para escribir un texto o realizar un proyecto.

Colloquialism/Expresión coloquial. Expresión informal y pintoresca que se utiliza en la conversación diaria.

Comparative degree/Grado comparativo. *Ver Adjective; Adverb.*

Comparison-and-contrast/Comparación y contraste. Manera de organizar ideas, señalando sus similitudes y diferencias.

Complement/Complemento (u objeto). Palabra o frase que complementa el significado de un verbo. Tres complementos son: **directo** (*direct object*), **indirecto** (*indirect object*) y **predicativo (atributo)** (*subject complement*).

Conceptual map/Mapa conceptual. Recurso gráfico que desarrolla un concepto central rodeándolo con ejemplos o ideas relacionadas a manera de red.

Conclusion/Conclusión. Afirmación que resume las ideas de una composición, antes de ponerle punto final.

Conflict/Conflicto. Lucha entre dos fuerzas opuestas que constituye el elemento central de la trama en un cuento u obra de teatro.

Conjunction/Conjunción. Palabra que une palabras o grupos de palabras.

> **Coordinating conjunction/Conjunción coordinante.** Las palabras *and, but, or, nor, for, yet* (*y, pero, o, no, para, aun*) unen palabras o grupos de palabras que tienen igual importancia gramatical.

> **Correlative conjunction/Conjunción correlativa*.** Las palabras *both . . . and, just as . . . so, not only . . . but also, either . . . or, neither . . . nor* (*tanto . . . como, así como, no sólo . . . sino, o . . . o*) son palabras en pares que vinculan palabras o frases en una oración.

Connotation/Connotación. Pensamientos y sentimientos relacionados con una palabra, más que con su definición de diccionario.

Constructive criticism/Crítica constructiva. Comentario sobre lo que escribe otra persona, con la intención de ayudar a que mejore el borrador.

Context/Contexto. Palabras y oraciones que vienen antes y después de una palabra y ayudan a explicar su significado.

Conventions/Reglas de escritura. Normas que regulan la ortografía, la gramática, el uso y la puntuación de un escrito.

Coordinating conjunction/Conjunción coordinante. *Ver Conjunction.*

Correlative conjunction/Conjunción correlativa*. *Ver Conjuntion.*

Credibility/Credibilidad. Cualidad de un hablante o escritor que hace creer sus palabras.

Declarative sentence/Oración afirmativa. Oración que declara algo.

Deductive reasoning/Razonamiento deductivo. Pensamiento o explicación que parte de una afirmación o principio generales y los aplica a casos específicos.

Definite article/Artículo definido. *Ver Article.*

Demonstrative adjective/Adjetivo demostrativo. *Ver Adjective.*

Denotation/Denotación. Definición de una palabra que da el diccionario.

Dependent clause/Proposición dependiente. *Ver Clause.*

Descriptive writing/Escritura descriptiva. Tipo de escritura que ofrece detalles sensoriales para comunicar la impresión de un escenario, persona, animal, etcétera.

Desktop publishing/Edición por computadora. Uso de programas de computadora para formar un documento con texto escrito, gráficas y/o imágenes.

Dialect/Dialecto. Variedad de lenguaje hablado que usa un grupo particular. Un dialecto puede ser regional (de un lugar) o étnico (de un grupo cultural).

Dialogue/Diálogo. Conversación entre personajes en un escrito.

Diction/Dicción. Palabras que escoge un escritor y cómo las utiliza en frases, oraciones o versos.

Direct object/Complemento directo. *Ver Complement.*

Documentation/Documentación. Identificación de las fuentes que se emplean para escribir un artículo u otros textos informativos; generalmente se ponen como notas al pie, al final del texto o entre paréntesis.

Drafting/Borrador. Paso del proceso de escritura; transformación de ideas, palabras y frases a oraciones y párrafos.

Editing/Edición. Paso del proceso de escritura en que se revisa que el borrador corregido tenga un lenguaje estándar, una estructura sintáctica variada y la elección adecuada de palabras.

Editorial/Editorial. Artículo en un periódico u otro medio que expresa una opinión sobre un tema de interés general.

Elaboration/Elaboración. Sustento o desarrollo de una idea principal con hechos, estadísticas, detalles sensoriales, incidentes, anécdotas, ejemplos o citas.

Ellipsis/Puntos suspensivos. Signo de puntuación que consiste en dejar tres puntos para indicar que se están suprimiendo una o varias palabras.

E-mail/Correo electrónico. Mensajes, generalmente textos, que se envían por computadora.

Evaluating/Evaluación. Juicio sobre las fallas y aciertos de un borrador en cuanto a contenido, organización y estilo.

Evidence/Evidencia. Datos o ejemplos de fuentes confiables que sirven para sustentar afirmaciones escritas o habladas.

Exclamatory sentence/Oración exclamativa. Oración que expresa una emoción fuerte o repentina.

Explanatory writing/Texto explicativo. *Ver Descriptive text.*

Expository writing/Texto descriptivo. Tipo de escritura que informa o explica, como artículos periodísticos, instrucciones y artículos de investigación.

Expressive writing/Texto expresivo. Texto que realza y transmite los sentimientos del escritor.

F

Fact/Hecho. Información que puede comprobarse.

Feedback/Retroalimentación. Respuesta del escucha o lector al mensaje de un hablante o escritor.

Figurative language/Lenguaje figurado. Palabras usadas con un efecto descriptivo que expresa una verdad más allá del nivel literal. Los tropos, como el símil, la metáfora y la personificación, son ejemplos de lenguaje figurado.

Formal language/Lenguaje formal. Lenguaje que utiliza una gramática correcta y omite contracciones y expresiones coloquiales. Es común en textos de no ficción, que no son de carácter personal.

Fragment/Fragmento. Oración incompleta con puntuación de oración completa.

Freewriting/Escritura libre. Búsqueda de ideas escribiendo durante un tiempo determinado, sin detenerse ni limitar el flujo de ideas.

Future tense/Tiempo futuro. *Ver Verb tense.*

G–H

Generalization/Generalización. Afirmación que presenta una conclusión sobre un tema sin dar detalles específicos.

Genre/Género. Clasificación literaria o de otro medio. Los principales géneros literarios son la prosa, la poesía y el drama. Cada uno se divide en subgéneros.

Graphic organizer/Organizador gráfico. Manera visual de organizar la información, como las tablas, las gráficas, las redes y los árboles de ideas.

Home page/Página principal. Página por medio de la cual un usuario entra normalmente a un sitio de Web. Por lo general, explica el sitio, resume el contenido y proporciona vínculos con otros sitios.

Hyperlink/Hipervínculo. Oraciones o palabras sombreadas o subrayadas en una página en red que al activarse con un clic conectan con otra parte de la página o con otra página de la red.

Hypertext/Hipertexto. Vínculos en textos electrónicos que llevan a otro documento o a una sección distinta del mismo documento.

I-J

Ideas/Ideas. En composición, el mensaje o tema y los detalles que lo elaboran.

Idiom/Modismo. Palabra o frase cuyo significado es diferente del significado estándar o de diccionario. (*Se le pegaron las sábanas* es un modismo que significa "se levantó muy tarde").

Imagery/Imaginería. Lenguaje que describe impresiones sensoriales para que el lector de un texto literario pueda ver, oír, sentir, oler y gustar las escenas descritas.

Imperative sentence/Oración imperativa. Oración que exige u ordena algo.

Indefinite article/Artículo indefinido. *Ver Article.*

Independent clause/Proposición independiente. *Ver Clause.*

Inductive reasoning/Razonamiento inductivo. Pensamiento o explicación que parte de varios ejemplos para llegar a una afirmación general.

Informative writing/Texto informativo. Texto que explica un proceso o una idea. *Ver también Descriptive text.*

Intensifier/Intensificador. Adverbio que refuerza un adjetivo u otro adverbio (*very* important, *quite* easily; *muy* importante, *bastante* fácil).

Interjection/Interjección. Palabra o frase que expresa un sentimiento muy fuerte. La interjección no tiene relación gramatical con las demás palabras de la oración.

Internet/Internet. Red mundial computarizada que permite comunicarse electrónicamente con cualquier computadora de la red para buscar información social, comercial, de investigación y de otro tipo.

Interpretation/Interpretación. Explicación del significado de un texto, de una representación visual o de cualquier otro tipo de comunicación.

Interview/Entrevista. Diálogo a base de preguntas y respuestas cuyo propósito es obtener información actualizada o de expertos.

Introduction/Introducción. Sección inicial de un texto en la que el escritor identifica el tema y da la idea general de lo que contendrá el cuerpo del mismo.

Inverted order/Orden invertido. Colocación del predicado antes del sujeto. En la mayoría de las oraciones en inglés, el sujeto va antes del predicado.

Irregular verb/Verbo irregular. *Ver Verb tense.*

Jargon/Jerga. Palabras y frases que usa un determinado grupo.

Journal/Diario. Libreta personal en la que con toda libertad se anotan ideas, pensamientos y experiencias.

Learning log/Registro de aprendizaje. Diario para aclarar ideas sobre conceptos tratados en varias clases.

Listing/Lista. Técnica para generar ideas a partir de las cuales se escribe un texto.

Literary analysis/Análisis literario. Examen de las diferentes partes de una obra literaria a fin de evaluarla.

Logical fallacy/Falacia lógica. Error de razonamiento que se encuentra con frecuencia en publicidad o en escritos persuasivos, como razonamientos con dos alternativas opuestas o generalidades muy llamativas.

Main clause/Proposición principal. *Ver Clause.*

Main idea/Idea principal. *Ver Thesis statement.*

Main verb/Verbo principal. La palabra más importante de una frase verbal.

Media/Medios. Formas de comunicación usadas para llegar a un público. Los periódicos, la radio, la televisión y la Internet llegan a públicos muy grandes, por lo que se conocen como medios de comunicación masiva.

Memoir/Memoria. Tipo de narrativa de no ficción que presenta el relato de un hecho o período de la historia, resaltando la experiencia personal del narrador.

Metaphor/Metáfora. Tropo que compara dos cosas aparentemente distintas sin usar las palabra *like* o *as (como)*. *(Él es una roca.)*

Mood/Atmósfera. Sentimiento o ambiente de un texto escrito.

Multimedia presentation/Presentación multimedia. Uso de una variedad de medios como video, sonido, texto escrito y artes visuales para presentar ideas e información.

Narrative writing/Narrativa. Tipo de escritura que narra sucesos o acciones que cambian con el paso del tiempo; por lo general tiene personajes, escenario y trama.

Nonfiction/No ficción. Texto en prosa acerca de personas, lugares y sucesos reales.

Noun/Nombre (o sustantivo). Palabra que nombra a una persona, lugar, cosa, o a una idea, cualidad o característica.

Number/Número. Forma del nombre, pronombre o verbo que indica si se refiere a uno (**singular**) o a más de uno (**plural**).

O

Object/Objeto. *Ver Complement.*

Onomatopoeia/Onomatopeya. Palabra o frase que imita o sugiere el sonido que describe (*rattle, boom;* en español: *pum, zas*).

Opinion/Opinión. Creencia o actitud; no puede comprobarse si es falsa o verdadera.

Oral tradition/Tradición oral. Literatura que se transmite de boca en boca de una generación a otra. Puede representar los valores culturales de un pueblo.

Order of importance/Orden de importancia. Forma de acomodar los detalles en un párrafo o en otro texto escrito según su importancia.

Organization/Organización. La disposición y el orden de los puntos principales y los detalles de apoyo en un escrito.

Outline/Esquema. Organización sistemática de ideas principales y secundarias con números romanos, letras y números arábigos para una presentación oral o escrita.

P

Paragraph/Párrafo. Una unidad de un texto que consta de oraciones relacionadas.

Parallelism/Paralelismo. Serie de palabras, frases y oraciones que tienen una forma gramatical similar.

Paraphrase/Parafrasear. Repetir las ideas de otro con palabras diferentes del original pero conservando las ideas, el tono y la longitud general.

Parenthetical documentation/Documentación parentética. Referencia específica a la fuente de la información que se pone entre paréntesis directamente después de ésta.

Peer response/Respuesta de compañeros. Sugerencias y comentarios que dan los compañeros de clase sobre un texto escrito u otro tipo de presentación.

Personal pronoun/Pronombre personal. *Ver Pronoun.*

Personal writing/Escritura personal. Texto que expresa los pensamientos y sentimientos del autor.

Personification/Personificación. Tropo que da cualidades humanas a un animal, objeto o idea.

Perspective/Perspectiva. *Ver Point of view.*

Persuasion/Persuasión. Tipo de escritura encaminado a convencer a pensar o actuar de cierta manera.

Phrase/Frase. Grupo de palabras que forma una unidad en una oración.

> **Prepositional phrase/Frase preposicional.** Comienza con una preposición y termina con un nombre o un pronombre.
> **Verb phrase/Frase verbal.** Consta de uno o más **verbos auxiliares** (*auxiliary verbs*) seguidos del verbo principal.

Plagiarism/Plagio. Presentación deshonesta de palabras o ideas ajenas como si fueran propias.

Plot/Trama. Serie de sucesos en secuencia en un cuento, novela u obra de teatro.

Plural/Plural. *Ver Number.*

Poetry/Poesía. Forma de expresión literaria compuesta por versos. La poesía tradicional contiene un lenguaje emotivo e imaginativo y un ritmo regular.

Point of view/Punto de vista. Ángulo o perspectiva desde el cual se cuenta una historia; por ejemplo, primera o tercera persona.

Portfolio/Portafolio. Colección de varias obras escritas de un estudiante, que puede tener obras terminadas y otras en proceso.

Predicate/Predicado. Verbo o frase verbal y sus modificadores que hacen una afirmación esencial sobre el sujeto de la oración.

Predicate adjective/Adjetivo predicativo. *Ver Adjective.*

Preposition/Preposición. Palabra que muestra la relación de un nombre o pronombre con otra palabra en la oración.

Prepositional phrase/Frase preposicional. *Ver Phrase.*

Presentation/Presentación. La forma en que se ven en una página las palabras y los elementos de diseño.

Presenting/Publishing Presentación/ Publicación. Ultimo paso del proceso de escritura que implica compartir con otros lo que se ha escrito.

Prewriting/Preescritura. Primer paso del proceso de escritura: decidir sobre qué se va a escribir, reunir ideas y detalles, y elaborar un plan para presentar las ideas; usa estrategias como lluvia de ideas, organizadores gráficos, notas y registros.

Prior knowledge/Conocimiento previo. Hechos, ideas y experiencias que un escritor, lector u observador lleva a una nueva actividad.

Progressive form/Durativo. *Ver Verb tense.*

Pronoun/Pronombre. Palabra que va en lugar del nombre; grupo de palabras que funcionan como un nombre u otro pronombre. La palabra o grupo de palabras a que se refiere un pronombre se llama **antecedente** (*antecedent*).
    Personal pronoun/Pronombre personal. Se refiere a una persona o cosa específica.

Pronoun case/Caso del pronombre. *Ver Case.*

Proofreading/Corrección de pruebas. Último paso del proceso editorial en que se revisa el texto en busca de errores tipográficos y de otra naturaleza**.**

Propaganda/Propaganda. Información encaminada a influir en los pensamientos o acciones; en general es de naturaleza política y puede distorsionar la verdad.

Proper adjective/Adjetivo propio*. *Ver Adjective.*

Prose/Prosa. Escritura similar al lenguaje cotidiano tanto oral como escrito, a diferencia de la poesía y el teatro.

Publishing/Publicación. Presentación de una obra escrita terminada mediante el uso de la tecnología, para darla a conocer a un público amplio.

Purpose/Finalidad. Objetivo de la escritura: expresar, descubrir, registrar, desarrollar o reflexionar sobre ideas, resolver problemas, entretener, influir, informar o describir.

Regular verb/Verbo regular. *Ver Verb tense.*

Representation/Representación. Forma en que se presenta información o ideas al público.

Research/Investigación. Proceso de localizar información sobre un tema.

Review/Reseña. Análisis e interpretación de un tema presentado por lo general a través de los medios de comunicación masiva.

Revising/Revisión. Paso del proceso de escritura en que el autor repasa el borrador, cambia el contenido, la organización y el estilo para mejorar el texto. Las técnicas de revisión son agregar, elaborar, eliminar, combinar y reacomodar el texto.

Root/Raíz. Parte de una palabra que contiene el significado principal.

Run-on sentence/Oración mal puntuada. Dos o más oraciones o proposiciones seguidas, cuyo significado es confuso debido a su inadecuada puntuación.

Sensory details/Detalles sensoriales. Lenguaje que apela a los sentidos; los detalles sensoriales son elementos importantes de la escritura descriptiva, sobre todo en la poesía.

Sentence/Oración. Grupo de palabras que expresa un pensamiento completo. Cada oración tiene **sujeto** (*subject*) y **predicado** (*predicate*). *Ver también Subject; Predicate; Clause.*

> **Simple sentence/Oración simple.** Consta de una proposición principal y no tiene proposiciones subordinadas.
>
> **Compound sentence/Oración compuesta.** Tiene dos o más proposiciones principales, cada una con su propio sujeto y predicado; por lo general van unidas por una coma y una conjunción coordinante, o por un punto y coma.
>
> **Complex sentence/Oración compleja.** Tiene una proposición principal y una o más proposiciones subordinadas.

Sentence fluency/Fluidez oracional. El ritmo suave y suelto de las oraciones que varían en longitud y estilo.

Sentence variety/Variedad de oraciones. Uso de diferentes tipos de oraciones para agregar interés al texto.

Setting/Escenario. Tiempo y lugar en que ocurren los sucesos de un cuento, novela u obra de teatro.

Simile/Símil. Tropo que compara dos cosas esencialmente distintas, usando las palabras *like* o *as* (*como*). (*Su pelo era como hilo de seda.*)

Simple predicate/Predicado simple. *Ver Predicate; Sentence; Subject.*

Simple sentence/Oración simple. *Ver Sentence.*

Spatial order/Orden espacial. Forma de presentar los detalles de un escenario según su ubicación: de izquierda a derecha o de arriba hacia abajo.

Standard English/Inglés estándar. La forma más ampliamente usada y aceptada del idioma inglés.

Style/Estilo. Forma en que un escritor elige y organiza las palabras y oraciones.

Subject/Sujeto. Nombre o pronombre principal que informa sobre quién o sobre qué trata la oración.

Subordinate clause/Proposición subordinada. *Ver Clause.*

Summary/Resumen. Breve explicación de la idea principal de una composición.

Supporting evidence/Sustento. *Ver Evidence.*

Suspense/Suspenso. Recurso literario que genera interés y emoción para llegar al clímax o desenlace de una historia. Un escritor crea suspenso al proporcionar pistas sobre el desenlace pero sin revelar demasiada información.

Symbol/Símbolo. Objeto, persona, lugar o experiencia que representa algo más, por lo general, abstracto.

Tense/Tiempo. *Ver Verb tense.*

Theme/Tema. Idea o mensaje principal de una obra escrita.

Thesis statement/Exposición de tesis. Exposición de la **idea principal** o finalidad de una obra en una o dos oraciones.

Time order/Orden temporal. Organización de detalles en un texto escrito según el momento en que ocurrieron.

Tone/Tono. Reflejo de la actitud del escritor o hablante hacia un sujeto.

Topic sentence/Oración temática. Oración que expresa la idea principal de un párrafo.

Transition/Transición. Palabra o frase de enlace que aclara las relaciones entre los detalles, oraciones o párrafos.

U–V

Unity/Unidad. Integridad de un párrafo o composición; coherencia entre todas las oraciones o párrafos para expresar o sustentar una idea principal.

URL/URL. Forma estándar de una dirección de Internet. (Son iniciales de *Uniform Resource Locator.*)

Venn diagram/Diagrama de Venn. Organizador gráfico que consta de dos círculos que se traslapan, usado para comparar dos cosas con características comunes y diferentes.

Verb/Verbo. Palabra que expresa acción o estado y que es necesaria para hacer una afirmación.

Verb phrase/Frase verbal. *Ver Phrase.*

Verb tense/Tiempo verbal. El tiempo de un verbo indica cuándo ocurre la acción.

> **Present tense/Presente.** Indica una acción que sucede regularmente.
> **Past tense/Pasado.** Indica una acción que ya sucedió.
> **Future tense/Futuro.** Indica una acción que va a suceder.
> En inglés todos los tiempos verbales están formados por las cuatro partes principales del verbo: **base derivativa** (*base form*) (*freeze, congelar*), **participio presente** (*present participle*) (*freezing, congelando*), **pretérito simple** (*simple past form*) (*froze, congeló*) y **participio pasado** (*past participle*) (*frozen, congelado*).
> Un **verbo regular** (*regular verb*) forma su

pretérito simple y su participio pasado agregando la terminación *ed* al infinitivo. Los verbos que forman su pretérito y participio pasado de otra forma se llaman **verbos irregulares** (*irregular verbs*). Además de los tiempos presente, pasado y futuro hay tres tiempos perfectos: **presente perfecto** (*present perfect*), **pretérito perfecto** (*past perfect*) y **futuro perfecto** (*future perfect*).
Cada uno de los seis tiempos tiene una forma **durativa** (*progressive form*) que expresa acción continua.

Voice/Voz. La forma única que tiene un escritor o escritora de usar el tono y el estilo para comunicarse con los lectores.

Web site/Sitio Web. Sitio de World Wide Web que puede ser alcanzado mediante vínculos o una dirección Web o URL. *Ver también URL; World Wide Web.*

Word choice/Léxico. El vocabulario que selecciona una escritora o escritor para presentar un significado.

Word processing/Procesador de palabras. Programa de computadora para escribir y editar un texto.

World Wide Web/World Wide Web. Sistema global que usa Internet y permite a los usuarios crear, vincularse y entrar a campos de información. *Ver también Internet.*

Writing process/Proceso de escritura. Serie de pasos o etapas por los que atraviesa un escritor para desarrollar sus ideas y comunicarlas.

---

*Este término o explicación solamente se aplica a la gramática inglesa.

WRITING AND RESEARCH HANDBOOK

*W*hat are the basic tools for building strong sentences, paragraphs, compositions, and research papers? You'll find them in this handbook—an easy-to-use "tool kit" for writers like you. Check out the helpful explanations, examples, and tips as you complete your writing assignments.

Writing Good Sentences

A sentence is a group of words that expresses a complete thought. Every sentence has a subject and a predicate.

Using Various Types of Sentences

How you craft a sentence—as a statement, question, command, or exclamation—depends on the job you want the sentence to do.

Type	Job It Does	Ways to Use It
Declarative	Makes a statement	Report information *October is National Pizza Month.*
Interrogative	Asks a question	Make your readers curious *Why is pizza so popular?*
Imperative	Gives a command or makes a request	Tell how to do something *Spread the toppings on the pizza dough.*
Exclamatory	Expresses strong feeling	Emphasize a surprising fact *Every second, Americans eat about 350 slices of pizza!*

Varying Sentence Structure and Length

Many sentences in a row that look and sound alike can be boring. Vary your sentence openers to make your writing interesting.

- **Start a sentence with an adjective or an adverb.**
  Suddenly the sky turned dark.

- **Start a sentence with a phrase.**
  Like a fireworks show, lightning streaked across the sky.

- **Start a sentence with a clause.**
  As the thunderstorm began, people ran for cover.

Many short sentences in a row make writing sound choppy and dull. To make your writing sound pleasing, vary the sentence length.

- **Combine short sentences into longer ones.**

  Tornadoes are also called twisters. They are spinning clouds. The clouds are funnel shaped.

  Tornadoes, also called twisters, are spinning funnel-shaped clouds.

- **Alternate shorter sentences with longer sentences.**

  Tornado winds are powerful. They can hurl cows into the air, tear trees from their roots, and turn cars upside down.

Check It Out

For more about how to vary sentence length and structure, review Unit 20, Sentence Combining, pages 516–523.

Using Parallelism

Parallelism is the use of a pair or a series of words, phrases, or sentences that have the same grammatical structure. Use parallelism to call attention to the items in the series and to create unity in writing.

Not Parallel Gymnasts are strong, flexible, and move gracefully.
Parallel Gymnasts are strong, flexible, and graceful.

Not Parallel Do warm-up exercises to prevent sports injuries and for stretching your muscles.
Parallel Do warm-up exercises to prevent sports injuries and to stretch your muscles.

Not Parallel Stand on one leg, bend the other leg, and you should pull your heel.
Parallel Stand on one leg, bend the other leg, and pull your heel.

Revising Wordy Sentences

Revise wordy sentences to make every word count.

- **Cut needless words.**

  Wordy We need to have bike lanes in streets due to the fact that people like to ride their bikes to work and school, and it's not safe otherwise.
  Concise We need bike lanes in streets so that people can safely ride to work and school.

- **Rewrite sentences opening with the word *there*.**

  Wordy There are many kids riding their bikes in the street.
  Concise Many kids ride their bikes in the street.

- **Change verbs in passive voice to active voice.**

  Wordy Bikes are also ridden by grown-ups who want to keep fit.
  Concise Grown-ups who want to keep fit also ride bikes.

Write four sentences, one of each type—declarative, interrogative, imperative, and exclamatory—about food, sports, or another topic that interests you.

Writing Good Paragraphs

A paragraph is a group of sentences that relate to one main idea. A good paragraph develops a single idea and brings that idea into sharp focus. All the sentences flow smoothly from the beginning to the end of the paragraph.

Writing Unified Paragraphs

A paragraph has **unity** when the sentences belong together and center on a single main idea. One way to build a unified paragraph is to state the main idea in a topic sentence and then add related details.

Writing Topic Sentences A **topic sentence** gives your readers the "big picture"—a clear view of the most important idea you want them to know. Many effective expository paragraphs (paragraphs that convey information) start with a topic sentence that tells the key point right away.

Elaborating Topic Sentences Elaboration gives your readers a specific, more detailed picture of the main idea stated in your topic sentence. Elaboration is a technique you can use to include details that develop, support, or explain the main idea. The following chart shows various kinds of elaboration you might try.

Revising Tip

To make a paragraph unified, leave out details that do not relate to the topic sentence.

Topic Sentence: The state of Florida is known for its alligators.	
Descriptions	Alligators look like dinosaurs from millions of years ago.
Facts and statistics	Alligators can weigh as much as six hundred pounds.
Examples	Alligators eat a wide variety of foods, such as fish, insects, turtles, frogs, and small mammals.
Anecdotes	Silvia almost fainted when she came home to find an alligator paddling around in her swimming pool.
Reasons	Face-to-face encounters with alligators are now common because people have built golf courses over the animals' habitat.

Writing Coherent Paragraphs

A paragraph has **coherence** when all the sentences flow smoothly and logically from one to the next. All the sentences in a paragraph *cohere*, or "stick together," in a way that makes sense. To be sure your writing is coherent, choose a pattern of organization that fits your topic and use transition words and phrases to link ideas.

Organizing Paragraphs A few basic patterns of organization are listed below. Choose the pattern that helps you meet your specific writing goal.

- Use **chronological order,** or time order, to tell a story or to explain the steps in a process.
- Use **spatial order** to order your description of places, people, and things. You might describe the details in the order you see them— for example, from top to bottom or from near to far.
- Use **order of importance** to show how you rank opinions, facts, or details from the most to least important or the reverse.

Using Transitions Linking words and phrases, called **transitions,** act like bridges between sentences or between paragraphs. Transitions, such as the ones shown below, can make the organization of your paragraphs stronger by showing how ideas are logically related.

To show time order or sequence
after, at the beginning, before, finally, first, last year, later, meanwhile, next, now, second, sometimes, soon, yesterday

To show spatial relationships
above, ahead, around, at the top, below, beyond, down, here, inside, near, on top of, opposite, outside, over, there, under, within

To show importance or degree
above all, first, furthermore, in addition, mainly, most important, second

✓ Check It Out

For more about transitions, see page 120.

TRY IT OUT

Copy the following paragraph on your paper. Underline the topic sentence. Cross out the sentence that is unrelated to the topic sentence. Add a transition to make a clear connection between two of the sentences.

A local artist creates weird and funny sculptures from fruits and vegetables. First he uses a sharp knife to carve faces that look like animals, such as bears and pigs. He glues on tiny beans to make eyes. Finally he uses beet juice to paint the mouth. Although the process sounds easy, it requires great imagination. The octopus sculpted from a banana is the silliest work of art I've ever seen.

Writing Good Compositions

A composition is a short paper made up of several paragraphs, with a clear introduction, body, and conclusion. A good composition presents a clear, complete message about a specific topic. Ideas flow logically from one sentence to the next and from one paragraph to the next.

Making a Plan

The suggestions in the chart below can help you shape the information in each part of your composition to suit your writing purpose.

Introductory Paragraph

Your introduction should interest readers in your topic and capture their attention. You may

- give background
- use a quotation
- ask a question
- tell an anecdote, or brief story

Include a **thesis statement,** a sentence or two stating the main idea you will develop in the composition.

Body Paragraphs

Elaborate on your thesis statement in the body paragraphs. You may

- offer proof
- give examples
- explain ideas

Stay focused and keep your body paragraphs on track. Remember to

- develop a single idea in each body paragraph
- arrange the paragraphs in a logical order
- use transitions to link one paragraph to the next

Concluding Paragraph

Your conclusion should bring your composition to a satisfying close. You may

- sum up main points
- tie the ending to the beginning by restating the main idea or thesis in different words
- make a call to action if your goal is to persuade readers

Drafting Tip

Sometimes you'll need two paragraphs to introduce your topic. For example, the first paragraph can tell an anecdote; the second can include your thesis statement.

Drafting Tip

A good conclusion follows logically from the rest of the piece of writing and leaves the reader with something to think about. Make sure that you do not introduce new or unrelated material in a conclusion.

Using the 6+1 Trait® Model

What are some basic terms you can use to discuss your writing with your teacher or classmates? What should you focus on as you revise and edit your compositions? Check out the following seven terms, or traits, that describe the qualities of strong writing. Learn the meaning of each trait and find out how using the traits can improve your writing.

Ideas The message or the theme and the details that develop it

Writing is clear when readers can grasp the meaning of your ideas right away. Check to see whether you're getting your message across.

✔ Does the title suggest the theme of the composition?

✔ Does the composition focus on a single narrow topic?

✔ Is the thesis, or main idea, clearly stated?

✔ Do well-chosen details elaborate the main idea?

Revising Tip

Use the cut-and-paste features of your word processing program to experiment with the structure—the arrangement of sentences or paragraphs. Choose the clearest, most logical order for your final draft.

Organization The arrangement of main points and supporting details

A good plan of organization steers your readers in the right direction and guides them easily through your composition—from start to finish. Find a structure, or order, that best suits your topic and writing purpose. Check to see whether you've ordered your key ideas and details in a way that keeps your readers on track.

✔ Are the beginning, middle, and end clearly linked?

✔ Is the order of ideas easy to follow?

✔ Does the introduction capture your readers' attention?

✔ Do sentences and paragraphs flow from one to the next in a way that makes sense?

✔ Does the conclusion wrap up the composition?

Voice A writer's unique way of using tone and style

Your writing voice comes through when your readers sense that a real person is communicating with them. Readers will respond to the **tone,** or the attitude, that you express toward a topic and to the **style,** the way that you use language and write sentences. Read your work aloud to see whether your writing voice comes through.

✔ Does your writing sound interesting when you read it aloud?

✔ Does your writing show what you think about your topic?

✔ Does your writing sound like you—or does it sound like you're imitating someone else?

6+1 Trait® is a registered trademark of Northwest Regional Educational Laboratory, which does not endorse this product.

Word Choice The vocabulary a writer uses to convey meaning

Words work hard. They carry the weight of your meaning, so make sure you choose them carefully. Check to see whether the words you choose are doing their jobs well.

✔ Do you use lively verbs to show action?

✔ Do you use vivid words to create word pictures in your readers' minds?

✔ Do you use precise words to explain your ideas simply and clearly?

Sentence Fluency The smooth rhythm and flow of sentences that vary in length and style

The best writing is made up of sentences that flow smoothly from one sentence to the next. Writing that is graceful also sounds musical—rhythmical rather than choppy. Check for sentence fluency by reading your writing aloud.

✔ Do your sentences vary in length and structure?

✔ Do transition words and phrases show connections between ideas and sentences?

✔ Does parallelism help balance and unify related ideas?

Conventions Correct spelling, grammar, usage, and mechanics

A composition free of errors makes a good impression on your readers. Mistakes can be distracting, and they can blur your message. Try working with a partner to spot errors and correct them. Use this checklist to help you.

✔ Are all words spelled correctly?

✔ Are all proper nouns—as well as the first word of every sentence—capitalized?

✔ Is your composition free of sentence fragments?

✔ Is your composition free of run-on sentences?

✔ Are punctuation marks—such as apostrophes, commas, and end marks—inserted in the right places?

Presentation The way words and design elements look on a page

Appearance matters, so make your compositions inviting to read. Handwritten papers should be neat and legible. If you're using a word processor, double-space the lines of text and choose a readable font. Other design elements—such as boldfaced headings, bulleted lists, pictures, and charts—can help you present information effectively as well as make your papers look good.

Revising Tip

Listen carefully to the way your sentences sound when someone else reads them aloud. If you don't like what you hear, revise for sentence fluency. You might try adding variety to your sentence openers or combining sentences to make them sound less choppy.

✔ **Check It Out**

See the Troubleshooter, pages 248–267, for help in correcting common errors in your writing.

Evaluating a Composition Read this sample composition, which has been evaluated using the 6+1 Trait® model.

Ideas The introduction hooks readers by connecting to their experience. It includes a thesis statement, which is developed in the following paragraphs with an example.

Organization The body paragraphs are arranged in order of importance.

Sentence Fluency A variety of sentence types helps the writing flow smoothly.

Organization Transitions effectively link ideas within and between paragraphs. Ideas flow naturally from one to the next.

Word Choice Nouns and verbs are strong and precise.

Voice The personal voice reveals something about the writer's personality.

Conventions The composition is free of errors in grammar, spelling, usage, and mechanics.

Joining the Team

It's not always easy to take a risk and try something new. It's much easier to play it safe and to keep doing the same things you always do. But sometimes having just a little curiosity about something is all you need to make a decision that can change your life for the better.

Last fall I made such a decision, and I haven't regretted it for a moment. I decided to join the school track team, even though I've never competed in any sport before. I like to run with my dog in the park, and I wondered what it would be like to run as part of a team. So how do I know I made the right decision? I made a list of three questions—from the least important to the most important—to help me think through my decision. Did becoming a member of the track team give me a sense of pride? Did I improve my physical fitness? Did I find running competitively enjoyable? Here's what I discovered as I answered these questions.

First, I feel proud of what I have contributed to the team. I haven't finished first or second or even third in a race yet. But I like and admire my teammates, and cheering them on at track meets makes them feel good. And that makes me feel good about myself too.

Second, joining the track team has made me more physically fit. I used to hate running laps and doing crunches. After a while, though, I started to see the results of doing my exercises, and now I don't mind. My strength and endurance have increased, and my time is improving in every event. Better physical fitness is giving me more energy for other activities, such as babysitting for my little brother.

Above all, I know I made a wise decision to join the track team because I enjoy running more than I ever imagined I could. I've discovered that I have a competitive streak in me. I want to win, and I know I can win if I keep practicing. My dog definitely appreciates the fact that I can keep up with him now, and we run together in the park nearly every day. That's fun for both of us!

All kinds of benefits can come with trying something new. So if there's something you're curious about—learning to cook like a gourmet, performing in a school play, or raising money for charity, for example—I strongly recommend that you give it a try!

Writing Good Research Papers

A research paper reports facts and ideas gathered from various sources about a specific topic. A good research paper blends information from reliable sources with the writer's original thoughts and ideas. The final draft follows a standard format for presenting information and citing sources.

Exploring a Variety of Sources

Once you've narrowed the topic of your research paper, you'll need to hunt for the best information. You might start by reading an encyclopedia article on your topic to learn some basic information. Then widen your search to include both primary and secondary sources.

- **Primary sources** are records of events by the people who witnessed them. Examples include diaries, letters, speeches, photos, posters, interviews, and radio and TV news broadcasts that include eyewitness interviews.
- **Secondary sources** contain information that is often based on primary sources. The creators of secondary sources conduct original research and then report their findings. Examples include encyclopedias, textbooks, biographies, magazine articles, Web site articles, and educational films.

When you find a secondary source that you can use for your report, check to see whether the author has given credit to his or her sources of information in **footnotes, endnotes,** or a **bibliography.** Tracking down such sources can lead you to more information you can use.

If you're exploring your topic on the Internet, look for Web sites that are sponsored by government institutions, famous museums, and reliable organizations. If you find a helpful site, check to see whether it contains links to other Web sites you can use.

Evaluating Sources

As you conduct your research, do a little detective work and investigate the sources you find. Begin by asking some key questions so you can decide whether you've tracked down reliable resources that are suitable for your purpose. Some important questions to ask about your sources are listed in the box on the next page.

Research Tip

Look for footnotes at the bottom of a page. Look for endnotes at the end of a chapter or a book. Look for a bibliography at the end of a book.

Ask Questions About Your Sources

✔ **Is the information useful?**
Find sources that are closely related to your research topic.

✔ **Is the information easy to understand?**
Look for sources that are geared toward readers your age.

✔ **Is the information new enough?**
Look for sources that were recently published if you need the most current facts and figures.

✔ **Is the information trustworthy and true?**
Check to see whether the author documents the source of facts and supports opinions with reasons and evidence. Also check out the background of the authors. They should be well-known experts on the topic that you're researching.

✔ **Is the information balanced and fair?**
Read with a critical eye. Does the source try to persuade readers with a one-sided presentation of information? Or is the source balanced, approaching a topic from various perspectives? Be on the lookout for **propaganda** and for sources that reflect an author's **bias,** or prejudice. Make sure that you learn about a topic from more than one angle by reviewing several sources of information.

Giving Credit Where Credit Is Due

When you write a research paper, you support your own ideas with information that you've gleaned from your primary and secondary sources. But presenting someone else's ideas as if they were your own is **plagiarism,** a form of cheating. You can avoid plagiarism by citing, or identifying, the sources of your information within the text of your paper. The chart below tells what kinds of information you do and don't need to cite in your paper.

DO credit the source of . . .	DON'T credit the source of . . .
• direct quotations	• information that can be found in many places—dates, facts, ideas, and concepts that are considered common knowledge
• summaries and paraphrases, or restatements, of someone else's viewpoints, original ideas, and conclusions	
• photos, art, charts, and other visuals	• your own unique ideas
• little-known facts or statistics	

Citing Sources Within Your Paper The most common method of crediting sources is with parenthetical documentation within the text. Generally a reference to the source and page number is included in parentheses at the end of each quotation, paraphrase, or summary of information borrowed from a source. An in-text citation points readers to a corresponding entry in your **works-cited list**—a list of all your sources, complete with publication information, that will appear as the final page of your paper. The Modern Language Association (MLA) recommends the following guidelines for crediting sources in text.

✓ **Check It Out**

To see the relationship between parenthetical documentation and a works-cited list, study the sample research paper on pages 689–690.

- **Put in parentheses the author's last name and the page number where you found the information.**

    Sundiata would later be known by such titles as "Lord Lion," "Lion of Mali," and "Father of the Bright Country" (Koslow 12).

- **If the author's name is mentioned in the sentence, put only the page number in parentheses.**

    According to Philip Koslow, Sundiata would be known by such titles as "Lord Lion," "Lion of Mali," and "Father of the Bright Country" (12).

- **If no author is listed, put the title or a shortened version of the title in parentheses. Include a page number if you have one.**

    The facts of his life as a king are known, but many details about his early life are uncertain ("Sundiata").

Preparing the Final Draft

Ask your teacher how to format the final draft. Most English teachers will ask you to follow the MLA guidelines listed below.

- Put a heading in the upper left-hand corner of the first page with your name, your teacher's name, and the date on separate lines.
- Center the title on the line below the heading.
- Number the pages one-half inch from the top in the right-hand corner. After page one, put your last name before the page number.
- Set one-inch margins on all sides of every page; double-space the lines of text.
- Include an alphabetized, double-spaced works-cited list as the last page of your final draft. All sources noted in parenthetical citations in the paper must be listed.

On the next page, you'll find examples of how the sources you use for your research paper should be written and punctuated in a works-cited list, the final page of your paper.

MLA Style

MLA style is most often used in English and social studies classes. Center the title *Works Cited* at the top of your list.

Source	Style
Book with one author	Price-Groff, Claire. *The Manatee*. Farmington Hills: Lucent, 1999.
Book with two or three authors	Tennant, Alan, Gerard T. Salmon, and Richard B. King. *Snakes of North America*. Lanham: Lone Star Books, 2003. [If a book has more than three authors, name only the first author and then write "et al." (Latin abbreviation for "and others").]
Book with an editor	Follett, C. B., ed. *Grrrrr: A Collection of Poems About Bears*. Sausalito: Arctos, 2000.
Book with organization or group as author or editor	National Air and Space Museum. *The Official Guide to the Smithsonian Air and Space Museum*. Washington: Smithsonian Institution Press, 2002.
Work from an anthology	Soto, Gary. "To Be a Man." *Hispanic American Literature: An Anthology*. Ed. Rodolfo Cortina. Lincolnwood: NTC, 1998. 340–341.
Introduction in a published book	Weintraub, Stanley. Introduction. *Great Expectations*. By Charles Dickens. New York: Signet, 1998. v–xii.
Encyclopedia article	"Whales." *World Book Encyclopedia*. 2003.
Weekly magazine article	Trillin, Calvin. "Newshound." *New Yorker* 29 Sept. 2003: 70–81.
Monthly magazine article	Knott, Cheryl. "Code Red." *National Geographic* Oct. 2003: 76–81.
Online magazine article	Rauch, Jonathan. "Will Frankenfood Save the Planet?" *Atlantic Online* 292.3 (Oct. 2003). 15 Dec. 2003 <http://www.theatlantic.com/issues/2003/10/rauch.htm>.
Newspaper article	Bertram, Jeffrey. "African Bees: Fact or Myth?" *Orlando Sentinel* 18 Aug. 1999: D2.
Unsigned article	"Party-Line Snoops." *Washington Post* 24 Sept. 2003: A28.
Internet	"Manatees." *SeaWorld/Busch Gardens Animal Information Database*. 2002. Busch Entertainment Corp. 3 Oct. 2003 <http://www.seaworld.org/infobooks/Manatee/home.html>.
Radio or TV program	"Orcas." *Champions of the Wild*. Animal Planet. Discovery Channel. 21 Oct. 2003.
Videotape or DVD	*Living with Tigers*. DVD. Discovery, 2003. [For a videotape (VHS) version, replace "DVD" with "Videocassette."]
Interview	Salinas, Antonia. E-mail interview. 23–24 Oct. 2003. [If an interview takes place in person, replace "E-mail" with "Personal"; if it takes place on the telephone, use "Telephone."]

Evaluating a Research Paper Read this sample research paper, which has been evaluated using the 6+1 Trait® model.

The Early Life of King Sundiata of Mali

In the beginning of the thirteenth century, a boy named Sundiata Keita was born near the kingdom of Kangaba, a region of West Africa. Sundiata was no ordinary boy. In fact, he grew up to become the founder and first king of the West African empire of Mali. The facts of his life as a king are known, but many details about his early life are uncertain ("Sundiata"). To find out more about Sundiata as a boy, historians have had to play the role of detectives searching for clues.

Some historians have had to get their information about Africa's past from storytellers, called *griots*. Griots are like living history books, because they tell stories about things that happened a long time ago. These stories are passed down from generation to generation. In the 1960s, West African historian D. T. Niana wrote down Sundiata's story. This story was told to him by Djeli Mamoudou Kouyata, a griot from the nation of Guinea (Koslow 12). Kouyata's version of Sundiata's life as a child may be based on fact, but no one knows for sure if the events he described really happened.

Kouyata said that Sundiata's father was named Maghan Kon Fatta and his mother was named Sogolon. Maghan Kon Fatta was king of the Mandingo people, who lived in and near present-day Mali. Sogolon was one of his many wives. When Sundiata was born, a prediction was made that he would rise to greatness someday. However, many obstacles stood in his way.

Sundiata faced one of his biggest challenges when he was a young child. He had been born with a disability. He crawled around like a baby until he was seven years old (McKissack and McKissack 49). People teased him and called him names, but Sundiata showed incredible courage. One day Sundiata announced to his mother that he was going to walk. According to the griot Kouyata's story, "Sundiata then told a blacksmith to make him the heaviest possible iron rod, and then, with trembling legs and a sweaty brow, he proceeded to lift himself up, bending the rod into a bow in the process" ("Mali," Part I, 3). People were amazed that Sundiata had accomplished such an incredible feat.

However, Sundiata's troubles were not over. Kouyata tells that Sundiata and his mother were in danger after Maghan Kon Fatta died. Sundiata's half-brother had become the king of Kangaba, and he thought that Sundiata would be a threat to him. To escape certain death, Sundiata and his mother went into exile.

(continued)

Ideas The title suggests the paper's theme. The central idea is clearly expressed in the introduction.

Word Choice Special terms are defined. Carefully chosen words show that the truth of the story is not certain.

Sentence Fluency A variety of sentence lengths and structures helps the writing flow smoothly.

Ideas Parenthetical citations (using MLA style) give credit to the source of ideas.

Conventions Writing is free of errors in spelling, grammar, usage, and mechanics.

Organization Information is organized in chronological order.

Organization The conclusion sums up the information and ties the ending to the beginning.

Voice The writer sounds curious and fascinated about the topic.

Presentation Like every good research paper, this one ends with a properly formatted list of works cited. There's an entry for every work used as a source of information. Remember to put your works-cited list on a separate sheet of paper.

The story goes that over the next few years, Sundiata grew stronger and wiser. He became an excellent hunter and warrior. By the time he was fifteen years old, Sundiata had fought his first major battle. His heroism and leadership in battle caught the attention of Mansa Tankura, king of Mema. When Sundiata was eighteen years old, he became an adviser to this king. Kouyata describes the teenage Sundiata this way: "He was a tall young man with a fat neck and a powerful chest. Nobody could bend his bow. Everyone bowed before him and he was greatly loved" (Koslow 14).

Sundiata would grow up to be the founder and first king of the empire of Mali. He would be known by such titles as "Lord Lion," "Lion of Mali," and "Father of the Bright Country" (Koslow 12). These are facts about Sundiata's adult life. However, the legends about his early life are more interesting than the facts. As a young boy, did Sundiata really overcome a disability and miraculously learn to walk? As a teenager, did Sundiata really become a military hero and a royal adviser? The answers to these questions remain a mystery.

Works Cited

Koslow, Philip. *Mali: Crossroads of Africa*. New York: Chelsea, 1995.

"Mali: Africa's Empire of Empires." *Kennedy Center African Odyssey Interactive*. John F. Kennedy Center for the Performing Arts. 2 Nov. 2000 <http://artsed.kennedycenter.org/aoi/events/theater/empire.html>.

McKissack, Patricia, and Fredrick McKissack. *The Royal Kingdoms of Ghana, Mali, and Songhay*. New York: Holt, 1994.

"Sundiata Keita." *Encyclopedia of World Biography*. Detroit: Gale Research, 1998.

INDEX

A

A, an, the, 381
A lot, 455
Abbreviations
   correct use of, 503
   periods in, 503
   for states, 503
   of units of measure, 503
Accept, except, 455
Action verbs, 333
Addresses
   abbreviations in, 503
   commas in, 495
   numbers in, 505
Adjective phrases, 421
Adjectives
   adverbs modifying, 397
   articles as, 381
   comparative form of, 383,
      385, 658
   definition of, 379
   demonstrative, 381, 658
   in descriptive writing, 123
   diagraming, 468
   distinguishing, from adverbs,
      401
   good and *well,* 401
   after linking verb, 401
   possessive, 658
   predicate, 337, 379, 401, 469,
      658
   proper, 379, 658
   superlative form of, 383, 385,
      658
   Troubleshooter for, 260–262
Adverb phrases, 421
Adverbs
   comparative form of, 399, 658
   definition of, 395, 658
   diagraming, 468
   distinguishing, from
      adjectives, 401
   distinguishing, from
      prepositions, 423
   and double negatives, 403

in modifying adjectives and
   adverbs, 397
   positioning of, 395
   superlative form of, 399, 658
Advertisements, 638–639,
   642–643
Affirmative words, 403
Agreement. See Pronoun-
   antecedent agreement;
   Subject-verb agreement
All ready, already, 455
All together, altogether, 455
Allusion, 658
Among, between, 455
Analogies in standardized tests,
   588–590
Analysis, 190–193, 658
   Internet sources, 651–652
   media, 290–293, 635–639
Analyzing media messages,
   635–639
   advertisements, 638
   movies, 637
   music videos, 637
   television, 637
Anecdote, 658
Antecedents for pronouns, 365
Antonyms, 553
Application forms, 278–281
   creating, 279, 281
   example, 278, 280
   online, 281
   parts, 280, 281
   purpose, 278, 279
   signature, 278, 280, 281
   style, 280
   types, 279
   word processing, 281
Appositive, 658
Apostrophes
   in contractions, 501
   in possessive nouns, 382
   Troubleshooter for, 264–265
Argument, 658
Art
   list of works herein, xxvii

writing topics in, 65, 159, 197,
   225
Articles, 381, 658
   definite, 658
   indefinite, 658
Atlases, 535
Audience, 658
   knowing your prompts, 97
   winning over, in persuasive
      writing, 228
   See also Writing
Autobiography, literature selec-
   tion in, 28–33
Auxiliary verbs, 663. See also
   Helping verbs, 663

B

Bad, badly, 401
Bad, comparative, 399
Bandwagon, 620, 638
Bar graphs, 580
Base word. See Root words
Be
   as helping verb, 341
   as linking verb, 337
Beside, besides, 455
Between, among, 455
Bias, 231, 658, 686
Bibliography, 658
Biography
   dialogue in, 156–159
   responding to, 164–167
   writing, 167
Body
   of business letter, 272
   of paper, 658
Book reports, 202–205
   parts of, 203
Bookmarks/favorites, 648, 659
Books
   fiction, 531, 533
   nonfiction, 527–531, 533
   See also Library; Reference
      works
Borrowed words, 542–543, 546

Brainstorming, 25, 131, 659
Brake, break, 555
Brand names, capitalizing of, 479
Break, brake, 555
Business letters, 269–272
  colon after salutation in, 269, 272, 273, 497
  commas in, 493
  format, 273–274
  parts, 272–273
  purpose, 269, 270
  style, 269–270, 271
  tone, 270
  types, 270–271
Businesses, capitalizing names of, 479

C

Calendar items, abbreviations for, 503
Capitalization
  of abbreviations, 475
  of academic degrees following persons name, 475
  of brand names, 479
  of buildings and structures, 477
  of cities, countries, states, etc., 477
  of compass points, 477
  of first word in sentence, 473
  of geographical names, 477
  of historical events, periods, 479
  of interrupted quotation, 473
  of monuments and awards, 477
  of names of places, 477
  of names and titles of people, 475
  of nationalities, races, etc., 479
  of pronoun *I,* 475
  of proper adjective, 379, 479
  of proper nouns, 475–480
  of quotations, 473
  of salutations, 473
  of sentences, 473
  of street names, 477
  of titles of books, movies, magazines, 479
  of titles of persons, 475

Troubleshooter for, 266–267
  of words showing family relationship, 475
Card catalog, 528, 533
Cartoon, 640–641
Case, 659
  See also Pronouns
Cause-and-effect chain, 659
Characterization, 659
Choose, chose, 455
Chronological (time) order, 659
  explaining a process, 154
  in narration, 154
Chronological organization, 154, 155
Clarity, 659
Classification system in library, media center, 530, 531
Clause
  dependent, 659
  independent, 252–253, 659
Cliché, 659
Closing of a letter, 473, 493
Clubs, capitalizing names of, 479
Clustering, 48, 49, 52, 53, 55, 131, 169, 207, 659
Coherence, 62–65, 66–69, 659
  in paragraphs, 680
Cohesive writing, 89–99, 659
Collaboration, 659
Collective nouns, 321
Colloquialism, 659
Colons
  to introduce list, 497
  after salutation in business letter, 272, 273, 497
  in time expressions, 497
Combining sentences. *See* Sentence combining
Commas
  in addresses, 495
  with *and, or,* or *but,* 493
  and combining sentences, 517, 519
  in compound sentences, 493, 517
  in dates, 495
  with direct quotations, 495
  with interjections, 427
  after introductory words, 491
  in letter writing, 269, 272, 493

  with names in direct address, 491
  with nonessential elements, 491
  with personal titles, 495
  with prepositional phrases, 491
  to prevent misreading, 493
  in series, 116, 263
  with *too,* 495
  Troubleshooter for, 262–263
Common nouns, 319, 475
Comparative form of an adjective, 383, 385, 658
Comparative form of an adverb, 399, 658
Compare-and-contrast essay, 190–193
  drafting in, 191, 192
  logical order in, 192
  prewriting in, 183
  revising in, 191
  Venn diagram 191–192
Comparison-and-contrast, 659
Comparison of modifiers
  comparative degree 383, 385, 399
  irregular, 385
  positive degree, 383, 385, 399
  superlative degree, 383, 385, 399, 658
Compass points, capitalizing names of, 477
Complement, 659
Complete predicates, 301
Complete subjects, 301
Complex sentence, 664–665
Composition. *See* Writing prompts
Compound elements, 519
Compound nouns, 501
Compound numbers, 505
Compound objects, object pronoun in, 363
Compound predicates, 305–306, 307
  diagraming, 466–471
Compound sentences, 307, 517, 664–665
  commas in, 493
  diagraming, 471
  semicolons in, 497
  Troubleshooter for, 252–253

Compound subjects, 305, 306, 307, 443
  diagraming, 471
  subject pronoun in, 363
  and subject-verb agreement, 443
Compound words, 501
Computer catalog, 532–533
Computers, 645–657
  CD-ROM, 656
  diskettes, 656–657
  DVD, 656
  e-mail, 654–655
  history, 645
  hyperlinks, 649
  for multimedia presentations, 292
  removable storage, 657
Conceptual map, 659
Conclusion of narrative, 162, 659
Conflict, 659
Conjunctions
  in compound sentences, 305
  coordinating, 425, 659
  correlative, 425, 659
  definition of, 425, 659
  Troubleshooter for, 253
Connotation, 660
Constructive criticism, 660
Context clues, 544–545, 660
Contexts for writing. See Writing prompts
Contractions, apostrophes in, 501
  distinguished from possessive pronouns, 501
  double negatives and, 403
Conventions, 34, 133, 660, 683–684, 690
Cooperative Learning, 49, 61, 65, 69, 73, 109, 117, 121, 151, 163, 167, 193, 205, 233
Coordinating conjunctions, 425, 659
Correlative conjunctions, 425, 659
Creative writing, 11, 22, 23, 49, 57, 73, 78–81, 159, 167, 221
Credibility, 635–636, 660
Critical listening, 617–620
Critical thinking

drawing conclusions, 178, 214, 246
evaluating characters, 87
interpreting, 140
making inferences, 34
Cross-curricular writing
  in architecture, 23
  in art, 57, 65, 141
  in geography, 11, 117, 247
  in history, 189, 215
  in mathematics, 35, 197
  in music, 155
  in science 88, 113
  in social studies, 53, 179
Cryptograms, 564

D

Dates
  capitalizing of, 479
  commas in, 495
  numbers in, 505
Declarative sentences, 297, 489, 660
  diagraming, 466
Deductive reasoning, 660
Definite article, 658
Definition
  as context clue, 544
  in dictionary, 539
Demonstrative adjectives, 381, 658
Demonstrative pronouns, 381
Denotation, 660
Dependent clause, 659
Descriptive writing, 100–141
  describing place in, 122–125
  details in, 110–113, 117
  drafting, 104, 108, 112, 119, 124, 131, 132
  editing, 116, 120, 123, 128, 133
  exploring places in, 126–129
  focusing on details in, 114–117
  literature models in, 106, 107, 110, 114, 118, 124, 126, 134–139
  note taking for, 109, 110–113
  ordering details in, 118–121
  organization in, 119
  presenting, 124, 133

  prewriting, 103, 105, 131
  revising, 112, 132
  transitions in, 120, 121
  uses of, 108
  word choice in, 106–109
Desert, dessert, 566
Desktop publishing, 660
Details
  checking, in editing, 70–73
  choosing, 56, 116, 153
  in descriptive writing, 102–103, 110–121, 123, 127
  listening for, 617–618
  in narrative writing, 153
  order of importance, 52, 118, 153
  organizing, 50, 52, 153
  in personal writing, 25
Dewey decimal system, 530–531, 532
Diagraming sentences, 465–471
  adjectives, 468
  adverbs, 468
  direct objects, 467
  indirect objects, 467
  predicate adjectives, 469
  predicate nouns, 469
  predicates, compound, 471
  predicates, simple, 465
  prepositional phrases, 470
  sentences, compound, 471
  sentences, four kinds of, 466
  subjects, compound, 471
  subjects, simple, 465
Dialect, 660
Dialogue, in narrative, 660
  punctuating, 473
  writing, 156–159
Diction, 660
Dictionary, 536
  definition in, 539
  entry word in, 539
  guide words, 537
  organization of entry, 537, 539–540
  illustrations in, 537
  parts of speech labels, 540
  pronunciation key, 537, 540
  sample entry, 537, 540
  synonyms, 540
  types of, 536
  usage information in, 540

word origin, 540
Direct address, commas to set off words or names in, 491
Direct objects, 333, 659
 diagraming, 467
 pronoun as, 361
Direct quotations, 447
 capitalization of, 473
 commas with, 495
 quotation marks for, 499
Directions
 giving, 622
 listening to, 617
Documentation, 198–201, 648, 660
Double negatives, 403
Drafting, 660
 descriptive writing, 104, 108, 112, 119, 124, 131–132
 expository writing, 183–185, 191, 192, 196, 200, 207–208
 narrative writing, 145–147, 154, 158, 169–170
 oral reports, 624
 personal writing, 4–5, 25–26
 persuasive writing, 220, 223, 236, 239–240
 TIME Facing the Blank Page, 90, 94–95
 writing process, 39, 43, 54–57, 61, 79–80
Drawing, 207
 in responding to poem, 21

E

Editing, 660
 checklist for, 71, 81, 133, 171, 209, 241
 descriptive writing, 116, 120, 128, 133
 dialogue, 158
 expository writing, 184, 188, 209
 for grammar, 116, 128
 narrative writing, 149, 162, 171
 personal writing, 27
 persuasive writing, 227, 235, 236, 241
 TIME Facing the Blank Page, 91, 98

in writing process, 40, 44, 70–73, 81
 See also Proofreading; Revising
Editor, role of, 96
Editorial, 660
ei and *ie,* spelling rule for, 558
Elaboration, 114–115, 117, 125, 660
Electronic resources, 645–657
Ellipsis, 660
E-mail, 654–655, 660
 attachments, 654
 etiquette, 655
 domain name, 654
 spam, 654
 user name, 654
Encyclopedias, 534–535
End marks, 489
 defined, 489
 exclamation mark, 489
 period, 489
 question mark, 489
 and run-on sentence, 252–253
Endorsement, 619
English language
 history of, 542–543
 See also Vocabulary
Essays. *See* Expository writing
Ethnic groups, capitalizing names of, 479
Evaluation, of writing, 660, 684
Evidence, 231–232, 660
Exaggeration, 619
Examples
 as context clues, 544
Exclamation points
 to end exclamatory sentences, 297, 489
 with interjections, 427, 489
 quotation marks with, 499
Exclamatory sentences, 297, 489, 661
 diagraming, 466
Explanatory writing. *See* Expository writing
Expository writing, 180–215, 661
 compare-and-contrast essay in, 190–193
 describing a process, 194–197, 214

drafting, 183–184, 192, 207–208
 editing, 184, 188, 199, 209
 illustrating, 183–184
 literature models in, 186, 207, 210–213
 meaning of, 187
 presenting, 203, 209
 prewriting, 183, 203, 207
 research for, 183–184
 research reports as, 198–201
 revising, 184, 192, 208
 transitions in, 196
 types of, 188
Expressive writing, 661. *See also* Descriptive writing; Personal writing

F

Fact, 97, 231, 661
 distinguishing from opinions, 230–233, 619–620, 635–636
Feedback, 661
Fiction books
 arrangement in library, media center, 531, 533
 card catalog cards for, 533
Figurative language, 661
Film, 633
Fine art. For a complete list of fine art see p. xxvii
Folk etymology, 551
Formal language, 661
Fragments, sentence, 250–251, 299, 661
Freewriting, 9, 10, 11, 23, 25, 661
Friendly letters, parts, 16–19, 224
Future tense, 339, 666

G

Gender, pronoun-antecedent agreement in, 365
Generalization, 661
Genre, 661
Geographical names, capitalizing of, 477
Geography, writing topics in, 117

Giving directions
    instructions, 622
Glossary, 569, 570. *See also*
    Dictionary
Government agencies, abbreviations for, 503
Grammar Link, 7, 11, 15, 19, 23, 41, 45, 49, 53, 57, 61, 65, 69, 77, 105, 109, 113, 117, 121, 125, 129, 147, 151, 155, 159, 163, 167, 185, 189, 193, 197, 201, 205, 221, 225, 229, 233, 237
Graphic organizers, 661
    creating, 237
    graphs in, 580
    maps in, 582
    tables in, 579
    time lines in, 581

H

Hear, here, 556
Helping verb, 341, 663
Here, beginning sentence with, 441
Here, hear, 556
Hidden fears, 620
Historical events, capitalizing names of, 479
Home page, 648, 661
Homographs, 554
Homonyms, 555–556
"How-to" paper, 194–197
Hyperlink, 649, 661
Hypertext, 648, 661
Hyphens
    in compound nouns, 501
    in compound numbers, 501
    to divide words at end of line, 501

I

I, capitalization of, 475
Ideas, 108, 246, 661, 682, 684, 689
    ordering of, 50–53
Idiom, 661
ie and *ei* spelling rule for, 558
Imagery, 661
Imperative sentences, 297, 489, 661
    diagraming, 466
In, into, 455
Incident reports, 286–289
    format, 289
    model, 286, 288
    parts, 289
    purpose, 286
    style, 288
    types, 287
Indefinite article, 658
Indefinite pronouns, 369
    list of, 369
    plural, 369
    singular, 369
Independent clause, 659
Index, 569, 570
Indirect objects, 335, 659
    diagraming, 467
    position of, in sentences, 335
    pronoun, 361
Indirect quotations, 473
Inductive reasoning, 661
Inferring word meaning, 544
Informal discussion, taking part in, 622–623
Information. *See* Details
Informative writing, 661. *See also* Expository writing
Initials, capitalization of, 475
Instructions
    following, 617
    giving, 282–285, 622
    model, 282, 284
    parts, 285
    style, 283–284, 285
    types, 283
    word processing, for organizing, 285
Intensifier, 662
Interjections, 427, 662
    commas with, 427
    exclamation points with, 427, 489
Internet, 645–655, 662
    addresses, 647
    bookmarks/favorites, 648
    browser, 647
    domain name, 648
    e-mail, 654
    etiquette, 655
    evaluating sources, 651
    home page, 648, 661
    hyperlinks, 649, 661
    hypertext transfer protocol, 648
    message board, 647
    search engine, 649–650
    smiley, 655
    spam, 654
    subject directory, 649
    Troubleshooting Guide, 652
    URL, 647, 665
    Web site, 647–648, 650–653, 666
    World Wide Web, 645–653, 666
Interpretation, 662
Interrogative sentences, 297, 489
    diagraming, 466
Interrupters, with quotations, 473, 491, 499
Interview, 79–80, 662
Into, in, 455
Intransitive verbs, 333
Introductions, in writing, 55–56, 149, 662
Introductory words, commas with, 463
Inverted order of sentences, 662
Irregular verbs, 347, 349, 666
Italics, with titles of works, 499
Items in a series, 262, 491
Its, it's, 367, 455, 556

J

Jargon, 662
Journal, 662
Journal writing, 7, 9, 12, 13, 15, 17, 21, 25, 43, 47, 51, 55, 59, 63, 67, 71, 75, 107, 111, 115, 119, 123, 127, 149, 153, 157, 161, 165, 169, 187, 191, 195, 199, 203, 223, 227, 231, 235
    secured files on computer for, 15
    tips for, 13
    See also Prewriting

L

Languages, capitalizing
    names of, 479
Lay, lie, 457
Learn, teach, 457
Learning log, 662
Leave, let, 457
Legibility, 75, 247
Letter writing, 99
    business, 497
    capitalization in, 473
    commas in, 493
    friendly, 16–19, 224
Library
    card catalog, 528, 533
    computer catalog, 528,
        532–533
    finding books in, 533
    obtaining information at,
        198–199, 239, 527
    organization of books in,
        530–531
    references in, 534–535
    sections in, 527–529
Lie, lay, 457
Line graphs, 580
Linking verbs, 337
    as action verbs, 337
    defined, 337
    list of, 337
    and predicate adjective, 337
Listening
    analyzing persuasive tech-
        niques and propaganda,
        619–620
    evaluating commercials, 619
    following instructions, 617
    organizing spoken ideas, 618
    to persuasive speech, 618
    purpose for, 618
    taking notes, 618
    See also Speaking
Listening and speaking, 11, 19,
    45, 49, 61, 73, 109, 113, 121,
    129, 151, 155, 159, 163, 167,
    193, 197, 201, 205, 225, 233
Listing, 47, 49, 53, 61, 71, 107,
    109, 111, 121, 127, 151,
    187, 191, 203, 215, 662
Lists
    colons to introduce, 497
    commas with, 491

Literary analysis, 662
Literature. For a complete list-
    ing of the literature in the
    book, *see* p. xxv
Literature, responding to, 34,
    87, 140, 178, 214, 246
    See also Writing about
        literature
Logical fallacy, 662

M

Magazine writing, 90–99
Main clause, 659
Main idea and supporting
    details
    organization of, 50–53
    in paragraphs, 62–65
Main verbs, 341, 662
Maps, 127
    keys for, 582
    scales for, 582
Mass media, 629–634
Matching tests, 586–587
Measure, abbreviations for
    units of, 503
Mechanics. *See* Capitalization;
    Punctuation
Media, 662
    critical listening, 222–223
Media messages, 635–643
    analyzing, 635
    producing, 640
Memoir, 662
Memory
    devices, using, to learn prob-
        lem words, 567
Memos, 274–277
    format, 277
    model, 274, 276
    parts, 276, 277
    purpose, 275
    style, 276
    tone, 274, 275
    types, 275
    word processing template,
        276
Metaphor, 662
Misreading, commas to
    prevent, 493
Modifiers
    adjectives, 379
    adverbs, 395, 397

articles, 381
    good and *well,* 401
    predicate adjectives, 337
    See also Adjectives; Adverbs
Months, capitalization of, 479
Mood, 662
Movies, 633, 634
Multimedia presentation,
    290–293, 662
    creating with computer soft-
        ware, 292
    example, 290, 292
    parts, 293
    to persuade, 291
    style, 292
    types, 291
Multiple-choice tests, 586
Music, writing topics in, 155

N

Names, capitalization of, 473
Narrative writing, 142–179, 662
    conclusion for, 162
    details in, 153
    developing real-life story in,
        148–151
    dialogue in, 156–159
    drafting, 145–146, 154, 158,
        169–170
    editing, 149, 162, 171
    keeping story on track in,
        152–155
    literature models in, 149, 156,
        172–178
    organizing, 152–155
    presenting, 158, 171
    prewriting, 145, 161, 165, 169
    revising, 146, 153, 166, 170
    writing about real events in,
        160–163
Nationalities, capitalizing
    names of, 479
Negatives, double, 403
Nominative case, 361–362, 659
Nonessential elements,
    commas with, 491
Nonfiction, 662
    classification of, 533
Note cards for report, 576
Notes
    in descriptive writing, 109,
        110–113

in editing report, 199
in personal writing, 21
taking, 42, 165, 199, 576–577,
    620
Nouns
    collective, 321
    common, 319
    compound, 501
    definition of, 301, 319, 663
    of direct address, 491
    distinguishing between pos-
        sessive and plural, 323
    forming plurals of, 561–562
    plural, 321
    possessive, 323
    predicate, 337, 469
    proper, 128, 319, 475–480
    singular, 321
    suffixes, 549
Number, 663
    pronoun-antecedent agree-
        ment in, 365
    subject-verb agreement
        in, 439
Numbers
    compound, 501
    hyphen with, 501
    ordinal, 505
    spelling out, 505
Numerals, 505

O

Object of the preposition, 419
    compound, 419
Object pronouns, 363, 419
Objective case, 659
    See also Pronouns
Objective test
    matching questions, 586
    multiple-choice questions,
        586
    studying for, 584
Objects
    direct, 333, 335
    indirect, 335
Onomatopoeia, 663
Opinion, 663
    distinguishing from facts,
        230–233, 619–620, 635–636
Oral presentations, 81
Oral reports
    audience, 627

drafting, 624
presenting, 627
prewriting, 626
revising, 626
Oral tradition, 663
Order of importance, 52, 118,
    153, 663
Organization, 152, 154, 191,
    214, 663, 682, 684, 690
    chronological, 154, 155
    in descriptive writing, 119
    of details, 50, 52, 153
    transitions in, 120, 121
Organizations
    abbreviations for, 503
    capitalizing names of, 479
Outlines, 93, 577–578, 663
    correct form for, 577–578
    note taking and, 577–578
    in persuasive writing, 220

P

Paragraphs, 663
    developing main idea in,
        63–64
    organization of, 680
    topic sentence in, 63, 679
    transitions in, 64, 680
    writing unified, 679
Parallelism, 110, 663, 678
Paraphrase, 663
Parenthetical documentation,
    663
Participle
    past, 341, 666
    present, 341, 666
Past participle, 341, 666
Past perfect tense, 345, 666
Past progressive form of
    verb, 343
Past tense, 339, 666
Peer review, 59, 61, 153, 663
Percentages, numbers in,
    505
Perfect tenses, 345, 666
Periods
    in abbreviations, 503
    to end declarative sen-
        tence, 297, 489
    to end imperative sen-
        tence, 297, 489
    quotation marks with, 499

Personal pronouns, 361
Personal writing, 2–35, 663
    confidence in, 12–15
    drafting, 5–6, 24–25
    editing, 27
    literature models in, 8, 16,
        28–33
    making personal connections
        in, 16–19
    presenting, 6, 27, 171
    prewriting, 5, 25, 169
    responding to poem in,
        20–23
    revising, 26
    self-expression in, 8–11
Personification, 663
Persuasive speech, 618–620
    types of, 619–620
Persuasive writing, 216–249,
    663
    drafting, 219–220, 223,
        239–240
    editing, 227, 236, 241
    facts in, 231
    kinds of, 224
    literature models in, 222, 230,
        242–245
    opinions in, 231
    presenting, 220, 228, 231, 241
    prewriting, 219, 233
    revising, 220, 231, 232, 240
    stating position in, 226–229
    taking stand in, 222–225
    using facts and opinions in,
        230–233
Phrase, 663
    prepositional, 417, 663
    verb, 341, 663
Piece, peace, 555
Plagiarism, 663, 686
Plot, 663
Plural nouns, forming, 321,
    561–562
    nouns ending in *o*, 321,
        561–562
    nouns ending in *s, x, z, ch, sh,*
        321, 561–562
    nouns ending in *y*, 321,
        561–562
    nouns same in singular and
        plural, 321
Poetry, 663
    responding to, 20–23

writing, 22, 23
Point of view, 9, 663
Political parties, capitalizing names of, 479
Portfolio, 35, 88, 141, 179, 215, 247, 663
Possessive adjective, 658
Possessive case, 323, 659
Possessive nouns, 323
   apostrophes in, 501
Possessive pronouns, 367
   distinguishing from contraction, 367
Practicing oral reports, 627
Predicate adjectives, 337, 379, 401, 658
   diagraming, 469
Predicate nominative, 337
Predicate nouns, 337
   diagraming, 469
Predicates, 299, 664
   complete, 301
   compound, 305–307
   diagraming, 465–469
   simple, 301
Prefixes, 547, 548
Prepositional phrases, 417, 663
   as adjectives and adverbs, 421
   in combining sentences, 521
   commas with, 491
   diagraming, 470
Prepositions
   composed of more than one word, 415
   commonly used, 415
   definition of, 415, 664
   distinguishing, from adverbs, 423
   list of, 415
   object of, 417
   pronouns after, 419
Present perfect tense, 345, 666
Present progressive form of a verb, 343
Present tense, 339, 666
Presentation, 664, 683–684
Presenting, 664
   descriptive writing, 124, 133
   expository writing, 203, 209
   of oral reports, 627
   personal writing, 6, 27
   persuasive writing, 220, 228, 241

TIME Facing the Blank Page, 91, 99
in writing process, 40, 44, 74–77
Prewriting, 664
   brainstorming in, 25, 131
   charts in, 235
   clustering, 48, 49, 52, 53
   descriptive writing, 102–103, 131
   drawing in, 207
   expository writing, 191, 195, 198–199, 203, 207
   finding topics in, 46–49
   freewriting in, 9, 10, 11, 23, 25, 129, 131, 145, 169
   narrative writing, 161, 165, 169
   note taking in, 39, 165, 199, 576–577, 620
   oral reports, 624
   ordering ideas in, 50–53
   personal writing, 4, 25
   persuasive writing, 218–220, 231, 234, 239
   TIME Facing the Blank Page, 90, 92–93
   Venn diagrams in, 191
   in writing process, 39, 43, 46–53
   See also Journal writing
Principal parts of verbs, 341
Principal, principle, 556, 566
Prior knowledge, 664
Process, explaining, 194–197
Progressive verb forms, 343, 666
Prompts. See Writing prompts
Pronoun-antecedent agreement in number and gender, 365
Pronouns
   antecedent for, 365, 664
   in compound objects, 363
   definition of, 301, 361, 664
   demonstrative, 381
   indefinite, 369
   object, 361, 363, 419
   personal, 361, 664
   possessive, 367
   after prepositions, 419
   selecting proper, 227
   subject, 361, 363, 439
   Troubleshooter for, 258–259

Proofreading, 70–73, 664
   symbols for, 72, 267
   TIME Facing the Blank Page, 91, 98
Propaganda, 619–620, 638–639, 664, 686
Proper adjectives, 379, 658
   capitalization of, 479
Proper nouns, 319
   capitalization of, 475–480
Prose, 664
Publishing, 664
   TIME Facing the Blank Page, 91, 99
   See also Presenting
Punctuation
   apostrophes, 501
   colon, 497
   comma, 491, 493, 495
   end marks, 489
   exclamation point, 489
   hyphens, 501
   italics, 499
   period, 489
   question mark, 489
   quotation marks, 499
   semicolons, 497
Purposes for writing, 50, 664
   to describe, 106–109, 123–125
   to explain a process, 186–189, 194–197
   to express, 8–11
   to inform, 186–189, 198–201
   to persuade, 222–229, 233
   to tell a story, 149–151

Q

Question marks
   to end interrogative sentences, 297, 489
   quotation marks with, 499
Questions, 297, 489
   diagraming, 466
Quotation marks
   commas with, 499
   for dialogue, 499
   for direct quotations, 499
   with other marks of punctuation, 499
   with titles of short works, 499
Quotations
   capitalization of, 473

commas with, 499
direct, 473
indirect, 473
in note taking, 576, 577
punctuating, 499

R

Real-life story, developing, 148–149
Reference works
  atlas, 535
  dictionary, 536–537, 539–540
  encyclopedias, 534–535
  thesaurus, 538
Reflecting, 27, 81, 133, 171, 209, 241
Regular verb, 341, 666
Representation, 664
  See also Viewing and Representing
Research, 664
Research reports
  drafting, 200
  editing, 199
  prewriting, 198–199
  sources, 685–687
Responding to literature. *See* Literature, responding to
Review, 664
Revising, 664
  checklist for, 27, 59, 80, 132, 170, 208, 240
  compare-and-contrast essay, 192
  descriptive writing, 112, 132
  expository writing, 184, 192, 208
  narrative writing, 146, 153, 166, 170
  oral reports, 624
  personal writing, 24
  persuasive writing, 220, 231, 232, 240
  thesaurus in, 112
  TIME Facing the Blank Page, 91, 96–97
  wordy sentences, 678
  in writing process, 40, 44, 58–61, 62–65, 66–69
Root words, 547, 664
Run-on sentences, 307, 664
  Troubleshooter for, 252–253

S

Salutation, capitalization of, 473
Science, writing topics in, 113
Search engine, 649
Semicolons, 497–498
Sensory details, 20, 110–113, 122–124, 126, 664
Sentence combining
  compound sentences, 517
  compound elements, 519
  prepositional phrases, 521
Sentence fluency, 66, 87, 665, 683–684, 690
Sentence fragments, 299
  Troubleshooter for, 250–251
Sentence variety, 517–522, 665
Sentences
  capitalization of, 473
  clear sentences, 307
  complex, 664–665
  compound, 307, 517, 664–665
  declarative, 297, 489, 660
  definition of, 297, 664–665
  diagraming, 466–471
  exclamatory, 297, 489, 661
  imperative, 297, 489, 661
  interrogative, 297, 489
  predicate in, 299, 301, 303, 305
  run-on, 252–253, 307
  simple, 307, 664–665
  subject in, 299, 301, 303, 305
  topic, 63–64
  types of, 677
  varying, 66–68, 677
  word order in, 303
Series, commas in, 116, 491
Setting, 122–125, 665
Silent *e*, spelling and, 557
Simile, 665
Simple predicates, 301, 465
Simple sentences, 307, 664–665
Simple subjects, 301, 465
Singular indefinite pronouns, 369
Singular nouns, 321
6+1 Trait® writing, 682
Social studies, writing topics in, 11, 69, 189
Spatial order, 665

Speaking
  giving directions, 622
  giving oral reports, 75, 624–627
  taking part in informal discussion, 622–623
  using telephones, 621
  in writing conference, 26, 59, 88, 141, 247
Spelling
  building skills in, 563
  changes in, 557–562
  compound words, 560
  dictionary used for, 539
  doubling the final consonant and, 559
  of easily confused words, 566
  of foreign words, 546
  forming plurals and, 561–562
  ie and *ei*, 558
  problem words in, 565–567
  roots, 547–550
  suffixes and the final *y* and, 558
  suffixes and the silent *e* and, 557
  syllable boundaries, 559–560
  syllables and, 539
  words commonly misspelled, 565
SQ3R study method, 573–575
Standard English, 665
Standardized tests, 588–590
Stanzas, 22
States, abbreviations for, 503
Story writing. *See* Narrative writing
Storytelling, 625–627
Student models, 9, 22, 122, 160, 165, 236
Study skills
  book parts, 569–570
  graphic aids, 579–582
  outlining, 577–578
  setting study goals, 571
  SQ3R study method, 573–575
  taking notes, 576–577
  time management, 572
Style sheet MLA, 668
Style, 665

Subject complement, 659
Subject pronouns, 361, 363
  subject-verb agreement with, 439
Subjects, 299, 664, 665
  complete, 301
  compound, 305, 307, 443
  defined, 299
  diagraming, 465, 466
  finding, 303
  in complete sentence versus fragment, 250–251
  position in sentence of, 303, 441
  simple, 301
  understood, 303, 466
Subject-verb agreement
  with compound subjects, 443
  with interrupting words and phrases, 441
  with noun subjects, 439
  with subject pronouns, 439
  Troubleshooter for, 254–255
Subordinate clause, 659
Suffixes, 547, 548–550
  and the final *y,* 558
  and the silent *e,* 557
Summary, 162, 233, 665
Superlative form of an adjective, 383, 385, 658
Superlative form of an adverb, 399, 658
Support, for argument
  See Evidence
Suspense, 665
Symbol, 665
Symbols, for revising and proofreading, 72
Synonyms, 538, 540, 552, 590

T

Table of contents, 569, 570
Tables, 579
Teach, learn, 457
Technical writing, 269–289
Technology presentations, 290–293
Telephones, using, 621
Television program, Case study of, 218–221
Tenses, of verbs, 339

  using, 339
Tests
  grammar usage, and mechanics on, 590
  matching items in, 586–587
  multiple-choice items in, 586
  preparing for, 584–585
  standardized, 588–590
  time management for, 585
  true-false items in, 586
  See also Study skills
Than, then, 457
Their, they're, 457, 556
Theme, 665
Then, than, 457
There, beginning sentence with, 441
There, their, they're, 556
Thesaurus, 538
  electronic, 125
  in revising, 112
Thesis statement, 665, 681
They're, their, 457, 556
Thinking skills, *See* Critical thinking
Third-person pronoun, 361
Time expressions
  abbreviations in, 503
  colons in, 497
  numbers in, 505
TIME Facing the Blank Page, 90–99
Time lines, 581
Time management
  as study skill, 572
  for tests, 585
Time order, 665
Titles of persons
  abbreviations in, 503
  commas with, 495
Titles of works
  capitalizing, 479
  italics with, 499
  quotation marks with, 499
Tone, 665
Too, comma with, 495
Topic, finding, 46–49
Topic sentences, 63, 65, 95, 665
  elaborating, 679
  and main idea, 63
  placement, 63
Transitions
  in descriptive writing, 120,

  121, 132
  in expository writing, 196
  list of, 120
  in paragraphs, 64, 680
Transitive verbs, 333
Travel brochures, creating, 128, 129
True-false tests, 586
TV reviews, 234–237
  drafting, 236
  editing, 235
  prewriting, 235
Two, to, too, 457, 556, 566

U

Underlining. *See* Italics
Understood subject, 303, 466
Unity, 665
URL, 647, 665
Usage
  glossary of problem words, 455, 457
  glossary of special usage problems, 459–462
Using Computers
  copy function, 61
  comparing Web sites, 193
  composing paragraphs on, 69, 109
  creating charts on, 45, 237
  creating graphic organizers, 121
  desktop publishing, 201
  drawing program, 49
  electronic thesaurus, 125
  e-mail, 229
  grammar checker, 73, 77
  line-spacing function, 163
  modems, 647
  page-layout option, 129
  researching famous people, 167
  secured files, 15
  spelling checker, 73
  word processing program, 69
  writing poetry on, 23
  See also Computers; Word processing

V

Variety, in sentences, 66–69
Venn diagrams, 191, 193, 665
Verb phrases, 341, 663
Verb tenses and forms, 339, 666
 base, 666
 future, 339, 666
 future perfect, 666
 past, 339, 666
 past participle, 666
 past perfect, 345, 666
 past progressive, 343, 666
 present, 339, 666
 present participle, 666
 present perfect, 345, 666
 present progressive, 343, 666
 simple past, 666
 Troubleshooter for, 256–257
Verbs, 665
 action, 333
 helping, 341
 intransitive, 333
 irregular, 347, 349, 666
 linking, 337
 main, 341
 principal parts of, 341
 regular, 666
 simple predicate, 301, 465
 transitive, 333
Viewing and Representing, 15,
 23, 53, 57, 65, 69, 77, 117,
 125, 151, 189, 229, 237,
 629–643
Visual learning. *See* Graphic
 organizers
Visual messages, 629–643
 composition, 629–634
 film 633
 mass media, 629–634
 producing, 640–643
 visual design, 629–634
Vocabulary
 antonyms, 553
 borrowed words, 542–543,
 546
 compound words, 560
 context clues for, 544–545
 homographs, 554
 homonyms, 555–556
 prefixes, 547–548
 root words, 547
 suffixes, 547–549

 synonyms, 552
 See also Dictionary
Voice, 140, 666, 682, 684, 690

W

Weather, whether, 566
Web site, 647–648, 650–653,
 666
Webbing. *See* Clustering
Well and *good,* 401
Whether, weather, 566
Who, whom, 419
Who's, whose, 457, 556
Word choice, 122, 178, 666,
 683–684
Word parts
 prefixes of, 547–548
 roots of, 547
 suffixes of, 547, 548–550
Word processing, 666
 memo template, 276
 for creating application
 forms, 281
 for writing instructions, 285
Words
 affirmative, 403
 borrowed, 542–543, 546
 choice of, 106–109
 compound, 560
 difficult, 565
 double negative, 403
 easily confused, 566–567
 homographs, 554
 See also Vocabulary
World Wide Web, 645–653, 666
Writing about art, 57, 65, 141,
 159, 193, 225, 229
Writing about literature
 responding to biography,
 164–167
 responding to poem, 20–23
 writing book report, 202–205
 writing about places,
 126–129
 writing TV review, 234–237
Writing across the curriculum
 in art, *See* Cross-curricular
 writing
Writing portfolios
 See Portfolios
Writing process, 38–88, 666
 drafting, 87, 90, 94–95

 editing, 27, 91, 98, 133, 171,
 249, 326
 presenting, 27, 91, 99, 133,
 171
 prewriting, 29, 87, 90, 92–93,
 140, 183, 246
 revising, 26, 88, 91, 96–97,
 132, 170
 *See also specific types of
 writing*
Writing prompts, 11, 15, 19, 23,
 45, 49, 53, 57, 61, 65, 69,
 73, 77, 109, 113, 117, 121,
 125, 129, 151, 155, 159,
 163, 167, 189, 193, 197,
 201, 205, 225, 229, 233, 237
Writing Rubrics, 11, 15, 19, 23,
 45, 49, 53, 57, 61, 65, 69,
 73, 77, 109, 113, 117, 121,
 125, 129, 151, 155, 159,
 163, 167, 189, 193, 197,
 201, 205, 225, 229, 233,
 237, 273, 277, 281, 285,
 289, 293
Writing skills and strategies
 audience, adapting to, 228
 choosing details, 114–116,
 153
 chronological order, 50, 154
 classifying, 188
 comparing and contrasting,
 190–192
 conclusions, 162, 200
 creating a clear picture,
 106–108
 dialogue, 156–158
 fact and opinion, 230–231
 introductions, 200
 main idea paragraphs, 62–64
 order of importance, 50, 52,
 232
 sensory details, 20, 110–113,
 122–124, 126
 spatial order, 51, 118–120,
 124
 stating a goal, 223
 step-by-step order, 195–196
 support statements, 223–224,
 227, 230–231
 topic sentence, 63–64
 transitions, 120
 varying sentences, 66–68

TIME Facing the Blank Page,
    90–99
See also Writing process

You, understood as subject,
    303, 466
Your, you're, 556

ACKNOWLEDGMENTS

Text

UNIT ONE "This is Just to Say" by William Carlos Williams, from *Collected Poems: 1909-1939, vol. I.* Copyright 1938 by New Directions Publishing Corporation. Reprinted by permission of New Directions Publishing Corp.

From *The Invisible Thread* by Yoshiko Uchida. Copyright 1991 by Yoshiko Uchida. Courtesy of the Bancroft Library, University of California, Berkeley.

UNIT TWO From "The Empire Builder" by Curtis Katz. Reprinted by permission.

From *Coast to Coast* by Betsy Byars. Copyright 1992 by Betsy Byars. Used by permission of Delacorte Press, a division of Random House, Inc.

UNIT THREE From "Attacking the Nunataks" by John Boulanger. *International Wildlife,* November/December 1993. Reprinted with permission.

From *Julie of the Wolves* by Jean Craighead George. Copyright 1972 by Jean Craighead George. Reprinted by permission of HarperCollins Publishers, Inc.

From *Morning Girl* by Michael Dorris. Copyright 1992 by Michael Dorris. Published by Hyperion Books for Children.

UNIT FOUR From *W.E.B. DuBois: A Biography* by Virginia Hamilton. Copyright © 1992 by Virginia Hamilton. Reprinted by permission of Arnold Adoff.

"The Jacket" by Gary Soto, is reprinted by permission from the publisher of *Small Faces* (Houston: Arte Publico Press— University of Houston, 1992).

UNIT FIVE From "How Does Michael Fly?" by Julie Sheer. Copyrighted Chicago Tribune Company. All rights reserved. Used with permission, 1990.

From "Bathing Elephants" from *Keepers and Creatures at the National Zoo* by Peggy Thomson. Copyright 1988 by Peggy Thomson. Reprinted by permission of the author.

UNIT SIX From "A Popular Little Planet" by Douglas Anderson. Copywrited © 1992 Children's Television Workshop. Reprinted by permission.

"Thanking the Birds" by Joseph Bruchac, from *Keepers of the Earth: Native American Stories and Environmental Activities for Children* by Michael Caduto and Joseph Bruchac. Fulcrum Publishing, 350 Indiana St., #350, Golden, CO 80401. 303-277-1623. Reprinted by permission.

Photo

Cover KS Studio; **vi** Copyright © The Detroit Institute of Arts, City of Detroit Purchase; **vii** (t)Photodisc, Inc., (b)Ralph J. Brunke; **viii** (l)© Time, Inc., (r)Movie Still Archive; **ix** Edition Leipzig, Germany. Courtesy of the Library of the Academy of Sciences of St. Petersburg, Russia; **x** (t)From the Collection of the Portland Art Museum, (b)Courtesy of Carmen Garza; **xi** © DC Comics, Inc; **xii** Art Wise; **xiii** © DC Comics, Inc; **xiv** ©1983 Andy Warhol/Ronald Feldman Fine Arts, courtesy Ronald Feldman Arts, NY; **xvi** Robert Miller Gallery, New York; **xvii** Collection of Lois Mailou Jones; **xviii** Courtesy of Nancy Schutt; **xx** Artville; **xxi** Ralph J. Brunke; **xxiii** Photodisc, Inc.; **xxiv** Scala/Art Resource, NY; **xxv** Art Wise; **xxvii** Los Angeles County Museum of Art, gift of Mrs. Homer Kripke; **xviii xxix** file photo; **xxxii-1** Philadelphia Museum of Art/CORBIS; **2-3** Jim Sugar Photo/CORBIS; **4** Art Wise; **8 through 14** Ralph J. Brunke; **16** Ralph A. Deinhold/Animals Animals; **18** Ralph J. Brunke; **21** Nathaniel Bruns; **23** Erich Lessing/Art Resource, NY; **24** Bob Daemmrich/Stock Boston; **27** Seth Resnick/Stock Boston; **30** *Farmhouse and Chestnut Trees at Jas-de-Bouffan,* c. 1885. Paul Cezanne (1839-1906). Oil on canvas, 36x29 inches. F. 1969.38.2.P The Norton Simon Museum; **32** Copyright © 1980, Helen Oji. Collection of Prudential Insurance Co., Newark, NJ; **35** Jim Sugar Photo/CORBIS; **36-37** Mike Dwyer/ Stock Boston/PictureQuest; **42** Allan Landau; **46 48 50 54** Ralph J. Brunke; **57** Courtesy of Tina Dunkley; **58 59** Ralph J. Brunke; **60** Historical Pictures/Stock Montage; **65** Private collection, photo courtesy of Joshua Baer & Company, Sante Fe, NM; **66** Steven Frame/Stock Boston; **67** Ralph J. Brunke; **70** Allan Landau; **72 74** Ralph J. Brunke; **78** FPG; **81** FPG; **83** Giraudon/Art Resource, NY. Copyright © 1992 ARS, New York/ADAGP, Paris; **84** Scala/Art Resource, NY; **88** Mike Dwyer/Stock Boston/PictureQuest; **100-101** Pal Hermansen/Tony Stone Images; **102** John Boulanger; **106** Lawrence Migdale/Stock Boston; **107** Matthew McVay/Stock Boston; **110** Ralph J. Brunke; **111** Janice Fried; **112** Allan Landau; **113** Edition Leipzig, Germany. Courtesy of the Library of the Academy of Sciences of St. Petersburg, Russia; **114** Thomas R. Fletcher/ Stock Boston; **115 116** Allan Landau; **117** Tony Shafrazi Gallery, New York. Collection Mr. & Mrs. K. Scharf; **118** Culver Pictures; **121** Salander-O'Reilly Galleries; **122** Jose Carrillo/Stock Boston; **126** Allan Landau; **127** Ralph J. Brunke; **128** Allan Landau; **130** Myrleen Ferguson/PhotoEdit; **133** Stephen Frisch/Stock Boston; **135** Giraudon/Art Resource, NY. Copyright © 1992 ARS, New York/SPADEM, Paris; **138** Scala/Art Resource, NY; **141** Pal Hermansen/Tony Stone Images; **142-143** Alan Detrick/ Photo Researchers; **148** Allan Landau; **152** (t)Frans Lanting/Minden Pictures, (b)From the Collection of the Portland Art Museum, photo by Edward S. Curtis; **156** Bill Aron/PhotoEdit; **157** Calvin and Hobbes. Copyright © 1992 Watterson. Reprinted with permission of Universal Press Syndicate. All rights reserved; **159** Scala/Art Resource, New York; **160** Charles Palek/Animals Animals; **164 166** UPI/Bettmann/CORBIS; **168** Tony Freeman/ PhotoEdit; **173** Acervo Partrimonial de la Secretario de Haciende y Credito Publico, Mexico, D.F; **174** Courtesy of Carmen Garza; **179** Alan Detrick/ Photo Researchers; **180-181** Staffan Widstrand/CORBIS; **182** Allan Landau; **186** Peter L. Chapman/Stock Boston; **187** Allan Landau; **190** © DC Comics, Inc; **194** © AFP; **197** Los Angeles County Museum of Art, gift of Mrs. Homer Kripke; **202** Janice Fried; **204** Allan Landau; **206** Diane Graham-Henry/Tony Stone Images; **209** Tony Stone Images; **213** ©1983 Andy Warhol/Ronald Feldman Fine Arts, New York; **215** Staffan Widstrand/CORBIS; **216-217** Jim Brandenburg/Minden Pictures; **222 223 224** Art Wise; **225** ©Japser Johns/VAGA, New York 1992. Collection Albright-Knox Art Gallery, Buffalo, NY; **228** (t)Mike Okoniewski/The Image Works, (b)Myrleen Ferguson/PhotoEdit; **230-231 232** Allan Landau; **234** Art Wise; **241** David Young-Wolf/PhotoEdit; **243** Courtesy Elaine Horwitch Galleries, Scottsdale, Arizona; **247** Jim Brandenburg/ Minden Pictures; **248-249** Randy Faris/CORBIS; **294-295** SuperStock;

297 Murray Close/TriStar Pictures, Inc./PhotoFest; **315** Giraudon/ Art Resource, NY; **329** file photo; **357** Courtesy of Nancy Schutt; **363** David Young-Wolff/Photo Edit; **375** National Museum of American Art, Washington, DC/Art Resource, NY; **391** Collection of the Artist; **411** Phyllis Kind Gallery, New York/Chicago; **423** Allan Landau; **427** Calvin and Hobbes. © 1986 Watterson, reproduced with permission of Universal Press Syndicate; **435** Robert Miller Gallery, New York; **451** National Museum of American Art, Smithsonian Institution/Art Resource, Bequest of Henry Ward Ranger through the National Academy of Design; **461** Courtesy Frumkin/Adams Galler, New York; **485** The Phillips Collection, Washington, DC; **493** Library of Congress; **513** Evans-Tibbs Collection, Washington, DC; **524-525** Archivo Iconografico, SA/CORBIS; **527** Allan Landau; **528** Cathy Ferris; **534** From The World Book Encyclopedia. Copyright © 1992 World Book, Inc. By permission of World Book, Inc; **535** Hammond Incorporated, Maplewood, NJ, photo by Allan Landau; **537** Courtesy of Macmillan Publishing; **542** (l)Bob Daemmrich/The Image Works, (c)E. R. Degginger/Earth Scenes, (r)Bob Daemmrich/Stock Boston; **546** Ralph J. Brunke; **551** Neal Mishler/Natural Selection; **555** (t)Bettmann/CORBIS, (b)Vernon Doucette/Stock Boston; **546 through 564** (gears)VCG/FPG; **569** Ralph J. Brunke; **571** Mark Burnett/Stock Boston; **572** Allan Landau; **581**(t)UPI/Bettmann/ CORBIS, (bl)Bill Gallery/Stock Boston, (br)NASA; **584** Allan Landau; **619** GARFIELD © Paws, Inc. Reprinted with permission of UNIVERSAL PRESS SYNDICATE. All rights reserved; **621 624** Allan Landau; **631** Excerpt from LISTEN, BUDDY by Helen Lester. Text © 1995 by Helen Lester. Illustrations © 1995 by Lynn Munsinger. Reprinted by permission of Houghton Mifflin Company. All rights reserved; **632** The Boston Globe; **634** (t)Photofest, (b)Movie Still Archive; **639** Stephen Simpson/FPG; **646** Jeffrey Muir Hamilton/Liaison; **650** file photo.

Acknowledgments